AF656539

A competition book for

FOOD SAFETY OFFICER

(Main Subject: An Objective Approach)

Dr. Suresh Chandra

Assistant Professor (Agric. Process and Food Engg)

Department of Agricultural Engineering and Food Technology

SV Patel University of Agriculture and Technology, Meerut (UP)

Dr. Durvesh Kumari

Manager-3 (Quality Assurance)

GDUSS (Parag Dairy), Meerut (UP)

Dr. S. K. Goyal

Assistant Professor (Farm Engineering)

Institute of Agricultural Sciences, RGDC (BHU),

KVK Barkachha (Mirzapur)

2026

JAIN BROTHERS (New Delhi)

16/873, East Park Road, Near Dr. N. C. Joshi Hospital,

Karol Bagh, New Delhi - 110 005

Phones : 011- 23618426, 45097398

E-mail : jain_bros@hotmail.com

Website : www.thejainbrothers.com

Published by :

Shri Sunil Kumar Jain
for
Jain Brothers (New Delhi)
16/873, East Park Road, Karol Bagh, New Delhi-110 005
Phones : 011-23618426, 45097398

Branch Office at :

1. **M/s Sunil Book Service**
   Fatima Nagar, Opp. Andhra Bank,
   KAZIPET-506004 (A.P.)
   Ph. : 0870-2459617, Mob. : 9390115435
   E-mail : kpkulshrestha@yahoo.com
2. **M/s Jain Brothers**
   Vidya Vihar, Pilani (Rajasthan)
   Phone : 01596-242144

Available at:
Pusa Agricultural Book Service
Shishir Hostel, IARI, PUSA
New Delhi
Ph.: 011-25841048

First Edition	:	Oct., 2014
Second Edition	:	Sept., 2015
Third Edition	:	March, 2016
Fourth Edition	:	April, 2017
Fifth Edition	:	May, 2018
Sixth Edition	:	May, 2019
Reprinted with corrections and additions	:	Jan., 2020
Reprinted with corrections	:	Oct., 2021
Reprinted with corrections	:	Feb., 2022
Seventh Edition	:	Dec, 2022
Eighth Edition	:	April, 2025
Ninth Edition	:	April, 2026

Price: ₹ 450.00

***ISBN*: 978-81-8360-213-6**

Laser Typesetting by :

NIYATI *Graphics*
754/23 Khajoor Road,
Karol Bagh, New Delhi

Printer by :
BALAJI OFFSET PRINTERS, New Delhi-110035

Preface

The overall goal of the food processing industry is to convert raw materials into high valued finished products at the lowest cost. Due to significant variations in raw material properties, the main challenge of the food process engineer/food technologist is to produce a final product of consistent quality. It is extremely important that the food engineer be aware of the latest scientific advances that would allow for the production of the highest quality products. The processing of food is no longer as simple or straightforward as in the past. It is now moving from an art to a highly interdisciplinary science. A number of new preservation techniques are being developed to satisfy current demands of economic preservation and consumer satisfaction in nutritional and sensory aspects, convenience, absence of preservatives, low demand of energy, and environmental safety. Better understanding and manipulation of these conventional and sophisticated preservation methods could help to develop high-quality, safe products by better control of the processes and efficient selection of ingredients.

Food processing needs to use preservation techniques ranging from simple to sophisticated; thus, any food process must acquire requisite knowledge about the methods, the technology, and the science of mode of action. Keeping this in mind, this book has been developed to discuss the fundamental and practical aspects of most of the food preservation methods important to practicing industrial and academic food scientists, technologists, and engineers as well as **Food Safety Officer**. Innovative technology in preservation is being developed in the food industry that can extend shelf life; minimize risk; is environment friendly; or can improve functional, sensory, and nutritional properties. The large and ever-increasing number of food products and new preservation techniques available today creates a great demand for an up-to-date handbook of food preservation methods.

This book contains a huge accumulation of objective type questions. It is very much hoped that the subject matter will create a confidence among the candidates and the books will help them like an ideal teach.

Though the book are sure to make more useful to the reader as syllabus but the authors and it is earnestly hoped that suggestions to improve the book shall be forthcoming from the readers. Grate acknowledges are assured. In last, authors are thanks to Mr. S.K. Jain for The Jain Brothers, New Delhi; give us a opportunity to publish this important book in the favor of student's keen interest.

(SURESH CHANDRA)

Date: 10th April, 2026

Place: Meerut

MPPSC Food Safety Officer Syllabus 2025

UNIT-I :

1. Phenols
2. Aldehydes
3. Ketones
4. Carboxylic acids
5. Nitro compounds and amines
6. Chemical bonds and forces
7. Concept of pH and buffer
8. Thermochemistry
9. Chemical equilibrium
10. Different methods of purification
11. Qualitative and quantitative analysis
12. Solutions-concentration terms
13. Liquid-properties surface tension
14. Viscosity and its applications
15. Chemical kinetics
16. Aliphatic and Aromatic hydrocarbons-concept of aromaticity
17. Methods of preparation and chemical properties of alcohols
18. Surface chemistry-adsorption homogeneous and heterogeneous catalysis colloids and suspension\

UNIT-II :

1. Some important food spoilage microorganisms
2. Fermentation-definition and types
3. Microorganisms used in food fermentation
4. Dairy fermentation
5. Fermented foods-types
6. Methods of manufacture for vinegar
7. Sauerkraut
8. Soya sauce
9. Types of microorganism associated with food their morphology and structure
10. Factors affecting their growth
11. Microbiological standards
12. Sources of microorganisms in food
13. Beer
14. Wine and traditional Indian foods

UNIT-III:

1. Metabolism and calorific value
2. Enzymes-classification
3. Kinetics factors controlling enzyme activities
4. Enzymes used during food processing
5. Modification of food by endogenous enzymes
6. Vitamins and their types
7. Biomolecules – carbohydrates
8. Proteins
9. Lipids and nucleic acids
10. Their classification
11. Structure
12. Biosynthesis
13. Minerals-important minerals and their functions in the human body
14. Plant alkaloids and their uses
15. Animal and plant toxins
16. Toxic substances and their metabolism-pesticides
17. Metals food additives

UNIT-IV :

1. Respiration-respiratory pigment transport and gaseous exchange
2. Excretion-structure of kidney and urine formation
3. Circulatory system-Heart Blood vascular system blood and its components
4. Nervous system conduction of impulses
5. Muscular system types of muscles and muscle contraction
6. Reproductive system Endocrine system hormones and their role
7. Classification-five kingdom system up to phylum plants and animal products used as food by a human
8. Culture of animals used as a food
9. Eukaryotic and Prokaryotic cells
10. Types of cells animal tissues and organs
11. Human physiology-Nutrition and Digestion
12. Immune system-types of immunity antigen-antibody reaction
13. Diseases-deficiency diseases communicable diseases and diseases caused by animals (protozoan's helminths arthropods)

UNIT – V :

1. Environmental bio technology-pollutants
2. Standard deviation
3. Regression and correlation
4. T-test variance
5. Biomagnification and microbial bioremediation
6. Statistical analysis-mean
7. Genetically modified plants and animals
8. Plant and animal tissue culture and its application
9. Importance of GM-crops and their products
10. Median
11. Mode

UNIT-VI :

1. Horticultural crops (Citrus, Mango, Guava, Ber, Onion, Tomato, Cucurbits, Chilli, Rose, etc.)
2. Spices and Medicinal crops Cumin, Fenugreek, Fennel, Coriander, Isabgol, Aloe vera
3. Salient features of agriculture with special reference to Rajasthan
4. Soil Fertility and Management of Problematic Soils in Rajasthan
5. Introduction to Dryland Farming and Agro-forestry
6. Introductory knowledge about Production Techniques of important field crops (Wheat, Mustard
7. Groundnut, Pulses, Bajra, and Maize)
8. Important diseases and Pests of major Crops and their Management
9. Importance of agriculture marketing
10. General awareness about Seed science and Crop Physiology

UNIT-VII :

1. Laboratory diagnostics
2. Important diseases of livestock and their management
3. Present status of Milk and Milk Products
4. Milk production and quality of milk
5. Importance of Livestock in Economy of Rajasthan
6. Fundamentals of Livestock and Poultry Production
7. Artificial insemination and pregnant animal management
8. Milk processing and packaging
9. Dairy equipment and utility Introduction to livestock products

UNIT-VIII :

1. Postharvest Physiology and handling of fruits and vegetables
2. Types and functions of Packaging materials used in fresh and processed food
3. Food laws -a brief review of regulatory status in India (FPO Prevention of Food adulteration Act Food
4. Safety and Standard Act Testing Food for its Safety AGMARK)
5. Present status of Food Technology in India and Rajasthan
6. General methods of food preservation and food processing
7. Importance of Postharvest technology of fruits and vegetables
8. Technology for processed products like Squash Jelly Sauce Pickles
9. Hygiene and Sanitation HACCP Good Manufacturing Practices Good Laboratory Practices

UNIT-IX :

1. The emergence of Modern MP: factors of Socio-Political awakening of 19th century
2. Peasants and tribal movements of 20th century
3. Pre & Early history of MP
4. Age of Raj put Major dynasties of MP and the achievements of prominent rulers
5. The political struggle of the 20th century and the integration of Rajasthan

UNIT-X :

1. Performing Art of MP -Folk music and musical instruments of MP
2. Visual Art of MP-Architecture of forts and temples of MP
3. Sculpture traditions of MP and various schools of painting of MP
4. Folk dance and folk drama of MP

UNIT-XI :

1. Various religious cults
2. Saints and folk deities of MP
3. Various dialects and their distribution in MP literature of the MP language

UNIT-XII :

1. Droughts & Floods
2. Deforestation
3. Environmental Pollution and Ecological Concerns
4. Climate and Agro-climatic regions
5. Major soil types and distribution
6. Major forest types and distribution
7. Broad physical features-Mountains
8. Plateaus Plains & Desert
9. Major rivers and lakes
10. Demographic characteristics
11. Desertification

UNIT-XIII :

1. Major agro-based industries-Textile Sugar Paper & Vegetable oil
2. Poverty and Unemployment
3. Agro-food parks
4. Major Minerals-Metallic & Non-Metallic
5. Power Resources-Renewable and Non-Renewable

UNIT-XIV :

1. National and International events of importance
2. National and International Organisations- (BIS ICMR ICAR Council for Social Welfare APEDA Export inspection Council FAO WHO ISO WTO)
3. Important Persons
4. Places and Current events of the State

SYLLABUS (UP)

The competitive examination comprises two successive stages viz:-

Paper-I General Studies	**75 Questions**	**150 Marks**	**01 Hour**	**9.30A.M. to 10.30A.M.**
Paper-II Main Subject	**125 Questions**	**250 Marks**	**02 Hours**	**2.30 P.M. to 4.30 P.M.**

Personality Test will be of 50 marks.

This test will relate to the matter of General Interest keeping in view of general awareness, intelligence, character, personality, expression power and general suitability for the service.

The paper of General Studies will include questions on the following topics:-

1. General Science
2. Current Events of National and International Importance
3. History of India
4. Indian National Movement
5. Indian Polity and Economy
6. World Geography and Population.

Question on **General Science** will cover general appreciation and understanding of Science, including matters of everyday observation and experience, as may be expected of a well educated person who has not made a special study of any scientific discipline.

In History of India emphasis should be on broad understanding of economic, Social, Cultural and Political aspects of Indian History. In Indian National Movement, the candidates are expected to have a synoptic view of the nature and character of the Indian freedom movement, growth of nationalism and attainment of Independence. In Indian Polity and Economy questions will test knowledge of the candidate pertaining to Indian Polity including the Indian Constitution, Panchayati Raj and community Development, broad features of Indian economy and planning. In world geography and population, only General understanding of the subject will be expected with emphasis on physical/ecological, economic and socio-demographic aspects of Geography of India.

Candidates are expected to have general awareness about the above topics with special reference to Uttar Pradesh.

The paper of **main subject** will include questions on the following topics:-

Desirable and Potentially undesirable food constituents and their importance. Water, Carbohydrates, Lipids, Proteins, Vitamins, Minerals: Classes, Nomenclature, structure and their chemistry.

Enzymes: Nomenclature, Classification and specificity of enzymes, enzyme Kinetics, enzymes and their role in modification of foods. Single cell protein (SCP). Metabolic Pathways: Carbohydrates, proteins and fats, catabolism and anabolism, Digestion and absorption, Assimilation and Transport of nutrients in human beings.

General characteristics of microorganism: Classification, morphology, physiology, growth, nutrition and reproduction; Pure culture techniques and maintenance of cultures, control of microorganism. Sources of contamination. Microbiological standards of foods. Food poisoning and food borne infections, Food toxins, food plant sanitation, inspection and control, personnel hygiene, beneficial microorganisms and their utilization in food fermentation.

Balance diet, Recommended Dietary Allowances (RDA), Dietary utilization and disturbances, Functions and energy values of foods, Basal energy metabolism: BV, NPU, BMR, PER calculations, Protein quality as reference protein. Dietary allowances and standards for different age groups, Techniques for assessment of human nutritional status, Causes and preventions of malnutrition. Biochemical, clinical manifestation & preventive measures due to vitamins deficiency. Diseases caused due to food adulteration.

Basic knowledge of major Indian crops, their total production, losses in storage, storage of perishable and non-perishable foods, Storage requirements: Storage environment and its interaction with stored product; temperature and moisture migration. Storage practices (including fumigation and aeration of stored product). Storage structures for Perishable and non perishables: bulk storage structures (bins and silos) Modified and Controlled atmosphere storage systems.

Technology of fruits and vegetable products: Juices, pulp, Puree, Paste, Ketchup, Sauce, soup, concentrates and powders, Squashes and cordials. Beverage: Still and carbonated. James, Jellies and Marmalades. Preserves, candies and crystallized fruits.

Processing of oilseeds Pretreatments of oilseeds, oil milling, solvent extraction, impurities present in oils and fats. Vegetable oil refining, hydrogenation, enter esterification, processing of de-oiled cake into protein products, textured protein. Peanut butter, Margarine and Spread. Different quality parameters: Peroxide value, Saponification value, Iodine value, acid value, RM value, Polanski value, Adulteration and its detection in oils and fats. Rancidity, auto oxidation and anti-oxidants.

Fluid Milk: Physico-chemical properties, Production and collection, cooling and transportation of milk. Clarification and filtration of milk, pasteurized and homogenized milk.: Whole, Standardized, Toned, Double toned, skim and special milks, Test for milk quality and detection of dairy adulterant. Milk products: cream, butter, Butter oil/Ghee, Cheeses, Curd and Yoghurt, Sweet meat, Ice cream. Evaporated and Condensed milk, milk powders. Indian Dairy Products, Manufacture of casein, and Lactose. Causes and prevention of defects in dairy products.

Scientific slaughtering, Tendering and curing of meat, Beef Mutton, Pork Sausages and other meat products. Fish and poultry processing. Physical, Chemical Nutritional and Functional characteristics of Egg. Processing of Egg and egg products.

Principle underlying spoilage and preservation of foods: Low and high temperature, drying and dehydration, chemical, salt and sugar, Radiation, HHP, hurdle technology,

Parboiling and Milling of paddy, Quality characteristics, Curing and aging of rice. Processed rice products. Wheat milling into flour and semolina, Flour grades and their suitability for baking purposes, Flour quality, Macaroni products, Baked products: Bread, Biscuits and cakes, Breakfast cereals. Dry and Wet milling of corn, Starches and its conversion products, Malting of barely, beer, wine, cider, vinegar, Milling of legume-pulses.

Spices: Composition, Structure and characteristics. Preservation and processing of spices, Processing of Tea and coffee, cocoa processing, chocolate and confectionary products.

Concept of food packaging, polymeric, glass, metal packaging materials, Aseptic Packaging. Newer trends, Package printing, Packaging Laws and Regulations, Evaluation of food packaging materials and package performance.

Quality Control/Quality Assurance, Legislation for food safety: National and International criteria, sampling, records, risk analysis and management. Microbial contamination, Nutritional imbalance. Pesticide residues, permitted food additives. Relevant Foods laws: PFA, FPO, SWMA, MPO, AG Mark, and BIS Standards. Food Safety and Standard Act (FSSA). Testing food for its safety. The HACCP system and food Safety management systems used in Controlling microbiological hazards. Food standards and Specifications, NABL and ISO certification requirements.

Contents

Chapter 1

Role of Food Safety Officer

MINISTRY OF LAW AND JUSTICE (Legislative Department) New Delhi, the 24th August, 2006 Bhadra 2, 1928 (Saka)

The following Act of Parliament received the assent of the President on 23rd August, 2006, and is hereby published for general information:-

FOOD SAFETY AND STANDARDS ACT, 2006

No. 34 OF 2006

[23rd August, 2006]

An Act to consolidate the laws relating to food and to establish the Food Safety and Standards Authority of India for laying down science based standards for articles of food and to regulate their manufacture, storage, distribution, sale and import, to ensure availability of safe and wholesome food for human consumption and for matters connected therewith or incidental thereto.

Food Safety Officer

1. The Commissioner of Food Safety shall, by notification, appoint such persons as he thinks fit, having the qualifications prescribed by the Central Government, as Food Safety Officers for such local areas as he may assign to them for the purpose of performing functions under this Act and the rules and regulations made there-under.
2. The State Government may authorize any officer of the State Government having the qualifications prescribed under sub-section (1) to perform the functions of a Food Safety Officer within a specified jurisdiction.

Powers of Food Safety Officer

1. The Food Safety Officer may –

a. take a sample –

i. of any food, or any substance, which appears to him to be intended for sale, or to have been sold for human consumption; or

ii. of any article of food or substance which is found by him on or in any such premises; which he has reason to believe that it may be required as evidence in proceedings under any of the provisions of this Act or of the regulations or orders made thereunder; or

(*b*) seize any article of food which appears to the Food Safety Officer to be in contravention of this Act or the regulations made thereunder; and

(*c*) keep it in the safe custody of the food business operator such article of food after taking a sample; and in both cases send the same for analysis to a Food Analyst for the local area within which such sample has been taken:

Provided that where the Food Safety Officer keeps such article in the safe custody of the food business operator, he may require the food business operator to execute a bond for a sum of money equal to the value of such article with one or more sureties as the Food Safety Officer deems fit and the food business operator shall execute the bond accordingly.

2. The Food Safety Officer may enter and inspect any place where the article of food is manufactured, or stored for sale, or stored for the manufacture of any other article of food, or exposed or exhibited for sale and where any adulterant is manufactured or kept, and take samples of such articles of food or adulterant for analysis.
3. Where any sample is taken, its cost calculated at the rate at which the article is usually sold to the public shall be paid to the person from whom it is taken.
4. Where any article of food seized under clause (b) of subsection (1) is of a perishable nature and the Food Safety Officer is satisfied that such article of food is so deteriorated that it is unfit for human consumption, the Food Safety Officer may, after giving notice in writing to the food business operator, cause the same to be destroyed.
5. The Food Safety Officer shall, in exercising the powers of entry upon, and inspection of any place under this section, follow, as far as may be, the provisions of the Code of Criminal Procedure, 1973 (2 of 1974) relating to the search or inspection of a place by a police officer executing a search warrant issued under that Code.
6. Any adulterant found in the possession of a manufacturer or distributor of, or dealer in, any article of food or in any of the premises occupied by him as such and for the possession of which he is unable to account to the satisfaction of the Food Safety Officer and any books of account or other documents found in his possession or control and which would be useful for, or relevant to, any investigation or proceeding under this Act, may be seized by the Food Safety Officer and a sample of such adulterant submitted for analysis to a Food Analyst:

   Provided that no such books of account or other documents shall be seized by the Food Safety Officer except with the previous approval of the authority to which he is subordinate.
7. Where the Food Safety Officer takes any action under clause (a) of sub-section (1), or sub-section (2), or sub-section (4) or sub-section (6), he shall, call one or more persons to be present at the time when such action is taken and take his or their signatures.
8. Where any books of account or other documents are seized under sub-section (6), the Food Safety Officer shall, within a period not exceeding thirty days from the date of seizure, return the same to the person from whom they were seized after copies thereof or extracts there from as certified by that person in such manner as may be prescribed by the Central Government have been taken:

   Provided that where such person refuses to so certify and a prosecution has been instituted against him under this Act, such books of account or other documents shall be returned to him only after copies thereof and extracts there from as certified by the court have been taken.
9. When any adulterant is seized under sub-section (6), the burden of proving that such adulterant is not meant for purposes of adulteration shall be on the person from whose possession such adulterant was seized.
10. The Commissioner of Food Safety may from time to time issue guidelines with regard to exercise of powers of the Food Safety Officer, which shall be binding:

    Provided that the powers of such Food Safety Officer may also be revoked for a specified period by the Commissioner of Food Safety.

Chapter 2

Role of Food Standards

Prevention of Food Adulteration Act, 1954

The size of the food industry in India is worth more than Rs.250, 000 crore and accounts for 26 percent of the GDP. This makes it far larger than entire manufacturing sector. With an increase in the population, it is forecasted that the food processing industry shall be one of the major growing areas in India, in the years ahead. Therefore, it is incumbent that any government should control and ensure the supply of hygienic, wholesomeness and nutritious food lest it may become a source of ill health to human beings. With this in view, the government of India enacted the Prevention of Food Adulteration Act, 1954 and rules were framed under it. The act and rules have been undergone several changes during 57 years and more than 200 amendments have been made. These cover the standards of various foods, the restrictions on the type and quantity of pesticide residues, use of food additives in addition to the procedures for the working of food enforcement staff and other regulatory authorities. In addition to the Prevention of Food Adulteration (PFA) Act, There are other laws enacted time to time in India are as follows:

- Essential Commodities Act, 1955
- Standards of Weights and Measures Act, 1976
- Consumer Protection Act, 1986
- Agricultural Produce Grading and Marketing Act, 1973 (APGM)
- Indian Standards Institution Act, 1952 as amended (ISI),
- Bureau of Indian Standard Act, 1986
- Fruit and Vegetables Products Order (FPO)
- Meat Food Products Order (MFPO)
- Milk and Milk Products Order (MMPO)
- Solvent Extracted Vegetable Oils Control Order

Consumer Protection Act 1986

This act protect the interest of consumers and help in for the settlement of disputes of the consumers with the service provider or product manufacturer / provider.

Rights of consumers

1. Right to the service and quality of product, 2. Right to choose, 3. Right to be informed, 4. Right to safety, 5. Right to be heard, 6. Right to seek compensation

Role of the developmental agencies in ensuring food quality and safety

APEDA: Agricultural and Processed Food Export Development Authority (Ministry of Commerce and Industry) HQ. New Delhi (1985) came into effect on 13th Feb., 1986.

- Promote export of Agricultural and Processed Foods
- Overcome various constraints inhibiting export growth
- Undertake special export promotion efforts
- Safeguard Intellectual Property Rights
- Financial assistance for food safety measures
- Rewards for achievements
- Issuance of certificate for export as per schedule

MPEDA: Marine Product Export Development Authority (Ministry of Commerce and Industry) HQ. Kochi (1972)

- Promote export of Marine Products
- Provide Training in safe handling of Marine Product
- Overcome various constraints inhibiting export growth including quality issues
- Undertake special export promotion efforts of marine products
- Financial assistance for food safety measures
- Identification and mapping of marine products
- Quality product promotion growth through international fair and online trading

BIS: Bureau of Indian Standards : HQ- New Delhi (1986)

- Formulating standards and guidelines
- Ensuring the quality and safety of products
- Ensuring the quality and safety of food products under compulsory certification
- Product certification
- Quality systems certification
- Contact point for WTO matters

EICI: Export Inspection Council of India. HQ- New Delhi (1963)

- India's official export certification body
- Notify commodities for pre shipment quality control and inspection
- Establish quality standards for above
- Certification of quality of export items via inspection, quality control and self certification
- Issue certificate for origin and health
- Mutual agreements for equivalence

AGMARK: Agricultural Marketing: AGMARK is a certification mark employed on agricultural products in India, assuring that confirm to set standards approved by the Directorate of Marketing and Inspection an agency of GoI. Certifying Agency Directorate of M&I (Ministry of Agricultural and Farmers Welfare) Central Agmark laboratory at Nagpur. Agmark enforced in India by act in 1937 and amended in 1987. The present AGMARK Standards cover quality guidelines for 224 different commodities.

- System of post harvest grading of agriculture produce
- Product quality certification
- Ensuring safety of products
- Network of quality control laboratories
- Ensuring quality of imported products
- Assist in marketing and fair trade practices

FPO: Fruit Product Order (1955)

- Establish quality and safety standards
- Certification and monitoring the quality of notify products under order
- Ensuring Good Handling Practice (GHP) and Good Manufacturing Practice (GMP)
- Promotion of quality systems- HACCP
- Financial assistance for installing quality systems
- Promotion of Research and Developments (R&D)

MMPO: Milk and Milk Product Order (1972)

- Issue license for dairy industry
- Ensuring minimum hygienic practices in dairy industry
- Continuous monitoring of Good Manufacturing Practice (GMP)
- Regular inspection of dairy industry
- Safe Handling, Storage and Transport of dairy products

MFPO: Meat Food Product Order (1973)

- Establish quality and safety standards for meat products
- Ensuring minimum hygienic practices in meat industry
- Continuous monitoring of Good Manufacturing Practice (GMP)
- Regular inspection of meat industry
- Safe slaughtering, handling, storage and transport of meat products

NHB: National Horticultural Board (Ministry of Agriculture and Farmers Welfare) (1984) HQ : Gurugram

- Promote productivity of horticultural produces
- Ensure measures to reduce post harvest losses
- Production of processable varieties
- Overcome various constraints inhibiting production and marketing of horticultural produces
- Undertake special export promotion efforts
- Development of high tech commercial horticulture.

Spices Board (Ministry of Commerce and Industry) 1987

- Quality certification and control
- Promote productivity of spices
- New product developments
- Ensure measures to reduce post harvest losses
- Production of process able varieties and quality upgradation.
- Overcome various constraints inhibiting production and marketing of spices
- Post harvest improvement of all spices

Coffee Board (Ministry of Commerce and Industry) HQ: Bengaluru (1942)

- Establish quality and safety standards for coffee
- Promote productivity of coffee
- New product developments
- Ensure measures to reduce post harvest losses
- Production of process able varieties
- Overcome various constraints inhibiting production and marketing of coffee
- Undertake special export promotion efforts

Coconut Development Board (Ministry of Agri. and Farmers Welfare) 1981 Kochi

- Establish quality and safety standards for coconut
- Promote productivity of coconut
- New product developments
- Ensure measures to reduce post harvest losses
- Production of process able varieties
- Overcome various constraints inhibiting production and marketing of coconut
- Undertake special export promotion efforts

NBB: National Bee Board Ministry of Agriculture and Farmers Welfare, New Delhi (2000)

National Bee Board has taken following initiatives:

- Promotion of scientific beekeeping in the country.
- Setting up of Integrated Beekeeping Development Centres
- (IDBCs)/Centres of Excellences (CoEs)
- Registration of Beekeepers.
- Facilitation of SHGs of beekeepers
- Also, Integrated Development of Scientific Beekeeping (IDSB) Programme has been proposed under RKVY

QCI: Quality Council of India New Delhi 1997

- Apex body to establish national accreditation
- Promote, coordinate, guide and implement a national quality building confidence in Indian product and service
- NABCEB-for certification bodies
- NABAT- for auditors training
- NABL- for laboratory accreditation

NABL: National Accreditation Board for Testing and Calibration Laboratories (A Constituent Board of Quality Council of India) 1992

- NCTCF- National co-ordination of testing & calibration facilities (1982) – NABL (1992)
- Testing Laboratories as per ISO/IEC 17025 : 2005
- Calibration Laboratories as per ISO/IEC 17025 : 2005
- Medical Laboratories as per ISO 15189 : 2012
- Proficiency Testing Providers (PTP) as per ISO/IEC 17043
- Reference Material Producers (RMP) as per ISO 17034
- Certified laboratories under Section 43(1) of FSS Act, 2006

Chapter 3

Specification of Food Products

Table 1: Products prepared from fruits and vegetables

S. No.	*Name of fruit/ vegetable*	*Products prepared*
		Fruits
1	Aonla	Preserve, jam, candy, syrup, pickle, chutney, dried shreds, triphala, chyawanprash
2	Apple	Jam, preserve, juice, chutney, cider
3	Apricot	Jam, chutney, canned and dried apricot
4	Banana	Canned banana, dried banana, toffee
5	Bael	Preserve, nector, squash, canned bael, cider
6	Ber	Candy, preserve, canned ber, jam
7	Citrus fruits	Juice, pickle, marmalade, squash, cordial, barley water, candy
8	Cherry	Jam, candy, canned cherry, dried cherry
9	Date	Dried
10	Guava	Jelly, cheese, toffee, nector, canned guava, squash, vinegar
11	Grape	Wine, juice, raisin, munakka
12	Jamun	Jelly, syrup, vinegar
13	Jackfruit	Pickle
14	Karonda	Pickle, jelly, candy, preserve
15	Litchi	Juice, syrup, canned litchi
16	Loquat	Jam, jelly, canned loquat
17	Mango	Juice, RTS, nector, squash, jam, toffee, pickle, amchur, chutney, canned mango, mango powder, mango concentrate, preserve, ampapad
18	Mulberry	Juice, squash
19	Papaya	Jam, candy, nectar, pickle, sauce, canned papaya, papain
20	Peach	Jam, chutney, canned and dried peach
21	Pomegranate	Juice, squash, syrup, anardana (dried product)
22	Pineapple	Canned pineapple, juice, squash, syrup, jam
23	Plum	Jam, chutney, sauce, dried plum
24	Strawberry	Jam, juice

	Vegetables
1 Ash gourd (Petha)	Candy
2 Beans	Canned and dried beans
3 Beetroot	Pickle, canned beat root
4 Bitter gourd	Pickle, dried bitter gourd, juice
5 Brinjal	Pickle
6 Carrot	Jam, preserve, pickle, candy, canned carrot
7 Cabbage	Sauerkraut, dried cabbage
8 Cucumber	Pickle,
9 Garlic	Pickle, powder, paste
10 Ginger	Pickle, preserve, candy, dried ginger, paste, RTS, syrup
11 Green chilli	Pickle, paste
12 Musk melon	Juice, squash
13 Mushroom	Pickle, sauce, canned mushroom, dried mushroom powder
14 Onion	Pickle, dried onion, salad
15 Potato	Chips, french-fries, finger chips, papad, starch, canned potato, salad
16 Pointed gourd (Parwal)	Canned and dried parwal
17 Radish	Pickle, salad
18 Spinach	Canned spinach
19 Turnip	Pickle, canned and dried turnip
20 Watermelon	Juice, squash

Table 2: Different types of microbial contaminants founds in fruits and vegetables

Foods	*Types of spoilage*	*Microorganism involved*
Bread	Moldy	*Rhizopus nigricans, Penicillium, Aspergillus niger*
Syrups	Ropy	*Bacillus subtilis, Enterobacter aerogenes,*
	Yeasty	*Saccharomyces, Zygosaccharomyces*
	Pink	*Micrococcus roseus*
	Moldy	*Penicillium, Aspergillus*
Fresh fruits and vegetables	Soft rot	*Rhizopus, Erwinia*
	Gray mold rot	*Botrytis*
	Black mold rot	*Aspergillus niger*
Pickles	Film yeast and pink yeast	*Rhodotorula*
Fresh meat	Putrefaction	*Alcaligenes, Clostridium, Proteus vulgaris, Pseudomonas flourescens*
Fish	Moldy	*Penicillium, Aspergillus, Rhizopus*
	Souring	*Pseudomonas, Micrococcus*
	Greening, slime	*Lactobacillus, Leuconostoc*
	Disclouration	*Pseudomonas*
	Putrefaction	*Alcaligenes, Flavobacterium*
Eggs	Green rot	*Pseudomonas flourescens*
	Colourless rots	*Pseudomonas, Alcaligenes*
	Black rots	*Proteus*
Concentrated orange juice	Off flavor	*Lactobacillus, Leuconostoc, Acetobacter*
Poultry	Slime, odour	*Pseudomonas, Alcaligenes*

Table 3: Regulatory standard for permitted artificial sweeteners

Food article	*Maximum limit of artificial sweetener (ppm)*				*Regulatory body*
	Aspartame	*Acesulfame-K*	*Saccharin*	*Sucralose*	
Sweet (carbohydrates based and milk products based): halwa, mysore pak, Boondi ladoo, jalebi, khoa burfi, peda, gulabjamun, rasgolla and similar product based sweets sold by any name	200	500	500	750	PFA, 2004
Dairy based drinks, flavored and/or fermented (*e.g.* chocolate milk, cocoa, eggnog)	600	500	400	300	CODEX, 2005 (draft standards
Dairy based desserts (*e.g.* ice cream, ice milk, pudding, fruit or flavored yoghurt)	3000	1000	100	250	CODEX, 2005 (draft standards)

Table 4: Some of the microorganisms responsible for the production of fermented foods

Fermented product	*Microorganisms responsible*	*Description*
Sour cream	*Streptococcu sp., Leuconostoc sp.*	Cream is inoculated and incubated until the desired acidity develops.
Cultured butter milk	*Streptococcu sp., Leuconostoc sp.*	Made with skimmed or partly skimmed pasteurized.
Bulgarian butter milk	*Lactobacillus bulgaricus*	Product differs from commercial butter milk in having higher acidity and lacking aroma.
Acidophilus milk	*Lactobacillus acidophilus*	Milk for propagation of *L. acidophilus* and the milk to be fermented are sterilized and then inoculated with *L. acidophilus.* This milk product is used for its medicinal therapeutic value.
Yoghurt	*Streptococcus thermophilis* *Lactobacillus bulgaricus*	Made from milk in which solids are concentrated by evaporation of some water and addition of skim milk solids. Product has consistency resembling custard.
Kefir	*Streptococcus lactis* *Lactobacillus bulgaricus* Yeast	A mixed lactic acid and alcoholic fermentation: bacteria produce acid and yeast produce alcohol.

Table 5: Chemical composition of Ghee

Constituents	*Cow ghee*	*Buffalo ghee*
Fat, %	99-99.5	99-99.5
Moisture, %	<0.5	<0.5
Carotene, mg/g	3.2-7.4	-
Vitamin A, IU/g	19-34	17-38
Cholesterol, mg/100g	302-362	209-312
Tocopherols, mg/g	26-48	18-31
Free fatty acid, %	2.8	2.8

Table 6: Physico-chemical characteristics of ghee

S. No.	*Parameters*	*Cow ghee*	*Buffalo ghee*
1.	RM Value	26.7	32.3
2.	Polenske value	1.76	1.41
3.	Iodine Number	33.7	29.4
4.	Butryorefractometer reading	42.3	42.0
5.	Saponification Number	227.3	230.0
6.	Kirscher Value	22.1	28.4
7.	Melting Point, °C	28-41	32-43
8.	Refractive Index at 60 °C	1.4465	-
9.	Specific Gravity at 60 °C	0.887	0.887
10.	Unsaponifiable matter, %	0.4	-
11.	Smoking Point, °C	20.8	

Table 7: The common organic acids used in food preservation, their occurrence and action

S. No.	*Organic acids*	*Occurrence*	*Action*
1.	Benzoic acid	Raspberries, Can berries, plum	Antifungal agent, prevent amino acid uptake by microbial cells
2.	Citric acid	Citrus fruits	Lowers pH, chelates metals ions, interferes with glucose utilization in cell walls
3.	Lactic acid	Lactic acid bacteria	Spores inhibitors below pH 5.0, lower pH of the system
4.	Maleic acid	Apple, tamarind	Multifunctional additives
5.	Propionic acid	Swiss cheese	Mold inhibitors

Table 8: Relative sweetness of some intensively sweet substances

Artificial sweetener	*Relative value (sucrose = 1, wt. basis)*
Acesulfame-K	200
Advantame	2000
Alitame	2000
Aspartame	180-200
Brazzein (Natural)*	500-2000
Cyclamate	30
Glycyrrhizin	50-100
Monellin (Natural)**	1500-3000
Neohesperidin dihydrochalcone	1600-2000
Neotame (Newest) $CO_2H_3N_2O_5$	7000-13000 (Approved in 2010 for use in foods)
Saccharine	300-400
Stevioside (Stevia)	300
Sucralose	600-800
Thaumatin (Natural Sweetener)***	1600-3000
Thevmatin	1600-2000

*Brazzein is generally GRAS (Fruit derived) **Monellin is found in berry plant

***Thaumatin is found in fruits of Katemfe plant

Table 9: Analytical values of some fats and oils:

Fats/ oils	*Sapon. Number (mg KOH/g)*	*Iodine value (g I_2/100 g)*	*RM Number*	*Acetal Number*	*Acid value (mg KOH/g)*
		Animal fat			
Halibut liver oil	170-180	120-135	-	-	1.0
Cod liver oil	180-190	140-180	-	-	0.5-5.0
Human fat	194-198	65-69	0.4	-	-
Lard	195-203	47-66	0.5-0.8	2.6	-
Beef fat	196-200	35-42	-	2.7-8.6	-
Butter	210-230	25-40	17-35	1.9-8.6	0.5-3.0
Cow's milk	216-235	26-45	-	-	-
		Vegetable fat			
Castor oil	175-187	80-90	1.4	146-150	0.2-4.0
Corn oil	187-195	104-128	-	-	1.0-2.0
Linseed oil	188-195	170-195	1.0	4.0	1.04-4.0
Olive oil	190-195	80-90	0.6-1.5	10-11	0.2-3.0
Coconut oil	254-262	7-10	0.6-7.5	2.0	2.5-6.0

Table 10: The iodine number of common oils or fats

S. No.	*Fats or oils*	*Iodine number*
1.	Coconut oil	7-10
2.	Butter	25-28
3.	Palm oil	45-55
4.	Olive oil	80-85
5.	Ground nut oil	85-100
6.	Cotton seed oil	100-110
7.	Sunflower oil	125-135
8.	Linseed oil	175-200

Table 11: Maximum levels of some GRAS chemical food preservatives permitted in foods

Preservatives	*Maximum concentrations allowed*	*Organisms affected*	*Foods*
Benzoic acids	0.1%	Yeasts and molds	Jams, jellies, salad dressings, apple cider, soft drinks, pickles, tomato catsup
Propionic acid	0.32%	Molds	Bread, cakes, Swiss cheese
Sorbic acid	0.2%	Molds and yeast	Hard cheeses, baked goods, fruit cocktails, syrups, fruit juices, jams and jellies, dried fruits, margarine
Nitrites and nitrates	100-120 ppm	Clostridia and molds	Meat and meat products as a meat curing agent
Nisin (bio-preservative)	100 ppm	Gram+ve spore formers	Processed cheeses, canned fruits and vegetables, condensed milk

Table 12: Yeasts causing food spoilage

S. No.	*Yeast*	*Product spoiled*
1	*Brettanomyces*	Beers and wines
2	*Candida*	High acid foods, salty foods, butter
3	*Debaryomyces*	Meat brine, cheese, sausages, etc.
4	*Hansenula*	Beers
5	*Hanseniospora*	Fruits juices
6	*Pichia*	Wines
7	*Rhodotorula*	Meat, sauerkraut
8	*Saccharomyces*	Low-sugar products
9	*Trichosporon*	Chilled beer
10	*Torulopsis*	Milk products, fruit juices, acid foods
11	*Zygosaccharomyces*	Honey, syrups, molasses, wines, soy sauce
12.	*Saccharomyces cerevisiae*[*]	Maple syrup or sugar rich foods.
13.	*Pichia Kudriavzevii*	Kimchi drink

[*] Fermenting yeasts, such as *Saccharomyces*, *Zygosaccharomyces* and *Debaromyces* species, convert fruit sugars to ethanol, causing a variety of off-aromas.

Table 13: Minimum water activity (a_w) for growth of microorganisms

S. No.	*Microorganisms*	*Minimum water activity (a_w)*
1	Bacteria	0.91
2	Halophilic bacteria	0.75
3	Moulds	0.80
4	Osmophilic	0.60
5	Xerophilic fungi	0.65
6	Yeasts	0.88

Table 14: Summary of different food spoilages and their causative organisms

Disease	**Causal organism**
Ropiness in bread	***Bacillus subtilis***/ *B. licheniformis*/ *B. mesentricus*
Bacterial soft rot	*Erwinia carotovora*
Mold rot	*Rhizopus, Botrytis*
Blue mold rot	*Penicillum digitatum*
Anthracnose	*Colletotrichum*
Greening of sausage	Peroxides produced by heterofermentative lactic acid bacteria
Surface slime	Lactic acid bacteria, *Pseudomonas etc.*
Phosphorescence	*Photorhabdus, Photobacterium*
Red spot in meat	*Serratia marcescens*
Musty flavour of meat	Actinomycetes
Yellow pigmentation of meat	*Flavobacterium, Micrococcus*
Black spots of meat	*Cladosporium herbarum*
White spots of meat	*Sporotrichum carnis*
Whiskers in meat	*Thamnidium chaetocladioides*
Green patches in meat	*Penicillium expansum*
Green rot of egg	*Pseudomonas fluorescens*
Black rot of egg	*Proteus* sp. and *Cladosporium* sp.
Pink rot of egg	*Pseudomonas* sp. and *Sporotrichum* sp.
Red rot of egg	*Serratia* sp.
Hay odour in eggs	*Enterobacter cloacae*
Fishy flavours in eggs	*Escherichia coli*
Ropiness in milk	*Alcaligenes viscolactis*
Soapiness in milk	Ammonia producers like *Pseudomonas sapolactica*
Fishiness in milk	*Aeromonas hydrophila*
Blue Milk	*Pseudomonas syncyanea*
Yellow Milk	*Pseudomonas synxantha*
Red Milk	*Brevibacterium erythrogenes*
Brown Milk	*Pseudomonas putrefaciens*
Black smudge in butter	*Pseudomonas nigrificans*
Flat Sour Spoilage in canned foods	*Bacillus coagulans*
Sulfide spoilage	*Desulfatomaculum nigrificans*
TA spoilage (Thermophilic Anaerobe not producing H_2S)	*C. thermosaccharolyticum*

Table 15: Sugar quantity used to make syrup of different concentrations

Sugar (kg)	*Syrup concentration (%)**
0.250	20
0.333	25
0.428	30
0.538	35
0.666	40
0.818	45
1.000	50
1.222	55

*Dissolve in 1 litre of water

Table 16: Salt quantity used* to make brine of different concentrations

Salt (g)	*Brine concentration (%)**
10.00	1
20.40	2
30.92	3
41.66	4
47.33	5
111.11	10
176.47	15

*Dissolve in 1 litre of water

Table 17: Classification of fruits and vegetables according to pH value

Class	*pH*	*Product*
Low acid (non-acid)	Above 5.0	Vegetables such as peas, lima bean, asparagus, cauliflower, potato, spinach, beet, corn, French bean
Medium acid	4.5 – 5.0	Turnip, carrot, okra, cabbage, pumpkin, beet, green bean, etc. and products like soups and sauces
Acid	3.7 – 4.5	Tomato, pear, banana, mango, jackfruit, pineapple, sweet cherry, peach, apple, etc.
High acid	Below 3.7	Citrus juice, rhubarbe, prune, sauerkraut, pickles, chutney, etc.

Table 18: Standards of water for various products

Water characteristics	*Maximum tolerance limit (ppm)*		
	Canning	*Carbonated beverages*	*Beverages*
Turbidity	1	1	5
Colour	-	10	-
Taste and odour	None	None	None
Iron and manganese	0.2	0.3	0.1
Sulphates (as SO_4)	-	250	-
Chlorides (as Cl)	-	250	-
Alkalinity (as $CaCO_3$)	-	30-85	50
Hardness (as $CaCO_3$)	85	-	150
Total dissolved solids	-	850	500
Organic matter	-	None	None
Fluoride	1.0	1.0	1.0

Table 19: General standards of water for fruit and vegetable processing plants

Water characteristics	*Maximum tolerance limit (ppm)*	*Typical effect when in excess of maximum tolerance*
Turbidity	1 – 10	Deposits on product and equipment
Colour	5 – 10	Possible discolouration from organic matter
Taste and odour	Noticeable	Corresponding or intensified taste or odour in product
Iron and manganese	0.2 - 0.3	Staining, discolouration, off taste and possible growth of iron bacteria
Alkalinity	30 – 250	Neutralization of acid constituents, possible inhibition of bacteria action, deposits or white butts in ice
Hardness (as $CaCO_3$)	10 – 250	Deposits, absorption by some products, precipitation with alkaline constituents
Total dissolved solids	850	Perceptible taste and possible inhibition of chemical reduction
Organic matter	Generally any	Off-taste, sediment, spoilage, undesirable reactions
Fluoride	1.0	Mottling of tooth enamel in children

Table 20: FPO specifications for fruit and vegetable products

Product	*Specifications*	
Prepared from any suitable fruit and variety	*Minimum % of TSS in final product (w/w)*	*Minimum % of fruit juice or prepared fruit in final product (w/w)*
Barley water	30	25 (min % of barley starch 0.25)
Cordial	30	25
Crush	55	25
Fruit syrup	65	25
Fruit nectars (excluding orange and pineapple nectars)	15	20
Fruit juice concentrate	32	100
Fruit preserve	68	55
Fruit jelly and marmalade	65	45
Fruit chutney	50	40
Jam and fruit cheese	68	45
Mango nectar	15	20
Orange and pineapple hectors	15	40
RTS beverages including aerated water containing fruit juice	10	10
Sweetened juice	10	85
Synthetic syrup / sherbet (prepared from herbs, flowers or essences)	65	-
Unsweetened juice	Natural	100

Table 21: FPO specifications for candied and crystallized or glazed fruits

Product (Prepared from any suitable fruit and variety)	*Specifications*	
	Total Sugar (%)	Reducing sugar as % of total sugar
Candied and crystallized or glazed fruits and peel	Not less than 70	Not less than 25

Table 22: FPO Specifications for bottled or canned fruits and vegetables

S. No.	*Product*	*Specifications*
1	Bottled or canned fruits	(a) Head space in can shall not be more than 1.6 cm. (b) The drained weight of the fruit shall not be less than 50 % and the fruit should be firm. (c) No preservative shall be added. (d) No artificial colour shall be present / added. (e) The can shall not show any positive pressure at sea level and shall not show any sign of bacterial growth when incubated at 37°C for a week.
2	Bottled or canned vegetables	(a) Head space in can shall not be more than 1.6 cm. (b) The drained weight of the vegetable shall not be less than 55 % (50 % in case of tomatoes). (c) No preservative shall be added. (d) No artificial colour shall be present, except in case of peas where permitted colour may be added. (e) The can shall not show any positive pressure at sea level and shall not show any sign of bacterial growth when incubated at 37°C for a week.

Table 23: FPO specifications for tomato products

Product prepared from any suitable fruit and variety	*Minimum TSS (%)*	*Mould count*
Juice	5	Not in excess of 30 % of the field examined
Soup	7	
Puree	9	Not in excess of 60 % of the field examined
Paste	25	
Ketchup / Sauce	25 (min acidity as acetic acid 1.0%)	Not in excess of 40 % of the field examined. (Yeast and spores not in excess of 125 per 1/60 cc, bacteria not in excess of 100 million per cc)

Table 23a: Potential Chemical Indicators of Food Quality

Ammonia	Indole
Trimethylamine	Ethanol
Dimethylamine	Furfural
Total volatile bases	Hydrogen sulfide
Total volatile acids	Total reducing substances
Free fatty acids	Volatile reducing substances
Water insoluble acids (oleic, palmitic)	Histamine
Organic acids (acetic, lactic, pyruvic, succinic)	Hypoxanthine
	Diacetyl
	Acetylmethylcarbinol

Table 24: Permissible limits of preservatives used in food products

Food product	*Preservative*	*Parts per million (ppm)*
Fruit, fruit pulp or juice (not dried) for conversion into jam or crystallized, glazed or çured fruit or other products		
(i) Cherries	Sulphur dioxide	3000
(ii) Strawberries and raspberries	Sulphur dioxide	2000
(iii) Other fruits	Sulphur dioxide	1000
Fruit juice concentrate	Sulphur dioxide	1500
Dried fruits		
(i) Apricots, peaches, apples, pears and other fruits	Sulphur dioxide	2000
(ii) Raisins and sultanas	Sulphur dioxide	750
Squashes, crushes, fruit syrups, cordials, fruit juices and barley waters	Sulphur dioxide or Benzoic acid	350 600
Jam, marmalade, preserve, canned cherry and fruit jelly	Sulphur dioxide or Benzoic acid	40 200
Crystallized, glazed or cured fruit (including candied peel)	Sulphur dioxide	150
Fruit and fruit pulp not otherwise specified in the schedule	Sulphur dioxide	350
Sweetened RTS beverages	Sulphur dioxide or Benzoic acid	70 120
Pickles and chutneys made from fruits or vegetable	Sulphur dioxide or Benzoic acid	100 250
Tomato and other sauces	Benzoic acid	750
Dehydrated vegetables and dried ginger	Sulphur dioxide	2000
Tomato puree and paste	Benzoic acid	250
Syrups and sherbats	Sulphur dioxide or Benzoic acid	350 600
Cider	Sulphur dioxide	200
Wines	Sulphur dioxide	450
Beer	Sulphur dioxide	70
Brewed ginger beer	Benzoic acid	120
Sugar, glucose, gur and khandsari	Sulphur dioxide	70
Corn flour and suchlike starch	Sulphur dioxide	100
Corn syrup	Sulphur dioxide	450
Gelatin	Sulphur dioxide	1000
Coffee extract	Sulphur dioxide	450
Cheese or processed cheese	Sorbic acid or its sodium, potassium and calcium salts (calculated as sorbic acid) or nisin	1000
Flour confectionary	Sorbic acid or its sodium salt	1500
Hard boiled sugar confectionary	Sulphur dioxide	350
Sausages and sausage meat containing raw meat, cereals and condiments	Sulphur dioxide	450
Cooked pickle meat including ham and bacon	Sodium or potassium nitrate or commercial saltpetre (calculated as sodium nitrate)	200 500
Smoked fish (in wrappers)	Sorbic acid	Only wrappers may be impregnated with sorbic acid

Table 25: Common food adulterants

S. No.	*Foodstuff*	*Adulterants*
A	**Beverages**	
1	Coffee powder	Exhausted coffee powder, starch, roasted dates tamarind seeds, chicory powder
2	Tea	Other leaves with added colour
B	**Cereals**	
1	Wheat and rice	Stones of similar colours
2	Wheat flour	Tapioca flour, talc, chalk powder
3	semolina	Tapioca semolina
C	**Milk and milk products**	
1	Milk	Water refined oil or fat after removal of milk fat, skim milk reconstituted from skim milk powder
2	Milk powder	Starch, dextrins
3	Cream	Other fats
4	Ice cream	Non-permitted colour, artificial sweeteners, other fats and jelling agents
5	Butter and ghee	Hydrogenated fats
D	**Pulses**	
1	Bengal gram dhal	Khesari dhal
2	Red gram dhal	Khesari dhal coloured yellow with dye
3	Bengal gram flour	Tapioca flour or starch coloured yellow with dye
E	**Spices and condiments**	
1	Whole turmeric	Coating with lead chromate or coal tar dye
2	Turmeric powder	Coal tar colour, yellow earth, starch or talc coloured yellow with coal tar dye
3	Curry powder	Starch coloured brown with coal tar dye
4	Coriander seed	Other seeds coloured green
5	Coriander seed powder	Powdered barn or sawdust coloured green with dye
6	Chilli powder	Starch coloured red with coal tar dye
7	Mustard seed	Argemone seeds
E	**Sweetening agents and soft drinks**	
1	Honey	Coloured invert sugar syrup
2	Soft drinks	Artifical sweeteners (saccharine), mineral acid other than phosphoric acid
F	**Miscellaneous**	
1	Processed arecanut	Other seeds or nuts broken and coloured

Table-26: Tests* for common food adulterants

S. No.	*Foodstuff*	*Adulterant*	*Test*
1	Coffee powder	Starch (toasted bread crumbs, rye, wheat, peas, etc.)	Make decoction of the coffee, decolourize it by adding potassium permanganate and then add a drop of iodine solution. Blue colour indicates starch.
		Roasted dates, tamarind seeds, chicory roots, etc.	Shake powder with 2% sodium hydroxide (or washing soda) solution. Formation of reddish colour indicates tamarind seeds.
2	Edible oils	Argemone oil	Shake 5 ml of filtered oil with 2 ml of con. HCl in a test tube and warm the mixture for 5 minutes in a water bath with occasional shaking. Decant off the oil from the top and add to the remaining acid layer 1 ml of 10% ferric chloride solution, gently. Rotate the tube between the plams of the hands to mix the solutions and heat the mixture in boiling water bath for 10 minutes. Formation of a reddish brown precipitate or crystals indicates argemone oil.
		Mineral oil	Mix 2 ml of oil with 2 ml of 3% alcoholic potassium hydroxide, heat in boiling water bath for 15 minutes, add 10 ml of water. Any turbidity indicates mineral oil.
		Caster oil	Dissolve oil in petroleum ether in a test tube and cool the test tube in ice-salt mixture. Turbidity within 5 minutes indicates caster oil.
3	Ghee or butter	Vegetable oils (Vanaspati)	Dissolve a pinch of cane sugar in 10 ml conc. HCl taken in a glass stoppered test tube. Add 10 ml of melted ghee, stopper the bottle and shake vigorously for two minutes. Allow to stand till 2 layers separate. If the lower layer turns pink or red, the ghee contains vanaspati.
4	Honey	Commercial invert sugar (mixture of glucose and fructose)	*Fiehe's test*: Mix about 5 g of honey with 10 ml of ether in a mortar, using a pestle. Decant off the ether extract into a china dish. Repeat extraction twice with more ether and collect all the extracts in the same dish. Allow the ether to evaporate off at room temperature. To the residue in the dish, add a large drop of 1% solution of freshly sublimed resorcinol in conc. HCl. Immediate appearance of a cherry-red colour indicates invert sugar.

5	Milk, curd, khoa, ghee, butter	Starch	Add a drop of iodine solution to a little of the sample. Blue colour indicates added starch in any from. (Iodine solution is prepared by dissolving 2.5 g of iodine crystals and 3 g of potassium iodide in sufficient water to make the volume 100 ml).
6	Milk or curd	Cane sugar	Add 0.1 g of resorcin and 1 ml of conc. HCl acid to 10 ml of the sample and boil. A rose-red colour indicates sugars.
7	Mustard and rai seeds	Argemone seed	Examination under magnifying glass shows small seeds resembling mustard but blacker, more rough and not uniformly smooth and round.
	Mustard, rai, cumin seeds, khus-khus, etc	Stones and foreign matter	Visual examination
8	Powdered spices (turmeric, chilli, coriender, garam masala, curry powder, etc)	Sand, grits and talc	Shake up a little of the sample in a dry test tube with 5 ml of carbon tetrachloride. Allow to settle. Sand, talc and grit will sink to the bottom, leaving spice on top.
9	Split and dehusked pulses (tur dhal and Bengal gram dhal)	Khesari dhal Metanil yellow	Visual examination Shake portion of sample with cold or warm water. The water becomes yellowish and on treatment with a few drops of conc. HCl acid turns magenta red.
10	Soft drinks	Mineral acid other than phosphoric acid	Soak a strip of filter paper in a 0.1% solution of metanil yellow and then dry. Dip one end of paper into the soft drink. Wetted portion turns violet if mineral acid is present.
11	Tea (dust/leaves)	Artificially coloured foreign matter or exhausted tea leaves	Sprinkle the tea on a sheet of wet white paper. Pink or red spots appearing on the paper indicate added colour.
12	Turmeric (whole and powdered) and mixed spices (powdered)	Metanil yellow	Shake sample with some water. Dilute water till it is almost colourless and then add a few drops of conc. HCl. Magneta red colour seed if dye present.
13	Wheat flour, semolina (suji), Bengal gram flour (Besan)	Sand and grit Chalk powder	To a little of the sample in a dry test tube add 5 ml of carbon tetrachloride and shake well. Sand and grit will settle at the bottom, leaving flour on top. Treat sample with hot dilute HCl acid. Bubbling of gas indicates CO_2 from chalk or other carbonates.

Note: Adulteration detected as above needs to be confirmed by analysis by a recognized food testing laboratory; the above tests in no way replace the prescribed laboratory tests.

Table- 27: Common food additives to be used with caution

Additive	*Use*	*Possible adverse effects*
Artificial flavourings	In soft drinks, breakfast cereals, baked goods, vegetable and fruit products, ice creams, custards, desserts, alcoholic beverages	Hyperactivity in some children; not adequately tested for safety
Butylated hydroxyanisole (BHA)	Antioxidant in cereals, chewing gum, potato chips, edible oils, etc.	Appears to be safer than BHT but needs more testing
Butylated hydroxytoluene (BHT)	Antioxidant in cereals, chewing gum, potato chips, edible oils, etc.	Cancer; allergic reactions; stored in body fat
Caffeine	Stimulant in soft drinks	Insomnia and other adverse effects at high levels of intake. Not recommended for children and pregnant mothers
Coal tar dyes	Colourant in vegetable and fruit products, soft drinks, candy, deserts, pastry, sausage, baked food, ice cream, hot dogs, hamburgers, sweetmeats, snacks, confectionary, alcoholic and other beverages	Allergic reactions, cancer and pathological lesions in vital organs
Monosodium glutamate	Flavour enhancer for soup, poultry, meat preparations, sauces, stews and cheese	Damages brain cells in infant mice, so not recommended for children; headache, tightness of head, neck and arms in sensitive adults (Chinese Restaurant Syndrome)
Phosphoric acid and phosphates	Acidifier, chelating agent, buffer, emulsifier, nutrient, discoloration inhibitor used in baked goods, cheese, cured meat, soft drinks, dried potatoes	Dietary imbalance that may cause bone thinning (osteoporosis) on prolonged use
Saccharin	Non- calorie sweetener in food products, also as adulterant	Bladder cancer reported in animals, Not recommended for normal people (not suffering from diabetes, obesity)
Sodium nitrite and nitrate	Preservative to prevent growth of bacillus, *Closridium botulinum* and colourant for bacon, ham, meat smoked fish, corned beef	Formation of small amounts of cancer producing nitrosamines
Sulphur dioxide and bisulphites	Preservative and bleach for sliced fruit, wine grape juice, dried potatoes, dried fruit, vegetables and fruit products, etc.	Destroys vitamin B_1, but otherwise safe at prescribed levels
Talc and kaolin	Making dry powdery foods free-flowing and as dusting agent for rice, confectionary, chewing gum	Absorbed and stored in vital organs; cancer if asbestos is present

Table 28: Functions and sources of availability of various nutrients

Nutrient	*Functions*	*Sources of availability*
Carbohydrates	• To supply energy • To help assimilate other nutrients	Cereal products including rice, chapatti, bread, potato, corn, yam, sugar, syrup, jam, honey, jaggery, dried fruits, banana, cashew nut, mango, beal, date, pea, tapioca, arvi, sweet potato, etc.
Fats	• To supply energy in concentrated form • To supply essential fatty acids for transport and absorption of fat-soluble vitamins	Edible oils, ghee, butter, cream, vanaspati, cashew nut, almond, etc.
Fibers	• To improve digestion • To prevent constipation • To reduce cholesterol	Banana, mango, apple, guava, potato, brinjal, spinach, sweet potato, cabbage, beans, etc.
Proteins	• To maintain body structure and composition • To build and repair tissues • To help formation of antibodies to fight infections • To form enzymes and hormones to regulate body processes • To provide energy	Milk, curd, cheese, pulses, beans, pea, groundnut and other oilseeds, egg, fish, meat, bread, cereals, cashew nut, almond, coconut, green vegetables, etc.
Minerals		
(*a*) Calcium	• To build bones and teeth • To help clotting of blood • To help normal functioning of muscles and nerves	Milk, curd, cheese, fish, ragi, sesame seeds, tomato, pea, almond, raspberry, coconut, pomegranate, banana, guava, amaranth, leaves of colocasia, chaulai, drumstick, fenugreek, radish, etc.
(*b*) Iron	• To form haemoglobin	Egg, shellfish, leafy vegetables, cereal products, ragi, bajra, pulses, beans, banana, date, papaya, mango, guava, karonda, tomato, cabbage, etc.
Vitamins		
(*a*) Vitamin A	• To help growth • To help keep skin and mucous membrane healthy and resistant to infection	Leafy vegetables, amaranth, chaulai, radish tops, spinach, fenugreek, carrot, mango, papaya, ghee, butter, vanaspati, egg, etc.
	• To protect against night blindness	Wheat products, pulses, parboiled rice, fresh

(*b*) Thiamine (B_1)	• To maintain appetite and keep the nervous system healthy • To help release energy for the body	pea and beans, egg, milk, pomegranate, bael, plum, jamun, pumpkin, cabbage, etc.
(*c*) Riboflavin (B_2)	• To help cell respiration which is essential for growth • To help keep clear vision • To help maintain the skin around mouth and nose smooth	Milk, curd, cheese, egg, fish, banana, litchi, cowpea and other pulses, papaya, colocasia, bael, radish tops, pineapple, etc.
(*d*) Niacin or Nicotinic acid (B_5)	• To help growth • To help in energy release	Groundnut, meat, prawn, pulses, green vegetables, peach, cherry, banana, strawberry, etc.
(*e*) Vitamin C	• To make cementing substance to hold cells together and to strengthen walls of blood vessels to help resist infection • To help healing of wounds • To help absorption of iron	Aonla, guava, cashew apple, drumstick leaves, cabbage, radish tops, amaranth, orange, grapefruit, pummelo, tomato, barbados cherry, carrot, green chillies, etc.
(*f*) Vitamin D	• To help absorption of calcium • To help in building strong bones and teeth	Cabbage, carrot, fish, oil, butter, egg, etc.
Water	• To maintain body structure and composition • To help digest and absorb food • To regulate body temperature and pH	Water and water based beverages such as tea, coffee, juice, sherbet, coconut water, etc.

Differences between pasteurization and sterilization

Parameter	*Pasteurization*	*Sterilization*
Extent of microbial destruction	Partial	Complete
Temperature	<100°C	100°C and above
Applicable to	Fruits	Vegetables

Chapter 4

Proximate Analysis of Foods Products

1. ***Determination of moisture content:*** A thin layer of finely divided asbestos (gooch grade) is spread over a flat bottom metallic dish and dried at 110°C in hot air oven for one hour then covered, cooled and weighed. Sample of 20 g was taken and its weight is recorded as initial weight of sample (M_0). The samples are spread uniformly over the asbestos layer in a metallic dish and weight was recorded as M_1. Weighing is done quickly as possible to avoid of moisture. The dish-containing sample was then placed in the hot air oven maintained at 100 ± 1°C temperature for 16-18 hours. The covei of dish is removed before placing the dish. The drying is conducted upto 16-18 hours. After drying, the dish is taken out of the oven, covered with lids and cooled into the desiccators containing activated silica gel. When dish get cool to the room temperature which generally took about one hour. It is weighed and its weight was recorded as M_2. The moisture content tests are carried out in triplicate and weighing was done to the nearest ±1mg. Moisture content of sample was calculated using following equation.

$$\text{Moisture content }(\%) = \frac{M_1 - M_0}{M_0} \times 100$$

where,

MC = Moisture content of sample, % (wb)

M_0 = Initial weight of sample taken, 20 g

M_1 = Weight of sample before oven drying and weight of dish with cover, g

M_2 = Weight of the dish with cover containing dried and desiccated sample, g

2. ***Determination of total soluble solids (TSS):*** Among the various constituents of fresh fruits and vegetables, minerals, acids, sugars, vitamins B and constitute 80-85 percent of the soluble in water. Sugars constitute 80-85 percent of the soluble solids. The TSS value is defined as the amount of sugar and soluble minerals present in fruits and vegetables. The method for its determination by means of a hand refractometer is given below. A hand refractometer is based on the principle of total refraction. The refractometer should be checked for accuracy before use. This is done by placing a few drops of distilled water on the prism in the specimen chamber of the back the cover.

By looking through the eye-piece with the projection inlet facing towards light the point on the scale is noted when the boundary line of the shaded area eyepiece is rotated to either side for clear reading. The distilled water reading should be zero. If it is not so, it should be set to zero with the scale correction knob. The specimen chamber is now cleaned with muslin cloth or tissue paper. For determining the TSS, a drop of sample (juice, syrup, etc.) is placed on the prism and the percentage of dry substance in it read directly at temperature of 20°C for proper accuracy.

3.*Determination of acidity as (citric and acetic acids)*

Citric acid: Dissolve a known volume or weight of sample in a known volume of distilled water. From this, take an aliquot and titrate with 0.1 N NaOH using phenolphthalein as indicator. The end point is denoted by the appearances of pink colour.

Acetic acid: Dilute 10 ml of sample with water in a porcelain dish (about 5 inches in diameter). All phenolphthalein as indicator and titrate with 0.5 NaOH.

Calculation

$$\text{Titrable acidity} = \frac{\text{ml NaOH} \times \text{N NaOH} \times \text{meq. Weight of acid} \times 100}{\text{ml juice titrated}}$$

***Note :** meq = milli equivalent

meq wt. of citric acid = 0.06404

meq wt. of acetic acid = 0.06005

meq wt. of malic acid = 0.067

meq wt. of tartaric acid = 0.075

4. *pH Measurement:* It is important to accurately measure and control the acidity or alkalinity of any solution. The degree of acidity and/or alkalinity of a solution are denoted by using a scale, termed as pH scale. The pH value is based on the actual measurement of the hydrogen ion concentration in gm/litre of the solution. Example, the hydrogen ion concentration for pure water, which is neutral solution at 25°C, is 0.0000001 or 1×10^{-7} gm/litre. The pH is the measurement of the reciprocal logarithm of hydrogen ion concentration in a solution. It may be noted that the acid solution increase in strength, the pH value decrease from 7 to 0 and alkalinity solution increase in strength as the pH value increase in value above 7.00.

$$pH = 1/\log(H^+), \quad \text{or} \quad pH = -\log(H^+)$$

where,

(H^+) is hydrogen ion concentration (g/lit)

$pH = 1/\log(10^{-7}) = \log(10^7) = 7 \log 10 = 7 \times 1 = 7$

Procedure: The digital pH meter is kept at stand by position firstly then calibrating the pH 7 and pH 4 standard buffer solutions. The electrode of pH meter is dipped in test solution and the temperature knob was placed at 0°C control to the temperature of test solution. The function selector switch is set to pH and reading of digital display was allowed to stabilize before it was grind with 100 ml water and filtered through what man filter paper No.1. The filtered sample is used for pH measurement

5. *Fat estimation*

Apparatus used: Soxhlet apparatus

Solvent Used: Petroleum ether as extraction medium (b.p. 46-60°C)

Procedure: A 15 g of sample is taken in a thumble, which is of porous paper for fat estimation. The thumble is placed in the extracting tube and tube is connected with the weighed flask and the condenser too. The heat vaporizes the volatile solvent, which passes up the side arm and is condensed in the condenser. The condensed solvent fell drop by drop into the thumble. When sufficient amount of solvent had thus been transferred to the extracting tube to fill the siphon arm, it siphoned back over into the weighed flask. This processed was continued for 20 hr until extraction was completed. Then the bottom flask was removed, the volatile solvent was evaporated and fat extracted was obtained as residue. The following formula was used to express fat content of then sample.

$$\text{Fat content (\%)} = \frac{\text{Weight of residue left after evaporation of slvent}}{\text{Initial weight of the food sample}} \times 100$$

6. *Protein estimation:* In this method protein is analytically estimated by determining the amount of total nitrogen in the samples.

Reagent used:

- **Mixed indicator:** Prepare 0.1% bromocresol green and 0.1% methyl red indicators in 95% alcohol separately. Mix 10 ml of the bromocresol green with 2 ml of the methyl red solution in a bottle provided with a dropper which will deliver about 0.05 ml per 4 drops.
- **2% Boric acid:** Dissolve 10 g of boric acid (crystal) in 500 ml of boiling distilled water. After cooling, transfer the solution into glass stoppered bottle. It keeps indefinitely.
- **0.01 N Hydrochloric acid:** Check the concentration of the final solution against pure sodium carbonate.
- **30% Sodium hydroxide:** Dissolve 150 g of sodium hydroxide pellets in 350 ml of distilled water. Store the solution in a bottle closed with a rubber stopper.
- **Catalysts for digestion:** Mix 2.5 g of powdered selenium dioxide (SeO_2); 100 g of potassium sulphate (K_2SO_4) and 20 g of copper sulphate ($CuSO_4.5H_2O$).
- **Conc. Sulphuric acid: 98 % pure**

Apparatus used: Kjel-dahl apparatus

Procedure: A 5 g of product sample and 2 g of catalyst mixture is taken into a digestion flask. Then 10 ml Conc. H_2SO_4 is poured into the mixture and kept for gently heating. The heating was continued until frothing was ceased and the mixture become light greenish coloured liquid. The complete digestion required at least 2 hour. The flask is cooled after digestion and the digestion liquid is maintained upto 100 ml with DMU in a standard 100 ml flask.

A 10 ml aliquot of sample is taken and transferred into the digestion flask through the small funnel and 30 ml of 30% NaOH is also added into the digestion flask and now again heat the two liquid mixture which evolves. Nitrogen gas which is collected into a small 100 ml conical flask which contains 100 ml of 2% boric acid and one or two drops of mixed indicator. This process continued until the bubble formation stops in the boric acid solution. This process is repeated at least three times.

Now this collected solution is titrated against 0.1 N HCl. The blank is run in the second test of the experiment and the titration is done in a similar way.

Calculations:

$$\text{Nitrogen (\%)} = \frac{(\text{Sample titre} - \text{Blank titre}) \times \text{N NCl} \times 14 \times \text{Volume made up of digest} \times 100}{\text{Aliquot of digest taken} \times \text{Weight of the food sample taken} \times 1000}$$

Protein (%) = Nitrogen (%) × 6·25

7. *Estimation of sugars by Shaffer–Somogyi micro method*

Reagents

- **Copper sulphate solution (10%):** Dissolve 100g of copper sulphate in water and make upto 1000 ml.
- **Potassium iodate solution (0.1 N):** Dissolve 0.567 g of potassium iodate in water and make upto 1000 ml.
- **Shaffer–Somogyi carbonate reagent:** Dissolve 25 g each of a hydrous sodium tartrate) in approximately 500 ml of water in a beaker. Add with stirring 75 ml of copper sulphate solution and 20 g of sodium bicarbonate. After dissolving, add 5 g of potassium iodide. Transfer the solution to a 1 litre volumetric flask; add 250 ml of 0.1 N potassium iodate solution. Make upto volume, filter and store overnight before use.
- **Iodide–potassium oxalate solution:** Dissolve 2.5 g each of potassium iodide and potassium oxalate in water and dilute to 100 ml. Prepare afresh every week.
- **Thiosulphate solution (0.005 N):** Prepare daily from standard stock of 0.1 N solutions.
- Sulphuric acid solution (2 N)
- Potassium oxalate solution (22%)
- Lead acetate solution 45%

Procedure

(1) Preparation of sample: Take 2.5 to 5.0 g sample in a 250 ml of beaker, add about 50 ml of water. Heat to boiling, cool and transfer to a 250 ml volumetric flask. Add 2 ml lead acetate solution, shake and allow standing for 10 minutes. Precipitate excess lead by adding 2 ml of potassium oxalate solution. Make up the volume with water and filter.

(2) Reducing sugars: Take 5 ml of filtrate in a test tube, add 5 ml of Shafer – Somogyi reagent and mix well. Simultaneously prepare blank using 5 ml of water and 5 ml of reagent. Place the two tubes in a water bath for 15 minutes. Remove the tubes carefully without disturbing the contents and cool in running water for 4 minutes. Along the side of each tube, add 2 ml of iodide – oxalate solution and then 3 ml of 2 N sulphuric acid and allow both tubes to stand in cold water for 5 minutes. Then titrate against 0.005 N thiosulphate solution using starch as indicator. Subtract the titre value of the test solution from that of a blank and determine the amount of dextrose in 5 ml of solution from the table given below.

(3)Total sugars: Take 25 ml of filtrate in a 50 ml volumetric flask and add 5 ml of HCI (1:1). Allow to stand for 24 hours at room temperature. Neutralize exactly with NaOH using phenolphthalein as indicator and make upto volume with water. Take an aliquot and determine the total invert sugars as in case of reducing sugars.

Calculation

$$\text{Reducing sugar (\%)} = \frac{\text{mg of Dextrose} \times \text{Volume made up} \times 100}{5 \times \text{Weight of food sample taken} \times 100}$$

$$\text{Total sugars as invert sugar (\%)} = \frac{\text{mg of Dextrose} \times \text{Volume made up} \times 100}{\text{Titre} \times \text{Weight or Volume of food sample taken} \times 1000}$$

Sucrose (%) = (% Total invert sugars – % Reducing sugar originally present) × 0·95 % Total sugars = % Reducing sugars + % Sucrose.

8.*Estimation of starch:* After the sugars present in the sample have been leached out, starch is hydrolyzed and estimated as invert sugars.

Reagents

(*i*) Ethanol (95%)

(*ii*) Ethanol (50%)

(*iii*) HCI

(*iv*) NaOH

Procedure: To a weighed sample (100 g in case of barley water) add a little water and heat to 60°C. Allow to stand for some time, add about 100 ml of 95% ethanol and centrifuge till the precipitate settles at bottom, and filter. Wash the residue with 50% ethanol and transfer to a 500 ml conical flask with about 100 ml of water. Add 20 ml of concentrated HCI and place a funnel in the neck of the flask to prevent evaporation and heat in a boiling water bath for 2½ hours. Cool, neutralize with NaOH using phenolphthalein as indicator and make up to a definite volume with water. Determine the reducing sugars as described earlier.

Calculation

Starch (%) = Reducing sugars (%) × 0·90

9.*Determination of vitamin C (ascorbic acid) by titration:* In the absence of interfering substance that may reduce the dye of oxidize ascorbic acid during sample preparation. The capacity of a sample is to reduce a standard dye solution. As determined by titration, is directly proportional to the ascorbic acid content.

Reagents

(*i*) **Metaphosphoric acid** (HPO_3) solution (3%)

(*ii*) **Dye solution:** Dissolve 50 mg of mately 150 ml of hot distilled water containing 42 mg of sodium bicarbonate. Cool and dilute with distilled water to 200 ml. Store solution in brown bottle in a refrigerator at about 3°C, standardize every day and prepare a fresh every week.

(*iii*) **Standard ascorbic acid solution:** Dissolve 100 mg of L-ascorbic acid in a small volume of 3% metaphosphoric acid solution and make up to 100 ml with same solution. Dilute 10 ml this of stock solution to 100 ml with 3% metaphosphoric acid (0.1 mg ascorbic acid per ml.)

Procedure

(*i*) **Standardization of dye:** Dilute 5 ml of standard ascorbic acid solution with 5 ml of solution till pink colour persists for 10 seconds. Calculate the dye factor (mg of ascorbic acid per ml of dye) as follows:

$$\text{Dye Factor (D.F.)} = \frac{0{\cdot}50}{\text{Titre}}$$

(*ii*) **Preparation of sample and titration:** In case of a liquid or juice sample, take 10 ml sample and make upto 100 ml with 3% HPO_3 and filter. In case of a semi-solid or solid product, blend 10 g of sample with 3% HPO_3 and then make up to 100ml and filter. Pipette 10 ml of filtrate in to a conical flask and titrate with the standard dye to a pink end point. If a sample contains sulphur dioxide which reduces the dye and thus interferes with the ascorbic acid estimation, the following procedure is followed.

Take 10 ml of filtrate; add 1 ml of 40% formaldehyde and 0.1 ml of HCI. Allow to stand for 10 minutes and then titrate.

Calculation

$$\text{Ascorbic Acid} = \left(\frac{\text{mg}}{100\text{g}}\right) = \frac{\text{Titre} \times \text{Dye factor} \times \text{Volume made up} \times 100}{\text{Volume of filtrate taken} \times \text{Weight or volume of sample taken}}$$

10. *Estimation of ash content in food samples*

Procedure: Weigh 2-3 g of food sample in a previously weighed, silica crucible. Heat crucible first over a low flame to volatilize as much of the organic matter as possible (until no more smoke is given off by the material), and then heat in a muffle furnace (temperature controlled) at about $600^{O}C$ for 3-4 hours. Cool in desiccators and weigh. To ensure complete ashing, the crucible is again heated in the furnace for 30 minutes, cooled and weighed.

Calculation

$$\text{Percent Ash (total minerals)} = \frac{\text{Weight of ash}}{\text{Initial weight of the sample}} \times 100$$

11.*Determination of Non-enzymatic browning*

Preparation of sample

(*i*) **Liquids and juices:** Centrifuge the sample at 4000 rpm for 15 minutes. To 20 ml of centrifugate add 30 ml of 60 percent alcohol mix thoroughly and filter.

(*ii*) **Semi-solids and solids (pulp, jam, etc.):** Blend the sample and to 10 g of blended sample add 10 ml of distilled water and 30 ml of 60 ml percent alcohol. Mix thoroughly and filter.

(iii) **Dried fruits and vegetables:** Soak 5 g of sample in 100 ml of 60 percent alcohol for 12 hours and filter.

In the case of chlorophyll containing sample, shake filtrate thrice with 50 ml of benzene each time to remove chlorophyll, before measurement.

Observation: Record the absorbance of the filtrate at 440 nm using 60 percent alcohol as blank and express as optical density (O.D.).

12. *Determination of pigments in food*

(1) Chlorophyll II

Reagent: Acetone (80%)

Procedure: Take 1 g of fresh sample, cut into small pieces, add about 5 ml of water and homogenize in blender. Make up homogenate to 10 ml with water and centrifuge solution. Take 0.5 ml aliquot and add 4.5 ml of 80% acetone to it to extract pigments. Centrifuge, remove the supernatant and record its optical density (O.D.) at 480, 645 and 663 nm, and using 80% acetone as a blank.

Calculation

Total chlorophyll (g/litre) = (0.0202) (O.D. at 645) + (0.00802) (O.D. at 663)

Chloriphyll a (g/litre) = (0.0127) (O.D. at 663) – (0.00269) (O.D. at. 645)

Choloriphyll b (g/litre) = (0.0229) (O.D. at 645) – (0.00488) (O.D. at 663)

Carotene (g/litre) = (O.D. at 480) – (0.114) (O.D. at 663) – (0.638) (O.D. at 645)

(2) Lycopene

Reagents

Procedure

Take of 5 to 10 g of sample and crush repeatedly in acetone in a pestle and mortar until the residue is colourless. Transfer the acetone extracts to a separatory funnel containing 10 to 15 ml of petroleum ether. Mix gently to take up the pigments in to the petroleum ether phase. Transfer the lower (acetone) phase to a 100 ml volumetric flask and extract it repeatedly with petroleum ether until colourless. Combine the petroleum ether extracts and dry over a small quantity of anhydrous sodium sulphate. Make up to 100 ml with petroleum ether and measure the O.D. of the solution at 503 nm using petroleum ether as blank.

Calculation

O.D. of 1.0 = 3.1206 μg of lycopene /ml

$$\text{Lycopene}\left(\frac{\text{mg}}{\text{100g}}\right)=\frac{3\cdot 1206\times \text{O.D. of sample}\times \text{Volume made up}\times \text{Dilution}}{\text{Weight of sample}\times 1000}$$

(3) Beta – carotene

Reagents

Acetone, anhydrous sodium sulphate, petroleum ether

Procedure

Take 5 g of fresh sample and crush in 10-15 ml acetone, adding a few crystals of anhydrous sodium sulphate, with the help of pestle and mortar. Decant the supernatant in to a beaker. Repeat the process twice and transfer the combined supernatant to a separatory funnel add 10-15 ml petroleum ether and mix thoroughly. Two layers will separate out on standing. Discard the lower layer and collect upper layer in a 100 ml volumetric flask, make up the volume to 100 ml with petroleum ether and record optical density at 452 nm using petroleum ether as blank.

Calculation

$$\beta\text{—Carotene}\left(\frac{\mu g}{100g}\right) = \frac{O.D \times 13 \cdot 9 \times 10^4}{\text{Weight of sample} \times 560 \times 1000} \times 100$$

$$\text{Vitamin A (I.U.)} = \frac{\beta - \text{Carotene}\left(\frac{\mu g}{100g}\right)}{0 \cdot 6}$$

(4) Anthocyanin

(i) In skins

Reagents

(*i*) Ethanal (95%)

(*ii*) HCI

Procedure: 10 discs of 5 mm each are taken in a screw cap culture tube containing 20 ml of 95 percent ethanol to which 0.1 ml of concentrated HCI is added. Tubes are tightly capped, placed in a water bath for 5 minutes and then kept in the dark for 2 hours. Now record the absorbance at 530nm as O.D. /10 discs.

(ii) In Pulp

Reagents

Ethanolic HCI solution: Prepare by mixing 95% ethanol and 1.5 N HCI in the ratio of 85:15.

Procedure: Blend 10 g of sample with 10 ml of ethanolic HCI and transfer to a 100 ml volumetric flask and make up to volume. Store overnight in a refrigerator at 4°C, filter through Whatman No. 1 filter paper and record optical density (O.D.) of filtrate at 535 nm.

Calculation

$$\text{Total O.D./100 g} = \frac{\text{O.D.} \times \text{Volume made up} \times 100}{\text{Weight of sample}}$$

$$\text{Total Anthocyanins}\left(\frac{mg}{100g}\right) = \frac{\text{Total O.D./100g}}{98 \cdot 2}$$

(iii) In Juice

Reagents: 0.1 N HCI

Procedure: Dilute 10 ml of juice to 50 ml with 0.1 N HCI and allow equilibrating in the dark for 1 hour. Record the absorbance (O.D.) at 510 nm.

Calculation

$$\text{Total O.D./ 100 g} = \frac{\text{O.D.} \times \text{Volume made up} \times 100}{\text{ml of juice taken}}$$

$$\text{Total Anthocyanins}\left(\frac{\text{mg}}{\text{100g}}\right) = \frac{\text{Total O.D./100g}}{87 \cdot 3}$$

13. *Determination of total pectin as calcium pectate:* Pectin extracted from the plant material is saponified with alkali and precipitated from an acid solution as calcium pectate by the addition of calcium chloride.

Reagents

(*i*) 1 N acetic acid: Prepared by dissolving 30 ml of glacial acetic acid in a little water a making up the volume to 500 ml with water.

(*ii*) 1 N calcium chloride: Prepared by dissolving 27.5 g of anhydrous calcium chloride in water and making upto 500 ml volume.

(*iii*) 0.05 N HCI

(*iv*) 1 N NaOH

(*v*) Phenolphthalein indicator

Procedure: Take 50 g of blended sample in 1000 ml beaker. Add about 400 ml of 0.05 N HCI and heat the contents for 2 hours at 80-90°C (in case of jam, jelly and marmalade. acid is not added, the sample is boiled in 400 ml of water only with stirring). Replace water lost by evaporation. Cool and transfer to a 500 ml volumetric flask, make up the volume and filter.

Pipette a 100 ml aliquot into a conical flask and add 250 ml of distilled water. Neutralize the acid with 1 N NaOH using phenolphthalein as indicator. Add another 10 ml of 1 N NaOH and allow standing overnight. Now add 50 ml of 1N acetic acid followed by 25 ml of 1 N calcium chloride. Allow to stand for 1 hour, boil for 1-2 minutes and filter through a previously weighed filter paper (wet the filter paper in hot water, dry in oven at 100°C for 2 hours, cool in dissicator and weigh). Wash the precipitate free of chloride with hot water. Dry the precipitate, cool in dessicator and weigh again.

Calculation

$$\text{\% Pectin (as Calcium pectate)} = \frac{\text{Weight of precipitates} \times 500 \times 100}{\text{ml of filtrate} \times \text{Weight of sample estimation}}$$

14. *Determination of rehydration ratio:* According to Ranganna (1994), there is no standarc time for rehydration of dried fruits and vegetables. It varies from product to product. Rehydration time was, therefore, standardized through trial runs. Dehydrated material weighing 5 g was placed in 500-ml beaker containing 150 ml of boiled distilled water. Beaker was covered with a watch glass and continued to boil for 20 min. Then samples were transferred into a 7.5 cm Buchner funnel covered with a coarsely porous Whatman filter paper No.4. After filtration, samples were removed from funnel and weighed immediately. Rehydration ratio was calculated using the following equation.

$$\text{Rehydration Ratio} = \frac{A}{B}$$

where,

A = Weight of mushrooms samples after rehydration, g

B = Weight of dehydrated mushrooms samples before rehydration, g

15. *Determination of browning index:* Browning index (OD) of dehydrated mushroom sample was determined by using method recommended by Srivastava and Kumar (1994). A brief description is given below:

A 5 g of dried sample was soaked in 100 ml of 60% ethyl alcohol solution for 12 hours and filtered through what man No.1 filter paper. After the filtration, absorbance of the filtrate was measured at 440 nm by the digital spectrophotometer using 60% ethyl alcohol as blank and expressed as optical density.

16. *Microbiological analysis of foods*

Microbial analysis: Microbial analysis is done to determine the total plate count on the sample on Nutrient Agar (NA) for bacterial count and on Potato Dextrose Agar (PDA) for yeast and mold count.

Procedure:

Preparation of media: The various compositions of media are as follows:-

Nutrient Agar Media (NA)

Peptone	= 5 g
Agar-Agar	= 20 g
Beef extract	= 1.5 g
Yeast extract	= 1.5 g
NaCl	= 5 g
Distilled water	= 1000 ml

Potato Dextrose Agar (PDA)

Peptone	= 20 g
Dextrose	= 40 g
Agar-Agar	= 50g
Chlorum fenicol	= 3 mg (capsule)
Distilled water	= 1000ml

Normal Saline Solution (NSS)

Distilled water	= 1000ml
NaCl	= 8.6 g

Sterilization: All the necessary glass wares, required numbers of Petri -dishes, Nutrient agar media, potato dextrose agar media, 9 ml of NSS distributed in 7 test tubes, microbial tips (1 ml and 0.5 ml), and spreader were heated for 15 min in an autoclave maintained at 15 psi for sterilization. The autoclave is then switched off and the steam was allowed to escape.

Pouring: This is the transfer of media into the Petri-dishes. This is done in laminar flow chamber. The flame was lighted and the Petri-dishes were slightly opened near the flame and the media was poured in the Petri-dished. The Petri-dishes with media were kept undisturbed for solidification.

Preparation of sample (Serial dilution): One gram of the sample is taken and transfer to the test tube with 9 ml of NSS. It is marked as 10^{-1} and other as 10^{-2}, 10^{-3}, 10^{-4}, 10^{-5} and 10^{-6}. The test tube containing sample is homogenized with the help of cyclo-mixer. One ml of sample suspended in saline solution from 10^{-1} test tube is transferred to test tube marked as 10^{-2} with the help of micro-pipette and homogenized. The tip is then discarded. One ml sample from 10^{-2} marked tube is transferred to 10^{-3} with a sterilized 1 ml micro pipette. Similarly, the sample is transferred till the test tube marked as 10^{-6}.

Inoculation of sample: This is also done aseptically in the laminar flow chamber. 0.5 ml of the sample suspended in saline solution from 10^{-1}, was taken with micro pipette and transferred to Petri dishes marked as 10^{-1} of NA media and PDA media. The microbial tip is discarded and another sterilized tip was used to transfer sample from 10^{-2} saline solution to 10^{-2} NA and PDA plates. Precautions are taken in inoculation so that contamination should not take place. Similarly, the entire samples suspended in saline solution are transferred to the respective Petri dishes of both NA and PDA media. For each dilution, two replications are taken. A control of both NA and PDA media was also kept without inoculation.

The inoculated Petri dishes are incubated in BOD incubator for 48 hours where the temperature was maintained at 37°C. After 24 hour and 48 hours, total plate count is taken for both NA and PDA plates.

Observation for TPC and yeast and molds. Example:

Sample	10^{-1}	10^{-2}	10^{-3}	10^{-4}	10^{-5}	10^{-6}	Average
1.	128	5	3	2	1	0	
2.							
3.							
4.							

Calculations: The number of organism per ml of original culture is calculated by multiplying the number of colonies counted by the dilution factor.

No. of cell per ml (TPC) = Number of colony × Dilution factor

$$\text{Total plate count (cfu/g)} = 128 \times \frac{1}{10^{-1}} = 128 \times 10 = 1280$$

17. *Sensory Evaluation*: Sensory evaluation of food uses our senses to assess and comprehend the attributes of food products. It involves a comprehensive taste, smell, sight, touch, and sometimes hearing analysis. By harnessing these senses, experts can objectively judge different food items' quality, acceptability, and overall consumer experience.

The Role of Sensory Analysis of Food

Sensory analysis of food provides valuable insights into the organoleptic characteristics of various food items. "Organoleptic" refers to the attributes of food that our senses can perceive. The analysis helps identify the factors contributing to a food product's success or failure in the market. For example, by conducting sensory evaluation, the chefs can gauge whether the level of spiciness is appropriate, whether the aroma complements the flavours, and whether the overall appearance is visually appealing..

Basic Methods for Sensory Evaluation of Food

Difference Tests: These tests are designed to determine if there is a detectable difference between two or more products.

Triangle Test: Participants are given three samples, two of which are identical, and asked to identify the odd one out.

Duo-Trio Tests: Participants are presented with a reference sample and then two other samples (one identical to the reference and one different) and are asked to pick the one that matches the reference.

Paired Comparison Test: Participants are given two samples and asked to determine which one has more of a specific attribute.

Descriptive Tests: These tests provide detailed information about the specific attributes of a product.

Flavour Profile Test: A trained panel describes and quantifies the flavours in a product.

Texture Profile Test: A method used to quantify textural attributes such as hardness, chewiness, and grittiness.

Qualitative Test: Provides descriptive data about a product without quantification. It can be narrative or through focus groups.

Free Choice/Consumer Based: Participants can use their own words to describe a product.

Affective Tests: These tests measure consumers' preferences or feelings towards products.

Paired Preference Test: Participants are given two samples and asked which one they prefer.

Ranking Test: Participants rank multiple products based on a specific attribute or preference.

Hedonic Test: Participants rate products on a scale ranging from "dislike extremely" to "like extremely" to gauge overall acceptance.

Latest Technologies Used for Sensory Evaluation

E-nose: This electronic device mimics the human olfactory system. It detects and identifies odours and flavours using a variety of sensors, making it helpful in detecting off-flavours or verifying flavour profiles.

E-tongue: Similar to the E-nose, the E-tongue mimics human taste receptors. It can detect and measure different taste attributes in food and drink samples, helping to provide objective data on taste profiles.

Sensory Mapping: Utilizing advanced statistical methods and data visualization tools, sensory mapping allows for the graphical representation of sensory data, highlighting product relationships and differences.

Computer-Assisted Sensory Evaluation: Software applications streamline the process of data collection, analysis, and reporting in sensory evaluation.

Time-Intensity Profiling: Instruments that continuously monitor and track the intensity of a sensory perception over time.

Virtual Reality (VR) and Augmented Reality (AR): Emerging technologies where panellists are exposed to controlled virtual environments, allowing researchers to study the influence of context on sensory perception.

Texture Analyzers: Machines that measure physical properties of food, such as hardness, chewiness, and springiness, providing objective data on texture attributes.

Chapter 5

Cereals, Pulses and Oilseed Processing

1. The major carbohydrate of rice is
   (*a*) Glucose (*b*) Fructose
   (*c*) Starch (*d*) Pectin

2. The fibre of rice is the hemicelluloses made up of the
   (*a*) Pentose (*b*) Arabinose
   (*c*) Xylose (*d*) All

3. Glutelin (Oryzenin) is the principal protein of
   (*a*) Rice (*b*) Milk
   (*c*) Wheat (*d*) Pulse

4. The nutritive value of rice protein is superior than
   (*a*) Wheat (*b*) Barley
   (*c*) Oat (*d*) All

5. The rice protein is richer in
   (*a*) Arginine (*b*) Lysine
   (*c*) Threonine (*d*) All

6. Lysine and Threonine is absent in
   (*a*) Rice (*b*) Wheat
   (*c*) Barley (*d*) All

7. The polished rice is poor in
   (*a*) Ca and Fe (*b*) Ca and P
   (*c*) P and Fe (*d*) Fe and Mn

8. The activity of ______________ in fresh rice is probably responsible for its sticky consistency after cooking.
   (*a*) α-Amylase
   (*b*) Protease
   (*c*) Lipase
   (*d*) Oxidase

9. The pigments of coloured rice are
   (*a*) Anthocyanin
   (*b*) Carotenoid
   (*c*) Both (*a*) and (*b*)
   (*d*) None

10. Parboiling of rice is originated in
    (*a*) Pakistan
    (*b*) India
    (*c*) Bhutan
    (*d*) USA

11. High proportion of amylopectin is available in
    (*a*) Flint corn
    (*b*) Dent corn
    (*c*) Waxy corn
    (*d*) Pop corn

12. The major lipids of maize oil is
    (*a*) Triglycerides
    (*b*) Diglycerides
    (*c*) Amylose
    (*d*) Phospholipid

13. The triglycerides of corn oil have high proportion of ______________ and ______________ acid.
    (*a*) Lysine and Valine
    (*b*) Alanine and Proline
    (*c*) Oleic and Linoleic
    (*d*) Tryptophan and Methionine

14. Corn is deficient in the vitamin
    (*a*) Niacin
    (*b*) Calciferol (B_{12})
    (*c*) Thiamine (B_1)
    (*d*) Tocopherol (E)

15. The phosphorus in corn is found in the form of
    (*a*) Phytin
    (*b*) Glutamine
    (*c*) Histidine
    (*d*) Glycine

16. The keeping quality of breakfast cereals is depended on the
    (*a*) Fat content
    (*b*) Protein
    (*c*) Starch content
    (*d*) Vitamin

17. South Indian breakfast food (Upma) is made from
    (*a*) Flour
    (*b*) White flour
    (*c*) Semolina
    (*d*) Grits

18. The cooking time of farina (Payasam) is reduced by adding of
    (*a*) Disodium phosphate
    (*b*) Sodium benzoate
    (*c*) Salt
    (*d*) Sugar

19. Bread flour is milled from
(*a*) Soft wheat (*b*) Hard wheat
(*c*) Winter wheat (*d*) (*b*) and (*c*) both

20. Pudding, cake, pastries etc. are made from
(*a*) Self raising flour (*b*) Bread flour
(*c*) Biscuit flour (*d*) Cake flour
(Cake flour produces soft and tender texture and have low protein content which creates less gluten)

21. A slight excess of bicarbonate gives rise to an unpleasant odour and a brownish yellow colouration in
(*a*) Self raising flour (*b*) Bread flour
(*c*) All purpose flour (*d*) Pastry flour
(It turns yellow with higher CO_2 content due to excess bicarbonates)

22. One of the following is not a leavening agent for baking products
(*a*) Air (*b*) CO_2
(*c*) Steam (*d*) Baking soda

23. One of the following gas is generated during leavening process of baking product by action of chemical leaveners or action of microorganisms on sugars.
(*a*) O_2 (*b*) CO_2
(*c*) NH_3 (*d*) SO_2

24. The most important chemical agent used in leavening process is
(*a*) caustic soda (*b*) sodium hydrogen carbonate (Baking Powder)
(*c*) salt peter (*d*) sodium benzoate

25. Baking powder contains an inert filler used in leavening process is
(*a*) Corn starch (*b*) Potato starch
(*c*) Arrowroot (*d*) Egg powder

26. Corn starch acts as buffering agent between
(*a*) Baking soda and acids (*b*) CO_2 and acid
(*c*) O_2 and CO_2 (*d*) None

27. Baking powder is a compound of
(*a*) Sodium bicarbonate and tartrates (*b*) Sodium bicarbonate and corn starch
(*c*) Corn starch and tartrates (*d*) None

28. Tartrates in baking powder is implemented in the form of
(*a*) Tartaric acid (*b*) Potassium hydrogen tartrate
(*c*) (*a*) and (*b*) (*d*) None

29. Yeast used form leavening is marketed in the form of
(*a*) Compressed yeast
(*b*) Active dry yeast
(*c*) Both (*a*) and (*b*)
(*d*) None

30. The activity and shelf life of compressed yeast at 1ºC to 3ºC remains up to
(*a*) One week
(*b*) Two week
(*c*) Four week
(*d*) Five week

31. The shelf life of dry yeast is more than two years, if stored at temperature of
(*a*) 5 ºC
(*b*) 10 ºC
(*c*) 15 ºC
(*d*) 32 ºC

32. Small volume of bread may be due to
(*a*) Tight dough
(*b*) Lower or high temperature
(*c*) Under proofing
(*d*) All of these

33. In countries where rice is staple diet, continuous and exclusive use of polished rice causes *beriberi* due to deficiency of
(*a*) Thiamine
(*b*) Riboflavin
(*c*) Pyridoxine
(*d*) Cobalamin

34. Flaked rice is made from
(*a*) Raw rice
(*b*) Brown rice
(*c*) Parboiled rice
(*d*) Bulgur

35. Malting is a basic operation employed in
(*a*) Wheat
(*b*) Rice
(*c*) Barley
(*d*) Pulse

36. Aleurone layer in grains of wheat contain
(*a*) Higher protein
(*b*) Lower protein
(*c*) No protein
(*d*) None of these

37. Wheat flour when mixed with the appropriate amount of water forms dough which have a rheological property
(*a*) Elastic
(*b*) Plastic
(*c*) Visco-elastic
(*d*) None

38. In South India, Idli is a fermented food item made from
(*a*) Wheat and rice
(*b*) Black gram and rice
(*c*) Semolina and milk
(*d*) White flour and semolina

39. A favourable temperature for fermentation in the making of 'Idli' should be
(*a*) 10-20 ºC
(*b*) 20-25 ºC
(*c*) 25-30 ºC
(*d*) 30-35 ºC

40. The basic purpose of fermentation in Idli is
(*a*) To increase nutritive value
(*b*) Digestibility
(*c*) To decrease the acceptability
(*d*) Both (*a*) and (*b*)

41. For Idli making both ground lentil and rice batter is mixed and kept for fermentation for about
(*a*) 8-9 hrs
(*b*) 2025 hrs
(*c*) 15-120 hrs
(*d*) 24 hrs

42. The appropriate moisture of barley for malting purpose should be between
(*a*) 8-10 %
(*b*) 10-14 %
(*c*) 14-17 %
(*d*) 20-22 %

43. In milling, cleaned oats are subjected to kiln drying to inactivate lipase. This process is known as
(*a*) Drying
(*b*) Sterilization
(*c*) Stabilization
(*d*) Dehydration

44. When the proteins in the flour combine with water, a complex between gliadin and glutenin is formed resulting in the development of
(*a*) Gluten
(*b*) Casein
(*c*) Oryzenin
(*d*) Lactoalbumin

45. During bread making, the elasticity of gluten is controlled by
(*a*) Glutenin
(*b*) Gliadin
(*c*) Water
(*d*) Yeast

46. Loaf volume of bread during preparation is adjusted by
(*a*) Gliadin
(*b*) Glutenin/Gliadin ratio
(*c*) Gluten
(*d*) Yeast

47. High levels of flour amylase enzyme is responsible for
(*a*) Adverse affect on quality of bread
(*b*) Decrease loaf volume
(*c*) Decrease attractiveness in colour
(*d*) All of the above

48. The quantities and quality of gluten which a flour can yield is observed by the following instruments
(*a*) Mixograph and farinograph
(*b*) Amylograph
(*c*) Extensograph
(*d*) Alveogragh

49. The brown colour of crust of bread during baking is due to the maillard reaction between
(*a*) Protein and sugar
(*b*) Sugar and vitamin
(*c*) Sugar and salt
(*d*) Damage starch and amino acid

50. The activity of yeast fermentation during bread making is controlled by
(*a*) Flour (*b*) Water
(*c*) Sugar (*d*) Salt

51. Propionates are added in bread to inhibit the
(*a*) Mold growth (*b*) Bacterial growth
(*c*) Enzyme reaction (*d*) All

52. Enzyme used in bread making is protease acting on the gluten to alter
(*a*) Dough extensibility (*b*) Loaf volume
(*c*) Colour (*d*) Texture

53. Ammonium sulphate and phosphate in bread making are used as a
(*a*) Yeast nutrient (*b*) Oxidize agent
(*c*) Antioxidant (*d*) Emulsifier

54. Maize is deficient in the following amino acids
(*a*) Methionine and lysine (*b*) Methionine and arginine
(*c*) Lysine and arginine (*d*) Lysine and tryphtophane

55. In rice polishing
(*a*) A coating is applied on the outer surface of brown rice
(*b*) A layer of bran is removed from brown rice
(*c*) A layer of starch is removed
(*d*) Only husk is removed

56. Shelling out turn of (in percentage) of ground nut is
(*a*) 40 (*b*) 60
(*c*) 75 (*d*) 90

57. Terminal velocity of particle is equal to air velocity for which
(*a*) Particle remains in the bottom (*b*) Particle is carried away
(*c*) The particle remains in suspended state (*d*) None of these

58. Scalping is also known as
(*a*) Grading (*b*) Rough cleaning
(*c*) Separating (*d*) Dust removal

59. The value of moisture content determined on dry basis is
(*a*) lower than that determined on wet basis (*b*) higher than moisture content on wet basis
(*c*) equal to moisture content on wet basis (*d*) none of the above

60. In dry milling process prior to treatment with oil, in pulse the following operation is done
(*a*) grading (*b*) polishing
(*c*) conditioning (*d*) pitting

61. The edible portion of paddy is called
(*a*) Rice (*b*) Bran
(*c*) Endosperm (*d*) Husk

62. In paddy grain, the weight of hull is about
(*a*) 18-22 kg (*b*) 18-22 gm
(*c*) 18-22 % (*d*) 20-22 %

63. Removal of bran layer from the brown rice is done by
(*a*) Polisher (*b*) Bran aspirator
(*c*) Whitener (*d*) both (*a*) and (*c*)

64. The basic requirement of parboiling in paddy is done to
(*a*) increase the moisture content (*b*) minimize breakage during milling
(*c*) minimize the recovery of head rice (*d*) none of them

65. Rubber roll sheller shelled up the paddy about
(*a*) 85 % (*b*) 87 %
(*c*) 96 % (*d*) 95 %

66. Horizontal jet pearler is used in paddy milling for
(*a*) Polishing (*b*) Whitening
(*c*) Pearling (*d*) None of them

67. Glazing is done on rice for
(*a*) Polishing (*b*) Whitening
(*c*) Transparent look (*d*) Pearling

68. The soaking of cleaned wheat for milling is done at the temperature of
(*a*) 65-75 °F (*b*) 65-75 °C
(*c*) 75-80 °K (*d*) 80-85 °B

69. In pulse milling, pulse is treated with linseed oil with range of
(*a*) 1.0-2.0 kg/ton (*b*) 1.5-2.5 kg/ton
(*c*) 1.5-2.5 kg/quintal (*d*) 1.5-2.0 kg/ton

70. In CFTRI method of pulse milling, Pre conditioning of pulse is done at
(*a*) 120 °C (*b*) 125 °C
(*c*) 110 °C (*d*) 100 °C

71. After the oil treatment, the pulses are kept for about 12 hours to allow proper penetration to take place in the pulse kernel is called
(*a*) Conditioning (*b*) Oil penetration
(*c*) Tempering (*d*) Saponification

72. The moisture content of pulse for dehusking should not be more than
(*a*) 8-10 % (*b*) 10-20 %
(*c*) 20-25 % (*d*) 20-30 %

73. The efficiency of Gota machine for pulse in single pass is to about
(*a*) 50 % (*b*) 60 %
(*c*) 80 % (*d*) 90 %

74. The LSU is a
(*a*) Evaporator (*b*) Drier
(*c*) Washer (*d*) Polisher

75. The full name of LSU drier
(*a*) Ludhiana state university (*b*) Laos state university
(*c*) Lebanon state university (*d*) Louisiana state university

76. Saturated fatty acid increases
(*a*) Cancer (*b*) AIDS
(*c*) Heart problems (*d*) Diabetes

77. The boiling poirt of *n*-hexane for oil recovery should be
(*a*) 70.5 °C (*b*) 65.0 °C
(*c*) 65.5 °C (*d*) 60.5 °C

78. Removal of fibre from cotton seed is known as
(*a*) Flaking (*b*) Shelling
(*c*) Dehusking (*d*) Delinting

79. A thin layer grain drying is one in which grain thickness should be
(*a*) 20 cm (*b*) more than 20 cm
(*c*) less than 50 cm (*d*) less than 100 cm

80. Break rolls have
(*a*) Smooth surface (*b*) Corrugated surface
(*c*) Rough surface (*d*) Hole in surface

81. Reduction rolls have
(*a*) Smooth surface (*b*) Corrugated surface
(*c*) Rough surface (*d*) Hole in surface

82. The differential speed ratio of break rolls or reduction rolls is about
(*a*) 3.5:1 (*b*) 2.25:1
(*c*) 2.5:1 (*d*) 2.0:1

83. The purpose of hydrothermal treatment in wheat is for
(*a*) Loosening of hull (*b*) Loosening of endosperm
(*c*) Loosening of bran layer (*d*) None of them

84. The tempering of wheat is done for
(*a*) 18-72 h (*b*) 18-62 h
(*c*) 18-74 h (*d*) 18-50 h

85. The optimum temperature for conditioning of wheat is subjected at
(*a*) 45 °C (*b*) 47 °C
(*c*) 40 °C (*d*) 50 °C

86. Drying is a __________ operation.
(*a*) Thermo-physical (*b*) Physio-chemical
(*c*) Thermo-physical and physico-chemical (*d*) None of them

87. Grading refers to
(*a*) Classification of cleaned product (*b*) Classification of uncleaned product
(*c*) Separation of cleaned product (*d*) Separation of large impurities

88. Screening is a method of separating grains into two or more fractions according to
(*a*) Size alone (*b*) Shape alone
(*c*) Colour alone (*d*) Texture alone

89. Conditioning means
(*a*) Wetting (*b*) Drying
(*c*) Steaming (*d*) Wetting and drying

90. Pure starch, pure germ and feed are prepared from
(*a*) Corn dry milling (*b*) Corn wet milling
(*c*) Above both (*d*) None

91. Rotary steam tube in corn milling are used for the
(*a*) Drying (*b*) Washing
(*c*) Cooling (*d*) Steaming

92. Corns are treated at temperatures of 75°C during drying in
(*a*) dry milling (*b*) wet milling
(*c*) Above both (*d*) None

93. Hull is the synonyms of
(*a*) Endosperm (*b*) Bram
(*c*) Husk (*d*) Germ

94. Brokens in rice may be separated by
(*a*) Plan Sifter or trieur (*b*) Shellers
(*c*) Rubber separator (*d*) None of these

95. During shelling, the speed of faster roll of rubber roll sheller has about
(*a*) 8-10 m/s (*b*) 10-13 m/s
(*c*) 9-10 m/s (*d*) 12-15 m/s

96. Semolina is milled product containing coarse particles of endosperm with a diameter of
(*a*) 5-50 μm (*b*) 300-750 μm
(*c*) 100-130 μm (*d*) None of thee

97. The kernel of paddy is enclosed by
(*a*) Hull (*b*) Germ
(*c*) Bran (*d*) a and c

98. During polishing, bran from brown rice is removed approximately
(*a*) 4-6 % (*b*) 2-3 %
(*c*) 5-6 % (*d*) 3-4 %

99. In paddy grain, the weight of bran is about
(*a*) 2-3 % (*b*) 5-6 %
(*c*) 4-6 % (*d*) 3-4 %

100. The main products of corn dry milling is
(*a*) Pure starch (*b*) Germ
(*c*) Grits (*d*) Bulgur

101. The percent endosperm is present in corn kernel is about
(*a*) 82 % (*b*) 85 %
(*c*) 89 % (*d*) 87 %

102. The wet and soften corn kernel attain the moisture in wet milling is about
(*a*) 14 % (*b*) 22 %
(*c*) 27 % (*d*) 45 %

103. Moisture content in pegion pea (arhar) is about
(*a*) 10.25 % (*b*) 10.52 %
(*c*) 10.35 % (*d*) 15.54 %

104. The oil treatment in pulse is done to loosen the
(*a*) Bran
(*b*) Germ
(*c*) Husk
(*d*) Aleurone layer

105. The machine used for making scratch over whole grain of pulse is
(*a*) Gota machine
(*b*) Emery roller
(*c*) Concave type machine
(*d*) Screw conveyor

106. For dehusking and splitting, the moisture content in pulse should be
(*a*) 5-10 %
(*b*) 10-20 %
(*c*) 15-25 %
(*d*) 25-30 %

107. The pearler is also called
(*a*) Degermer
(*b*) Dehusker
(*c*) Polisher
(*d*) Debranner

108. Per capita consumption of edible oil per year in India is
(*a*) 5 kg
(*b*) 8 kg
(*c*) 10 kg
(*d*) 19.7 kg

109. Oil percent in soybean is approximately
(*a*) 18-20 %
(*b*) 30-35 %
(*c*) 45-50 %
(*d*) 20-25 %

110. The term disintegration is related to
(*a*) Paddy processing
(*b*) Pulse processing
(*c*) Corn milling
(*d*) Oil processing

111. In solvent extraction of oil, the solvent is
(*a*) n-hexane
(*b*) iso-hexane
(*c*) n-butane
(*d*) hot water

112. Separating of grains or seeds in two or more fraction according to the size alone is called
(*a*) Sorting
(*b*) Screening
(*c*) Scalping
(*d*) Grading

113. At the time of harvesting, the moisture content in paddy should not more or less than
(*a*) 12-14 %
(*b*) 16-18 %
(*c*) 20-22 %
(*d*) 24-28 %

114. Reduction of food grains in to various edible end products is called
(*a*) grinding
(*b*) milling
(*c*) shelling
(*d*) splitting

115. Bulgur is the product, popular in Egypt is made of the
(*a*) Rice (*b*) Corn
(*c*) Wheat (*d*) Pulse

116. Talcum powder or glucose are used in the unit operation of
(*a*) Polishing (*b*) Whitening
(*c*) Glazing (*d*) Shining

117. Separation of broken rice and head rice is known as
(*a*) Scalping (*b*) Screening
(*c*) Sorting (*d*) Grading

118. Removal of hull or husk from the cereal grain is called
(*a*) Dehusking (*b*) Splitting
(*c*) Degerming (*d*) Polishing

119. Beall degermer are used for processing of
(*a*) Paddy (*b*) Wheat
(*c*) Oat (*d*) Corn

120. One hundred kg of paddy grain would yield husk about
(*a*) 30 kg (*b*) 25 kg
(*c*) 22 kg (*d*) 72 kg

121. Composition of endosperm, bran and germ in wheat (in percent) is approximately
(*a*) 82, 14, 4 (*b*) 75, 10, 15
(*c*) 85, 12, 3 (*d*) 80, 5, 15

122. The yield of white flour and by product in wheat processing is
(*a*) 80 % and 20 % (*b*) 70 % and 30 %
(*c*) 85 % and 15 % (*d*) 90 % and 10 %

123. Wheat is harvested at the moisture content of
(*a*) 35 % (*b*) 25 %
(*c*) 20 % (*d*) 15 %

124. Husk separators are used in
(*a*) Pulse processing (*b*) Wheat processing
(*c*) Paddy processing (*d*) Vegetable processing

125. The main purpose of hydrothermal treatment in wheat processing is
(*a*) Remove of moisture content (*b*) Remove of germ
(*c*) Loosening of bran (*d*) Increase the temperature

126. Food processing involving the application of
(*a*) Chemistry and biochemistry
(*b*) Biophysics, nutrition and microbiology
(*c*) All branches of engineering
(*d*) Above all

127. Grading refers to
(*a*) Cleaning of product
(*b*) Separation of cleaned products according of physical properties
(*c*) Classification of cleaned products according commercial values and usages
(*d*) Both (*b*) and (*c*)

128. Milling refers to the
(*a*) Cleaning and grading
(*b*) Dehusking, splitting
(*c*) separating, size reduction and polishing
(*d*) Overall operations in mill

129. Dehydration means removal of moisture content to
(*a*) Very high level
(*b*) Medium level
(*c*) Vey low level
(*d*) Bone dry condition

130. Environmental factors such as ____________ will spoil the food.
(*a*) O_2 and water vapour
(*b*) O_2 and H_2
(*c*) H_2 and N_2
(*d*) N_2 and C

131. The ____________ makes the food products suitable for storage.
(*a*) Scalping
(*b*) Sorting
(*c*) Screening
(*d*) Drying

132. Clean and good quality paddy can give a yield of ________ rice.
(*a*) 70 %
(*b*) 76 %
(*c*) 74 %
(*d*) 87 %

133. The ____________ is done to achieve maximum recovery of head rice and to minimize breakage.
(*a*) Shelling
(*b*) Cleaning
(*c*) Polishing
(*d*) Parboiling

134. Moisture of paddy during milling should be
(*a*) 20-22 %
(*b*) 10-12 %
(*c*) 12-14 %
(*d*) 15-20 %

135. Disc Sheller consists of ____________ coated with emery.
(*a*) Two horizontal iron discs
(*b*) Two vertical iron discs
(*c*) One horizontal and one vertical disc
(*d*) Two vertical stone discs

136. Grading in rice milling usually refers to the separation of
(*a*) Small weed seed
(*b*) Broken from head rice
(*c*) Husk particles
(*d*) Bran particles

137. The weight of hull is ________ of the total weight of paddy grain.
(*a*) 20-22 %
(*b*) 12-14 %
(*c*) 14-16 %
(*d*) 18-22 %

138. Rice bran contains about ________ percent fat
(*a*) 10-12 %
(*b*) 12-15 %
(*c*) 15-17 %
(*d*) 17-19 %

139. Pulses contain following percent of protein by weight
(*a*) 5-10 %
(*b*) 10-15 %
(*c*) 17-25 %
(*d*) 30-35 %

140. Parboiling of paddy is following treatment
(*a*) Cooling
(*b*) Heating
(*c*) Hydrothermal
(*d*) None of these

141. In most of the wheat mills, the yield of flour can be obtained about
(*a*) 25 %
(*b*) 50 %
(*c*) 75 %
(*d*) 90 %

142. Shelled groundnut contains following percent oil content
(*a*) 10-20 %
(*b*) 20-30 %
(*c*) 30-40 %
(*d*) 45-50 %

143. Soybean contains ________ % protein and ________ % oil content.
(*a*) 30 and 10
(*b*) 40 and 20
(*c*) 50 and 30
(*d*) 60 and 30

144. The percentage of germ in wheat grain or the composition of germ in wheat is
(*a*) 5 %
(*b*) 1 %
(*c*) 2 %
(*d*) 3 %

145. During conditioning of wheat, the temperature of wheat grain should not be
(*a*) Less than 40 °C
(*b*) Less than 47 °C
(*c*) More than 47 °C
(*d*) None of the above

146. In wheat mills, the rolls that have smooth surface are
(*a*) Reduction roll
(*b*) Break roll
(*c*) plan sifter
(*d*) Scratch roll

147. The differential speed of the pair of break rolls is
(*a*) 1:2 (*b*) 2:1
(*c*) 2.5:1 (*d*) 1:2.5

148. Which one of the following can be said as the extension of break roll is
(*a*) Reduction roll (*b*) Purifier
(*c*) Plan sifter (*d*) Scratch roll

149. The purpose of tempering of wheat through tempering bin is employed to
(*a*) Raise the moisture (*b*) Reduce the moisture
(*c*) Equalize the moisture in whole grain (*d*) Raise the temperature

150. The number of baking quality of the flour depend on the percentage of
(*a*) Germ (*b*) Bran
(*c*) Gluten (*d*) Grits

151. The number of break rolls which are employed to accomplished the proper breaking of grain is
(*a*) 3 to 4 (*b*) 8 to 10
(*c*) 1 to 3 (*d*) 6 to 8

152. The oils and fats are composed of different mixture of
(*a*) Glycerin (*b*) Glucose
(*c*) Glycerides (*d*) Glycerol

153. What are the main constituents of vegetable oils?
(*a*) 16 and 18 carbon acids (*b*) 11 and 12 carbon acids
(*c*) 16 and 18 carbonic acids (*d*) 13 and 17 carbon acids

154. The recommended value of oil consumption in India per annum per capita is about
(*a*) 6 MT (*b*) 19.4 MT
(*c*) 5 kg (*d*) 18 kg

155. The amount of energy released by oils and fats is more than protein and carbohydrate by
(*a*) 2.25 times (*b*) 2.5 times
(*c*) 2.00 times (*d*) remains same

156. The essential fatty acid provided by the oils is
(*a*) Carbonic acid (*b*) Linoleic acid
(*c*) Lactic acid (*d*) Gluconic acid

157. Which of the following is not a method of oil processing?
(*a*) Bullock driven ghani (*b*) Mechanical expression
(*c*) Chemical lye method (*d*) Solvent oil extraction method

158. The process of mechanically pressing liquid containing solid liquid to leach out of liquid is called
(*a*) Pressing (*b*) Expression
(*c*) Compression (*d*) Disintegration

159. The optimum moisture content of corn for degerming in the Baell Degermer should be
(*a*) 20-23 % (*b*) 25-30 %
(*c*) 21-25 % (*d*) 10-15 %

160. In which unit operation, germ is detached from the other component of corn kernel
(*a*) Tempering (*b*) Degerming
(*c*) Rolling (*d*) Flaking

161. Which one of the following, is not an example of equipment used in expression of oil seed :
(*a*) Screw press (*b*) Screw conveyor
(*c*) Hydraulic press (*d*) Pasteurizer

162. The process of separating a liquid from liquid solid medium with the help of solvent is known as:
(*a*) Expression (*b*) Pressing
(*c*) Extraction (*d*) Disintegration

163. The deoiled cake that comes out from the oil extraction unit has a weight of total mass is
(*a*) 25 to 40 % (*b*) 20 to 25 %
(*c*) 15 to 20 % (*d*) 30 to 35 %

164. Stone-separator is a form of
(*a*) Specific gravity separator (*b*) Velvet roll separator
(*c*) Magnetic separator (*d*) Disc separator

165. Disc separator separates material on the basis of
(*a*) Surface area (*b*) Length
(*c*) Density (*d*) Roundness

166. Separation on the basis of roundness is accomplished by
(*a*) Tray separator (*b*) Inclined dapper
(*c*) Spiral separator (*d*) Aspiration separator

167. If the separation on the basis of relative length of grain, disc separator is equivalent to
(*a*) Spiral separator
(*b*) Cyclone separator
(*c*) Indented cylinder separator
(*d*) Magnetic separator

168. 'R-Pockets' are present to separate desirable grains in
(*a*) Velvet roll separator
(*b*) Disc separator
(*c*) Indented cylinder separator
(*d*) Spiral separator

169. Dissimilar materials like wheat, barley and mustard from oat are separated by
(*a*) Cyclone separator
(*b*) Velvet roll separator
(*c*) Spiral separator
(*d*) Disc separator

170. In destoner, separation can be controlled by adjusting
(*a*) Feed rate
(*b*) Air flow rate
(*c*) Slope of the deck and its vibration
(*d*) All of these

171. In spiral separator, the adjustable component for separation is
(*a*) Slope of deck
(*b*) Rate of feeding
(*c*) Air flow rate
(*d*) None of these

172. Lack of flexibility is the main limitation of
(*a*) Spiral separator
(*b*) Velvet roll separator
(*c*) Disc separator
(*d*) Magnetic separator

173. Pneumatic separation is based on
(*a*) Difference in relative length
(*b*) Difference in aerodynamic properties
(*c*) Difference in density
(*d*) All of the above

174. The performance factor ($S = Cf/W$) is related with
(*a*) Spiral separator
(*b*) Magnetic separator
(*c*) Disc separator
(*d*) Cyclone separator

175. Larger crops seeds like peas and beans are separated by
(*a*) Disc separator
(*b*) Cyclone separator
(*c*) Colour separator
(*d*) Velvet roll separator

176. Magnetic separator performs separation on the basis of
(*a*) difference in aerodynamic properties
(*b*) relative length of grains
(*c*) surface texture and stickiness property of the grain
(*d*) all of these

177. Separation on the basis of difference in shape and surface texture is done by
(*a*) destoner and magnetic separator
(*b*) pneumatic and aspirator separator
(*c*) spiral and disc separator
(*d*) inclined draper and velvet roll separator

178. The device which is simple, inexpensive and quite useful for seed cleaning purposes
(*a*) Disc separator (*b*) Magnetic separator
(*c*) Spiral separator (*d*) Velvet roll separator

179. The high pressure air blast separates the material in
(*a*) Pneumatic separator (*b*) Aspirator
(*c*) Both of these (*d*) None of these

180. The function of cyclone separator is to
(*a*) collect the end products (dust and wastes) during processing of grains
(*b*) separate grains on the basis of relative length
(*c*) separate grains on the aerodynamic properties
(*d*) separate the grains with rough seed coat from smooth surface grain

181. A rice mill has to separate 40 tones of rice and paddy (long grain) per hour using a compartment type paddy separator. Calculate (*i*) the number of compartment required to carry out this separation (*ii*) the number of compartment per deck if number of decks are 4.
(*a*) 250, 1000 (*b*) 1000, 250
(*c*) 100, 25 (*d*) 667, 167

182. How many magnetic drums are used to increase the efficiency in magnetic separator generally,
(*a*) 1 or 2 (*b*) 2 or 3
(*c*) 3 or 4 (*d*) 4 or 5

183. Roll mill separator is also known as
(*a*) Disc separator (*b*) Spiral separator
(*c*) Cyclone separator (*d*) Velvet roll separator

184. Fractioning aspirator is a
(*a*) Dehusker (*b*) Sheller
(*c*) Huller (*d*) Separator

185. On which factor, the particles are acted upon by a cyclone separator
(*a*) Centrifugal force (*b*) Weight of the particle
(*c*) Shape of the particle (*d*) Both (*a*) and (*b*)

186. Tray separator is generally used for separating
(*a*) Wheat (*b*) Paddy
(*c*) Pulse (*d*) All of these

187. Husk aspirator separates immature grains from shelled paddy by which of the following action
(*a*) Gravity flow (*b*) Perforating sieve
(*c*) Winnowing action (*d*) Blowing action

188. The table inclination in case of fixed stroke separator is
(*a*) 2–3°
(*b*) 3–4°
(*c*) 4–5°
(*d*) 5–6°

189. How many strokes and with what speed of the fixed stroke separator is adjusted in case of long grain rice
(*a*) 90-96, 114 rpm
(*b*) 86-92, 120 rpm
(*c*) 75-80, 124 rpm
(*d*) 95-100, 110 rpm

190. Which separators separate the grain on the basis of length
(*a*) Disc separator and magnetic separator
(*b*) Indented cylinder separator and disc separator
(*c*) Indented cylinder separator and spiral separator
(*d*) Velvet roll separator and inclined separator

191. The inclination of the deck in the compartment type paddy separator depends on
(*a*) Percentage paddy and brown rice
(*b*) Percentage of brown rice
(*c*) Percentage of paddy
(*d*) None of these

192. The shape of steel flanks and impact angle in compartment type paddy separator is
(*a*) *Z* and 60°
(*b*) *Z* and 30°
(*c*) *V* and 30°
(*d*) *V* and 60°

193. The efficiency of hullers doesn't depend upon
(*a*) Husking machine
(*b*) Operator skill
(*c*) Uniformity of paddy
(*d*) None of these

194. The distance between indented trays of tray separator is
(*a*) 4 cm
(*b*) 5 cm
(*c*) 7 cm
(*d*) 9 cm

195. Separation on the basis of smooth surface and higher bulk density of brown rice from paddy is done by
(*a*) Disc separator
(*b*) Tray separator
(*c*) Spiral separator
(*d*) Velvet roll separator

196. The velocity of fixed stroke separators in compartment type paddy separator is
(*a*) 114/100 rpm
(*b*) 100/100 rpm
(*c*) 124/100 rpm
(*d*) 105/100 rpm

197. The pockets/indentations in disc separator capture
(*a*) Small sized grains
(*b*) Large sized grains
(*c*) Bothe of these
(*d*) None of these

198. The shape of indent in inclined cylinder separator is
(a) Hemispherical
(b) Circular
(c) Spherical
(d) Triangular

199. Size of all indents particularly in indented cylinder separator should be
(a) Variable
(b) Same
(c) Adjustable
(d) None of these

200. The separator in which centrifugal force is involved for the separation of grain is
(a) Indented cylinder separator
(b) Cyclone separator
(c) Spiral separator
(d) All of these

201. Mustard is separated from wheat mainly by
(a) Disc separator
(b) Magnetic separator
(c) Spiral separator
(d) None of these

202. The power requirement of tray separator is ____________ than the compartment type separator.
(a) Equal
(b) Half
(c) Less
(d) More

203. Performance factor 'S' in cyclone separator is equal to
(a) $V^2/g\ R^2$
(b) $V/g\ R^2$
(c) $V^2/g\ R$
(d) $V/g\ R$

204. The motion of belt in inclined drapper separator is
(a) in upward direction
(b) in downward direction
(c) opposite direction
(d) none of these

205. The roller of velvet roll separator rotate in
(a) Opposite direction
(b) Same direction
(c) In arbitrary direction
(d) None of these

206. Maximum percentage of oil is found in
(a) Ground nut
(b) Mustard
(c) Linseed
(d) Coconut

207. Cracked debranned parboiled wheat is called as
(a) Maida
(b) Bulgur
(c) Semolina
(d) Flour

208. Cleaning of agricultural materials is performed by
(a) Washing
(b) Screening
(c) Hand picking
(d) All of these

209. Classification of cleaned products into various quality fractions on the basis of commercial values is called
(*a*) Sorting
(*b*) Grading
(*c*) Cleaning
(*d*) Scalping

210. Separation of cleaned products into various quality fractions on the basis of any one physical property is known as
(*a*) Sorting
(*b*) Grading
(*c*) Cleaning
(*d*) Scalping

211. Removal of few large particles involved in the process is called
(*a*) Screening
(*b*) Cleaning
(*c*) Grading
(*d*) Scalping

212. The material which retained over a screen surface is called
(*a*) Over size or plus materials
(*b*) Undersize or minus material
(*c*) Intermediate materials
(*d*) Undesirable material

213. The vibratory screens are agitated by
(*a*) Eccentric unit
(*b*) Belt and pulley
(*c*) Chain and sprocket
(*d*) None

214. A screen is capable of accurate and complete separation of very fine sizes but its capacity is limited.
(*a*) Shaking screen
(*b*) Vibratory screen
(*c*) Rotary screen
(*d*) Horizontal screen

215. The inclination of cylinder sorter for dry granular materials is kept upto
(*a*) 125 mm/m
(*b*) 145 mm/m
(*c*) 135 mm/m
(*d*) 155 mm/m

216. The effective screening area in cylinder sorter is calculated by the formula
(*a*) 1/3 length × diameter
(*b*) Length × 1/3 diameter
(*c*) Length × 1/2 diameter
(*d*) 1/2 length × diameter

217. Cylinder sorter is a type of
(*a*) Rotary screen
(*b*) Shaking screen
(*c*) Revolving screen
(*d*) Vibratory screen

218. The effectiveness of which screen is higher than others.
(*a*) Rotary screen
(*b*) Horizontal screen
(*c*) Revolving screen
(*d*) Vibratory screen

219. The technique useful in coarse sifting is
(*a*) Horizontal reciprocating motion
(*b*) Combined vertical and horizontal motion
(*c*) Inclined reciprocating motion
(*d*) Horizontal rotary motion

220. In perforated metal screens, the diameter of round opening having unit in
(*a*) mm
(*b*) Inch
(*c*) Above both
(*d*) None

221. In groundnut grader, the part used to avoid clogging is called
(*a*) Spreader
(*b*) Brushes
(*c*) Both
(*d*) None

222. The two oscillating sieves in groundnut grader are oscillated by
(*a*) Eccentric mechanism
(*b*) Vertically motion
(*c*) Offcentric mechanism
(*d*) Downward/horizontal motion

223. The length of screen surface should be
(*a*) 1-2 times its width
(*b*) 2-3 times its width
(*c*) 3-4 times its width
(*d*) Equal to width

224. The common range in pitch adjustment (angle of inclination) in air screen grain cleaner is
(*a*) 3 to 8°
(*b*) 4 to 12°
(*c*) 12 to 20°
(*d*) 16 to 24°

225. During screening in air screen grain cleaner, the bed thickness can be reduced by
(*a*) Increasing the screen slope at constant feed rate
(*b*) Increasing the feed rate at constant screen slope
(*c*) Decreasing the screen slope at constant feed rate
(*d*) Decreasing the feed rate at constant screen slope

226. Which statement is true?
(*a*) Smallest possible perforation is used for scalping
(*b*) Largest possible perforation is used for grading
(*c*) Both
(*d*) None

227. Drying is a
(*a*) Thermo-physical process
(*b*) Physic-chemical process
(*c*) Both
(*d*) None

228. The specific heat of a product is not dependent on
(*a*) Mass density
(*b*) Specific gravity
(*c*) Weight density
(*d*) All of these

229. To determine the heat transfer rates in solid agricultural product of any shape, thermal diffusivity formula is as

(*a*) $\alpha = k/\rho C_p$ (*b*) $\alpha = C_p / k\rho$
(*c*) $\alpha = k\rho/ C_p$ (*d*) $\alpha = \rho/ k C_p$

230. The heat content of a material is called as

(*a*) Specific heat (*b*) Enthalpy
(*c*) Thermal conductivity (*d*) Entropy

231. Thermal conductivity is determined by the formula

(*a*) $Q = AK (T_1 - T_2) / t$ (*b*) $Q = AK (T_1 - T_2)^2 / t$
(*c*) $Q = AK (T_2 - T_1) / t^2$ (*d*) $Q = AK (T_2 - T_1) / t$

232. Thermal conductivity depends on ______________ of materials.

(*a*) Mass density (*b*) Specific gravity
(*c*) Weight density (*d*) All of these

233. Thermal conductivity of single grain is

(*a*) 0.1 to 0.2 kcal/m-h-°C (*b*) 0.1 to 0.2 kcal/m²-h-°C
(*c*) 0.3 to 0.6 kcal/m-h-°C (*d*) 0.3 to 0.6 kcal/m²-h-°C

234. Advantages of drying in favour of farmers are

(*a*) Drying permits early harvest of crops
(*b*) It helps in proper planning of harvesting season
(*c*) Drying of agricultural products to optimum moisture content results in safe storage of products for a longer period
(*d*) All of above

235. W/m-°C is the unit of

(*a*) Enthalpy (*b*) Entropy
(*c*) Thermal diffusivity (*d*) Thermal conductivity

236. At 18 % moisture content, the sample of grain contains 18 kg (100 × 0.18) of water and 82 kg of dry matter. The same amount is dried to 13 % moisture content, and then final weight of water will be

(*a*) 12.25 kg (*b*) 30.25 kg
(*c*) 5.75 kg (*d*) 25.25 kg

237. If moisture content (wet basis) is 14 %. Then, moisture content dry basis will be

(*a*) 14.30 % (*b*) 9.28 %
(*c*) 16.27 % (*d*) 19.22 %

238. Henderson equation for determination of EMC is based on
(*a*) Gibbs adsorption equation
(*b*) Chung-pfost equation
(*c*) Kelvin equation
(*d*) Harkins –Jura equation

239. The difference between desorption and adsorption curve of drying is known as
(*a*) Hysteresis effect
(*b*) Cooling effect
(*c*) Chilling effect
(*d*) Refrigeration effect

240. The ratio of actual vapour pressure in air water mixture and the saturated water vapour at same temperature is known as
(*a*) Percentage humidity
(*b*) Relative humidity
(*c*) Absolute humidity
(*d*) None of these

241. Which statement is correct?
(*a*) Drying is convection process in which moisture from a product is removed.
(*b*) Dehydration is a process in which products are dried to very low moisture level.
(*c*) Both (*a*) and (*b*)
(*d*) None of these

242. When the atmospheric vapour pressure is greater than grain vapour pressure, transfer of moisture is from
(*a*) Grain to atmosphere
(*b*) Grain absorbs moisture from atmosphere
(*c*) There is no transfer of moisture
(*d*) Moisture is completely removed from grain.

243. The critical moisture of wheat varies between
(*a*) 50-60 % (db)
(*b*) 85-90 % (db)
(*c*) 69-85 % (db)
(*d*) 80-90 % (db)

244. The moisture content of agricultural products at which constant rate drying ceases and falling rate starts is called
(*a*) Equilibrium moisture content
(*b*) Critical moisture content
(*c*) Moisture content on dry basis
(*d*) Hysteresis effect

245. The type of dryer used in big rice mills.
(*a*) Recirculating dryer
(*b*) Deep bed dryer
(*c*) LSU dryer
(*d*) Continuous flow dryer

246. The process of cooling the oil to a low temperature for long time and filtering the solid material from the oil is called
(*a*) Deodourization
(*b*) Decolouration
(*c*) Winterization
(*d*) Bleaching

247. The oil content in raw rice bran is
(*a*) 10-12 % (*b*) 12-18 %
(*c*) 20-28 % (*d*) 28-30 %

248. The oil content of parboiled rice bran is
(*a*) 20-28 % (*b*) 12-18 %
(*c*) 30-35 % (*d*) 43-48 %

249. The refined crude bran oil for edible purpose is uneconomic if FFA content is above
(*a*) 5 % (*b*) 20 %
(*c*) 12 % (*d*) 10 %

250. Bran oil is a rich source of
(*a*) Vitamin D (*b*) Riboflavin
(*c*) Vitamin E (*d*) Tocopherol

251. Tocopherol content in crude bran oil is about
(*a*) 2-4 % (*b*) 4-5 %
(*c*) 1-2 % (*d*) 6-8 %

252. A significant amount of tocopherol is lost during processing of crude oil. This loss occurs during
(*a*) Winterization (*b*) Deodourization
(*c*) Decolouration (*d*) None of these

253. Which one of the following is a liquid fumigant?
(*a*) Hydrogen phosphide (*b*) Methyl bromide
(*c*) Hydrogen cyanide (*d*) Ethyl bromide

254. The transfer of moisture from interior of grain faster towards surface during drying due to
(*a*) Osmotic pressure (*b*) Vapour pressure
(*c*) Surface tension (*d*) Conduction

255. The amount of moisture removed from grain by drying air depends upon the
(*a*) Length of grain (*b*) Chemical properties of air
(*c*) Psychometric properties of air (*d*) Amount of air

256. Drying process means removal of moisture due to simultaneous __________ and ________ transfer.
(*a*) Heat, mass (*b*) Volume, shape
(*c*) Moisture, vapour (*d*) Density, specific gravity

257. In which drying process heat is supplied to wet products by conduction
(*a*) Radiation drying (*b*) Freeze drying
(*c*) Superheated steam drying (*d*) Contact drying

258. The sensible heat of heated air is transferred to the wet product by convection in
(*a*) Osmotic drying (*b*) Convective drying
(*c*) Fluidized bed drying (*d*) Desiccated air drying

259. Sublimation of frozen moisture from wet product is employed in
(*a*) Freeze drying (*b*) Dehydro-freezing
(*c*) Spray drying (*d*) Drum drying

260. The wavelength of electromagnetic radiation in radiation drying of foods ranges between
(*a*) 0.76–400 μm (*b*) 100–200 μm
(*c*) 1–200 μm (*d*) 400–1000 μm

261. The wave length of 0.76 to 400 μm radiation is known as
(*a*) *x*-rays (*b*) infrared radiation
(*c*) γ-rays (*d*) none of these

262. Recommended air flow rate for deep bed drying of grain is
(*a*) 2.94–3.92 m^3/min per ton (*b*) 2.94–3.43 m^3/min per ton
(*c*) 3.43–3.92 m^3/min per ton (*d*) 50–95 m^3/min per ton

263. The lower limit of air flow rate of 2.94–3.43 m^3/min per ton in deep bed drying is recommended for the __________ region .
(*a*) Hot (*b*) Rainy
(*c*) Cool and dry (*d*) Hot and humid.

264. For hot and dry condition, recommended higher limit of air flow rate in deep bed drying is
(*a*) 2.94–3.92 m^3/min per ton (*b*) 3.43–3.92 m^3/min per ton
(*c*) 2.94–3.43 m^3/min per ton (*d*) 50–60 m^3/min per ton

265. For uneven deep bed drying, recommended air flow rate for the grain is
(*a*) 4.92 m^3/min per ton (*b*) 3.92 m^3/min per ton
(*c*) 3.43 m^3/min per ton (*d*) 2.94 m^3/min per ton

266. If the moisture content of grain is upto 18%, the layer depth of grain for deep drying should not be more than
(*a*) 3.0 m (*b*) 2.0 m
(*c*) 4.5 m (*d*) 1.0 m

267. For grain whose moisture content is 18 %, the recommended maximum depth for deep bed drying is
(*a*) 3.0 m (*b*) 2.5 m
(*c*) 2.0 m (*d*) 1.0 m

268. The net perforated drying area of deep bed dryer should be __________ of the total flour area.
(*a*) 10 % (*b*) 15 %
(*c*) 25 % (*d*) 40 %

269. Grains are spread 0.6 to 1.2 m deep over perforated flour in
(*a*) Deep bed dryer (*b*) Flat bed dryer
(*c*) Continuous flow dryer (*d*) LSU dryer

270. The capacity of flat bed dryer is usually
(*a*) 2-5 ton (*b*) 1-2 ton
(*c*) 50-60 ton (*d*) 5-50 ton

271. The main advantage of flat bed dryer is
(*a*) Whole batch is dried quickly (*b*) Less chance of mold spoilage
(*c*) Less over drying of grain (*d*) Need of lower air pressure
(*e*) All of the above

272. Which dryer is classified in to mixing and non mixing method?
(*a*) Deep bed dryer (*b*) Flat bed dryer
(*c*) Continuous flow dryer (*d*) LSU dryer
(*e*) Recirculating dryer

273. In which dryer, baffles are employed for proper mixing of grain during drying?
(*a*) Deep bed dryer (*b*) Continuous flow dryer
(*c*) LSU dryer (*d*) Recirculating dryer

274. The temperature of hot air at which grain is dried in mixing type continuous flow dryer
(*a*) 60ºC (*b*) 50ºC
(*c*) 65ºC (*d*) 47ºC

275. Drying air temperature used in non mixing type continuous flow dryer is about
(*a*) 54ºC (*b*) 47ºC
(*c*) 45ºC (*d*) 65ºC

276. A popular drier used in paddy processing industry originated in USA is
(*a*) Recirculating dryer (*b*) LSU dryer
(*c*) Deep bed dryer (*d*) Flat bed dryer

277. For continuous mixing of grain, inverted V-shaped channels are installed in
(*a*) Deep bed dryer (*b*) Recirculating dryer
(*c*) Fluidized bed dryer (*d*) LSU dryer

278. Safe storage of grains is essential
(*a*) To prevent losses and disease
(*b*) To prevent from the attack of birds, insects, pest, rodents and microorganisms
(*c*) To maintain good quality of products
(*d*) All of the above

279. The estimated losses of world food production damaged by insects during storage is about
(*a*) 1–3 % (*b*) 5–10 %
(*c*) 10–15 % (*d*) 20–40 %

280. The estimated losses of total food grains of India due to insect is about
(*a*) 1–3% (*b*) 5–10%
(*c*) 10–15 % (*d*) 20–40 %

281. How much grain is contaminated by rodent of own actual weight?
(*a*) Two times (*b*) Five times
(*c*) Ten times (*d*) Twenty times

282. In India, Morai storage structure is commonly used in the rural area of
(*a*) Southern region (*b*) Eastern region
(*c*) Central region (*d*) Both (*a*) and (*b*)

283. Morai structure is generally suitable for
(*a*) Paddy, maize and sorghum (*b*) Paddy, potato and tobacco
(*c*) Mustard, soybean and wheat (*d*) Maize, bazra and oat

284. The capacities of morai storage structure varies between
(*a*) 3.5–18 tonnes (*b*) 9–35 tonnes
(*c*) 10–15 tonnes (*d*) 1–2 tonnes

285. One of the following structures has inverted truncated cone shape.
(*a*) Bukhari (*b*) Kothari
(*c*) Pusa bin (*d*) Morai

286. A wooden floor surrounded by 22 gauge corrugated metal cylinder upto height of 90 cm is in__________.
(*a*) Pusa bin (*b*) Kothari
(*c*) Morai (*d*) Bukhari

287. The height of grain loaded in morai structure is about
(*a*) 75 cm (*b*) 90 cm
(*c*) 120 cm (*d*) 100 cm

288. Bukhari storage structure generally has capacities between
(*a*) 2–4 tonnes (*b*) 4–5 tonnes
(*c*) 3.5–18 tonnes (*d*) 9–35 tonnes

289. Kothar structure is used to store the paddy, maize, sorghum and wheat, their capacities varies between
(*a*) 2–4 tonnes (*b*) 4–5 tonnes
(*c*) 3.5–18 tonnes (*d*) 9–35 tonnes

290. 'Muda' is a popular grain storage structure of
(*a*) Bihar
(*b*) West Bengal
(*c*) Orissa
(*d*) UP

291. 'Kanaj' is a type of
(*a*) Grain storage structure
(*b*) Drying method
(*c*) Food products
(*d*) Grain separator

292. The 'Kanaj storage structure is very common in the rural area of
(*a*) Jammu and Kashmir
(*b*) Punjab and Haryana
(*c*) UP and Bihar
(*d*) Karnataka and Maharashtra

293. The capacity of 'Kanaj' varies between
(*a*) 1 to 20 tonnes
(*b*) 3.5 to 18 tonnes
(*c*) 9 to 35 tonnes
(*d*) 35 to 40 tonnes

294. In which states, Kuthla for grain storage is very commonly used in the rural areas.
(*a*) UP and Bihar
(*b*) Bihar and Jharkhand
(*c*) MP and Chhattisgarh
(*d*) Rajasthan and Gujarat

295. One of the following is not a grain storage structure.
(*a*) Kuthla
(*b*) Kanaj
(*c*) Muda
(*d*) Bellows

296. In which of grain storage structure, plastic film of 700 gauges is used
(*a*) Kothar
(*b*) Morai
(*c*) Pusa bin
(*d*) Bukhari

297. The size of an open space on top of Pusa bin for loading should be
(*a*) 60 cm × 60 cm
(*b*) 50 cm × 50 cm
(*c*) 50 cm × 50 mm
(*d*) No open space

298. One of the following is not improved grain storage structure.
(*a*) Pusa bin
(*b*) Bunker storage
(*c*) Cover and plinth storage structure
(*d*) Muda

299. The height of stack in CAP grain storage structure should not be more than
(*a*) 10 bags
(*b*) 15 bags
(*c*) 18 bags
(*d*) 20 bags

300. The capacity of CAP storage structure is
(*a*) 10 tonnes
(*b*) 100 tonnes
(*c*) 1000 tonnes
(*d*) 2000 tonnes

301. The word 'CAP' used for grain storage is also known as
(*a*) Cover and plinth
(*b*) Controlled atmospheric packaging
(*c*) Both of the above
(*d*) None of them

302. High moisture and warm climate for stored grain is responsible for
(*a*) Mold growth
(*b*) Insect growth
(*c*) Increase respiration of grain
(*d*) All of the above

303. At present in India, most quite grain storage structures used are
(*a*) Mild steel bin and RCC bin
(*b*) Fibre glass and asbestos sheet bin
(*c*) Plain or corrugated galvanized sheet bin
(*d*) Aluminium sheet and mild black sheet

304. The advantages of modern grain storage bins are
(*a*) Less expansive, less space requirement and easy quality control
(*b*) Protection from losses due to birds and rodents
(*c*) Provision of automation and mechanization
(*d*) All of the above

305. A bin whose relative dimensions are such that the plane of rupture meets the grain surface before it strikes the opposite side is called
(*a*) Deep bin
(*b*) Shallow bin
(*c*) Silo
(*d*) CAP

306. A bin in which plane of rupture meets the opposite side before it emerges from the grain is called
(*a*) Deep bin
(*b*) Shallow bin
(*c*) CAP
(*d*) Silo

307. If Φ is the angle of repose of material, then the angle of rupture may be taken as $(90 + \Phi)/2$ with the horizontal as per
(*a*) Airy's theory
(*b*) Jenssion theory
(*c*) Rankine theory
(*d*) Henderson equation

308. If L and h be breadth and depth of the grain storage structure, then the structure can be taken to shallow if
(*a*) $h < L \tan (90+ \Phi)/2$
(*b*) $h > L \tan (90+ \Phi)/2$
(*c*) $h < L \tan (90-\Phi)/2$
(*d*) $h > L \tan (90-\Phi)/2$

309. If L and h be breadth and depth of the grain storage structure, then the structure is deep, if
(*a*) $h < L \tan (90 + \Phi)/2$
(*b*) $h < L \tan (90 - \Phi)/2$
(*c*) $h > L \tan (90 + \Phi)/2$
(*d*) $h > L \tan (90 - \Phi)/2$

310. A grain bin referred to as shallow bin when the depth of the grain is ______ to the equivalent diameter

(*a*) Less (*b*) Equal
(*c*) Greater (*d*) Less or equal

311. In a deep bin, depth of grain is ______________ than equivalent diameter.

(*a*) Less (*b*) Equal
(*c*) Greater (*d*) Less or equal

312. The equivalent diameter is taken ____________ times the hydraulic radius of the circular bin.

(*a*) Two (*b*) Four
(*c*) Eight (*d*) Sixteen

313. If H_d is depth of grain and 'R' is hydraulic radius, the relationship for deep bin will be

(*a*) $H_d = 4R$ (*b*) $H_d < 4R$
(*c*) $H_d = 8R$ (*d*) $H_d > 4R$

314. If H_d is depth of grain and 'R' is hydraulic radius, the relationship for shallow bin will be

(*a*) $H_d = 4R$ (*b*) $H_d < 4R$
(*c*) $H_d = 8R$ (*d*) $H_d > 4R$

315. As per definition given by Issacson and Boyd, deep bin is calculated by

(*a*) $H_d/D < 0.75\ (1/\mu K)$ (*b*) $H_d/D = 0.75\ (\mu/K)$
(*c*) $H_d/D = 0.75\ (K/\mu)$ (*d*) $H_d/D = 0.75\ (1/\mu K)$

316. A good quality storage structure should be

(*a*) Structurally adequate (*b*) Durable and hygienic
(*c*) Gas sealable for fumigation (*d*) All

317. Vertical grain silo may be

(*a*) Circular (*b*) Hexagonal
(*c*) Square or rectangular (*d*) All

318. Qne of the following is not a permanent grain storage structure.

(*a*) Shed (*b*) Vertical silo
(*c*) Squat silo (*d*) CAP

319. Rankine's coefficient (K) for silo designing is equivalent to

(*a*) $(1 - \sin \Phi)/(1 + \sin \Phi)$ (*b*) $(1 + \sin \Phi)/(1 - \sin \Phi)$
(*c*) $(1 - \sin \Phi)/(1 - \cos \Phi)$ (*d*) $(1 - \sin \Phi)/(1 + \cos \Phi)$

320. The Rankine's formula is used for determination of pressure induced by granular materials against retaining wall in

(*a*) Deep bin (*b*) Shallow bin
(*c*) Squat bin (*d*) Shed

321. The process of moving air through stored grain at low flow rates to maintain or improve its quality is called
(*a*) Ventilation
(*b*) Aeration
(*c*) Fumigation
(*d*) Migration

322. Aeration can provide major profit in the storage of grain if
(*a*) It cools the grains and slowdown insect activity
(*b*) Prolongs the effectiveness of pesticides by cooling
(*c*) It can provide an appreciable drying function
(*d*) All of the above

323. Aeration has some minor benefits like
(*a*) It prevents storage odour
(*b*) It reduces moisture accumulation
(*c*) Application of fumigation
(*d*) All of the above

324. The most common air flow rates for aerating paddy range varies from
(*a*) 0.07-0.28 m^3/min/tonne
(*b*) 0.01-0.04 m^3/min/tonne
(*c*) 0.80-1.00 litre/sec/tonne
(*d*) 1.20-1.60 litre/sec/tonne

325. The perforation in duct for aeration should be uniformly spaced with minimum area of
(*a*) 10%
(*b*) 15%
(*c*) 18%
(*d*) 20%

326. Recommended perforation of aeration in grain storage shall be
(*a*) 10%
(*b*) 15%
(*c*) 20%
(*d*) 35%

327. Methyl bromide or phosphine are used as
(*a*) Germicide
(*b*) Pesticide
(*c*) Fungicide
(*d*) Fumigant

328. The protection of food by packaging means safeguard against
(*a*) Physical activity
(*b*) Chemical activity
(*c*) Biological activity
(*d*) All of them

329. Stored food products have the main source of heats *i.e.*
(*a*) Sensible heat of products
(*b*) Heat of respiration
(*c*) Specific heat
(*d*) Both (*a*) and (*b*)

330. The heat loads in cold storage system are classified like
(*a*) Chilling load
(*b*) Freezing load
(*c*) Cooling load
(*d*) All of the above

331. For increasing safe storage period of fruits and vegetables under CAP conditions by
(*a*) Increasing CO_2 level (*b*) Decreasing O_2 level
(*c*) Decreasing the temperature (*d*) All of these

332. Air tight storages are normally used
(*a*) To arrest the insect infestation
(*b*) To protect the wet grain from mold attack
(*c*) To decrease the oxygen content (*d*) Both (*a*) and (*b*)

333. In winter season, grain stored in bin will be spoiled at
(*a*) Top (*b*) Bottom
(*c*) Centre (*d*) Near walls of bin

334. Spoilage of grain in bin during warm season takes place due to moisture accumulation at
(*a*) Top (*b*) Centre
(*c*) Bottom (*d*) Inner surface of walls

335. Grain is spoiled in bin due to accumulation of
(*a*) Temperature (*b*) Moisture
(*c*) Heat (*d*) Relative humidity

336. By controlling insect and moisture levels, the losses in Bunker structure can be reduced upto
(*a*) 0-0.5% (*b*) 1-3%
(*c*) 10-20% (*d*) 20-40%

337. The granular material behave as composite mass having the characteristics of
(*a*) Liquid and solid (*b*) Liquid and gel
(*c*) Solid and gas (*d*) Semi solid and semi liquid

338. The size of food grains is represented by
(*a*) Length (*b*) Width
(*c*) Diameter (*d*) Equivalent diameter

339. The equivalent diameter of a granular particle can be determined by the following formula
(*a*) $(abc)^{1/3}$ (*b*) $(abc)^{2/3}$
(*c*) $(abc)^{3/2}$ (*d*) $(abc)^3$

340. The diameter of a sphere having same ratio of surface to volume as actual particle is called
(*a*) Equivalent diameter (*b*) Spherecity
(*c*) Roundness (*d*) Roundness ratio

341. The ratio of largest projected area of the particle when it is in natural rest position (A_p) and area of smallest circumscribing circle (A_c) is called
(*a*) Roundness (*b*) Spherecity
(*c*) Geometric mean diameter (*d*) Perimeter

342. The ratio of radius of curvature (r) of the sharpest corner and mean radius of particle (R) is known as
(*a*) Geometric mean diameter (*b*) Equivalent diameter
(*c*) Roundness ratio (*d*) Spherecity

343. The ratio of diameter of a sphere of the same volume as that of the particle and the diameter of the smallest circumscribing sphere or generally the largest diameter of particle is defined as
(*a*) Roundness ratio (*b*) Roundness
(*c*) Spherecity (*d*) Equivalent mean diameter

344. Drying takes place in
(*a*) Fruits (*b*) Vegetables
(*c*) Food grains (*d*) All

345. Which of the following is not a food processing operation?
(*a*) Harvesting (*b*) Cleaning
(*c*) Screening (*d*) Sorting

346. Removal of large few foreign materials from food grains comes under
(*a*) Sorting (*b*) Cleaning
(*c*) Scalping (*d*) Screening

347. The package does not include
(*a*) Attracting the buyers (*b*) Identifying the products
(*c*) Information about use of product (*d*) To improve the flavour

348. Which of the following is a not food constituent?
(*a*) Carbohydrate (*b*) Fat
(*c*) Minerals (*d*) Enzyme

349. The removal of colour of rice is called
(*a*) Blanching (*b*) Bleaching
(*c*) Parboiling (*d*) Polishing

350. Heat energy supplied to wet material by electromagnetic wave length of 0.76-400 μm in
(*a*) Radiation drying (*b*) Fluidized drying.
(*c*) Freeze drying (*d*) Osmotic drying

351. Moisture content of substance is expressed in
(*a*) ml (*b*) litre
(*c*) gm (*d*) percentage

352. The process of water absorption by food material is a
(*a*) Diffusion process (*b*) Osmosis
(*c*) Capillary process (*d*) Migration

353. Which scientist expressed the relation between swelling and moisture content?
(*a*) B. Bandyopadhyaya and NC Raj
(*b*) B. Bandyopadhyaya and TK Ghose
(*c*) Ali and Ojha
(*d*) KR Bhattacharya and UP Subbarao

354. Vitamin B in milled parboiled rice than milled raw rice is
(*a*) Lower
(*b*) Equal
(*c*) Higher
(*d*) None

355. Oil content in raw rice bran is
(*a*) 10-15%
(*b*) 15-25%
(*c*) 20-25%
(*d*) 10-20 %

356. During parboiling, the tank is filled with water heated by steam injection of
(*a*) 95ºC
(*b*) 85ºC
(*c*) 70ºC
(*d*) 90ºC

357. For complete gelatinization of starchy endosperm by open steaming process, the moisture content of wheat is increased upto the level of
(*a*) 85% (db)
(*b*) 75% (db)
(*c*) 80% (db)
(*d*) 70% (db)

358. The hardness of barley endosperm is
(*a*) 7.0-9.0 kg/mm^2
(*b*) 6.0-9.0 kg/mm^2
(*c*) 8.0-10.0 kg/mm^2
(*d*) 5.0-6.0 kg/mm^2

359. The preheating treatment process in bulgur production, moisture content of wheat is raised upto
(*a*) 10-20 % (db)
(*b*) 10-50% (db)
(*c*) 20-30% (db)
(*d*) 50-70% (db)

360. Optimum moisture content (db) for milling of parboiled paddy should be
(*a*) 30%
(*b*) 40%
(*c*) 50%
(*d*) 60%

361. Soaked wheat is conditioned at a temperature between
(*a*) 10–20ºC
(*b*) 30–35ºC
(*c*) 40–50ºC
(*d*) 50–60ºC

362. The percentage of endosperm in mature corn is about
(*a*) 65%
(*b*) 70%
(*c*) 82%
(*d*) 85%

363. Optimum moisture content for degerming of corn in Baell Degermer should be
(*a*) 10-15%
(*b*) 15-20%
(*c*) 21-25%
(*d*) 30-35%

364. Raw pulses may contain impurities
(*a*) 2-5% (*b*) 5-10%
(*c*) 20-25% (*d*) 30-35%

365. Residual oil in the cotton seed deoiled cake is
(*a*) 2-4% (*b*) 4-5%
(*c*) 5-10% (*d*) 10-12%

366. Which machine is used for the cleaning/washing of corn?
(*a*) Whizzer (*b*) Washer
(*c*) Degermer (*d*) Blancher

367. The moisture content at which the drying rate ceases to constant is known as
(*a*) EMC (*b*) CMC
(*c*) MC (db) (*d*) MC (wb)

368. Development of drying equation for heating or cooling is based on
(*a*) Newton's law (*b*) Arrhenius equation
(*c*) Henderson equation (*d*) Kick's law

369. The moisture content at which grain should not be dried in natural air is
(*a*) >20% (*b*) 20%
(*c*) 18% (*d*) < 20%

370. The relationship between heat utilization factor (HUF) and coefficient of performance (COP) of a drier.
(*a*) HUF = 1 – COP (*b*) HUF = 1 + COP
(*c*) HUF = 1/COP (*d*) HUF = COP

371. Natural air drying can not be used if the ambient relative humidity of air exceed
(*a*) 60% (*b*) 65%
(*c*) 70% (*d*) 75%

372. Recommended air flow rate for drying of parboiled paddy is
(*a*) 50-60 m^3/min/tonne (*b*) 60-70 m^3/min/tonne
(*c*) 70-80 m^3/min/tonne (*d*) 80-90 m^3/min/tonne

373. About how much paddy in India is converted in to parboiled of the total production
(*a*) 45% (*b*) 50%
(*c*) 60% (*d*) 65%

374. Deep bed drying theory is given by
(*a*) Becker (*b*) Hukill
(*c*) Huston (*d*) Ives

375. Oil content in parboiled paddy bran is
(*a*) 20-30% (*b*) 25-30%
(*c*) 30-45% (*d*) 40-50%

376. Hardness of rice endosperm is
(*a*) 8.5–10.5 kg/mm^2 (*b*) 11.5–14.5 kg/mm^2
(*c*) 14.5–16.5 kg/mm^2 (*d*) 18.5–19.5 kg/mm^2

377. Coconut shell contains lignin about
(*a*) 20% (*b*) 26%
(*c*) 30% (*d*) 36%

378. At which moisture content cereals grain should be stored for longer period?
(*a*) 10% (*b*) 12%
(*c*) 13% (*d*) 14%

379. Melting point of the rice bran wax is
(*a*) 20-30°C (*b*) 44-52°C
(*c*) 72-84°C (*d*) 90-96°C

380. Corn syrups are produced by the hydrolysis of
(*a*) corn starch (*b*) corn sweetener
(*c*) corn flour (*d*) corn grits

381. High intensity sweetener are used in confectionary to reduce
(*a*) quantity of sugar (*b*) Calorific value
(*c*) Cost of sweetener (*d*) Above all

382. The term 'food dehydration' refers to
(*a*) artificial drying by thermal means under controlled conditions
(*b*) sun drying under controlled conditions
(*c*) both above
(*d*) none

383. Lower drying temperature and short time are especially important in case of
(*a*) heat sensitive foods (*b*) highly perishable food
(*c*) staple foods (*d*) none

384. Thermoplastic foods by heat treatment, become
(*a*) Harder (*b*) Soften
(*c*) Discolouration (*d*) Burn

385. How many types of yeasts are used in baking?
(*a*) 2 (*b*) 3
(*c*) 4 (*d*) 5

386. Percentage of carbohydrate in wheat grain is
(*a*) 50% (*b*) 62%
(*c*) 69% (*d*) 70%

387. Typical food label shows
(*a*) Principal display (*b*) Nutrition information
(*c*) Panel and mandatory information (*d*) Above all

388. The temperature at which denaturation of protein in cereals takes place
(*a*) 30°C (*b*) 40°C
(*c*) 50°C (*d*) 70°C

389. Porosity percent in wheat is
(*a*) 40–45 (*b*) 50–55
(*c*) 65–70 (*d*) 48–53

390. Percentage of bran in wheat milling is
(*a*) 5% (*b*) 10%
(*c*) 12% (*d*) 15%

391. Percent recovery of white flour in wheat milling is
(*a*) 30% (*b*) 63%
(*c*) 80% (*d*) 85%

392. Oil percentage in parboiled rice bran is
(*a*) 20–28% (*b*) 10–12%
(*c*) 13–17% (*d*) 20–40%

393. Rice bran oil contains saturated fatty acids about
(*a*) 25–35% (*b*) 30–42%
(*c*) 35–48% (*d*) 42–50%

394. The respiratory rate of stored grain depends largely on
(*a*) Moisture content and temperature
(*b*) Relative humidity and temperature
(*c*) Pressure and temperature
(*d*) Relative humidity and moisture content

395. Modern rice milling machine *i.e.* single scalper drum cleaner is developed in
(*a*) Japan (*b*) Australia
(*c*) India (*d*) Germany

396. Fat percentage in corn is
(*a*) 3.0% (*b*) 3.5%
(*c*) 4.0% (*d*) 4.5%

397. Barley has indigestible fibre percentage
(*a*) 6 (*b*) 7
(*c*) 8 (*d*) 9

398. Viscosity of oil is measured in terms of___
(*a*) Its resistance to flow (*b*) Its cooling effect
(*c*) Both above (*d*) None

399. Glucose is added to rice as glazing substance with water solution in the ratio of
(*a*) 1:1 (*b*) 1:2
(*c*) 2:1 (*d*) 1:3

400. Spiral separator separates the grain on the basis of
(*a*) size (*b*) length
(*c*) Roundness (*d*) Spherecity

401. Cleaning of materials is performed by
(*a*) Washing (*b*) Screening
(*c*) Hand picking (*d*) All

402. The boiling point of *n*-hexane used as solvent for oil extraction is
(*a*) 60.5°C (*b*) 65.5°C
(*c*) 70.5°C (*d*) 90.5°C

403. For grinding operation, the operating speed of hammer mill should be
(*a*) 700-800 rpm (*b*) 1000-1100 rpm
(*c*) 1400-1500 rpm (*d*) 1500-1600 rpm

404. Hammer mill and Burr mill are used for the grinding of
(*a*) Grain (*b*) Oil seed
(*c*) Fruit powder (*d*) Milk powder

405. Natural drying needs dehumidification if atmospheric humidity exceeds than
(*a*) 30% (*b*) 60%
(*c*) 70% (*d*) 80%

406. In batch type dryer, the air temperature seldom exceeds
(*a*) 35°C (*b*) 40°C
(*c*) 45°C (*d*) 50°C

407. In single boiling method of paddy parboiling, paddy is soaked upto
(*a*) 12–18 hrs (*b*) 12–24 hrs
(*c*) 24–48 hrs (*d*) 24–72 hrs

408. The storage life of non-perishable fruits exceed by
(*a*) 8 weeks (*b*) 10 weeks
(*c*) 12 weeks (*d*) 14 weeks

409. Percentage starch in wheat grain is about
(*a*) 48–55% (*b*) 56–59%
(*c*) 60–68% (*d*) 75–78%

410. In attrition mills, the size reduction of grains is accomplished due to
(*a*) impact and shear (*b*) shear and crushing
(*c*) impact only (*d*) impact and crushing

411. The shelling of paddy by centrifugal dehusker is due to
(*a*) Shear (*b*) Crushing
(*c*) Rubbing (*d*) Impact

412. Brewing and malting is related to
(*a*) Beer (*b*) Juice
(*c*) Milk (*d*) Sausage

413. Generally in thin layer drying, thickness of grain bed with recommended air grain ratio is
(*a*) 10 cm (*b*) 15 cm
(*c*) 20 cm (*d*) 25 cm

414. The moisture contained by a substance in excess of the equilibrium moisture is known as
(*a*) Free moisture (*b*) Bound moisture
(*c*) Unbound moisture (*d*) Critical moisture

415. Fuel consumption per kg of moisture evaporated in convection drying is always ________ than conduction drying.
(*a*) Lower (*b*) Equal
(*c*) Higher (*d*) Unknown

416. Wheat is dried under constant rate drying period when its moisture content exceeds
(*a*) 50% (*b*) 60%
(*c*) 72% (*d*) 75%

417. The drying method particularly suitable for drying of small quantity of seed with respect to conserving strain purity and viability is
(*a*) Sun drying (*b*) Radiation drying
(*c*) Freeze drying (*d*) Sack drying

418. Natural air drying can not be used if the ambient relative humidity exceeds
(*a*) 60% (*b*) 70%
(*c*) 80% (*d*) 85%

419. The parboiled paddy is required to dry the moisture content for desirable milling and storage is
(*a*) 10-12% (*b*) 14-16%
(*c*) 16-18% (*d*) 20-22%

420. Broken in raw rice is about 50%, whereas in parboiled rice the broken is about
(*a*) 10% (*b*) 20%
(*c*) 80% (*d*) 90%

421. Parboiled rice takes __________ time to cook to the same degree of softness than raw rice.
(*a*) Less (*b*) Equal
(*c*) More (*d*) Unknown

422. Addition of moisture and heat to grain for improving their quality and quantity of end product is known as
(*a*) Radiation treatment (*b*) Hydrothermal treatment
(*c*) Blanching (*d*) None

423. The water impregnated with sulphur dioxide for arresting certain fermentation is practiced in the process of
(*a*) Degerming (*b*) Steeping
(*c*) Conditioning (*d*) Thermal treatment

424. The average processing capacity of pulses mills in India varies between
(*a*) 2-5 tonnes/day (*b*) 5-10 tonnes/day
(*c*) 10-20 tonnes/day (*d*) 20-30 tonnes/day

425. In pulses, during pitting process the subsequently applied substance to facilitate loosing of husk is
(*a*) Water (*b*) Red earth
(*c*) Oil (*d*) $NaHCO_3$

426. The clean pulses contain husk about
(*a*) 10–15% (*b*) 15–20%
(*c*) 20–25% (*d*) 25–30%

427. The highest amount of carbohydrate in the form of starch, cellulose etc. present in
(*a*) Pericarp (*b*) Endosperm
(*c*) Aleurone layer (*d*) Germ

428. Maximum moisture content of wheat for safe storage in leak proof environment for one year is
(*a*) 8-10% (*b*) 12-13%
(*c*) 16-18% (*d*) 18-20%

429. For drying of cereals grains, which is best suitable is
(*a*) Spray drier
(*b*) Tray drier
(*c*) Tunnel drier
(*d*) Rotary drier

430. The optimum moisture content for harvesting of paddy is
(*a*) 10-12%
(*b*) 14-18%
(*c*) 20-22%
(*d*) 24-26%

431. Drying medium in desiccated air drying to absorb the RH of air is
(*a*) Silica gel
(*b*) Common salt
(*c*) Baking powder
(*d*) Electric heater

432. The mature corn kernel is composed of
(*a*) Endosperm (82%), germ (12%), Pericarp (5%) and tip cap (1%)
(*b*) Endosperm (80%), germ (10%), Pericarp (7%) and tip cap (3%)
(*c*) Endosperm (70%), germ (12%), Pericarp (10%) and tip cap (5%)
(*d*) Endosperm (82%), germ (7%), Pericarp (8%) and tip cap (5%)

433. The optimum moisture content of corn for degerming in Beall Degermer is
(*a*) 15-20%
(*b*) 12-14%
(*c*) 21-25%
(*d*) 25-30%

434. Steeping of corn in wet milling, water is impregnated with ______ for arresting fermentation.
(*a*) SO_2
(*b*) SO_3
(*c*) NO_2
(*d*) CO_2

435. The steeping of corn is carried out at 50°C for a period of
(*a*) 10-18 hrs
(*b*) 20-25 hrs
(*c*) 28-48 hrs
(*d*) 40-50 hrs

436. Corn attains moisture content during steeping in wet milling process at 50°C temperature about
(*a*) 20%
(*b*) 40%
(*c*) 45%
(*d*) 50%

437. Emery roller known as gota machine are used for dehusking of
(*a*) Conditioned paddy
(*b*) Conditioned wheat
(*c*) Splitted pulse
(*d*) Conditioned pulse

438. According to Simmond's rate of drying of wheat is sharply depended upon the temperature of air varying from
(*a*) 15-65°C
(*b*) 37-96°C
(*c*) 21-77°C
(*d*) 28-80°C

439. In dielectric drying, heat is generated within a solid by placing it in a
(a) Fixed light frequency magnetic field
(b) Fixed high frequency current
(c) Varying frequency magnetic field
(d) Low frequency current

440. Modern rice milling machine-single scalper drum cleaner is developed in
(a) USA
(b) India
(c) Japan
(d) China

441. Indented tray type paddy separator (Japan) is made up of
(a) Iron
(b) Steel
(c) Aluminium
(d) Copper

442. The raw corn for wet milling should have moisture content of
(a) 10-12%
(b) 12-14%
(c) 15-16%
(d) 18-20%

443. The husking capacity of a impact type paddy husker (Japan) with a disc of 30 cm in diameter is about
(a) 300 kg/h
(b) 175 kg/h
(c) 280 kg/h
(d) 225 kg/h

444. The optimum peripheral speeds of rubber roll husker for paddy and oats respectively are
(a) 16 m/s and 20 m/s
(b) 14 m/s and 20 m/s
(c) 20 m/s and 12 m/s
(d) 10 m/s and 16 m/s

445. The pneumatic separation of different compounds is based on the
(a) Thermodynamic properties
(b) Physical properties
(c) Magnetic properties
(d) Aerodynamic properties

446. Siddha, a traditional method of paddy parboiling is originated in
(a) Bengal
(b) Gujrat
(c) Japan
(d) Pakistan

447. Recommended air flow rate of drying of parboiled paddy is
(a) 60-70 m^3/min/tonne
(b) 70-80 m^3/min/tonne
(c) 16-28 m^3/min/tonne
(d) 56-62 m^3/min/tonne

448. Swelling capacity is expressed as the ratio of
(a) Final to initial volume of rice
(b) Initial to final volume of rice
(c) Initial to final weight of rice
(d) Final to initial volume or weight of rice

449. Composition of unsaturated fatty acid in rice bran oil is
(a) 80-84%
(b) 40-50%
(c) 20-42%
(d) 16-20%

450. Paddy, corn, wheat, buck wheat seeds are specially rich source of
(*a*) Vitamin
(*b*) Fat
(*c*) Oil
(*d*) Carbohydrate

451. The endosperm of cereals grain contains the highest amount of carbohydrates in the form of
(*a*) Pectin
(*b*) Dextrin
(*c*) Starch
(*d*) Sugar

452. The temperature at which denaturation and coagulation of cereals protein take place above
(*a*) 50°C
(*b*) 60°C
(*c*) 75°C
(*d*) 40°C

453. Useful storage life of dried fruit and dried seed is upto
(*a*) 100 days
(*b*) 200 days
(*c*) 300 days
(*d*) 360 days or more

454. Screening refers to
(*a*) Separation of cleaned products into various quality fractions by any one physical property
(*b*) Removal of few large particles
(*c*) Classification of cleaned products into various quality fractions by commercial values
(*d*) Separating grains into two or more fraction according to size alone.

455. MAQ is defines as
(*a*) Minimum acceptable quality
(*b*) Moderate acceptable quality
(*c*) Modified atmospheric quality
(*d*) Maximum acceptable quality

456. The date beyond which the product is no longer acceptable
(*a*) Pack value
(*b*) Expiration date
(*c*) Manufacturing date
(*d*) Selling date

457. FDA is termed as
(*a*) Fruit and Drug Administration
(*b*) Food and Drug Administration
(*c*) Fruit and dietary allowance
(*d*) Foundation of drug administration

458. The machine used for removal of bran layers from brown rice is known as
(*a*) Polisher
(*b*) Bran aspirator
(*c*) Husk aspirator
(*d*) Paddy sheller

459. The system used for separating husk from the paddy grain is called
(*a*) Husk aspirator
(*b*) Paddy separator
(*c*) Husk separator
(*d*) Rubber roll sheller

460. The equipment applied for separation of husk from the product mixture obtained from sheller.
(*a*) Husk aspirator
(*b*) Paddy separator
(*c*) Husk separator
(*d*) Rubber roll sheller

461. The machines used for separating of broken rice from head rice is known as
(*a*) Rubber roll sheller
(*b*) Polisher
(*c*) Grader
(*d*) Whitener

462. The foreign materials in paddy processing can be grouped in
(*a*) Big impurities like stems, paddy ear heads, stone and iron particles
(*b*) Small impurities like weed seeds, dust, mud particles
(*c*) Equal size impurities like immature grain, stones
(*d*) All of the above

463. Parboiling of paddy is carried out by
(*a*) Soaking
(*b*) Steaming
(*c*) Drying
(*d*) All of them

464. One of the following is not a rice whitener
(*a*) Vertical whitening cone
(*b*) Horizontal abrasive whitener
(*c*) Jet pearler
(*d*) Horizontal polisher

465. The separation of brokens from head rice (grading) is not accomplished by
(*a*) Tray separator
(*b*) Rotating reel grader
(*c*) Rotating indented cylinder
(*d*) Oscillating grading sieves

466. Milling recovery of rice mill is calculated by
(*a*) Weight of head rice × 100 / weight of milled rice
(*b*) Weight of milled rice × 100 / Weight of head rice
(*c*) Weight of brokens × 100 / weight of paddy
(*d*) Weight of total rice × 100 / total weight of paddy

467. Milling efficiency (%) of rice mill is expressed as
(*a*) Coefficient of hulling × coefficient of wholeness of kernel × 100
(*b*) Weight of brown rice × 100 / weight of feed to machine
(*c*) Weight of brown head rice/weight of total brown rice
(*d*) Weight of total rice × 100 / total weight of paddy

468. Coefficient of hulling is formulated as
(*a*) Coefficient of hulling × coefficient of wholeness of kernel × 100
(*b*) Weight of brown rice × 100 / weight of feed to machine
(*c*) Weight of brown head rice/weight of total brown rice
(*d*) Weight of total rice × 100 / total weight of paddy

469. Coefficient of wholeness is expressed as
(*a*) Coefficient of hulling × coefficient of wholeness of kernel × 100
(*b*) Weight of brown rice × 100 / weight of feed to machine
(*c*) Weight of brown head rice/weight of total brown rice
(*d*) Weight of total rice × 100 / total weight of paddy

470. The peripheral speed of vertical whitening cone for whitening of rice should be about
(*a*) 5 m/s (*b*) 7 m/s
(*c*) 10 m/s (*d*) 13 m/s

471. The process used to remove the bran layer from brown rice by the procedure of
(*a*) Shearing and friction (*b*) Impact and cutting
(*c*) Abrasion and friction (*d*) Compression and friction

472. Recovery of dal varies from
(*a*) 40-45% (*b*) 50-60%
(*c*) 60-75% (*d*) 75-80%

473. Pulses are
(*a*) Monocotyledons (*b*) Dicotyledons
(*c*) Multicotyledons (*d*) Polycotyledons

474. The protein content in pulse is about ____________ than cereals.
(*a*) Equal (*b*) Double
(*c*) Triple (*d*) Five times

475. The protein efficiency ratio (PER) of pulses varies
(*a*) 0.1–0.22 (*b*) 0.3–0.41
(*c*) 0.7–2.1 (*d*) 2.9–3.11
(Protein efficiency ratio is a measure of quality of protein in food and infant formula and is given by weight gained per unit by a subject by the amount of protein intake)

476. The main objective of conditioning of pulses is
(*a*) to loose the husk (*b*) to facilitate its separation from the kernel
(*c*) reduce the milling losses (*d*) All of the above

477. Conditioning of grain can be achieved by
(*a*) Water treatment (*b*) Hydrothermal treatment
(*c*) Use of salt and chemicals (*d*) Thermal treatment
(*e*) All of the above

478. The pulse milling means
(*a*) Conditioning of pulse (*b*) Dehusking and splitting
(*c*) Polishing and grading (*d*) All of the above

479. The process by which to impart desirable shine and lusture to dal is called
(*a*) Conditioning (*b*) Dehusking and splitting
(*c*) Grading (*d*) Polishing

480. One person by hand operated stone chakki can be produced about ________ of dal in eight hours.
(*a*) 10-20 kg (*b*) 15-25 kg
(*c*) 25-30 kg (*d*) 30-40 kg

481. An average dal recovery of pigeon pea by wet milling method is reported as
(*a*) 50% (*b*) 55%
(*c*) 65% (*d*) 70%

482. The objective of red earth treatment to whole grain dal is
(*a*) To impart yellow colour (*b*) To provide mild abrasiveness
(*c*) Help in the removal of husk from cotyledons (*d*) All of the above

483. Which chemical used for preservation of wet paddy is
(*a*) Sodium chloride (*b*) Calcium propionate
(*c*) Copper or ferrous sulphate (*d*) Urea
(*e*) All of them

484. When wet paddy is treated with common salt, water is removed from the rice kernel by
(*a*) Diffusion (*b*) Osmosis
(*c*) Reverse osmosis (*d*) Osmotic dehydration

485. The method is particularly suitable for drying of small quantity of seed to prevent mixing of varieties and conserve strain purity and variability is known as
(*a*) Dielectric drying (*b*) Vacuum drying
(*c*) Sack drying (*d*) Convective drying

486. Natural air drying for in-bin or in-storage drying can not be used if the ambient relative humidity exceeds
(*a*) 60 % (*b*) 70 %
(*c*) 80 % (*d*) 90 %

487. The food grains containing moisture higher than ________ percent should not be dried with natural air.
(*a*) 10 % (*b*) 18 %
(*c*) 20 % (*d*) 24 %

488. For continuous flow dryer, thickness of grain layer exposed to the heated air is generally restricted to
(*a*) 10 cm (*b*) 15 cm
(*c*) 20 cm (*d*) 22 cm

489. Which one of the flow of drying air is preferred to the grain drying?
(*a*) Cross flow
(*b*) Counter flow
(*c*) Co-current flow
(*d*) All of the above

490. A hydrothermal treatment followed by drying before milling for the production of milled parboiled grain is called
(*a*) Parboiling
(*b*) Soaking
(*c*) Steaming
(*d*) None

491. The most important change takes place during parboiling in paddy are
(*a*) Gelatinization of starch
(*b*) Disintegration of protein bodies in the endosperm
(*c*) Destruction of antioxidants
(*d*) All of them

492. Processes in sequence applied in parboiling of paddy are
(*a*) Soaking, steaming and drying
(*b*) Steaming, soaking and drying
(*c*) Drying, soaking and steaming
(*d*) Drying, steaming and soaking

493. Steaming process during parboiling of grain helps in the
(*a*) Swelling of grain
(*b*) Gelatinization of starch
(*c*) Reducing the moisture content
(*d*) All

494. The process of water absorption by grain during parboiling is known as
(*a*) Soaking
(*b*) Steeping
(*c*) Imbibation
(*d*) All

495. Soaking of water in parboiling process to the grain is the result of
(*a*) Molecular absorption
(*b*) Capillary absorption
(*c*) Hydration
(*d*) All of them

496. The volume of paddy increases due to soaking. But the volume of soaked paddy is always _____ than the sum of the initial volume of paddy and the volume of water absorbed.
(*a*) Less
(*b*) Higher
(*c*) Equal
(*d*) Unknown

497. The moisture at which the second phase of soaking starts may be called
(*a*) Initial moisture content
(*b*) Critical moisture content
(*c*) Equilibrium moisture content
(*d*) Final moisture content

498. The parboiled paddy is required to be dried to a moisture content of __________ percent to obtain the desirable milling and storing properties.
(*a*) 8–10 %
(*b*) 12–14 %
(*c*) 14–16 %
(*d*) 10–12 %

499. Parboiled rice requires _______ to _________ times as much abrasive load as raw rice to obtain the same degree of polish.
(*a*) One to three (*b*) Two to three
(*c*) Sixth to eighth (*d*) Three to four

500. Swelling capacity of grain is expressed as the ratio of
(*a*) Final length to the initial length (*b*) Final mass to the initial mass
(*c*) Final volume to the initial volume (*d*) Both (*b*) and (*c*)

501. Expansion ratio is the ratio of
(*a*) The dimension of cooked and uncooked rice both along the length and width
(*b*) Length to width after cooking
(*c*) Width to length after cooking
(*d*) All of the above

502. Disclouration of rice during parboiling is mainly caused by
(*a*) High temperature (*b*) High moisture content
(*c*) Fermentation (*d*) Non-enzymatic maillard browning

503. The water content of paddy after soaking increases to about ________on dry basis.
(*a*) 10-20 % (*b*) 20-40 %
(*c*) 40-50 % (*d*) 50-55 %

504. Which traditional method of paddy parboiling is not originated in Bengal?
(*a*) Atapa (*b*) Balam
(*c*) Josh (*d*) Siddha

505. Which method of paddy parboiling is originated at Saharanpur (UP)?
(*a*) Sela (*b*) Josh
(*c*) Balam (*d*) Siddha

506. In which method of paddy parboiling, sand is used as drying medium?
(*a*) Atapa (*b*) Sela
(*c*) Siddha (*d*) Josh

507. Which improved method of paddy parboiling is originated in India?
(*a*) Sodium chromate method (*b*) Brine solution method
(*c*) Pressure parboiling method (*d*) RPEC method
(*e*) All of the above

508. Maek process of paddy parboiling was originated at
(*a*) UK (*b*) USA
(*c*) Italy (*d*) Surinam

509. Schule process of paddy parboiling is developed at
(*a*) Italy (*b*) India
(*c*) Germany (*d*) UK

510. Avorio process of parboiling of paddy is patented in
(*a*) Italy (*b*) Indonesia
(*c*) USA (*d*) Germany

511. Debranned, polished and cracked parboiled wheat is known as
(*a*) Sela (*b*) Bulgur
(*c*) Pasta (*d*) Milled wheat

512. Bulgur takes about __________ minutes to cook fully.
(*a*) 10–15 (*b*) 15–20
(*c*) 25–30 (*d*) 30–45

513. Soaking temperature of parboiling of wheat above ________ should not be used so as to minimize the bursting of wheat kernel and leaching losses as well.
(*a*) 40°C (*b*) 45°C
(*c*) 70°C (*d*) 75°C

514. How much percentage of moisture is added during steaming of soaked wheat containing 83 % percent moisture (db)?
(*a*) 1–3% (*b*) 3–5%
(*c*) 5–8% (*d*) 10–13%

515. From the stand point of drying time and quality of parboiled wheat, the drying air temperature should not be more than
(*a*) 45°C (*b*) 65°C
(*c*) 75°C (*d*) 85°C

516. Production of bulgur is done by the method of
(*a*) Batch type (*b*) Preheating treatment process
(*c*) Continuous process (*d*) Chemical lye peeling process
(*e*) All of them

517. To increase the milling quality of the food grains or to improve the quality and quantity of their end products or to facilitate milling operations for desired products, food grains are some times subjected to hydrothermal treatment prior to milling is called
(*a*) Hysteresis (*b*) Reverse osmosis
(*c*) Conditioning (*d*) Product development

518. The aerodynamic properties of a particle depends on the
(*a*) Shape
(*b*) Dimension and weight of the particles
(*c*) The state and position of the particles with respect to the air current
(*d*) All of them

519. The husk of grain is removed by the action of
(*a*) Compression and shear (*b*) Abrasion and friction
(*c*) Impact and friction (*d*) All of them

520. Concave type husking machine and rubber roll husker are designed on the basis of
(*a*) Compression and shear (*b*) Impact and friction
(*c*) Abrasion and friction (*d*) None of them

521. Centrifugal type paddy sheller works on the principle of
(*a*) Abrasion and friction (*b*) Impact and friction
(*c*) Compression and shear (*d*) None of them

522. The minimum clearance between the roll and concave must be ________ than the dimensions of the grain kernel; otherwise the kernel will be crushed.
(*a*) Less (*b*) Greater
(*c*) Equal (*d*) None

523. The clearance between rubber roll sheller is ______ than the mean diameter of the paddy.
(*a*) Smaller (*b*) Greater
(*c*) Equal (*d*) None

524. Length of husking zone (l_h) for rubber roll sheller can be expressed as follows if d = diameter of rolls (cm), b = size of grain (cm) and C = clearance between rolls (cm).
(*a*) $l_h = (2\pi d/360).\cos^{-1}(d + C/d + b)$
(*b*) $l_h = (2\pi d/360).\cos^{-1}(d + b\ /d + c)$
(*c*) $l_h = (2\pi d/360).\cos^{-1}(dC/d + b)$
(*d*) $l_h = (2\pi d/360).\cos^{-1}(d + C/db)$

525. The length of the husking zone (l_h) for rubber roll sheller depends on the
(*a*) Diameter of the rolls (*b*) Thickness of grain to be husked
(*c*) Linear distance between the centres of the rolls
(*d*) All of these

526. In rubber roll sheller, the size of the grain (b) and the clearance (c) are fixed, then the length of husking zone (l_h) increases with ________ in diameter of the roll.
(*a*) Decrease (*b*) Increase
(*c*) No change (*d*) Unknown

527. In under runner disc husker, the effective width of the abrasive coating should not be more than _______ of the stone diameter.
(*a*) 1/2th (*b*) 1/3rd
(*c*) 1/4th (*d*) 1/6th

528. The coefficient of hulling ($E_{hulling}$) is expressed as if n_1 = amount of grain before hulling, and n_2 = amount of unhulled grain after hulling.
(*a*) $(n_1 - n_2) / n_1$ (*b*) $(n_2 - n_1) / n_2$
(*c*) $n_1 n_2 / n_2$ (*d*) $n_1 n_2 / n_1$

529. How much power consumption for grinding varies _________ percent of the total power required for all operation.
(*a*) 10-20% (*b*) 20-35%
(*c*) 35-40% (*d*) 50-80%

530. Which grain parameter is affected the characteristics of grinding operation?
(*a*) Type and variety of cereal grain
(*b*) Moisture content and mechanical properties
(*c*) Extent of hydrothermal treatment given to the grain
(*d*) All of these

531. Hardness of rice endosperm is as
(*a*) 11.5 to 14.5 kg/mm² (*b*) 10.5 to 11.5 kg/mm²
(*c*) 6.0 to 9.0 kg/mm² (*d*) 20.0 to 30.15 kg/mm²

532. Hardness of barley kernel varies from
(*a*) 11.5 to 14.5 kg/mm² (*b*) 10.5 to 11.5 kg/mm²
(*c*) 6.0 to 9.0 kg/mm² (*d*) 20.0 to 30.15 kg/mm²

533. Degree of grinding is expressed as
(*a*) S_a/S_b (*b*) S_b/S_a
(*c*) $S_a - S_b$ (*d*) $S_b - S_a$

534. The difference between the percentage of undersized particles (C_1) in the final ground product and the percentage of undersized particles (I) in the initial feed entering the grinder is also known as
(*a*) Overall extraction (*b*) Effectiveness of grinding
(*c*) Coefficient of grinding (*d*) Grinding efficiency

535. The factor affecting the effectiveness of roller mills is /are
(*a*) Clearance between rolls (*b*) Geometrical parameter of rolls
(*c*) Kinematic parameter of rolls
(*d*) Capacity of roller mills and power consumption for their operation
(*e*) All of them

536. The hydrothermal treatment can be used for
   (*a*) Improving shelling efficiency
   (*b*) Nutritional quality and milling quality of paddy
   (*c*) Facilitating degermination and dehulling of corn and wheat
   (*d*) All of them

537. Which type of changes occurs in grain due to the hydrothermal treatments?
   (*a*) Physico-thermal
   (*b*) Physico-chemical
   (*c*) Biochemical
   (*d*) All

538. Physico-thermal properties of grain is classified into
   (*a*) Strength or hardness
   (*b*) Density and hardness
   (*c*) Hysteresis
   (*d*) Thermal properties
   e) All of them

539. Which is not the thermal property of the grain?
   (*a*) Specific heat
   (*b*) Specific gravity
   (*c*) Thermal conductivity
   (*d*) Thermal diffusivity

540. Thermal properties like specific heat, thermal conductivity and thermal diffusivity of grain increase with increase in
   (*a*) Temperature
   (*b*) Moisture content
   (*c*) Relative humidity
   (*d*) Both (*a*) and (*b*)

541. The residual oil percentage in the deoiled cake obtained from mechanical expression is about
   (*a*) 1-2 %
   (*b*) 2-4 %
   (*c*) 4-5 %
   (*d*) 6-8 %

542. The deoiled cake obtained from solvent extraction has the residual oil content of about
   (*a*) 1%
   (*b*) 2%
   (*c*) 4%
   (*d*) 6%

543. Oil content in raw bran varies between
   (*a*) 2-4%
   (*b*) 4-8%
   (*c*) 10-12%
   (*d*) 12-18%

544. Oil content in parboiled rice bran is about
   (*a*) 5-10%
   (*b*) 12-18%
   (*c*) 20-28%
   (*d*) 30-40%

545. After extraction of oil from raw and parboiled bran, the deoiled cake contains about __________ % oil only.
   (*a*) 1-3%
   (*b*) 3-5%
   (*c*) 6-8%
   (*d*) 8-11%

546. Immediately after milling rice, the FFA content in bran is normally bellow
(*a*) 1% (*b*) 3%
(*c*) 8% (*d*) 10%

547. After milling of rice, the rate of increase of FFA in bran may be as high as ________ per hour under favourable conditions.
(*a*) 0.5% (*b*) 1.0%
(*c*) 2.5% (*d*) 4.0%

548. The main problem in processing of rice bran oil for edible purpose and defatted bran for food and feed are
(*a*) Rapid hydrolysis of oil into FFA and glycerol
(*b*) Oxidation of fat (*c*) Flavour reversion
(*d*) High refining losses (*e*) All of the above

549. The main advantages of stabilization of rice bran are
(*a*) It impart hardening effect to the bran for better extrability
(*b*) It increases the particles size and reduces the problem of fines and filtration
(*c*) It increases the bulk density and reduces the hardening problem
(*d*) All of them

550. The factors affecting the rate of formation of FFA in rice bran during storage are
(*a*) Storage temperature and RH (*b*) Moisture content of bran
(*c*) Variety, type and particle size of bran
(*d*) Contamination of bran with microflora or insects
(*e*) All of them

551. In the refining process of bran oil, neutralization process is used for
(*a*) Removing hard wax (*b*) Removal of FFA
(*c*) Removal of colouring matter (*d*) Removal of odours

552. The role of winterization in the rice bran oil refining process is
(*a*) Removal of hard wax, gum, mucilage (*b*) Removal of soft wax
(*c*) Removal of odours matter and unsaponifiable matter
(*d*) Removal of colouring matter

553. A cyclone separator is used for
(*a*) Particles from liquids (*b*) Liquid droplets from gases
(*c*) Fine particles from solids (*d*) All of the above

554. If d_1 and d_2 are average initial and final sizes of material and K is a constant, then E, energy requirement for size reduction of the unit mass is given by
(*a*) $E = K [(d_1 - d_2)/ (d_1.d_2)]$ (*b*) $E = K [(d_1.d_2) / (d_1 - d_2)]$
(*c*) $E = K [(d_2 - d_1)/ (d_1.d_2)]$ (*d*) $E = K [(d_1.d_2) / (d_2 - d_1)]$

555. In a ball mill if '*R*' is the radius of mill, '*g*' is acceleration due to gravity and '*r*' is the radius of ball, then the critical speed is given by

(*a*) $Yc = (1/2\pi)\ \sqrt{g/(R-r)}$
(*b*) $Yc = 2\pi\ \sqrt{g/(R-r)}$
(*c*) $Yc = (1/2p)\ \sqrt{(R-r)/g}$
(*d*) $Yc = 2\pi \sqrt{(R-r)/g}$

556. A machine which removes surface moisture from grain after washing by centrifugal force and impact is called

(*a*) Hammer mill
(*b*) Ball mill
(*c*) Whizzer
(*d*) Degermer

557. Sketch roll system in wheat milling is extension of

(*a*) breaking roll system
(*b*) reduction roll system
(*c*) Sieving
(*d*) All of these

ANSWER KEY

(CEREALS, PULSES, AND OILSEED PROCESSING)

1.C	2.D	3.A	4.D	5.A	6.A	7.A	8.A	9.C	10.B
11.C	12.A	13.C	14.A	15.A	16.A	17.C	18.A	19.D	20.A
21.A	22.B	23.B	24.B	25.A	26.A	27.A	28.C	29.C	30.D
31.A	32.D	33.A	34.C	35.C	36.A	37.C	38.B	39.C	40.D
41.A	42.B	43.C	44.A	45.A	46.B	47.D	48.A	49.A	50.D
51.A	52.A	53.A	54.D	55.B	56.C	57.C	58.B	59.B	60.D
61.A	62.C	63.D	64.B	65.D	66.B	67.C	68.B	69.B	70.A
71.C	72.B	73.A	74.B	75.D	76.C	77.C	78.D	79.A	80.B
81.A	82.C	83.C	84.A	85.B	86.C	87.A	88.A	89.D	90.B
91.A	92.B	93.C	94.A	95.B	96.A	97.D	98.A	99.C	100.C
101.A	102.D	103.C	104.C	105.B	106.B	107.C	108.D	109.A	110.D
111.A	112.B	113.C	114.B	115.C	116. C	117.D	118.D	119.D	120.C
121.C	122.C	123.C	124.C	125.C	126.D	127.C	128.D	129.D	130.A
131.D	132.C	133.D	134.C	135.A	136.B	137.D	138.D	139.C	140.C
141.C	142.D	143.B	144.D	145.C	146.A	147.C	148.D	149.C	150.C
151.A	152.C	153.A	154.D	155.A	156.B	157.C	158.B	159.C	160.B
161.D	162.C	163.A	164.A	165.B	166.C	167.C	168.B	169.D	170.D
171.B	172.A	173.B	174.D	175.C	176.C	177.D	178.C	179.A	180.A
181.B	182.B	183.D	184.D	185.D	186.B	187.D	188.B	189.A	190.B
191.C	192.B	193.D	194.B	195.B	196.B	197.A	198.A	199.B	200.D
201.C	202.B	203.C	204.A	205.A	206.D	207.B	208.D	209.B	210.A
211.D	212.A	213.A	214.C	215.A	216.B	217.C	218.B	219.B	220.C
221.B	222.A	223.B	224.B	225.A	226.C	227.C	228.D	229.A	230.B
231.A	232.A	233.C	234.D	235.D	236.C	237.C	238.A	239.A	240.B
241.C	242.C	243.C	244.B	245.C	246.C	247.B	248.A	249.D	250.C

251.A	252.B	253.D	254.A	255.C	256.A	257.D	258.B	259.A	260.A
261.B	262.A	263.C	264.B	265.B	266.A	267.B	268.B	269.B	270.B
271.E	272.C	273.B	274.C	275.A	276.B	277.D	278.D	279.B	280.A
281.C	282.D	283.A	284.A	285.D	286.C	287.B	288.C	289.D	290.A
291.A	292.D	293.A	294.A	295.D	296.C	297.B	298.D	299.C	300.C
301.A	302.D	303.A	304.D	305.B	306.A	307.C	308.A	309.C	310.D
311.C	312.B	313.A	314.B	315.D	316.D	317.D	318.D	319.A	320.B
321.B	322.D	323.D	324.A	325.A	326.B	327.D	328.D	329.D	330.D
331.D	332.D	333.A	334.C	335.B	336.A	337.A	338.D	339.A	340.A
341.A	342.C	343.C	344.C	345.A	346.C	347.D	348.D	349.B	350.A
351.D	352.A	353.A	354.C	355.D	356.B	357.C	358.B	359.B	360.C
361.C	362.C	363.C	364.A	365.B	366.A	367.B	368.A	369.D	370.A
371.C	372.B	373.B	374.B	375.B	376.B	377.D	378.B	379.C	380.A
381.D	382.A	383.A	384.B	385.A	386.C	387.D	388.C	389.B	390.C
391.D	392.A	393.B	394.A	395.A	396.C	397.B	398.A	399.A	400.C
401.D	402.B	403.C	404.A	405.C	406.C	407.C	408.C	409.C	410.B
411.D	412.A	413.C	414.A	415.C	416.C	417.D	418.B	419.B	420.A
421.C	422.B	423.B	424.C	425.C	426.A	427.B	428.B	429.D	430.C
431.A	432.A	433.C	434.A	435.C	436.C	437.D	438.C	439.B	440.C
441.B	442.C	443.A	444.B	445.D	446.A	447.A	448.D	449.A	450.D
451.C	452.A	453.D	454.D	455.A	456.B	457.B	458.A	459.D	460.A
461.C	462.D	463.D	464.D	465.A	466.D	467.A	468.B	469.C	470.D
471.C	472.C	473.B	474.B	475.C	476.D	477.E	478.D	479.D	480.D
481.D	482.D	483.E	484.B	485.C	486.B	487.C	488.C	489.A	490.A
491.D	492.A	493.B	494.D	495.D	496.A	497.B	498.C	499.D	500.A
501.A	502.D	503.D	504.C	505.A	506.B	507.E	508.B	509.C	510.A
511.B	512.C	513.D	514.B	515.C	516.E	517.C	518.D	519.D	520.A
521.B	522.B	523.A	524.A	525.D	526.B	527.D	528.A	529.D	530.D
531.A	532.C	533.A	534.A	535.E	536.D	537.D	538.E	539.B	540.D
541.C	542.A	543.D	544.C	545.A	546.B	547.B	548.E	549.D	550.E
551.B	552.B	553.C	554.A	555.A	556.C	557.A			

Chapter 6

Fruits and Vegetable Processing

1. Milk and fruit juices are deaerated before they are allowed to flow through pasteurizer. This is done by
   (*a*) Reducing fouling of pasteurizer
   (*b*) Increasing rate of heat transfer
   (*c*) Reducing oxidative deterioration
   (*d*) All of them

2. Jelly is ____________ food product.
   (*a*) Solid
   (*b*) Liquid
   (*c*) Semi-solid
   (*d*) Syrup

3. The end point of cooking of jelly/jam is tested by
   (*a*) Alcohol test
   (*b*) Temperature test
   (*c*) Flake test
   (*d*) both (*b*) and (*c*)

4. How many kinds of marmalade are prepared
   (*a*) One
   (*b*) Two
   (*c*) Three
   (*d*) Four

5. Sweetened juice contains the ______ percent juice.
   (*a*) 85
   (*b*) 20
   (*c*) 25
   (*d*) 45

6. RTS contains the acid content (%) about
   (*a*) 1.5
   (*b*) 0.3
   (*c*) 2.5
   (*d*) 1.0

7. The percentage of fresh juice in fruit squash is added about
   (*a*) 15-20%
   (*b*) 20-25%
   (*c*) 30-35%
   (*d*) 40-45%

8. Iron and copper equipments should not be used in the preparation of
   (*a*) Chutney
   (*b*) Sauce
   (*c*) Ketchup
   (*d*) All

9. Blanching refers to
(*a*) Inactivate the enzyme
(*b*) Cooking the food
(*c*) Sterilization of food
(*d*) Drying of food

10. Invert sugar in Fruit jam should not be more than
(*a*) 40 %
(*b*) 50 %
(*c*) 60 %
(*d*) 70 %

11. Premature setting of jelly is caused by
(*a*) Low TSS
(*b*) High TSS
(*c*) Low Acidity
(*d*) Low pectin

12. Best quality jelly is made from the __________ fruit.
(*a*) Apricot
(*b*) Guava
(*c*) Strawberry
(*d*) Mango

13. A clear sugar solution which has artificial flavour is known as
(*a*) Syrup
(*b*) Cordial
(*c*) Sherbet
(*d*) Squash

14. A good quality chutney should be
(*a*) Palatable
(*b*) Appetizer.
(*c*) Digestive
(*d*) All

15. In sauce/ketch up, tamarind pulp and pomegranate seed powder is used to increase
(*a*) Acidity
(*b*) Digestion
(*c*) Palatability
(*d*) Sweetness

16. Water soluble vitamins are
(*a*) *A*, *D*
(*b*) *E*, *K*
(*c*) *a* and *b*
(*d*) none

17. Oil and fat soluble vitamins are
(*a*) *A*, *D*
(*b*) *E*, *K*
(*c*) *a* and *b*
(*d*) none

18. The process preservation of fruits and vegetable with common salt and vinegar is called
(*a*) Pickling
(*b*) Fermentation
(*c*) Steeping
(*d*) Asepsis

19. Lactic acid forming bacteria is beneficial and grown in
(*a*) Sauce
(*b*) Ketchup
(*c*) Jelly
(*d*) Pickle

20. Mango pickles are kept for proper curing in sun for
(*a*) One week (*b*) Two week
(*c*) Two days (*d*) One day

21. The by product of apple is
(*a*) Rags (*b*) Pomace
(*c*) Peel (*d*) Stones

22. Rags is the by product of
(*a*) Apple (*b*) Citrus fruit
(*c*) Apricot (*d*) Grape

23. Rags (by product of citrus fruits) is used for preparation of
(*a*) Candy (*b*) Vinegar
(*c*) Jam (*d*) Marmalade

24. For the prevention of black neck, sauce should be filled hot in bottle at the temperature of
(*a*) 80 °C (*b*) 85 °C
(*c*) 90 °C (*d*) 75 °C

25. Soy sauce is known by the following name in China
(*a*) Ching-yu (*b*) Kecap
(*c*) Kanjang (*d*) Shoyu

26. Soy sauce is made by fermentation of a combination of
(*a*) Soybean and wheat (*b*) Rice and pulse
(*c*) Milk and sugar (*d*) Soybean and fruits

27. A paste like product made by fermenting cereals, soybeans and salt with molds, yeasts and bacteria is famous in Japan is known as
(*a*) Tempeh (*b*) Miso
(*c*) Kefir (*d*) Koumiss

28. Acidophilus milk is produced by fermentation of milk by
(*a*) *Lactobacillus acidophilus* (*b*) *Saccharomyces rouxii*
(*c*) *Torulopsis* yeasts (*d*) *Lactobacillus caucasicus*

29. Kefir is the main fermented food product of
(*a*) USA (*b*) Russia
(*c*) China (*d*) Japan

30. Which microorganisms is not used in the preparation of cultured butter milk
(*a*) *Streptoccus lactis* (*b*) *Streptoccus cremoris,*
(*c*) *S. lactis subsp. Diacelylactis* (*d*) *Saccharomyces rouxii*

31. Jam contains ______ per cent acid and invert sugar should not be more than ____ per cent.
(*a*) 0.2-0.3 and 40
(*b*) 0.5-0.6 and 40
(*c*) 0.1-0.3 and 45
(*d*) 0.5-0.6 and 45

32. Protopectin is converted into pectin by the enzyme
(*a*) Protopectinase
(*b*) Pectinase
(*c*) Lipase
(*d*) Catalase

33. Sugar content in jelly is
(*a*) 75 %
(*b*) 70 %
(*c*) 72 %
(*d*) 65 %

34. Large quantity of acid in jelly may cause
(*a*) Syneresis
(*b*) Crystallization
(*c*) Gelation
(*d*) Premature setting

35. When sugar is boiled with an acid it is hydrolyzed into
(*a*) Dextrose
(*b*) Fructose
(*c*) Above both
(*d*) None

36. Temperature test is not used to judge the end-point of
(*a*) Jam
(*b*) Jelly
(*c*) Kefir
(*d*) Marmalade

37. Sauce is _________ than ketchup.
(*a*) Thinner
(*b*) Thicker
(*c*) Similar
(*d*) None of these

38. Formation of blackening in the neck of sauce bottles is known
(*a*) Round neck
(*b*) Black neck
(*c*) Gray neck
(*d*) All of these

39. How many carbon is constituted in vegetable oils?
(*a*) 12 & 14
(*b*) 16 & 18
(*c*) 18 & 20
(*d*) None of above

40. Vitamin A, D, E and K are soluble in
(*a*) Water
(*b*) Fat
(*c*) Alcohol
(*d*) Paraffin

41. Rich source of fatty acid is
(*a*) Milk
(*b*) Cereals
(*c*) Pulse
(*d*) Dry vegetables

42. Which items contain varying quantity of alcohol?
(*a*) Fruit juice
(*b*) Fermented beverage
(*c*) Fruit juice powder
(*d*) Syrup

43. The grape juice can be preserved by adding of
(*a*) Potassium meta bisulphate
(*b*) Sodium benzoate
(*c*) Sulpher dioxide
(*d*) Sodium chloride

44. The ratio of sweet orange and khatta orange in jelly marmalade is subjected to
(*a*) 2:1
(*b*) 1:2
(*c*) 1:1
(*d*) 3:1

45. The amount of sugar per kg pulp in the preparation apple jam is subjected to
(*a*) 0.75 kg
(*b*) 1.00 kg
(*c*) 1.25 kg
(*d*) 1.50 kg

46. In pickles, yeast and molds can be easily grown in the ____________.
(*a*) Basic
(*b*) Alkali
(*c*) Acidic
(*d*) Salty

47. Lactic acid bacteria are most active at the temperature of
(*a*) 20 ºC
(*b*) 23 ºC
(*c*) 30 ºC
(*d*) 40 ºC

48. Microbial spoilage in pickles can be prevent at salt concentration of
(*a*) 15 %
(*b*) 10 %
(*c*) 5 %
(*d*) 3 %

49. Aroma of over ripe fruit of banana is due to
(*a*) Isopenttanol
(*b*) Allicin
(*c*) Isothiocyanate
(*d*) capsaicin

50. Richest source of vitamin C among the fruits
(*a*) Lemon
(*b*) Barbados cherry
(*c*) Aonla
(*d*) Guava

51. The ______________ fruit is also known as butter fruit.
(*a*) Banana
(*b*) Mango
(*c*) Avacado
(*d*) Papaya

52. Zero energy chamber operates on the principle of
(*a*) Evaporative cooling
(*b*) Charle's law
(*c*) Second law of thermodynamics
(*d*) Boyle's law

53. Garlic contain amino acid
(*a*) Allicin
(*b*) Alliin
(*c*) Allinage
(*d*) Diallyl disulphide

54. Onion Bulbs are stored well at
(*a*) 20-25 ºC
(*b*) 15-20 ºC
(*c*) 10-15 ºC
(*d*) 0-10 ºC

55. Pungency in onion is due to the presence of
(*a*) Capacin
(*b*) Diallyl disulphide
(*c*) Isothiocyanate
(*d*) Allyl propyl disulphide

56. Potato contains solanine per 100 gram of fresh weight is considered safe for human consumption
(*a*) 20 mg
(*b*) 20 g
(*c*) 12 mg
(*d*) 8 g

57. Pungency in reddish is due to volatile compound of
(*a*) Diallyl disulphide
(*b*) Isothiocyanate
(*c*) Euric acid
(*d*) Acetic acid

58. Lime is good source of vitamin
(*a*) A
(*b*) K
(*c*) E
(*d*) C

59. Cluster bean contains mucilaginous substance is
(*a*) Glutamine
(*b*) Asparagine
(*c*) Mannogalacton
(*d*) Galactoronic acid

60. Red colour in tomato is due to pigment
(*a*) Capsaicin
(*b*) Capsanthin
(*c*) Isothiocyanate
(*d*) Lycopene

61. Balanced diet includes at least gram of vegetables
(*a*) 300
(*b*) 200
(*c*) 100
(*d*) 400

62. Which fruit is richest source of riboflavin?
(*a*) Ber
(*b*) Bael
(*c*) Orange
(*d*) Mango

63. Flavour in cabbage leaves is due to the glycoside
(*a*) Oleoresin
(*b*) Euric acid
(*c*) Sinigrin
(*d*) Cucubitacin

64. Coagulating vitamin is
(*a*) A (*b*) B
(*c*) C (*d*) K

65. Exhausting temperature of canned fruit and vegetables is
(*a*) 80-82 ºC (*b*) 90-92 ºC
(*c*) 100-102 ºC (*d*) 110-112 ºC

66. The ________________ is richest source of iron.
(*a*) Green pea (*b*) Spinach
(*c*) Parsley (*d*) Celery

67. Papaya is rich source of Vitamin
(*a*) E (*b*) B
(*c*) A (*d*) C

68. Storage temperature to extend shelf life of banana is
(*a*) –10 ºC (*b*) 2-5 ºC
(*c*) 8-10 ºC (*d*) 12-15 ºC

69. Fruit for making jelly should be rich in
(*a*) Pectin and acids (*b*) Acids and proteins
(*c*) Protein and sugars (*d*) Sugars and acids

70. Controlled atmosphere storage (CAS) of fruits and vegetables is done to
(*a*) Maintain higher concentration of ethylene than the normal atmosphere
(*b*) Maintain higher concentration of CO_2 than the normal atmosphere
(*c*) Maintain higher concentration of N_2 than the normal atmosphere
(*d*) None of these

71. The anti-sterility vitamin is
(*a*) A (*b*) B
(*c*) E (*d*) D

72. Fruits on the basis of respiration can be classified as
(*a*) Non climacteric (*b*) Parthenocarpic
(*c*) Climacteric (*d*) Climacteric and Non climacteric

73. Sweetest sugar in fruit is
(*a*) Fructose (*b*) Sucrose
(*c*) Glucose (*d*) Galactose

74. The yellow pigment in papaya is
(*a*) Xanthophylls (*b*) Anthocyanin
(*c*) Caricaxanthin (*d*) Carotene

75. Fruits and vegetables stored in a cold chamber enhance storage life because
(*a*) There is an increase in humidity
(*b*) CO_2 concentration in the environment is increased
(*c*) Exposure to sun light is prevented
(*d*) Rate of respiration is decreased

76. Sodium benzoate is used for preservation of fruit juices in the range of
(*a*) 0.01–0.5 % (*b*) 0.06–0.10 %
(*c*) 1.1–1.5 % (*d*) 1.6–2.0 %

77. Which one of the following fruits is a rich source of fat
(*a*) Cashew nut (*b*) Mango
(*c*) Walnut (*d*) Guava

78. Rich source of protein is
(*a*) Banana (*b*) Almond
(*c*) Mango (*d*) Cashew nut

79. Agriculture and processed products development authority (APEDA) was came in existence in the year
(*a*) 1975 (*b*) 1985
(*c*) 1995 (*d*) 2005

80. The yellow colour in onion is due to the pigment of
(*a*) Lycopene (*b*) Caraotene
(*c*) Quereitin (*d*) Anthocyanin

81. Wax coating treatment enhance the shelf life of fruits because it block the
(*a*) Ripening process (*b*) Respiration
(*c*) Evaporation (*d*) Transpiration

82. Yellow coloured fruits and vegetables are rich source of
(*a*) Vitamin A (*b*) Vitamin B
(*c*) Vitamin C (*d*) Vitamin D

83. Fruit not suitable for jam making is
(*a*) Banana (*b*) Lemon
(*c*) Aonla (*d*) Mango

84. Fruits are blanched before canning at temp.
(*a*) 70 °C (*b*) 90 °C
(*c*) 80 °C (*d*) 100 °C

85. Refractometer is used to determine the
(*a*) Minerals (*b*) Vitamins
(*c*) Acidity (*d*) TSS

86. Vegetables are canned in the
(*a*) Brine (*b*) Syrup
(*c*) Vinegar (*d*) Distilled water

87. Which fruit is a rich source of iron?
(*a*) Datepalm (*b*) Karonda
(*c*) Apple (*d*) None of these

88. Preservative used for preparation of tomato ketchup is
(*a*) Citric acid (*b*) KMS
(*c*) Sodium benzoate (*d*) Sodium bisulphate

89. Redness in apple is due to
(*a*) Carotene (*b*) Anthocyanin
(*c*) Xanthophylls (*d*) Lycopene

90. CIPHET is situated at
(*a*) Bhopal (*b*) Ludhiana
(*c*) Mysore (*d*) Cochin

91. CIAE is located at
(*a*) Nagpur (*b*) Ludhiana
(*c*) Bhopal (*d*) Budhani

92. Which of the following is a non-reducing carbohydrate?
(*a*) Maltose (*b*) Lactose
(*c*) Glucose (*d*) Sucrose

93. Fat soluble vitamins are
(*a*) A, D, E and K (*b*) A and D
(*c*) A, D and C (*d*) B and C

94. Cryo-preservation is done in liquid nitrogen at a temperature of
(*a*) –196 ºC (*b*) 0 ºC
(*c*) 200 ºC (*d*) 50 ºC

95. Recommended temperature for storage of potatoes in cold storage is
(*a*) 0-2 ºC (*b*) 3-7 ºC
(*c*) 8-10 ºC (*d*) 10-15 ºC

96. To avoid bruising, the onion should not be stored than
(*a*) 4 m (*b*) 10 m
(*c*) 6 m (*d*) 8 m

97. The acid percentage in jam varies
(*a*) 2.0% (*b*) 0.5-0.6 %
(*c*) 65 % (*d*) 30-50 %

98. Moulds which causes of microbial spoilage in jam when humidity is
(*a*) Less than 90 % (*b*) More than 90%
(*c*) Equal to 90 % (*d*) None of these

99. The jam becomes sticky or gummy because of
(*a*) More citric acid (*b*) Low TSS
(*c*) More pectin content (*d*) High TSS

100. Which of the following is best suitable for jelly making?
(*a*) Apricot (*b*) Apple
(*c*) Strawberry (*d*) Pine apple

101. The effective concentration of sugar in jelly is
(*a*) 65 % (*b*) 80 %
(*c*) 40 % (*d*) 75 %

102. The pectin content for producing good jelly is
(*a*) 1% (*b*) 2 %
(*c*) 20 % (*d*) 10 %

103. The optimum pH for jelly containing 1 % pectin and 65 % TSS should be
(*a*) 3.0 (*b*) 3.4
(*c*) 3.2 (*d*) 3.1

104. The suitable temperature for judging the end point or proper setting of jelly containing 65 %TSS is
(*a*) 105 ºC (*b*) 85 ºC
(*c*) 82 ºC (*d*) 65ºC

105. In jelly making, which one of the following does not lead to syneresis:
(*a*) Low concentration of sugar (*b*) Insufficient pectin
(*c*) Less acid (*d*) Fermentation

106. Which one of the following, there is not a problem of jam making?
(*a*) Syneresis (*b*) Crystallization
(*c*) Premature setting (*d*) Microbial spoilage

107. Causes of browning and blackness formation in sauce /ketch and chutney is due to the presence

(*a*) Head less clove
(*b*) Flower head of clove
(*c*) All spice except clove
(*d*) Vinegar only

108. Tannin is responsible for browning and blackness formation in sauce /ketch up and chutney is found in

(*a*) Clove
(*b*) Red chili
(*c*) Cardamom
(*d*) Cinnamon

109. Addition of 100 ppm SO_2 or 100 mg ascorbic acid in sauce /ketch up or chutney to prevent the

(*a*) Black neck ring formation and Browning
(*b*) Blackness
(*c*) Browning
(*d*) Fermentation

110. Fermented beverage undergone in alcoholic fermentation with help of

(*a*) Yeast
(*b*) Mold
(*c*) Bacteria
(*d*) Virus

111. The fruit beverage which contains 20 % juice/pulp, 15 % TSS and 0.3 % acid is called

(*a*) Squash
(*b*) Cordial
(*c*) Syrup
(*d*) Nectar

112. Which one of the following beverage prepared by dissolving 200 g sugar and 1.0 g citric acid in 800 ml water ?

(*a*) Squash
(*b*) Syrup
(*c*) Cordial
(*d*) Sherbet

113. Which fruits are used in the preparation of cordial?

(*a*) Apple and guava
(*b*) Mango and apple
(*c*) Bael and papaya
(*d*) Lime and lemon

114. The problem likes cloudiness and foggy in jelly happens by

(*a*) Use of immature fruits
(*b*) Over cooking
(*c*) Use of non-clarified juice or extract
(*d*) All of the above

115. The kefir is foamy and fizzy in appearance due to its

(*a*) CO_2 content
(*b*) SO_2 content
(*c*) O_2 content
(*d*) O_3 content

116. Aroma in coffee is created due to

(*a*) Fermentation
(*b*) Drying
(*c*) Roasting
(*d*) None

117. In litchi, which portion is edible?
(*a*) Endocarp (*b*) Epicarp
(*c*) Mesocarp (*d*) Rind

118. Minimum TSS required for Jam is
(*a*) 68 % (*b*) 70 %
(*c*) 85 % (*d*) 80 %

119. Vinegar from coconut today is prepared by
(*a*) Yeast (*b*) Bacteria
(*c*) Fermentation (*d*) Fungi

120. The ideal relative humidity (%) for onion storage is
(*a*) 60-65 (*b*) 70-75
(*c*) 80-85 (*d*) 90-95

121. The 'Champaigne' is a type of
(*a*) Juice (*b*) Wine
(*c*) Beverage (*d*) Pod

122. Which are the following used for preparing best Jelly is
(*a*) Jamun (*b*) Guava
(*c*) Mango (*d*) Aonla

123. The Jelly in which fruits pieces are suspended is called as
(*a*) Jam (*b*) Jelly
(*c*) Marmalade (*d*) Candy

124. The sparkling clear liquid free from all suspended solids is called as
(*a*) Concentrate (*b*) Cordial
(*c*) Squash (*d*) Beverage

125. Jelly with high sugar and low acid is called as
(*a*) Weeping jelly (*b*) Crystallized jelly
(*c*) Soft jelly (*d*) Cloudy jelly

126. The preservative recommended by FPO are
(*a*) SO_2 and sodium benzoate (*b*) KMS and KNO_3
(*c*) Acetic acid (*d*) None

127. Chilies are good source of
(*a*) Protein (*b*) Fat
(*c*) Carbohydrates (*d*) Vitamin A & C

128. Guava is a rich source of
(*a*) Carbohydrates (*b*) Vitamin C
(*c*) Vitamin A (*d*) β-carotene

129. Dry fruits like cashew and almond are richest source of
(*a*) Vitamin B (*b*) Fat
(*c*) Vitamin K (*d*) Carbohydrates

130. Ripe papaya fruits contain
(*a*) Vitamin A (*b*) Vitamin B
(*c*) Vitamin C (*d*) Vitamin D

131. Vitamin C is maximum in
(*a*) Guava (*b*) Aonla
(*c*) Papaya (*d*) Mango

132. Carrot is a rich source of
(*a*) Vitamin A (*b*) Vitamin B
(*c*) Vitamin C (*d*) Vitamin D

133. Pink colour of onion is due to
(*a*) Qucertin (*b*) Anthocyanin
(*c*) Carotene (*d*) None

134. Preservative used in tomato ketchup is
(*a*) Sodium benzoate (*b*) SO_2
(*c*) Both (*d*) None

135. Low temperature preservation prevent growth of microorganisms due to
(*a*) Reduction in growth of microorganisms (*b*) Increase in growth of microorganisms
(*c*) Killing of microorganisms (*d*) All of the above

136. Pectin test is done by
(*a*) Jelmeter (*b*) Alcohol
(*c*) Acid (*d*) None

137. Crystal formation in Jelly is due to
(*a*) Excess of sugar (*b*) Over cooking
(*c*) Both (*d*) None

138. Treatments of fruits and vegetables by slight temperature for small time is known as
(*a*) Sterilization (*b*) Blanching
(*c*) Pasteurization (*d*) None

139. After preservation, nutrients, vitamins and minerals are
(*a*) Less than before preservation
(*b*) More than before preservation
(*c*) Constant
(*d*) None

140. Good storage require
(*a*) High temperature and high humidity
(*b*) Low temperature and high humidity
(*c*) High temperature and low humidity
(*d*) None

141. Good source of carbohydrate, vitamins, fat, minerals and protein is
(*a*) Vegetables
(*b*) Egg
(*c*) Milk
(*d*) None

142. For packing of spinach, cauliflower and sweet potato which type of can is used
(*a*) AR cans
(*b*) SR cans
(*c*) Plain
(*d*) All

143. Papaya contain __________ unit of vitamin A.
(*a*) 2500 IU
(*b*) 2020 IU
(*c*) 3000 IU
(*d*) 4000 IU

144. Standard error formula is
(*a*) σ/n
(*b*) σ^2/n
(*c*) $\sigma/\sqrt{n}$
(*d*) none

145. Pigment in Jamun is due to
(*a*) Anthocyanin
(*b*) Carotene
(*c*) Xanthophylls
(*d*) None

146. Potato is the rich source of
(*a*) Fat
(*b*) Starch
(*c*) Vitamin
(*d*) Minerals

147. Potato contain ______________ percentage of protein.
(*a*) 1.8
(*b*) 2.2
(*c*) 1.4
(*d*) 3.2

148. Which product is made by yeast fermentation?
(*a*) Apple cider
(*b*) Mango pulp
(*c*) Citrus nectar
(*d*) All

149. Guava Jelly is preserved by
(*a*) Pectin
(*b*) Sugar
(*c*) Sodium benzoate
(*d*) None

150. Storage temperature of banana is
(*a*) 2-3 ºC (*b*) 10-13 ºC
(*c*) 4-5 ºC (*d*) 15-20 ºC

151. Storage temperature of cucumber is
(*a*) 0 ºC (*b*) 4-5 ºC
(*c*) 6-7 ºC (*d*) 10 ºC

152. Ripening fruits exist which gas is
(*a*) NH_3 (*b*) Ethylene
(*c*) Methane (*d*) All

153. Capacity of refrigeration is measured in the term of
(*a*) Gram (*b*) Ton
(*c*) Pascal (*d*) Lux

154. Bacteria are involved in production of
(*a*) Nectar (*b*) Vinegar
(*c*) Jam (*d*) Squash

155. Yeast is used in the production of
(*a*) Nectar (*b*) Cordial
(*c*) Syrup (*d*) Cider

156. Why does blanching in vegetables?
(*a*) microorganism removal (*b*) inactivate enzyme
(*c*) for softening the vegetables (*d*) all

157. Non-climacteric fruit is
(*a*) which ripe after the maturity (*b*) which ripe before the maturity
(*c*) which ripe at time of maturity (*d*) none

158. How much juice is required in making of fruit jelly?
(*a*) 10 % (*b*) 20 %
(*c*) 25 % (*d*) 30 %

159. How much sugar is recommended for making Jam?
(*a*) Above 30 % (*b*) Above 40 %
(*c*) Above 70 % (*d*) Above 60 %

160. Which of the following is responsible for sourness of reddish?
(*a*) Iso thiocynate (*b*) Anthocyanin
(*c*) Auxin (*d*) All

161. Lactic acid bacteria is used in preparation of
(*a*) Pickle (*b*) Chutney
(*c*) Marmalade (*d*) Jelly

162. Which of the following fruit contain maximum fat?
(*a*) Avocado (*b*) Walnut
(*c*) Apricot (*d*) peanut

163. Which is the rich source of vitamin?
(*a*) Cabbage (*b*) Tomato
(*c*) Chili (*d*) All

164. Rich source fruit of Vitamin A is
(*a*) Ber (*b*) Pomegranate
(*c*) Indian goose berry (*d*) Mango

165. In which product, TSS is 30° Brix
(*a*) Cordial (*b*) Squash
(*c*) Jam (*d*) jelly

166. The pungency of chili is due to
(*a*) Capsanthin (*b*) Capsacin
(*c*) Isothiocynate (*d*) none

167. The pungency of onion is due to
(*a*) Allyl propyl disulphide (*b*) Diallyl disulphide
(*c*) Both (*d*) None

168. Which of the following is class one preservative?
(*a*) Silver nitrate (*b*) KMS
(*c*) Sugar (*d*) Vinegar

169. For measurement of TSS, which instrument is used?
(*a*) Dendrometer (*b*) Thermometer
(*c*) Refractometer (*d*) Spectrophotometer

170. Sugar used as preservative have concentration of
(*a*) 60 % (*b*) 70 %
(*c*) 40 % (*d*) 50 %

171. Most commonly used oil extraction method from flower is
(*a*) Distillation (*b*) Maceration
(*c*) Solvent extraction (*d*) None

172. Time and temperature for vegetable processing in canning depend upon
(*a*) Amount of microbes present in food
(*b*) Texture of foods
(*c*) Nutrient
(*d*) None

173. Which cucurbit has highest vitamin A?
(*a*) Bitter guard
(*b*) Cucumber
(*c*) Pumpkin
(*d*) All

174. Protein content in ground nut is
(*a*) 22 %
(*b*) 25 %
(*c*) 40 %
(*d*) 43 %

175. Most suitable radiation for disinfection of food is
(*a*) UV- rays
(*b*) g-rays
(*c*) a-rays
(*d*) b-rays

176. TSS of Watermelon is
(*a*) 10-12 °Brix
(*b*) 14-16 °Brix
(*c*) 18-22 °Brix
(*d*) 20-22 °Brix

177. Pungency of garlic is due to
(*a*) Allyl propyl disulphide
(*b*) Diallyl disulphide
(*c*) Isothiocynate
(*d*) None

178. According to BIS, tomato has been specialized into
(*a*) 4 grades
(*b*) 3 grades
(*c*) 2 grades
(*d*) Only 1 grade

179. Fruit which is rich in pectin and acid is
(*a*) Jamun
(*b*) Apple
(*c*) Pear
(*d*) Pomegranate

180. Permissible limit of SO_2 in jam is
(*a*) 300 ppm
(*b*) 40 ppm
(*c*) 70 ppm
(*d*) 100 ppm

181. Acetic acid is present in
(*a*) Nectar
(*b*) Sweet chutney
(*c*) Vinegar
(*d*) Apple cider

182. Vitamin C is commonly known as
(*a*) Citric acid
(*b*) Acetic acid
(*c*) Lactic acid
(*d*) Ascorbic acid

183. Standard unit used in expressing refrigeration capacity is
(*a*) Calorie (*b*) Ampere
(*c*) Ton (*d*) Joule

184. Ideal storage temperature of papaya is
(*a*) 8–9 °C (*b*) 9–11 °C
(*c*) 11–13 °C (*d*) 5–6 °C

185. Ideal storage temperature of Brinjal is
(*a*) 10–11 °C (*b*) 14–15 °C
(*c*) 8–9 °C (*d*) 17–18 °C

186. The pigment present in watermelon is
(*a*) Carotenoid (*b*) Anthocyanin
(*c*) Lycopene (*d*) Both b and c

187. Identify the mango cultivar suitable for canning
(*a*) Alphonso (*b*) Amarapalli
(*c*) Neelum (*d*) Bombay green

188. Potato variety more suitable for chips making
(*a*) Kufri Jyoti (*b*) Kufri Naveen
(*c*) Kufri Badshah (*d*) Kufri Chipsona

189. Softness of Pea is measured by
(*a*) Derometer (*b*) Refractometer
(*c*) Alanometer (*d*) Tenderometer

190. In fruit jelly, pectin and sugar is present in the ratio of
(*a*) 1:65 (*b*) 65:1
(*c*) 65:33 (*d*) 33:65

191. Daily requirement of vitamin D for a healthy adult is
(*a*) 200 IU (*b*) 400 IU
(*c*) 600 IU (*d*) 800 IU

192. Cashew nut contains following % of protein
(*a*) 21 % (*b*) 22.7 %
(*c*) 27 % (*d*) 47 %

193. Yellow colour of onion is due to
(*a*) Qucertin (*b*) Myrcetin
(*c*) Allicin (*d*) Malvelin

194. Wine is preserved at
(*a*) 10 % alcohol
(*b*) 14 % alcohol
(*c*) 8 % alcohol
(*d*) 5 % alcohol

195. Cryo-preservation of foods is done by liquid N_2 at the temperature of
(*a*) 200 °C
(*b*) 0 °C
(*c*) –196 °C
(*d*) 4 °C

196. High sugar containing variety of muskmelon may contain TSS of
(*a*) 80 %
(*b*) 2 %
(*c*) 17 %
(*d*) 4 %

197. Vegetables are called as protective food because they are rich source of
(*a*) Fat
(*b*) Vitamins and minerals
(*c*) Proteins
(*d*) Sugars

198. In general, fruit and vegetables are not rich source of
(*a*) Vitamin A
(*b*) Vitamin B_1
(*c*) Vitamin C
(*d*) Minerals

199. Which of following is used as antioxidant?
(*a*) Fat
(*b*) Protein
(*c*) Carbohydrate
(*d*) Vitamin C

200. Fruit and vegetable are rich source in dietary fibers which protect human body from
(*a*) Colon cancer
(*b*) Protein deficiency
(*c*) Fat deficiency
(*d*) Sugar deficiency

201. Benzoic acid and SO_2 are added to preserve fruit and vegetable product to check
(*a*) Microorganism's activity
(*b*) Ethylene production
(*c*) Reduce rancidity
(*d*) None

202. MAP of fruits and vegetables prevent the building up of the following
(*a*) Sugar
(*b*) Protein
(*c*) CO_2 and ethylene
(*d*) None

203. Vegetable of the 20th century is
(*a*) Cluster bean
(*b*) Amaranths
(*c*) Winged bean
(*d*) Chikurmanis

204. Which vegetable has high calorific value?
(*a*) Fenugreek
(*b*) Amaranths
(*c*) Potato
(*d*) Tomato

205. Which vegetables are rich source of niacin
(*a*) Spinach
(*b*) Cow pea
(*c*) Radish
(*d*) Sweet potato

206. Daily requirement of vegetable per capita/day is
(*a*) 150 g
(*b*) 200 g
(*c*) 285 g
(*d*) 400 g

207. Which is non-pungent when uncooked?
(*a*) Lettuce
(*b*) Radish
(*c*) Onion
(*d*) Chili

208. Onion stored at temperature of
(*a*) 4–5 ºC
(*b*) 0 ºC
(*c*) 6–8 ºC
(*d*) 10 ºC

209. Jam should contain at least nearby percent of sugar
(*a*) 60 %
(*b*) 70 %
(*c*) 50 %
(*d*) 80 %

210. TSS of jam should be minimum at time of end point
(*a*) 68.5 %
(*b*) 70 %
(*c*) 50 %
(*d*) 80 %

211. Which is not used as food preservative?
(*a*) KMS
(*b*) Sodium benzoate
(*c*) Acetic acid
(*d*) Bendate

212. Inactivation of enzyme is done by
(*a*) Canning
(*b*) Freezing
(*c*) Blanching
(*d*) Dehydration

213. Lye peeling of fruit and vegetables is done by
(*a*) 1 % caustic soda + cool
(*b*) 5 % caustic soda + cool
(*c*) 1 % caustic soda + hot
(*d*) 5 % caustic soda + hot

214. Curcumin is extracted from
(*a*) Cucumber
(*b*) Capsicum
(*c*) Turmeric
(*d*) Cashew nut

215. The ideal concentration of sodium benzoate for preserving fruit juice
(*a*) 0.01 - 0.05 %
(*b*) 0.06 - 0.10 %
(*c*) 1.1 – 1.5 %
(*d*) 1.6 - 2.0 %

216. Chemical formula of potassium meta bisulphate is
(*a*) KMS (*b*) K_2SO_4
(*c*) KSO_2 (*d*) $K_2S_2O_5$

217. Vinegar concentration in finished pickle should not be
(*a*) Less than 10% (*b*) Less than 5%
(*c*) Less than 2 % (*d*) More than 50 %

218. Degree Brix is an unit for measurement of
(*a*) Salt content in juice (*b*) Sucrose content in juice
(*c*) Total solids in juice (*d*) Juice content of fruits

219. The cheapest method of preservation is
(*a*) Canning (*b*) Freezing
(*c*) Drying (*d*) Preserving

220. Palmolein is a/an
(*a*) Anti trasnpirant (*b*) Protein
(*c*) Edible oil (*d*) Essential oil

221. Which is an anti-hemorrhagic vitamin?
(*a*) Vitamin A (*b*) Vitamin K
(*c*) Vitamin K (*d*) Vitamin C

222. 'Essential oil' is extracted from ________________ fruit.
(*a*) Chili (*b*) Mangostein
(*c*) Olive (*d*) Almond

223. An equipment used for removing moisture from fruit and vegetable by evaporation
(*a*) Evaporator (*b*) Transpirator
(*c*) Auto clave (*d*) Dehydrator

224. The most common method of grape preservation is
(*a*) Jam making (*b*) Jelly making
(*c*) Dehydration (*d*) Pickling

225. Flame peeling is useful for
(*a*) Onion and garlic (*b*) Mango and guava
(*c*) Pea and tomato (*d*) Apple and carrot

226. The process of removal of air from cans is known as
(*a*) Appertizing (*b*) Exhausting
(*c*) Brining (*d*) Syruping

227. Which is diluted before serving?
(*a*) Jam (*b*) Jelly
(*c*) RTS (*d*) Squash

228. Canned vegetable is dipped in brine solution is made up from
(*a*) Common salt (*b*) Black salt
(*c*) Sugar (*d*) Salt and sugar

229. RTS stands for
(*a*) Ready to safe (*b*) Ready to serve
(*c*) Ready to store (*d*) Ready to sale

230. Colouring additives are added to foods for
(*a*) Improving shelf life (*b*) Improving appearance
(*c*) Easily processing (*d*) Improving taste

231. Father of food preservation is
(*a*) Lavoisier (*b*) Nicholas Appert
(*c*) Needham (*d*) Luis Pasteur

232. Food product order was established by GOI in the year
(*a*) 1950 (*b*) 1985
(*c*) 1945 (*d*) 1955

233. First food processing industry was started at
(*a*) Bombay (1935) (*b*) Lucknow (1934)
(*c*) Mysore (1945) (*d*) Delhi (1950)

234. World food day is celebrated on
(*a*) 15th July (*b*) 20th July
(*c*) 16th October (*d*) 10th July

235. Monoglycerides (GMS) emulsifier is used in
(*a*) Tomato juice (*b*) Bakery items
(*c*) Ice-cream (*d*) Fruit juice

236. Field to plate of food process is so called
(*a*) Food processing (*b*) Food engineering
(*c*) Food technology (*d*) Food nutrition

237. The process for prevention of decay or spoilage of food is called
(*a*) Preservation (*b*) Sanitization
(*c*) Filtration (*d*) Sterilization

238. The KMS of 350 ppm is mostly used in which food products?
(*a*) Juice (*b*) Jelly
(*c*) Jam (*d*) Pickle

239. Phosphoric acid is added in
(*a*) Soft drink (*b*) Jam
(*c*) Jelly (*d*) Juice

240. Ethylbutyrate, a flavouring compound is found in
(*a*) Strawberry and pineapple (*b*) Mango and grape
(*c*) Guava and banana (*d*) None

241. During sealing of can, temperature should not be less than
(*a*) 70°C (*b*) 74°C
(*c*) 84°C (*d*) 89°C

242. The lye peeling of fruits and vegetables is done at the temperature of
(*a*) 75°C (*b*) 93°C
(*c*) 80°C (*d*) 100°C

243. Enzymatic browning in apple is due to
(*a*) Oxidase (*b*) Catalase
(*c*) Poly phenol oxidase (*d*) Protease

244. Salt concentration in pickle is measured by
(*a*) Salometer (*b*) pH meter
(*c*) Lactometer (*d*) Refractometer

245. Water core is a serious disorder of
(*a*) Grape (*b*) Mango
(*c*) Apple (*d*) Ber

246. Syrup or brine in can is filled at the temperature of
(*a*) 90-100°C (*b*) 79-82°C
(*c*) 50-70°C (*d*) 45-53°C

247. Pricking is related to the processing of
(*a*) Papaya (*b*) Apple
(*c*) Mango (*d*) Aonla

248. Cold process is also known as
(*a*) Pre cooling (*b*) Freezing
(*c*) Cold storage (*d*) Ultra filtration

249. Cold sterilization of food is so called as
(*a*) Freezing (*b*) Irradiation
(*c*) Waxing (*d*) Chilling

250. Good quality of pectin is found when guava is at
(*a*) Green stage (*b*) Dark yellow in colour
(*c*) Over ripe (*d*) Ripe but green stage

251. Most of the enzymes are inactivate at the temperature of
(*a*) 80ºC (*b*) 85ºC
(*c*) 90ºC (*d*) 70ºC

252. The coconut shells contain cellulose
(*a*) 40% (*b*) 35%
(*c*) 34% (*d*) 30%

253. Orange juice contain approximately solid about
(*a*) 5% (*b*) 12%
(*c*) 20% (*d*) 25%

254. Fermentation was discovered by
(*a*) Lavoisier (*b*) Benjamin
(*c*) Funk (*d*) Louise Pasteur

255. Fruit preservation and canning institute is located at
(*a*) Hyderabad (*b*) Mumbai
(*c*) Lucknow (*d*) Allahabad

256. Jelly is pasteurized at temperature of
(*a*) 90-95ºC (*b*) 82-85ºC
(*c*) 70-75ºC (*d*) 60-65ºC

257. Which vitamin destroyed during freezing due to oxidation?
(*a*) Vitamin D (*b*) Vitamin C
(*c*) Vitamin B (*d*) Vitamin A

258. Honey wine is known as
(*a*) Mead (*b*) Brandy
(*c*) Bear (*d*) Whisky

259. Which pickle is known as 'National Pickle of India?'
(*a*) Mango pickle (*b*) Chili pickle
(*c*) Lime pickle (*d*) garlic pickle

260. Density of liquid is measured by
(*a*) Hydrometer (*b*) Hygrometer
(*c*) Lactometer (*d*) Refractometer

261. Food packaging foils consist of pure
(*a*) Iron (*b*) Aluminium
(*c*) Zinc (*d*) Lead

262. How much pectin should be present in finished jelly?
(*a*) 2.0% (*b*) 3.0%
(*c*) 2.5% (*d*) 1.0%

263. What should be pH of good Jelly?
(*a*) 2.50 (*b*) 3.46
(*c*) 4.73 (*d*) 4.59

264. Basic principle of freeze drying is
(*a*) Water evaporate from ice crystal without ice melting
(*b*) Water evaporate after melting ice crystals
(*c*) Both above
(*d*) None

265. Dry ice sublime at which temperature and pressure
(*a*) 0°C and 2 bar (*b*) 1°C and 15 bar
(*c*) At room temperature and atmospheric pressure
(*d*) None of these

266. The percentage of sucrose in solution prevents the growth of all microorganisms in foods.
(*a*) 30% (*b*) 45%
(*c*) 60% (*d*) 70%

267. The percentage of salt in solution prevents the growth of all microorganisms in foods.
(*a*) 18-25% (*b*) 25-30%
(*c*) 30-40% (*d*) 10-15%

268. Atmospheric drying foams is also known as
(*a*) Natural drying (*b*) Foam mat drying
(*c*) Both above (*d*) None

269. Heat sensitive foods are mostly concentrated with low temperature by
(*a*) Vacuum evaporator (*b*) Natural evaporator
(*c*) Flash evaporator (*d*) Thin film evaporator

270. The freeze drying generally works at pressure of
(*a*) 2 mm to about 0.1 mm Hg (*b*) 3 mm to about 1.0 mm Hg
(*c*) 1 mm to about 0.3 mm Hg (*d*) None

271. At one atmosphere, pure water boils at
(*a*) 30ºC (*b*) 82ºC
(*c*) 70ºC (*d*) 100ºC

272. At 250 mm Hg, pure water boils at
(*a*) 72ºC (*b*) 82ºC
(*c*) 70ºC (*d*) 100ºC

273. The kiln drier cannot reduce moisture content of food below
(*a*) 10% (*b*) 12%
(*c*) 15% (*d*) 20%

274. Kiln drier is used for drying of
(*a*) Vegetable slices (*b*) Potato slice
(*c*) Cereals (*d*) Apple slices

275. Cabinet, tray and pan drier are best suited for the drying of
(*a*) Fruit and vegetable (*b*) Cereals grains
(*c*) Meat (*d*) Fish

276. In vacuum drying, temperature of foods and rate of water removal is controlled by
(*a*) Degree of vacuum (*b*) Intensity of heat input
(*c*) Both above (*d*) None

277. In vacuum drier, heat transfer from foods takes place by
(*a*) Only conduction (*b*) Only radiation
(*c*) Both above (*d*) Only convection

278. Freeze drying is used for the drying/dehydration of
(*a*) High value liquid foods like coffee, juices etc.
(*b*) Fruit slices
(*c*) Cereals grains (*d*) Live stock products

279. Sugar and salt concentrated solution have
(*a*) High diffusion pressure (*b*) High atmospheric pressure
(*c*) High osmotic pressure (*d*) All above

280. Sodium benzoate is added for preservation to fruit juice at the rate of
(*a*) 0.01-0.5% (*b*) 0.06-0.10%
(*c*) 1.1-1.5% (*d*) 1.6-2.0%

281. Jelly in appearance is
(*a*) Transparent (*b*) Opaque
(*c*) Colloid (*d*) None

282. One of the following preservative is used in squash
(*a*) Formaldehyde (*b*) NaCl
(*c*) KMS (*d*) Sodium benzoate

283. In freeze drying, the liquid phase comes at the pressure above
(*a*) 1.7 mm (*b*) 2.7 mm
(*c*) 4.7 mm (*d*) 3.7 mm

284. In conventional freeze drying, dehydration temperature are kept between
(*a*) 10.6-30.8°C (*b*) 30.2-69.5°C
(*c*) 35.5-75.0°C (*d*) 37.8-93.3°C

285. The heating of infrared drying in comparison to convection drying is higher by
(*a*) 5 times (*b*) 8 times
(*c*) 10 times (*d*) 12 times

286. The toxicant formed by Clostridium botulinum in foods is destroyed in 10 minutes if exposed to moist heat of the temperature of
(*a*) 50°C (*b*) 100°C
(*c*) 200°C (*d*) 300°C

287. Sterilization frequently requires a thermal treatment at least at
(*a*) 100°C (*b*) 121°C
(*c*) 135°C (*d*) 149°C

288. Sterilization increases _______________ of foods.
(*a*) Shelf life (*b*) Taste
(*c*) Protection form pathogens (*d*) All

289. Commercially sterilized food has a shelf life more than
(*a*) 3 month (*b*) 6 month
(*c*) 1 year (*d*) 2 years

290. Which combination is required to inactivate the pathogen in particular foods?
(*a*) Time and temperature (*b*) Moisture and temperature
(*c*) RH and temperature (*d*) RH and moisture

291. Acid foods generally having pH of
(*a*) More than 6 (*b*) 4.6 or less
(*c*) 7.5 (*d*) 8.6

292. Lemon juice are generally classified under
(*a*) Low acid food (*b*) Medium acid food
(*c*) Very low acid food (*d*) High acid food

293. The juices are pasteurized at 88°C for a period of
(*a*) 60 seconds (*b*) 900 seconds
(*c*) 30 seconds (*d*) 50 seconds

294. Typically acid fruit juices are first heated in the range of
(*a*) 77-100°C (*b*) 50-80°C
(*c*) 200-225°C (*d*) None

295. Freezing and refrigeration were started in year of
(*a*) 1850 (*b*) 1875
(*c*) 1900 (*d*) 1901

296. Cool storage generally refers to store the foods at temperature of
(*a*) 16°C down to –2°C (*b*) 4°C to – 4°C
(*c*) 0°C (*d*) 10°C

297. Commercial and house hold refrigerators are usually operated at
(*a*) 7.5°C (*b*) 4.5 to 7.0°C
(*c*) 0°C (*d*) –4°C

298. The freezing point of pure water is
(*a*) 0°C (*b*) 4°C
(*c*) – 4°C (*d*) –2°C

299. Storage life of fruits at 0°C is
(*a*) 2-180 days (*b*) 10 days
(*c*) 1 week (*d*) none

300. Air freezing method was introduced around the year
(*a*) 1905 (*b*) 1910
(*c*) 1860 (*d*) 1850

301. Which gas is helpful for freezing of foods at –196°C?
(*a*) Oxygen (*b*) Hydrogen
(*c*) Nitrogen (*d*) Ozone

302. The full form of FDA
(*a*) Food development authority (*b*) Food dehydration agency
(*c*) Food and drugs administration (*d*) None of the above

303. Non carbonated stimulating beverage is
(*a*) Nectar (*b*) Tea and coffee
(*c*) Milk (*d*) Mead

304. Roasting process is employed in making of
(*a*) Coffee (*b*) Milk
(*c*) Jam (*d*) Chips

305. Instant coffee is technically known as
(*a*) Solubilized coffee (*b*) Dry coffee
(*c*) Heated coffee (*d*) Boiled coffee

306. Coffee is made from the
(*a*) Beans (seed) (*b*) Leaves
(*c*) Buds (*d*) Roots

307. Tea is prepared from the
(*a*) Young leaves (*b*) Matures leaves
(*c*) Yellow leaves (*d*) Buds

308. Tea plant is a type of
(*a*) Evergreen (*b*) Herbaceous
(*c*) Annual (*d*) None

309. Tannin compound is found in
(*a*) Tea leaves (*b*) Coffee
(*c*) Fruits (*d*) Milk

310. For the preparation of black tea, air temperature for drying is employed at about
(*a*) 27ºC for 2-5 hrs (*b*) 40ºC for 2-5 hrs
(*c*) 10ºC for 2-5 hrs (*d*) 80ºC for 2-5 hrs

311. Caffeine percentage in Indian black tea is
(*a*) 2-3% (*b*) 4-5%
(*c*) 10-11% (*d*) 12-13%

312. Coffee is the major source of
(*a*) Caffeine (*b*) Nicotine
(*c*) Tannin (*d*) Saponin

313. 150 ml coffee beverage contain caffeine about
(*a*) 75-150 mg (*b*) 100-200 mg
(*c*) 75-150 ml (*d*) None of these

314. Full form of FSIS is
(*a*) Food supply and inspection system
(*b*) Food safety and inspection system
(*c*) Food safety and inspection service
(*d*) Food service and inspection scheme

315. One of the following equipment is used for ash determination.
(*a*) Soxlet
(*b*) Macro Jeldhal
(*c*) Micro Kjeldhal
(*d*) Muffle furnace

316. Micro Kjeldahl apparatus is used for the estimation of
(*a*) Ash
(*b*) Fat
(*c*) Protein
(*d*) Vitamin

317. Function of pulper is to
(*a*) grind the pulp
(*b*) dry the pulp
(*c*) cook the pulp
(*d*) slice the vegetables

318. To estimate the fat content in food which apparatus is employed?
(*a*) Soxlet
(*b*) Macro Kjeldahl
(*c*) Microwave oven
(*d*) Muffle furnace

319. To determine the rheological properties of food which apparatus is used?
(*a*) Shaker
(*b*) Mixograph
(*c*) Sedimentation apparatus
(*d*) Texture analyzer

320. Size analysis of flour/powder is done with the help of
(*a*) Pulper
(*b*) Grader
(*c*) Sieve shaker
(*d*) Attrition mill

321. Tray drier is facilitate to
(*a*) cook the food
(*b*) sterilize the food
(*c*) dry the food
(*d*) control the RH

322. The enzyme used as a emulsifying agent is
(*a*) Casein
(*b*) Leucine
(*c*) Rennin
(*d*) Lysine

323. To separate two liquids from their mixture is performed by
(*a*) Double distillation column
(*b*) BOD
(*c*) Spray drier
(*d*) Centrifuge

324. Suitable variety for processing of mango is
(*a*) Chausa
(*b*) Alphanso
(*c*) Amarpalli
(*d*) Malika

325. Grape is rich source of
(*a*) Citric acid (*b*) Malic acid
(*c*) formic acid (*d*) Tartaric acid

326. Food adulteration committee was set up in the year
(*a*) 1944 (*b*) 1945
(*c*) 1943 (*d*) 1946

327. Codex Alimetariuos commission was set up in the year
(*a*) 1962 (*b*) 1663
(*c*) 1985 (*d*) 1972

328. Establishment of International Organization for Standards was done in the year
(*a*) 1454 (*b*) 1955
(*c*) 1944 (*d*) 1947

329. Agricultural produce (grading and marketing Act) was started in the year
(*a*) 1935 (*b*) 1937
(*c*) 1947 (*d*) 1955

330. Food product order (FPO) was started in the year
(*a*) 1955 (*b*) 1937
(*c*) 1947 (*d*) 1962

331. Export (quality control and inspection) act was established in the year
(*a*) 1952 (*b*) 1956
(*c*) 1945 (*d*) 1963

332. Solvent extraction oil deoiled meal and edible flour (control) order started in the year
(*a*) 1955 (*b*) 1963
(*c*) 1967 (*d*) 1956

333. Meat product order was set up in the year
(*a*) 1973 (*b*) 1975
(*c*) 1955 (*d*) 1980

334. Quality of Agricultural commodity divided into ___________ categories.
(*a*) One (*b*) Two
(*c*) Three (*d*) Four

335. The Central Food Advisory Board was established in the year
(*a*) 1955 (*b*) 1937
(*c*) 1956 (*d*) 1938

336. Which chemical is used for controlling sprouting of onion during storage?
(*a*) Malic hydrazide (*b*) Ethylene
(*c*) GA_3 (*d*) All of these

337. For low sugar content, potato should be stored at
(*a*) 5ºC (*b*) 10ºC
(*c*) 15ºC (*d*) 20ºC

338. For long term storage potato should be stored at
(*a*) 0-5ºC (*b*) 5-10ºC
(*c*) 10-15ºC (*d*) 15-20ºC

339. Ratio of sugar to acid determine the
(*a*) pH of fruit (*b*) sweetness
(*c*) tartness and flavour of fruit (*d*) all of these

340. Which compound is highly sensitive to pH for changing the colour?
(*a*) Betaloins (*b*) Carotenoid
(*c*) Anthocyanin (*d*) Tannins

341. Ascorbic acid (vitamin C) reduces which activities in fruits?
(*a*) Oxidation (*b*) Dehydration
(*c*) Respiration (*d*) Decay of fruit by microorganisms

342. The level of vitamin C (%) in apple syrup or peach syrup mixture for acting as antioxidant is
(*a*) 0.05-0.20 (*b*) 0.20-0.50
(*c*) 0.50-1.00 (*d*) 1.00-1.20

343. A fine grind coffee may have a bulk density of
(*a*) 0.29-0.37 (*b*) 0.39-0.47
(*c*) 0.19-0.27 (*d*) 0.49-0.57

344. Instant coffee typically has a moisture content of
(*a*) 1-2 % (*b*) 2-4 %
(*c*) 4-6 % (*d*) 6-8 %

345. When roasted whole coffee beans are placed within a closed packaged which gas is released.
(*a*) CO_2 (*b*) O_2
(*c*) NH_3 (*d*) None

346. After picking black tea leaves are placed on trays to wither or dry for about
(*a*) 8 hrs (*b*) 10 hrs
(*c*) 18 hrs (*d*) 25 hrs

347. Initial moisture content of black tea is
(*a*) 1-3% (*b*) 3-4%
(*c*) 4-6% (*d*) 7-10%

348. The can must be able to withstand continual internal pressure of upto
(*a*) 1 atm (*b*) 3 atm
(*c*) 5 atm (*d*) 7 atm

349. Malted barley is crushed and mashed by mixing with water upto the temperature of
(*a*) 65°C (*b*) 67°C
(*c*) 68.5°C (*d*) 69.7°C

350. The desserts and appetizer wine contains alcohol about
(*a*) 10-15% (*b*) 15-21%
(*c*) 20-24% (*d*) 5-11%

351. Rate of oxygen uptake by wine may be
(*a*) 0.17 ppm day $^{-1}$ (*b*) 0.18 ppm day $^{-1}$
(*c*) 0.10 ppm day $^{-1}$ (*d*) 0.38 ppm day $^{-1}$

352. Owing to the natural limit of sugar present in grape wine, the alcohol content of such wine is normally about
(*a*) 8 % (*b*) 12%
(*c*) 13.5% (*d*) 18.6 %

353. The initial concentration of SO_2 in wine is
(*a*) 100 ppm (*b*) 200 ppm
(*c*) 350 ppm (*d*) 600 ppm

354. The amount of sodium chloride added upto saturation of cauliflower for making of sauerkraut may vary from
(*a*) 1.0-1.5 % (*b*) 1.5-2.0 %
(*c*) 2.0-2.5 % (*d*) 2.25-2.50 %

355. The lower concentration of salt in sauerkraut permit an
(*a*) Acid fermentation (*b*) Alcoholic fermentation
(*c*) Both (*d*) None

356. The percent of salt increases, the rate of acid production becomes
(*a*) Lower (*b*) Higher
(*c*) Remain same (*d*) None

357. Irradiation can be delay of sprouting for
(*a*) Potato (*b*) Onion
(*c*) Garlic (*d*) All

358. During of preparation of fruits for freezing, undesirable changes may take place such as
(*a*) Darkening
(*b*) Deterioration in flavour
(*c*) Spoilage by molds
(*d*) All of the above

359. The lactic acid fermentation of sugar in apples mostly by heterofermentative lactic acid bacteria such as
(*a*) Lactobacillus pastorianus
(*b*) L. brevis
(*c*) Leuconostoc mesenteroides
(*d*) All

360. The fermentation of organic acid of fruit juices by LAB e.g.
(*a*) Lactobacillus pastorianus
(*b*) L. brevis
(*c*) Leuconostoc mesenteroides
(*d*) All

361. Heat processing kills the bacteria but freezing
(*a*) prevent the growth of bacteria
(*b*) freeze the DNA of bacteria
(*c*) increase the multiplication of bacteria
(*d*) destroy the bacteria

362. Concentration of CO_2 and O_2 for apple in CA storage should be maintained at
(*a*) 1.5 -10 %, 2.5 %
(*b*) 2.5 %, 2.5 %
(*c*) 5-10 %, 3 %
(*d*) 5.0 %, 0%

363. One of the following is predominant mold organisms in frozen fruits is
(*a*) Aspergillus and Penicillium
(*b*) Mucor aad Rhizopus
(*c*) Botrytis, Fusarium and Alternaria
(*d*) All of the above

364. Yeasts are mostly likely to grow in food during
(*a*) Fast thawing
(*b*) Slow thawing
(*c*) Fast freezing
(*d*) Slow drying

365. The number of microorganisms in frozen fruits juices depend on the
(*a*) Condition of fruits and washing process
(*b*) Method of juice filtration
(*c*) Opportunity of contamination and growth
(*d*) All of the above

366. The deterioration of raw vegetable and fruits may results from
(*a*) Physical factor
(*b*) Enzyme activity
(*c*) Microbial action
(*d*) All of the above

367. Low moisture content syrup containing a small quantity of invert syrup has been rapidly cooled so that the sugar crystals are small in size is also called
(*a*) Cane sugar
(*b*) Fondants
(*c*) Syrup
(*d*) Sherbet

368. A mixture of dextrose and levulose made by inverting sucrose with acid or enzymes is called
(*a*) Reducing sugar
(*b*) Non-reducing sugar
(*c*) Invert sugar
(*d*) All of them

369. The process of blending together fat and fat solution of ingredients to produce a stable mixture which will not separate on standing is called
(*a*) Fermentation (*b*) Emulsification
(*c*) Fortification (*d*) Condensation

370. The chemical changes of an organic compound due to the action of living organisms (yeast or bacteria) usually producing a leavening gas is called
(*a*) Dough (*b*) Fortification
(*c*) Fermentation (*d*) Stabilization

371. A combination of fruit juice and sugar, stiffened by the action of the pectin of the fruit, as a result of heating is called
(*a*) Jam (*b*) Marmalade
(*c*) Cordial (*d*) Jelly

372. Food industry as a separate department of Government of India was established in the year
(*a*) 1960 (*b*) 1965
(*c*) 1980 (*d*) 1995

373. Titrable acidity (TA) can be determined by titrating a known volume of fruit juice with
(*a*) 0.1N NaOH (*b*) 0.01N NaOH
(*c*) 1N NaOH (*d*) 10N NaOH

ANSWER KEY

(FRUITS AND VEGETABLE PROCESSING)

1.D	2. C	3.D	4.B	5.A	6.B	7.D	8.D	9.A	10.A
11.A	12.B	13.C	14.D	15.A	16.D	17.C	18.A	19.D	20.A
21.B	22.B	23.D	24.B	25.A	26.A	27.B	28.A	29.B	30.D
31.B	32.A	33.D	34.A	35.C	36.C	37.B	38.B	39.B	40.B
41.A	42.B	43.B	44.A	45.A	46.C	47.C	48.A	49.A	50.B
51.C	52.A	53.A	54.D	55.D	56.A	57.B	58.D	59.C	60.D
61.A	62.B	63.C	64.D	65.A	66.B	67.C	68.D	69.A	70.B
71.C	72.D	73.A	74.C	75.D	76.B	77.C	78.D	79.B	80.C
81.D	82.A	83.B	84.C	85.D	86.A	87.B	88.C	89.B	90.B
91.C	92.D	93.A	94.A	95.B	96.A	97.B	98.A	99.D	100.B
101.A	102.A	103.C	104.A	105.C	106.A	107.B	108.A	109.A	110.A
111.D	112.B	113.D	114.D	115.A	116. C	117.C	118.A	119.C	120.B
121.B	122.B	123.C	124.B	125.B	126.A	127.D	128.B	129.B	130.A
131.B	132.A	133.A	134.A	135.A	136.A	137.C	138.B	139.A	140.B
141.A	142.B	143.B	144.C	145.A	146.B	147.C	148.A	149.B	150.B

151.D	152.B	153.B	154.B	155.D	156.D	157.C	158.C	159.D	160.A
161.A	162.B	163.C	164.D	165.A	166.B	167.A	168.C	169.C	170.A
171C	172.B	173.C	174.A	175.B	176.A	177.B	178.A	179.A	180.B
181.C	182.D	183.C	184.B	185.B	186.D	187.A	188.D	189.D	190.A
191.A	192.A	193.A	194.B	195.C	196.C	197.B	198.B	199.D	200.A
201.A	202.C	203.C	204.C	205.C	206.C	207.A	208.B	209.B	210.A
211.D	212.C	213.B	214.C	215.B	216.D	217.C	218.C	219.C	220.C
221.C	222.A	223.A	224.C	225.A	226.B	227.D	228.A	229.B	230.B
231.B	232.D	233.A	234.C	235.C	236.A	237.A	238.A	239.A	240.A
241.B	242.B	243.C	244.A	245.C	246.B	247.D	248.D	249.B	250.D
251.D	252.C	253.B	254.A	255.C	256.B	257.B	258.A	259.C	260.A
261.B	262.D	263.B	264.A	265.C	266.D	267.A	268.B	269.A	270.A
271.D	272.A	273.A	274.D	275.A	276.C	277.C	278.A	279.C	280.B
281.A	282.C	283.C	284.D	285.C	286.B	287.B	288.D	289.D	290.A
291.B	292.D	293.B	294.A	295.B	296.A	297.B	298.A	299.A	300.C
301.C	302.C	303.B	304.A	305.A	306.A	307.A	308.A	309.A	310.A
311.A	312.A	313.A	314.B	315.D	316.C	317.A	318.A	319.D	320.C
321.C	322.C	323.D	324.B	325.D	326.C	327.A	328.D	329.B	330.A
331.D	332.C	333.A	334.B	335.B	336.A	337.B	338.C	339.C	340.C
341.A	342.A	343.B	344.B	345.A	346.C	347.B	348.C	349.B	350.B
351.A	352.B	353.A	354.D	355.A	356.A	357.D	358.D	359.D	360.A
361.A	362.A	363.D	364.B	365.D	366.D	367.B	368.C	369.B	370.C
371.D	372.D	373.A							

Chapter 7

Dairy Product Processing

1. HTST milk pasteurization destroys
   (*a*) all bacteria
   (*b*) all disease producing pathogens
   (*c*) only selected disease producing bacteria
   (*d*) no bacteria

2. Milk sugar is
   (*a*) Lactose
   (*b*) Glucose
   (*c*) Sucrose
   (*d*) Maltose

3. The yellow colour of cow milk is due to the presence of
   (*a*) Vitamin B
   (*b*) Carotene
   (*c*) Anthocyanin
   (*d*) None of these

4. Cow milk's protein is
   (*a*) Albumin
   (*b*) Zein
   (*c*) Casein
   (*d*) Lactoalbumin

5. Temperature of LTLT pasteurization is
   (*a*) 42-49 ºC
   (*b*) 51-65 ºC
   (*c*) 62-65 ºC
   (*d*) 61-63 ºC

6. Element defecient in milk is
   (*a*) Fe
   (*b*) Mg
   (*c*) P
   (*d*) Ca

7. National Dairy Research Institute is located at
   (*a*) Delhi
   (*b*) Izzatnagar
   (*c*) Jhansi
   (*d*) Karnal

8. Casein is ______________ % of total milk protein
   (*a*) 80-83
   (*b*) 70-71
   (*c*) 60-65
   (*d*) 42-45

9. Pasteurization kills
   (*a*) Bacteria +virus
   (*b*) Bacteria spores alive
   (*c*) Bacteria along spores
   (*d*) None of these

10. Most successful example of cooperative in milk processing is
   (*a*) Raksha
   (*b*) Proagro
   (*c*) Syngenta
   (*d*) Anand

11. Operation flood is related to
   (*a*) Milk
   (*b*) Rice
   (*c*) Potato
   (*d*) None of these

12. White revolution is related to
   (*a*) Cotton
   (*b*) Milk
   (*c*) Sheep
   (*d*) Rice

13. The most suitable temperature for separation of cream by centrifugal cream separator is
   (*a*) 40 °C
   (*b*) 30 °C
   (*c*) 20 °C
   (*d*) 10 °C

14. The moisture content of paneer is not less than
   (*a*) 65 %
   (*b*) 70 %
   (*c*) 60 %
   (*d*) 50 %

15. Better quality Khoa is prepared from
   (*a*) Sheep milk
   (*b*) Cow milk
   (*c*) Buffalo milk
   (*d*) None of these

16. Specific gravity of milk is
   (*a*) 1.03
   (*b*) 1.05
   (*c*) 0.85
   (*d*) 0.93

17. The fat content of double toned milk is
   (*a*) 1.5 %
   (*b*) 2.0 %
   (*c*) 2.5 %
   (*d*) 3.0 %

18. Better quality chhana is prepared from
   (*a*) Camel milk
   (*b*) Cow milk
   (*c*) Sheep milk
   (*d*) Buffalo milk

19. Paneer is a
   (*a*) Concentrated milk product
   (*b*) Dried milk product
   (*c*) Coagulated milk product
   (*d*) Fermented product

20. Ash content of human milk is
(*a*) 0.8 % (*b*) 0.7 %
(*c*) 0.5 % (*d*) 0.2 %

21. Lactic acid content in fresh milk is
(*a*) 0.10 % (*b*) 0.20 %
(*c*) 0.30 % (*d*) 0.40 %

22. Flavouring component for butter is
(*a*) Acetyl methyl carbinol (*b*) Diacetyl
(*c*) Lactic acid (*d*) Protein

23. UHT milk is heated to a temperature of
(*a*) 100 °C (*b*) 130 °C
(*c*) 145 °C (*d*) 165 °C

24. Enzyme coagulated milk product is
(*a*) Dahi (*b*) Paneer
(*c*) Chhana (*d*) Cheese

25. Curd tension of dahi
(*a*) is lower than milk (*b*) remains constant
(*c*) is higher than milk (*d*) None of these

26. The time temperature combination in plate pasteurization is
(*a*) 60 °C for 30 minutes (*b*) 72 °C for 15 seconds
(*c*) 72 °C for 15 minutes (*d*) 121 °C for 15 seconds

27. Protein in milk exits in the form of
(*a*) Solution (*b*) Emulsion
(*c*) Colloidal (*d*) None of these

28. The fat content of plain ice cream is
(*a*) 6 % (*b*) 8 %
(*c*) 12 % (*d*) 10 %

29. Lactose in milk exist in the form of
(*a*) Solution (*b*) Emulsion
(*c*) Colloidal (*d*) Nine of these

30. Fat in separated milk is not more than
(*a*) 0.1 % (*b*) 0.5 %
(*c*) 1.0% (*d*) 1.5 %

31. Khoa contains milk fat not less than
(*a*) 10 % (*b*) 20 %
(*c*) 30 % (*d*) 40 %

32. The SNF content of toned milk is
(*a*) 6.0 % (*b*) 7.0 %
(*c*) 8.5 % (*d*) 9.0 %

33. Methylene blue reduction test is conducted to know the efficiency of
(*a*) Sterilized milk (*b*) Toned milk
(*c*) Double toned milk (*d*) Pasteurized milk

34. The optimum temperature for making dahi is
(*a*) 22 °C (*b*) 18 °C
(*c*) 15 °C (*d*) 10 °C

35. Gerber method is used for testing the following
(*a*) Lactose (*b*) Fat
(*c*) Vitamins (*d*) Protein

36. A good quality dahi should have acidity less than
(*a*) 0.3 % (*b*) 0.5 %
(*c*) 0.8 % (*d*) 1.0%

37. Buffalo milk is rich source of following minerals
(*a*) Calcium and iron (*b*) Iron and copper
(*c*) Copper and phosphorus (*d*) Calcium and phosphorus

38. Buffer value of milk is due to
(*a*) Protein (*b*) Lipid
(*c*) Fat (*d*) Carbohydrate

39. Polenske value of milk fat is due to
(*a*) Fats (*b*) Water insoluble fatty acids
(*c*) Protein nitrogen (*d*) Water soluble fatty acids

40. Lactose is a disaccharide made of
(*a*) Glucose and fructose (*b*) Maltose and fructose
(*c*) Glucose and galactose (*d*) Maltose and glucose

41. Average pH of normal milk is
(*a*) 3.6 (*b*) 4.6
(*c*) 5.6 (*d*) 6.6

42. Most variable of all constituents present in milk is
(*a*) Fat
(*b*) Protein
(*c*) Minerals
(*d*) Carbohydrate

43. Which vitamin remains most resistant on heat treatment of milk
(*a*) Vitamin C
(*b*) Vitamin A
(*c*) Vitamin B_1
(*d*) Vitamin B_{12}

44. The normal size of fat globules in raw milk is
(*a*) 0.5-1.0 µm
(*b*) 1.0-1.5 µm
(*c*) 2.0-6.0 µm
(*d*) 6.0-8.0 µm

45. The pasteurization process was developed by
(*a*) Louis Pasteur
(*b*) Alexander Fleming
(*c*) Newton
(*d*) Robert Hook

46. Good milk dryer expose the milk to ______________ temperature for a very ________ time.
(*a*) High, high
(*b*) High, short
(*c*) Low, short
(*d*) None of these

47. The separation of milk powder from air may be accomplished by
(*a*) Cyclone separator
(*b*) Indented cylinder
(*c*) Compartment separator
(*d*) None of these

48. The cheese and curd of milk is used for ______________ the curd to proper size.
(*a*) recusing
(*b*) increasing
(*c*) freezing
(*d*) none of these

49. Butter is an emulsion of
(*a*) Water in oil
(*b*) Oil in oil
(*c*) Water in water
(*d*) Oil in water

50. The lactometer will sink __________ in milk without cream when compared to whole milk.
(*a*) more
(*b*) less
(*c*) no change
(*d*) none of these

51. According to PFA, table butter should not contain fat less than
(*a*) 50 %
(*b*) 60 %
(*c*) 70 %
(*d*) 80 %

52. Table butter contains minimum _________ % fat and maximum ________ % moisture.
(*a*) 80, 16
(*b*) 70, 10
(*c*) 60, 15
(*d*) 50, 20

53. Milk – milk serum =
(*a*) Skim milk
(*b*) Milk fat
(*c*) Coagulation
(*d*) Casein

54. Casein is present in milk as which of the following form
(*a*) Emulsion
(*b*) Colloidal suspension
(*c*) True solvent
(*d*) Homogenized

55. Fat is present in milk as which of the following form
(*a*) Emulsion
(*b*) Colloidal suspension
(*c*) True solvent
(*d*) Homogenized

56. Which of the following is the protein of milk?
(*a*) 3.1
(*b*) 3.2
(*c*) 3.3
(*d*) 3.4

57. Which of the following is known as spoon eating milk?
(*a*) Recombined milk
(*b*) Tattoo milk
(*c*) Standard milk
(*d*) Toned milk

58. Milk viscosity is due to which constituent of milk
(*a*) Albumin
(*b*) Globulin
(*c*) Casein
(*d*) Phospholipids

59. Which of the following is milk protein?
(*a*) α- casein
(*b*) β-casein
(*c*) γ-casein
(*d*) All of these

60. Which of the following have maximum casein in its milk?
(*a*) Buffalo
(*b*) Cow
(*c*) Human
(*d*) None

61. Fishy odour of milk is due to
(*a*) γ- casein
(*b*) kephalin
(*c*) α- casein
(*d*) β-casein

62. Which of the following milk does not have 8.5 % SNF?
(*a*) Toned
(*b*) Double toned
(*c*) Combined
(*d*) Standardized

63. Standard fat percentage in toned and double toned milks are
(*a*) 3.5 and 1.5
(*b*) 1.5 and 3.0
(*c*) 3.0 and 1.5
(*d*) 1.5 and 3.5

64. Milk boils _______ than water.
(*a*) Slowly (*b*) Equally
(*c*) Quickly (*d*) Not compared

65. Effect of addition of water in milk on the specific gravity is that specific gravity
(*a*) increases (*b*) decreases
(*c*) irregular (*d*) no effect

66. Effect of addition of fat in milk on specific gravity
(*a*) increase (*b*) decrease
(*c*) irregular (*d*) no effect

67. Phosphatase test for standardized milk
(*a*) Positive (*b*) Negative
(*c*) Neutral (*d*) Depend upon temperature

68. Maximum pesticide tolerance (mg/kg of milk fat) is for
(*a*) Lindane (*b*) Chlorane
(*c*) DDT (*d*) Finitrothin

69. Minimum pesticide tolerance (mg/kg of milk fat) is for
(*a*) Chlorane (*b*) Finitrothin
(*c*) Both (*a*) and (*b*) (*d*) None of these

70. Ratio of milk powder and water in recombined milk is
(*a*) 1:3 (*b*) 1:2
(*c*) 1:5 (*d*) 1:7

71. Soft curd milk is low in water of the following
(*a*) Calcium (*b*) Casein
(*c*) Both (*a*) and (*b*) (*d*) None of these

72. In pasteurization and sterilization which vitamin get lost
(*a*) A and D (*b*) B_1 and C
(*c*) B_2 and B_{12} (*d*) E and K

73. Yellow colour of cow milk is due to the presence of
(*a*) Fat (*b*) Casein
(*c*) Lactochrome (*d*) Carotene

74. Greenish colour of skim milk is due to
(*a*) Lacto-chrome (*b*) Fat
(*c*) Carotene (*d*) Casein

75. Surface tension of milk (dyne/cm) is which of the following
(*a*) 60 (*b*) 55
(*c*) 50 (*d*) 45

76. Milk acidity is
(*a*) 0.10 % (*b*) 0.11 %
(*c*) 0.12 % (*d*) 0.13 %

77. Albumin and globulin occur in milk in the state of
(*a*) Colloidal suspension (*b*) Colloidal solution
(*c*) True solution (*d*) None of these

78. Flavour is composed of
(*a*) Smell (*b*) Odour
(*c*) Smell and taste (*d*) None of these

79. The curd tension of human milk is
(*a*) 3.0 (*b*) 0.0
(*c*) 55.0 (*d*) 14.5

80. Which one of the following is not an essential fatty acid?
(*a*) Oleic acid (*b*) Linoleic acid
(*c*) Linolenic acid (*d*) Arachidonic acid

81. Milk is a rich source of
(*a*) Iron (*b*) Iodine
(*c*) Calcium (*d*) Copper

82. Which of the following is yellowish in colour?
(*a*) Buffalo milk (*b*) Goat milk
(*c*) Human milk (*d*) None of these

83. Which one of the following is not a major constituent of milk?
(*a*) Ash (*b*) Fat
(*c*) Lactose (*d*) Vitamins

84. Which one of the following is not a minor constituent of milk?
(*a*) Enzyme (*b*) Vitamins
(*c*) Ash (*d*) Phospholipids

85. Which one of the following has the smallest size of fat globules?
(*a*) Cow milk (*b*) Buffalo milk
(*c*) Goat milk (*d*) None of these

86. Which one of the following does not furnish any energy to the body?
(*a*) Fat (*b*) Carbohydrate
(*c*) Vitamins (*d*) Proteins

87. Which one of the following is not a protein?
(*a*) Casein (*b*) Globulin
(*c*) Glycine (*d*) Albumin

88. Acidity of milk is expressed as
(*a*) Oleic acid (*b*) Lactic acid
(*c*) Butyric acid (*d*) Citric acid

89. Which one of the following is the heaviest constituent of milk?
(*a*) Proteins (*b*) Lactose
(*c*) Casein (*d*) Mineral salts

90. The pH of normal fresh milk is
(*a*) 6.6 (*b*) 6.8
(*c*) 7.0 (*d*) None of these

91. Oxytocin remains effective for
(*a*) 10 to 15 min (*b*) 5 to 7 min
(*c*) 20 to 30 min (*d*) None of these

92. Which of the following contains the higher number of bacteria?
(*a*) Fore milk (*b*) Middle milk
(*c*) Stripping (*d*) None of these

93. Which of the following contains highest percentage of fat?
(*a*) Fore milk (*b*) Middle milk
(*c*) Stripping (*d*) None of these

94. The cholesterol content of a single egg-yolk is
(*a*) 112 mg (*b*) 224 mg
(*c*) 300 mg (*d*) 448 mg

95. Which of the following contribute to the hardness of milk?
(*a*) Short chain saturated fatty acids (*b*) Unsaturated fatty acid
(*c*) Long chain saturated fatty acids (*d*) None of these

96. Which one of the following contains cobalt?
(*a*) Vitamin B_1 (*b*) Riboflavin
(*c*) Folic acid (*d*) Vitamin B_{12}

97. Which one of the following is stored in the body?
(a) Vitamin B_1 (b) Vitamin B_6
(c) Vitamin B_{12}. (d) Vitamin C

98. Which one of the following contains the highest percentage of lactose?
(a) Cow milk (b) Buffalo milk
(c) Goat milk (d) Human milk

99. One litre cow milk provides calcium
(a) 1 gm (b) 2 gm
(c) 3 gm (d) None of these

100. Maximum clumping of fat globules takes place at
(a) 7 °C (b) 11 °C
(c) 4 °C (d) 21 °C

101. Triglycerides of milk fat occur in
(a) Fat globules (b) Milk serum
(c) Fat globules membrane (d) None of these

102. Which one of the following is an unsaponificable constituent of milk fat?
(a) Triglyceride (b) Phospholipids
(c) Cholesterol (d) None of these

103. Cholesterol content in buffalo ghee is
(a) 330 mg % (b) 275 mg %
(c) 400 mg % (d) None of these

104. Melting point of cholesterol is
(a) 150 °C (b) 114 °C
(c) 117 °C (d) None of these

105. Vitamin A content in buffalo ghee on an average is
(a) 9.5 μg/g (b) 15.0 μg/g
(c) 7.00 μg/g (d) None of these

106. Which one of the following is responsible for the characteristic pleasing flavour of ghee?
(a) Lactic acid (b) Butyric acid
(c) Lactones (d) None of these

107. The number of essential amino acids is
(a) 6 (b) 8
(c) 10 (d) 12

108. Which one of the following is not a sulphur containing amino acid?
(*a*) Methionine (*b*) Cystine
(*c*) Lysine (*d*) None of these

109. Which one of the following contains the lowest percentage of ash?
(*a*) Cow milk (*b*) Buffalo milk
(*c*) Goat milk (*d*) Human milk

110. Which one of the following is known as vitamin M?
(*a*) Biotin (*b*) Choline
(*c*) Folic acid (*d*) None of these

111. The disease 'Pellagra' in man is caused due to the deficiency of
(*a*) Vitamin B_1 (*b*) Vitamin B_2
(*c*) Ascorbic acid (*d*) None of these

112. 'Fatty liver' is caused due to the deficiency of
(*a*) Cobalamin (*b*) Pantothenic acid
(*c*) Choline (*d*) None of these

113. Adequate heating of milk is indicated by
(*a*) Phosphatase test (*b*) Baudoin test
(*c*) Hansa test (*d*) None of these

114. Which of the following organisms produces red colour in milk?
(*a*) *B. cyanogenes* (*b*) *B. synxanthus*
(*c*) *Serratia marcescens* (*d*) None of these

115. Acidity of ghee is expressed as
(*a*) % lactic acid (*b*) % butyric acid
(*c*) % oleic acid (*d*) None of these

116. The optimum size of container for packaging ghee is
(*a*) 16 kg (*b*) 5 to 10 kg
(*c*) Not more than 4 kg (*d*) None of these

117. The optimum temperature for storing ghee is
(*a*) 5 °C (*b*) 7 °C
(*c*) 21 °C (*d*) None of these

118. The most sensitive method for detecting added water in milk is the determination of
(*a*) Specific gravity (*b*) Refractive index
(*c*) Freezing point (*d*) None of these

119. One I.U. of vitamin A is equal to
(*a*) 0.3 μg of vitamin A acetate
(*b*) 0.6 μg of vitamin A acetate
(*c*) 0.9 μg of vitamin A acetate
(*d*) None of these

120. The Vieth ratio between lactose, total protein and ash contents of milk is
(*a*) 9 : 13 : 2
(*b*) 13 : 9 : 2
(*c*) 13 : 2 : 9
(*d*) 9 : 13 : 2

121. Addition of cane sugar to milk can be detected by
(*a*) Hansa test
(*b*) Cotton's test
(*c*) Holde's test
(*d*) None of these

122. The following amount of formalin is sufficient as milk preservative
(*a*) 1 drop/100 ml of milk
(*b*) 2 drop/100 ml of milk
(*c*) 4 drop/100 ml of milk
(*d*) None of these

123. The density of water is maximum at
(*a*) 15.5 ºC
(*b*) 20 ºC
(*c*) 4 ºC
(*d*) None of these

124. The amount of cream taken for fat test by Gerber's method is
(*a*) 11 gram
(*b*) 10 gram
(*c*) 5 gram
(*d*) None of these

125. The specific gravity of Gerber's sulphuric acid is
(*a*) 1.091
(*b*) 1.082
(*c*) 1.815
(*d*) None of these

126. If cream is removed from milk sample and water is added thereafter the specific gravity of the sample will
(*a*) increase
(*b*) decrease
(*c*) will become normal
(*d*) none of these

127. Boiling point of buffalo milk is
(*a*) 100 ºC
(*b*) 117 ºC
(*c*) 100.17 ºC
(*d*) 100.55 ºC

128. In India, "milk' means:
(*a*) Cow milk
(*b*) Buffalo milk
(*c*) Cow milk or buffalo milk or a mixture thereof
(*d*) None of these

129. Mixed milk means a mixture of :
(*a*) Cow milk, buffalo milk and goat milk
(*b*) Milk of all the species
(*c*) Cow and buffalo milk
(*d*) None of these

130. There is no formation of cream when the following is allowed to stand overnight?
(*a*) Cow milk (*b*) Buffalo milk
(*c*) Goat milk (*d*) None of these

131. Cow or buffalo body fat is called
(*a*) Lord (*b*) Pork
(*c*) Tallow (*d*) None of these

132. Pig body fat is called
(*a*) Lord (*b*) Pork
(*c*) Tallow (*d*) None of these

133. Presence of sesame oil in genuine ghee can be detected by
(*a*) Nickel test (*b*) Valenta test
(*c*) Holde's test (*d*) Baudoin's test

134. Presence of cotton seed oil in genuine ghee or the genuine ghee from cotton tract areas may be detected by
(*a*) B.N. Ghosh's test (*b*) Boudoin's test
(*c*) Halphen's test (*d*) None of these

135. Addition of any vegetable oil or vegetable fat to genuine ghee can be detected by
(*a*) Nickel test (*b*) Boudoin's test
(*c*) Bomer's phytosterol test (*d*) None of these

136. Which of the following test can be used to detect the adulteration of genuine ghee with Dalda (vanaspati ghee)
(*a*) Bomer's phytosterol test (*b*) Nickel test
(*c*) Holde's test (*d*) Nitric acid test

137. The B.R. Reading of animal body fats range from,
(*a*) 40 to 50 (*b*) 50 to 60
(*c*) 44 to 51 (*d*) None of these

138. R.M. value of a ghee sample indicates:
(*a*) Saturation of fatty acid (*b*) Unsaturation of fatty acid
(*c*) Steam-volatile water-soluble fatty acids (*d*) None of these

139. Iodine value of ghee sample is the indication of
(*a*) Saturation of fatty acid (*b*) Unsaturation of fatty acid
(*c*) Average molecular weight of the fatty acids (*d*) None of these

140. Saponification value indicates
(*a*) Average molecular weight of the fatty acids (*b*) Saturation of fatty acid
(*c*) Steam-volatile water-insoluble fatty acids (*d*) None of these

141. Which of the following in not found in the adulterant fats?
(*a*) Oleic acid
(*b*) Linolenic acid
(*c*) Butyric acid
(*d*) None of these

142. Which of the following is not found in the milk fat?
(*a*) Butyric acid
(*b*) Caproic acid
(*c*) Oleic acid
(*d*) Cyclopropenoic acid

143. Cyclopropenoic acid is found in
(*a*) Milk fat
(*b*) Animal body fat
(*c*) Cotton seed oil
(*d*) None of these

144. Which of the following can reduce methylene blue to colourless?
(*a*) Animal body fat
(*b*) Cotton seed oil
(*c*) Milk fat
(*d*) None of these

145. Which one of the following is a volumetric method for determining % fat in milk?
(*a*) Gerber's method
(*b*) Werner-Schmidt method
(*c*) Adam's paper-coil method
(*d*) Roese-Gottlieb method

146. Which one of the following is a gravimetric method for determining fat in milk?
(*a*) Gerber's method
(*b*) Babcock method
(*c*) Roese-Gottlieb method
(*d*) None of these

147. Which of the following test can not be used for detection of adulteration of genuine ghee with animal body fat?
(*a*) Valenta test
(*b*) Carbolic test
(*c*) Opacity test
(*d*) Holde's test

148. Which one of the following milk preservative is not an official preservative?
(*a*) Formalin
(*b*) Potassium permanganate
(*c*) Hydrofluoric acid
(*d*) β-naphthol

149. Which one of the following milk preservative is an official preservative?
(*a*) Salicylic acid
(*b*) β-naphthol
(*c*) Mercuric chloride
(*d*) Hydrogen peroxide

150. Addition of formalin to milk interferes with the following test:
(*a*) Fat test
(*b*) % total solids
(*c*) % Ash
(*d*) None of these

151. The specific gravity of amyl alcohol used in the fat test by Gerber's method is
(*a*) 1.081
(*b*) 1.810
(*c*) 0.810
(*d*) 0.081

152. Ashing of milk in muffle furnace is done at:
(*a*) 200°C ± 10°C for 4-5 hrs
(*b*) 300°C ± 10°C for 4-5 hrs
(*c*) 550°C ± 10°C for 4-5 hrs
(*d*) 400°C ± 10°C for 4-5 hrs

153. Which one of the following milk preservative is most suitable for fat test in milk?
(*a*) Formalin
(*b*) Potassium di-chromate
(*c*) Hydrogen peroxide
(*d*) None of these

154. The most accurate method of determining the specific gravity of milk is by:
(*a*) Lactometer
(*b*) R.D. Bottle
(*c*) Westphal balance
(*d*) None of these

155. "Zero point" is:
(*a*) Freezing point of milk
(*b*) Freezing point of water
(*c*) Freezing point of ice cream
(*d*) None of these

156. Lactostar (automatic milk analyzer) analyses fat, solid non fat, lactose, protein percentage and freezing point of milk within:
(*a*) 2 minutes
(*b*) 4 minutes
(*c*) 6 minutes
(*d*) None of these

157. The Butyro-Refractometer reading of milk fat ranges from:
(*a*) 45 to 50
(*b*) 40 to 45
(*c*) 50 to 60
(*d*) None of these

158. The Butyro-Refractometer reading of vegetable fat and oils ranges from:
(*a*) Above 50
(*b*) Above 60
(*c*) Above 70
(*d*) None of these

159. Which one of the following does not increase the Butyro-Refractometer reading when added to milk fat?
(*a*) Sesame oil
(*b*) Ground nut oil
(*c*) Coconut oil
(*d*) None of these

160. Dry ice is:
(*a*) Frozen water
(*b*) Frozen milk
(*c*) Frozen carbon dioxide
(*d*) None of these

161. Fishiness flavour in cream and butter is developed due to
(*a*) Aeromonas hydrophila
(*b*) P. fragi
(*c*) P. mephitica
(*d*) Alternaria

162. Freezing point of milk (°C) is
(*a*) – 0.50
(*b*) – 0.54
(*c*) – 0.60
(*d*) – 0.65

163. Average specific gravity of milk is
(*a*) 1.030 (*b*) 1.035
(*c*) 1.040 (*d*) 1.045

164. Refractive index of milk at 20°C is
(*a*) 1.31 (*b*) 1.32
(*c*) 1.33 (*d*) 1.34

165. Boiling point of milk (°C) is
(*a*) 100.5 (*b*) 110.5
(*c*) 120.5 (*d*) 115.5

166. Which colour of milk is due to which of the following
(*a*) Carotene (*b*) Lactochrome
(*c*) Calcium sensitive a_s casein (*d*) Calcium insensitive k casein

167. Water soluble protein of milk is which of the following
(*a*) α-Lactoalbumin (*b*) β-Lactoglobulin
(*c*) α-Casein (*d*) β-Casein

168. Milk from which cream can not be separated
(*a*) Frozen milk (*b*) Soft curd milk
(*c*) Homogenized milk (*d*) Fermented milk

169. Bacterial count in machine milking in comparison to hand milking is
(*a*) Lower (*b*) Equal
(*c*) Higher (*d*) Zero

170. Melting point of milk fat (°C) is
(*a*) 25-35 (*b*) 30-36
(*c*) 36-40 (*d*) 40-45

171. Pressure required for machine milking (mm of Hg)
(*a*) 15-25 (*b*) 25-40
(*c*) 40-50 (*d*) 50-60

172. Pulsation rate of machine milking (cycle/min)
(*a*) 10-20 (*b*) 30-40
(*c*) 40-120 (*d*) 120-200

173. Maximum limit of SPC/ml for pasteurized milk is
(*a*) 10,000 (*b*) 20,000
(*c*) 30,000 (*d*) 40,000

174. Maximum limit of SPC/ml for market milk is
(*a*) 1,00,000
(*b*) 2,00,000
(*c*) 3,00,000
(*d*) 4,00,000

175. Lactogenic is also known as
(*a*) Chloretic
(*b*) Galactopaietic
(*c*) Cholacgagoue
(*d*) Mammogenic

176. Which of the following is/are emulsifiers of milk?
(*a*) Milk protein
(*b*) Phospholipids
(*c*) Both (*a*) and (*b*)
(*d*) None of these

177. Which of the following is volumetric method for determination of fat % of milk?
(*a*) Soxhlet method
(*b*) Wast fall balance
(*c*) Richmond sliding method
(*d*) Gerber method

178. Which of the following is method for determination of specific gravity of milk?
(*a*) Wast fall balance
(*b*) Soxhlet method
(*c*) Richmond sliding method
(*d*) Gerber method

179. Which of the following is gravimetric method for determination of fat % of milk?
(*a*) Wast fall balance
(*b*) Soxhlet method
(*c*) Richmond sliding method
(*d*) Gerber method

180. Which of the following is gravimetric method for determination of total solids % of milk?
(*a*) Wast fall balance
(*b*) Soxhlet method
(*c*) Richmond sliding method
(*d*) Gerber method

181. Richmond formula is
(*a*) $TS = 0.25\ L + 1.2$ Fat $+ 0.41$
(*b*) $TS = 0.25\ L + 0.14$ Fat $+ 1.20$
(*c*) $TS = 1.25\ L + 1.2$ Fat $+ 0.14$
(*d*) $TS = 0.25\ L + 1.2$ Fat $+ 0.14$

182. Curding of milk by admixture of acid in milk is known as
(*a*) Sour curding
(*b*) Sweet milk
(*c*) Acid curding
(*d*) Milk curding

183. Curding of milk by admixture of rennet in milk is known as
(*a*) Sour curding
(*b*) Sweet milk
(*c*) Acid curding
(*d*) Milk curding

184. Ordinary souring of milk is due to citrate produced by
(*a*) Butter
(*b*) Chhana
(*c*) Paneer
(*d*) Cheese

185. Instruments used for measurement of refractive index
(*a*) Babcock bottle
(*b*) Soxhlet apparatus
(*c*) Lactometer
(*d*) Zeiss refractometer

186. Flavouring agent of butter is which of one the following
(*a*) Diacetyl
(*b*) Volatile fatty acid
(*c*) Butter protein
(*d*) All of these

187. Specific heat of milk
(*a*) Higher than water
(*b*) Lower than water
(*c*) Equal to water
(*d*) Independent

188. Which fungi are used for ripening of butter from unpasteurized sweet cream at room temperature?
(*a*) Oidium
(*b*) Oospora
(*c*) Both (*a*) and (*b*)
(*d*) None of these

189. Instrument used for vacuum pasteurization
(*a*) Pasteurized bottle
(*b*) Vacuum creator
(*c*) Flasher
(*d*) Henristassanao bottle

190. Efficiency of pasteurizer is measured by which test
(*a*) Phosphatase test
(*b*) MBR test
(*c*) Reductase test
(*d*) Resazurine test

191. Bacteriological status of milk is judged by which of the following
(*a*) Alizarine test
(*b*) COB test
(*c*) Reductase test
(*d*) Catalase test

192. In starter of the butter and the cheese bacteriophase fed on which of the following
(*a*) Acetate bacteria
(*b*) Propionate bacteria
(*c*) Lactate bacteria
(*d*) Butyrate bacteria

193. Is tetanus toxin appear in milk?
(*a*) Never
(*b*) Some time
(*c*) Depend upon symptom
(*d*) Always

194. Organoleptic test (platform test) is which of the following
(*a*) Smell and appearance of milk
(*b*) Acidity and temperature of milk
(*c*) Sediment and lactometer reading
(*d*) All above

195. Preheating temperature (°C) of milk before pasteurization is
(*a*) 30-35
(*b*) 35-40
(*c*) 40-45
(*d*) 45-50

196. Temperature and time combination for LTLT pasteurization
(*a*) 63°C and 30 min (*b*) 63°C and 30 sec
(*c*) 72°C and 15 sec (*d*) 72°C and 15 min

197. Temperature and time combination for HTST pasteurization
(*a*) 63°C and 30 min (*b*) 63°C and 30 sec
(*c*) 72°C and 15 sec (*d*) 72°C and 15 min

198. Casual agent of which disease is used as index for pasteurization
(*a*) Rabies (*b*) Small pox
(*c*) TB (*d*) Cholera

199. Organism of TB destroyed at what temperature
(*a*) 138°F (*b*) 142°F
(*c*) 143°F (*d*) 144°F

200. Temperature of cream line reduction test
(*a*) 138°F (*b*) 142°F
(*c*) 143°F (*d*) 144°F

201. Which of the following is true?
(*a*) LTLT is batch process (*b*) LTLT is continuous process
(*c*) HTST is batch processes (*d*) None of these

202. Uperization temperature and time is (°C and seconds) (UHT pasteurization)
(*a*) 74 and 7 (*b*) 150 and 3/4
(*c*) 72 and 15 (*d*) 63 and 15

203. Test for accessing sweet/soft curding of milk
(*a*) Curd test (*b*) Hill curd test
(*c*) Tension test (*d*) Hill curd tension test

204. Test for mixing of the cow milk and buffalo milk
(*a*) Sediment test (*b*) Hansa test
(*c*) COB test (*d*) Alizarine test

205. Lecithin is a component of which of the following
(*a*) Milk protein (*b*) Milk vitamin
(*c*) Milk lipid (*d*) Milk pigment
(Average amount of lecithin present in the milk is about 0.075 %)

206. Flavoured milk contains _______________ fat %.
(*a*) Above 2 % (*b*) 5 %
(*c*) 1-2 % (*d*) 2-5 %

207. Temperature and time for frozen concentrated milk is
(*a*) 4°C and 12 hr (*b*) 0°C and 12 hr
(*c*) 4°C and 24 hr (*d*) 0°C and 24 hr

208. Milk gel oxidized if it is pored in container of following metal
(*a*) Bronze (*b*) Copper
(*c*) Nickel (*d*) Steel

209. Taint due to improper homogenization is
(*a*) Fishy (*b*) Oily
(*c*) Rusty (*d*) None of these

210. Skim milk contains approximately ________________ of water
(*a*) 70 % (*b*) 80 %
(*c*) 90 % (*d*) 50 %

211. Nature of fermentation by yeast in milk is
(*a*) Acidic (*b*) Alcoholic
(*c*) Alkaline (*d*) Neutral

212. Carotene in cow milk (μg/gm)
(*a*) 26 (*b*) 30
(*c*) 34 (*d*) 40

213. Cow milk is used for making which of the following
(*a*) Butter (*b*) Cheese
(*c*) Paneer (*d*) All of these

214. Sheep milk is used for making
(*a*) Butter (*b*) Cheese
(*c*) Paneer (*d*) Roquefort cheese

215. Best substitute of human milk is
(*a*) Goat milk (*b*) Cow milk
(*c*) Buffalo milk (*d*) Camel milk

216. Minimum fat % required for two stage homogenization is
(*a*) Less than 6% (*b*) Above 6 %
(*c*) Above 10 % (*d*) Above 20 %

217. Specific gravity of milk is reduced one hour after milking is known as
(*a*) Ham burg phenomenon (*b*) Rackangel phenomenon
(*c*) Donnan phenomenon (*d*) None of these

218. Effect of fat admixture on specific gravity of milk
(*a*) Decreased (*b*) Increased
(*c*) Irregular (*d*) Not affected

219. Which of the following is/are preservatives for milk?
(*a*) Boric acid (*b*) Formalin
(*c*) Sodium carbonate (*d*) All above

220. Byproduct of cheese and cream making is
(*a*) Whey and skim milk (*b*) Whey and butter milk
(*c*) Skim milk and butter (*d*) All of these

221. Enzyme required for cheese formation from milk is
(*a*) Rennin (*b*) Amylase
(*c*) Alkaline phosphatase (*d*) All above

222. Which mineral element is found maximum in cow milk?
(*a*) Sodium (*b*) Calcium
(*c*) Phosphorus (*d*) Iron

223. Which sugar is present in milk?
(*a*) Lactose (*b*) Fructose
(*c*) Glucose (*d*) Sucrose

224. Casein protein is found in which of the following
(*a*) Egg (*b*) Milk
(*c*) Meat (*d*) Cereals

225. Table sugar is
(*a*) Lactose (*b*) Maltose
(*c*) Sucrose (*d*) Fructose

226. Total solids percentage in milk can be calculated by the formula
(*a*) CLR/4 +2.2 F + 1.4 (*b*) CLR/5 +1.2 F +0.14
(*c*) CLR/4 +1.2 F + 1.4 (*d*) CLR +1.2 F + 1.4

227. The milk sugar is
(*a*) Monosaccharide (*b*) Disaccharides
(*c*) Oligosaccharides (*d*) Polysaccharides

228. Which of the following milk is best for infant?
(*a*) Goat (*b*) Buffalo
(*c*) Cow (*d*) Sheep

229. Protein are composed of a series of
(*a*) Nucleic acid (*b*) Amino acid
(*c*) Nucleotide (*d*) None of these

230. National Dairy Development Board (NDDB) is located
(*a*) Punjab (Ludhiana) (*b*) Haryana (Karnal)
(*c*) Madhya Pradesh (Bhopal) (*d*) Gujarat (Anand)

231. The most important factor in determination the milk quality is
(*a*) SNF (*b*) Fat
(*c*) Both above (*d*) Lactose

232. Average total solids in milk is
(*a*) 8.5 % (*b*) 10.2 %
(*c*) 15.0 % (*d*) 12.5 %

233. Average ash percent in milk is
(*a*) 0.8 % (*b*) 1.8 %
(*c*) 2.8 % (*d*) 3.8 %

234. Taste of milk is
(*a*) Sour (*b*) Sweet
(*c*) Above both (*d*) None of these

235. Buffalo milk is not yellow because
(*a*) It contains more fat (*b*) It contains no lactose
(*c*) It contains no carotene (*d*) It contains more calcium

236. The freezing point of milk is about
(*a*) – 029°C (*b*) – 0.10°C
(*c*) – 4.5°C (*d*) – 0.55°C

237. Milk is deficient in which of the following
(*a*) Iron (*b*) Copper
(*c*) Calcium (*d*) Potassium

238. Milk – milk serum =
(*a*) Milk fat (*b*) Skim milk
(*c*) Coagulum (*d*) Casein

239. Milk – milk fat =
(*a*) Milk fat (*b*) Skim milk
(*c*) Coagulum (*d*) Casein

240. Casein is present in milk as which of the following
(*a*) Colloidal suspension (*b*) Emulsion
(*c*) True solvent (*d*) Homogenized

241. Fat is present in milk as which of the following form
(*a*) Colloidal suspension (*b*) Emulsion
(*c*) True solvent (*d*) Homogenized

242. Which constituent is critical for milk yield
(*a*) Milk fat (*b*) Milk casein
(*c*) Milk lactose (*d*) Calcium

243. Which of the following is known as spoon eating milk?
(*a*) Toned milk (*b*) Standard milk
(*c*) Tattoo milk (*d*) Recombined milk

244. Milk viscosity is due to which constituent of milk
(*a*) Casein (*b*) Albumin
(*c*) Globulin (*d*) Phospholipids

245. Which of the following is milk protein?
(*a*) Alpha casein (*b*) Beta casein
(*c*) Gamma casein (*d*) All above

246. Which of the following have maximum casein in its milk?
(*a*) Cow (*b*) Buffalo
(*c*) Human (*d*) Camel

247. Two carbonyl compounds are responsible for flavour in blue cheese.
(*a*) 2-heptanone and 2-nonanone (*b*) Trans-2-hexenal and Benzaldehyde
(*c*) Trans -2-hexenall and trans-2-cis-nonadienal (*d*) None of these

248. The freshly drawn milk turns the red litmus to blue and blue litmus to red due to the presence of
(*a*) Amino acid (*b*) Carbohydrates
(*c*) Lactic acid (*d*) None of these

249. Riboflavin is present in
(*a*) Butter milk (*b*) Skim milk
(*c*) Milk fat (*d*) All of these

250. At which temperature, the specific gravity of milk is determined?
(*a*) 25ºC (*b*) 10ºC
(*c*) 15ºC (*d*) 20ºC

251. Specific gravity of milk is
(*a*) >1 (*b*) 1
(*c*) <1 (*d*) 1.5

252. The average freezing point of milk is
(*a*) – 0.545ºC (*b*) – 0.535ºC
(*c*) – 0.550ºC (*d*) – 0.555ºC

253. The instrument used for determining of freezing point of milk is known as
(*a*) Cryogenic (*b*) Cryoscope
(*c*) Lactometer (*d*) Psychrometer

254. The thermal conductivity of milk should be
(*a*) 13.5×10^4 (*b*) 2.0×10^5
(*c*) 1.5×10^4 (*d*) None of these

255. Which component of milk imparts immunological properties to milk?
(*a*) Lactobacillus (*b*) Lactoglobulin
(*c*) Amino acid (*d*) Tryptophan

256. On an average, what is the ratio of calcium and phosphorus in milk?
(*a*) 1.43:1 (*b*) 2.43:1
(*c*) 1.7:1.5 (*d*) 1.6:1.4

257. Which vitamin is responsible for eye sight?
(*a*) D (*b*) B
(*c*) A (*d*) C

258. The alternative name of vitamin is
(*a*) Antirichetic (*b*) Calcitonic
(*c*) Keratin (*d*) None

259. What is the daily requirement of milk per capita in India?
(*a*) 280 g (*b*) 256 g
(*c*) 312g (*d*) 250 g

260. One litre of buffalo milk yield energy about
(*a*) 800 calorie (*b*) 900 calorie
(*c*) 1100 calorie (*d*) 1000 calorie

261. One litre of cow milk yield energy about
(*a*) 720 calorie (*b*) 750 calorie
(*c*) 1100 calorie (*d*) 980 calorie

262. The temperature, at which milk is cooled?
(*a*) Less than 10ºC (*b*) Above 10ºC
(*c*) 10ºC (*d*) 25ºC

263. Which method of chilling is less expensive, simple and suited for small scale operation?
(*a*) Can cooling (*b*) Can immersion
(*c*) Surface cooler (*d*) Tubular cooler

264. Which operations are performed to clean the milk?
(*a*) Straining (*b*) Filtration
(*c*) Clarification (*d*) All of these

265. When HTST pasteurization is performed, the milk is heated at
(*a*) 70ºC (*b*) 60ºC
(*c*) 85ºC (*d*) 71.5ºC

266. The sterilization of milk is done at
(*a*) 115ºC for 15 minutes (*b*) 125ºC for 10 minutes
(*c*) 130ºC for 12 minutes (*d*) 118ºC for 8 minutes

267. The process of homogenization was first time employed in 1892 for the manufacturing of
(*a*) Milk (*b*) Margarine
(*c*) RTS (*d*) Fruit juice

268. According to WHO and FAO, the percentage of milk fat in double cream is
(*a*) >18 % (*b*) >28 %
(*c*) >35 % (*d*) >45 %

269. The percentage of lactic acid in special cream grade is
(*a*) 0.1% (*b*) 0.2%
(*c*) 0.3% (*d*) 0.4%

270. Which milk was first made in India?
(*a*) Skim milk (*b*) Cream milk
(*c*) Toned milk (*d*) Double cream milk

271. The conversion of milk into curd takes place with the help of
(*a*) Bacteria (*b*) Molds
(*c*) Yeasts (*d*) None of them

272. Which of the following is capable of to freeze the food at –196ºC?
(*a*) LPG (*b*) Frozen CO_2
(*c*) LN_2 (*d*) LH_2

273. Muffle furnace is used for the estimation of
(*a*) Protein
(*b*) Sugar
(*c*) Salt
(*d*) Ash

274. Texture analyzer is employed to determine the ___________ properties of foods.
(*a*) Physical
(*b*) Mechanical
(*c*) Rheological
(*d*) Aerodynamic and hydrodynamic

275. Packaging material for food should be
(*a*) Non toxic
(*b*) Transparent
(*c*) Economically sound
(*d*) All above

276. Which of the following is not considered as a food additives?
(*a*) Vitamins
(*b*) Flavouring agent
(*c*) Emulsifier
(*d*) Antioxidants

277. Sugar and salt is used as
(*a*) Antioxidant
(*b*) Sequestrant
(*c*) Emulsifier
(*d*) Preservative

278. Cottage cheese is an example of
(*a*) High fat
(*b*) Low fat
(*c*) Both
(*d*) none

279. Which of the following is the substitute of butter?
(*a*) margarine
(*b*) enzyme
(*c*) cholesterol
(*d*) ester

280. Dairy products such as cheese and butter milk is
(*a*) Fermented products
(*b*) Main products
(*c*) Byproducts
(*d*) None of these

281. Swiss cheese also known as
(*a*) Brown cheese
(*b*) White cheese
(*c*) Emmental cheese
(*d*) None of these

282. Salt added at a level about 2.5 % of the final butter constitutes flavour and also act as a
(*a*) Preservative
(*b*) antioxidant
(*c*) Catalyst
(*d*) Colouring agent

283. Which bacteria is responsible for conversion of lactose into lactic acid
(*a*) Aspergillus spp.
(*b*) Theujunasis
(*c*) Byssachlamyc fulva
(*d*) Streptococcus lactis

284. Fat percentage in milk cream is
(*a*) 25 (*b*) 40
(*c*) 35 (*d*) 40

285. First time secreted milk from cattle is known as
(*a*) Colustrum (*b*) Clostridium
(*c*) Cholesterol (*d*) None

286. Sterilized canned cream has fat percentage nearly
(*a*) 20% (*b*) 40%
(*c*) 60% (*d*) 80%

287. Frozen cream has fat percentage about
(*a*) 20% (*b*) 40%
(*c*) 60% (*d*) 80%

288. Fruit cream may have fat % approximately
(*a*) 20-25% (*b*) 40-45%
(*c*) 60-65% (*d*) 80-85%

289. Which of the following is responsible for better flavour in cream?
(*a*) Diacetyl (*b*) Propionic acid
(*c*) Acetyl methyl carbinol (*d*) All of the above

290. Separeta refers to
(*a*) Milk without cream (*b*) Milk after separated fat
(*c*) Milk with cream (*d*) All of the above

291. How much percentage of Khoa can be prepared from cow milk?
(*a*) 15.5% (*b*) 18.3%
(*c*) 21.6% (*d*) None

292. Mother dairy in Delhi was established in the year
(*a*) 1974-75 (*b*) 1976-77
(*c*) 1977-78 (*d*) 1978-79

293. Rancidity in cheese is caused by
(*a*) Lipolytic organisms (*b*) Low salts
(*c*) High acidity (*d*) None

294. Condensed milk means
(*a*) Milk with 30 % water (*b*) Milk with 30 % total solids
(*c*) Milk with 9 % fat (*d*) All of the above

295. Condensed milk may be made of
(*a*) Sugar free milk (*b*) Sweet milk
(*c*) Both above (*d*) None of the above

296. Pasty cheese is caused by
(*a*) High moisture and acidity (*b*) Low moisture and acidity
(*c*) High salt percentage (*d*) All of these

297. Evaporated milk may be made from
(*a*) Sugar free milk (*b*) Sweet milk
(*c*) Both above (*d*) None of the above

298. Evaporated milk is homogenized at
(*a*) 45-50°C (*b*) 55-60°C
(*c*) 60-65°C (*d*) 80-82°C

299. Milk powder may be prepared from
(*a*) Milk (*b*) Sepreta
(*c*) Cream (*d*) All of the above

300. Pure ghee should have RM value about
(*a*) >28 (*b*) <24
(*c*) >15 (*d*) None

301. Chhana refers to
(*a*) It is milk product (*b*) It is prepared after curdling of milk
(*c*) The solid particles are separated from paneer water
(*d*) All of the above

302. Which of the following component is found in paneer?
(*a*) Ca (*b*) Vitamin B
(*c*) Protein (*d*) All of the above

303. Export quality chedder paneer contains water about
(*a*) <36% (*b*) >36%
(*c*) <10% (*d*) None

304. Under UHT the milk is heated to
(*a*) 132°C for 1 sec (*b*) 132°C for 1 min
(*c*) 132°C for 1 hour (*d*) None

305. Evaporated milk is accomplished by removing the water upto
(*a*) 50 % (*b*) 60%
(*c*) 80% (*d*) 90%

306. Skim milk contain usually about __________ percent fat.
(*a*) 0.1 (*b*) 1.0
(*c*) 0.9 (*d*) 0.01

307. Moisture content in cow and buffalo milk khoa is respectively about
(*a*) 25.6 and 19.2% (*b*) 25.6 and 25.6%
(*c*) 10.6 and 20.5% (*d*) 35.1 and 18.9%

308. The position of India in milk production globally is
(*a*) First (*b*) Second
(*c*) Third (*d*) Fourth

309. Full name of SNF is
(*a*) Soluble non fat (*b*) Solid non fat
(*c*) Saturated non fat (*d*) Synthetic non fat

310. Rapid heating of cream is accomplished by injecting steam or by a combination of steam injection and evacuation in a process known as
(*a*) Flash pasteurization (*b*) Vat pasteurization
(*c*) Vacreation (*d*) Aseptic processing

311. The most popular of the UHT system are the direct heating methods include
(*a*) Steam injection technique (*b*) Steam infusion technique
(*c*) Bactofugation (*d*) Both (*a*) and (*b*)

312. Steam injection technique of UHT system is referred as
(*a*) Milk injected into steam process (*b*) Steam injected into milk process
(*c*) Vacreation (*d*) None

313. Milk injected into steam process of UHT method is also known as
(*a*) Steam injected technique (*b*) Steam infusion technique
(*c*) Milk injected technique (*d*) Milk infusion technique

314. The efficiency of milk pasteurization or the percentage of reduction of numbers of microorganisms in milk during pasteurization depends on
(*a*) Temperature of pasteurization (*b*) Holding time
(*c*) Total numbers of bacteria
(*d*) The proportion of the total microbial load that are spore-formers or thermoduric organisms
e) All of the above

315. The shelf life of pasteurized milk depends on the
(*a*) Temperature of storage (*b*) Number of microorganisms
(*c*) Types of microorganisms (*d*) All of the above

316. Sealed cans of evaporated milk are processed at about
(*a*) 115 to 118ºC for 14-18 min
(*b*) 93 to 100ºC for 14-18 min
(*c*) 71.1 to 82ºC for 30 min
(*d*) 71 to 100ºC for 10-30 min

317. During the manufacturing of processed cheese from cheese, one of the following is used as emulsifiers.
(*a*) Phosphates
(*b*) Citrates
(*c*) Tartrates
(*d*) All of the above

318. Refrigeration temperature are recommended for milk or related products during
(*a*) Storage in the plant and during delivery
(*b*) Retail market
(*c*) Home or restaurant until consumption
(*d*) All of the above

319. Butter should be stored at
(*a*) –17 to –18ºC or lower
(*b*) 0 to 5ºC
(*c*) –5 to –10ºC
(*d*) None

320. Evaporated milk is made by removing about _______ percent of the water from whole milk.
(*a*) 20
(*b*) 40
(*c*) 60
(*d*) 80

321. Among the dairy products prepared in the dry form are
(*a*) Milk, skim milk
(*b*) Cream, ice cream milk
(*c*) Whey, butter milk and malted milk
(*d*) All of the above

322. Most of dry milk is prepared by
(*a*) Roller process with vacuum
(*b*) Roller process without vacuum
(*c*) Spray drying process
(*d*) All of the above

323. Milk is preheated before drying to __________ for the roller process and to _________ for the spray process.
(*a*) 65 to 85ºC, 68.8 to 93.3ºC
(*b*) 60 to 70ºC, 65 to 75ºC
(*c*) 50 to 80ºC, 60 to80ºC
(*d*) None

324. In dry process of milk involve an instantization step, in which the dry powder is
(*a*) Wetted and re-dried
(*b*) Added the steam and dried
(*c*) Dried and wetted
(*d*) None

325. The microbial content of the heat dried dairy product depends on
(*a*) Content of liquid product to be dried
(*b*) Temperature and time of preheating and method of drying
(*c*) Contamination and growth in storage tank, pipes and drying source (air)
(*d*) All of them

326. The high temperature of the roller process of drying milk without vacuum destroyed almost all microorganisms
(*a*) Fungus (*b*) Mold
(*c*) Bacterial spores (*d*) All

327. The use of sorbic or propionic acid or one of their salts is permitted in
(*a*) Cottage cheese (*b*) Yogurt
(*c*) Hard cheese and processed cheese (*d*) All of them

328. The primary objective in adding a preservative to hard cheese or processed cheese is to prevent
(*a*) Surface growth of mold (*b*) Surface growth of bacteria
(*c*) Surface growth of yeast (*d*) All of them

329. Added sugar acts as a preservative and reduces the water activity in
(*a*) Toned milk (*b*) Skim milk
(*c*) Sweetened condensed milk (*d*) Evaporated milk

330. Sodium chloride (common salt) is usually used in the cheese making for
(*a*) Increase digestibility (*b*) Flavour enhancement
(*c*) Controlling the growth of microorganisms (*d*) Both (*b*) and (*c*)

331. Mold spoilage of cheese is usually delayed or prevented when ________ are added or incorporated in the wrapper.
(*a*) Sorbic acid (*b*) Sorbates
(*c*) Propionic acid or propionates (*d*) All of these

332. Milk is an excellent culture medium for much kind of microorganisms because of
(*a*) High in moisture content (*b*) Neutral in pH
(*c*) Rich in microbial foods (*d*) All of the above

333. In raw milk at temperature from 10 to 37°C, which microorganisms are most likely to cause the souring?
(*a*) Streptococcus lactic (*b*) S. faecalis
(*c*) Lactobacillus bulgaricus (*d*) L. thermophilus

334. Butyric acid may be produced in the milk by the action of
(*a*) Coliform bacteria (*b*) Streptococcus spp.
(*c*) Clostridium spp. (*d*) Bacillus spp.

335. The chief gas formers in milk and milk products are
(*a*) Coliform bacteria (*b*) Clostridium spp.
(*c*) Gas forming bacillus spp. (*d*) All of the above

336. The hydrolysis of milk protein by microorganisms usually accompanied by production of bitter flavour caused by some of the peptides release is called
(*a*) Proteolysis
(*b*) Hydrogenation
(*c*) Stabilization
(*d*) Sterilization

337. The ropiness usually decreases as the acidity of milk or cream
(*a*) Decreases
(*b*) Increases
(*c*) Constant
(*d*) Increase than decrease

338. Ropiness and sliminess in milk, cream and whey is caused by
(*a*) Enterobacter
(*b*) LAB
(*c*) Micrococcus, streptococcus and bacillus
(*d*) All of the above

339. The change in milk fat occurs by microbial decomposition are
(*a*) Oxidation of unsaturated fatty acid
(*b*) Hydrolysis of the butter fat
(*c*) Combined oxidation and hydrolysis to produce rancidity
(*d*) All of the above

340. Oxidation of the unsaturated fatty acids of milk may results
(*a*) Aldehydes
(*b*) Acids
(*c*) Ketones
(*d*) Tallow odour and taste
e) All of the above

341. Hydrolysis of the butterfat to fatty acid and glycerol may occur by the enzyme is
(*a*) Lipase
(*b*) Lactase
(*c*) Amylase
(*d*) Catalase

342. Which one of the following, colour of milk is not changed due to microorganisms.
(*a*) Blue milk
(*b*) Yellow
(*c*) Brown milk
(*d*) Red milk
e) Green milk

343. Which one of the following produces a bluish gray to brownish colour in milk in pure culture?
(*a*) Pseudomonas syncyanea
(*b*) Pseudomonas synxantha
(*c*) Serratia spp.
(*d*) Micrococcus roseus

344. Pseudomonas synxantha may cause a ________ colour in the cream layer of milk.
(*a*) Blue
(*b*) Yellow
(*c*) Red
(*d*) Green

345. In red milk, a red layer at the top of milk is caused by
(*a*) Brevibacterium erythrohenes
(*b*) Flavobacterium
(*c*) Geotrichum
(*d*) All of the above

346. At refrigeration temperature, proteolysis may be initiated by psychrotophic bacteria such as
(*a*) Pseudomonas
(*b*) Leuconostoc
(*c*) Shiggela
(*d*) Salmonella

347. Spoilage of evaporated milk from leakage, as indicated by the presence of non spore formers may result in gas and swelling caused by
(*a*) Coliform bacteria or yeast
(*b*) Coagulation by streptococci
(*c*) Bitterness caused by cocci
(*d*) All of them

348. The main kind of spoilage in sweetened condensed milk is due to
(*a*) Gas forming fermentating yeasts or more rarely by Coliform bacteria
(*b*) Thickening caused by micrococci which probably produced rennin like enzyme
(*c*) Button's which are mold colonies growing on the milk surface
(*d*) All of the above

349. Cheesiness flavour defect in cream is caused by
(*a*) Lactobacilli
(*b*) Enterobacter
(*c*) Yeast
(*d*) Coliform bacteria

350. Musty flavour in cream is caused by
(*a*) Bacteria
(*b*) Mold and anctinomycetes
(*c*) Pseudomonas
(*d*) None of these

351. Milk is a good source of all water-soluble vitamins except for _____
(*a*) Cyanocobalmin
(*b*) Riboflavin
(*c*) Ascorbic Acid
(*d*) Thiamine

352. _________ is a milk process that makes milk more easily digested by those with a sensitive digestive system.
(*a*) Ionization
(*b*) Evaporation
(c) Pasteurization
(*d*) Homogenization

353. ______ amino acids are commonly found in milk proteins, including the essential amino acids.
(*a*) 7
(*b*) 12
(*c*) 14
(*d*) 19

354. Summer milk has been estimated to contain 1.6 times as much vitamin ____ as winter milk.
(*a*) A
(*b*) B
(*c*) C
(*d*) D

355. The milk becomes the property of the buyer once ?
(*a*) The transport truck reaches the plant
(*b*) It is loaded into the transport truck on the farm
(*c*) The transport truck leaves the farm
(*d*) It is unloaded into the processor's bulk tanks

356. Discolouration of milk powder during storage is due to
(a) Carnelization
(b) Maillard browning
(c) Autoxidation
(d) Moisture content

ANSWER KEY

(DAIRY PRODUCT PROCESSING)

1.A	2. A	3.B	4.C	5.D	6.A	7.D	8.A	9.B	10.D
11.A	12.B	13.A	14.B	15.C	16.D	17.A	18.B	19.C	20.D
21.A	22.B	23.C	24.D	25.A	26.B	27.C	28.D	29.A	30.A
31.B	32.C	33.D	34.A	35.B	36.C	37.D	38.A	39.B	40.C
41.D	42.A	43.B	44.C	45.A	46.B	47.A	48.A	49.A	50.B
51.D	52.A	53.C	54.B	55.A	56.C	57.B	58.C	59.D	60.A
61.B	62.B	63.C	64.C	65.B	66.B	67.B	68.C	69.C	70.D
71.C	72.B	73.D	74.A	75.D	76.D	77.B	78.C	79.B	80.A
81.C	82.D	83.D	84.C	85.C	86.C	87.C	88.B	89.D	90.A
91.B	92.A	93.C	94.D	95.C	96.D	97.C	98.D	99.A	100.A
101.A	102.C	103.B	104.A	105.A	106.C	107.C	108.C	109.D	110.C
111.D	112.C	113.A	114.C	115.C	116. C	117.C	118.C	119.A	120.B
121.B	122.B	123.C	124.C	125.C	126.C	127.D	128.C	129.C	130.C
131.Ç	132.A	133.D	134.C	135.C	136.B	137.C	138.C	139.B	140.A
141.C	142.D	143.C	144.B	145.A	146.C	147.D	148.D	149.C	150.A
151.C	152.C	153.B	154.C	155.B	156.A	157.B	158.A	159.C	160.C
161.A	162.B	163.A	164.D	165.A	166.C	167.A	168.C	169.C	170.B
171.B	172.C	173.C	174.A	175.B	176.B	177.D	178.A	179.B	180.C
181.D	182.A	183.B	184.C	185.D	186.A	187.B	188.C	189.B	190.A
191.C	192.C	193.D	194.D	195.B	196.A	197.C	198.C	199.A	200.D
201.A	202.B	203.D	204.B	205.C	206.C	207.A	208.B	209.B	210.C
211.B	212.A	213.B	214.D	215.A	216.B	217.B	218.A	219.D	220.A
221.A	222.B	223.A	224.B	225.C	226.C	227.B	228.A	229.B	230.D
231.C	232.D	233.A	234.B	235.C	236.D	237.A	238.C	239.B	240.A
241.B	242.C	243.C	244.A	245.D	246.B	247.A	248.A	249.B	250.C
251.A	252.A	253.B	254.A	255.B	256.A	257.C	258.A	259.A	260.C
261.A	262.A	263.B	264.D	265.D	266.A	267.B	268.D	269.B	270.C
271.A	272.C	273.D	274.C	275.D	276.A	277.D	278.B	279.A	280.C
281.C	282.A	283.D	284.A	285.A	286.A	287.B	288.B	289.A	290.D
291.B	292.A	293.A	294.D	295.C	296.A	297.A	298.A	299.D	300.A
301.D	302.D	303.A	304.A	305.B	306.A	307.A	308.A	309.B	310.C
311.D	312.B	313.B	314.E	315.D	316.A	317.D	318.D	319.A	320.C
321.D	322.D	323.A	324.A	325.D	326.C	327.D	328.A	329.C	330.D
331.D	332.D	333.A	334.C	335.D	336.A	337.B	338.D	339.D	340.E
341.A	342.E	343.A	344.B	345.A	346.A	347.D	348.D	349.A	350.B
351. C	352. D	353. D	354. A	355. B	356. B				

Chapter **8**

Livestock, Fish and Poultry Product Processing

1. NRC on meat and meat products is located at
   (*a*) Hyderabad (*b*) Aligarh
   (*c*) Izzatnagar (*d*) Puttur

2. NRC on cold water fisheries is at
   (*a*) Srinagar (*b*) Nainital
   (*c*) Dehradun (*d*) Shimla

3. Central Institute of Fisheries Technology is established at
   (*a*) Kolkata (*b*) Mumbai
   (*c*) Cochin (*d*) Chennai

4. Blue revolution is related to
   (*a*) Crops (*b*) Oilseeds
   (*c*) Energy source (*d*) Fisheries

5. Quality of egg can be judged by
   (*a*) pH (*b*) Candling
   (*c*) Annealing (*d*) Temperature test

6. Egg shell is made up of
   (*a*) CaO (*b*) $Ca_3(PO_4)_2$
   (*c*) $CaCO_3$ (*d*) $Ca(OH)_2$

7. Yellow colour of egg is due to
   (*a*) Carotene (*b*) Vitamin B
   (*c*) Xanthophyll (*d*) None of these

8. Meat of sheep is known as
   (*a*) Chicken (*b*) Pork
   (*c*) Beef (*d*) Mutton

9. Buffalo meat contains white fat as
(*a*) WBC (*b*) RBC
(*c*) Yellow pigment (*d*) Carotene covered to vitamin A

10. Minimum weight of extra large A grade Egg is
(*a*) 45 g (*b*) 55 g
(*c*) 60 g (*d*) 70 g

11. Oiling of egg present the escape of following gas
(*a*) CO_2 (*b*) O_2
(*c*) Water vapour (*d*) H_2

12. Egg shell contributes about how much percent of egg
(*a*) 11 (*b*) 20
(*c*) 30 (*d*) 35

13. To differentiate between fresh and old eggs which of the following method is used?
(*a*) Breakage of egg (*b*) Rotation of egg
(*c*) Candling of egg (*d*) All above

14. In white albumin, how much fat is present?
(*a*) 0 % (*b*) 17 %
(*c*) 30 % (*d*) 55 %

15. In yolk, how much protein is present?
(*a*) 0 % (*b*) 17 %
(*c*) 30 % (*d*) 50 %

16. Which is major fat in yolk?
(*a*) Phosvitin (*b*) Conalbumin
(*c*) Ovalbumin (*d*) Livetin

17. In which albumin, which protein is in maximum amount (54%)
(*a*) Phosvitin (*b*) Ovalbumin .
(*c*) Livetin (*d*) Conalbumin

18. Major bactericidal protein in albumin is
(*a*) Phosvitin (*b*) Ovalbumin
(*c*) Livetin (*d*) Conalbumin

19. Which protein of albumin, binds with biotin
(*a*) Ovamucin (*b*) Ovamucoid
(*c*) Lysozyme (*d*) Avidin

20. Energy provided per egg is about (Weight of egg about 60 gm)
(*a*) 75 kcal
(*b*) 90 kcal
(*c*) 100 kcal
(*d*) 150 kcal

21. Fat content per egg is
(*a*) 5.5 gm
(*b*) 6.6 gm
(*c*) 600 IU
(*d*) 20 mg

22. Cholesterol content per egg is about in egg yolk
(*a*) 213 mg
(*b*) 240 gm
(*c*) 600 IU
(*d*) 2.0 mg

23. Vitamin A content per egg is
(*a*) 540 IU
(*b*) 300 IU
(*c*) 600 IU
(*d*) 450 IU

24. Safe storage temperature of egg should be
(*a*) 20 °F or below
(*b*) 30 °F or below
(*c*) 40 °F (7°C) or below
(*d*) 40 °F or below

25. Freezing temperature of chicken is
(*a*) 0 °F
(*b*) –10°F to –20°F.
(*c*) –20 °F to –40°F
(*d*) –60°F to –80°F

26. Chilling of carcass (poultry) done at which temperature
(*a*) 0 °F or below
(*b*) 15 °F or below
(*c*) 25 °F or below
(*d*) 40 °F or below

27. Removal of filoplume from carcass is known as
(*a*) Singeing
(*b*) Pinning
(*c*) Plucking
(*d*) Scalding

28. Removal of feather from scaled bird is known as
(*a*) Singeing
(*b*) Pinning
(*c*) Plucking
(*d*) Scalding

29. Removal of pin feather from carcass is known as
(*a*) Singeing
(*b*) Pinning
(*c*) Plucking
(*d*) Scalding

30. Time and temperature combination for bird scalding is
(*a*) 120–130°F for 20-40 sec
(*b*) 100°F
(*c*) 180 – 190°F for 6-8 sec
(*d*) Any one of these

31. Semi-scalding is done at
(*a*) 120 -130°F for 20-40 sec
(*b*) 100°F
(*c*) 180 – 190°F for 6-8 sec
(*d*) Any one of these

32. Which is ISI grade of quality of egg?
(*a*) A to F
(*b*) 1 to 5
(*c*) I to V
(*d*) Any one

33. According ISI, the weight of extra large egg
(*a*) 70 gm and above
(*b*) 60 gm and above
(*c*) 50 gm and above
(*d*) 47 gm and above

34. According to USDA grade, the size of extra large egg is
(*a*) 70 gm
(*b*) 65 gm
(*c*) 56 gm
(*d*) 49 gm

35. In good egg, air space should be
(*a*) 1/8 inch
(*b*) 1/16 inch
(*c*) 3/36 inch
(*d*) 5/16 inch

36. Egg quality judge by
(*a*) External appearance
(*b*) Candling experiment
(*c*) Broken out examination
(*d*) All

37. Cocking test include
(*a*) Chemical test of egg
(*b*) Biological test of egg
(*c*) Bacterial test of egg
(*d*) All

38. Specialties of cold storage for egg is
(*a*) Temperature 29 - 30°F, humidity 80-90 %
(*b*) Temperature 30 - 40°F, humidity 60-80 %
(*c*) Temperature 0 -10°F, humidity 90 %
(*d*) Temperature 4 -6°F, humidity 100 %

39. Shell treatment of egg is done for
(*a*) Checking escape of CO_2
(*b*) Checking escape of O_2
(*c*) Checking escape of moisture
(*d*) Checking escape of N_2

40. In shell treatment spraying is done by
(*a*) Liquid
(*b*) Coconut oil
(*c*) Both ((*a*) and ((*b*)
(*d*) Mustard oil

41. Pasteurizing of egg is done by
    (*a*) Immersing egg in water at 72°F for 30 minutes
    (*b*) Immersing egg in water at 100°F for 15 minutes
    (*c*) Immersing egg in water at 130°F for 30 minutes
    (*d*) None of these

42. Dirty egg can be cleaned by washing with
    (*a*) NaOH (*b*) Warm water
    (*c*) Cold water (*d*) Both ((*a*) and ((*b*)

43. Almost all vitamins are present in eggs except vitamin
    (*a*) A (*b*) B
    (*c*) C (*d*) E

44. The colour of meat is due to the pigment
    (*a*) Heamoglobin (*b*) Myoglobin
    (*c*) Lycopene (*d*) None of these

45. Egg shell is a rich source of
    (*a*) Phosphorus (*b*) Calcium
    (*c*) Sodium (*d*) Zinc

46. Number of layer of outer membrane of egg is made by
    (*a*) Eight (*b*) Ten
    (*c*) Six (*d*) Seven

47. Number of layer of inner membrane of egg is made by
    (*a*) Three (*b*) Ten
    (*c*) Six (*d*) Seven

48. Two carbohydrates are found in meat is ______________ and ______________.
    (*a*) Glucose and fructose (*b*) Glycogen and glucose
    (*c*) Maltose and fructose (*d*) Chitin and lignin

49. Natural emulsifier *i.e.* lecithin is found in
    (*a*) Egg (*b*) Meat
    (*c*) Apple (*d*) Cereals

50. Fish protein concentrate contain the high quality protein of about
    (*a*) 30-40% (*b*) 50-59%
    (*c*) 62-67% (*d*) 85-92%

51. Roasted white meat without skin contain fat percent about
    (*a*) 1.8 (*b*) 2.5
    (*c*) 3.5 (*d*) 4.0

52. Composition of an egg is
    (*a*) 70 % water, 7% protein and 11 % fat
    (*b*) 65 % water, 12% protein and 11 % fat
    (*c*) 80 % water, 10% protein and 11 % fat
    (*d*) 62 % water, 10% protein and 11 % fat

53. Meat preservative agents are
    (*a*) Nitrite and nitrate
    (*b*) Sugar
    (*c*) Acetic acid
    (*d*) Benzoic acid

54. The major protein of muscles fibre in meat is
    (*a*) Myosin
    (*b*) Elastin
    (*c*) Gyosin
    (*d*) None

55. When an animal is well fed, fat percentage between the muscle fibre bundles is called
    (*a*) Fat reduction
    (*b*) Fat marbling
    (*c*) Fat budding
    (*d*) Fat bundling

56. The substance added to meat as mild preservative and flavour enhancer is
    (*a*) Common salt
    (*b*) Sugar
    (*c*) Vinegar
    (*d*) Brine

57. The chief muscle pigment in meat protein is called
    (*a*) Myosin
    (*b*) Cyoglobin
    (*c*) Hemoglobin
    (*d*) Myoglobin

58. The ideal temperature of meat smoke room is
    (*a*) 52°C
    (*b*) 55°C
    (*c*) 57°C
    (*d*) 60°C

59. The smoking of meat is done for the period of
    (*a*) 15-20 hrs
    (*b*) 18-24 hrs
    (*c*) 20-25 hrs
    (*d*) 30-35 hrs

60. According to USFDA, freezing of meat is done at the temperature of
    (*a*) 0°C
    (*b*) – 10°C
    (*c*) –15°C
    (*d*) – 20°C

61. Nutritive value of beef meat is
    (*a*) Protein (18%), fat (23%), water (58%), and ash (0.5%)
    (*b*) Protein (17.5%), fat (22%), water (60%), and ash (0.9%)
    (*c*) Protein (21%), fat (20%), water (55%), and ash (0.9%)
    (*d*) Protein (25%), fat (18%), water (58%), and ash (0.5%)

62. Amount of protein in an egg
(*a*) 5.5 gm (*b*) 6.6 gm
(*c*) 600 IU (*d*) 20 mg

63. The washed poultry chilled to prevent bacterial spoilage and preserve quality at temperature of
(*a*) 32 to 2°C (*b*) – 35 to – 5°C
(*c*) – 40 to – 1°C (*d*) – 20 to – 10°C

64. A grade quality of egg can be maintained as long as
(*a*) 6 month (*b*) 12 month
(*c*) 18 month (*d*) 24 month

65. Pasteurization of egg should be done at the temperature of
(*a*) 60-62°C (*b*) 60-65°C
(*c*) 40-50°C (*d*) 70-75°C

66. The water activity of chilled meat is
(*a*) Very high (*b*) Very low
(*c*) Moderate (*d*) Low

67. Unprotected meat will lose weight by
(*a*) Evaporation (*b*) Respiration
(*c*) Transpiration (*d*) Refrigeration

68. Oxymyoglobin has a colour of
(*a*) Black (*b*) White
(*c*) Red (*d*) Bright red

69. The colour of meat surface will become some what brighter when stored at
(*a*) Lower temperature (*b*) Higher temperature
(*c*) Any temperature (*d*) None

70. The first observation regarding the effect of carbon dioxide on retarding bacterial growth were made in
(*a*) 1982 (*b*) 1882
(*c*) 1873 (*d*) 1802

71. The boxed beef concept was introduced in
(*a*) 1950 (*b*) 1870
(*c*) 1967 (*d*) 1913

72. Shrink bath method was developed by
(*a*) W.R. Grace (*b*) C.M. Davidson
(*c*) V.R. Robert (*d*) G. Moun

73. Vacuum packaged beef of normal pH can be stored at chiller temperature for
(*a*) One month
(*b*) 10 weeks
(*c*) 15 weeks
(*d*) 30 weeks

74. The use of carbon dioxide (CO_2) enriched atmosphere for extending the shelf life of poultry meat was carried out in
(*a*) Germany (1951)
(*b*) USA (1915)
(*c*) USA (1951)
(*d*) Newzeland (1915)

75. Sea foods have a much higher content of
(*a*) Poly unsaturated fat
(*b*) Lipid
(*c*) Protein
(*d*) Vitamin A, D, E, K

76. Heat products sufficiently to inactivate the non proteolytic spores and than keep the product well at
(*a*) 0°C
(*b*) 12°C
(*c*) Below 10°C
(*d*) Below 0°C

77. The partial pressure of oxygen in air is
(*a*) 160 mm Hg
(*b*) 200 mm Hg
(*c*) 150 mm Hg
(*d*) 760 mm Hg

78. The meat is the good culture media for the growth of microorganisms due to
(*a*) High in moisture
(*b*) Nearly neutral pH
(*c*) High in nutrients
(*d*) All of the above

79. After slaughtering, meat undergo undesirable changes occurs in
(*a*) Moisture content
(*b*) Appearance
(*c*) Flavour
(*d*) Both (*b*) and (*c*)

80. Long storage of meat at __________ temperature may allow increase in the number of microorganisms.
(*a*) Drying
(*b*) Freezing
(*c*) Chilling
(*d*) Curing

81. Most meat products are
(*a*) Low acid foods
(*b*) Medium acid foods
(*c*) High acid foods
(*d*) None of them

82. Chemicals added during curing of meat such as
(*a*) Spices
(*b*) Salt
(*c*) Nitrates and nitrites
(*d*) All of the above

83. One of the following ingredients in meat helps to kill spores of anaerobic bacteria by heat and inhibit germination of surviving spores.
(*a*) Salt (*b*) Spices
(*c*) Nitrates (*d*) Nitrites

84. The processing temperature for shelf stable canned cured meats is
(*a*) 65 °C (*b*) 72 °C
(*c*) 98 °C (*d*) 100 °C

85. The non shelf stable cured meats are packed in container upto 22 lb are processed at temperature of about
(*a*) 65 °C (*b*) 72 °C
(*c*) 98 °C (*d*) 100 °C

86. Mostly meat is preserved under low temperature in
(*a*) Freezing (*b*) Chilling
(*c*) Cold storage (*d*) Refrigeration

87. Increasing amounts of CO_2 in the atmosphere inhibits microorganisms but also
(*a*) Hasten the formation of metamyoglobin (*b*) Loss of bloom
(*c*) Loss of natural colour (*d*) All of the above

88. Optimal concentration of CO_2 under chilled condition for most of meat vary from
(*a*) 5-7 % (*b*) 5-15%
(*c*) 10-30% (*d*) Upto 100 %

89. Storage time of meat under chilling can be increased in the presence of ozone in atmosphere varying from
(*a*) 1-2% (*b*) 3-7%
(*c*) 2.5-3.0% (*d*) 10-30%

90. Ozone is an active oxidize agent that may cause tallow flavour to
(*a*) Fat (*b*) Protein
(*c*) Carbohydrates d) β-carotene

91. The fish is most susceptible to
(*a*) Autolysis (*b*) Oxidation
(*c*) Hydrolysis of fat (*d*) Microbial spoilage
(*e*) All of these

92. Rigor mortis is especially important in the preservation of fish to retard
(*a*) Postmortem autolysis (*b*) Bacterial decomposition
(*c*) Hydrolysis of fat (*d*) Both ((*a*) and ((*b*)

93. The best antioxidant used to retard oxidative rancidity of fat or oil of fish is
(*a*) Nordihydroguaiaretic acid
(*b*) Ethyl gallet
(*c*) Ascorbic acid
(*d*) All of the above

94. To differentiate between fresh and old eggs which of the following method is used?
(*a*) Breakage of egg
(*b*) Rotation of egg
(*c*) Candling of egg
(*d*) All above

95. Scalding of poultry may be done at the temperature of
(*a*) 60°C for 15 minutes
(*b*) 70°C for 5 seconds
(*c*) 60°C for 45 seconds
(*d*) 80°C for 2 seconds

96. Internal quality of egg is measured in unit
(*a*) Haugh unit
(*b*) Reynold unit
(*c*) Haber unit
(*d*) None of the above

97. The pink colour characteristic of cured meat is due to :
(a) Myoglobin
(*b*) Nitrosyl myoglobin
(c) Haemoglobin
(*d*) Nitrosyl hemochrome

98. PSE condition of pork is caused due to :
(*a*) Short term pre-slaughter stress
(*b*) Chronic stress
(*c*) Rapid decline of muscle pH
(*d*) Both (*a*) and (*c*)
(PSE = Pale, soft, exudative meat)

ANSWER KEY

LIVESTOCK, FISH AND POULTRY PRODUCT PROCESSING

1. A	2. B	3. C	4. D	5. B	6. C	7. C	8. D	9. D	10. C
11. B	12. A	13. A	14. B	15. D	16. D	17. B	18. D	19. D	20. B
21. A	22. A	23. C	24. C	25. C	26. D	27. A	28. C	29. B	30. C
31. A	32. A	33. B	34. A	35. A	36. D	37. B	38. A	39. A	40. C
41. C	42. D	43. C	44. B	45. B	46. C	47. A	48. B	49. A	50. D
51. C	52. B	53. A	54. A	55. B	56. A	57. D	58. C	59. B	60. C
61. B	62. B	63. A	64. A	65. A	66. A	67. B	68. D	69. A	70. B
71. C	72. A	73. B	74. C	75. A	76. C	77. A	78. D	79. D	80. C
81. A	82. D	83. C	84. C	85. A	86. B	87. D	88. C	89. C	90. A
91. E	92. D	93. D	94. C	95. C	96. A	97. D	98. D		

Chapter 9

Food Preservation and Microbiology

1. Which fungus is used for lactic acid production?
   (*a*) *Fusarium moniliforme* (*b*) *Rhizopus oryzae*
   (*c*) *Aspergillus terreus* (*d*) *Aspergillus niger*
2. The microorganism used for meat preservation is
   (*a*) Mesophilic bacteria (*b*) Thermophylic bacteria
   (*c*) Psychrophylic microorganisms (*d*) Hydrophilic microorganisms
3. pH of acid found in Banana
   (*a*) 5.0 (*b*) 2.3
   (*c*) 7.3 (*d*) 8.0
4. pH range of vegetables is around
   (*a*) 5 to 5.5 (*b*) 5.0 to 7.0
   (*c*) 7.0 to 12.0 (*d*) 2.0 to 3.0
5. Microorganisms found in milk is classified on the basis of their major characteristics are
   (*a*) Biochemical types (*b*) Temperature response
   (*c*) Ability to cause infection and diseases (*d*) All of the above
6. Vitamin C is not present in
   (*a*) Banana (*b*) Apple
   (*c*) Lemon (*d*) Milk
7. Canning is the basic method of food preservation is done at
   (*a*) 100°C for high acidic foods (*b*) 121°C for low acidic foods
   (*c*) Both above (*d*) None
8. The phosphatase test is done for purpose of
   (*a*) Pasteurized milk testing (*b*) Sterilized milk testing
   (*c*) Aseptic processing of milk (*d*) Osmotic pressure testing

9. Derivatives of lactic acid is used in the treatments of
(*a*) Tuberoculosis and Asthma
(*b*) Neurological problems
(*c*) Calcium deficiency and anemia
(*d*) Pneumonia and diabetes

10. Which amino acid has two chiral carbons
(*a*) Leucine
(*b*) Isolucine
(*c*) Glycine
(*d*) Valine

11. Riboflavin is obtained from
(*a*) Ashbya gossypii and Eremthecium ashbyii
(*b*) Aspergillus oyyzae and A. niger
(*c*) Rhizopus niveus and rhyzopus stolinerfer
(*d*) None

12. Non protein part of enzyme is called
(*a*) Haloenzymes
(*b*) Prosthetic part
(*c*) Apoenzyme
(*d*) Nanoenzyme

13. Which of the following enzyme was 1st isolated and purified in the form of crystal
(*a*) Urease
(*b*) Pepsin
(*c*) Amylase
(*d*) Ribonuclease

14. Urease enzyme is extracted 1st time from
(*a*) Jack bean
(*b*) Yeast
(*c*) Tomato
(*d*) Jack fruit

15. One of the following, potable water is rich in nitrate caused disease
(*a*) Methaneglobenemia
(*b*) Pneumonia
(*c*) Monomofia disease
(*d*) Loss of appetite

16. Germinating barley seeds are used in preparation of
(*a*) Cheese
(*b*) Wine
(*c*) Beer
(*d*) Lactic acid

17. Whey is the residual part of cheese formation (curd) used for the production of
(*a*) Acetic acid
(*b*) Citric acid
(*c*) Lactic acid
(*d*) Gluconnic acid

18. Wonder drug is also known as
(*a*) Penicillin
(*b*) Streptomycin
(*c*) Insulin
(*d*) Griseoflavin

19. Industrial production of ethanol from starch is brought about by a certain species of
(*a*) Saccharomyces
(*b*) Penicillium
(*c*) Azatobacter
(*d*) Lactobacillus

20. Rennin used in cheese manufacturing is an
(*a*) Antibiotic (*b*) Alkoid
(*c*) Enzyme (*d*) Inhibitor

21. Shikonin is the name of
(*a*) Vitamin (*b*) Enzyme
(*c*) Steroids
(*d*) A red dye used in the manufacturing of cosmetics

22. Which organism is useful in the preparation of Roquefort cheese ?
(*a*) Aspergillus (*b*) Penicillium
(*c*) Rhizopus (*d*) Yeast

23. Which one of these participates in the manufacturing of dextrin ?
(*a*) Leuconostoc (*b*) Pseudomonas
(*c*) Lactobacillus (*d*) Mucor

24. Maximum quantity of alcohol is obtained from
(*a*) Maize (*b*) Sugarcane
(*c*) Wood (*d*) Tapioca

25. The first acid to be produced by fermentation was
(*a*) Lactic acid (*b*) Citric acid
(*c*) Acetic acid (*d*) Malic acid

26. Which enzymes are used for converting corn starch into high fructose syrup?
(*a*) Glucoisomerase (*b*) Glucoamylase
(*c*) Amylase (*d*) All of above

27. The main advantages of waxing on fruits are
(*a*) Reduced moisture loss (*b*) Improved appearances
(*c*) Reduce spoilage due attack of microörganisms
(*d*) All of the above

28 Fungi can produced by the following items
(*a*) Antibiotics (*b*) Vitamins
(*c*) Acid (*d*) All

29. The sour taste of vinegar is due to
(*a*) Acetic acid (*b*) Lactic acid
(*c*) Formic acid (*d*) Citric acid

30. Canning is the method of
(*a*) Spoilage of foods (*b*) Preservation of foods
(*c*) Making plant free from disease (*d*) Isolating bacteria from soils

31. Enzymes are basically
(*a*) Vitamin (*b*) Protein
(*c*) Minerals (*d*) Fat

32. Golden rice is rich source of
(*a*) Vitamin C (*b*) Vitamin A
(*c*) Vitamin D (*d*) Vitamin B_{12}

33. High lysine content is found in
(*a*) Wheat (*b*) Maize
(*c*) Rice (*d*) Bajara

34. Clove is the part of
(*a*) Flower (*b*) Thalamus of flower
(*c*) Auxiliary bud (*d*) Seed

35. Cryopreservation is done at
(*a*) 273 ºC (*b*) –196 ºC
(*c*) 0 ºC (*d*) 273 ºK

36. Geocarpic fruit is
(*a*) Onion (*b*) Water melon
(*c*) Ground nut (*d*) Carrot

37. Lactic acid is produced from one of the following raw material
(*a*) Whey (*b*) Curd
(*c*) Cheese (*d*) Butter

38. Pulses not have the amino acid
(*a*) Methionine, Glycine (*b*) Cysteine, Methionine
(*c*) Lysine, Cysteine (*d*) Tryptophan, Lysine

39. Millets and cereals not have the amino acid
(*a*) Tryptophan, Lysine (*b*) Cysteine, Methionine
(*c*) Lysine, Glycine (*d*) Cysteine, Tryptophan

40. The enzyme is capable of lysising (dissolving) the cell wall of bacteria.
(*a*) Lysozyme (*b*) Lipase
(*c*) Rennin (*d*) Protease

41. The factors, by which the growth of microorganisms are influenced.
(*a*) Moisture (*b*) Oxygen
(*c*) Food supply (*d*) All of the above

42. Which one of the following group of bacteria can not tolerate relatively low and high temperature?
(*a*) Psychrophytic (*b*) Mesophyllic
(*c*) Thermodiuric (*d*) Thermophyllic

43. The first and most important change occurs in milk due to bacterial activity is making of
(*a*) Lactic acid (*b*) Citric acid
(*c*) Butyric acid (*d*) Malic acid

44. Botulism is an example or type of
(*a*) Food intoxication (*b*) Food infection
(*c*) Both of these (*d*) None of these

45. The microorganism responsible for botulism in food intoxication is
(*a*) Streptococcus botulinum (*b*) Salmonella botulinum
(*c*) Clostridium botulinum (*d*) All of these

46. In botulism, the toxin produced in food which is ingested by *Clostridium botulinum* is a
(*a*) Mycotoxin (*b*) Aflatoxin
(*c*) Neurotoxin (*d*) Haemotoxin

47. Clostridium botulinum is
(*a*) Aerobic bacteria (*b*) Anaerobic bacteria
(*c*) Facultative anaerobic (*d*) Facultative aerobic

48. Which of the following bacterium are not involved in spoilage of the finished cheese?
(*a*) Cladosporium (*b*) Penicillium pubervulum
(*c*) PM nigra (*d*) Pseudomonas fragae

49. Sauerkraut is a fermented product made from the
(*a*) Tomato (*b*) Cabbage
(*c*) Cauliflower (*d*) Barley

50. The best quality sauerkraut should contain ___________ percent salt by weight.
(*a*) 3.0-4.0 (*b*) 2.25-2.5
(*c*) 2.0-2.25 (*d*) 1.0-2.0

51. Slimy or ropy kraut is caused by
(*a*) *Lactobacillus plantarum* (*b*) *Lactobacillus brewis*
(*c*) *Leuconostoc* (*d*) *Lactobacillus aceti*

52. Blackening of pickles is caused due to the formation of
(*a*) Ferrous sulphate (*b*) Ferric sulphate
(*c*) Lead tannate (*d*) None of these

53. Blackening of pickles is also caused due to black pigmented bacteria which is
(*a*) *Bacillus nigrificans* var. subtilis
(*b*) *Pseudomonas nigrificans* var. subtilis
(*c*) *Leuconostoc*
(*d*) *None of these*

54. Among the following which bacteria is rod-shaped?
(*a*) Streptococcus
(*b*) Micrococcus
(*c*) Sarcina
(*d*) Capsulated

55. Which bacteria can transmit food borne infection and also capable of causing human diseases?
(*a*) Clostridium perfringens
(*b*) Salmonella
(*c*) Shigella
(*d*) All of above

56. Name of the bacteria causes neurotoxicity is
(*a*) Clostridium botulinum
(*b*) Campylobacter jejuni
(*c*) Shigella dysenterial
(*d*) Bacillus cercus

57. Name of important food borne parasite is
(*a*) Tape worm
(*b*) Trichinosis nematode
(*c*) Flat worm
(*d*) Bug

58. The temperature which double the chemical reaction takes place in food products is
(*a*) 10ºC
(*b*) 20ºC
(*c*) 30ºC
(*d*) 40ºC

59. How much concentration of nitrogen and oxygen in air is?
(*a*) 79% and 20%
(*b*) 69% and 30%
(*c*) 50% and 50%
(*d*) 75% and 23%

60. Among the following which are destroyed by sun light?
(*a*) Riboflavin
(*b*) Vitamin A and C
(*c*) Food colour
(*d*) All of above

61. What is the optimum temperature for the growth of microorganisms?
(*a*) 12-14ºC
(*b*) 16-32ºC
(*c*) 16-18ºC
(*d*) 16-38ºC

62. What is the important feature of 'Psychrtrophs'?
(*a*) Can grow at 4ºC
(*b*) Are parasites
(*c*) Can grow down to 0ºC
(*d*) None of these

63. The higher humidity produce
(*a*) Lower population of microorganisms
(*b*) Higher population of microorganisms
(*c*) Average population of microorganisms
(*d*) None of these

64. The term 'water activity' is related to
(*a*) Absolute Humidity
(*b*) Equilibrium Relative humidity
(*c*) Action of water on food
(*d*) All of these

65. How an acid affect the microorganism when combined with heat
(*a*) Destruction of microorganisms
(*b*) Provide good condition for growth of microorganism
(*c*) Increase the aerobic reaction
(*d*) Denaturates of their food protein

66. Smoke acts as
(*a*) Good preservative
(*b*) Poor preservative
(*c*) Very poor preservative
(*d*) None of these

67. Smoke used as colour enhancer in
(*a*) Meat processing
(*b*) Milk processing
(*c*) Vegetable processing
(*d*) Cereal processing

68. What is the main role of FDA?
(*a*) Ensure how much chemical to be used in food
(*b*) The temperature at which food is kept
(*c*) How to increase the growth of food
(*d*) Both (*a*) and (*b*)

69. In which food product, sorbic acid is used as inhibitor to control the growth of mould.
(*a*) Mushroom
(*b*) Cheese
(*c*) Leafy vegetables
(*d*) Fruits

70. Heat preservation of food is generally done in the form of
(*a*) Dehydration/drying
(*b*) Pasteurization/sterilization
(*c*) Canning
(*d*) All the above

71. Among the following, the most heat resistance pathogens found in food.
(*a*) Clostridium botulinum
(*b*) Bacillus stearothermophilus
(*c*) Micrococcus
(*d*) Both (*a*) and (*b*)

72. Heat energy is transferred by
(*a*) Conduction
(*b*) Convection
(*c*) Radiation
(*d*) All of the above

73. In natural convection, the heated portion of food becomes
(*a*) Lighter in density
(*b*) Higher in density
(*c*) Higher in mass
(*d*) Both (*a*) and (*c*)

74. At which temperature the best quality juice is retained after pasteurization.
(*a*) 63ºC for 30 min
(*b*) 88ºC for 1 min
(*c*) 100ºC for 12 sec
(*d*) 121ºC for 2 sec

75. HTST stands for
(*a*) Hot temperature short time
(*b*) High temperature short time
(*c*) High time short temperature
(*d*) None of them

76. GMP stands for
(*a*) Good manufacturing practices
(*b*) Gene modified products
(*c*) Gas modified packaging
(*d*) None of them

77. Aseptic packaging is generally used in
(*a*) Food pasteurization
(*b*) Food sterilization
(*c*) Food fermentation
(*d*) Food sanitization

78. What should be the temperature of commercial and house hold refrigerator?
(*a*) 6-8ºC
(*b*) 4.5-7ºC
(*c*) 6-10ºC
(*d*) 5-7ºC

79. Air blast freezers are typically operated at temperature of ________ with forced air velocity is of ________.
(*a*) –30 to – 45ºC and 10-15 m/s
(*b*) – 10 to – 35ºC and 10-15 m/s
(*c*) –2 to – 10ºC and 10-15 m/s
(*d*) 30 to 45ºC and 10-15 m/s

80. The principal requirements of effective refrigerator storage are
(*a*) Controlled temperature
(*b*) Air circulation
(*c*) Humidity control
(*d*) Modification of gas atmosphere
(*e*) All of these

81. The freezing rate will be faster when
(*a*) The temperature difference between food and refrigerant is greater
(*b*) The thinner the food piece or greater the heat transfer rate of the food package
(*c*) The greater the velocity of refrigerated air
(*d*) The more intimate the contact between the food and cooling medium
(*e*) All of the above

82. The term 'food dehydration' generally refers
(*a*) To artificial drying under controlled condition
(*b*) To remove the water upto predetermined level
(*c*) To dry food upto bone dry condition
(*d*) Both (*a*) and (*c*)

83. Dehydrated foods will be
(*a*) Dry
(*b*) Hygroscopic
(*c*) Bone dry
(*d*) Having high relative humidity

84. In the principal cereals, the percentage of carbohydrate is about
(*a*) 10-14%
(*b*) 58-72%
(*c*) 8-13%
(*d*) 2-5 %

85. IRRI is related to________________ and located at________________.
(*a*) Rice, Mexico
(*b*) Rice, Philippines
(*c*) Rape seed, Bharatpur
(*d*) Rice, Rome

86. The protein content is higher in
(*a*) Cereals
(*b*) Pulses and legumes
(*c*) Oil seeds
(*d*) Fruit and vegetables

87. Peanut is a
(*a*) Cereal
(*b*) Pulse
(*c*) Oil seed
(*d*) Legume

88. The water content is comparatively
(*a*) Lower in milk, higher in apple
(*b*) Higher in milk, lower in apple
(*c*) Similar in milk as well as in apple
(*d*) None of these

89. Among the following which pigment is termed as flavonoid
(*a*) Chlorophyll
(*b*) Carotenoid
(*c*) Anthocyanin
(*d*) Anthoxanthens
(*e*) Both (*c*) and (*d*)

90. Betalains are
(*a*) Green water soluble pigment
(*b*) Green water in soluble pigment
(*c*) Red water in soluble pigment
(*d*) Red water soluble pigment

91. Flavonoids are
(*a*) pH sensitive
(*b*) pH resistant
(*c*) tending toward deeper yellow in alkaline medium
(*d*) both (*a*) and (*c*)

92. The mild stimulant used in cola flavour is
(*a*) Opium
(*b*) Caffeine
(*c*) Nicotine
(*d*) Solanine

93. Starches are
(*a*) Sweet
(*b*) Readily soluble in cold water
(*c*) They form paste and gel in hot water
(*d*) They not occur in cereals.

94. Fats are
(*a*) Gradually softer on heating
(*b*) Not form emulsion with water and air
(*c*) as lubricant in foods
(*d*) Both (*a*) and (*c*)

95. Lecithin are
(*a*) Structurally like fats
(*b*) Contain phosphoric acid
(*c*) They have a polar and a non polar end
(*d*) All of the above

96. Lipase enzyme are used as
(*a*) Chill proofing of buns and related products
(*b*) Classification of fruit juices
(*c*) Removal of glucose from egg white before drying
(*d*) Improvement in whipping quality of dried egg white and flavour production in cheese and chocolate.

97. Which vitamin is also called α-tocopherol?
(*a*) Vitamin E
(*b*) Vitamin B
(*c*) Vitamin C
(*d*) Vitamin K

98. Among the following which one is known as nicotinamide in the United Kingdom
(*a*) Riboflavin
(*b*) Folacin
(*c*) Niacin
(*d*) Biotin

99. Vitamin B_6 is the name given to closely related substances such as
(*a*) Pyridoxine
(*b*) Pyridoxal
(*c*) Pyridoxamine
(*d*) All of the above

100. Those foods, do not spoil unless handled carelessly are called
(*a*) Highly perishable
(*b*) Semi perishable
(*c*) Perishable
(*d*) Non-perishable

101. Those foods are properly handled and stored; they will remain unspoiled for a fairly long period are known as
(*a*) Highly perishable
(*b*) Semi perishable
(*c*) Perishable
(*d*) Non-perishable

102. The group includes important daily foods that spoils readily unless special preservatives methods are used and termed as
(*a*) Highly perishable
(*b*) Semi perishable
(*c*) Perishable
(*d*) Stable foods

103. The flour and sugar are classified as
(*a*) Highly perishable
(*b*) Semi perishable
(*c*) Perishable
(*d*) Stable foods

104. Leafy vegetables is recommended as
(*a*) Highly perishable (*b*) Semi perishable
(*c*) Perishable (*d*) Non-perishable

105. A dry food such as bread is most likely to be spoiled by
(*a*) Bacteria (*b*) Yeast
(*c*) Molds (*d*) Virus

106. The moist or neutral foods such as milk, meat, fish and egg ordinarily are spoiled by
(*a*) Molds (*b*) Yeast
(*c*) Bacteria (*d*) Virus

107. In which process, microorganisms are not destroyed?
(*a*) Drying and dehydration (*b*) Irradiation
(*c*) Sterilization (*d*) Freezing

108. Which one of the process is the reverse of freezing?
(*a*) Drying (*b*) Thawing
(*c*) Blanching (*d*) Aseptic processing

109. In growth of microbial culture, the phase in which, there is no growth or even a decline in numbers of microorganisms is called
(*a*) Lag phase (*b*) Exponential phase
(*c*) Death phase (*d*) Positive acceleration phase

110. The phase in which the rate of growth is continuously increasing is termed as
(*a*) Lag phase (*b*) Exponential phase
(*c*) Positive acceleration phase (*d*) Logarithmic phase

111. The phase in which the rate of multiplication is most rapid and is constant is known as
(*a*) Lag phase (*b*) Exponential phase
(*c*) Death phase (*d*) Survival phase

112. The phase during which no cell division occurs but remaining cells survive on endogenous nutrients is called
(*a*) Lag phase (*b*) Logarithmic phase
(*c*) Survival phase (*d*) Death phase

113. In special conditions, removal of microorganisms from food may be accomplished by
(*a*) Filtration
(*b*) Centrifugation or sedimentation or clarification
(*c*) Washing or trimming
(*d*) All of these

114. The foods contain pH above 5.3 are known as
(*a*) Low acid foods (*b*) Medium acid foods
(*c*) Acid foods (*d*) High acid foods

115. One of the following is on example of low acid foods.
(*a*) Peas (*b*) Asparagus
(*c*) Pears (*d*) Cape goose berry

116. The pH of high acidic foods should be
(*a*) Above 5.3 (*b*) 3.7 and below
(*c*) 5.3 – 4.5 (*d*) 4.5-3.7

117. Tomato, pears and pine apples are acid foods contain the pH value between
(*a*) 5.3-4.5 (*b*) 3.7 and below
(*c*) 4.5-3.7 (*d*) Above 5.3

118. Medium acid foods like spinach and pumpkin having pH between
(*a*) 3.7 and below (*b*) 4.5-3.7
(*c*) 5.3-4.5 (*d*) Above 5.3

119. Most of the molds and their spores are killed by moist heat at
(*a*) 60°C in 5 to 10 min. (*b*) 60°C in 15 to 20 min.
(*c*) 50°C in 5 to 10 min. (*d*) None of these

120. The thermal death time of bacterial spore of *Clostridium botulinum* at 100°C is
(*a*) 10-20 min (*b*) 50-100 min
(*c*) 100-330 min (*d*) 20-50 min

121. Generally TDT curve is plotted on
(*a*) Simple graph paper (*b*) Semi log paper
(*c*) Log-log paper (*d*) Plain paper

122. The symbol 'D' in thermo-bacteriology is indicated for
(*a*) Dehydration (*b*) Drying
(*c*) Diffusion (*d*) Decimal reduction time

123. The time of heating at a specified temperature required to destroy 90 percent of organisms in a population is known as
(*a*) F-value (*b*) D-value
(*c*) Z-value (*d*) F_0- value

124. The D-value, decimal reduction time decreased the surviving population by
(*a*) One log cycle (*b*) Two log cycle
(*c*) Ten log cycle (*d*) None of these

125. The time in minutes required to destroy the organisms in a specified medium at 250°F (121.1°C) is referred as
(*a*) F-value (*b*) Z-value
(*c*) D-value (*d*) None of these

126. The degree Fahrenheit required to reduce the TDT tenfold is called
(*a*) F-value (*b*) Z-value
(*c*) D-value (*d*) None of these

127. Heat penetration into container for sterilization is dependent on
(*a*) Size, shape and material of container
(*b*) Temperature of food and retort
(*c*) Consistency of can content and size and shape of foods
(*d*) All of the above

128. The monograph method is most rapid for the estimation of
(*a*) Thermal process time (*b*) Drying time
(*c*) Freezing time (*d*) Blanching time

129. The heat treatment that kills part but not all of microorganisms below 100°C temperature is referred as
(*a*) Sterilization (*b*) Pasteurization
(*c*) Heat at about 100°C (*d*) Blanching

130. Temperature and time combination in ultra pasteurization method employed for milk is
(*a*) 62.8°C for 30 min (*b*) 71.7°C for 15 sec
(*c*) 137.8°C for at least 2 sec (*d*) 121.1°C for 30 min

131. The average heat treatment for carbonated juice would be
(*a*) 65.6°C for 30 min (*b*) 62.8°C for 30 min
(*c*) 60°C for 30 min (*d*) 85 to 87.8°C for 30 sec

132. Thermal treatment for apple juice in can and bulk form would be done at
(*a*) 65.6°C for 30 min (*b*) 62.8°C for 30 min
(*c*) 60°C and 85 to 87.8°C for 30 to 60 sec (*d*) none

133. Dried fruits usually are pasteurized in the packaged at
(*a*) 65.6°C to 85°C for 30-90 min (*b*) 72°C for 15 sec
(*c*) 68.2°C for 30 min (*d*) 85 to 87.8°C for 30 sec

134. The process of hermetically sealing of foods in container and sterilizing by heat treatment for long period of storage is known as
(*a*) Canning (*b*) Aseptic packaging
(*c*) Dehydration (*d*) Irradiation

135. The father of canning is
(*a*) Spllanzani
(*b*) Nicolas Appert
(*c*) Robert Kotch
(*d*) Louise Pasteur

136. Tomato juice may be pasteurized to kill spores of *Bacillus coagulaus* before canning at
(*a*) 121 to 132°C
(*b*) 121°C
(*c*) 137.8°C
(*d*) 71.7°C

137. Carbon dioxide under pressurize packaged food inhibit various microorganism like
(*a*) Aerobic bacteria and molds
(*b*) Yeasts
(*c*) LAB
(*d*) None

138. Mold infection in bread can be prevented by adding of
(*a*) Salts
(*b*) Sugar
(*c*) Sodium benzoate
(*d*) Sodium and calcium propionate

139. Ropiness of bread can be eliminated by adding of
(*a*) Citrate
(*b*) Sorbate
(*c*) Pectate
(*d*) Propionate

140. The basic purpose of smoking in foods is
(*a*) Adding desired flavour
(*b*) Preserving the food
(*c*) Improvement in colour
(*d*) Tenderizing action on meat
(*e*) All of the above

141. Smoking temperature for meat vary between
(*a*) 20-30°C
(*b*) 30-42°C
(*c*) 43-71°C
(*d*) 71-85°C

142. Wood smoke used for food contains a large number of volatile compounds that may have
(*a*) Bacteriostatic effect
(*b*) Bacteriocidal effect
(*c*) Fungicidal effect
(*d*) Both (*a*) and (*b*)

143. The rate of germicidal action of smoke increases with
(*a*) Its concentration
(*b*) Temperature
(*c*) Above both
(*d*) None of these

144. Wood smoke is more effective against vegetative cells than
(*a*) Bacterial spore
(*b*) Fungi
(*c*) Yeast and molds
(*d*) None of these

145. The concentration of mycostatic material from wood smoke necessary to prevent mold growth increases with in the
(*a*) Humidity of storage
(*b*) Temperature of storage
(*c*) Gas composition of storage
(*d*) Oxygen concentration

146. Mustard flour and the volatile oil of mustard are very effective against
(*a*) *Saccharomyces cerevisiae* (*b*) *Clostridium botulinum*
(*c*) *Aspergillus* (*d*) *Salmonella*

147. One of the following is most effective against yeast
(*a*) Volatile oil of mustard (*b*) Oil of cinnamon and cloves
(*c*) Oil of thyme and bay leaves (*d*) None of them

148. Halogen kill organism during washing of foods or equipments by
(*a*) Oxidation (*b*) Injury to cell membranes
(*c*) Direct combination with cell proteins (*d*) All of the above

149. Hypochlorite treated water in food processing plants is used for
(*a*) Drinking (*b*) Processing
(*c*) Cooling (*d*) Washing
(*e*) All of the above

150. An oxidizing agent like hydrogen peroxide (H_2O_2) is employed as a preservative along with
(*a*) Water (*b*) Humidity
(*c*) Heat (*d*) Acid

151. One of the following bacteria are destroyed in the processing of sugar by a combination of heat and hydrogen peroxide
(*a*) Thermoduric (*b*) Thermophiles
(*c*) Osmophilic (*d*) Saccharolytic

152. One of the following is used as an inert gas over foods that should not be exposed to air.
(*a*) Hydrogen dioxide (*b*) Hydrogen peroxide
(*c*) Nitrogen (*d*) Sulphur dioxide

153. Antifungal antibiotics include
(*a*) Grisefulvin (*b*) Pimaricin
(*c*) Fulcine and actidione (*d*) Rimacidin and nystalin
(*e*) All of the above

154. Antimycotics permitted in food packaging materials (under specified conditions) are
(*a*) Na and Ca propionate (*b*) Na benzoate
(*c*) Sorbic acid and sorbates (*d*) Methyl and propyl parabens
(*e*) All of these

155. Which one antibiotic has been used in Europe to suppress anaerobes in cheese and cheese products?
(*a*) Nisin (*b*) Natamycin
(*c*) Neomycin (*d*) Bacitracin

156. Natamycin is effective against
(*a*) Bacteria
(*b*) Vegetative spore
(*c*) Yeast and molds
(*d*) None of above

157. Microbial destruction without the generation of high temperature suggest the term
(*a*) Cold sterilization
(*b*) Oxidation
(*c*) Chemical sterilization
(*d*) None of the above

158. The factors that influence the effectiveness of UV rays on foods are
(*a*) Time
(*b*) Intensity
(*c*) Penetration
(*d*) All of the above

159. The quantity or dose of irradiation actually absorbed by an organism or products thus is expressed by the product of
(*a*) Time and intensity
(*b*) Time and specific gravity
(*c*) Mass and intensity
(*d*) Moisture content and intensity

160. The UV rays affect only ____________ of most irradiate food directly to the UV lamp.
(*a*) Inner surface
(*b*) Outer surface
(*c*) Front side of UV rays
(*d*) Whole product

161. One of the following is most resistant against the rays of UV lamp.
(*a*) Bacteria
(*b*) Mold
(*c*) Yeast
(*d*) None

162. The resistance of mold in comparison to bacteria exposed to UV rays is more than
(*a*) 2 to 5 times
(*b*) 5 to 15 times
(*c*) 1 to 3 times
(*d*) Equal

163. Which one ionizing radiation is used to preserve food economically?
(*a*) x-rays
(*b*) γ-rays
(*c*) β-rays
(*d*) photon

164. The quantity of γ-rays or x-radiations which produces one electrostatic unit of electric charge of either sign in a cubic centimeter of air under standard condition is termed as
(*a*) Roentgen (r)
(*b*) Roentgen-equivalent- physical (rep)
(*c*) 1 rad
(*d*) 1MeV

165. The unit of radiation dosage, being equivalent to the absorption of 100 erg per gram of irradiated material is called
(*a*) rad
(*b*) Mrad
(*c*) Krad
(*d*) MeV

166. The radiation dose like 1Krad is equivalent to
(*a*) 100 rad
(*b*) 1000 rad
(*c*) 10000 rad
(*d*) 100000 rad

167. An electron volt (eV) is the energy gained by a/an __________ in moving through a potential difference of 1 volt.
(*a*) Neutron
(*b*) Electron
(*c*) Proton
(*d*) Photon

168. A MeV is the measurement of
(*a*) Intensity of irradiation
(*b*) Absorbed energy
(*c*) Dose of irradiation
(*d*) All of these

169. A rep is a measure of the __________ that is effective within the foods.
(*a*) Intensity of irradiation
(*b*) Dose of irradiation
(*c*) Absorbed energy
(*d*) None of these

170. Radiation sterilization which would imply high dose treatment, with the resulting product being shelf life stable is also known as
(*a*) Radurization
(*b*) Radicidation
(*c*) Radappertization
(*d*) Picowaved

171. 'Commercially sterile' means
(*a*) Kill all microorganisms but some are unable to grow during storage
(*b*) Completely destruction of all microorganisms
(*c*) Partially killing of microorganisms by thermal treatment
(*d*) Any one (*b*) or (*c*)

172. Pressurized packaged liquids or paste are packed under pressure of a propellant gas is called
(*a*) Aerosols
(*b*) Tetra pack
(*c*) Ultra pack
(*d*) Vacuum pack

173. Carbon dioxide under pressure inhibit various microorganism including
(*a*) Aerobic bacteria and molds
(*b*) Anaerobic bacteria and molds
(*c*) Yeast and molds
(*d*) None of these

174. Low temperature preservation are used to
(*a*) Retard biochemical reaction
(*b*) Retard of enzymatic activity
(*c*) Slow down or stop the growth and activity of microorganisms
(*d*) Above all

175. Which one of the following prevents the growth of most food borne microorganisms?
(*a*) Freezing
(*b*) Refrigeration
(*c*) Commercial refrigeration
(*d*) All of the above

176. Refrigeration temperature is used to
(*a*) Prevent the growth of microorganisms
(*b*) Slow down the growth rates
(*c*) Increase the growth rate
(*d*) No change in growth rate

177. Commercial refrigeration temperature retards the growth of various food borne pathogens at
(*a*) Lower than 5 to 7.2°C
(*b*) More than 7.2°C
(*c*) 10°C
(*d*) 121°C

178. *Clostridium botulinum* type E which has a minimum temperature for growth of about
(*a*) 0°C
(*b*) –3.3°C
(*c*) 3.3°C
(*d*) 10°C

179. The use of temperature above or below freezing, although the application of mechanical refrigeration is implied in
(*a*) Cold storage
(*b*) Freezing
(*c*) Refrigeration
(*d*) Commercial sterile

180. Most commercial storage freezer are used
(*a*) At or below –18°C
(*b*) Above –18°C
(*c*) At 18°C
(*d*) At –10°C

181. A high alcohol yielding variety of yeast used to produce industrial alcohol, wine and distilled liquors is
(*a*) *S. cerevisiae var. ellipsoideus*
(*b*) *S. uvarum*
(*c*) *S. fragilis*
(*d*) *S. lactis*

182. Yeast grow in soy sauce with its high content of salt of
(*a*) 18 %
(*b*) 20 %
(*c*) 3 %
(*d*) 1 %

183. Osmophilic yeasts grow well in food which has
(*a*) High concentration of sugar or salt
(*b*) Low concentration of sugar or salt
(*c*) Normal concentration of sugar or salt
(*d*) All of the above

184. The range of temperature for growth of most yeasts are, in general to that molds, with the optimum around __________ and the maximum about__________.
(*a*) 25-30°C and 35-47°C
(*b*) 10-15°C and 25-30°C
(*c*) 15-20°C and 30-35°C
(*d*) None of these

185. Enzymatic and microbial changes due to chilling in food is
(*a*) Prevented
(*b*) Not prevented
(*c*) Slowed considerably
(*d*) Both (*b*) and (*c*)

186. The chilling temperature for any food is selected on the basis of
(*a*) Kind of food
(*b*) Time of storage
(*c*) Condition of storage
(*d*) All

187. The banana should be kept in the refrigerator; it keeps best at temperature of
(*a*) 13.3 to 16.7°C (*b*) 8 to 10°C
(*c*) 0 to 8°C (*d*) 10 to 20°C

188. Too low relative humidity, what would be happen in foods?
(*a*) Loss of moisture and weight (*b*) Wilting and softening of the vegetables
(*c*) Shrinkage of fruits (*d*) All of these

189. Changes in humidity as well as in temperature during low temperature storage of foods may cause
(*a*) Sweating or precipitation of moisture (*b*) Shrinkage of fruits
(*c*) Drying of foods (*d*) None of these

190. In the presence of optimal concentration of CO_2 or O_3 in CAP with chilling storage,
(*a*) A food will remain unspoiled for a longer period
(*b*) A higher RH can be maintained without harm to keeping quality of certain foods
(*c*) A high storage temperature can be used without shortening the keeping time of the food than is possible with ordinary chilling storage
(*d*) All of the above

191. The rate of freezing of food depends upon
(*a*) Method employed and freezing temperature (*b*) Circulation of air or refrigerant
(*c*) Size and shape of package (*d*) Kind of food
(*e*) All of the above

192. Temperature and time combination in sharp freezing for foods are as
(*a*) –15 to –29°C and 3-72 hr (*b*) –17.8 to – 45.6°C and 2hr
(*c*) –17.8 to –34.4°C and 10 hr (*d*) None

193. Quick freezing of food is accomplished by
(*a*) Direct immersion of food or packaged foods in a refrigerant
(*b*) Indirect contact with refrigerant
(*c*) Air blast
(*d*) All of the above

194. Optimum temperature of sharp freezing used to frozen the food is
(*a*) –23.3°C (*b*) – 45.6°C
(*c*) –17.8°C (*d*) 34.4°C

195. In indirect contact method of quick freezing, the temperature of refrigerant is
(*a*) –23.3°C (*b*) –17.8 to –45.6 °C
(*c*) –17.8 to –34.4°C (*d*) None

196. Air blast freezing method freeze the food at the temperature of
(*a*) –17.8 to –34.4°C (*b*) –15 to –29°C
(*c*) –23.5°C (*d*) –17.8 to – 45.6°C

197. The freezing method in which half moisture is removed from food before freezing is called
(*a*) Freeze drying (*b*) Dehydro-freezing
(*c*) Dehydration (*d*) Osmotic dehydration

198. The advantages of quick freezing over slow freezing are
(*a*) Smaller ice crystal formation (*b*) Shorter period of solidification
(*c*) Quick prevention of microbial growth (*d*) Rapid slow down of enzyme activity
(*e*) All of these

199. When ice crystal of frozen food evaporate from an area at the surface, the defect is called
(*a*) Freezer burn (*b*) Chilling injury
(*c*) Freezing injury (*d*) Cold shock

200. The pink or reddish liquid that comes from meat during thawing is called
(*a*) Drip or bleeding (*b*) Metacryotic liquid
(*c*) Leakage (*d*) Cold shock

201. The liquid oozing out from fruits or vegetables on thawing is referred as
(*a*) Drip (*b*) Sweating
(*c*) Leakage (*d*) Seepage

202. Rapid cooling of cells from an optimal temperature to 0°C can also results in death referred as
(*a*) Freezer burn (*b*) Chilling injury
(*c*) Cold shock (*d*) Freezing injury

203. Best quality dried product of coffee, milk, tea and fruits puree is obtained by using the one following drier
(*a*) Drum drier (*b*) Rotary drier
(*c*) Spray drier (*d*) Freeze drier

204. Liquid food should be comparatively dried at
(*a*) low temperature and under vacuum (*b*) high temperature and under vacuum
(*c*) low temperature and high RH (*d*) high temperature and high RH

205. Case hardening in food takes place by
(*a*) Freezing (*b*) Improper drying
(*c*) Chilling (*d*) Drying

206. The factors that affect the drying of any food products are
(*a*) Temperature and RH of hot air
(*b*) Velocity of air
(*c*) Drying time and drying method
(*d*) All of the above

207. Before drying, fruits are treated by SO_2 with the amount of
(*a*) 100-200 ppm (*b*) 350-600 ppm
(*c*) 600-905 ppm (*d*) 1000-3000 ppm

208. Most foods are packed just after drying from the protection against
(*a*) Moisture (*b*) Microbial Contamination
(*c*) Infestation with insect (*d*) All of the above

209. The predominant kinds of organisms in dry milk are
(*a*) Thermoduric streptococci (*b*) Micrococci
(*c*) Sporeformers (*d*) All of these

210. The foods which contain 20 to 40 percent moisture and have non refrigerated shelf stability is referred as
(*a*) Flesh product (*b*) Protective product
(*c*) Colloid (*d*) Intermediate moisture foods

211. Which one of the following is not a intermediate moisture foods.
(*a*) Jam (*b*) Jelly
(*c*) RTS (*d*) Honey

212. The effect of water activity (a_w) on microorganisms in foods is influenced by
(*a*) pH and temperature (*b*) oxygen level
(*c*) nutritional concentration (*d*) all of the above

213. The water activity (a_w) of most intermediate moisture foods would be between
(*a*) 0.10-0.30 (*b*) 0.32-0.45
(*c*) 0.46-0.72 (*d*) 0.75-0.85

214. The water activity (a_w) of foods usually adjusted by
(*a*) Drying (*b*) Additives (sugar or salt)
(*c*) Combination of drying and additives (*d*) All

215. Those foods additives which are specifically added to prevent the deterioration or decomposition of a food have been referred to as
(*a*) Physical preservatives (*b*) Chemical preservatives
(*c*) Biological preservative (*d*) None

216. The additives in food are added when deterioration may be caused by
(*a*) Microorganism (*b*) Food enzymes
(*c*) Purely Chemical reaction (*d*) All of the above

217. The inhibition of growth and activity of microorganisms is the one of the main purpose of the use of
(*a*) Pasteurization (*b*) Blanching
(*c*) Chemical preservatives (*d*) None of these

218. Preservative may inhibit microorganism by interfering with their
(*a*) cell membrane (*b*) enzyme activity
(*c*) genetic mechanism (*d*) all of the above

219. The effectiveness of chemical preservatives depend upon
(*a*) Concentration of chemical (*b*) Kind and number of organisms
(*c*) Time and temperature
(*d*) Physical-chemical characteristics of substrate in which organism is found
(*e*) All of these

220. Physio-chemical characteristic of substrate means
(*a*) Moisture and pH (*b*) Kind and amount of solute
(*c*) Surface tension (*d*) Colloids and other protective substance
(*e*) All of the above

221. A chemical preservative have a wide range of antimicrobial activity and should be
(*a*) Non toxic and economic
(*b*) No effect on flavour, taste or aroma of original food
(*c*) Should not encourage the development of resistant strain
(*d*) All

222. Antimicrobial preservative added to foods can be classified on the basis of
(*a*) Those added preservative not defined as such by low
(*b*) Substances generally recognized as safe for addition to foods
(*c*) Chemical considered to be food additives
(*d*) Chemical proved safe and approved by the USFDA
(*e*) All of these

223. Preservatives added to inhibit or kill microorganisms may be classified on their
(*a*) Chemical composition (*b*) Mode of action
(*c*) Specificity or effectiveness (*d*) Legality
(*e*) All of the above

224. Sugar, salt, oil, spices and essence are classified into
(*a*) Preservative class I
(*b*) Preservative class II
(*c*) Both above
(*d*) None

225. One of the following organic acids is used in syrup, drinks, jam and jelly as substitute for fruit flavour and preservation
(*a*) Lactic acid
(*b*) Citric acid
(*c*) Benzoic acid
(*d*) Acetic acid

226. Lactic acid or acetic acid are used in foods along with
(*a*) Brine
(*b*) Sugar syrup
(*c*) Corn syrup
(*d*) None

227. Na or Ca propionate is used extensively in the
(*a*) Cheese and spreads
(*b*) Baked items
(*c*) Dairy confectionary foods
(*d*) All of the above

228. The basic purpose of Na or Ca propionate to be used in food for
(*a*) Prevention of mold growth
(*b*) Prevention of rope development
(*c*) Regulation of acidity
(*d*) Both (*a*) and (*b*)

229. The effectiveness of Na or Ca propionate decreases with
(*a*) increase in pH
(*b*) increase in acidity
(*c*) decrease pH
(*d*) increase relative humidity

230. The effectiveness of sodium benzoate increases with
(*a*) increase in pH
(*b*) increase in acidity
(*c*) constant pH
(*d*) increase relative humidity

231. The pH at which sodium benzoate is most effective against growth of bacteria is
(*a*) 2.5 – 4.0
(*b*) 4.0 – 4.5
(*c*) 5.0 – 6.5
(*d*) Above 7.0

232. Sorbic acid and its salts are used as direct antimicrobial additives in food in the form of
(*a*) Spray
(*b*) Dip
(*c*) Coating on packaging material
(*d*) All of these

233. Sorbic acid and its salts are known to inhibit the
(*a*) Yeast
(*b*) Molds
(*c*) Bacteria
(*d*) Both (*a*) and (*b*)

234. Sorbets are more effective than sodium benzoate at the pH value above
(*a*) 2.0
(*b*) 4.0
(*c*) 6.0
(*d*) 7.0

235. One of the following is not added in fruits juices.
(*a*) Propionate (*b*) Benzoate
(*c*) Sorbate (*d*) Sulpher dioxide

236. One of the following is mostly used in pickles and sauce/ketchup
(*a*) Calcium Propionate (*b*) Sodium benzoate
(*c*) Potassium sorbate (*d*) Acetic acid

237. Which antimicrobial preservative is not added in jam and jelly?
(*a*) Propionate (*b*) Benzoate
(*c*) Sorbate (*d*) Acetate

238. The combination of nitrates and nitrites used in curing of
(*a*) Pickles (*b*) Cheese
(*c*) Meat (*d*) Egg

239. Nitrite can react with secondary and tertiary amines to form nitrosamine which is known as
(*a*) Carcinogenic (*b*) Oxidation
(*c*) Flocculation adsorption (*d*) None

240. The problem of possible carcinogenic nitrosamine may be greatest in
(*a*) Bacon (*b*) Beef
(*c*) Pork (*d*) Mutton

241. Sulphur dioxide are used in food to prevent
(*a*) Microbial load
(*b*) Prevent enzymatic and non enzymatic reaction
(*c*) Disclouration of some foods
(*d*) All of these

242. Ethylene oxide and propylene oxide used for
(*a*) Sterilizing packaging material (*b*) Fumigation of ware house
(*c*) Cold sterilization of surgical items (*d*) All of these

243. The FDA restricted the used of ethylene oxide in
(*a*) Spices (*b*) Processed natural seasoning
(*c*) Both (*a*) and (*b*) (*d*) None

244. Effect of sugar and salt on water activity of foods
(*a*) Decreased (*b*) Increased
(*c*) Remain same (*d*) Increased then decreased

245. High sugar concentration as preservatives is used in
(*a*) Sweetened condensed milk (*b*) Fruit in syrup
(*c*) Jam, jelly and candies (*d*) All of the above

246. Ethanol is most germicidal in the concentration between
(*a*) 5-10% (*b*) 10-25%
(*c*) 25-70% (*d*) 70-95%

247. Flavour extract e.g., vanilla and lemon extract are preserved along with
(*a*) Ethanol (*b*) Formaldehyde
(*c*) Glycerol (*d*) Propylene glycol

248. The effectiveness of NaCl in foods varies directly with its
(*a*) Concentration (*b*) Temperature
(*c*) Salinity (*d*) Both (*a*) and (*b*)

249. Most bacteria, yeast and molds grow best in the temperature range of about
(*a*) 10-20°C (*b*) 30-40°C
(*c*) 16-38°C (*d*) Above 40°C

250. Bread is prepared by
(*a*) Yeast (*b*) Bacteria
(*c*) Fungus (*d*) Molds

251. Most of the bacteria are killed at temperature range of
(*a*) 80-90°C (*b*) 82-93°C
(*c*) 95-100°C (*d*) 100-105°C

252. The greatest drawback at present to the use of x-rays in food preservation is
(*a*) Low efficiency (*b*) High cost
(*c*) High penetration (*d*) Both (*a*) and (*b*)

253. Gamma rays have good penetration, but their effectiveness decreases exponentially with
(*a*) Depth (*b*) Volume
(*c*) Mass (*d*) Area

254. The bactericidal efficiency of a given dose of irradiation to food depends upon
(*a*) Kind, species and number of organisms or species
(*b*) Composition and physical state of food
(*c*) The presence or absence of oxygen
(*d*) All of the above

255. Low level irradiation (1kGy) can be used to kill insects and to inhibit spoilage in
(*a*) Fresh fruits and vegetables (*b*) Dried vegetables
(*c*) Pickles (*d*) Stored grains

256. Dry or dehydrated vegetables (herbs and spices) can be irradiated to kill insects and bacteria by the dose of

(*a*) 0.8 kGy
(*b*) 10 kGy
(*c*) 30 kGy
(*d*) 30 Gy

257. Radiation dose (kGy) for inhibiting sprouting of potato, onions and garlic is used about

(*a*) 0.05-0.15
(*b*) 0.08-0.15
(*c*) 0.25-0.35
(*d*) 0.1-1.0

258. Meat foods, sea foods and baked foods are irradiated by the dose of

(*a*) 8-30 kGy
(*b*) 1-10 kGy
(*c*) 20-70 kGy
(*d*) 1-4 kGy

259. Bacteria in wheat flour include

(*a*) Spores of bacillus
(*b*) Coliform bacteria
(*c*) Achromyces, micrococcus, alcaligenes and other
(*d*) All of the above

260. Species of *Fusarium* and *Pencillium* are the dominant mold which contaminate to the

(*a*) Corn meal
(*b*) Corn flour
(*c*) Corn sweetener
(*d*) Both (*a*) and (*b*)

261. During slicing of bread, contamination may take place from the microorganism by

(*a*) Air
(*b*) Knives
(*c*) Wrapper
(*d*) All

262. Spores of bacteria able to cause ______________ in bread will survive in the baking process.

(*a*) Ropiness
(*b*) Bitterness
(*c*) Mustiness
(*d*) All of the above

263. *Aspergillus flavus* and *A. parasiticus* molds are responsible to produce a toxin in food is known as

(*a*) Aflatoxin
(*b*) Mycotoxin
(*c*) Neurotoxin
(*d*) Enterotoxin

264. A storage temperature for dry food products is recommended about

(*a*) 1-3°C
(*b*) 4.4-7.2°C
(*c*) 10-15°C
(*d*) 37°C

265. The moisture content of corn at which aflatoxin formation by mold take place

(*a*) 15%
(*b*) 20%
(*c*) More than 20%
(*d*) None

266. One of the following chemicals can be reduce the mold growth in high moisture corn.
(*a*) Ammonia (2%) and propionic acid (1%) (*b*) SO_2 (2%) and citric acid (0.25%)
(*c*) Sodium benzoate (0.06%) (*d*) All of the above

267. The major factor involved in the spoils of stored grain by mold including
(*a*) Microbial load
(*b*) pH, temperature and moisture above 12-13%
(*c*) Physical damage
(*d*) All of the above

268. One of the following molds spoils the cereals grains.
(*a*) Aspergillus (*b*) Penicillium and fusarium
(*c*) Mucor and rhyzopus (*d*) All of the above

269. A moisture content of wheat flour is less than ________ percent has been reported to prevent the growth of all microorganisms.
(*a*) 15% (*b*) 13%
(*c*) 17% (*d*) 10%

270. Optimum moisture content of wheat flour, at which mold grows very well.
(*a*) 10% (*b*) 13%
(*c*) 15% (*d*) 17%

271. Population of both mold and bacteria in flour increased if moisture content is over than
(*a*) 10% (*b*) 13%
(*c*) 15% (*d*) 17%

272. Ropiness of bread is caused by a mucoid variant of
(*a*) *Bacillus subtilis or B. licheniformis* (*b*) *Serratia marcescens*
(*c*) *Monilia (Neurosporca) sitophila* (*d*) *Geotrichum aurantiacum*

273. The red colour on bread results the growth of pigmented bacteria usually
(*a*) *Geotrichum aurantiacum* (*b*) *Bacillus subtilis*
(*c*) *Serratia marcescens* (*d*) *Monilia (Neurospora) sitophila*

274. Chalk like spots has been blamed on the growth of yeast like fungi is
(*a*) *Endomycopsis fibuligera* (*b*) *Trichosporon variable*
(*c*) *Aspergillus* (*d*) Both (*a*) and (*b*)

275. The detèrioration of breads, cakes, pies and other bakery products due to mostly by physical changes during holding without microorganisms is called
(*a*) Physical injury (*b*) Mechanical shock
(*c*) Staling (*d*) Proofing

276. Approximate bacterial load in raw cane juice is between
(*a*) $10^2 - 10^8$ per gram (*b*) $10^2 - 10^4$ per ml
(*c*) $10^4 - 10^8$ per gram (*d*) $10^4 - 10^8$ per ml

277. Raw sugar contain number of bacteria in the range of
(*a*) $10^2 - 10^4$ per gram (*b*) $10^2 - 10^4$ per ml
(*c*) $10^4 - 10^8$ per gram (*d*) $10^4 - 10^8$ per ml

278. Bacterial counts in maple sap are usually less than
(*a*) 1000 per ml (*b*) 10000 per gram
(*c*) 10000 per ml (*d*) 100000 per gram

279. The chief sources of microorganisms in honey are
(*a*) Nectar of flower (*b*) Honey bees
(*c*) Both above (*d*) None

280. An enzyme of honey contain a bacteriostatic as well as a lytic effect on most of the gram positive bacteria is
(*a*) Apoenzyme (*b*) Lysozyme
(*c*) Lipase (*d*) Peroxidase

281. The main groups of bacteria present during maturation of nectar to honey are
(*a*) Gluconobacter (*b*) Lactobacillus
(*c*) Salmonella (*d*) Both (*a*) and (*b*)

282. Liquid sugar with sugar content as high as 67 to 72°Brix will support the growth of yeasts like
(*a*) Saccharomyces (*b*) Candida
(*c*) Rhodotorula (*d*) All of the above

283. The percentage of sugar content in honey with the range of
(*a*) 75-90% (*b*) 70-80%
(*c*) 20-30% (*d*) 40-60%

284. The honey is rich source of
(*a*) Glucose and fructose (*b*) Glucose and levulose
(*c*) Glucose and maltose (*d*) Sucrose and levulose

285. The pH value of honey lies between
(*a*) 1.2-2.2 (*b*) 2.2-3.0
(*c*) 3.2-4.2 (*d*) 5.0-5.6

286. Chief source of spoilage of honey is
(*a*) Osmophilic yeast (*b*) Osmophilic bacteria
(*c*) Mesophilic molds (*d*) All of the above

287. The critical moisture content of honey for the initiation of yeast growth has been placed at
(*a*) 15% (*b*) 17%
(*c*) 21% (*d*) 25%

288. Smallest and largest enzyme, respectively is
(*a*) Urease and zymase (*b*) Catalase and isomerase
(*c*) Peroxidase and catalase (*d*) Amylase and pectinase

289. Spoilage of fresh fruits and vegetables usually occurs during
(*a*) Harvesting (*b*) Transportation and Storage
(*c*) Processing (*d*) All of the above

290. Pre-cooling and refrigeration during storage of the fresh fruits and vegetables will _________ the growth of microorganisms.
(*a*) Increase (*b*) Decrease
(*c*) No effect (*d*) None

291. Washing of foods with detergent or germicidal solution will ________ microbial load.
(*a*) Reduce (*b*) Increase
(*c*) No effect (*d*) None

292. Added ingredients such as sugar and starch to foods may add spoilage organisms especially spores of
(*a*) Thermophiles (*b*) Psychotrophs
(*c*) Thermoduric (*d*) Halophiles

293. Adequate control of temperature and RH of environment of foods will _______ growth of microorganisms.
(*a*) Increase (*b*) Reduce
(*c*) Constant (*d*) None

294. Contamination from equipment at the processing plant can be reduced by adequate
(*a*) Cleaning (*b*) Sanitization
(*c*) Both (*a*) and (*b*) (*d*) Sanitation

295. Cooling of fruits and vegetables before normal cold storage after harvesting by use of cold water is referred as
(*a*) Hydro cooling (*b*) Air cooling
(*c*) Chilling (*d*) Refrigeration

296. The blanching of foods at (86 to 98ºC) brings about a great reduction in the number of microorganisms as much as
(*a*) 20-40% (*b*) 50-60%
(*c*) 80-90% (*d*) 90-99%

297. The kind of bacteria in vegetables most likely to grow on thawing will depends upon
(*a*) Temperature
(*b*) Elapsed time
(*c*) Moisture content
(*d*) Both (*a*) and (*b*)

298. Most bacteria multiple best at the temperature of 16-38°C, is called
(*a*) Psychrophilic
(*b*) Mesophilic
(*c*) Thermophilic
(*d*) All of the above

299. Under favourable conditions, bacteria can ______________ their number after every 30 minutes.
(*a*) Five times
(*b*) Triple
(*c*) Double
(*d*) Remain same

300. Bacteria can grow under aerobic and anaerobic conditions is called
(*a*) Aerobic
(*b*) Anaerobic
(*c*) Facultative
(*d*) Putrefactive

301. The temperature at which thermophilic bacteria can grow very well is
(*a*) 52-62°C
(*b*) 66-82°C
(*c*) 62-72°C
(*d*) 80-100°C

302. 'Neurotoxicity' is caused by which pathogenic microorganisms.
(*a*) Salmonella sps
(*b*) Shigella sps
(*c*) Clostridium botulinum
(*d*) Clostridium perfringens

303. Microorganisms cause food deterioration and found in intestinal tracts of human and animal.
(*a*) Vibrio cholera
(*b*) Bacillus cereus
(*c*) Salmonella sps
(*d*) Escherichia coli

304. Most of bacteria are killed at the temperature range of
(*a*) 66-82°C
(*b*) 50-70°C
(*c*) 82-93°C
(*d*) 93-110°C

305. The acid effective against the growth of several molds
(*a*) H_2SO_4
(*b*) HCl
(*c*) Sorbic acid
(*d*) Acetic acid

306. The water activity equals to
(*a*) $T/100$
(*b*) RH × 100
(*c*) $T \times 100$
(*d*) RH/100

307. Most bacteria requires water activity in the range of
(*a*) 0.50-0.60
(*b*) 0.60-0.80
(*c*) 0.90-1.00
(*d*) 1.80-2.00

308. An ice cream mix inoculated with typhoid bacteria still retained ________ bacteria per milliliter after one year frozen is
(*a*) 2,00,000 (*b*) 5,00,000
(*c*) 6,00,000 (*d*) 10,00,000

309. If sufficient acid is present, to gain sterility in food requires
(*a*) 93°C temperature for 15 min (*b*) 66°C temperature for 2 min
(*c*) 100°C temperature for 40 min (*d*) 82°C temperature for 10 min

310. The moderate temperature ranges over which most of foods are handled.
(*a*) 5-10°C (*b*) 20-50°C
(*c*) 30-60°C (*d*) 10-38°C

311. *Entamoeba histolytica* is a parasite contaminant of food responsible for
(*a*) Bacterial dysentery (*b*) Fungal dysentery
(*c*) Amoebic dysentery (*d*) Histolic dysentery

312. Diarrhoea is caused by
(*a*) Vibrio cholera (*b*) *Bacillus cereus*
(*c*) *Yersinia enterocolitica* (*d*) Shigella sps

313. To destroying insect eggs in flour, a centrifuge type machine used named as
(*a*) Centoleter (*b*) Mycoleter
(*c*) Insectoleter (*d*) Entoleter

314. Food spoilage can be reduced by
(*a*) Pasteurization and sterilization (*b*) Canning
(*c*) Blanching (*d*) All of the above

315. The factor influencing the kind and rate of spoilage of fish is/are
(*a*) Kind of fish (*b*) Condition of catching of fish
(*c*) Contaminants
(*d*) Temperature and use of an antibiotic ice or dip
(*e*) All of them

316. Salt fish are spoiled by salt tolerant or halophilic bacteria of genus
(*a*) Serratia (*b*) Micrococcus and bacillus
(*c*) Alcaligene and pseudomonas (*d*) All of the above

317. The shell and membrane of an egg can prevent itself from
(*a*) Microbial invasion (*b*) Water and RH
(*c*) Temperature (*d*) All of the above

318. The shell and the thin surface layer of proteinaceous material of egg is known as
(*a*) Cuticle or bloom
(*b*) Pericarp
(*c*) Seed coat
(*d*) Chalaza

319. The rate of physical and chemical changes in the eggs depends on the
(*a*) Time and temperature of holding
(*b*) Relative humidity
(*c*) Composition of the atmosphere about the eggs
(*d*) All of the above

320. The frozen eggs should be stored at
(*a*) 0 to 5°C
(*b*) 10 to 12°C
(*c*) –10 to 0°C
(*d*) –17.8 to – 20.5°C

321. An especially black colouration in the yolk and a dark colour in white is caused by
(*a*) Pseudomonas
(*b*) Acromonas
(*c*) Proteus melanovogenes
(*d*) Alcaligenes

322. Pink rot in eggs are caused by the strain of
(*a*) Pseudomonas
(*b*) Alcaligenes
(*c*) Flavobacterium
(*d*) Paracolobactrum

323. Pin spot molding in egg is caused due to
(*a*) Mold growth
(*b*) Bacterial growth
(*c*) Moisture
(*d*) Low temperature

324. In storage atmosphere of high humidity, a variety of molds may cause
(*a*) Pin spot molding
(*b*) Superficial fungal spoilage
(*c*) Fungal spoilage
(*d*) Off flavour development

325. Fishy flavours are produced in egg by certain strains of
(*a*) Escherichia coli
(*b*) Enterobacter cloacae
(*c*) Streptomyces
(*d*) None

326. The coliform bacteria, anaerobes and yeast can cause gassiness and off-flavour in which milk products.
(*a*) Fermented milk
(*b*) Cheese
(*c*) Ice cream
(*d*) Both (*a*) & (*b*)

327. The centrifugal procedure used for removing bacteria from milk is known as
(*a*) Bactofugation
(*b*) Centrifuge
(*c*) Ultra filtration
(*d*) Homogenization

328. The presence of heat resistant microorganisms or spores may be potential source of spoilage in
(*a*) Cheese (*b*) Butter
(*c*) Evaporated and sweetened condensed milk (*d*) Double toned milk

329. Pasteurization should be accomplished without deleteriously affecting
(*a*) Flavour and appearance (*b*) Nutritional properties
(*c*) Creaming of the milk (*d*) All of these.

330. The heat treatment of cream also destroys ____________that may cause deterioration of butter during storage.
(*a*) Lipase (*b*) Amylase
(*c*) Lactase (*d*) PPO

331. Spoilage of heated foods may have
(*a*) Physical cause (*b*) Chemical cause
(*c*) Biological cause (*d*) Both (*b*) and (*c*)

332. The most important kind of chemical spoilage of canned foods is
(*a*) Hydrogen swell (*b*) Oxygen swell
(*c*) Sulphur dioxide swell (*d*) None

333. Hydrogen swell in canned foods are favoured by
(*a*) Increasing acidities of foods and Increasing temperature of storage
(*b*) Imperfection in the tinning and lacquering of the interior of the can
(*c*) A poor exhaust
(*d*) Presence of soluble sulphur and phosphorus compounds
(*e*) All of them

334. The defect caused by interaction between the steel base of the can and the contained food include
(*a*) Discolouration of the inside of the can and foods
(*b*) Production of off flavour in foods
(*c*) Cloudiness of liquors or syrup and loss in the nutritive value
(*d*) Corrosion or perforation of the metals
(*e*) All of the above

335. Acid foods such as fruits are processed at temperature of ________, which killing all vegetative cells of bacteria, yeasts and molds and their spores and some bacterial spores.
(*a*) 72ºC (*b*) 80ºC
(*c*) 100ºC (*d*) 121ºC

336. A __________ has flat ends, one of which will become convex when the side of the can is struck sharply or the temperature of contents is increased.
(*a*) Flats
(*b*) Flipper
(*c*) Soft swell
(*d*) Breather

337. A __________ has both ends of can bulged, but one or both ends will stay concave if pushed in or if a swollen ends in pushed in, an opposite flat end will pop out.
(*a*) Flipper
(*b*) Springer
(*c*) Hard swell
(*d*) Soft swell

338. When both ends of the can bulged, but the gas pressure is low enough to permit the ends to be dented by manual pressure is called
(*a*) Breather
(*b*) Hard swell
(*c*) Springer
(*d*) Soft swell

339. A __________ has such high gas pressure from within that the ends are too hard to dented by hand.
(*a*) Soft swell
(*b*) Hard swell
(*c*) Flat
(*d*) Flipper

340. A __________ is a can with a minute leak that permits air to move in or out but does not necessarily allow microorganisms to enter.
(*a*) Springer
(*b*) Flipper
(*c*) Breather
(*d*) None

341. The __________ of canned foods is important in determining the heat process necessary for their sterilization.
(*a*) pH
(*b*) acidity
(*c*) water content
(*d*) optical density

342. The classification of kind of spoilage of canned foods is based on the kinds of changes produced in the food *i.e.*
(*a*) Putrefaction
(*b*) Acid formation
(*c*) Gas formation
(*d*) All of the above

343. The most important kinds of biological spoilage of commercial canned foods are
(*a*) Flat sour spoilage
(*b*) TA spoilage
(*c*) Putrefaction
(*d*) All of the above

344. A fourth important kind of spoilage caused by action of acid of foods on iron of can results in a
(*a*) Flat sour spoilage
(*b*) TA spoilage
(*c*) Hydrogen swell
(*d*) Putrefaction

345. The ends of the can of food remain flat during souring, or the development of lactic acid in the food by the flat sour bacteria is known as
(*a*) Flat sour spoilage
(*b*) TA spoilage
(*c*) Hydrogen swell
(*d*) Putrefaction

346. The flat sour spoilage occurs chiefly in low acid foods, such as peas or corn and is caused by species of
(*a*) Bacillus
(*b*) Lactobacillus
(*c*) Clostridium
(*d*) All

347. The ability of B. coagulans in flat sour spoilage to grow in tomato juice depends on
(*a*) No. of spores present
(*b*) The availability of oxygen
(*c*) pH
(*d*) All

348. TA spoilage is the short form of
(*a*) Thermophilic anaerobe
(*b*) Thermal allowance
(*c*) Thermal absorption
(*d*) None

349. TA spoilage is caused due to
(*a*) Clostridium botulinum
(*b*) Clostridium thermosaccharolyticum
(*c*) B. coagulant
(*d*) B. stearothermophilus

350. Sulfide or sulphur stinker spoilage in low acid food is caused by
(*a*) Dusulfotomaculum nigrificans
(*b*) Clostridium thermosaccharolyticum
(*c*) B. stearothermophilus
(*d*) None of them

351. Mesophilic clostridium species spoiled the canned foods when the pH is
(*a*) 2.5-4.5
(*b*) 4.5
(*c*) Above 4.5
(*d*) Below 2.5

352. Home canned foods heated to 100°C may be spoiled by the saccharolytic bacteria with production of
(*a*) Butyric acid
(*b*) Carbon dioxide
(*c*) Hydrogen
(*d*) All of the above

353. Under spoilage of mesophilic clostridium species, the putrefactive anaerobic produces CO_2 and hydrogen causing the can to
(*a*) Flat
(*b*) Swell
(*c*) Burst
(*d*) Breather

354. The presence of viable non spore forming bacteria in heated processed canned foods indicates
(*a*) Flipper
(*b*) Springer
(*c*) Swell
(*d*) Leakage of container

355. Canned fruits, jam, jellies, fruit juices, syrups and sweetened condensed milk spoiled by fermentative yeast with swelling of can by the production of
(*a*) Hydrogen (*b*) Carbon dioxide
(*c*) Sulphur dioxide (*d*) Hydrogen sulfide

356. Jam, jellies, marmalade and fruit butters will permit mold growth when sugar concentration is as high as
(*a*) 60 % (*b*) 65 %
(*c*) 70 % (*d*) 75 %

357. Strain of Aspergillus, Penicillium and Citromyces found growing in jelly and canned fruits are able to grow in sugar concentration upto
(*a*) 65.0 % (*b*) 67.5 %
(*c*) 70.0 % (*d*) 72.5 %

358. One of the following is pectin fermenting molds in bottled and canned fruits and have caused spoilage.
(*a*) Aspergillus (*b*) Penicillium
(*c*) Byssochlamys fulva (*d*) Citromyces

359. Low acid canned foods with a pH above 5.3 are subjected to
(*a*) Flat sour spoilage (*b*) Putrefaction
(*c*) TA spoilage (*d*) Both (*a*) and (*b*)

360. Canned foods with a pH between 5.3 and 4.5 are likely to undergo
(*a*) Flat sour spoilage (*b*) TA spoilage
(*c*) Sulfide spoilage (*d*) Putrefaction

361. High acid canned foods with a pH between 4.5 and 3.7 usually are spoiled by a
(*a*) Special flat sour bacterium (*b*) Saccharolytic anaerobe
(*c*) TA spoilage (*d*) Both (*a*) and (*b*)

362. High acid canned foods with a pH below 3.7 ordinarily do not undergo spoilage by microorganisms but in cans may become
(*a*) CO_2 swell (*b*) H_2 swell
(*c*) NH_3 swell (*d*) H_2S swell

363. Spoilage in canned meats and fish without gas production with souring and changes in colour and texture may be caused by
(*a*) Bacillus sps. (*b*) Homo-fermentative LAB (faecalis)
(*c*) Both (*a*) and (*b*) (*d*) None

364. One of the following species can produce bitterness, acidity and curdling in canned milk, cream and evaporated milk.
(*a*) Bacillus sps.
(*b*) Lactobacillus sps.
(*c*) Clostridium sps.
(*d*) Streptococcus sps.

365. The spoilage of fatty foods (fats or oils) due to oxidation, chemical or microbiological is termed as
(*a*) Oxidative rancidity
(*b*) TA spoilage
(*c*) Halogenation
(*d*) Maceration

366. Any change in fats or oils that is accomplished by undesirable flavour is known as
(*a*) Spoilage
(*b*) Rancidity
(*c*) Hydrolysis
(*d*) Adsorption

367. The change in fat or oil or fatty foods resulting from hydrolysis, or by lipase originally present or by those from microorganisms causing
(*a*) Oxidative rancidity
(*b*) Hydrolytic rancidity
(*c*) Ketonic rancidity
(*d*) Flavour reversion

368. Hydrolytic rancidity in fatty foods is due to
(*a*) Hydrolysis
(*b*) Lipase
(*c*) Microorganisms
(*d*) All of the above

369. The appearance of objectionable flavour from less oxidation than is needed to produce rancidity is called
(*a*) Auto oxidation
(*b*) Ketonic rancidity
(*c*) Flavour reversion
(*d*) Oxidative rancidity

370. The oxidation of fats and oils may be catalyzed by
(*a*) Metals and rays
(*b*) Moisture
(*c*) Microorganisms
(*d*) All of the above

371. Some of the pigments produced by microorganisms are fat soluble and therefore can diffuse into fat producing discoloration ranging through
(*a*) Yellow
(*b*) Red
(*c*) Purple
(*d*) Brown
(*e*) All of the above

372. The types of spoilage of mayonnaise and similar dressing is/are
(*a*) Separation of the oil or water from emulsion
(*b*) Oxidation and hydrolysis of the oils by chemical or biological action
(*c*) Growth of microorganisms to produce gas, off-flavour, or other defects
(*d*) All of the above

373. The decomposition of salad dressing and related products can be caused by
(*a*) Bacteria (*b*) Yeast
(*c*) Molds (*d*) All of the above

374. Molds can grow on salad dressing if air is available and are favored by the addition of
(*a*) Starch or pectin (*b*) Pectin
(*c*) Edible salt (*d*) None

375. The yeasts are most likely causes of spoilage of soft drinks for such beverages are acid and contain sugar
(*a*) Toruplosis and candila (*b*) Saccharomyces
(*c*) Zygosaccharomyces (*d*) All of the above

376. Types of spoilage of soft drinks is
(*a*) Cloudiness (*b*) Ropiness
(*c*) Gassiness (*d*) Both (*a*) and (*b*)

377. The cloudiness in soft drink takes place due to the growth of various
(*a*) Yeast (*b*) Mold
(*c*) Bacteria (*d*) Both (*a*) and (*c*)

378. Ropiness in soft drink is caused by capsulated bacteria belongs to
(*a*) Bacillus sps. (*b*) Lactobacillus sps.
(*c*) Clostridium sps. (*d*) Streptococcus sps

379. Treatment of spices with ______________ greatly reduces their content of microorganisms.
(*a*) Sulphur dioxide (*b*) Propylene oxide
(*c*) Carbon dioxide (*d*) Nitrogen oxide

380. Which salt is used in foods
(*a*) Solar salt (*b*) Mined or rock salt
(*c*) Welled salt (*d*) All of the above

381. One of the following microorganisms may produce mycotoxin on nuts such as aflatoxin production in pea nut.
(*a*) Yeast (*b*) Mold
(*c*) Bacteria (*d*) Parasite

382. Butterfat and meat fat becomes "tallowy" as the result of
(*a*) Oxidation (*b*) Dehydration
(*c*) Frying (*d*) Freezing

383. A mixed lactic acid culture is used in the manufacturing of
(*a*) Cultured butter milk (*b*) Yogurt
(*c*) Several types of cheese (*d*) All of the above

384. Spray dried or lyophilized culture of *Propionibacterium freudenreichii* are added to milk used in the manufacture of ______________ to improve the flavour.
(*a*) Chedder cheese (*b*) Cottage cheese
(*c*) Swiss cheese (*d*) All of the above

385. Activity of culture for food fermentation depends on
(*a*) Condition of mother or intermediate culture (*b*) Culture medium
(*c*) Incubation time and temperature (*d*) All of the these

386. The food fermentation may take place by
(*a*) Yeast (*b*) Molds
(*c*) Bacteria (*d*) Combination of the microorganisms
(*e*) All of the above

387. The bread, beer, wine and distilled liquors is fermented products made by with the help of
(*a*) Yeast (*b*) Mold
(*c*) Bacteria (*d*) All

388. Fermented milk is produced by
(*a*) Yeast fermentation (*b*) Mold fermentation
(*c*) Bacterial fermentation (*d*) All of the above

389. Yeast and bacteria are involved in the manufacturing of __________ from sugar bearing materials.
(*a*) Vinegar (*b*) Sugar
(*c*) Syrup (*d*) Alcohol

390. Molds are important in the preparation of
(*a*) Pickles (*b*) Sauerkraut
(*c*) Cheese and oriental foods (*d*) Vinegar

391. Dough is usually leavened by ______________ which ferment the sugars in dough and produce mainly CO_2 and alcohol.
(*a*) Bread yeast (*b*) Bacterial culture
(*c*) Mold (*d*) Citric acid

392. Dough conditioner or yeast foods added in dough to improve the dough characteristics are
(*a*) $KBrO_3$ (*b*) KIO_3
(*c*) CaO_2 (*d*) $(NH_4)_2\ S_2O_8$
(*e*) All of them

393. The rate of gas production by yeast in dough is increased by adding
(*a*) More yeast (*b*) Sugar or amylase bearing malt
(*c*) Dough conditioner within limit (*d*) All of them

394. In the sponge method of bread making, some of the ingredients are mixed at ________ temperature and allowed to ferment to the desired maturity.

(a) 23-24°C
(b) 25-30°C
(c) 30-34°C
(d) 35-45°C

395. In the straight dough method of bread making, all the ingredients are mixed at ________temperature.

(a) 23-24°C
(b) 24-25°C
(c) 26-28°C
(d) 30-32°C

396. The fermentation room where the dough is held for most of the leavening process is usually held at the temperature of about

(a) 20°C
(b) 25°C
(c) 27°C
(d) 30°C

397. Leavening of dough takes place by

(a) Bread yeast
(b) Microorganisms
(c) Chemicals
(d) All of the above

398. Thermal treatment in baking process serves as to

(a) kill the yeast
(b) inactivate the enzyme
(c) expand the gas
(d) set the structure of the loaf
(e) All of the above

399. "Set" of bread under baking process, ____________ gives structural support in the dough, but ____________ support the structure of baked bread.

(a) Starch, gluten
(b) Gluten, starch
(c) Yeast, salt
(d) Yeast, sugar

400. The amount of salt by weight is added to shredded cabbage for manufacturing of sauerkraut.

(a) 1.0-1.5%
(b) 1.5-2.0%
(c) 2.25-2.5%
(d) 2.5-3.5 %

401. Dextran, a gummy poly saccharide is a neutral glucan made by *Leuconostoc mesenteroides* from

(a) Molasses or refined sucrose medium
(b) Cereals waste
(c) Starch
(d) Dextrose

402. Dextran is used as __________ for sugar syrup, ice cream and confections.

(a) Antioxidant
(b) Stabilizer
(c) Gelling agent
(d) Preservatives

403. The protein, a biocatalysts called

(a) Protein enhancer
(b) Dough conditioner
(c) Enzyme
(d) Preservative

404. The principal mold used in citric acid production is
(*a*) Aspergillus niger (*b*) Mucor
(*c*) Penicillum (*d*) Rhyzopus

405. In food industries, citric acid is used as
(*a*) Flavouring agent (*b*) Adjust the pH
(*c*) To prevent discolouration or browning (*d*) Synergists with antioxidants for oils
(*e*) All of them

406. The food borne illness caused by the presence of a bacterial toxin formed in the food is referred as
(*a*) Bacterial food intoxication (*b*) Bacterial food infection
(*c*) Both (*d*) None

407. The food borne illness caused by the entrance of bacteria into the body through ingestion of contaminated foods and the reaction of the body to their presence or to their metabolites is known as
(*a*) Bacterial food intoxication (*b*) Bacterial food infection
(*c*) Both (*d*) None

408. Botulism is a disease caused by the ingestion of food containing the neurotoxin produced by
(*a*) Clostridium botulinum (*b*) Clostridium perfringens
(*c*) Salmonella (*d*) Escherichia coli

409. Staphylococcal intoxication caused by a toxin in the food by
(*a*) Clostridium botulinum (*b*) Salmonella sps
(*c*) Shigella (*d*) Staphylococcus aureus

410. Mycotoxins are
(*a*) Fungal metabolites (*b*) Bacterial metabolites
(*c*) Plant parasites (*d*) Enzyme

411. The syndrome resulting the ingestion of toxin in a mold containing food is referred as
(*a*) Mycotoxicosis (*b*) Aflatoxin
(*c*) Neurotoxin (*d*) Botulism

412. Aflatoxin is resulting of
(*a*) Aspergillus flavus (*b*) Alternaria
(*c*) Fusarium (*d*) Helminthosporium

413. Optimal conditions for the production of aflatoxin would be
(*a*) a_w (0.85), temperature (25-40°C) (*b*) a_w (0.65), temperature (30-35°C)
(*c*) a_w (0.90), temperature (20-25°C) (*d*) a_w (0.75), temperature (10-30°C)

414. Food borne disease take place in human by the consumption of
(*a*) Solid foods
(*b*) Milk
(*c*) Water or other beverage
(*d*) All of the above

415. The strength of the sewage or food waste containing organic matter is expressed in term of
(*a*) BOD (*b*) COD
(*c*) DO (*d*) TDS

416. FAO is primary concerned with food production through improved method of
(*a*) Production (*b*) Processing and preservation
(*c*) Distribution of foods (*d*) All of the above

417. WHO activities are more related to the
(*a*) Health of consumer (*b*) Maintenance of food wholesomeness
(*c*) Processing and preservation (*d*) Both (*a*) and (*b*)

418. The joint FAO/WHO Food Standard Commission is a forum for the cooperation among nations to develop or agree upon various international standards for
(*a*) Agriculture industry (*b*) Health industry
(*c*) Food industry (*d*) Sugar industry

419. The maximum acceptable number of microorganisms or specific types of microorganisms, as determined by prescribed method, in a food being purchased by a firm or agency for it own use is known as
(*a*) Microbiological standard (*b*) Microbiological specification
(*c*) Microbiological guideline (*d*) Microbiological hazard

420. That part of a law or administrative regulation designating the maximum acceptable number of microorganisms or of specific types of microorganisms, as determined by prescribed methods, in a food produced, packed or stored or imported into the area of jurisdiction of an enforcement agency is called
(*a*) Microbiological standard (*b*) Microbiological specification
(*c*) Microbiological guideline (*d*) Microbiological hazard

421. That level of bacteria in final products or in a shipped product that requires identity and correction of causative factors in a current and future production, or in handling after production.
(*a*) Microbiological standard (*b*) Microbiological specification
(*c*) Microbiological guideline (*d*) Microbiological hazard

422. The chilling of foods is accomplished by the use of
(*a*) Cold water or ice (*b*) Mechanical refrigeration
(*c*) Vacuum cooling (*d*) All

423. Most spoilage bacteria grow at
(*a*) acidic pH
(*b*) alkaline pH
(*c*) neutral pH
(*d*) any of the pH

424. The microbiological examination of coliform bacteria in foods preferably use
(*a*) MacConkey broth
(*b*) Violet Red Bile agar
(*c*) Eosine Methylene blue agar
(*d*) All of these

425. Which of the following is not true for the thermal resistance of the bacterial cells?
(*a*) Cocci are usually more resistant than rods
(*b*) Higher the optimal and maximal temperatures for growth, higher the resistance
(*c*) Bacteria that clump considerably or form capsules are difficult to kill
(*d*) Cells low in lipid content are harder to kill than other cells

426. Water activity can act as
(*a*) an intrinsic factor determining the likelihood of microbial proliferation
(*b*) a processing factor
(*c*) an extrinsic factor
(*d*) all of the above

427. Enumeration of microorganism refers to
(*a*) either spiral plating, pour plate or spread plate of a food suspension on to a suitable selective agar, or non-selective plate, depending on the test
(*b*) either spiral plating, pour plate or spread plate of a food suspension on to a suitable selective agar
(*c*) non-selective plating, depending on the test
(*d*) none of the above

ANSWER KEY

(FOOD PRESERVATION AND MICROBIOLOGY)

1.A	2. C	3.A	4.B	5.D	6.D	7.C	8.A	9.C	10.B
11.A	12.B	13.A	14.A	15.A	16.C	17.C	18.A	19.A	20.C
21.D	22.B	23.A	24.B	25.A	26.D	27.D	28.D	29.A	30.B
31.B	32.B	33.C	34.A	35.B	36.C	37.A	38.B	39.A	40.A
41.D	42.B	43.A	44.A	45.C	46.C	47.B	48.D	49.B	50.B
51.A	52.A	53.A	54.A	55.D	56.A	57.B	58.B	59.A	60.D
61.D	62.C	63.B	64.B	65.A	66.B	67.A	68.A	69.B	70.D
71.D	72.D	73.D	74.D	75.B	76.A	77.B	78.B	79.A	80.E
81.E	82.D	83.C	84.B	85.B	86.B	87.D	88.C	89.E	90.D

91.D	92.B	93.C	94.D	95.D	96.D	97.A	98.C	99.D	100.D
101.B	102.C	103.D	104.A	105.C	106.C	107.D	108.B	109.A	110.C
111.B	112.C	113.D	114.A	115. A	116. B	117.C	118.C	119.A	120.C
121.B	122.D	123.B	124.A	125.A	126.B	127.D	128.A	129.B	130.C
131.A	132.C	133.A	134.A	135.B	136.A	137.A	138.D	139.D	140.E
141.C	142.D	143.C	144.A	145.A	146.A	147.A	148.D	149.E	150.C
151.B	152.C	153.E	154.E	155.A	156.C	157.A	158.D	159.A	160.B
161.B	162.B	163.B	164.A	165.A	166.B	167.B	168.A	169.C	170.C
171.A	172.A	173.A	174.D	175.A	176.B	177.A	178.C	179.A	180.A
181.A	182.A	183.A	184.A	185.D	186.D	187.A	188.D	189.A	190.D
191.E	192.A	193.D	194.A	195.B	196.A	197.B	198.E	199.A	200.A
201.C	202.C	203.C	204.A	205.B	206.D	207.D	208.D	209.D	210.D
211.C	212.D	213.D	214.D	215.B	216.D	217.C	218.D	219.E	220.E
221.D	222.E	223.E	224.A	225.B	226.A	227.D	228.D	229.A	230.B
231.A	232.D	233.D	234.B	235.A	236.D	237.D	238.C	239.A	240.A
241.D	242.D	243.C	244.A	245.D	246.D	247.A	248.D	249.C	250.A
251.B	252.D	253.A	254.D	255.A	256.C	257.A	258.C	259.D	260.D
261.D	262.A	263.A	264.B	265.C	266.A	267.D	268.D	269.B	270.C
271.D	272.A	273.C	274.D	275.C	276.D	277.A	278.C	279.C	280.B
281.D	282.D	283.B	284.B	285.C	286.A	287.C	288.C	289.D	290.B
291.A	292.A	293.B	294.C	295.A	296.D	297.D	298.B	299.C	300.C
301.B	302.C	303.D	304.C	305.C	306.D	307.C	308.C	309.A	310.D
311.C	312.C	313.D	314.D	315.E	316.D	317.A	318.A	319.D	320.D
321.C	322.A	323.A	324.B	325.A	326.D	327.A	328.C	329.D	330.A
331.D	332.A	333.E	334.E	335.C	336.B	337.B	338.D	339.B	340.C
341.B	342.D	343.D	344.C	345.A	346.A	347.D	348.A	349.B	350.A
351.C	352.D	353.B	354.D	355.B	356.C	357.B	358.C	359.D	360.B
361.D	362.B	363.C	364.A	365.A	366.B	367.B	368.D	369.C	370.D
371.E	372.D	373.D	374.A	375.A	376.D	377.D	378.A	379.B	380.D
381.B	382.A	383.D	384.C	385.D	386.E	387.D	388.C	389.A	390.C
391.A	392.E	393.D	394.A	395.C	396.C	397.D	398.E	399.B	400.C
401.A	402.B	403.C	404.A	405.E	406.A	407.B	408.A	409.D	410.A
411.A	412.A	413.A	414.D	415.A	416.D	417.D	418.C	419.B	420.A
421.C	422.D	423. C	424. D	425. D	426. D	427. A			

Chapter 10

Metabolism

1. Number of ATP produced from one pyruvic acid during conversion to acetyl Co-A
   (*a*) 6 (*b*) 3
   (*c*) 12 (*d*) 15
2. The link between glycolysis and Krebs's cycle is
   (*a*) Citric acid (*b*) Malic acid
   (*c*) Fumaric acid (*d*) Acetyl co-enzyme
3. Succinyl Co-A is related to
   (*a*) Krebs's cycle (*b*) Calvin cycle
   (*c*) Glycolate cycle (*d*) HMP-cycle
4. The formation of Acetyl Co-A from pyruvic acid is the result of its
   (*a*) Reduction (*b*) Dehydration
   (*c*) Phosphorylation (*d*) Oxidative decarboxylation
5. Which of the following is link between carbohydrate and fat metabolism
   (*a*) CO_2 (*b*) Acetyl Co-A
   (*c*) Pyruvic acid (*d*) Citric acid
6. Pyruvate dehydrogenase complex is used in converting
   (*a*) Pyruvate to glucose (*b*) Glucose to pyruvate
   (*c*) Pyruvic acid to lactic acid (*d*) Pyruvate to acetyl Co-A
7. The first compound of TCA cycle is
   (*a*) Oxalo succinic acid (*b*) Oxalo acetic acid
   (*c*) Citric acid (*d*) Cis aconitic acid
8. Which of the following is coenzyme-II
   (*a*) NAD (*b*) NADP
   (*c*) FAD (*d*) None of the above

9. End product of glycolysis is

(*a*) Citric acid (*b*) Glyceraldehydes

(*c*) Phosphoglyceraldehyde (*d*) Pyruvic acid

10. First reaction in pentose phosphate pathway is

(*a*) Oxidation of glucose-6-phosphate (*b*) 6-phosphogluconic acid

(*c*) Ribose-5-phosphate (*d*) Fructose-5-phosphate

11. Alternate name of Krebs's cycle is

(*a*) Glyoxylate cycle (*b*) Glycolate cycle

(*c*) Citric acid cycle (*d*) EMP pathway

12. Complete oxidation of 1 g mol of glucose gives rise to

(*a*) 6860000 calories (*b*) 686000 calories

(*c*) 68600 calories (*d*) 6860 calories

13. Energy obtained by a cell from catabolic reaction is stored immediately in the form of

(*a*) Glucose (*b*) Pyruvic acid

(*c*) ADP (*d*) ATP

14. ATP is

(*a*) A hormone (*b*) A protein

(*c*) An enzyme which brings about oxidation

(*d*) A molecule which contain high energy band

15. The net gain of ATP molecules in glycolysis

(*a*) Zero (*b*) Two

(*c*) Four (*d*) Eight

16. Most of the energy of the carbohydrates is released by oxidation when

(*a*) Pyruvic acid is converted into CO_2 and H_2O

(*b*) Pyruvic acid is converted into acetyl Co-A

(*c*) Sugar is converted into pyruvic acid

(*d*) Glucose is converted into alcohol and CO_2

17. Glycolysis takes place in

(*a*) Cytoplasm (*b*) Chloroplast

(*c*) Ribosomes (*d*) Mitochondria

18. The universal hydrogen acceptor is

(*a*) NAD (*b*) ATP

(*c*) Co-A (*d*) FMN

19. Citric acid is produced by

(*a*) Bacterial episome (*b*) Krebs's cycle

(*c*) Calvin cycle (*d*) Calvin+ HSK cycle

20. The number of ATP molecules produced from one Krebs's cycle are

(*a*) 15 (*b*) 30

(*c*) 38 (*d*) 40

21. How many molecules of ATP are produced per molecule of $FADH_2$ oxidized

(*a*) One (*b*) Two

(*c*) Three (*d*) Four

22. The amount of energy given by one ATP molecule is

(*a*) 67 kcal (*b*) 6.7 kcal

(*c*) 7.6 kcal (*d*) 75 kcal

23. The full form of NAD is

(*a*) Nicotine adenosine diphosphate (*b*) Nicotinamide adenosine dinucleotide

(*c*) Nicotinamide adenine dinucleotide (*d*) Nicotinamide adenine diphosphate

24. How many ATP molecules produced from the complete oxidation of a molecule of active acetate or acetyl Co-A

(*a*) 38 ATP (*b*) 15 ATP

(*c*) 12 ATP (*d*) 4 ATP

25. Which of the following is 5-carbon compound of Krebs's cycle

(*a*) Citric acid (*b*) Fumaric acid

(*c*) Oxalosuccinic acid (*d*) α-ketoglutaric acid

26. Which of the following is a coenzyme

(*a*) NAD (*b*) NADP

(*c*) FAD (*d*) All the above

27. What is NADP

(*a*) An enzyme (*b*) An ion carrier

(*c*) H_2 acceptor coenzyme (*d*) A part of t-RNA

28. Energy for ATP synthesis is obtained from
(*a*) Oxygen ion gradient (*b*) Heavy water gradient
(*c*) Uranium ion gradient (*d*) Hydrogen ion gradient

29. Direct gain of ATP from one mole of glucose during glycolysis or EMP pathway
(*a*) 2 ATP (*b*) 6 ATP
(*c*) 36 ATP (*d*) 38 ATP

30. $FADH_2$ produced in Krebs's cycle from
(*a*) Isocitrate (*b*) á-ketoglutarate
(*c*) succinate (*d*) malate

31. Which 5-carbon organic acid of TCA cycle is key compound in N_2 metabolism
(*a*) Citric acid (*b*) Fumaric acid
(*c*) OSA (*d*) α-ketoglutarate

32. One mole of glucose when oxidized through EMP & TCA cycle would yield
(*a*) 30 ATP gross (*b*) 40 ATP net
(*c*) 36 or 38 ATP net (*d*) 38 ATP only

33. What is true for Krebs's cycle
(*a*) GTP/ATP is formed (*b*) 2 Decarboxylation
(*c*) Acetyl Co-A acceptor is OAA (*d*) All of the above

34. Link between glycolysis and TCA cycle is
(*a*) Pyruvic acid (*b*) Acetyl Co-A
(*c*) Citric acid (*d*) None

35. Accepter of acetyl Co-A in krebs's cycle
(*a*) Malic acid (*b*) Fumaric acid
(*c*) á-ketoglutaric acid (*d*) Oxalo acetic acid

36. Pyruvic acid is the end product of which process
(*a*) Krebs's cycle (*b*) Calvin cycle
(*c*) Pentose phosphate pathway (*d*) Glycolysis

37. 1molecule glucose + 6 molecule of O_2 and 38 ADP combined to form $6H_2O + 6CO_2$ + ____________
(*a*) 38 molecule of ATP (*b*) 28 ATP
(*c*) 38ADP (*d*) 28ADP

38. Number of ATP obtained at the end of Krebs's cycle

(*a*) 2 ATP (*b*) 4 ATP

(*c*) 36 ATP (*d*) 38 ATP

39. In which one of the following do the two names refer to one and the same thing

(*a*) Krebs's cycle and Calvin cycle

(*b*) Tricaboxylic acid cycle and citric acid cycle

(*c*) Citric acid cycle and Calvin cycle

(*d*) Tricaboxylic acid cycle and urea cycle

40. In glycolysis, during oxidation electrons are removed by

(*a*) Molecular oxygen (*b*) ATP

(*c*) Glycereldehyde (*d*) NAD^+

41. During which stage in the complete oxidation of glucose are the greatest number of ATP molecules formed from ADP

(*a*) Conversion of pyruvic acid to acetyl Co-A

(*b*) Electron transport chain

(*c*) Glycolysis

(*d*) Krebs's cycle

42. In glycolysis in addition to pyruvic acid and ATP two molecules are made of

(*a*) ATP (*b*) ATP and NADH

(*c*) $NADH_2$ (*d*) NADH

43. In order for glycolysis to continue NAD must be generated through

(*a*) Fermentation (*b*) Respiration

(*c*) Both above (*d*) Fermentation or respiration

44. Phosphofructose kinase I is inhibited only by

(*a*) ATP only (*b*) Hexokinase

(*c*) ATP & citrate both (*d*) Isocitrate dehydrogenase

45. The cycle of reaction that includes glucose conversion to lactate in muscle and lactate conversion to glucose in liver is called

(*a*) Glucogenesis (*b*) Lactogenesis

(*c*) Allosteric regulation (*d*) Cori cycle

46. The entire spectrum of chemical reactions occurring in the living system are collectively referred to as
(a) Metabolism (b) Assimilation
(c) Digestion (d) absorption

47. A series of enzymatic reaction to produce specific products in the living system is called
(a) Respiration chain (b) Electron transportation chain
(c) Metabolic pathway (d) None of them

48. Metabolism is broadly divided into ———— category
(a) Two (b) Three
(c) Four (d) None

49. Catabolism and Anabolism is classification of
(a) Digestion (b) Assimilation
(c) Biosynthesis (d) Metabolism

50. The derivative processers concerned with the breakdown of complex molecules to similar ones is called
(a) Metabolism (b) Catabolism
(c) Anabolism (d) None of them

51. The biosynthetic reactions involving the formation of complex molecules from simple precursor is known as
(a) Metabolism (b) Catabolism
(c) Anabolism (d) None of them

52. The basic purpose o catabolism is to trap energy of the biomolecules in the form of ————
(a) ADP (b) ADP + Pi
(c) ATP (d) Glucose

53. In which stages, catabolism occurs
(a) Conversion of complex molecules into their building block
(b) Formation of simple intermediate
(c) Final oxidation of acetyl CoA
(d) All of them

54. Poly saccharides are broken down by catabolism into
(a) Monosaccharides (b) Disaccharides
(c) Oligosaccharides (d) None

55. By catabolism, fat or lipid is breakup into

(*a*) FFA (*b*) Oils

(*c*) Glycerides (*d*) None

56. Protein is break down by catabolism into

(*a*) Amino acids (*b*) Glycerin

(*c*) Glycerol (*d*) FFA

57. Kreb cycle is also known as

(*a*) RL cycle (*b*) Citric acid cycle

(*c*) Calvin cycle (*d*) Futile cycle

58. Anabolism consume the energy in the form of

(*a*) ADP (*b*) ATP

(*c*) Glucose (*d*) None

59. The central molecule in carbohydrate metabolism is

(*a*) Glucose (*b*) Fructose

(*c*) Mannose (*d*) Maltos

60. The fasting blood glucose level in normal individuals is

(*a*) 10-20 mg/dl (*b*) 20-40 mg/dl

(*c*) 40-60 mg/dl (*d*) 60-100 mg/dl

61. The following substance is ketogenic

(*a*) Fatty acids (*b*) Leucine

(*c*) Lysine (*d*) All of them

62. The lipoprotein possessing the highest quantity of phospholipid

(*a*) HDL (*b*) LDL

(*c*) VLDL (*d*) Chylomicrons

63. Hypercholesterolemia is observed in the disorder

(*a*) Hypothyroidism (*b*) Diabetes mellitus

(*c*) Nephritic syndrome (*d*) All of them

64. The two final products in the β-oxidation of odd chain fatty acids are

(*a*) Acetyl CoA and malonyl CoA (*b*) Acetyl CoA and Acetyl CoA

(*c*) Acetyl CoA and propionyl CoA (*d*) Acetyl CoA and succinyl CoA

65. The oxidation of glucose to pyruvate and lactate is referred as
(*a*) Glycolysis (*b*) Citric acid cycle
(*c*) Gluconeogenesis (*d*) Glycogenesis

66. Glycolysis is also termed as
(*a*) TCA cycle (*b*) EM pathway
(*c*) RL Cycle (*d*) None

67. The synthesis of glucose from non-carbohydrates precursors (*e.g.* amino acid, glycerol etc.) is called
(*a*) Glycolysis (*b*) Citric acid cycle
(*c*) Gluconeogenesis (*d*) Glycogenolysis

68. The formation of glycogen from glucose is known as
(*a*) Glycolysis (*b*) Glycogenesis
(*c*) Gluconeogenesis (*d*) Glycogenolysis

69. The breakdown of glycogen to glucose and then lactate and pyruvate is termed as
(*a*) Glycolysis (*b*) Glycogenesis
(*c*) Gluconeogenesis (*d*) Glycogenolysis

70. Glycolysis is very essential for ——— which is dependent on glucose for energy
(*a*) Heart (*b*) Kidney
(*c*) Lungs (*d*) Brains

71. Glycolysis may be summarized by the net glucose + 2ADP + 2Pi $\rightarrow$ 2Lactare + _____ATP reaction
(*a*) 2 (*b*) 3
(*c*) 4 (*d*) 6

72. Glucose is phosphorylated to glucose 6-phosphate by
(*a*) Amylase (*b*) Hexokinase or glucokinase
(*c*) Invertase (*d*) None

73. Glycolysis takes place in the
(*a*) Cytosol (*b*) Lysosome
(*c*) Peroxisome (*d*) Ribosomes

74. Which enzyme regulate the glycolysis process
(*a*) Hexokinase (*b*) Phosphofructokinase
(*c*) Pyruvate kinase (*d*) All the above

75. The inhibition of glycolysis by oxygen (aerobic condition) is known as

(*a*) Crabtree effect (*b*) Pasteur effect

(*c*) Both above (*d*) None

76. The phenomenon of inhibition of oxygen consumption by the addition of glucose to tissues having high aerobic Glycosis is known as

(*a*) Crabtree effect (*b*) Pasteur effect

(*c*) Both above (*d*) None

77. Citric acid cycle essentially involves the oxidation of acetyl CoA to CO_2

(*a*) Glucose (*b*) H_2O

(*c*) NaCl (*d*) Pyruvate

78. Citric acid cycle is the final common oxidative pathway for

(*a*) Carbohydrates (*b*) Fats

(*c*) Amino acids (*d*) All the above

79. When a molecule of glucose is burnt in calorimeter __________ KJ of heat is liberated

(*a*) 2580 (*b*) 2680

(*c*) 2780 (*d*) 2880

80. Which enzyme(s) are catalyzed the three irreversible steps of glycolysis

(*a*) Hexokinase (*b*) Pyruvate kinase

(*c*) Phosphofructokinase (*d*) All the above

81. The GN ratio represents the ratio between glucose (dextrose) to ____________ excreted in urine

(*a*) Nitrogen (*b*) Ninhydrin

(*c*) NaCl (*d*) None

82. The GN ratio is 3.65 it means that 3.65 g of glucose is synthesized from 1 g of nitrogen of

(*a*) Sodium nitrate (*b*) Proteins

(*c*) Vitamins (*d*) Minerals

83. The prime function of liver glycogen is to maintain the blood _________ level particularly between meals.

(*a*) Sugar (*b*) Water

(*c*) Salt (*d*) Temperature

84. Glycogen, the storage from in animal is of

(*a*) Fructose (*b*) Maltose

(*c*) Mannose (*d*) Glucose

85. The compound implicated in the development of cataract in diabetic patient is

(*a*) Mannitol (*b*) Sorbitol

(*c*) Fructose (*d*) Sucrose

86. Synthesis of 2-3 bisphosphoglycerate occurs in the tissue namely

(*a*) Liver (*b*) Kidney

(*c*) Erythrocytes (*d*) Brains

87. The number of ATP produced when a molecule of acetyl CoA is oxidized through citric acid cycle

(*a*) 12 (*b*) 24

(*c*) 38 (*d*) 15

88. The storage form of glycogen in plant is

(*a*) Glucose (*b*) Pectin

(*c*) Starch (*d*) Amylopectin

89. Triacylglycerols (TG) is highly concentrated forms of energy yielding

(*a*) 4 cal/g (*b*) 6.5 cal/g

(*c*) 9 cal/g (*d*) 13 cal/g

90. One gram of glycogen combines with 2g ________ for storage.

(*a*) Water (*b*) Oxygen

(*c*) Nitrogen (*d*) Hydrogen

91. The triglycerides are in nature

(*a*) Non polar (*b*) Polar

(*c*) Dipole (*d*) None

92. The oxidation of fatty acids on the β carbon atom is define as

(*a*) β-Oxidation (*b*) α-Oxidation

(*c*) ω-Oxidation (*d*) All the above

93. Which sequence is correct for β-oxidation?

(*a*) clearage ⟶ oxidation ⟶ hydration ⟶ oxidation

(*b*) oxidation ⟶ hydration ⟶ clearage ⟶ hydration

(*c*) hydration ⟶ oxidation ⟶ oxidation ⟶ clearage

(*d*) oxidation ⟶ hydration ⟶ oxidation ⟶ clearage

94. An unexpected death of healthy infants usually overnight is
(*a*) SIDS (*b*) HIV
(*c*) Starvation (*d*) Ketosis

95. The removal of one carbon unit at a time by the oxidation of α-carbon atom of fatty acid is known as
(*a*) β-Oxidation (*b*) α-Oxidation
(*c*) ω-Oxidation (*d*) Starvation

96. The most predominant lipid components of chylomicrons is
(*a*) Triacylglycerols (*b*) Glucose
(*c*) Protein (*d*) HDL

97. Cholesterol synthesis is controlled by feedback inhibition of the enzymes
(*a*) β-ketoacyl CoA thiolase (*b*) Thiokinase
(*c*) Phosphodiesterase (*d*) HMG CoA reductase

98. A compound possessing hydrophobic and hydrophilic groups in its structure is known as
(*a*) Anomers (*b*) Ampipathic
(*c*) Epimers (*d*) None

99. The lipoprotein involved in the reverse cholesterol transport is
(*a*) HDL (*b*) VLDL
(*c*) LDL (*d*) CHD

100. The total no. of ATP produced by the oxidation of a molecule of palmitic acid is
(*a*) 109 (*b*) 119
(*c*) 129 (*d*) 139

101. A plasma lipoprotein that is inversely correlated with coronary heart disease is
(*a*) VLDL (*b*) LDL
(*c*) CHD (*d*) HDL

102. The fatty acid that is commonly found in the C_2 of triacylglycerols is
(*a*) Unsaturated fatty acids (*b*) Saturated fatty acids
(*c*) Both above (*d*) None

103. The removal of amino group from the amino acids as NH_3 is called
(*a*) Deamination (*b*) Transamination
(*c*) Translation (*d*) Transcription

104. The transfer of an amino ($-NH_2$) group from an amino acid to a keto acid is known as
(*a*) Deamination (*b*) Transamination
(*c*) Translation (*d*) Transcription

105. Which out of the following statements is true about regulation of metabolic pathway?
(*a*) Most of the metabolic pathways are regulated
(*b*) Most of the metabolic pathways are not regulated
(*c*) Regulation of metabolic pathways always involves changing the amount of enzymes
(*d*) Metabolic regulation always depends on control by hormones

106. The rate of breakdown of metabolites is termed as
(*a*) Metabolic state (*b*) Metabolism
(*c*) Steady state (*d*) Homeostasis

107. Diminished delivery of oxygen to tissues is termed as
(*a*) Hypoxia (*b*) Ischemia
(*c*) Homeostasis (*d*) Metabolism

108. Diminished flow of blood to tissues is termed as
(*a*) Hypoxia (*b*) Ischemia
(*c*) Homeostasis (*d*) Metabolism

109. Which of the following statements is true about the control of muscle glycogen phosphorylase?
(*a*) It is activated by phosphorylation by an active phosphorylase kinase
(*b*) It is allosterically activated by ATP
(*c*) It is allosterically activated by cAMP
(*d*) Normally it exists in active form

ANSWER KEY

(METABOLISM)

Q.	Ans.	Q.	Ans.	Q.	Ans.	Q.	Ans.	Q.	Ans.	Q.	Ans.
1.	b	21.	b	41.	b	61.	d	81.	a	101.	d
2.	d	22.	c	42.	d	62.	a	82.	b	102.	a
3.	a	23.	c	43.	d	63.	d	83.	a	103.	a
4.	d	24.	a	44.	c	64.	c	84.	d	104.	b
5.	b	25.	d	45.	d	65.	a	85.	b	105.	a
6.	d	26.	d	46.	a	66.	b	86.	c	106.	c
7.	c	27.	c	47.	c	67.	c	87.	d	107.	a
8.	b	28.	d	48.	a	68.	b	88.	c	108.	b
9.	d	29.	a	49.	d	69.	d	89.	c	109.	a
10.	a	30.	c	50.	b	70.	d	90.	a		
11.	c	31.	d	51.	c	71.	a	91.	a		
12.	b	32.	c	52.	c	72.	b	92.	a		
13.	d	33.	d	53.	d	73.	a	93.	d		
14.	d	34.	b	54.	a	74.	d	94.	a		
15.	d	35.	d	55.	a	75.	b	95.	b		
16.	a	36.	d	56.	a	76.	a	96.	a		
17.	a	37.	a	57.	b	77.	b	97.	d		
18.	a	38.	d	58.	b	78.	d	98.	b		
19.	b	39.	b	59.	a	79.	c	99.	a		
20.	a	40.	d	60.	d	80.	d	100.	c		

Chapter 11

Digestion and Absorption

1. Vitamin B_1 is present in one of these molecules

(*a*) TPP (*b*) FMN

(*c*) NAD (*d*) ATP

2. The pH of stomach is 1.6, and then which enzyme will digest protein?

(*a*) Trypsin (*b*) Pepsin

(*c*) Amylase (*d*) Erypsin

3. Which of the following is an essential fatty acids in mammals?

(*a*) Stearic acid (*b*) Acetic acid

(*c*) Palmitic acid (*d*) Gamma linolenic acid

4. Brunner's gland is present in

(*a*) Liver (*b*) Duodenum

(*c*) Oesophagus (*d*) Stomach

5. Which of the following enzymes carries out the initial step in the digestion of milk in humans?

(*a*) Rennin (*b*) Lipase

(*c*) Trypsin (*d*) Pepsin

6. Root present in the upper molars are

(*a*) Four (*b*) Three

(*c*) Two (*d*) One

7. Epiglottis is meant for protecting

(*a*) Oesophagus from entry of air

(*b*) Nasal chambers from entry of food

(*c*) Larynx from entry of food

(*d*) Teeth from carriers

8. Among mammals a significant role in the digestion of milk is played by
   (*a*) Rennin (*b*) Invertase
   (*c*) Amylase (*d*) Intestinal bacteria
9. Sucrase converts sucrose in to glucose and
   (*a*) Fructose (*b*) Ribose
   (*c*) Curd (*d*) Maltose
10. Transverse rugae occur on
   (*a*) Hard palate (*b*) Soft palate
   (*c*) Tongue (*d*) Stomach
11. Frenulum is
   (*a*) Adenoid present on pharyngeal walls
   (*b*) Tonsil found on lateral walls of soft palate
   (*c*) V-shaped sulcus dividing tongue into pharyngeal and oral parts
   (*d*) Fold attaching tongue
12. A person suffering from the deficiency of the visual pigment rhodopsin in advised to take more of
   (*a*) Radish and potato (*b*) Apple and grapes
   (*c*) Carrot and ripe papaya (*d*) Guava and ripe banana
13. Monophyodont teeth occur in
   (*a*) Humans (*b*) Frog
   (*c*) Whale (*d*) Rat
14. Teeth of most reptiles and amphibians are
   (*a*) Acrodont (*b*) Thecodont
   (*c*) Heterodont (*d*) Diphyodont
15. Bunodont teeth occur in
   (*a*) Elephant (*b*) Sheep
   (*c*) Carnivores (*d*) Humans
16. Bile can be prevented to pass into duodenum by
   (*a*) Phloric valve (*b*) Sphincter of boyden
   (*c*) Sphincter of Oddi (*d*) Cardiac sphincter
17. Teeth of carnivores arȇ
   (*a*) Solenodont (*b*) Secodont
   (*c*) Lophodont (*d*) Pleurodont

18. Odotoblasts produce

(*a*) Dentine
(*b*) Cement
(*c*) Enamel
(*d*) Periodontal membrane

19. Precursor of trypsin is secreted by

(*a*) Stomach
(*b*) Intestine
(*c*) Pancreas
(*d*) Liver

20. The main bulk of tooth is formed of

(*a*) Dentine
(*b*) Enamel
(*c*) Bone
(*d*) Calcium

21. Bile pigments are

(*a*) Haemocyanin
(*b*) Biliverdin
(*c*) Bilirubin
(*d*) Both *b* and *c*

22. The important salts of bile are

(*a*) Sodium carbonate
(*b*) Sodium glycocholate
(*c*) Sodium taurocholate
(*d*) All of above

23. The greenish colour of bile is due to

(*a*) Biliverdin and bilirubin
(*b*) Melanin
(*c*) Haematochrome
(*d*) All of these

24. Epithelial cells of the intestine involved in food abosroption have on their surface

(*a*) Pinocytic vessels
(*b*) Phagocytic vesicles
(*c*) Zymogen granules
(*d*) Microvilli

25. In gluconeogenesis

(*a*) Glucose is converted into glycogen
(*b*) Glycogen is converted into glucose
(*c*) Sugars are converted into fats
(*d*) Glucose is formed from non –carbohydrates

26. Cholecystokinin stimulates

(*a*) Pancreas
(*b*) Kidney
(*c*) Gall bladder
(*d*) Liver

27. Phagocytic cells lining blood sinuses of liver are known as

(*a*) Enterochromaffin cells
(*b*) Kupfer cells
(*c*) Oxyntic cells
(*d*) Zymogen cells

28. Dental formula of a child is

(a) $\frac{2102}{2102}$ (b) $\frac{2120}{2120}$

(c) $\frac{2123}{2123}$ (d) $\frac{2111}{2111}$

29. A patient is generally advised to specially, consume more meat, lentils, milk and eggs in diet only when he suffer from

(a) Kwashiorkor (b) Rickets

(c) Anaemia (d) Scurvy

30. Chewing is required for

(a) Solubilisation of food (b) Enjoying the taste of food

(c) Decreasing surface area of food (d) Increasing surface area of food

31. Insulin is secreted by

(a) α-cells of pancreas (b) β-cells of pancreas

(c) γ- cells of pancreas (d) acini of pancreas

32. α-cells of pancreas secrete

(a) Insulin (b) Glucagon

(c) Trypsinogen (d) Amylase

33. Secretin and cholecystokinin are digestive hormones. They are secreted in

(a) Oesophaggus (b) Ileum

(c) Duodenum (d) Pyloric stomach

34. The protein deficiency disease is known as

(a) Scurvy (b) Addison's disease

(c) Kwashiorkor (d) Pellagra

35. In an empty stomach, the mucosa is thrown into folds called

(a) Rugae (b) Villi

(c) Alveoli (d) None of these

36. Glottis is opening in the floor of

(a) Diaphragm (b) Buccopharyngeal cavity

(c) Trachea (d) None of these

37. The terminal portion of the small intestine is the

(a) Ileum (b) Caecum

(c) Duodenum (d) Jejunum

38. The large intestine lacks

(*a*) Goblet cells (*b*) Epiploic appendages

(*c*) Plicae circulars (*d*) Haustra

39. HCl is secreted by

(*a*) Zymogen cells (*b*) Peptic cells

(*c*) Oxyntic cells (*d*) None of these

40. The hormone 'secretin' stimulates secretion of

(*a*) Bile juice (*b*) Pancreatic juice

(*c*) Both a and b (*d*) Gastric juice

41. Pepsin is secreted by

(*a*) Zymogen (*b*) Epithelial cell

(*c*) Liver (*d*) Pancreas

42. Oxyntic cells secrete

(*a*) HCl (*b*) NaOH

(*c*) Trypsin (*d*) Pepsin

43. The daily dietary requirement of a moderately active adult individuals is approximately

(*a*) 1000 kcal (*b*) 4000 kcal

(*c*) 8000 kcal (*d*) 2500 kcal

44. a disorder of digestive system associated with liver is

(*a*) Diarrhoea (*b*) Constipation

(*c*) Jaundice (*d*) Vomiting

45. Amylase converts starch into

(*a*) Fructose (*b*) Glucose

(*c*) Maltose (*d*) Lactose

46. Crown of teeth is covered by

(*a*) Dentine (*b*) Enamel

(*c*) Both (*a*) and (*b*) (*d*) None of these

47. Wisdom tooth are

(*a*) Last molars (*b*) Last premolars

(*c*) Incisors (*d*) Canines

48. The duct of gall bladder along with the hepatic duct from the liver forms

(*a*) Pancreatic duct (*b*) Common bile duct

(*c*) Common hepatopancreatic duct (*d*) None of the above

49. The enzymes trypsin is found in
(*a*) Pancreatic juice (*b*) Mucus
(*c*) Saliva (*d*) Intestinal juice

50. The chief function of bile is to
(*a*) Regulate the process of digestion
(*b*) Eliminate the waste products
(*c*) Emulsify fats for digestion
(*d*) Digest fat by enzymatic action

51. Digestion of cellulose in rabbit takes place in
(*a*) Caecum (*b*) Colon
(*c*) Rectum (*d*) Ileum

52. Which of the following statement is incorrect?
(*a*) Bile helps in emulsification of fats
(*b*) Bile contains bilirubin, biliverdin, bile salts, cholesterol and phospholipids
(*c*) Bile contains proteolytic enzymes
(*d*) Bile activates lipases

53. 'Kwashiorkor' and 'beri-beri' are
(*a*) Communicable disease (*b*) Infectious diseases
(*c*) Deficiency diseases (*d*) None of these

54. Formation of gallstones is referred to as
(*a*) Jaundice (*b*) Cirrhosis
(*c*) Hepatitis (*d*) Cholelithiasis

55. Which of the following is not a function of saliva?
(*a*) To initiate protein digestion
(*b*) To aid in cleansing the teeth
(*c*) To lubricate the pharynx
(*d*) To assist in the formation of a bolus

56. Which of the following is not a major gastrointestinal hormone?
(*a*) Epinephrine (*b*) Secretin
(*c*) Gastrin (*d*) cholecystokinin

57. Peristalsis moves food material
(*a*) In the stomach and small intestine
(*b*) In the intestine
(*c*) In the stomach and intestine
(*d*) From the pharynx to the anal canal

58. Most enzymes involved in protein digestion are

(*a*) Secreted by the pancreas
(*b*) Activated by HCl
(*c*) Present in the stomach
(*d*) Secreted in an inactive form

59. Amylase in saliva initiates digestion of

(*a*) Lipids
(*b*) Proteins
(*c*) Carbohydrates
(*d*) Fats

60. Pancreatic juice contains a protein-splitting enzyme called

(*a*) Trypsin
(*b*) Zymogen
(*c*) Pepsin
(*d*) Amylase

61. Duodenum has characteristic Brunner's glands, which secrete two hormones called

(*a*) Kinase and estrogen
(*b*) Secretin and cholecystokinin
(*c*) Prolactin and parathormone
(*d*) Estradion and progesterone

62. Which of the following ducts is not associated with the digestive system?

(*a*) Cystic duct
(*b*) Parotid duct
(*c*) Pancreatic duct
(*d*) Lacrimal duct

63. Which of the following is not an energy source for cells?

(*a*) Glucose
(*b*) Protein
(*c*) Fats
(*d*) Vitamins

64. Number of teeth, which grow twice, is

(*a*) 8
(*b*) 12
(*c*) 14
(*d*) 20

65. The richest sources of vitamin-B12 is

(*a*) Goat's liver and *Spirulina*
(*b*) Chocolate and green gram
(*c*) Rice and hen's egg
(*d*) Carrot and chicken's breast

66. Reduced growth, hair loss and vomiting may results from a deficiency of

(*a*) Iron
(*b*) Copper
(*c*) Potassium
(*d*) Zinc

67. Which vitamin gets destroyed on heating

(*a*) Vitamin B (*b*) Vitamin C

(*c*) Vitamin D (*d*) Vitamin A

68. Night blindness is caused by the deficiency of

(*a*) Vitamin A (*b*) Vitamin B6

(*c*) Vitamin B12 (*d*) Vitamin C

69. Pepsin differs from trypsin in digesting

(*a*) Protein in acidic medium in duodenum

(*b*) Protein in alkaline medium in duodenum

(*c*) Protein in alkaline medium in stomach

(*d*) Protein in acidic medium in stomach

70. Mostly in the stomach of vertebrates which food is digested

(*a*) Carbohydrates (*b*) Fats

(*c*) Proteins (*d*) All of them

71. Role of HCl in stomach

(*a*) To change trypsinogen into active trypsin

(*b*) To increase food absorption

(*c*) To dissolve enzymes secreted from gastric glands

(*d*) To destroy bacteria in food

72. Amylase is found in

(*a*) Bile (*b*) Gastric juice

(*c*) Saliva (*d*) Saliva and pancreatic juice

73. Vitamin C is

(*a*) Folic acid (*b*) Nicotinic acid

(*c*) Ascorbic acid (*d*) Citric acid

74. Milk protein is

(*a*) Lactogen (*b*) Myosin

(*c*) Casein (*d*) Pepsin

75. The end product of carbohydrates digestion are

(*a*) Galactose, maltose, fructose

(*b*) Maltose, fructose, lactose

(*c*) Glycogen, glucose, Galactose

(*d*) Glucose, fructose, Galactose

76. Which disease is caused due to the prolonged deficiency of nicotinic acid?

(*a*) Pellagra (*b*) Rickets
(*c*) Scurvy (*d*) Beri-beri

77. Which of the following is different from the other three

(*a*) Glucagon (*b*) Secretin
(*c*) Gastrin (*d*) Ptyalin

78. The cells of the epithelial lining in the vertebrates stomach are not damaged by HCl because of

(*a*) Mucous secretion covering the epithelium
(*b*) Neutralization of HCl by alkaline gastric juice
(*c*) HCl being too dilute
(*d*) Epithelium being resistant to HCl

79. Our food mainly contains

(*a*) Carbohydrates (*b*) Cellulose
(*c*) Sucrose (*d*) Glucose

80. What is the source of ascorbic acid

(*a*) Banana (*b*) Potato
(*c*) Orange (*d*) Mango

81. Which enzyme is found in the saliva of mammals

(*a*) Ptyalin (*b*) Amylase
(*c*) Rennin (*d*) All of them

82. Gastric juice contain

(*a*) HCl (*b*) Pepsin
(*c*) Rennin (*d*) All of them

83. Digestion of carbohydrates, proteins and fats complete in

(*a*) Stomach (*b*) Liver
(*c*) Small intestine (*d*) Large intestine

84. Which enzyme changes milk protein in calcium paracasinate

(*a*) Rennin (*b*) Trypsin
(*c*) Lactase (*d*) Maltase

85. End product of carbohydrate digestion are

(*a*) Glycogen (*b*) Glycerol
(*c*) Monosaccharide's (*d*) Disaccharides

86. Herbivorous animals can digest cellulose because

(*a*) Gastric juice has suitable enzymes

(*b*) Alimentary canal is very long

(*c*) Bacteria found in caecum are helpful in it

(*d*) Premolar and molar teeth help in grinding

87. Which of following helps the most in growth and formation of new cells

(*a*) Protein (*b*) Carbohydrate

(*c*) Fats (*d*) Salts

88. Which group of enzymes are protein digesting

(*a*) Ptyalin, pepsin, erpsin (*b*) Trypsin, amylase

(*c*) Trypsin, pepsin, erepsin (*d*) None of them

89. Emulsification of fats by bile takes place in

(*a*) Duodenum (*b*) Intestine

(*c*) Stomach (*d*) Liver

90. Glycogen is stored in

(*a*) Blood (*b*) Liver

(*c*) Lungs (*d*) Kidney

91. Vitamin A is synthesized from carotene in

(*a*) Liver (*b*) Kidney

(*c*) Blood (*d*) Skin

92. Liver secretes

(*a*) No digestive juice (*b*) HCl

(*c*) No enzymes (*d*) No salts

93. In India, the best source for protein in herbivorous person is

(*a*) Pulses (*b*) Potato

(*c*) Egg (*d*) Meat

94. Proteins are broken down into amino acids in

(*a*) Buccal cavity (*b*) Stomach

(*c*) Intestine (*d*) Rectum

95. Man is said to be starving when
    (*a*) Food he eat meets the loss of energy
    (*b*) He begins to store reserve food
    (*c*) Food he eats does not meet the loss of energy
    (*d*) None of them

96. Starch is digested in
    (*a*) Duodenum (*b*) Stomach and duodenum
    (*c*) Buccal cavity and oesophagus (*d*) Buccal cavity and duodenum

97. A man who is chronic alcoholic may develop deficiency of
    (*a*) Vitamin B5 (*b*) Vitamin E
    (*c*) Vitamin C (*d*) Vitamin D

98. Which is sweet in taste, but is not sugar
    (*a*) Starch (*b*) Saccharine
    (*c*) Lactose (*d*) Protein

99. In mammals carbohydrates are stored in the form of
    (*a*) Lactic acid in muscles (*b*) Glycogen in liver and muscles
    (*c*) Glucose in liver and muscles (*d*) Glycogen in liver and spleen

100. To prevent entry of food into the trachea the opening is guarded by
    (*a*) Epiglottis (*b*) Glottis
    (*c*) Hard palate (*d*) Soft palate

101. Where is protein digestion accomplished in the body
    (*a*) Stomach (*b*) Ileum
    (*c*) Rectum (*d*) Duodenum

(*Explanation*: Protein digestion occurs in stomach, jejunum and ileum. It is completed in ileum).

102. Release of pancreatic juice is stimulated by
    (*a*) Enterokinase (*b*) Cholecystokinin
    (*c*) Trypsinogen (*d*) Secretin

103. Oxyntic cells in stomach secrete
    (*a*) Pepsin (*b*) Mucus
    (*c*) HCl (*d*) Rennin

104. Brunner's glands are found in
    (*a*) Stomach (*b*) Duodenum
    (*c*) Ileum (*d*) Large intestine

105. Xerophthalmia in children and night blindness in adults is caused by the deficiency of

(*a*) Vitamin A (*b*) Vitamin B
(*c*) Vitamin C (*d*) Vitamin K

ANSWER KEY

(DIGESTION AND ABSORPTION)

Q. No.	*Ans.*	*Q. No.*	*Ans.*	*Q. No.*	*Ans.*	*Q. No.*	*Ans.*	*Q. No.*	*Ans.*
1.	a	21.	d	41.	a	61.	b	81.	a
2.	b	22.	d	42.	a	62.	d	82.	d
3.	d	23.	a	43.	d	63.	d	83.	c
4.	b	24.	d	44.	c	64.	d	84.	a
5.	d	25.	d	45.	b	65.	a	85.	c
6.	b	26.	c	46.	b	66.	d	86.	c
7.	c	27.	b	47.	a	67.	b	87.	a
8.	a	28.	b	48.	b	68.	a	88.	c
9.	a	29.	a	49.	a	69.	d	89.	a
10.	a	30.	d	50.	c	70.	c	90.	b
11.	d	31.	b	51.	a	71.	d	91.	a
12.	c	32.	b	52.	c	72.	d	92.	c
13.	c	33.	c	53.	c	73.	c	93.	a
14.	a	34.	c	54.	d	74.	c	94.	c
15.	d	35.	a	55.	a	75.	d	95.	c
16.	c	36.	b	56.	a	76.	a	96.	d
17.	b	37.	a	57.	d	77.	d	97.	c
18.	a	38.	c	58.	d	78.	a	98.	b
19.	c	39.	c	59.	c	79.	a	99.	b
20.	a	40.	b	60.	a	80.	c	100.	a
101.	b	102.	b	103.	c	104.	b	105.	a

Chapter 12

Fill in the Blanks

Note: Fill in the blanks with appropriate words.

Section 1

1. In India, _________% of the total grain production is stored at farmer's level.
2. The main purpose of food processing is to _________ the qualitative and quantitative deterioration of the material after harvest.
3. Food Processing operations are undertaken to _________ to agricultural produce after their harvest.
4. The removal of undesirable matters from the desired grains is called _________.
5. The classification of cleaned products in various quality fractions depending upon the various commercial values and other usage is referred as _________.
6. The separation of cleaned product into various quality fractions by any one physical property is known as _________.
7. The rough cleaning of grain in initial process is defined as _________.
8. The separating grain/seeds into two or more fractions according to size alone are performed by _________.
9. _________means removal of moisture to very low levels usually to bone dry condition.
10. Removal of moisture from grains and other products to predetermined level is called _________.
11. Drying is a thermo-physical and _________operation by which the excess moisture from a product is removed.
12. Mechanical handling devices aim to the work of _________.
13. The role of packaging is to contain _________ and sell.
14. The weight of hull is _________% of the total weight of paddy grain.
15. The edible portion (endosperm) of paddy is called _________.
16. The outermost layer of the endosperm of rice is the _________.

17. The primary objective in rice milling is to remove the hull or husk and bran with minimum breakage of the endosperm to produce acceptable ____________.
18. After harvest, paddy grain is to be dried upto __________ % moisture content (wet basis).
19. Rice quality involves the head rice yield (HRY) and ________ rice yield (MRY).
20. The percent of rough rice that is left after complete milling operation is termed as ______.
21. Unbroken kernels of rice and broken kernel of rice that are at least three fourths of an unbroken kernel is defined as ___________.
22. Clean and good quality paddy can give a yield of __________% rice.
23. __________ is the percentage of rough rice remaining as milled rice that contains both head and broken kernels.
24. Rice with whole milled kernels having length breath ratio between 2.0 and 3.0 is called _________.
25. The outer covering of the brown rice is known as ___________.
26. The pieces of rice kernel that are less than ¾th of the size of full kernels is called _______.
27. Rice obtained from paddy after milling operation i.e. removal of husk and also removal of bran layers is defined as __________.
28. Rice kernel whole or broken which have 25% or more their surface having red pericarp is called __________.
29. Parboiling treatment given to paddy prior to its milling to achieve maximum recovery of head rice and to __________ breakage.
30. The paddy grain is mainly composed of ____________ starch granules.
31. During gelatinization process of paddy, __________ swell and fill the voids.
32. The temperature at which gelatinization of starch in paddy takes place is known as the ___________ temperature.
33. Gelatinization of starch in paddy during parboiling takes place in near hood to ______°C.
34. In rubber roll sheller, the clearance between rolls is kept __________than the thickness of paddy grain.
35. In rubber roll sheller, the faster roll should have a peripheral surface speed of __________ and while the slower roll speed is 8-10 m/s.
36. __________is a coating with talcum powder or/and glucose after polishing to give a transparent look to rice.
37. Glucose as glazing agent is added to the rice as __________solution with water.
38. One hundred kg of paddy would yield about ________of husk, 4 kg bran and about 74 kg of white rice.
39. The first part of the grinding process of wheat milling is properly carried out in corrugated rollers known as__________.
40. The break rolls are usually 60 to 75 cm in length and ________ cm diameter.
41. The differential speed ratio of break rolls of wheat mill are of about _________.
42. Debranned (polished) and cracked parboiled wheat is known as __________

43. Parboiled wheat resembles as _____ when it is debranned and split into two more pieces.
44. The process of _______ wheat production is more or less same as that of parboiled rice.
45. Soaking of wheat should be done at temperature ________ °C for best result.
46. Increasing the moisture content of wheat during parboiling to a desirable level of __________% (db).
47. The drying air temperature of _____°C is the optimum temperature for the drying of parboiled wheat.
48. Commercial dhal mills have a Dhal recovery of 65-70% where as modern Dhal mills yield about ________%.
49. Milling of pulses means removal of the _____ and splitting the grain in to two equal halves.
50. Pulses consumed as Dhal have about __________% protein.
51. Pulses are the major source of ____________ to vegetarian masses of the country.
52. The scratched/pitted pulses are treated with linseed oil of about _____ kg/tonnes.
53. An emery roller and concave type machine commonly is known as _______.
54. About _______ % of pulses are dehusked and splitted in single pass by Gota machine.
55. The purpose of ____________is to remove small size of husk adhering to cotyledons and to provide glazing look or glossy look for the dhal.
56. In CFTRI method of pulse milling, preconditioned pulses are dried at 120°C by __________dryer.
57. The process in which endosperm is separated (detached) from other component of corn kernels like germ, hull and tip cap is called _____________ .
58. The raw corn for wet milling should contain __________moisture.
59. The steeped corn in wet milling method attains a moisture content of about _________%.
60. The oils and fats are composed of different mixtures of ________ of various fatty acids.
61. Fat and oils generated ________times more energy than protein and carbohydrates.
62. Oils and fats are excellent source of ___________.
63. Oils provide the essential fatty acid like ________, which is needed for human health.
64. The ________is the process of mechanically pressing liquid out of liquid containing solids.
65. The advantage of mechanical expression system over chemical extraction is that it gives the liquid free of dissolved __________.
66. The most commonly used solvent for oil extraction in Indian plants is the________.
67. The boiling point of *n-hexane* used for oil extraction is about _________°C.
68. Casein is a phospho-protein which is found only in _________.
69. Lactose is a disaccharide carbohydrate found in the form of glucose and ________.
70. Lactose is easily changed by bacterial action to __________.
71. Carotene is mainly responsible for yellow colour of ___________.
72. The amount of cholesterol in milk varies directly with the _______ content of the milk.

73. The principal phospholipids found in milk are called ________
74. The enzyme Catalase of milk is destroyed at the temperature of ______ for 30 min.
75. The milk has natural acidity with the range from ________to ________ percent.
76. Normal fresh milk has a hydrogen ion concentration of approx. pH __________.
77. Oxidation-reduction potential or Redox-potential of milk is about ________ volt.
78. The sweet taste of milk comes from the flavour and aroma principally from __________ and buffer fat.
79. Buffalo have a tendency to convert all carotene into ________.
80. Jam contains ________ per cent invert sugar.
81. Corn syrup may be added in jelly along with the cane sugar to avoid ________.
82. Syneresis is major problem of jelly during ___________.
83. Fruit peels or slice are suspended in __________.
84. TSS of Jam marmalade should not be more than ________ per cent.
85. The microorganisms that cause food spoilage are moulds, yeasts and __________.
86. Aflatoxins produced by moulds growing on __________.
87. All enzymes are inactivated by temperature above ___________°C.
88. Antifungal food additives are basically chemicals that prevent the ________ growth.
89. Sorbates are generally used in foods at the concentrations of ________ to ________%.
90. Sorbic acid and its mineral salts are ________ agents often used as preservatives in food, cheese and drinks to prevent the growth of mold, yeast and fungi.
91. The efficacy of benzoic acid and benzoate is dependent on the ________ of the food.
92. Calcium propionate is the main preservative used in ________ and other bakery products.
93. Acetic acid and sodium or calcium propionate is also used for their __________ property in paneer, chhana, cheese, dried fish and other foods.
94. Generally, fatty acids are most effective as inhibitors of ________ bacteria and yeast.
95. Natamycin ($C_{33}H_{47}NO_{13}$) is a ________used to keep cheese from getting moldy.
96. As a food additive, Nisin has E number __________.
97. The optimum temperature for the growth and multiplication of insects in stored grain is __________°C.
98. The optimum temperature for the growth and multiplication of fungi in stored grain is __________°C.
99. The optimum temperature for the growth and multiplication of mites in stored grain is __________°C.
100. The growth rate of insect, fungi and mites decreases with ________ of temperature.

Section 2

101. Generally, insects do not develop below 15°C and nor mites below _____ °C.
102. Most of storage fungi in grain do not develop below _____ °C.
103. The metabolic heat produced exclusively by dry grain is about _______ cal/sec/cm^3.
104. The metabolic heat produced approximately by wet grain is ________ cal/sec/cm^3.
105. Moisture content of grain below _________ % arrest the growth of most of the microorganisms and mites.
106. Moisture content below _________% limit development of most of the stored insect pests.
107. The allowable storage time is defined as the maximum time before germination falls by _______% or visible mould appears.
108. The main objective of management during the grain storage period is to reduce the _______ of grains.
109. The increase of temperature above the level of food grains is an indication of ________.
110. Large bins maintain lower average temperature in stored grain during the _________than small bins.
111. No species of storage fungi can grow below _____ % equilibrium relative humidity.
112. The process of hermetically sealing of fruit and vegetable food stuffs in container and sterilizing by heat treatment for long period of storage is known as _____________.
113. The process of canning is invented by ___________ in France in 1804.
114. Ascorbic acid or acetic acid is used in canned fruit to create ___________ in finished product.
115. A process of sealing foods hermetically in containing and sterilizing them by heat is so called canning or __________.
116. A solution of sugar in water is called a ___________.
117. A solution of salt in water is called ___________.
118. Hot brine of _________to _________% concentration is used for covering of the vegetables.
119. Fruit and vegetables are covered with syrup or brine in can at the temperature of _________to_________°C, respectively.
120. Head space in canned food is left about __________.
121. The process of removal of air from cans is known as ___________.
122. During sealing of canned foods, the temperature should not fall below ___________.
123. Almost all fruits and acid vegetables can be processed satisfactorily at a temperature of ________°C in boiling water.
124. Blanching of fruits and vegetables is done by immersing them in hot/boiled water or by exposing them to live steam or hot air for a period of _______ minute followed by cooling.
125. Inactivation of most of plant enzymes which cause firmness, discoloration (polyphenal oxidase), off flavour (peroxidase), softening and loss of nutritive value during canning is caused by _______.

126. After processing, the cans are cooled rapidly to about ________ °C to stop the cooking process and to prevent stack burning.
127. During sealing of canned foods, the temperature should not fall below ________ °C.
128. Lye peeling of fruits and vegetables is done in aqueous solution of ________ in 1–2% strength.
129. Lye peeled fruit and vegetable is neutralized in 0.5% ________ upto few second.
130. Chilling is the unit operation in which the temperature of a food is reduced to between –1°C and ________ °C.
131. Fruits which undergo 'climacteric' ripening show a short but abrupt increase in the rate of ________ which occurs near to the point of optimum ripeness.
132. The most significant effect of chilling on the sensory characteristics of processed foods is hardening due to solidification of ________.
133. A cryogen is a ________ that changes phase by absorbing latent heat to cool the food.
134. The temperature of air may vary from –15°C to –30°C, and freezing may take place from 3 to 72 hr in ________ freezing.
135. The time in minutes at a specified temperature required to destroy 90% of the organisms in a population is known as ________.
136. The ________ is the number of degrees required for a specific thermal time curve to pass through one log cycle (change by a factor of 10).
137. The number of minutes at a specific temperature required to destroy a specified number of organism having a specific *Z*-value is defined as ________.
138. After processing of wheat flour, flour can separate into higher protein or higher starch fraction in a process known as ________.
139. The principal functional protein of wheat flour is ________.
140. A container that is sealed completely against the ingress of gases and vapors is referred as ________.
141. The primary objective of a heat treatment of foods is to decrease the initial microbial load and inactivate the ________.
142. The ________ point is defined as the point of electric neutrality or zero potential.
143. The ________ is defined as the number of gram equivalents of acid or base required to change the pH of one litre of buffer solution one unit of pH.
144. The buffer index of milk at pH of 6.6 is about ________.
145. The buffer index increases with decrease in pH but ________ again at pH of 5.5.
146. The best pH value for dough at time of baking should be ________.
147. The pH of fresh egg rapidly changes during ________.
148. Molds grow at lower pH values than ________.
149. If the vapour pressure of the moisture within the grain is higher than that of moisture in the atmosphere, the grains will ________ its moisture to the atmosphere.

150. If the vapour pressure of the moisture within the grain is lower than that moisture in the atmosphere, the grains will ____________ its moisture from the atmosphere.
151. The psychometric chart is a graphical representation of the physical and thermal properties of _________.
152. Most of bacteria, yeasts and mold grow best at temperature of __________.
153. Some microorganisms continue to grow even at low temperature. These are known as __________ organisms.
154. The retardation of microbial and bio-chemical activities at low temperature is the basis of preservation of food by _____________.
155. Household and commercial refrigerators usually run at _____________°C.
156. The management of objectives during the storage period is to reduce the _________ to such a low level that the grain mass is sufficiently stable with minimal deterioration.
157. Sterilization of foods in hermetically sealed containers by irradiation is called _______.
158. Sprouting in onion, garlic and potatoes are major problems during _________ at ambient temperature for long period of time is treated with 15 krad.
159. To make food last longer by destroying or inactivating insects, molds and yeasts that spoil food, delaying the ripening of fruits and vegetables, and limiting unwanted spouting of potatoes and other similar vegetables is done by ______________.
160. Irradiation with __________ doses could allow a much longer shelf life at refrigerator temperatures for fish and other sea foods and could improve the safety of poultry by eliminating potential dangerous organisms.
161. Primary aim of storage is simply to prevent __________ of quality of grain.
162. The electro-magnetic energy used in food irradiation is similar to ___________ but has shorter wave length, producing grater energy and penetration.
163. A post harvest ecosystem of stored grains is defined as a _____________ system that includes a group of interacting organism and their environment.
164. Grain has very ________ thermal conductivity and specific heat.
165. Hygroscopicity of grain is described by ________ which are generally sigmoidal curves.
166. In absence of forced circulation of air through inter-granular spaces, there may be the formation of hot zone localized within the grain mass, sphere heat generation due to biological (metabolic) activities are _________.
167. The creation of moisture content gradient without temperature gradient in grain mass results in a transfer of _________ from moist to dry grain.
168. No species of storage fungi in stored grain can grow below ________ % equilibrium relative humidity.
169. Common grain storage fungi grow mostly rapidly at ________°C.
170. Oxygen at less than ________% level retards the fungi development in stored grain.
171. The growth and reproduction of insect in stored grain ecosystem is greatly reduced at a temperature below ________ °C.

172. Insect development in grain storage system is enhanced by high moisture content above ________%.
173. Little or no insect activity in stored grain occurs below ________% moisture content.
174. The optimum relative humidity for the development of mites in grain storage is approximately at ________%.
175. One rat eats approximately ________kg of grain in a year.
176. Optimum moisture content for storage of paddy is ________% for longer period.
177. About ________% of total grain losses occurs due to activity of insect in India.
178. The maximum time before the germination falls by 5% or visible mould appears is called ________.
179. Generally, insect do not develop below 15°C and nor mites below ________°C.
180. The metabolic heat produced exclusively by dry grain is about ________ cal/sec/cm^3.
181. The growth rate of insect, fungi and mites decreases with ________ of temperatures.
182. Normal grain atmosphere consists of________% carbon dioxide.
183. Drying is the removal of ________ from food materials.
184. Dehydration means removal of moisture from foods to ________ condition.
185. Paddy needs to store at ________% moisture content for shorter period.
186. Normally, farmers harvest paddy at ________% moisture.
187. Moisture content of a substance is expressed in ________.
188. Direct methods of moisture determination are simple and accurate but ________ consuming.
189. The electrical conductivity or resistance of grain depends upon its ________
190. In Henderson equation, $1-rh = \exp(-CTM_e^n)$, M_e is ________.
191. In milling operation, the losses of about ________% occur.
192. If the moisture content on wet basis is 25 %, then the moisture content on dry basis shall be ________%.
193. Spiral separator is used for grading the seed on the basis of________.
194. The differential speed ratio of rolls of wheat mill is________.
195. The 'R' pocket type disc separator is used for ________.
196. A scalper is used for ________.
197. 100 kg of grain is dried from 18 % (wb) to 13 % (db). The amount of water removed ________kg.
198. The edible portion of paddy is called________.
199. Two by-products of paddy milling process are________ and ________.
200. The method of separating particles according to size alone is known as________.

Section 3

201. The scratch roll system is further extension of________.
202. If the moisture content on wet basis is 20 %, then the moisture content on dry basis is ________ %.
203. 100 kg of grain is dried from 24 % (wb) to 10 %(db). The wt. of dried grains is_______.
204. The powdered materials obtained from the outermost part of the brown rice are called________.
205. In 1 – *rh* = exp (– $KTMe^n$), rh means__________.
206. Pulses contain ____________percent of protein by weight.
207. Soybean consists of __________ percent oil content.
208. Lye solution is made from ____________.
209. Moromi is partial product of __________.
210. Acidophilus milk is heated at __________°C temperature for 30 min.
211. Milk of ___________ percent fat used for preparation of culture butter milk.
212. Wheat consists of bran (____ %.), germ (___ %) and endosperm (____ %).
213. Tempering of wheat is done for __________ hours in parboiling process.
214. Number of break rolls in wheat mill used are __________.
215. Kefir is foamy and fizzy in nature due to____________.
216. Plan sifter in wheat milling works as __________system.
217. Formation of black neck in sauce and ketchup is caused due to ____________.
218. Mechanical handling devices aim to __________ the work of labour.
219. The conveying device has to be selected according to __________.
220. The grain storage facility available with CWC is about ________million tonnes.
221. The ___________ is very efficient device for the vertical conveyance of bulk grain.
222. Bucket elevator with a belt carrier can be used at fairly high speeds of ______to______.
223. The capacity of kothari structure varies from ________to________ tonnes.
224. The gable roof is the part of___________ grain storage structure.
225. Circular steel bin is recommended for ___________storage of grain.
226. The size of outlet of Pusa Bin is recommended about ____________ cm.
227. Aluminium bin is constructed on _____________ cm high platform.
228. In rising film evaporator, __________ viscosity liquid food is allowed to boil.
229. The cost of down stream processing is often more than _________ percent of the manufacturing cost.
230. Membrane filtration achieves both concentration and separation of the products usually based on the ___________ of molecules.

231. The final step in the recovery of product is __________ which aims to obtain the product in highly purified state.

232. The unit used to measure the activity of a given source of radiation is __________.

233. The most useful supercritical fluid is __________ .

234. Extraction conditions for supercritical CO_2 are above the critical temperature of __________°C and critical pressure of ________ bar.

235. Supercritical Fluid Extraction is an alternative to liquid extraction using solvent such as __________.

236. The falling film evaporator is best suited for ________ products such as orange juice.

237. The properties of a supercritical fluid (CO_2) can be altered by varying the pressure and __________.

238. Supercritical Fluid Extraction is a __________ based process.

239. The quantity of radiation energy absorbed by a food is called __________.

240. The amount of radiation energy absorbed by foods equals the amount of heat required to raise the temperature of water to __________°C.

241. X-rays generated from machine sources operated at a maximum energy of ________ MeV.

242. Electron generated from machine sources operated at maximum energy of __________ MeV.

243. One (Gy) dose of radiation is equal to ________ joule of energy absorbed per kg of food material.

244. The process of separating one component (the extractant) from another (the matrix) using supercritical fluids as the extracting solvent is called ______________.

245. Food irradiation inhibited the ________ of bulbs, tubers and rhizomes.

246. Insect disinfection and elimination of food borne parasites in stored grains is accomplished by __________ dose irradiation.

247. Elimination of pathogenic microbes in fresh and frozen meat, poultry and sea foods is done by __________ dose irradiation.

248. Sterilization of packaged meat, poultry and their products which are shelf stable without refrigeration is accomplished by __________ dose irradiation.

249. Inactivation of harmful pathogens and viruses in food requires ________ irradiation doses.

250. Bacterial spores are ________ resistive to irradiation.

251. The sensitivity of microorganism to radiation is expressed as ____________ by analogy with thermal destruction.

252. The dose of radiation that reduces the microbial population to 10 % of its initial value is known as __________.

253. Ascorbic acid is ________ radio sensitive during irradiation.

254. Irradiation at ________ doses levels can delay ripening and over ripening of tropic fruits like banana, mangoes and papaya.

255. Radiation doses of ________kGy kill the adults and larvae of major insects infesting grain and cereals.

256. Gamma rays emitted by radioactive isotopes (Co-60) are used as a source of energy in ________ and in medical treatment.

257. Food irradiation is a ________ treatment in which food is exposed to ionizing radiation.

258. The optimum temperature for storage of ghee is ________ °C.

259. The partial removal of water from liquid food by boiling is called ________.

260. An increase in solid by evaporation ________ the water activity.

261. The increase in boiling point over that of pure water at a given pressure is called ________.

262. The rate of evaporation is determined by the rate of ________ transfer to the foods and the rate of ________ transfer of vapour from the foods.

263. Evaporation under ________ condition is to increase the rate of evaporation and reduce the boiling point.

264. During evaporation, the ________heat is transferred from the heating medium to the food to raise its temperature to boiling point.

265. The heat transfer area per unit volume in batch type pan evaporator is ________.

266. Heating of the liquid food in pan evaporator occurs due to ________ convection.

267. The poor heat transfer characteristics of batch type pan evaporator are substantially ________ the processing capacity.

268. In natural circulation evaporator, the vertical tubes are of 1-2 m and ________mm in diameter.

269. The various processes used for the actual recovery of useful product from fermentation or any other industrial process are called ________.

270. The length of vertical tubes in rising film evaporator varies with ________ meter.

271. A temperature difference of ________°C between the product and heating medium in rising film evaporator is necessary to obtain a well developed film on the inside the tubes.

272. Rising film evaporators achieved ________ convection heat transfer coefficients.

273. Falling film evaporator has a thin liquid film moving downward under ________ on the inside of vertical tubes.

274. The falling film evaporator allows a ________ number of effects than rising film evaporator.

275. The falling film evaporator can handle ________ liquid than rising film evaporator.

276. The volatile oils can be extracted by super critical fluid (CO_2) from a plant with ______ ________ pressures of 100 bar.
277. Typical residence time to food in falling film evaporator is ________ second against to the 3-4 minutes in rising film evaporator.
278. Per capita consumption of bakery products in India is just around _____ kg of bread and _____ kg of biscuit.
279. The growth rate of bakery industry in India is around _________ percent.
280. The ability of the material to store electrical energy in microwave heating is called _______ constant.
281. The ability of the material to dissipate electrical energy in microwave heating is defined as ________.
282. The degree to which an externally applied electrical field will be converted to heat in material during microwave heating is expressed as __________ factor.
283. The electromagnetic spectrum between the frequencies of 300 MHz to 300 GHz is represented by __________.
284. Microwave heating is depended upon _________ properties of foods.
285. Microwaves have certain similarities to _________.
286. Heat generation in food through microwave is done by mechanism of ________ and dipole rotation.
287. Food materials contain polar molecules such as _________.
288. Frozen storage refers to storage at temperatures that maintain food in ________ condition.
289. Good frozen storage generally requires temperature of ________ °C or below.
290. Pure water freezes at ________ °C temperature.
291. Extrusion cooking is a __________ process.
292. Farmers retain _____% of total wheat and ______% of paddy for personal utilization.
293. The total grain storage facility available with FCI is _______ million tonnes.
294. The _________ have a maximum feed on angle of 10° and conveying angle of 12°.
295. As much as ________% of the food industry is in organized sector and _______% in small scale, tiny and cottage sector in India.
296. The total storage facility available in country for perishable is ________ tonnes.
297. Maize products (dextrins, starch etc.) is prepared by_________ method.
298. Soybean has _____% protein with healthy amino acid profile and _____% oil content.
299. The process of hermetically sealing of fruit and vegetable food stuffs in container and sterilizing by heat treatment for long period of storage is known as ________.
300. Ascorbic acid or acetic acid is used in canned fruit to create _________ in product.

Section 4

301. A process of sealing foods hermetically in containing and sterilizing them by heat is so called canning or __________.
302. The grâding of fruits and vegetables in canning is done on the basis of ________ and ________ of products.
303. The purpose of peeling is to remove undesirable __________ of fruit or vegetable which provide hard texture and astringent flavour.
304. The purpose of peeling in root crop is to remove ________ and soil firmly adhering to the product.
305. Lye peeling is done in boiling caustic soda of _______ strength for about 2 to 5 minutes.
306. The lye peeled product is further dipped in 0.5% ______for few seconds for proper neutralization.
307. The main purpose of blanching is to inactivate most of the _________ which cause hardness, discoloration (poly phenol oxidase), off flavour (per oxidase), softening and loss of nutritive value.
308. Blanching of fruits and vegetables is to destroy the micro organisms about __________%.
309. Blanching enhance __________ of vegetables like peas, broccoli and spinach.
310. The time of blanching is depends on __________ of product.
311. A solution of sugar in water is called __________.
312. Syrup is added to improve the flavour and to serve as_________medium for facilitating processing.
313. In canning process, syruping is done only for__________.
314. In canning, the syrup or brine should be filled at about _________°C temperature.
315. The head space in canned food should be leave about ___________cm.
316. A solution of salt in water is called _________.
317. The objective of brining in canning process is similar to that of _________.
318. Strained and hot syrup concentration of ___________°brix is used for fruit canning.
319. Hot brine of ______% concentration is used for covering vegetables in canning process.
320. Clinching process in which the lid of can is __________ seamed.
321. The process of removal of air from cans is known as __________.
322. Exhausting minimizes disclouration of canned foods by preventing ________.
323. The time of exhausting varies from _________min., depending on the nature of product.
324. During sealing of cans, the temperature should not fall below ________°C.
325. Heating of foods for preserving is known as _________.
326. In canning, processing means heating or cooling of canned foods to inactivate ________.
327. Almost all fruits and acid vegetables can be processed satisfactorily at a temperature of ___________°C in boiling water.

328. Thermal processing time and temperature during canning should be adequate to eliminate all ______________.

329. The sourness of fruit and vegetables is due to their acid content (measured in pH) which has great influence upon the _____________ of microorganism.

330. Bacterial spores by heat can be more easily destroyed at pH of _________ for fruits and 5.0-6.0 for vegetables.

331. Bacterial spores do not grow or germinate below pH of _________.

332. After processing, the cans are cooled rapidly to about _________ °C to stop the cooking process and to prevent stack burning.

333. Preventing the entry of microorganisms is known as __________.

334. Pasteurization does not kill all _________ present in the foods.

335. Mould spores are destroyed by heating at __________ °C temperature for 5 to 10 min.

336. Usually fruit juice, RTS and nectar are pasteurized at about ________ °C temperature for 25 to 30 min. according to the nature of juice and the size of the container.

337. Acid fruit juices require a ___________ temperature and less time for pasteurization than the less acid ones.

338. The best way of preserving pure fruit juice is done by __________.

339. Juice can be kept in good condition for a long time in frozen form at ________ °C by excluding air.

340. Any substance which capable of inhibiting, retarding or arresting the process of fermentation, acidification or other decomposition of foods is called _________.

341. Two preservatives *i.e.* sulphur dioxide and ______ are mostly allowed with permissible limit in India according to Fruit Product Order (FPO) of 1955.

342. Potassium meta bisulphite ($K_2S_2O_5$) is commonly used as stable source of __________.

343. Sulphur dioxide retards the development of _________ browning or disclouration after killing enzyme of the food products.

344. Sulphur dioxide has a better preservative action than ____ against bacteria and moulds.

345. The pH for growth of moulds ranges from 1.5-8.5, that of yeast from 2.5-8.0 and bacteria from ________.

346. The toxicity of sulphur dioxide increases at high ___________.

347. According to FPO, the maximum permissible limits of SO_2 allowed in fruit juice are 700 ppm, in squash, crush and cordial 350 ppm and in RTS and nectar _______ ppm.

348. One part of sodium benzoate is soluble in ________ part of water at ordinary temperature.

349. Sodium benzoate is nearly __________ times more soluble as than benzoic acid.

350. Benzoic acid is more effective against yeast than __________.

351. According to FPO, permissible level of benzoic acid in RTS and nectar is _____ ppm and in squash, crush and cordial is 600 ppm.

352. By drying method, juices are preserved in the form of ____________.

353. Fruit juice powders are highly _______________ in nature.

354. The process of dissolving sufficient carbon dioxide in water or beverage is known as __________.

355. Fruit juice beverages are generally bottled with CO_2 content varying with _____ g/ litre.

356. The keeping quality of carbonated fruit beverage is enhanced by adding about ________ percent sodium benzoate.

357. Syrups containing __________ percent or more sugar which do not ferment.

358. Sugar acts as a preservative by ________________.

359. Fruit syrups, jam, jelly, marmalade, preserve, candy, crystallized fruit and glazed fruits are preserved by the addition of ____________.

360. Decomposition of carbohydrate by microorganisms or enzyme is called __________.

361. The keeping quality of fermented pickles depends upon the presence of __________.

362. About __________ percent alcohol acts as preservatives in wines against yeast.

363. Salt at a concentration of __________ percent is sufficient to preserve most food products.

364. Salt in the form of brine is used for _____________ of vegetable.

365. About ________ percent acetic acid prevents spoilage in many food products.

366. __________ acid is added to fruit squash, jam and jelly to increase the acidity and prevent mould growth.

367. __________ is added to impart the acidity to pickles, chutney, sauce and ketchup.

368. Spice like turmeric, pepper and asafoetida have little ________________ effect and their ability to prevent growth of microorganisms.

369. The primary function of spices is to impart their characteristic __________ to the food.

370. Nisin is commonly used in ___________ of mushroom, tomato and milk products.

371. Nisin is a ______ produced by *Steptococcus lactis,* an organism found in dairy products.

372. Nisin is widely used in the food industry especially for the preservation of ___________ foods in which it is more stable.

373. Subtilin, an antibiotic obtained from certain strains of __________ is used to preserve asparagus, corn and peas.

374. Subtilin and nisin effectively reduce the __________ process necessary to control the spoilage of several food products.

375. Canning industry for filling food products are preferred __________ container.

376. The coating of lacquer inside the tin container for preventing the corrosion and disclouration is called ______________.

377. R-enamel or AR cans are used for the packaging of ____________ foods.

378. C-enamel or SR cans are employed for packaging of __________foods.

379. Turnip, carrot, cabbage are classified in __________ acid foods.

380. The bulging of can is due to __________ internal pressure of gases created by microbial or chemical reaction.

381. Longer exhausting of can at 79°C gives better results than a short one at about _________°C.

382. A product made by boiling fruit pulp with sufficient sugar to a reasonably thick consistency, firm enough to hold the fruit tissues in position is known as __________.

383. Jam contains ______ % acid and invert sugar should not be more than ________%.

384. Corn syrup or glucose in jam may be added along with cane sugar to avoid ________.

385. Premature setting of jam can be prevented by adding more of ________.

386. Surface graining and shrinkage is caused by evaporation of moisture during _______ of jam.

387. Yeasts are not a serious problem in jam due to the high concentration of ________.

388. Microbial spoilage in Jam is prevented by adding of 40 ppm sulphur dioxide in the form of ________.

389. A semi-solid product prepared by boiling a clear, strained solution of pectin containing fruit extract, free from pulp, after the addition of sugar and acid is called __________.

390. Acid content in jelly should be _________ percent.

391. Pectin in the form of calcium pectate is responsible for the ________ of fruits.

392. Usually about 0.5–1.0% of ____________ of good quality in the fruit extract is sufficient to produce good quality jelly.

393. If the pectin content is __________, a firm and tough jelly is formed.

394. Proteins are made up of smaller compounds known as __________.

395. Each gram of protein supplies __________ kcal of energy.

396. Each gram of oil and fat supplies__________ kcal of energy.

397. Each gram of carbohydrate consumed provides __________ kcal of energy to body.

398. About _______ percent of the thiamine is destroyed in normal cooking.

399. Loss of water soluble vitamins may go upto ______ percent as a result of leaching and heating.

400. In modern food processing, nutrients losses are seldom in excess of _____ percent.

Section 5

401. The disease caused by the toxins of *Clostridium botulinum* is known as __________.

402. Mycotoxins produced by moulds such as *Aspergillus flavous* and *A. parasiticus* are ________.

403. The illness caused by the consumption of bacterial toxin formed in the foods is refered ________.

404. The illness caused by the entrance of bacteria into the body through ingestion of contaminated food is called ___________.

405. Lathyrism, a disease is associated with the consumption of _________.

406. Soaking, heating or fermentation of pulses can be eliminated most of the ______ factors.

407. Conduction is the method of transfer of heat by ________.
408. Radiation is the emission of heat in the form of ________ from a hot object.
409. A mixture of milk and milk fat of 10 to 12 percent is called ________.
410. Heat is used in broiling method of cooking in the form of ________.
411. Toasting of bread is essentially by ________ heat.
412. Roasting and baking are generally at ________°C and ________°C, respectively.
413. Boiling, simmering or stewing involves cooking of food in ________.
414. Simmering and poaching are methods of cooking of food by immersing in a hot liquid maintained at a temperature just below the ________.
415. Sauteing is cooking method of food used for the preparation of ________.
416. Microwaves penetrate food to a depth of ________cm.
417. Microwave cooking is ________ times faster than conventional cooking.
418. Electrical energy required for microwave cooking is ______ than that of the traditional method.
419. The principal effect of heat on protein is ________.
420. Interaction between the free amino groups of protein with reducing sugar or carbonyl groups formed by lipid oxidation results in ________ browning or maillard browning.
421. Starch molecules which are the main source of ________ in many diets.
422. In cooking, the loss of water soluble vitamins ranges ________ percent as a result of leaching and thermal destruction.
423. Vitamin A and carotene is ________ in water.
424. Vitamin A and carotene in frying and roasting cause their loss upto ______ percent.
425. Mineral losses in cooking methods of food are ________ percent.
426. Hydrolytic rancidity is catalyzed in food at ________ temperature and pressure.
427. Oxidative rancidity is responsible for more loss in the quality and nutritive value of ________ than any other changes.
428. The decrease of pH of egg white increases the stability of the ________.
429. The main substances for turbidity in cane juice is ________ etc.
430. The sugar industry is based on sugarcane and ________crop.
431. The ________ water is good for boiler as well as drinking purpose.
432. The required factory area for sugar industry should be about ______ to ______ acre.
433. The average length of cane stalk should not more be ____to ____feet.
434. The root, stalks and ________are the main part of sugarcane.
435. The soft, fibrous and central part of the cane is called ________.
436. The pith contains juice about ________% while in rind and node is ________%.
437. The approximate percentage of sugar in cane from ______ to ______%.
438. Succinic acid is main component of ________ other than sugar in sugarcane juice.

439. The powdered materials obtained from the outermost part of the brown rice are called_____.
440. A device which separates non-vegetative impurities from the grains is known as________.
441. The rapid removal of moisture to a very low level by applying external heat is called_____.
442. 1 $-rh$ = exp (_____________).
443. Pulses contain __________ percent of protein by weight.
444. Soybean consists of _________ percent oil content.
445. Lye solution is known as __________.
446. Moromi is partial product of__________.
447. Acidophilus milk is heated at__________°C for 30 min.
448. Milk of ___________percent fat used for culture butter milk.
449. Wheat consists of bran (12 %), germ (3%) and endosperm (________%)
450. Tempering of wheat is done for ____________hours.
451. Number of break rolls in wheat mill is used __________.
452. Plan sifter works as _________ system.
453. Kefir is foamy and fizzy in nature due to ___________.
454. Formation of black neck is caused due to _____________.
455. If the moisture content (db) is 25 %, then what would be the moisture content (wb) is __________%.
456. Velvet separator separates the seed on the basis of difference in _____ and surface texture.
457. The 'R' pocket type disc separator is used for removal of _______ from head rice.
458. A pearler is used for ___________.
459. All fats and oil are broadly classified into _________ and non-edible.
460. A bin whose relative dimensions are such that the plane of rupture meets the grain surface before it strikes the opposite side is called ____________.
461. Pressure cooking is a device to reduce the cooking time by increasing the __________.
462. A shear press is used to study the _______ of fruits and vegetables.
463. Sensory evaluation consists of judging the ________ of food by a panel of judges.
464. The ripeness of fruits is judged by _________.
465. The nose and mouth are utilized to obtain information on __________.
466. Flavour embraces the senses of taste, smell and a composite sensation known as ________.
467. The number of members in trained panel for sensory evaluation should be small, varying with________.
468. The semi-trained panel for sensory evaluation should consist of _________ members.
469. The methods of different testing in sensory evaluation commonly used are the paired comparison, __________ and triangle test.
470. The duo-trio test employs _________ samples, two identical and one different.
471. A hedonic rating testing is used to measure the degree of pleasurable and unpleasurable experience of the food product on a scale of ________ from like extremely to dislike extremely.

472. The best time of the day for sensory testing is ________ hour after normal meal.

473. The data of sensory evaluation are tabulated, averaged and __________ for the answer to the question posed in the experiments.

474. Tintometers are simple instruments used to determine the ________ and its depth in foods.

475. The tenderness of meat is an important quality for consumer's _________.

476. Tenderness of meat is tested by measurement of structure of meat with a _______.

477. A puncture testing is used to evaluate the ____________ of fruits.

478. Quality is the ______________ of the desirability of any food product.

479. Rheology is the science of flow and __________ of material.

480. Gel like those pectin, gelatin and starch, baked custard and rennet custard are examples of ___________.

481. The _________ of dough and batters determines the quality of finished products.

482. The consistency and stability of dough are measured with a __________.

483. A micrograph also gives information similar to that of ______________.

484. Textures of baked products such as pastries, cookies and crackers are evaluated by ______.

485. A compressimeter is used to evaluate the _________ of bread crumb or softness of a baked product.

486. Dried egg is stored at temperature much above freezing, the traces of glucose combines with egg proteins resulting in __________.

487. The functional properties of an egg are not adversely affected by __________.

488. Dried egg white is quite stable during ________.

489. Use of egg as thickening, binding and clarifying agents are all based on the ___________ its protein when heated.

490. Egg white protein begins to coagulate at _________°C under controlled conditions.

491. The coagulation of egg yolk begins at 65°C and is completed at ___________°C.

492. Acid, such as cream of tartar or lime juice reduce the coagulation temperature by helping reduce the pH of the egg mixture to the _________point.

493. The presence of salt ____________ the temperature of coagulation of egg mixture.

494. Egg yolk foam is a component of _________.

495. Egg white in nature is ________ in comparison with others foods.

496. The medium of cooking in steaming, waterless cooking and pressure cooking is ________.

497. The addition of water to egg white in an amount upto _________ percent by volume increases the volume of the foam but decrease the stability.

498. Salt added to egg white or whole egg before beating reduces the stability of ___________.

499. The volume and stability of egg white decrease but whipping time increase in the presence of _______.

500. Addition of ________ % of sugar to egg white more than doubles the time requires for foam formation.

ANSWER KEY

(FIIL IN THE BLANKS)

Section 1

S.No.	Answer	S. No.	Answer	S. No.	Answer	S. No.	Answer
1.	70%	26.	Brokens	51.	Protein	76.	6.5-6.7
2.	Minimize	27.	Milled rice	52.	1.5 to 2.5	77.	+0.2 to +0.3 volt
3.	Add value	28.	Red rice	53.	Gota machine	78.	Milk sugar
4.	Cleaning	29.	Minimize	54.	50%	79.	Vitamin A
5.	Grading	30.	Polygonal	55.	Polishing	80.	40%
6.	Sorting	31.	Starch	56.	LSU	81.	Crystallization
7.	Scalping	32.	Gelatinization	57.	degerming	82.	Storage
8.	Screening	33.	70°C	58.	15-16%	83.	Marmalade
9.	Dehydration	34.	Smaller	59.	45%	84.	65%
10.	Drying	35.	10 to 13 m/s	60.	Glycerides	85.	Bacteria
11.	Physico-chemical	36.	Glazing	61.	2.25	86.	Groundnut
12.	Human labour	37.	1:1	62.	Energy	87.	80°C
13.	Protect	38.	22 kg	63.	Linoleic acid	88.	Mold
14.	18-22%	39.	Break rolls	64.	Expression	89.	0.025- 0.10%
15.	Rice	40.	20 to 25 cm	65.	Chemical	90.	antimicrobial
16.	Aleurone layer	41.	2.5:1	66.	*n–hexane*	91.	pH
17.	White rice	42.	Bulgur	67.	65.5°C	92.	Bread
18.	12-13 %	43.	Rice	68.	Milk	93.	Bacteriostatic
19.	Milled	44.	Bulgur	69.	Galactose	94.	Gram positive
20.	HRY	45.	75°C	70.	Lactic acid	95.	Fungicide
21.	Head rice	46.	83-85% db	71.	Cow milk	96.	E234
22.	74%	47.	75°C	72.	Butter fat	97.	25-30°C
23.	MRY	48.	70-75%	73.	Lecithin	98.	30-32°C
24.	Bold rice	49.	Outer husk	74.	65-67°C	99.	25°C
25.	Bran	50.	17-25%	75.	0.13- 0.21%	100.	Decreases

Section 2

S.No.	Answer	S. No.	Answer	S. No.	Answer	S. No.	Answer
101.	5°C	126.	39°C	151.	Air	176.	12%
102.	0°C	127.	74°C	152.	16°C to 38°C	177.	3%
103.	1×10^{-7}	128.	NaOH	153.	Psychophysics or Cryophilic	178.	Allowable storage time
104.	1.3×10^{-5}	129.	Citric acid	154.	cold	179.	5°C
105.	13%	130.	8°C	155.	4.4 -7.2°C	180.	1×10^{-7}
106.	10%	131.	Respiration	156.	Metabolic activity	181.	Decrease
107.	5%	132.	Fats and oils	157.	Radappertizing	182.	0.03%
108.	Metabolic activity	133.	Refrigerant	158.	Storage	183.	Moisture
109.	Deterioration	134.	Slow or sharp	159.	Food Irradiation	184.	Bone dry
110.	Summer	135.	D-value	160.	Higher	185.	14%
111.	60%	136.	Z-value	161.	Deterioration	186.	16%
112.	Canning	137.	F-value	162.	X-rays	187.	Percentage
113.	Appert	138.	Turbo-milling	163.	Thermodynamic	188.	Time
114.	Flavour	139.	Gluten	164.	Low	189.	Moisture content
115.	Appertising	140.	Hermetic	165.	Sorption isotherm	190.	Equilibrium moisture content
116.	Syrup	141.	Enzyme	166.	High	191.	2-10%
117.	Brine	142.	Iso-electric	167.	Moisture	192.	20%
118.	1 - 3%	143.	Buffer index	168.	60%	193.	Roundness
119.	79 to 82°C	144.	0.0186	169.	30-32°C	194.	2.5:1
120.	0.3 to 0.5 cm	145.	Decreases	170.	1%	195.	Paddy
121.	Exhausting	146.	5.0	171.	20°C	196.	Rough cleaning
122.	74°C	147.	Storage	172.	14%	197.	7.8 kg
123.	100°C	148.	Bacteria	173.	10%	198.	Endosperm
124.	2-5 min	149.	Loose	174.	85%	199.	Husk and Bran
125.	Blanching	150.	Absorb	175.	10kg	200.	Screening

Section 3

S. No.	Answer	S. No.	Answer	S. No.	Answer	S. No.	Answer
201.	break rolls	226.	50×50 cm	251.	D_{10} Value	276.	Low
202.	25%	227.	60 cm	252.	D_{10} Value	277.	20-30 sec
203.	83.6 kg	228.	low	253.	More	278.	2.3 kg, 1.8 kg
204.	Bran	229.	50%	254.	Low	279.	17%
205.	relative humidity	230.	Size	255.	0.25 kGy	280.	Dielectric
206.	20-30%	231.	Purification	256.	Food irradiation	281.	Dielectric loss
207.	20%	232.	Becquerel	257.	Physical	282.	Dielectric loss
208.	Caustic soda	233.	Carbon dioxide	258.	21°C	283.	Microwave
209.	Soy sauce	234.	31°C, 74 bar	259.	Evaporation	284.	Dielectric
210.	98°C	235.	Hexane	260.	Reduces	285.	Visible light
211.	0.5-1.8%	236.	high heat sensitive	261.	Boiling point elevation	286.	Ionic polarization
212.	12 %, 3%, 85%	237.	Temperature	262.	Heat, mass	287.	Water
213.	18-72 hrs	238.	Diffusion	263.	Vacuum	288.	Frozen
214.	3 to 4	239.	Radiation dose	264.	Latent heat	289.	–18°C
215.	Carbon dioxide	240.	2.4°C	265.	Small	290.	0°C
216.	Scalping	241.	5 MeV	266.	Natural	291.	HTST
217.	Iron	242.	10 MeV	267.	Reduce	292.	44 %, 48%)
218.	Lighten	243.	One	268.	50-100mm	293.	27
219.	Characteristics of the products	244.	Supercritical fluid extraction	269.	Down stream processing	294.	Inclined conveyors
220.	18	245.	Sprouting	270.	10-15 meter	295.	42%, 33%
221.	Bucket elevator	246.	Low dose	271.	14°C	296.	8 lakh
222.	2.5-4.0 m/sec	247.	Medium dose	272.	High	297.	Wet milling
223.	9 to 35 tonnes	248.	High dose	273.	Gravity	298.	40%, 20%
224.	Kothar	249.	Higher	274.	Greater	299.	Canning
225.	Indoor	250.	Higher	275.	More viscous	300.	Flavour

Section 4

S.No.	Answer	S. No.	Answer	S. No.	Answer	S. No.	Answer
301.	Appertizing	326.	Bacteria	351.	100 ppm	376.	Lacquering
302.	Size, colour	327.	100°C	352.	Powder	377.	Acid
303.	Skin	328.	Bacterial growth	353.	Hygroscopic	378.	Non acid
304.	Root hairs	329.	Destruction	354.	Carbonation	379.	Medium
305.	1-2%	330.	3.0	355.	1-8 g/ litre	380.	Positive
306.	Citric acid	331.	4.5	356.	0.005%	381.	87°C
307.	Enzymes	332.	39°C	357.	66%	382.	Fruit jam
308.	99%	333.	Asepsis	358.	Osmosis	383.	0.5-0.6%, 40%
309.	Green colour	334.	Microorganisms	359.	Sugar	384.	Crystallization
310.	Characteristics	335.	79°C	360.	Fermentation	385.	Sugar
311.	Syrup	336.	85°C	361.	Lactic acid	386.	Storage
312.	Heat transfer	337.	Lower	362.	14%	387.	Sugar
313.	Fruits	338.	Freezing	363.	15-25%	388.	KMS
314.	79-82°C	339.	–12 to –17°C	364.	Canning	389.	Fruit Jelly
315.	0.3-0.5 cm	340.	Preservatives	365.	2%	390.	0.5-0.75%
316.	Brine	341.	Benzoic acid	366.	Citric	391.	Firmness
317.	Syruping	342.	Sulphur dioxide	367.	Vinegar	392.	Pectin
318.	20-50°Brix	343.	Non enzymatic	368.	Bacteriostatic	393.	Higher
319.	1 to 3%	344.	Sodium benzoate	369.	Flavor	394.	Amino acid
320.	Partially	345.	4.0-8.0	370.	Canning	395.	Four
321.	Exhausting	346.	Temperature	371.	Antibiotic	396.	Nine
322.	Oxidation	347.	100 ppm	372.	Acid	397.	Four
323.	9-10 min	348.	1.8	373.	*Bacillus subtilis*	398.	20%
324.	74°C	349.	170	374.	Thermal	399.	60%
325.	Processing	350.	Moulds	375.	Tin	400.	25%

Section 5

S.No.	Answer	S. No.	Answer	S. No.	Answer	S. No.	Answer
401.	Botulinum	426.	high	451.	3 to 4	476.	Penetrometer
402.	Aflatoxin	427.	lipids	452.	Scalping	477.	Firmness
403.	Food intoxication	428.	Foam formation	453.	Carbon dioxide	478.	Ultimate criterion
404.	Food infection	429.	Wax	454.	Iron	479.	Deformation
405.	Khesari dhal	430.	Beet sugar	455.	20%	480.	Elastic solids
506.	Anti-nutritional	431.	Potable	456.	Shape	481.	Texture
407.	Contact	432.	50 to 80	457.	Broken	482.	Farinograph
408.	Wave	433.	8-12	458.	Polishing	483.	Farinograph
409.	Half-and-half	434.	Leaves	459.	Edible	484.	Shortometer
410.	Radiation heat	435.	Pith	460.	Deep bin	485.	Firmness
411.	Radiation	436.	80%, 20%	461.	Pressure	486.	Browning
412.	120°C, 260°C	437.	8-16%	462.	Tenderness	487.	Drying
413.	Water	438.	Organic matter	463.	Quality	488.	Storage
414.	Boiling point	439.	Bran	464.	Colour	489.	Coagulation
415.	Dosa	440.	Destoner	465.	Flavour	490.	52°C
416.	2.5 to 7.5 cm	441.	Dehydration	466.	Mouth feel	491.	70°C
417.	Ten	442.	$-KTMe^{n}$	467.	5-10	492.	Iso electric
418.	Less	443.	20-30%	468.	25-30	493.	Lower
419.	Denaturation	444.	20%	469.	Duo-Trio	494.	Sponge cake
420.	Non enzymatic	445.	Caustic soda	470.	Three	495.	Alkine
421.	calories	446.	Soy sauce	471.	9-point	496.	Steam
422.	0 to 60 %	447.	98°C	472.	One	497.	40%
423.	Insoluble	448.	0.5-1.8 %	473.	Analyzed	498.	Foam
424.	20-40%	449.	85 %	474.	Colour	499.	Salt
425.	0 to 35%	450.	18 to 72	475.	Acceptability	500.	50

Chapter 13

True or False

Section 1

Note: Tick (✓) True or False against each statement

S. No.	***Questions /Statements***	***Tick T/F***
1.	The angle of repose increases with the materials when moisture content increase.	T/F
2.	Bulk density is less important than true density in drying and storage practices.	T/F
3.	Thermal conductivity of frozen foods is much less than that of foods at ordinary temperature.	T/F
4.	Liquids that do not follow Newtonian behaviour called non-Newtonian liquids.	T/F
5.	Sweetened condensed milk is not a thixotropic food.	T/F
6.	Surface heat transfer coefficient is a thermal property of food.	T/F
7.	Moisture content (wb) of food is always higher than moisture content (db) of food.	T/F
8.	The frontal area of food is a basic parameter for the determination of terminal velocity.	T/F
9.	Volume of prolate spheroid shape is calculated by $3/4\ (\pi ab^2)$.	T/F
10.	Coefficient of viscosity divided by the mass density is known as kinematic viscosity.	T/F
11.	For laminar flow, Reynolds number is less than 2100.	T/F
12.	Drop wise condensation usually occurs on coated surface.	T/F
13.	The convective coefficient for boiling and condensation usually lies in the range of 2500-10000 W/m^2K .	T/F
14.	The mean radius, r_m for a hollow cylinder of inner and outer radii for same radial heat flow rate is given by $\frac{r_2 - r_1}{\ln(r_2/r_1)}$	T/F

15. A radiation shield should have high transmissivity. T/F
16. For an ideal reflector, the energy distribution at higher temperature is at longer wavelength. T/F
17. Forced convection in a liquid bath is caused by density difference brought about by temperature gradient. T/F
18. Perishable foods have low moisture content. T/F
19. Green leafy vegetables are rich in vitamins and minerals. T/F
20. Farinograph measures water absorption. T/F
21. Freshly milled flour produces better dough for bread making. T/F
22. The measurement unit of viscosity is Nm^{-2}. T/F
23. Refrigerant absorbs heat through expansion. T/F
24. The vapour barrier in cold stores should be provided on the colder side of the insulation. T/F
25. The power required by the centrifugal pump varies as square of the speed. T/F
26. The efficiency of a pump increases as the viscosity increase. T/F
27. Storage tanks used in dairy plants maintain the milk at a temperature of 7°C or below. T/F
28. Citric acid may be used for curdling of milk. T/F
29. Pasteurization kills all microorganisms. T/F
30. The batch pasteurizers are costly. T/F
31. An increase in wet bulb temperatures of air indicates the lowering of relative humidity. T/F
32. Sensible cooling of air increases relative humidity of air. T/F
33. Dried onion and chilies being hygroscopic in nature have lot of sulphur T/F
34. Fish spoils at faster rate than other type of meat. T/F
35. Smoking improves the flavour of meat. T/F
36. Phosphorus content in rice is high but is not available to human being. T/F
37. After the death of animals, pH of the meat decreases. T/F
38. Fruits containing salts generally deteriorate the quality of jelly. T/F
39. Parboiling process protect the grain from rancidity. T/F
40. Vinegar is nothing but 4 % citric acid. T/F
41. Mango stones are used for extraction of protein T/F
42. Soft wheat is used for bread making. T/F
43. Foods are made up mostly from edible biochemical. T/F
44. Pectin is a type of carbohydrate. T/F
45. Simple carbohydrates are called starches. T/F

46. Milk sugar (lactose) is a combination of glucose and galactose T/F
47. Maltose or malt sugar is made from the two molecule of fructose only. T/F
48. Cane or beet sugar (sucrose) made from glucose and fructose. T/F
49. The disaccharides, Dextrins, starches, cellulose, hemicelluloses, pectin and gum are not composed by simple sugar or their derivatives. T/F
50. Sugars that possess free aldehyde or ketone group are known as non-reducing sugar. T/F
51. All monosaccharides are reducing sugars. T/F
52. When two or more monosaccharides are linked together through their aldehyde or ketone so that these reducing groups are not free, the sugar is non-reducing sugar. T/F
53. The disaccharide maltose is not a reducing sugar. T/F
54. The disaccharide sucrose is not a non-reducing sugar. T/F
55. Fermentation of carbohydrates by yeast and other microorganisms can not yield carbon dioxide and alcohol. T/F
56. Starches are usually used for their sweetness. T/F
57. Sugars form crystals when water is dried from their solution. T/F
58. Sugars prevent the growth of microorganisms in high concentration. T/F
59. Starches becomes darken colour or caramelize on heating T/F
60. Some sugar combine with protein to give dark colour known as browning reaction. T/F
61. Fructose is not sweeter than glucose or sucrose. T/F
62. Starches are soluble in cold water. T/F
63. Partial breakdown of starches yields dextrin. T/F
64. Gelatinization takes place only in starches. T/F
65. Cellulose and hemicelluloses are soluble in water and also digested by humans. T/F
66. Hard parts of coffee beans and nut shells are composed of cellulose and hemicelluloses. T/F
67. Cellulose and hemicelluloses can not break down to glucose units by certain enzymes and microorganisms. T/F
68. Pectin and gums are added to foods as thickener and stabilizer. T/F
69. Proteins are made up from amino acids. T/F
70. Proteins are not major constituents of blood, milk and egg white. T/F
71. In animals, protein help to form supporting and protective structure such cartilage, skin, nail, hair and muscles. T/F
72. Amino acid does not contains the $-NH_2$ or amino group. T/F
73. The amino and carboxyl groups themselves are basic and acidic in nature, respectively. T/F
74. Leucine, isoleucine and lysine are not essential amino acids. T/F

75. Cysteine and Cystine are essential amino acids. T/F
76. When the organized molecular or spatial configuration of a protein is disorganized by means of heat, chemical or enzyme is called gelatinization of protein. T/F
77. When milk is coagulated by acid and heat, protein precipitates forming cheese curd. T/F
78. Controlled cheese ripening involves a desirable degree of protein breakdown. T/F
79. Putrefaction of meat is not the result of excessive protein breakdown accompanying other charges. T/F
80. Proteins have some specific functional attributes like dispersibility, water sorption, elasticity, foamability and foam stability. T/F
81. Fats are not smooth and greasy substances that are soluble in water. T/F
82. Fat contains about 2.25 times the calories found in an equal dry weight of protein or carbohydrates. T/F
83. Ergosterol is an example of vegetable fat. T/F
84. Sterol and cholesterol are mostly occurring in animal fat. T/F
85. Glycerol and butyric acid is a common fatty acid not found in butter. T/F
86. A typical fat molecule consists of glycerol combined with free fatty acids. T/F
87. Glycerol has three reactive carboxyl groups and fatty acid has one reactive hydroxyl group. T/F
88. When free fatty acid molecules can combine with each glycerol molecule and eliminating three molecules of water is known as triglycerides. T/F
89. The unsaturated fatty acid is not a dietary essential for health. T/F
90. Diglycerides and monoglycerides have special emulsifying properties. T/F
91. The longer fatty acids yield softer fats and shorter fatty acids contribute to harder fats. T/F
92. Unsaturation of the fatty acids also contribute to softer the fats. T/F
93. An oil is simply a fat that is not liquid at room temperature. T/F
94. Hydrogen is added to saturated highly unsaturated fatty acids, this process is known a hydrogenation. T/F
95. Materials that keep fat globules dispersed in water or water droplets dispersed in fat are accompanied by an emulsifier. T/F
96. The darkening of dried milk on long storage is the example of browning reaction or maillard reaction. T/F
97. The darkening of foods by the action of heat on sugar is referred as Blackening. T/F
98. An amino group of a protein combines with an aldehyde or ketone group of a reducing sugar to produce a brown colour is not a mechanism of maillard reaction. T/F
99. A calorie is the amount of heat required to decrease the temperature of one gram of water at 1°C (from 14.5 to 15.5°C). T/F
100. The kilocalorie (1000 calorie) is the unit commonly used expressing energy values of foods. T/F

Section 2

101. One kilocalorie is 4.2 times of calories. T/F
102. Fat generally yield 2.5 times more calories as compared to protein or carbohydrate. T/F
103. α-carotene is the precursor of vitamin B. T/F
104. Fat soluble vitamins are B and C. T/F
105. Vitamins A, D, E and K are not fat soluble. T/F
106. Most of foods have less amount of vitamin D. T/F
107. Vitamin E is also known as α- tocopherol. T/F
108. Vitamin E has a strong antioxidant property. T/F
109. Vitamin C does not contains anti-scurvy properties. T/F
110. Vitamin C is easily lost during processing, storage and cooking. T/F
111. The foods rich in vitamin C must be protected against exposure to oxygen to prevent losses. T/F
112. Citrus fruits are not excellent source of ascorbic acid. T/F
113. Sulphur dioxide (a preservative) destroys the vitamin activity in foods which are major source of thiamin. T/F
114. Thiamin is heat stable only in acidic foods. T/F
115. Vitamin B12 is called the anti-pernicious anemia factor. T/F
116. Vitamin B12 does not contain cobalt molecule in own structure. T/F
117. Vitamin B12 is also recognized by cyanocobalamin. T/F
118. Vitamin B12 is synthesized by bacteria and molds and is a commercial by product of antibiotic production. T/F
119. Complete removal of water from foods under controlled conditions is known as food dehydration. T/F
120. Water is removed when potatoes are fried is an example of food dehydration. T/F
121. Removal of water from liquid food is a meaning of dehydration. T/F
122. Dried potato flakes, instant coffee and orange juice crystals are the example of food dehydration. T/F
123. At high pressure, carbon dioxide works as supercritical fluid. T/F
124. Decaffeinated product from coffee is made by supercritical fluid extraction. T/F
125. Crystallization is used to separate sugar from sugarcane juice. T/F
126. The operation by which large pieces of food converted into smaller particle are defined as disintegration. T/F
127. Cutting, grinding, pulping and homogenization is not the subgroup of disintegration. T/F
128. Grinding operation in food can partially denature the protein. T/F
129. Burned flavour in ground coffee is generated by grinding operation. T/F

130. Homogenization produces disintegration of fat globules in milk or cream from large globules and clusters into minute globules. T/F

131. Foods are not heated by conduction, convection, radiation or a combination of these. T/F

132. Microorganisms are more sensitive to rapid heating than chemical reaction. T/F

133. Baking, frying, concentration, dehydration are the unit operations of heating. T/F

134. Various kind of package closure for food is not used for the unit operation of heating. T/F

135. Heating is the removal of heat energy from foods while cooling is the addition of heat energy. T/F

136. Quality is defined as degree of excellence and includes such as taste, appearance and nutritional content. T/F

137. Appearance factors for quality evaluation include such as firmness, softness, juiciness and grittiness. T/F

138. Textural factors include size, shape, glossiness, transparency and colour etc. T/F

139. Wholeness refers to degree of whole and broken pieces. T/F

140. Colour is commonly not index of ripeness or spoilage. T/F

141. Colour measurement of food is measured by colorimeter or spectrophotometer. T/F

142. Value in colour measurement refers to lightness or darkness of the colour or the amount of white versus black. T/F

143. Hue determines the perceived colour like (red, green, yellow, blue etc.). T/F

144. Chroma refers to intensity strength of the colour. T/F

145. The value, hue and chroma is not related to Hunterlab colour or colour difference meter. T/F

146. The consistency of thick or thin liquid food can not measured by viscometer. T/F

147. A tenderometer applies compression and shear to measure the tenderness of peas. T/F

148. An universal testing machine cannot measure the firmness, crispiness and other textural parameters of foods. T/F

149. Flavour is not a combination of both taste and smell. T/F

150. The pH is the logarithm of hydrogen ion concentration. T/F

151. Deterioration may not include organoleptic desirability, nutritional value and aesthetic appeal. T/F

152. Meat, fish and poultry can become inedible in less than a day at room temperature. T/F

153. The shelf life of food is defined as the time it takes for a product to decline to an unacceptable level. T/F

154. Requirement of iron increases in lactation. T/F

155. Osteoporosis disease is common among pregnant ladies. T/F

156. Vitamin K is called as coagulation vitamin. T/F

157. Vitamin A is easily destroyed by heat. T/F

158. Carotene is the precursor of vitamin K. T/F

159. Vitamin E is an antioxidant. T/F

160. A tall thin person has more basal metabolic rate than fat short person. T/F

161. No energy is needed when person is asleep. T/F

162. Basal metabolic rate is related more to body weight than surface area. T/F

163. 5 gram of butter and sugar yield same amount of calories. T/F

164. A certain percentage of calories requested should come from fats. T/F

165. Bland diet is given in diabetes. T/F

166. An example of complete protein food is an egg protein. T/F

167. Protein requirement increases when a person is doing heavy task. T/F

168. With each °F rise in temperature basal metabolic rate increases. T/F

169. Pasteurization can make unclean milk clean. T/F

170. Bixin ($C_{25}H_{30}O_4$), a flavour compound is obtained from Annatto. T/F

171. Oils are saturated fats. T/F

172. Carotene ($C_{40}H_{56}$) is not a colouring matter or pigments which is present in carrot. T/F

173. Glucose is a disaccharide. T/F

174. Only carbohydrates, fat and protein provide energy to the body. T/F

175. Cochineal is a colouring matter of animal origin and is obtained from Coccus cacti insects. T/F

176. Hard studying require more energy. For this, one should take vitamin pills. T/F

177. Generally a person needs to drink 8-10 glasses of water in a day. T/F

178. Solid foods do not contain water. T/F

179. Cellulose cannot be digested; therefore it is not useful in the diet. T/F

180. Only starch can be obtained from grains and it is fattening. T/F

181. Milk is a complete food. T/F

182. Fats are less susceptible to microbial decomposition than are carbohydrates and proteins. T/F

183. None of the thiamine in vegetables leaks out into the water in which they are cooked. T/F

184. It is a good idea to add some baking soda to the water in which green vegetables are to be cooked, because it keeps them looking fresh and green. T/F

185. You should eat a daily serving of a food rich in vitamin C that has not been cooked or dried. T/F

186. Yellow and green vegetables have a high vitamin A value. T/F

187. Vitamin D is of no value to you when you are growing. T/F

188. The lack of vitamin D causes beri-beri. T/F

189. Vitamin pills can be a substitute for a balanced diet. T/F

190. Usually girls have a higher deposition of body fat as compared to boys of the same age but have a lesser percentage of muscle tissue. T/F

191. Triglycerides are the chief components of natural fats and oils. T/F

192. The date beyond which the food product is no longer acceptable is called expiration date. T/F

193. Enzymes and biochemical reactions are responsible for food deterioration. T/F

194. Lactic acid bacteria (LAB) are not responsible to make cheese and sauerkraut. T/F

195. Milk from a healthy cow is sterile as secreted. T/F

196. Bacteria are multi-celled organisms. T/F

197. Bacilli are found in spherical shape. T/F

198. Spiral in shape is possessed by the spirilla and vibrios. T/F

199. Bacteria, yeasts and molds can not attack virtually all food constituents. T/F

200. Most bacteria can not multiply best at temperatures between 16 to 38°C. T/F

Section 3

201. Some microorganisms will grow at temperature down to freezing point of water are called mesophilic. T/F

202. Microorganisms will grow at as high as 82°C is known as thermophilic. T/F

203. Some bacteria and molds require no oxygen for growth and are called aerobic. T/F

204. The organisms can grow under either aerobic or anaerobic conditions is called facultative. T/F

205. Bacteria are multiply by cell division process. T/F

206. Under favourable conditions, bacteria can double their number every 30 minutes. T/F

207. Staphylococcus aureus and Clostridium botulinum are not responsible for bacterial food poisoning by intoxication. T/F

208. Aflatoxin in foods is produced by Aspergillus flavous. T/F

209. Aflatoxin may be more toxic to man than domestic animal. T/F

210. When food is handled at 10-38°C, the rate of chemical reactions is approximately doubled for every 10°C rise in temperature. T/F

211. Moisture is not required for chemical reaction and for microbial growth. T/F

212. Thermophiles will grow in the temperature range of 66-82°C. T/F

213. Most of bacteria are killed in temperature range of 82-93°C. T/F

214. Bacteria and yeasts generally require more moisture than molds for growth and multiplication. T/F

215. Relative humidity is defined as the ratio of the partial temperature of water vapour in the air to vapour temperature of pure water at the same pressure. T/F

216. Water activity is the ratio of vapour pressure of the solution to the vapour pressure of pure water at the same temperature. T/F

217. Water activity is equal to ERH/100. T/F

218. Most bacteria for growth there is no need of water activity in range of 0.9-1.00. T/F

219. Acid combined with heat makes the heat more destructive to microorganisms. T/F

220. Solutions of high solute concentration have a high osmotic pressure and a low water activity. T/F

221. Dilute solutions are low in osmotic pressure and a low water activity. T/F

222. Yeasts and molds are more tolerant than most bacteria against osmosis, sugar and salt. T/F

223. The surface of cheese may not be treated with sorbic acid. T/F

224. Cottage cheese may have sorbic acid mixed directly in the product. T/F

225. Food irradiation is also known as cold sterilization. T/F

226. Cooking generally sterilize the food products. T/F

227. The toxin that can be formed by clostridium botulinum is destroyed by a 10 min exposure to moist heat at 100°C. T/F

228. Sterilization refers to incomplete destruction of microorganisms. T/F

229. Most canned or bottled food products are commercially sterile and have a shelf life of 2 years or more. T/F

230. Blanching is applied to fruits and vegetables to activate natural food enzymes. T/F

231. The time in minutes at a specified temperature required to destroy 90% of the organisms in a population is known as F_0 value. T/F

232. The Z-value is the number of degree required for a specified thermal death time curve to pass through one log cycle (change by a factor of 10). T/F

233. Different organisms in a given food will have same Z-value. T/F

234. F-value is defined as the number of minutes at a specified temperature required to destroy a specified number of organism having a specified Z-value. T/F

235. The F-value is not a measure of the capacity of heat treatment to sterilize. T/F

236. The F_0–value is also known as the 'sterilization value'. T/F

237. The retorts used in canning process, conduction and radiation play an important role. T/F

238. In natural convection, the heated portion of food becomes heavier in density and rises up. T/F

239. The point in a can or mass of food which is last to reach the final heating temperature is known as 'cold point'. T/F

240. HTST pasteurization of raw milk employs a temperature of at least 161°C for at least 15 seconds. T/F

241. Hydrogen peroxide is used in aseptic processing and packaging to sterilize the packaging materials. T/F
242. Rapid sterilization at extremely high temperature is referred as UHT sterilization. T/F
243. At a pH of 4.6, Clostridium botulinum will grow or produce toxin. T/F
244. Tomato juice under HTST heating is sterilized at 121°C for 0.7 min. T/F
245. In microwave heating of foods, heat transfer will not from outside to inside. T/F
246. Commercial and household refrigerators are usually operated at 4.5 to 7.0°C. T/F
247. Cool storage generally refers to storage the foods at temperature below freezing. T/F
248. Pure water will not starts to freeze at 0°C T/F
249. Ice cream is a frozen liquid food. T/F
250. Good frozen storage generally requires temperature of –18°C or below. T/F
251. Most foods store best at refrigeration temperature between when the relative humidity of air is lower than 75%. T/F
252. Hypobaric storage for fruits and vegetables is maintained under increased pressure and low humidity. T/F
253. At a pressure of 1 atm (760 mm Hg), no water boils at 100°C. T/F
254. At constant temperature, a decrease in pressure increases the rate of boiling. T/F
255. Although a large proportion of the microbial load is killed during drying operations but many bacterial spore remains to survive. T/F
256. More salt, sugar, minerals or proteins in a solution means higher freezing point. T/F
257. The freezing point of pure water is less than 0°C. T/F
258. When pure water freezes slowly, it forms minute ice crystals. T/F
259. Thawing is a reverse process of freezing. T/F
260. Faster the freezing rate, poorer the product quality. T/F
261. Enzyme reaction rates are faster in super-cooled water than in frozen water at the same temperature. T/F
262. Storage of foods at –18°C sufficiently retards the activity of many food enzymes to accelerate significant deterioration. T/F
263. Non enzymatic chemical reactions are not entirely stopped at –18°C, but proceed very slowly. T/F
264. Most of the fish are less stable in nature. T/F
265. The temperature at which eutectic mixture is formed is called eutectic point. T/F
266. A Btu is not a unit of heat energy. T/F
267. Thermal conductivity of ice is far greater than that of water. T/F
268. Air has a thermal conductivity far greater than that of water or fat. T/F
269. The oil-in-emulsion has greater thermal conductivity against water-in-oil emulsion under same chemical composition along with at different temperatures. T/F

270. Greater the temperature differences between the food and the refrigerant, slower the freezing rate. T/F

271. Thinner the food piece or greater the heat transfer rate of the food package, lower the freezing rate. T/F

272. The greater the refrigerating effect or heat capacity of the refrigerant, the faster is the freezing rate. T/F

273. Air blast freezers are operated at –30 to – 45°C with forced air velocities of 10-15 m/s. T/F

274. Egg yolk is a natural emulsifier. T/F

275. Liquid hydrogen is used as cryogenic liquid in immersion freezing of foods. T/F

276. Water is driven from the food as water vapour in drying/dehydration. T/F

277. Dehydrated foods are non hygroscopic in nature. T/F

278. The humidity at which the food products neither lose nor gains moisture is known as equilibrium moisture content. T/F

279. Cabinet, tray and pan driers are usually used for small scale operations. T/F

280. One Gray (Gy), a unit of radiation is equal to 10^5 rads. T/F

281. An electronic Volt (eV) is the energy equivalent to 1.6×10^{-19} Joule. T/F

282. The strength of gamma radiation is not expressed in terms of roentgens. T/F

283. Gamma rays have lesser penetrating power than beta (β) particles. T/F

284. Hydrogen peroxide is a strong oxidizing agent and a biological poison. T/F

285. Irradiation can be inhibited sprouting of potatoes and onions by specific doses. T/F

286. Sauerkraut is not an unfermented food which is made from cabbage. T/F

287. Vermouth is yeast fermenting alcoholic beverages made from vegetables only. T/F

288. Miso is a fermented food product of soybean. T/F

289. Breakdown of proteinaceous material by fermentation is known as lipolytic. T/F

290. Decomposition of fatty substance in food by fermentation is described as putrefactive. T/F

291. Industrial production of riboflavin and B12 is due to special fermentation process. T/F

292. Lactose (milk sugar) fermented by Streptococcus lactic bacteria is supported to yield cottage cheese. T/F

293. Protein in foods is breakdowned by proteolytic bacteria such as Alcaligenes lipotyticus. T/F

294. Lipids are broken down by lipolytic bacteria such as Proteus vulgaris. T/F

295. In the production of sauerkraut, approximately 2.0-2.5 % salt generally is added to the cabbage. T/F

296. Sauerkraut and pickles have no acidities range between the pH of 2.5-3.5. T/F

297. Fermented meat sausages commonly have acidities in the range of pH of 4.0-4.5. T/F

298. The milk solid non fat (MSNF) refers to total solid plus the fat. T/F
299. Milk solid non fat also is referred to as serum solids. T/F
300. One kg of butter is made from the 22.8 kg of milk. T/F

Section 4

301. 10 kg of milk is required to prepare one kg of cheese. T/F
302. The increase in volume caused by whipping air into the ice cream mix during the freezing is known as overrun. T/F
303. The MSNF contribute the flavour, to give body and desirable texture to ice cream. T/F
304. Egg yolk is a good•natural stabilizer due to its content of lecithin. T/F
305. Gelatin or gum gaur is used as emulsifier in ice cream. T/F
306. Milk fats do not give a rich flavour, smooth texture and body to the milk products. T/F
307. Vanilla is used as flavour enhancer in ice cream. T/F
308. Pasteurization temperature of ice cream is lower than the plain milk. T/F
309. Ice cream mix is pasteurized in continuous HTST process at 82°C for 25 seconds. T/F
310. After homogenization, the ice cream is cooled at 8.4°C. T/F
311. Semi solid ice cream is hardened at a temperature of about –34°C. T/F
312. Whey cheeses are high in β-lactoglobulin and α- lactalbumin. T/F
313. Cream cheese is high rich in fat content. T/F
314. Cottage cheese is an example of a high fat and soft cheese. T/F
315. Swiss cheese is soft in comparison to cottage cheese. T/F
316. Swish cheese is also known as Emmental cheese. T/F
317. Mold ripened cheese (Camembert) is originated in France. T/F
318. Acidophilus milk is a pasteurized milk or low fat milk which inoculated by Lactobacillus bulgaricus. T/F
319. Yoghurt is pasteurized or low fat milk coagulated with Lactobacillus acidophilus. T/F
320. Marbling is the deposition of fat within the lean muscle. T/F
321. A major protein of muscle fibre is myosin. T/F
322. The connective tissues of lean muscle contain two proteins is called collagen and elastin. T/F
323. Collagen on heating in the presence of moisture dissolves and yields elastin. T/F
324. Ageing or ripening of meat generally is done at 2°C. T/F
325. Curing refers to modification of meat that affects preservation, flavour, colour and tenderness due to added curing ingredients. T/F
326. Sodium nitrate or nitrite is helped to cure meat and have anti-botulinum activity. T/F
327. Sodium chloride for curing or pickling of meat is used a strong preservative and enhance the colour. T/F

328. Sugar in curing of meat helps to stabilize colour and add flavour. T/F

329. The chief muscle pigment is a protein called myoglobin. T/F

330. Smoking acts as a mild preservative in curing of meat. T/F

331. Frankfurters is also known as a type of meat pickles. T/F

332. Frankfurters which generally are mildly cured, cooked and smoked sausage. T/F

333. Italian salami which is uncooked, smoked and cured meat sausage. T/F

334. Freezing temperature can be used to destroy the trichinosis parasite in pork products. T/F

335. Poultry is raised only for egg. T/F

336. The washed birds are rapidly chilled from 32 to 2°C to prevent bacterial spoilage and to preserve quality. T/F

337. Poultry flesh is not a good source of vitamin B and minerals. T/F

338. Chicken flesh contains more protein, less fat and less cholesterol than red meat. T/F

339. The egg yolk is rich in fat soluble vitamin A, D, E & K and also lecithin. T/F

340. Egg contains about 300 mg of cholesterol. T/F

341. The most common method of grading of eggs is accomplished by candling. T/F

342. Storage of egg is best at a temperature of –1°C in warehouse. T/F

343. When eggs are dipped in hot water or oil for a short period to coagulate a thin layer of albumin is called thermo-stabilization. T/F

344. Pasteurization of eggs is not done at 60-62°C for 3.5-4.0 min. T/F

345. Freezing of eggs is done in sharp freezers at the temperature of –18°C. T/F

346. Prevention of browning disclouration in dried egg by removing glucose through fermentation by yeasts or enzymes is known as desugaring. T/F

347. Herring, Mackerel, Salmon, Tuna and Sardine is classified as Pelagic fish. T/F

348. Cod, Haddock and Shrimp is also known as demersal fish. T/F

349. Most of fish contain 0.2 to 20 % protein. T/F

350. The fat of fish is an excellent source of vitamin A & D. T/F

351. Canned fish with bone such as Salmon and Sardines are excellent sources of calcium and phosphorus. T/F

352. Fish tissue generally is less perishable than animal tissues. T/F

353. Fishy odour in fish is due to Trimethylamine. T/F

354. High quality, low fat fish stored in the frozen state at –21° to –23°C may retain its quality for as long as 2 years. T/F

355. Fish which contain more oil are not more suitable for canning. T/F

356. Canned fish products generally have a shelf-life of several years. T/F

357. Shrimp contained no natural polyphenol oxidase enzyme which is responsible for dark colour. T/F

358. The major portion of fat and oils are made up of fatty acid esters of glycerol. T/F
359. The fats that are liquid at room temperature are called oil. T/F
360. Hydrogenation which saturates the fat to make them less resistance to oxidation. T/F
361. Natural fats contain only one triglyceride molecule. T/F
362. The animal fat (tallow) is obtained from poultry. T/F
363. Lard contributes a fishy flavour in fish and meat. T/F
364. Butter contains not less than 80 per cent fat. T/F
365. Margarine is largely made from vegetable oils. T/F
366. The air screen cleaner usually called the fanning mill. T/F
367. The slope of the screen in air screen cleaner is adjustable to control the rate of downward movement of the grain. T/F
368. The horizontal rotating cylinder has indents on the outside surface. T/F
369. The density of the grain decides the size of screening surface. T/F
370. Copper carbonate and copper sulphate are used as insecticide. T/F
371. Mercuric chloride is not injurious to most seeds. T/F
372. High capacity belt conveyor has a conveying capacity less than 2000 tonnes per hour. T/F
373. The efficiency of belt conveyor is largely dependent on idlers. T/F
374. The moisture content of seed influenced the seed viability during storage. T/F
375. Fumigation is inefficient only in gas tight storage. T/F
376. Evaporation takes place at the falling rate. T/F
377. Packaging improves the quality of milk. T/F
378. The batch pasteurizers are costly. T/F
379. Cream separator rotates at recommended speed of 3000 to 3500 rpm. T/F
380. Moisture content on dry basis is always higher the moisture content on wet basis. T/F
381. Pasteurization of milk destroyed all microorganisms. T/F
382. Perishable foods have low moisture content. T/F
383. Due to the presence of casein, milk is adhesive in nature. T/F
384. Drying increases the packaging, handling and transportation cost. T/F
385. As the temperature increases, viscosity of air decrease. T/F
386. Food Processing may be defined as an activity which is performed to maintain or improve the quality or to change the form or Characteristics of an agricultural product. T/F
387. Processing operations are undertaken to reduce the value to agricultural produce after their harvest. T/F
388. The main purpose of food processing is to enhance the qualitative and quantitative deterioration of the material after harvest. T/F

389. The commercial value of agricultural products is depended on their grade factors. T/F

390. Grading may be done by washing, screening, hand pickling and winnowing etc. T/F

391. Grains with impurities provide higher price to the producers. T/F

392. Presence of foreign materials in the grains increases the bulk hence decrease the cost of processing, packaging, handling and transportation. T/F

393. Drying is a thermo-physical and physico-chemical operation by which the excess moisture to the product is added. T/F

394. Drying makes the attractive appearance of the food grains and other products for the attack of insects, molds and other microorganisms during storage. T/F

395. Milling means reduction of food grain in to various end products like meal, flour, splitted products (pulses) etc. T/F

396. Optimization of time and movement of material in a processing plant are necessary to minimize the cost of operation and maximize the profit. T/F

397. The aim of mechanical handling devices is to reduce the work of human labour. T/F

398. The role of packaging is not to contain, protect and sell the products. T/F

399. Packaging must protect against physical damage, chemical attack and contamination from biological vectors including microorganisms, insects and rodents. T/F

400. Environmental factors such as oxygen and water vapour will spoil food if they are allowed to enter packages freely. T/F

Section 5

401. Contamination of foods by microorganisms can not spoil foods or cause life threatening diseases. T/F

402. Storage is not an interim and a repeated phase during transit of agricultural products from producer to processor and its products from processor to consumer. T/F

403. Safe storage of agricultural products is essential to avoid losses due to rodents, insects, and diseases and to maintain good quality for a longer period. T/F

404. One hundred kg of paddy would yield about 22 kg of husk, 4 kg bran and about 74 kg of white rice. T/F

405. The kernel of paddy is not enclosed by hull or husk. T/F

506. The weight of hull is 4-6% of the total weight of paddy grain. T/F

407. The major constituent of the rice endosperm is starch (approx. 90 percent). T/F

408. The primary objective of rice milling is to remove the hull or husk and bran with minimum breakage of the endosperm to produce acceptable white rice. T/F

409. After harvest, paddy grain is to be dried upto 10-11 % moisture content (wet basis) for milling purpose. T/F

410. Rice quality involves the head rice yield (HRY) and milled rice yield (MRY). T/F

411. HRY is the percentage of rough rice that is left after complete milling operation. T/F

412. MRY is the percentage of rough rice remaining as milled rice that contains both head and broken kernels. T/F

413. Head rice is defined as 'unbroken kernels of rice and broken kernel of rice that are at least two fourths of an unbroken kernel'. T/F

414. Clean and good quality paddy can give a yield of 74% rice. T/F

415. Rice kernel that is less than ¾th of the size of full kernels is called brokens. T/F

416. Rice kernel whole or brokens which have 25% or more their surface having red pericarp is known as Brown rice. T/F

417. The outturn of rice after milling expressed in percentage with respect to clean paddy is called milling yield. T/F

418. Sorting refers to removal of all types of foreign matters and other impurities. T/F

419. Parboiling is an optional treatment given to paddy prior to its milling to achieve minimum recovery of head rice and to maximize breakage. T/F

420. The paddy grain is mainly composed of polygonal starch granules. T/F

421. The temperature at which gelatinization takes place is known as the swelling power temperature. T/F

422. Gelatinization temperature for paddy is specific far particular variety in the near hood of 70°C. T/F

423. Parboiling increases the total and head rice yield of paddy. T/F

424. Parboiling enhances the loss of nutrients during milling. T/F

425. In parboiling, paddy is soaked and the wet paddy is dried and then steamed. T/F

426. The purpose of rice huller is to remove the husk from paddy grain with minimum damage to the bran layer and as far as possible not to break the brown rice. T/F

427. Rubber roll sheller can shell up to 95% of paddy fed to it. T/F

428. In Rubber roll sheller, during shelling the faster roll should have a peripheral surface speed of 10 to 13 m/s, while the slower roll 8-10 m/s. T/F

429. Whitening is the removal of silver skin and bran layer of rice followed by polishing. T/F

430. Glazing is a coating with talcum powder and glucose after polishing to give a transparent look to rice. T/F

431. In glazing, about 1.0 kg glucose solution is required for 1000 kg of rice. T/F

432. Dry talc powder about 10-12% by weight is required for glazing of rice. T/F

433. Glucose is added to the rice as 1:3 solutions with water in glazing treatment. T/F

434. Grading in rice milling usually refers to the separation of unbroken from the head rice and the further classification of unbroken. T/F

435. Rice brokens may be separated either by a 'Plansifter' or by a 'Trieur'. T/F

436. Circular purifier is used for removing pieces of husk, bran and dust particles that remain adhering to milled rice after grading. T/F

437. The edible portion (endosperm) of paddy is called rice. T/F

438. Debranned (polished) and cracked parboiled wheat is known as bulgur. T/F

439. Parboiled wheat resembles rice when it is debranned and split into two more pieces. T/F

440. Bulgur production consists of milling (i.e. debranning and cracking) followed by soaking, steaming and drying. T/F

441. The hot air temperature of 60°C is to be optimum for the drying of parboiled wheat. T/F

442. In parboiling of wheat, 75°C temperature of soaking water gives to good compromises between advantages and disadvantages of high temperature soaking. T/F

443. In parboiling of wheat, only 13 to 15% moisture is added during steaming of soaked wheat containing 83% moisture (db). T/F

444. The protein from pulses is known to be inferior quality, due to the deficiency of sulphur containing amino acids. T/F

445. Pulses are poor in protein and are mainly consumed in the form of dehusked split pulses. T/F

446. Pulses consumed as Dhal have about 17-25% protein with Dhal yield potential of 80-85 %. T/F

447. Dhal mills have a Dhal recovery of 65-70% where as modern Dhal mills yield about 70-75%. T/F

448. Milling of pulses means removal of the outer husk and unsplitting the grain in to four equal halves. T/F

449. The yield of split pulses in traditional mills is only 65% to 70% while potential yield may be 80 to 85% and broken loss varies 15 to 20%. T/F

450. Pulses are the major source of proteins to vegetarian masses of the country. T/F

451. In general, pulses contain 20-30 percent protein. about 60 percent carbohydrates, 1.0-2.5 percent fat, and are fairly good source of thiamine, nicotinic acids, calcium and iron. T/F

452. The scratched or pitted pulses are treated with some edible oil like linseed oil of 2.5 to 2.75 kg/tonnes of pulse. T/F

453. An emery roller and concave type machine used in pulse milling is known as Gota machine. T/F

454. Milling of pulses is the operation in which to remove the outer husk as splitting and making of the pulse in two equal halves. T/F

455. About 75% of pulses are dehusked and splitted in single pass by Gota machine. T/F

456. The purpose of pulse polishing is to remove small size of husk adhering to cotyledons and to provide glazing look or glossy look for the dhal. T/F

457. A little amount of oil and / or water is used for proper polishing of pulses. T/F

458. Polishing of pulse is also carried out in gota machine. T/F

459. In Modern CFTRI Method of pulse milling, the pre conditioning is done in two pass, using a hot air of 120°C in the LSU type drier. T/F

460. Corn flakes are very popular breakfast cereals, popped corn and very popular snack food to even urban elite. T/F

461. The purpose of all dry degerming corn milling methods is to remove hull, germ and tip cap from the corn kernel as far as practicable and primarily produce corn grits with some meals and flours. T/F

462. The optimum moisture content for degerming of corn in the Baell Degermer is 25-30%. T/F

463. Degerming is a process in which endosperm is separated (detached) from other component of corn kernels is namely, germ, hull and tip cap. T/F

464. Baell corn degermer device which consists of a cone type rotor and cylinder. T/F

465. The raw corn for wet milling should contain 10-12% moisture and it should be physically sound. T/F

466. Humistor is the short form of humidity sensitive resister. T/F

467. All fats and oil are broadly classified into edible and non-edible. T/F

468. The main constituents of the vegetables oils are 20 and 28 carbon acids. T/F

469. Per capita consumption of edible oil per year in India is 5 kg, but recommended 18 kg oil per annum per capita. T/F

470. On weight basis, oil and fats furnish 2.25 times more energy than protein and carbohydrates. T/F

471. Oils provide the essential fatty acid i.e. linoleic acid, which is not needed for human health. T/F

472. Excessive intake of saturated fatty acids increases the level of serum lipids and the incidence of arteriosclerosis and heart disease. T/F

473. One bullock Ghani can operate six charges of sunflower per day or 80 kg of meal (approximately 160 kg of seed). T/F

474. Mechanical expression is the process of mechanically pressing liquid out of non liquid containing solids. T/F

475. Screw presses, roll presses and mill, collapsible plate and frame filler presses, disk mill are some of the example of a wide range of equipment used for oil solvent extraction method. T/F

476. The advantage of mechanical expression system over chemical extraction is that it gives the liquid free of dissolved chemical and thus a safer process. T/F

477. In hydraulic press, the oil samples are pressed at approximately 5 MPa for 15-20 minutes in first stage. T/F

478. Extraction is the process of separating a gas from a liquid solid system with the use of a solvent. T/F

479. Extraction may also be said as a process to extract oil from oil bearing materials through the process of diffusion with the help of low boiling point solvent. T/F

480. Extraction processing or solvent extraction is capable of adding nearly all of the available oil to oil seed meal or flakes. T/F

481. The most commonly used solvent in Indian oil extraction plants is the n–hexane. T/F

482. The boiling point of n-hexane is about 65.5°C used for solvent oil extraction. T/F

483. Milk solids such as fat, protein, lactose and minerals, all taken together are termed as total solids non fat (SNF) in milk. T/F

484. Milk fat is the lightest portion of milk. T/F

485. The size of fat globules in milk varies from 0.1 to 2 micron T/F

486. The Principal classes of milk proteins are not casein, lacto-globulin and lactalbumin. T/F

487. The casein account for 80% of total protein content, lactalbumin and lacto-globulin (whey proteins). T/F

488. Casein is a phospho-protein which is found only in milk. T/F

489. The casein is precipitate by acids at its iso-electric point of pH 6.6. T/F

490. Lactose is a disaccharide carbohydrate found only in milk in the form of glucose and galactose. T/F

491. Lactose in milk is easily changed by bacterial action to citric acid. T/F

492. The mineral constituents or salt of milk constitute 0.6 to 0.8 % of the total weight. T/F

493. Carotene is mainly responsible for yellow colour of buffalo milk. T/F

494. Milk contains two fat soluble pigments "carotene" and "xanthophylls" and water soluble "lactoflavin" (Lactochrome). T/F

495. The amount of cholesterol varies directly with the butter fat content of the milk. T/F

496. The principal phospholipids found in milk are called "lecithin". T/F

497. Lipase is an enzyme in milk fat that causes a strong or "rancid" flavor. T/F

498. The alkali nature of milk is due to the presence of phosphates, protein, citrates and dissolved dioxide. T/F

499. The acidity of milk ranges from 0.13% to 0.21% and expressed as percent lactic acid. T/F

500. Normal fresh milk has hydrogen ion concentration of approx. pH 6.5-6.7. T/F

ANSWER KEY

(TRUE / FALSE)

Section 1

S.No. Answer	S. No. Answer	S. No. Answer	S. No. Answer	S. No. Answer
1. T	21. F	41. F	61. F	81. F
2. F	22. F	42. F	62. F	82. T
3. F	23. F	43. T	63. T	83. T
4. T	24. F	44. T	64. T	84. T
5. F	25. F	45. F	65. F	85. F
6. T	26. F	46. T	66. T	86. T
7. F	27. T	47. F	67. F	87. F
8. T	28. T	48. T	68. T	88. T
9. F	29. F	49. F	69. T	89. F
10. T	30. F	50. F	70. T	90. T
11. T	31. F	51. T	71. T	91. F
12. T	32. T	52. T	72. F	92. T
13. F	33. F	53. F	73. T	93. F
14. T	34. T	54. F	74. F	94. T
15. F	35. T	55. F	75. F	95. T
16. F	36. F	56. F	76. F	96. T
17. F	37. T	57. F	77. T	97. F
18. F	38. T	58. T	78. T	98. F
19. T	39. F	59. F	79. F	99. F
20. T	40. F	60. T	80. T	100. T

Section 2

S.No. Answer	S. No. Answer	S. No. Answer	S. No. Answer	S. No. Answer
101. F	121. F	141. T	161. F	181. T
102. F	122. T	142. T	162. F	182. T
103. F	123. T	143. T	163. F	183. F
104. F	124. T	144. T	164. T	184. T
105. F	125. T	145. F	165. F	185. T
106. T	126. T	146. F	166. T	186. T
107. T	127. F	147. T	167. F	187. F
108. T	128. T	148. F	168. T	188. F
109. F	129. T	149. F	169. T	189. F
110. T	130. T	150. F	170. F	190. T
111. T	131. F	151. F	171. F	191. T
112. F	132. T	152. T	172. F	192. T
113. T	133. T	153. T	173. F	193. T
114. T	134. F	154. F	174. T	194. F
115. T	135. F	155. F	175. T	195. T
116. F	136. T	156. T	176. F	196. F
117. T	137. F	157. F	177. T	197. F
118. T	138. F	158. F	178. F	198. T
119. T	139. T	159. T	179. F	199. F
120. F	140. F	160. T	180. F	200. F

Section 3

S.No. Answer	S. No. Answer	S. No. Answer	S. No. Answer	S. No. Answer
201. F	221. T	241. T	261. T	281. T
202. T	222. T	242. T	262. F	282. F
203. F	223. F	243. F	263. T	283. F
204. T	224. T	244. T	264. T	284. T
205. T	225. T	245. T	265. T	285. T
206. T	226. F	246. T	266. F	286. T
207. F	227. T	247. F	267. T	287. F
208. T	228. F	248. F	268. F	288. T
209. F	229. T	249. F	269. T	289. F
210. T	230. F	250. T	270. F	290. F
211. F	231. T	251. F	271. F	291. T
212. T	232. T	252. F	272. T	292. T
213. T	233. F	253. F	273. T	293. F
214. T	234. T	254. T	274. T	294. F
215. F	235. F	255. T	275. F	295. T
216. T	236. T	256. F	276. T	296. F
217. T	237. F	257. F	277. F	297. T
218. F	238. F	258. F	278. F	298. F
219. T	239. T	259. T	279. T	299. T
220. T	240. F	260. F	280. F	300. T

Section 4

S.No. Answer	S. No. Answer	S. No. Answer	S. No. Answer	S. No. Answer
301. T	321. T	341. T	361. F	381. F
302. T	322. T	342. T	362. F	382. F
303. T	323. F	343. T	363. F	383. T
304. F	324. T	344. F	364. T	384. F
305. F	325. T	345. F	365. T	385. F
306. F	326. T	346. T	366. T	386. T
307. T	327. F	347. T	367. T	387. F
308. F	328. T	348. T	368. F	388. F
309. T	329. T	349. F	369. T	389. T
310. F	330. T	350. T	370. F	390. F
311. T	331. F	351. T	371. F	391. F
312. T	332. T	352. F	372. F	392. F
313. T	333. F	353. T	373. T	393. F
314. F	334. T	354. T	374. T	394. F
315. F	335. F	355. F	375. F	395. T
316. T	336. T	356. T	376. F	396. T
317. T	337. F	357. F	377. F	397. T
318. F	338. T	358. T	378. F	398. F
319. F	339. T	359. T	379. F	399. T
320. T	340. F	360. F	380. T	400. T

Section 5

S.No. Answer	S. No. Answer	S. No. Answer	S. No. Answer	S. No. Answer
401. F	421. F	441. F	461. T	481. F
402. F	422. T	442. T	462. F	482. T
403. T	423. T	443. F	463. T	483. F
404. T	424. F	444. T	464. F	484. T
405. F	425. F	445. F	465. F	485. T
506. F	426. T	446. T	466. T	486. F
407. T	427. T	447. T	467. T	487. T
408. T	428. T	448. F	468. F	488. T
409. F	429. T	449. T	469. T	489. F
410. T	430. T	450. T	470. T	490. T
411. T	431. T	451. T	471. F	491. F
412. T	432. F	452. F	472. T	492. T
413. F	433. F	453. T	473. T	493. F
414. T	434. F	454. T	474. F	494. T
415. T	435. T	455. F	475. F	495. T
416. F	436. T	456. T	476. T	496. T
417. T	437. T	457. T	477. T	497. T
418. F	438. T	458. F	478. F	498. F
419. F	439. T	459. T	479. T	499. T
420. T	440. F	460. T	480. F	500. T

IMPORTANT POINTS TO PONDER

FOOD CHEMISTRY

- **Fat** is a type of nutrient. Fats give you energy. Help **absorption of vitamins.** Contributes for blood cholesterol levels. **Avoid saturated fats and trans fats.**
- **Monounsaturated Fat** is found in **avocados, canola oil, nuts, olives, olive oil, seeds.** Eating food containing monounsaturated fat (or **healthy fat**) help to **lower cholesterol and reduce risk of heart disease. Contribute to weight gain** if you eat too much of it
- **Saturated Fat**: Solid at room temperature. Found in full-fat dairy products (like butter, cheese, cream, regular ice cream, and whole milk), coconut oil, lard, palm oil, ready-to-eat meats, and the skin and fat of chicken and turkey, among other foods.
- **Trans Fat** is a type of fat that is **created when liquid oils are changed into solid fats,** like shortening and some margarines. It makes them last longer without going bad. Found in crackers, cookies, and snack foods. Trans fat raises LDL (bad) cholesterol and lowers HDL (good) cholesterol. Unintentional by product in the industrial processing of vegetable and fish oils
- Sugar present in apple is **sorbitol**
- **Fatty acid** is a major component of fats that is used for energy and tissue development
- **Polyunsaturated Fat are of two types: 1. Omega 6:** Found in liquid vegetable oils (corn, safflower and soybean oil). **2. Omega 3:** Canola oil, flaxseed, soybean oil, walnuts and from fish and shellfish.
- **Polyunsaturated Fat and it is good for health** is **liquid at room temperature**
- **HDL** stands for high-density lipoproteins known as **good cholesterol.**
- **LDL** stands for **low density lipoproteins** known as **bad cholesterol.**
- Toxic chemicals produced by calcium carbide is **arsenic** and **phosphorus**
- **Triglycerides** are a type of fat found in blood. Higher triglycerides raise risk of coronary artery heart disease especially in women
- **Isoleucine** is essential for ensuring blood formation, is a oxygen-carrying pigment inside of red blood cells and helps to make hemoglobin.
- Non enzymatic browning observed in coffee beans **is millard browning**
- An example for water soluble pigment is **anthocyanin**
- Caramelization of sugar is due to **high temperature**
- Coloring compound present in annatto (food condiment) is **bixa orellana**
- **Electrolytes** are the minerals in body fluids
- Enzyme responsible for ethylene synthesis is **ACC (1-aminocyclo propane-1-carboxylate synthase**
- **Enzymes** are the substances that speed up chemical reactions in body
- Many fruits and vegetables have tendency to turn brown due to presence of enzyme **polyphenol oxidase**
- **Protein**: Obtained from foods - meat, dairy products, nuts, certain grains and beans. **Essential** to build and maintain bones, muscles, and skin. **Complete proteins**: Proteins from meat and animal products. They supply all the essential amino acids (the body can't make on its own). **Partially**

Incomplete proteins: Plant proteins (Lack of some essential amino acids).

- Pure water have water activity (a_w) of 1.00
- Water activity (a_w) is expressed as the ratio of vapour pressure in a food (P) to the vapour pressure of pure water (P_0) $a_w = P/P_0$
- The water activity of pure water is 1 (Water activity in an important consideration for food product design and safety). Microorganisms cannot grow in pure water
- Water is considered as one of the most important factor controlling the rate of deterioration of food by either microbial or non-microbial effects.
- Water activity of intermediate foods- **0.6- 0.9%**
- A small change in water activity produces a very large change in **osmotic pressure**
- Sublimation of pure water occurs below **triple point**
- **Sodium:** Table salt (sodium chloride) supplies Na. Essential for the function of nerves and muscles. Helps to keep the right balance of fluids in your body
- **Vitamin B** is a water soluble vitamin
- Vitamin D is also known as **calciferol**
- Compound highly sensitive to pH for changing colour is **Anthocyanin.**
- All enzymes are inactivated by temperature above **80°C.**
- The two vitamins, which are most affected by cooking are **thiamine** and **vitamin C.**
- Excess intake of carbohydrate is converted to **fat**
- In Vitamin A, **1 IU** (International Unit) = **0.3 mg retinol** or 1 IU = **0.6 mg beta-carotene** (1 μg = 1 millionth of gram)
- Chemical responsible for induction of senescence is **ABA** (Abscisic Acid)
- Most vitamins are not single vitamins, but groups of related molecules.
- Common materials used to **bind water are sugar, salt and hydrocolloids**
- Salt has six times more capacity to **bind water than sugar.**
- **Olestra lipid** has lowest energy value for humans. It is zero calorie replacement for dietary fat.
- Cereals and candies (sugar) have **low water activity (*aw*)**
- **Common salt** is used at 15-24%. It reduces *aw* (Water activity) and imparts flavor.
- **Sugar** is used as energy source for nitrate reducing bacteria
- Ragi has some good number of Essential Amino Acids (EAA) which are **Valine, Methionine, Isoleucine, Threonine** and **Tryptophan.**
- **Threonine** helps maintain protein levels in the body. It also helps formation of tooth enamel, also prevents formation of fat in the liver.
- **Tryptophan** which act as natural relaxant and help fight anxiety, depression and insomnia. They also help in treating migraine headaches. They reduce excess appetite and help control weight gain: they also release growth hormones.
- **Methionoine** which is a sulfur based amino acid which is essential for various activities in human body. It is said to help promote growth of healthy skin and hair.

- Most abundant amino acid found in nature is -**Leucine**
- **SDS (Sodium Dodecyl Sulfate)** molecules binds to hydrophobic region of the protein.
- Maltase converts maltose in **glucose**
- Invertase converts sucrose into **glucose and fructose**
- Liquids with high surface tension values also have high **latent heat values**
- The thermal conductivity of **ice** is more than **water**
- Latent heat of water is **580 cal**
- 1 cal is equal to **4.2 joules**
- Most abundant sugar found in nature is **Glucose.**
- Commercially sodium bicarbonate is known as **Baking soda.** (Formula is $NaHCO_3$)
- The moisture content at which the rate of drying changes is called **critical moisture content**
- For long term storage potato should be stored at **10-15°C.**
- Flattening of eye is an maturity indicator of **pineapple fruit.**
- During ripening, acids of fruits will be converted into **sugar**
- Epinasty in poinsettia is due to excess of **ethylene.** (Epinasty is characterized by downward bending or twin of leaves and bracts).
- Ethylene is produced in plants from amino acid methionine. Ethylene is formed in almost all plant parts.
- Garlic odour is due to- **diallele di sulphide**
- An increase in solid by evaporation decreases the **water activity**
- The enzyme which produce bad smelling aldehydes in vegetables is **Lipo-oxidase**
- Vitamins which are readily lost during cooking are – **water soluble vitamins**
- pH of fruits tissues is generally less than **-5**
- Surface pitting is a characteristic chilling injury in- **Citrus**
- Toxins produced during aerobic respiration of plant tissues that kills the cells if not removed are- **Ethyl Alcohol & acetaldehyde**
- Which antioxidant is abundant in citrus fruit- **Ascorbic acid**
- State of fat in milk is - oil in water emulsion
- Highest ethylene producing vegetable is - **Tomato**
- Highest ethylene producing fruits is - **Apples, Banana and Cantaloupe**

FOOD ANALYSIS AND TESTING

- Instrument used to measure pectin content is **jelly meter**
- Chemical used for NAOH standardization during acidity estimation is **potassium acid thalate**
- HPLC (High performance liquid chromatography) are preferred methods for quantitating simple sugars in a variety of food products.
- Instrument used to measure maturity of sweet corn **succulometer**
- **Yeast Assimilable Nitrogen (YAN)** analysis is used to measure nitrogen content in grape wine. YAN is combination of free amino nitrogen (FAN), ammonia and ammonium

- **Succulometer** is used to measure maturity of sweet corn and storage quality of apples.
- **Bellier temperature turbidity test** (BTTT) is used for assessing adulteration in groundnut oil with normal oil. In most cases the Bellier figure increases with the % of peanut oil in the mixture.
- Relative humidity is usually measured by **hygrometer**
- Salometer is used to test salt percent in brine solution
- Tintometer is used for measurement of coloured food. (Tintometer is a measuring instrument used in calorimetric analysis to determine the quantity of a substance from the colour it yields).
- Titratable acidity (TA) of juice can be determined by titrating a known volume of fruit juice with **0·1 N NaOH**
- Minimum standard size of sieve is **74 micron**
- Dynamometer is used to measure **torque**
- **Scoring/Numbering** in food evaluation is termed as **hedonic test.**
- One step resource for managing all activities of food testing through online interface is called as – INFLONet (Network of labs)

FOOD CROPS INCLUDING HORTICULTURE CROPS

- Highest ethylene producing fruit is **passion fruit**
- Taste of carrot is due to **glutamic acid**
- Good mango varieties have a TSS of 20%
- Fruits and vegetables are not good source of **calcium** (Except leafy vegetables likes spinach and rhubarb and dried fruit figs etc.).
- Kodo is **coarsest** among **food grains**
- Potato contains **2%** of protein, 0.2% of fat and 20% carbs. Potato contain **20 per cent** dry matter
- Pulpa crema (yellow pulp) is a physiological disorder of **banana.**
- Ripe banana contain **27% sugar.**
- Fruit giving highest calories per unit area is **banana**
- Aroma of guava is due to **beta-caryophyllene** and **limonene** including other volatile compounds
- Astringency in fruits are mainly due to **tannin**
- Beans variety suitable for canning is **contender**
- Dry Papain moisture content is **5 per cent** (Papain the dried latex obtained from the Papaya Fruit)
- For mango, the optimal storage condition is **10-20°C** temperature and **85 per cent** relative humidity
- **Gluten** is a protein found in wheat, rye, and barley
- Leafy vegetable are deficient in **methionine**
- Minimum ethylene producing fruit is **grape**
- Non fermented tea is **green tea and it does not undergo any oxidation hence the green appearance.**
- Pineapple variety suitable for canning is **kew**
- Term Tapka is associated with maturity of **mango**
- Tomato variety suitable for drying is **Pusa Ruby**

- Toxic compound found in cassava is **hydrocyanine**
- Saffron is obtained from **flowers.**
- Pulse crop which does not fix atmospheric nitrogen is **Rajmah and Tur dal**
- Golden rice is rich in **Vitamin A** (beta carotene)
- World's first hybrid of rice was developed by **Yuan Longping of China in 1976**
- ***T. durum*** is known as macaroni wheat. Durum wheat is used for making pasta
- The average protein content of dwarf wheat is **12%**
- Sapota fruit contains gummy chemical used in chewing gums- **Chickle**
- Maize is called the **queen** of cereals (because it has the highest genetic yield potential among the cereals).
- Maize contain **4% oil** and Maize grain contain **8-10%** protein
- **Zea mays everta** is pop corn variety of maize.
- Sorghum is rich in natural nutrients and is good source of vitamin-B (Thiamine), Vit B6 , copper. iron, magnesium, potassium, selenium and zinc. It is low in fat.
- **Due to high Leusine content** higher dose of sorghum in food causes **pellagra disease**
- **Barley** is used in soups and stews and in breads
- Basically Barley is a livestock feed and is a good source of **Protein.**
- **Pearl barley** is suited for kidney disorders
- **Kodo grain** is composed of 11% of protein an excellent source of fibre and also contain high amounts of polyphenols an antioxidant compounds.
- **Kutki** contain 7.7 g protein, 7.6 g fiber, 1.5 g minerals, 9.3 mg iron and 17 mg calcium.
- Ragi contain **carbohydrate 72.6%, protein 7.7%, 3.6 % fiber and 1.3% fat.**
- Ragi contain calcium **350 mg,** iron **3.9,** niacin **1.1,** thiamine **0.42** and riboflavin **0.19.** Ragi consist of high amount of calcium also.
- Ragi is a wonder cereal grain, good source of **iron**, excellent baby food, help in improving **haemoglobin**
- At present, the per capita availability of pulse in India is only **53.7 gm/day (2024)**
- The average protein available in pulses is **20-30%**
- Pulses are rich in **'Ca' and 'P'**
- Arhar contains **25% Protein**
- Green gram also known as **Mung, Mung been and Gold gram**
- The protein content in green gram is **24% and Vitamin C** is present in green gram
- Cowpea also known as **Lobhia,** Cowpea is also called **vegetable meat**
- Chickpea is also known as **Gram, Chana and Bengal gram and it contain 21% protein.**
- **Pungency** in mustard is due to **Isothiocynate**
- Sugarbeet is a **Sugar crop**
- In sugarbeet the sucrose is found in **roots** and in sugarbeet the sugar content is **15-16%**
- First man made cereal is **Triticale.**
- Potato contain water 72%, no cholesterol and sodium and more potassium than banana.

- Potatoes with skin are good source of vitamins and minerals.
- *Tomato has 5 forms:* 1. Cherry Tomato 2. Pear Tomato 3. Common Tomato 4. Potato Leaf Type 5. Upright Tomato.
- **Lycopene** is responsible for red colour in tomato and it is highest at 21–24°C. Production of this pigment drops rapidly above 27°C.
- Yellow pigment in Papaya- **Caricaxanthin**
- Guava is rich source of **Pectin (dietary fiber and also vitamin C)**
- Redness in Apple is due to **Antocyanin**
- Wheat variety used for manufacturing biscuits is **soft wheat**
- Barley is lacking in essential amino acid lysine Barley proteins- **albumin (2.9%), globulin (18.5%), prolamin (37.4%) and glutelin (41%).**
- Flavoring compound in banana is **Isopentyl acetate**
- Predominant sugar found in grape is **fructose**
- **Highest antioxidant fruits:** Blue berries, blackberry, strawberry, plums, rasp berries, Banana, Sweet orange, red grapes, cherries, kiwi fruit.
- **Highest antioxidant vegetables:** Black bean, kidney bean.

FOOD PROCESSING

- Degreening temperature is about **20-30 °C** (System for colouring fruits is called *degreening*)
- **Filtration** means removal of micro organisms
- Preferred fruits for making jelly: sour apples, sour berries, sour cherries, grapes, and cranberries.
- **Monosodium glutamate (MSG)** is a flavor enhancer.
- Main component of mango latex is **resorcinol**
- Predominant acid present in carambola is **oxalic acid.**
- Artificial curing of onion is done at temperature of **40 °C**
- Brining is treating food with salt which preserves and season the food.
- Brining is done only for **vegetables**
- Caustic soda or NaOH concentration is used as Lye peeling **1-2 per cent**
- Certain fruit tissues, such as orange rinds and apple flesh, contain heavy concentrations of pectin and can be used in powder form.
- Commercial pectin are produced from **citrus peel, apple pomace** and **sugar beet pulps** and **beet root** in smaller proportions.
- Concentration of CO_2 used for carbonation of beverages is **1-8 per cent**
- Dehydration method for peach and apricot is **vacuum dehydration**
- Flame peeling is done for **garlic** and **onion crop**
- **High pectin fruits** are quinces, apples, plums, blackberries crab apples and red currant and have enough naturally occuring pectin to act as a preservative and thickener.
- High pectin fruits release pectin when exposed to heat.
- Pectin has found to show **anticancer activity** in human prostate cancer cells at 1 and 3 mg/ml.

- Pectin in plants act as **binder** and keeps plant components together.
- Pectin is plant based polysaccharide which gelatinizes Jelly and jam, thickness sauces and give low sugar options.
- Highest riboflavin containing vegetable - **Potato**
- Highest riboflavin containing fruit is **Bael.**
- Jam has water activity of only 0.80 but have moisture content of 50-60%
- Kanji is prepared from **black carrot**
- Modern cooking uses additives like pectin to create structural and textural changes in other ingredients (powdered pectin increase the viscosity of dairy products and gives low fats or no fat yogurt). Powdered pectin can also be added at a rate ½ teaspoon per cup of low fat milk to make pudding.
- Moisture content of desiccated coconut is **5-6 per cent**
- Most important tea processing methods are **cut, tear** and **coil methods (CTC).**
- Off flavour in oranges is due to **ferulic acid**
- pH level of majority of fruit juice is **3.5-4.0**
- Prominent fatty acid present in cucurbits are **linoleic** and **linolenic acid**
- Protopectin is a component of the cementing material between plant cell walls also a part of cell wall themselves.
- Puree is prepared from vegetable **tomato**
- Rhizopus oligosporus is a fungus of **the family Mucoraceae** it is widely used as starter culture for the production of **tempeh.**
- **Sweet oranges** are preferred for marmalade preparation
- The first step in tea processing is **withering.** Withering process reduces the water content of the leaves by as much as **half.**
- The growth regulator used for bud opening in carnation is **gibberellin**
- The maturity index for Avocado is increase **oil content of fruit**
- The vascular sap collected from immature unopened coconut inflorescence is popularly known as "**Neera**". It is popular as delicious health drink.
- Tough jelly is due to more **pectin**
- TSS content of natural juice is **10 per cent**
- Which is the volatile compound which constitutes 50-75 per cent of carbon volatile during ripening? **ethylene**
- A combination of fruit juice and sugar stiffened by the action of pectin of the fruit, as a result of heating is called **jelly.**
- Percent of salt increases, the rate of acid production in food product becomes **lower.**
- A fine ground coffee may have bulk density of **0·39-0·47.**
- Ratio of sugar to acid determines the **tartness and flavour of fruit.**
- Raw eggs/milk may be carrier of **salmonalla** that's why both of them must be used after **boiling** upto 80°C for 10 minutes.
- **Gelatin** is used as the clarifying agent of fruit juice.
- Term neutraceutical was coined in 1989 by **F. DeFelice.**

- Yeast serves as **leavening agent** in bread production.
- **Tomato ketchup** is good example of **Non Newtonian fluid** and **pseudoplastic.**
- Sodium benzoate is effective in pH range of **2.5-4.0.**
- Tofu paneer is prepared from **soybean.**
- As per **FPO specifications,** the drained weight of canned fruits should not be less than 55%.
- As per **FSSAI,** maximum amount of moisture in wheat is 12 %.
- The permissible limit for **sulphur dioxide** in jams is – 40 ppm
- The unit of vacuum is **torr named by Italian Physicist Torricelli**
- **Cork** is a good insulator because it is **porous**
- Parboiling of paddy is a **hydrothermal treatment**
- Cryogenics can be effectively used for **spice milling** (It is the act of cooling or chilling a material and then reducing it into a small particle size.)
- Dipping cut fruits in pineapple juice with water (3:1) is used for controlling **enzymatic browning**
- **FIFO** stands for First in-First out
- IMF stands for **Intermediate Moisture Food** (These are shelf stable products with water activity of 0·6-0·84 with moisture content 15-40%).
- Commercial method of carrot peeling **lye peeling**
- **Cyanocobalamin** is synthetic form of **Vitamin B12 used for Vit. B_{12} deficiency ($C_{63}H_{88}CoN_{14}O_{14}P$)**
- What is the threshold level of ethylene in fruit? **0.01 mL/L**
- The enzyme responsible for the browning in cut fruits is called **polyphenol oxidase (or PPO).**
- The drying rate is affected by **relative humidity, surface area** and **air velocity**
- Acid percentage in jelly is - **0·5-1·0%**
- Suitable pH value of jelly- **3·2 to 3·4**
- Sabudana (sago) is prepared from roots of **Cassava /Topica**
- **Black neck** of bottle of ketchup is due to **ferric tannate; [Fe_2 ($C_{14}H_7O_9$)$(OH)_3$]**
- The meat of goat is called **chevon**
- Most efficient method to remove microorganisms from liquid is **Filtration.**
- **10% glycerol** is used to avoid freezing injury
- **Milling percent** of rice is 50-55% (Rough rice has optimum milling potential at moisture content of about 14%).
- **Propionic acid** is used to control molds in bakery products and cheese, especially against ropiness of bread. Used upto 1%.
- **Honey** is **pasteurized** at 71-77 °C for 10- 30 mins.
- Some types of sausages (finely ground meat) like Thuringer, bologna, salamis undergo **mixed lactic acid fermentation** during curing process
- For biscuit making wheat should be used having **low protein content**
- For preparing quality bread the protein content in wheat should be **more than 12%**
- For using chapatti purpose the protein content in wheat should be **10-12%**
- Malting barley requires moderate protein levels of between **9-12%**

- Cider-fermented wine is prepared from **Apple**
- Reynolds number is a **dimensionless** number. (Reynolds number = Inertial force /Viscous force)
- Sufficient amount of **pectin** and **acid** to gel is requirement of Jelly making.
- For the **good quality of food**, colour, sensory and texture is necessary.
- Sterlization refers to complete elimination of all **micro-organisms**
- **Acetic acid** can be used to prevent ropiness in bread
- KMS (Potassium metabisulfite) is used to control **moulds** in pickles and juices. It is potent antioxidant protecting with the colour and delicate flavours of the food.
- **Benzoic acid** is used in foods with high acidity like carbonated drinks, juices
- Scum formation in pickles is due to development of **wild yeast.** Scum retards the formation of lactic acid and helps the growth of putrefactive bacteria that cause vegetable to become soft and slippery.
- Sugar act as a preservative at a concentration of **62-65 per cent**
- Sugar act as a preservative by acting as a humectant (maintaining and stabilising the water content in foods). Sugar helps to prevent or slow the growth of bacteria in foods like jam and jelly.
- Syruping is done only for **fruit**
- ZECC (Zero energy cool chamber) was discovered by **S.K. Roy** and **S.R. Khurdiya**
- **Cold sterilization** preserves the most of nutrients.
- Eutectic temperature is the temperature at which product-No more freezable water is left
- Index enzyme in case of blanching of vegetables is – **Peroxidase**
- Most useful supercritical fluid is – **Carbon dioxide**
- **Sparkling water** consist of carbonated distilled water and salts in which CO_2 gas is added at the rate of - 4-5 volume
- The quality problem for sliced apple and potato is **Enzymatic Browning**
- Trans fats in food can be avoided by not using – **Vanaspati Ghee**
- Pectin contribute viscosity to tomato paste or puree and stabilize the fine particles in oramge juices from setting out.

FOOD SAFETY

- ICMR recommended daily diet of vegetable is **300g**
- Prevention of food adulteration act was passed in the year **1994**
- The ideal bactericide is **8-HQC**
- India witnessed green revolution in 1960's and 70's particularly through wheat crop. It was due to dwarfing gene **"Norin".**
- CFTRI (Central Food Technological Research Institute) is situated at **Mysore (1950)**
- FAO defines food security in four dimensions **food availability, access to food,** and **stability of food to supply** and **utilization of food.**
- State Institute of Food Processing Technology (SIFPT) is at **Lucknow** (Estd. in 1949).
- **Codex Alimentarius** comes under Non mandatory regulation.
- The percentage of **adulterated food** sold in various parts of India is about 30-35%.

- Insecticide rules were passed in **1971** (Pesticide act 2018) banned pesticide and toxicity
- Central Rice Research Institute (Now, National Rice Research Institute) at Cuttack was established during **1946.** New name is National Rice Research Institute
- Protein rich rice varities released by NRRI, Cuttack- **CR Dhan-310 and 311**
- India also witnessed **White revolution with milk. Blue revolution with aquaculture** and partial success of **Yellow revolution with oilseeds.**
- Food and Agriculture Organization is located at **Rome.**
- Food corporation of India came into existence in **1965.**
- HACCP stands for **Hazard Analysis** and **Critical Control Point**
- In HACCP 'P' refers to **point.**
- IFS (Indian Food standards) Quick system is developed by- FSSAI

FOOD MICROBIOLOGY

- **D-value:** Amount of time under specified conditions to reduce microbial population by one decimal **Z-value:** Measure of change in the rate of death due to change in temperature **F-value** is the duration of time in minutes required to kill a known population in a given food under specified conditions. F value is used to measure efficiency of canned foods.
- Mesoophile bacteria grow best at 32-37 °C
- For pickle preparation ***Lactobacillus plantarum*** microorganism is used.
- Fungus which is mostly grow on grape is **Botrytis (Bunch rot, Botrytis Cinerea or grey Mould of grape)**
- **Koji mold** is **also known as Aspergillus oryzae**, is a filamentous **fungus (a mold)** is used in East- Asia to **saccharify rice, sweet potato**, and **barley** in the making of **alcoholic beverages** such as *sake* and *shochu*, and also to **ferment soybeans** for making soy sauce and *miso*.
- Natural toxins found in cabbage are **goitrogens and thiocyanates**
- Preservative antibiotic subtilin is extracted from **Bacillus subtilis**
- Best pH for microbial growth is **6.6-7.5.**
- Best pH for molds growth is **4.0.**
- Thermophile bacteria grow best at 50-65 °C
- **Food poisoning microbes are:** (1) *Clostridium botulinum* – minimum pH 4.7 – 5.0. (2) *Clostridium perfringens*. (3) *Staphylococcus aures*. (4) *Bacillus cereus*.(5) *Aspergillus spp.*
- **Milk borne organisms** causing food poisoning are *Brucella, Mycobacteria, Beta Hemolytic, Streptococci, Corynebacteria.*
- Canned meat blackening is due to *Clostridium nigrificans.*
- **Microbial food spoilage** may be due to bacteria, yeast and mold.
- Microorganisms are also used in **preservation** of food products.
- **Bacteria** is present in large quantities in soil
- Q-fever is caused by ***Coxiella burtetti*** (It is spread to humans by animals most commonly sheep, goats and cattle).
- In pickle white cottony growth is due to **Rhizopus**
- Black rot of sweet potato is due to ***Certocystis fimbriata***

- Blue mould in citrus is due to ***Penicillium italicum***
- Blue mould in apple is due to ***Penicillium expansum***
- Green mould in citrus is due to ***Penicillium digitatum***
- Black mouldis caused by *Aspergillus sp.*
- **Water activity (a_w)** is an important parameter to be considered. Lowest ***aw*** for some organisms: Bacteria- 0.91; Yeasts- 0.88; Common food pathogens- 0.85; Molds- 0.80; Osmophilic yeasts- 0.60, Halophilic bacteria- 0.75
- **Optimum pH** for- Bacteria: **Neutral;** Fungi: **Acidic;** Actinomycetes: **Alkaline**
- **Generation time** nearly doubles at every 10 °C reduction of temperature.
- Viruses are the most resistant organisms against UV light. Gram Negative bacteria are more resistant to antimicrobial compounds than gram positive bacteria.
- **Nisin** is naturally produced antibiotic by *Streptococcus lactis.* It can be inactivated by other Lactobacilli
- Sodium nitrite is a **colour fixative** and bacteriostatic against anaerobes under acidic conditions
- *Clostridium* causes **butyric acid fermentation** in canned foods. Usually happens in foods of pH higher than 4.50.
- ***Acetobacter*** are associated with spoilage of alcoholic beverages.
- Off- flavours like diacetyl are produced by ***Pediococcus*** in beers (sarçina sickness)
- **Pediococcus** cause high acidity, buttery aroma and inhibit yeast growth, which results in decreased fermentation rates.
- **Pediococcus** has eight species currently only *pediococcus acidilactici* and *P. pentosaceus* are described as human pathogens causing **septicenia, hepatic absesses** and **bacteremia.**
- Lactic acid bacteria added to milk produce Lactic acid from Lactose
- Fat content of anhydrous milk fat should not be lower than **99.9%**
- Rhizopus oryzae was discovered by **Frits Went and Hendrik Coenraad Prinsen Geerligs** in 1895.
- Rhizopus stolonifer is common fungi is also called **black bread mold.**
- Bacterial growth is generally impossible when water activity reduces below — **0.90**
- Causative spoilage organisms of dried fruits and vegetables are- **Moulds**
- Fruits like banana, figs, grapes are more susceptible to development of "black mould rots" due to- *Aspergillus Niger*
- Full form of MRA is – **Microbiological Risk Assessment**
- In CA storage oxygen conc. is reduced from 21% to 10%
- Soft rot of citrus fruits is due to- **Rhizopus**
- Fermentation involved in mango pickle production is- **Lactic Acid**

MEAT PROCESSING

- **Delicing** is the process of removing of external parasites like lice, mites and fleas which suck the blood of the bird.
- **Deworming** is the process of removing worms from digestive track of the bird.
- **Pork** is the meat of swine

- A slaughter house is also called **abattoir.** (From French word Abattoir to strike down)
- **Meat and poultry products** stored at **– 5 to – 10 °C** develop black spots due to mold like *Cladosporium herbarum* while white spots caused by *Sporotrichum carnis*
- **Nitrite** can also be used to kill resistant spores of *C. botulinum* in **cured meats**
- Meats are cured using **common salt, sugar and/or sodium nitrite**
- **Lactic acid bacteria** dominate the microflora of **meats**
- Puffers (gassy hams) and souring are important problems in case of **ham** due to improper curing
- Meat cannot be **canned in cans with enamel coating containing zinc oxide**
- Yellow discoloration of meat with yellow pigmentation is usually caused by bacteria usually species of *micrococcus* and or *Flavobacterium*
- **Stamping ink** can cause discolouration in meats.
- Ageing or ripening of meat is done at 2°C
- Fat of fish is an excellent source of Vitamin A and D
- Fishy odour in fish is due to Trimethylamine (TMA)
- **Toughening of meat:** Rigor mortis (Rigor Mortis is the stiffening of muscle and the loss of extensibility

MILK PROCESSING

- Specific gravity of milk decreases with **rise of temperature**
- Milk can also be treated with **Ultra High Temperature** (130 °C for 2-3 secs)
- The pioneer of UHT milk processing is **Dr. Harold Burton**
- Milk is an **emulsion** of fat in water
- Freezing point of milk is **– 0.55 °C**
- Millard browning is also known as **non-enzymatic browning**
- Food industry as a separate department of GOI was established in the **year 1995.**
- Heat processing **kills** the bacteria and freezing **prevents** the growth of bacteria.
- Yeasts are most likely to grow in food during **slow thawing.**
- Psychrophile bacteria grow best at 15-20 °C
- Milk deemed pasteurized if it test negative for **alkaline phosphatase**
- **Phosphatase test** is used to check adequacy of pasteurization of milk.
- **Lactose** is the sugar found only in milk and is l/6th as sweet as sucrose.
- **Standardized milk** should contain a minimum of 4.5% fat and 8.5% SNF.
- **Toned milk** should contain a minimum of 3.0% fat and 8.5% SNF.
- **Double toned milk** should contain a minimum of 1.5% fat and 9.0% SNF.
- The fat content in **skim milk** should not be greater than **0.5 %**
- Sweet curdling of pasteurized milk is caused by ***Bacillus cereus***
- The component of milk which act as the food for the microbes producing acids is **lactose**
- The second stage in homogenization is used to **re-disperse fat globule**
- Curd is primarily a **coagulated protein** (The increased acidity causes the milk proteins to tangle into solid mass or curd.)

- **Bactofugation**: The process of removal of bacteria from milk through centrifugation
- Pasteurization temperature in milk is 62.8 °C for 30 mins in order to kill ***Coxiella burnetii*** (Rickettsia) that causes **Q fever.**
- 10 kg of milk is required to prepare 1 kg of cheese
- **Diacetyl** is present in butter. (It is a yellow liquid with an intensely buttery flavour).
- **Vacreation:** Rapid heating of cream along with injection of steam. It increase shelf life significantly.
- Iodine solution is used to test the presence of **starch** in the milk.
- Temperature range of UHT sterilization is **135-150 °C**
- Milk is pre-heated before UHT treatment to avoid **fouling**
- Milk plasma (Milk minus fat globules) is also called **skim milk**
- Milk serum is milk minus fat globules and casein micelles. Whey is that remains after protein is coagulated (with acid or enzymes) and removed. Whey may contain few fat globules.
- Caesin content of milk represent about 80% of milk proteins

NUTRITION

- PEM stands for **Protein Energy Malnutrition**
- **Dehydration** is a condition that happens when enough liquids is not taken by an individual to replace those that he lose
- **Digestion** is the process where body uses to break down food into nutrients. The body uses the nutrients for energy, growth, and cell repair.
- **(RDA) Recommended Dietary Allowance** for energy is expressed in Kcal. For proteins and fats in grammes, RDA for calcium, iron, vitamins and minerals in milligram or microgram. RDA for protein is based on body weight. RDA for vitamin A have been in terms of retinol or in beta-carotene.
- **Glycemic Index** measures how a carbohydrate-containing food raises blood sugar.
- **Metabolism** is the process by which body make energy from the food
- **Nutrition risk** is a health problem medical condition diet deficiency or other issue that refers to the field of study that focuses on foods and substances in foods that help animals (and plants) to grow and stay healthy Also includes behaviors and social factors related to food choices
- **Water intake**: Depends on your size, activity level and weather. 150 lbs person should drink

OILS SEED PROCESSING

- BOV stands for **Brominated Vegetable Oil**
- Rancidity in cooking oils is due to **Oxidation** and develop off taste, bad smell and texture
- Addition of Seasame oil in ghee as adulterant can be identified by **Baudouin test.**
- Adulteration of vanaspati oil in ghee is tested by **Baudouin test.**
- Oils are converted into fats by a process known as **hydrogenation**
- Butylated hydroxytoulene (BHT) is added to fats to prevent **rancidity**
- **Sunflower and Safflower** oils cannot be stored for longer periods
- Refined sunflower can be stored for 6 months in a cool place and unrefined sunflowr can be refrigerated and used for 4 months.

- Sunflower oil can be stored in a cool, dark place upto 2 years.
- Sunflower oil has high smokes point (232°C) and is more suitable for high heat cooking. It contains vitamin C and omega-6-fattyacids, supporting skin health and boost immunity.
- Mustard oil contains more 3-omega fatty acids beneficials for heart health and have pungent flavour.
- Unopened Mustard oil has a shelf life of 1 year if stored in a cool dark place. If opened can be used for 6 months.
- The **ratio of oleic to linoleic acid** affects the storage ability of edible oil and hence affects the nutritional quality.
- Good quality Sunflower oil have high level of Poly Unsaturated Fatty Acid **(PUFA)**
- Groundnut oil has very good stability due to the presence of **Tocopherols (Vitamin E)**

PRESERVATION AND STORAGE

- **Nisin** is a natural preservative for many food products. Nisin inhibits pathogenic bacteria *Listeria monocytogenes* and many other Gram-positive microorganisms in food. It can be used alone or in combination with other preservatives or also with several physical treatments. It is important for canned foods. It is present naturally in milk and in fermented dairy products.
- Two types of commercially available pectin 1. High methoxyl or sugar activated, and 2. Low methoxyl or calcium activated
- When high pectin fruits are first chopped and cooked on low heat for 1 to 1½ hrs or until reduces to preserves, they can be stored for six months.
- Ionization radiation used in sprout suppression is **10-15 K rad**
- Vinegar content in acetic acid is **5 per cent**
- According to WHO, irradiation of food upto **10 kGy** is permitted
- Ethylene ripening temperature is about **18-21 °C**
- Relative humidity required for storage of fruits and vegetables is **80-90 per cent**
- SO_2 concentration for preservation of cardinal is **350 ppm**
- ZECC storage temperature is **17-18 °C** (It uses no electricity)
- Zero energy cool chamber works under the principle of **evaporative cooling**
- "Kraft" used to mention the strength of paper and the word "Kraft" is derived from language **German**
- "To control post-harvest losses, chemical are heated to aid circulation" the process is known as **thermal fogging**
- Actual name used by Kid and West for CA storage is **gas storage**
- An example for cold process of storage is **irradiation**
- An example for potato sprout suppressant is **(Maleic and I-Tartaric acid)**
- **Asepsis** means keeping out of micro organisms
- Blanching temperature is **82.2-93.3 °C**
- **Broth** is a liquid culture medium.
- Cans of foods can swell due to two reasons : **1. Hydrogen swelling** happens to cans of acidic food such as tomatoes or citrus fruits. **2. CO_2 (Carbondioxide) swelling** in poorly processed foods cans.

- Cellar storage temperature is **15 °C**
- Chlorine concentration used in hydrocoolers is **200 ppm**
- Class I preservatives are **sugar, salt** and **vinegar**
- Class II preservatives are **sodium benzoate** and **potassium metabisulphite, glutamates and glycerides**
- Ethylene scrubber is **$KMnO_4$ or effective absorbent of ethylene**
- For delaying greening in potatoes **opaque packing** is used
- Heating, freeze drying, sun drying, freeze concentration and osmotic concentration methods are used to reduce water activity of foods.
- Home canning is safe method of **food preservation.**
- Hydrocooling is best cooling method for **leafy vegetables**
- Ionizing radiation which is harmful to human is **100-1000 K rad**
- Krafts are prepared from **Pinus spp.**
- Major storage pest of potato, **potato tuber moth**
- **Mature green** stage is suitable for long distance transport of tomatoes
- Most commonly used acidifying agent in vase solution is **citric acid**
- Presence of sodium ions in vase water is detrimental for **roses**
- Most commonly used oxygen absorbent in modified atmospheric storage is **FeO**
- Most commonly used refrigerant in refrigeration storage is **freon**
- Postharvest treatment for inactivation of enzyme is called **blanching**
- Pressure used in hypobaric storage is **1.3-13 kPA**
- Quick freezing is done at 0-4 °C for **30 min**
- Refrigeration temperature ranges from **1-5 °C**
- Salt act as preservative at concentration of **15-25 per cent**
- Salt is effective as a preservative because it reduces the water activity of food.
- **Silver thiosulphate** block the action of ethylene in plant cell cultures.
- Sodium benzoate is used to control **yeast**
- SR (Sulphur resistant) cans are not used for storing **pickles**
- Storage temperature for storing mature firm **ripe tomatoes** is **7-10 °C**
- Storage temperature for storing mature green tomatoes is **12.5-15 °C**
- Temperature for hot water treatment is **51-55 °C**
- Two important wax emulsions are: **Waxol-O and Waxol-W developed at CFTRI, MYSORE**
- **Wax coating** of apples skin reduce incidence of bitter pit during storage.
- Widely used sprout suppressant during storage is **CIPC** [N-(3-chlorophenyl) carbamate] at temp. of 15°C or below
- The example for **bio-preservation** used to preserve fruits and vegetables is called, Niacin and Pimaricin (Antimicrobial).
- Wet bulb temperature is always lower than **dry bulb temperature** except when there is 100% relative humidity
- Increasing the storage temperature of body by 10°C cuts the storage life by **half**
- Lower storage temperature of potatoes promote accumulation of **sugar**

- The most commonly used materials for metal cans is **tin plate**
- The 3 Ps of packaging are **protection, preservation** and **promotiom**
- An example for rapid method of cooling **hydro cooling**
- Sublimation is associated with **freeze drying** (Sublimation means conversion of solid material to gaseous state without becoming liquid wexamples are; Ammonium flouride, Iodine, Camphor, dry ice etc.)
- **Freezing** is the best technique for long term storage
- Cryopreservation is preservation technique at **–196 °C** using liquid nitrogen.
- Energy of irradiation increases with frequency and decreases with wavelength.
- Wavelength of UV radiation varies between 100-400 nm, with UVA (315-400 nm), UVB
- Gamma, X- rays and high energy electrons are **ionizing radiations.**
- **Radicidation** is low level ionizing radiation to complete elimination of specific pathogen through irradiation. **Radurization** aims mainly at enhancing the shelf-life of a product
- **Chemical preservative** is, "any chemical which, when added to food, tends to prevent or retard deterioration, but does not include common salt, sugars, vinegars, spices, or oils extracted from spices" **(Food Additives Amendment of 1958)**
- Organic acids like **sorbic acid**, acetic acid, lactic acid, citric acid, **benzoic acid** and their salts are important preservatives along with esters.
- **Sorbates** are widely used in jams, beverages, bakery foods *etc.* and are **ineffective** above **pH 6.5**
- Fruits and Vegetables are preserved by drying, freezing and addition of NaCl. Also Controlled Atmosphere by **increasing CO_2:O_2**
- Sprouting in potatoes can be delayed by using **irradiation.**
- Canned foods with **lesser acidity or pH** more than 5.30 are more susceptible to flat sour spoilage and putrefaction.
- **Flash 18** is a method that pasteurizes canned foods under high pressure of **18 psi.** It is mainly used for delicate foods like macaroni and cheese or meat dishes with sauce)
- CO_2 is the gas used as propellant in **canning**
- In fruits packed in cans, *Byssochlamys fulva* produces **ascospores**
- **Salicylates** are good alternatives for benzoates used for preservation of foods.
- "Bitter pit" a storage disorder of apple is caused by any one of the following deficiency of the tissue- calcium
- For storing different kinds of fruit together it is essential that their temperature requirement- should be same
- HP processing of fruit and vegetables mean- **High Pressure**
- In high oxygen modified atmosphere packaging the temperature should be in the range of – 0-3%
- Microwave Heating involves microwaves produced by magnetrons are directed toward reactants or heating medium, which absorb the electromagnetic energy volumetrically to achieve self-heating uniformly and rapidly.
- Potassium Sorbate a preservative is not affective against- **yeast/moulds**
- Radio frequency heating preservation method involves the transfer of Electromagnetic energy directly into the product
- The purpose of edible coating in minimally processed fruit and vegetables are – retards ethylene production, lower respiration and sealing flavour

- **AR (Acid resistant)** cans are used to pack acidic foods- Peaches, plumes, and tomatoes)
- **SR (Sulphur resistant)** cans are used to pack - Non acidic foods (Peas, Corn, lima beans etc.)
- Most suitable method for vegetable blanching is by- **Hot air**
- The volatile toxic substances accumulate in the tissue when fruit are stored in an environment of- Under poor ventilation condition
- Organic acid as preservative are particularly effective against putrefaction (Foul smell)
- Storage life of fruits and vegetables is extended by keeping them in an atmosphere- **High in CO_2 & low in oxygen**

WINE AND BEERS

- Alcohol percentage in wine is **13-20 per cent**
- TSS of grape fruit for wine preparation should be **> 20° brix**
- Important wine yeast is **Saccharomyces cerevisiae var. ellipsoideus**
- Mead an alcoholic drink made by fermenting honey with water.
- Vodka is prepared from **cereal grains** or **potatoes**
- **Sulphur dioxide gas** is used in wine making at around 100mg/*l* against wild yeast and acetic acid bacteria

OTHERS

- Harvesting index is a ratio of **economic yield to biological yield**
- Plants synthesize ethylene was first discovered by **Richard Gane in (1934)**
- The word nanotechnology was coined by **Norio Taniguchi**
- Acid content in nectarines (peach of the rose family) is **0.3 per cent**
- All fruits are acidic in nature and they are processed at temperature **100 °C**
- Blue colour of rose is due to presence of **delphinidin**
- Chilling injury temperature of beans is **< 5 °C** for **5-6 days**
- FDI per cent allowed for processing industries in India is **100 per cent**
- Fruit undergoing highest postharvest loss is papaya **60-100 per cent**
- In 1935 **Crocker** recognized ethylene as a **plant hormone.**
- National pickle of India is **lime pickle**
- Nitrogen fixation is carried out by the enzyme **nitrogenase**, which is found in microbes.
- Process of nitrification was discovered by **Theophile Schloesing and Müntz** in 1877.
- Sleepiness in carnation is due to increase in **ethylene concentration**
- The domestication of the microbe is thought to have occurred in **Indonesia** several centuries ago.
- The size of nanoparticles is between **1-100 nm**
- The "*Engine of Creations*" book was written by **K. Eric Drexler**
- The chicken breed **White leghorn** is famous for eggs production and laying average of 280 eggs per year.
- **Beautfort scale** is used to measure **wind pressure**
- Scientist who classified fruits into climacteric and non-climacteric are **Kid** and **West**
- At sea level atmospheric pressure equals to **101.325 kPa**

ABBREVIATIONS

ACABC : Agri-Clinics and Agri-Business Centres
AICRP : All India Coordinated Research Programmes
AKIS : Agriculture Knowledge Information System
AMFU : Agro -Meteorological Field Units
AMI : Agriculture Marketing Infrastructure
AOAC : Association of the official Analytical Chemists
AOCS : American Oil Chemists Society
APEDA : Agricultural and Processed Food Export Development Authority
ATIF : Agri-Tech Infrastructure Fund
BHT : Butylated hydroxytoluene
BIS : Bureau of Indian Standards
BD : Benchmark dose
BOT : Build, operate and transfer
BTT : Block Technology Team
CACP : Commission for Agricultural Costs and Prices
CCFAC : Codex Committee for Food Additives and Contaminants
CCI : Cotton Corporation of India (Ministry of Textiles)
CCP : Critical Control Point
CDM : Clean Development Mechanism
CFR : Code of Federal Regulations
CFSAN : Center for Food Safety and Applied Nutrition
CGDM : General Conference on Weights and Measures
CIP : Cleaned in Place
COP : Clean out of Place
CoS : Committee of Secretaries
CPC : Central Processing Centres
CPCB : Central Pollution Control Board
CWC : Central Warehousing Corporation
CWWG : Crop Weather Watch Group
DFPD : Department of Food and Public Distribution
DMC : Direct Microscopic count
DMI : Directorate of Marketing & Inspection
DSC : Differential Scanning Calorimetry
EAR : Estimated Average Requirement
EDEG : Entrepreneurship Development and Employment Generation
ELISA : Enzyme Linked Immunosorbent Assay
ESR : Electron Spin Resonance
EOPO : Edible Oil Packaging Oder (1998)
FAO : Food and Agriculture Organization
FASP : Food Additive Safety Profile
FCI : Food Corporation of India
FCN : Food Contact (Substance) Notification
FCS : Food Contact Substance
FDA : Food and Drug Administration
FID : Flame Ionization Detector
FIFO : First in First Out
FSSAI : Food Safety and Standards Authority of India
GAP : Good Agricultural Practices
GHP : Good Hygiene Practices
GMP : Good Manufacturing Practices
GRAS : Generally Recognized As Safe
GVA : Gross Value Added
HACCP : Hazard Analysis Critical Control Points
HMF : Hydroxy Methyl Furfural
ICMSF : International Commission on Microbiological Specifications for Foods
IDDP : Intensive Dairy Development Programme
INM : Integrated Nutrient Management
IPPO : International Plant Protection Organization.
ISO : International Organization for Standardization
JECFA : Joint (FAO/WHO) Expert Committee on Food Additives
LAB : Lactic Acid Bacteria
LOAEL : Lowest Observed Adverse Effect Level
MBRT : Methylene Blue Reduction Test
MIP : Market intervention price
MMPO : Milk and Milk Product Order
MoFPI : Ministry of Food Processing Industries
MPEDA : Marine Products Export Development Agency
MRL : Maximum Residue Limit
MSNF : Milk Solids Not Fat
MTD : Maximum Tolerance Dose
NARES : National Agricultural Research and Education System
NBS : Nutrient Based Subsidy
NCCF : National Cooperative Consumers' Federation
NDDB : National Dairy Development Board. Hyderabad
NDP : National Dairy Plan Phase
NDRI : National Dairy Research Institute. Karnal
NFDB : National Fisheries Development Board
NFSA : National Food Security Act
NFSM : National Food Security Mission
NIAM : National Institute of Agriculture Marketing
NLM : National Livestock Mission
NMFP : National Mission on Food Processing

NMOOP : National Mission on Oilseeds and Oil Palm
NMPS : National Mission for Protein Supplements
NPDD : National Programme for Dairy Development
NOAEL : No Observed Adverse Effect Level
OIML : International Organization of Legal Metrology
PFA : Prevention of Food Adulteration
PPC : Primary Processing Centres
PPP : Public private partnership
PERT : Project evaluation and review technique
PSS : Price Support Scheme
RDAs : Recommended Dietary Allowances
READY : Rural Entrepreneurship and Awareness Development Yojana
RNI : Reference Nutrient Intake
RQ : Respiratory Quotient
SCP : Single Cell Protein
SNF : Solids Not Fat
SOP : Standard Operating Procedure
SSOP : Sanitation Standard Operating Procedure
SWC : State Warehousing Corporations
SWMA : Standard Weight & Measure Act
T.E. : Triennium Ending
TLV : Threshold Limit Value,
TPDS : Targeted Public Distribution System
TQC : Total Quality Control
TQM : Total Quality Management
TSS : Total Soluble Solids
UHT : Ultra High Temperature
WDPSCA : Watershed Development Project in Shifting Cultivation Areas
WDRA : Warehousing Development and Regulatory Authority
WHO : World Health Organization
WPC : Whey Protein Concentration
WTO : World Trade Organization.

DEVELOPMENT OF FOOD MICROBIOLOGY

(1830-1890) Louis Pasteur Disapproved the theory of spontaneous generation laid the foundation of microbiology

1874–1914 Classic Golden Age of Microbiology

1872 – Ferdin and J. Cohn contributes to the founding of the science of bacteriology. In the publication *Ueber Bakterien*

1876 – *Robert Koch* established that microbes can cause disease

Food Preservation

1810 – Preservation of food by canning was patented by **Appert**, in France

1838 – Introduced the term bacteria **Ehrenberg**

1840 – Fish and fruits were first canned.

1842 – Patent was given to H. Benjamin for freezing foods by immersion in ice and salt brine.

1843 – I. Winslow attempted first to sterilize foods by steam.

1854 – Louis Pasteur investigated spoilage of wine and introduced commercially mild heating to eliminate spoilage microorganisms in food (1867-68).

1878 – Kuhne used the world enzyme

1880 – Pasteurization of milk was started in Germany.

1895 – Russell made first bacteriological study of canning.

1897 – Edward Buchner found that sugar was fermented by yeast extract even when there was no living yeast cells in the mixture.

1907 – E. Metchnikoff and coworkers isolated and named one of the yogurt bacteria, *Lactobacillus bulgaricus*.

1908 – Sodium benzoate given official sanction as a preservative in foods.

1916 – R. Plank, E. Ehrenbaum and K. Reuter achieved quick freezing of foods in Germany.

1929 – Food Irradiation Patent Published

1955 – The antibiotic chlortetracycline was approved for the use in fresh poultry meat.

Food Spoilage

1659 – **Kircher** demonstrated the presence of bacteria in the milk.

1809 – A parisian confectioner (Nicolas Appert) succeeded in preserving meat in glass bottles

1810 – Peter Durand developed canning on Nicolas Apperter's work

1836 – **Cogniard-Latour** discovered the existence of yeasts.

1857 – **Louis Pasteur** discovered the association of different organism other than yeasts in the conversion of sugars in the lactic acid
1860 – **Louis Pasteur** made important discovery that the fermentation process can proceed in the absence of oxygen (Pasteur effect).
1861 – Pasteur introduced the terms aerobic and anaerobic for yeasts.
1864 – **Louis pasteur** discovered that external microbial contamination causes food spoilage and described pasteurization.
1875 – **Carl ve Linde** developed practical and portable compression refrigeration system using methyl ether and later improved by Ammonia.
1876 – Charles Çhamberland developed first **Autoclave.**
1882 – **Krukowitsch** was the first to note the destructive effects of ozone on spoilage bacteria.
1888 – **Miquel studied** first thermophilic bacteria.
1902 – **Schmidt-Nielson** first named the microbes that grow at 0°C as psychrophiles.
1912 – **Ruther** coined the word osmophiles to describe yeasts that grow at high osmotic pressure.
1985 – Lister - Hurdle concept and published **Hurdle technology**

Food Poisoning

1820 – J. Kerner's description of sausage poisoning was probably due to botulism caused By *Clostridium botulinum.*
1888 – Gartner first isolated *Salmonella enteritidis* from meat that had caused food poisoning.
1896 – Van Ermengem first described *Clostridium botulinum.*
1960 – The production of aflatoxin by *Aspergillus flavus* was first reported.

Food Legislation

1890 – The first meat inspection law was enacted in U.S.A.
1906 – The US Federal Food and Drug Act was passed by Congress.
1939 – The new Food, Drug and Cosmetic Act became a law.
1958 – The Food additives amendments to Food, Drug and Cosmetic Act was passed.
1963 – CAC (Codex Alimentarius Commission (Jointly by FAO and WHO)

Indian Legislation

1930 – Sale of Goods Acts
1937 – AGMARK Act (Amended in 1986)
1947 – The Vegetable Oil Products (Control) Order
1948 – Minimum Wages Act
1954 – Prevention of Food Adulteration Act revised in 1968, 1973 and 1981.
1955 – The Fruit Products Order
1955 – Essential Commodities Act, (in relation to food)
1956 – Fo̧od products order Act
1963 – Export Quality Control and Inspection Act.
1967 – Vegetable Oil Product Act
1967 – The Solvent Extracted Oil, De oiled Meal, and Edible Flour (Control Order
1973 – Meat Food Products Order
1975 – Vegetable Oil Product (standard of quality) Order
1976 – Standard of Weights and Measures Act.
1986 – Consumer Protection Act
1986 – Bureau of Indian Standards
1987 – Dairy Development Board Act
1991 – Atomic Energy Rules
1992 – Milk and Milk product order
1998 – The Edible Oils Packaging (Regulation) Order, 1998
2002 – Agricultural Employees Protection Act
2005 – Right to Information Act
2006 – Food Safety and Standards Act, 2006
2013 – National Food Security Act.

GLOSSARY

A

Absorption: Uptake of moisture by dry foods.

Acid food: A food with a pH of less than 4.6 and a water activity (a_w) equal to or greater than 0.85.

Additives: Chemicals added to food to improve their eating quality or shelf life.

Adiabatic process: Processing in which no heat is added or removed from a system.

Adulterants: Chemicals that are intentionally added to food which are forbidden by law.

Aeration: It is the process of moving air through stored grain at low flow rate to maintain or improves its quality

Alkaline phosphatase: An enzyme in raw milk having a similar *D*-value to heat-resistant pathogens, used to test for effectiveness of pasteurization.

Allergy: Allergy is a hypersentivity reaction and defined as any unusual or exaggerated response to a particular substance, called an allergen, in a person sensitive to that substance.

Amino acids are organic compounds containing amine ($-NH_2$) and carboxyl ($-COOH$) functional groups, along with a side chain (R group) specific to each amino acid. Amino acids are the building blocks of proteins, there are 20 different amino acids in nature. All amino acids have five basic parts: 1. a central carbon atom, 2. a hydrogen atom, 3. an amino group-consisting of a nitrogen atom and two hydrogen atom, 4. a carboxyl (group) consisting of a nitrogen atom and two hydrogen, 5. an R-group or side chain consisting of varying atoms.

Antioxidant: A substance that retards the oxidative rancidity of fats in stored foods. Many fats, and especially vegetable oils, contain naturally occurring antioxidants, including vitamin E (E-306-309), which protect them against rancidity for some time.

Aseptic processing: Heat sterilization of foods before filling into pre-sterilized (aseptic) containers.

Atomiser: A device to form fine droplets of food (*e.g.* in a spray drier).

B

Bacteriocins: Naturally produced peptides that inhibit other micro-organisms, similar in effect to antibiotics.

Basal metabolic rate (BMR): The energy cost of maintaining the metabolic integrity of the body, nerve and muscle tone, respiration and circulation. For children the BMR also includes the energy cost of growth. It depends on the amount of metabolically active body tissue, and hence can be calculated from body weight, height and age.

Biological oxygen demand (BOD): A measure of the oxygen requirement by micro-organisms when breaking down organic matter, used as a measure of the polluting potential of materials in water.

Blancher: Equipment used to blanch foods.

Blanching: Heating foods, especially vegetables, to below 100°C for a short time, to both inactivate enzymes which would cause a loss of quality during storage and to remove air and soften the food.

Blinding: Blocking of a sieve by food particles.

Bloom: A thin layer of unstable forms of cocoa fat that crystallize at the surface of a coating to produce dullness or white specks.

Botulin: An exotoxin produced by *Cl. Botulinum*, able to cause fatal food poisoning.

Breading: The application of pre-prepared breadcrumbs to the surface of a food.

Brix: It is used to refer to the concentration of sugar syrups used in canned fruits. The specific gravity based on the balling tables, calculated in grams of cane sugar in 100g of solution at 20°C; degree Brix° percentage sugar.

Buffers: Solutions with stable hydrogen ion concentration and therefore usually with no change in pH which is almost independent of dilution and changing very little with small additions of a strong acid or alkali are called buffers.

Bulk density: The bulk density of a granular product is the density measured without the influence of any compression on the product. The bulk density depends on particle density, its shape and the manner in which the constituent particles are packed or positioned with respect to each other. Bulk density is also defined as weight of grains per unit bulk volume (including porosity/voids).

C

Caramelization or caramelisation is the oxidation of sugar, a process used extensively in cooking for the resulting nutty flavor and brown color. Caramelization is a type of non-enzymatic browning reaction.

Case hardening: Formation of a hard impermeable skin on some foods during drying, which reduces the rate of drying and produces a food with a dry surface and a moist interior.

Cavitation: Production of bubbles in foods by ultrasound and their rapid expansion/ contraction.

Chemical oxidation demand (COD): A chemical method used to measure the polluting potential of materials in water.

Chilling injury: Physiological changes to some types of fruits and vegetables caused by low temperatures which result in loss of eating quality.

Chilling: Reduction in the temperature of a food to between –1°C and 8°C.

Choke: Restriction of the outlet to a mill to retain particles until sufficiently small (or restriction of the outlet in an extruder).

Climacteric: Abrupt increase in respiration rate in some fruits during ripening.

Clinching: Partial sealing of can lids.

Collapse temperature: The maximum temperature of a frozen food before solute movement causes a collapse of the food structure and prevents movement of water vapour during freeze drying.

Commercial sterility:A term used in heat sterilisation to indicate that processing inactivates substantially all micro-organisms and spores which, if present, would be capable of growing in the food under defined storage conditions.

Compound coating: A coating material in which cocoa solids and hardened vegetable oils are used to replace cocoa butter.

Conjugated proteins: These are the proteins which consist of amino acids as well as other class of compounds *e.g.* Chromoprotein (Coloured pigment), Glycoprotein (Carbohydrate), Phosphoprotein (Phosphoric acid) etc.

Contaminant means any substance not intentionally added to food, which is present in such food as a result of the production (including operations carried out in crop husbandry, animal husbandry and veterinary medicine), manufacture, processing, preparation, treatment, packing, packaging, transport or holding of such food or as a result of environmental contamination. The term does not include insect fragments, rodent hairs and other extraneous matter.

Critical control point (CCP): A processing factor of which a loss of control would result in an unacceptable food safety or quality risk.

Critical moisture content: The moisture content of product from where constant rate drying ceases and falling rate drying starts is called as critical moisture content.

Crust: Hard surface layer on baked foods.

Cryogen: A refrigerant that absorbs latent heat and changes phase from solid or liquid to a gas, *e.g.* subliming or evaporating carbon dioxide or liquid nitrogen.

Cryogenic freezers: Equipment that uses subliming or evaporating carbon dioxide or liquid nitrogen directly in contact with food to freeze it.

D

Dead-folding: A crease or fold made in a material that will stay in place.

Density: The mass of a certain quantity of material divided by its volume. It is expressed in $kg.m^{-3}$ (SI units) or $g.ml^{-1}$

Derived Lipids: These are the substances derived from simple and compound lipids by hydrolysis. These includes fatty acids, alcohols, monoglycerides and diglycerides, steroids, terpenes, carotenoids.

Derived proteins: These represent various stages of hydrolytic cleavage of simple or conjugated proteins. *e.g.* proteoses, peptones, peptides, etc.

Detergents: Chemicals that reduce the surface tension of water and hence assist in the release of soils from equipment or foods.

Detoxication: The metabolism of (potentially) toxic compounds to yield less toxic derivatives that are more soluble in water and can be excreted in the urine or bile.

Dew point: Temperature at which an air–water vapour mixture becomes saturated with moisture, marking the onset of condensation.

Dicing: Cutting of materials, such as foods, into small cubes.

Dilatant material: Food in which the consistency increases with shear rate.

Dosimeter: A device that qualitatively or quantitatively measures the dose of irradiation received by a food.

Dry bulb temperature: Temperature measured by a dry thermometer in an air–water vapour mixture.

Dry weight basis (dwb): The composition of a wet food based on the mass of dry solids it contains.

Ductility is a measure of a material's ability to undergo significant plastic deformation before rupture, which may be expressed as percent elongation or percent area reduction from a tensile test.

Dynamic viscosity: It is the tangential force on unit area of one of two parallel planes at unit distance apart with the space between the planes filled with fluid and one of the planes moving relative to other with unit velocity in its place.

E

***E. coli* (*Escherichia coli*):** Group of bacteria including both harmless commensals in the human gut and strains that cause food poisoning by production of enterotoxins.

EDTA: Ethylene diamine tetra-acetic acid, a chelating agent that forms stable chelation complexes with metal ions. Also called versene, sequestrol and sequestrene. It can be used both to remove metal ions from a solution (or at least to remove them from activity) and also to add metal ions, for example in plant fertilisers (E-385).

Effective freezing time: Time required to lower the temperature of a food from an initial value to a predetermined final temperature

Electroporation: Use of high-voltage electric pulses at low-voltage gradients to exchange genetic information between protoplast cells of micro-organisms, plants or animals. At high-voltage gradients (up to 30kV/cm) used to sterilise or pasteurise food by permeabilisation of bacterial cell membranes.

Emulsification: Creation of an emulsion by the dispersion of one immiscible liquid (dispersed phase) in the form of small droplets in a second immiscible liquid (continuous phase).

Endemic: The usual cases of a particular illness in a community.

Endopeptidases: Enzymes that hydrolyse proteins (*i.e.* proteinases or peptidases), by cleaving peptide bonds inside protein molecules, as opposed to exopeptidases, which remove amino acids from the end of the protein chain. The main endopeptidases in digestion are chymotrypsin, elastase, pepsin and trypsin.

Energy drinks: Beverages containing glucose, vitamins, minerals, herb extracts and caffeine, and sometimes other ingredients, claimed to provide energy and to promote alertness and well-being. Some may contain artificial sweeteners instead of glucose, so negating the claims to be a source of (metabolisable) energy.

Entrainment: Oil droplets that are carried over in steam produced by vigorously frying foods, leading to loss of oil, or loss of concentrated droplets of product with vapour during evaporation by boiling.

Enzyme, immobilized: Enzyme bound physically to glass, plastic or other support, so permitting continuous flow processes, or recovery and re-utilisation of enzymes in batch processes.

Enzyme: An Enzyme is a biologic polymer that catalyse the chemical reactions. With the exception of a few catalytic RNA molecules, or ribozymes, the vast majority of enzymes are proteins.

Ethane: Hydrocarbon gas (C_2H_6) formed in small amounts by metabolism of oxidised linolenic acid and exhaled on the breath; used as an index of oxygen radical damage to tissue lipids, and indirectly as an index of antioxidant status. *See also* fatty acids; pentane.

Eutectic temperature (in freezing): The temperature at which a crystal of an individual solute exists in equilibrium with the unfrozen liquor and ice.

Evaporated milk: Product obtained from the cow milk having the consistency of thin milk with sterilization treatment.

Expeller: A horizontal barrel, containing a helical screw, used to extract oil from seeds or nuts.

Extraction: Process of separating a liquid from liquid solid system with the use of solvent.

Extractors: Equipment used to extract food components using solvents.

F

Filter cake: Solids removed by filtration.

Filtration: The separation of solids from liquids by passing the mixture through a bed of porous material.

Flash point: It is the lowest temperature at which the mixture of vapours of materials with air will ignite, when given an ignition source.

Flavour: The interaction of taste, odour and texture provide an overall sensation, known as flavour.

Food hygiene: comprises conditions and measures necessary for the production, processing, storage and distribution of food designed to ensure a safe, sound, wholesome product fit for human consumption.

Fortification: It refers to addition of nutrients to food which contained them in unimportant amount or not at all. For *e.g.* in some countries riboflavin and calcium is added to bread. It is also called supplementation.

Forming: Moulding of doughs and other materials into different shapes.

Fouling: Deposits of food or limescale on surfaces of heat exchangers.

Free moisture: Moisture in excess of the equilibrium moisture content at a particular temperature and humidity, and so free to be removed.

Freeze concentration: Concentration of liquid foods by freezing water to ice and removal of ice crystals.

Friability: The hardness of a food and its tendency to crack.

Functional food: It is a part of an everyday diet and is demonstrated to offer health benefits and to reduce the risk of chronic disease beyond the widely accepted nutritional effects.

***F*-value:** The time required to destroy a given percentage of micro-organisms at a specified reference temperature and *z* value.

G

Gels: Gels are defined as a substantially dilute cross linked system, which exhibits no flow in steady-state. Term was coined by Thomas Graham.

Grading: It refers to classification of cleaned products into various quality fraction depending upon the various commercial values and usages. or the assessment of a number of attributes to obtain an indication of overall quality of a food.

Gram staining : Gram staining is a common technique used to differentiate two large groups of bacteria based on their different cell wall constituents. The Gram stain procedure distinguishes between Gram positive and Gram negative groups by coloring these cells red or violet. Gram positive bacteria stain violet due to the presence of a thick layer of peptidoglycan in their cell walls, which retains the crystal violet these cells are stained with.

H

Hazard analysis: The identification of potentially hazardous ingredients, storage conditions, packaging, critical process points and relevant human factors which may affect product safety or quality.

Headspace: The space in a container between the surface of a food and the underside of the lid.

Heat sterilization: Destruction of the majority of micro-organisms in a food by heating.

Homogenization: It refers to the process of forcing the milk through a homogenizer with the object of sub-dividing the fat globules.

Homofermentative micro-organisms: Micro-organisms that produce a single main by product.

Hydrocooling: Immersion of fruits and vegetables in chilled water.

Hydrophile-lipophile balance (HLB value): The ratio of hydrophilic to hydrophobic groups on the molecules of an emulsifier.

Hydrostatic head: The pressure resulting from the weight of a column of liquid.

Hygroscopic foods: Foods in which the partial pressure of water vapour varies with the moisture content.

I

Ion exchange: The selective removal of charged molecules from a liquid by electrostatic adsorption, followed by their transfer to a second liquid using an ion-exchange material.

Ionisation: Breakage of chemical bonds (*e.g.* during irradiation).

Isoelectric point: The isoelectric point of a protein is that pH at which the net charge on the protein molecule is zero isomerization and polymerization of the sugars into various high molecular weight compounds.

Isostatic: Uniform pressure throughout a food.

L

Lamination: Bonding together of two or more packaging films, papers or foods.

Leaching: Washing out of soluble components from the food.

Lethality: Integrated effect of heating temperature and time on micro-organisms.

Lipid: It is a biomolecule that is soluble is nonpolar solvent. Non-polar solvents are typically hydrocarbons used to dissolve other naturally occurring hydrocarbons.

Liquid nitrogen: Nitrogen gas (N_2) that has been cooled to a temperature less than or equal to 77.4 K, thus existing in a liquefied state.

Low acid food: A food with a pH greater than 4.6 and a water activity (*a*w) equal to or greater than 0.85.

M

Mash: The soluble materials released from germinated grains and prepared as a microbial growth medium.

Mechanical refrigerators: Equipment which evaporates and compresses a refrigerant in a continuous cycle, using cooled air, cooled liquid or cooled surfaces to freeze foods.

Microfiltration: A pressure-driven membrane process using membranes with a pore size of 0.2–2 μ at lower pressures than ultrafiltration to seperate microorganisms and suspended particles from process liquid.

Mimetics: Low calorie fat substitutes.

Mycotoxins: These are the toxins produced by the fungi, *e.g.* Aflatoxin by Aspergillus flavus.

Moulders: Machines that form dough or confectionery into different shapes.

N

Newtonian liquid: where the relation between the shear stress and shear rate is a straight line passing through the origin.

Nip: The gap between rollers in a mill or a moulding/forming machine.

Non-hygroscopic foods: Foods that have a constant water vapour pressure at different moisture contents.

Non-Newtonian liquid: Food in which the viscosity changes with rate of shear.

Nutraceutical: It is a broad umbrella term that is used to describe any product derived from food sources with extra health benefits in addition to the basic nutritional value found in food product.

It is a product isolated from foods but sold in powders, pills and other medicinal forms not generally associated with food and is demonstrated to have physiological benefits or provide protection against chronic diseases.

O

Osmosis: Osmosis is the movement of solvent molecules through a selectively permeable membrane into a region of higher solute concentration, aiming to equalize the solute concentrations on the two sides.

Oxidation Reduction Potential: Oxidation Reduction Potential is a measure of the tendency of a chemical species to acquire electrons and thereby be reduced. Reduction potential is measured in volts (V), millivolts (mV), or Eh (1 Eh = 1 mV)

Oxidation: Oxidation is defined as the process, in which a substance takes up positive, or parts with negative charges.

P

Panning: The process of building up thin layers of sugar, sweetener or other coatings in a controlled way onto solid cores of nuts, fruit, etc.

Parboiling: Parboiling involves partial boiling of the paddy before milling in order to increase its nutritial value, to change the texture of cooked rice, and reduce the breakage in milling. Parboiling is done in three steps: Soaking, steaming and drying.

Pasteurisation: A relatively mild heat treatment in which food is heated to below 100°C to preserve it without substantial changes to sensory characteristics or nutritional value. In low acid foods, the main reason for pasteurisation is destruction of pathogens.

Pesticide residue: means any specified substance in food, agricultural commodities, or animal feed resulting from the use of a pesticide. The term includes any derivatives of a pesticide, such as conversion products, metabolites, reaction products, and impurities considered to be of toxicological significance.

pH: It refers to negative logarithm of hydrogen ion concentration of the system.

Plasticiser: Chemicals added to plastic films to make them more flexible.

Poise: Force in dynes/cm required to maintain a relative velocity of 1 cm per second between two parallel planes 1 cm apart. Centipoise is one hundredth of a poise.

Polymorphic fat: A fat that can crystallise into more than one form.

Popping: Process in which cereals and grains are expanded by heating until the outer skin of the kernels burst with a sudden sharp, explosive sound. Used particularly in the manufacture of popcorn.

Preforms: Small dense pellets made in an extruder from pre-gelatinised cereal dough, which are suitable for extended storage until they are converted to snackfoods by frying, toasting or puffing. (Also known as 'halfproducts'.)

Press cake: Solid residue remaining after extraction of liquid component from foods.

Pseudoplastic material: Food in which the viscosity decreases with increasing shear rate.

Psychrometrics: The study of inter-related properties of air–water vapour systems.

Q

Quality assurance (QA) is the set of activities which ensures that the quality levels of products and services are properly maintained and that the supplier and customer quality issues are properly resolved"

Quality control (QC) involves the set of activities used to ensure that the products and services meet/fulfill requirements for quality.

Quality management: Coordinated activities to direct and control an organization with regard to quality. It provides consistency & confidence to customers, management & staff.

Quality: is the totality of features and characteristics of a product or service that bear (determine) on its ability to satisfy stated or implied needs (requirements) of any product.

R

Recrystallisation: Physical changes to ice crystals (changes in shape, size or orientation) which are an important cause of quality loss in some frozen foods.

Redox potential: Oxidation/reduction potential of a food or microbial substrate.

Reduction: Reduction is the process in which a substance takes up negative or parts with positive charges

Refractive index: It refers to ratio of sines of angle of incidence and refraction of the light.

Refrigerant: A liquid that has a low boiling point and high latent heat of vaporisation so that it can change phase and absorb or lose heat in a refrigerator.

Regulatory enzyme: regulatory enzyme is an enzyme in a biochemical pathway which, through its responses to the presence of certain other bio-molecules, regulates the pathway's activity

Relative humidity: It is the ratio of mass of water vapour actually present in any volume of air at any temperature to the mass of water vapour required to saturate the same volume of air, at the same temperature. It is generally expressed as %.

Rennet: A complex of enzymes produced in the stomach of ruminant mammals which helps young mammals to digest their mothers' milk. Rennet can also be used to separate milk into solid curds for cheese making and liquid whey. Chymosin is key component of rennet.

Resistance: located 1 cm apart (*i.e.* the resistance of 1 cm 3 of product), having units of ohms cm^{-2} cm^{-1}.

Respiration: Metabolic activity of living animal or plant tissues.

Respiratory Quotent: Respiratory Quotient is the ratio of carbon dioxide produced to oxygen utilization and can be used to estimate fat and carbohydrates.

Retrogradation: The process of dissolved starch becoming less soluble is called retrogradation

Risk Analysis: means a process consisting of three components: risk assessment, risk management and risk communication

Risk Management: means the process of weighing policy alternatives, selecting an appropriate regulatory option, and implementing that option.

Risk: Means a function of the probability of an adverse event and the magnitude of that event, consequential to (a) hazard(s) in food

Rotting: Natural process in which animal or plant tissues decay or decompose due to microbial activity.

Roundness: It is a measure of sharpness of the corners of solid.

S

Saponify: Turning of oil or fat into soap by reaction with alkali.

Saponification value: No. of milligrams of KOH required to saponify 1 g of fat or oil is the Saponification value. It is the measure of the average molecular weight of the fatty acids. It is also called as *Koettstorfer number.*

Scalping: Removal of few large particle in an initial process

Screening: method of separating the grain into two or more fractions according to the size alone.

Shelf life: The length of time during which a material exhibits stability or continued conformance to specifications. The shelf life of a material begins from the date the material was manufactured.

Simple Lipids: These lipids are composed of fatty acids and alcohol components, and include fats, oils and wax esters. They can be hydrolyzed to two different components, usually an alcohol and an acid

Simple proteins: These are the proteins which consist of only amino.

Smart materials: Those materials which are able to sense the change in their environments and then respond to these changes in predetermined manners -traits that are also found in living organisms. Components of smart material (or systems) include some type of sensors and actuators.

Sorting: The separation of foods into categories on the basis of a measurable physical property.

Specific heat: Heat capacity of a substance per unit mass. The amount of energy required to raise the temperature of unit mass of an object by a unit increment in temperature (measured in Joules per Kelvin per kilogram).

Specific electrical: Electrical resistance of a food between two 1 cm 2 electrodes that are

Specific heat: Heat capacity of a substance per unit mass. The amount of energy required to raise the temperature of unit mass of an object by a unit increment in temperature (measured in Joules per Kelvin per kilogram).

Specific growth rate: The slope of the curve when the natural logarithm of microbial cell concentration is plotted against time.

Specific heat: The amount of heat that accompanies a unit change in temperature by a unit mass of material.

Sphericity: Ratio of the diameter of a sphere of the same volume as that of the particle and the diameter of the smallest circumscribing sphere or generally the largest diameter of the particle

Stabilisers: Hydrocolloids that dissolve in water to form viscous solutions or gels.

Sterilants: Chemicals that inactivate micro-organisms.

Sublimation: A change in state of water directly from ice to water vapour without melting.

Substrate: A growth medium for micro-organisms.

Supercooling: A phenomenon in which water remains liquid although the temperature is below its freezing point.

Supercritical carbon dioxide: Liquid CO_2 used to extract food components.

Surface tension: The force in dyne acting upon a line of a cm length on the surface of the liquid.

Susceptor: A packaging material that is used to create a localised high temperature in microwave ovens; usually made from lightly metallised polyethylene terephthalate.

T

Tempering: Cooling food to close to its freezing point, or a process of re-heating, stirring and cooling chocolate to remove unstable forms of polymorphic fats.

Thermal centre: The point in a food that heats or cools most slowly.

Thermal conductivity: It is a property of a material to conduct heat. It is measure of the ability of a material to transfer heat. Heat transfer occurs at a higher rate across materials of high thermal conductivity than those of low thermal conductivity.

Thermal death time (TDT) or *F*-value: The time required to achieve a specified reduction in microbial numbers at a given temperature.

Thermal shock: *Heating:* fracture to a glass container caused by rapid changes in temperature; *freezing:* a rapid reduction in temperature that causes foods to fracture.

Trimming: Making an item neat by cutting away irregular or unwanted parts. In the food industry, usually applied to removal of fats from meat.

Ton of refrigeration: The unit used for refrigeration is expressed as 'ton of refrigeration'. A ton of refrigeration may be defined as the quantity of heat required to be removed from one ton of water at 0°C within 24 hours to form one ton of ice. Latent heat of fusion is 335 kJ/kg. It means that 335 kJ heat is required to be removed from 1 kg of water at 0°C to convert it into ice at 0°C.

Thus one ton of refrigeration

$$= 1000 \times 335 \text{ kJ in 24 hours} = \frac{1000 \times 335}{24 \times 60} = 232.6 \text{ kJ/min}$$

In actual practice, one ton of refrigeration is taken as equivalent to 210 kJ/min or 3.5 kW or 3.5 kJ/s or 50 kcal/min.

U

Ultrafiltration: Unit operation in which solutes having molecular weights in the range of 1–200 kDA are selectively removed using a semi-permeable membrane operating at lower pressure than reverse osmosis.

Ultrasonication: Treatment of foods using ultrasound.

Unitised loads: Grouping of packages into larger loads.

V

Viscoelastic material: Food materials which exhibit viscous and elastic properties including stress relaxation, creep and recoil.

Viscosity: The tendency of a fluid (liquid or gas) by virtue of it suppose to flow is called viscosity. It arises due to opposing forces between layers on account of relative motion.

Water activity: Water activity may be defined as ratio of tendency of a solvent to escape from solution (f_0) to tendency of the solvent to escape from pure solvent (f).

Y

Yield: Weight of food after processing compared to weight before processing.

Z

Zero tillage (no tillage): In which new crops are planted in the residue of previous crop without any prior tillage or seed bed preparation.

Zinc: Essential trace element, chemical symbol Zn. Important for growth and is part of the active site of many enzymes, where it is usually required for activity.

Zone of aeration: In the surface strata, the openings are partially filled with water. It is divided into soil water zone, intermediate zone and capillary fringe.

SHORT NOTES

HACCP concept is a systematic approach to food safety management based on recognized principles that aim at any stage in the food supply chain and put into place controls that will prevent them from happening. It is a very logical and covers all stages of food production from the growing stage to the consumer, including all the intermediate processing and distribution activities.

HACCP concept was originated in 1960s by the Pillisbury company working along with NASA (National Aeronautics and Space Administration and US Army Laboratories. It was based on the engineering concept of failure mode and effect analysis (FEMA) which looks at what could potentially go wrong at each stage in an operation and puts effective control mechanism into place.

The system was launched publically in 1970s and received International acceptance from WHO as being the most effective means of controlling food borne diseases.

The seven(7) Basic principles of HACCP AS per the COD 2009 are as follow:

Principle 1: Conduct a hazard Analysis

Principle 2: Determine the critical control points (CCPs)

Principle 3: Establish the critical limits

Principle 4 : Establish a system to monitor control of the CCP

Principle 5: Establish the corrective action to be taken when monitoring indicates that a particular CCP is not under control

Principle 6 : Establish procedures for verification to confirm that the HACCP is working effectively

Principle 7 : Establish documentation concerning all procedures and records appropriate to these principles and their applications.

HACCP principle throughout the supply chain from raw material production through processing and distribution to final use by the consumer and can also be applied to non-foods such as primary packaging

HACCP is a preventive approach to food safety (not quality) management and works by

- Breaking a process down into individual process steps
- Analysing each step to find out whether a significant hazard might be introduced – a hazard analysis
- Deciding what control measures would prevent or eliminate the potential hazards or reduce them to acceptable level for use of product.
- Establishing where it is absolutely essential to control the safety of the food, *i.e.*, the CCPs at which the control measures are working
- Establishing what the critical operating specification as for the critical control points –the critical limits.
- Determining how to monitor the CCPs and what corrective measures and actions required in the event of any decision
- Establishing procedures to verify that the whole system is working properly *i.e.*, it will control food safety and its working in practice
- Documenting all the above (HACCP Plan) and keeping proper records.

Collagen: Collagen is a substantial part of connective tissue and is found in ligaments, tendons, skin and many other types of tissue serving mechanical and structural functions. Collagen accounts for almost one third of the total protein and is made from several different proteins. One of the major components is the amino acid hydroxyproline and this particular amino acid is present within collagen in a concentration of 12.5%. The amino acids proline and glycine are present at around 45–50% within collagen. The building blocks for collagen are units of tropocollagen, which is a right-handed triple helix made out of three intertwined proteins, and numerous molecules of tropocollagen align themselves next to each other to form collagen.

Tenderness is a quality of meat gauging how easily it is chewed or cut. Tenderness is a desirable quality, as tender meat is softer, easier to chew, and generally more palatable than harder meat. Consequently, tender cuts of meat typically command higher prices. The tenderness depends on a number of factors including the meat grain, the amount of connective tissue, and the amount of fat. Tenderness can be increased by a number of processing techniques, generally referred to as tenderizing or tenderization.

Tenderness is perhaps the most important of all factors impacting meat eating quality, with others being flavor, juiciness, and succulence.Techniques for breaking down collagens in meat to make it more palatable and tender are referred to as tenderizing or tenderization.

There are a number of ways to tenderize meat:

(1) Mechanical tenderization, such as pounding or piercing. (2) The tenderization that occurs through cooking, such as braising. (3) Tenderizers in the form of naturally occurring enzymes known as proteases, which can be added to food before cooking. Examples of enzymes used for tenderizing: **papain** from papaya, **trypsin** and **chymotrypsin** from honey, **bromelain** from pineapple and **actinidin** from kiwifruit. (4) Marinating the meat with vinegar, wine, lemon juice, buttermilk or yogurt. (5) Brining the meat in a salt solution (brine). (6) Dry aging of meat at 0 to 2 °C (32 to 36 °F). (7) Velveting and using Sodium bicarbonate.(Baking soda tenderizes meat because it has an alkaline pH, which helps break down the proteins and connective tissues in the meat.

Ageing of meat; Ageing is the holding of carcasses just above its freezing point so as to control microbial spoilage, and this process is accompanied by an enhancement in tenderness and flavour of meat.The enhancement in flavour is mainly attributed to inosine(inosine monophosphate), a breakdown product of ATP(adenosine monophosphate).

The breakdown of protein and fat during ageing resulting in formation of hydrogen sulphide, ammonia, actaldehyde, acetone, and di-acetyl and an increase in free amino acids also adds to the development of characteristic meat flavour.

The improvement in tenderness is on account of the subtle proteolytis that take place in the cytoskeletal proteins.Calpains are causally responsible for the proteolysis associated with ageing, which brings about the tenderness associated with ageing

Ageing period in different species of food animals

Cattle : 14 days, Sheep and Goats: 7 days. Pigs: 5 days, Chicken: 2 days

Techniques commonly adopted to decrease ageing periods include electrical stimulation of carcasses (should be within half an hour of slaughter, to be effective); Calcium chloride infusion into carcasses or• injection into meat

Pale, soft, exudative meat, or PSE meat, describes a carcass quality condition known to occur in pork, beef, and poultry. It is characterized by an abnormal color, consistency, and water holding capacity, making the meat dry and unattractive to consumers. The condition is believed to be caused by abnormal muscle metabolism following slaughter, due to an altered rate of glycolysis and a low pH within the muscle fibers. A mutation point in the ryanodine receptor gene (RYR1) in pork, associated to stress levels prior to slaughter are known to increase the incidence of PSE meat. Although the term "soft" may look positive, it refers to raw meat. When cooked, there is higher cook loss and the final product is hard, not juicy. PSE meat have high levels of lactic acid

PSE meat can be controlled on improving the processing characteristics of PSE meat especially protein and taking effective precautions to reduce the incidence of PSE meat.

RFN meat stands for "Red, Firm, and Non-exudative" meat. It is a term used to describe high-quality pork that has a desirable reddish-pink color, firm texture, and does not release excess water (non-exudative). This type of meat is considered ideal for consumers and processors because it has good water-holding capacity, minimal drip loss, and an appealing appearance.

Red,Soft, exudative (RSE) meat is pork but has exudative properties similar to Pale,soft and exudative(PSE) meat pork.. Cuses are (1) Poor post slaughter management can cause in pigs to red, firm and exudative (RFN) meat.Characteristics : RSE meat has higher glycolitic potential than RFN meat It also have highr rate of glycolysis than RFN-prone pigs but lower than PSE prone pigs. RSE meats have drip loss of 7% at least, which is double than RFN meat.

DFD meat stands for "Dark, Firm, and Dry" meat. It is a term used to describe a quality issue in meat, particularly in beef and pork. DFD meat has the following characteristics:

Dark Color: The meat appears darker than normal due to a higher pH level. This happens when animals experience prolonged stress before slaughter, leading to depletion of muscle glycogen.

Firm Texture: DFD meat is firmer and less tender compared to high-quality meat.

Dry Surface: The meat has a dry surface because it retains more water. This can make it less appealing to consumers and more difficult to process for certain products.

DFD meat is less desirable because it can have a shorter shelf life and may not be as flavorful or appealing as meat with ideal quality characteristics like RFN meat.

Thawing of meat: Thawing is the reverse process of freezing. The major difficulty when thawing is that the difference between the temperatures of the source of heat and the frozen meat cannot be too great for a prolonged period of time as this causes bacteria to grow at a fast rate, creating a microbiological risk. Thawing takes place at a slower rate than freezing as water displays less thermal conductivity than ice. During freezing, the layer of ice formed on the outside of the material to be frozen removes energy quickly from the water still present within the inner layers of the material and, as a result, the water turns fairly quickly into ice. During thawing, however, water is present first on the surface on the outer layers of the material to be defrosted. As water is a poor conductor of heat, the heat penetrates very slowly through the layer of surface water first before finally reaching the ice in the inner layers and core. This is why thawing takes place at a slower rate than freezing and also why a long period of time is required to thaw large pieces of meat fully; a large amount of water is already present in most areas of a large piece of meat, but water in the core remains as ice for a long time as the surrounding water acts as a barrier against heat.

Hydrocolloids: Hydrocolloids, also commonly referred to as gums, originate from various sources and most of these are not digested in the human digestive system. Carrageenan, alginate and agar originate from seaweed whilst materials such as guar gum, locust bean gum (LBG), cellulose, starch and pectin are of plant origin. Xanthan gum is produced by fermentation and gelatin is derived from animal collagen. Xanthan and guar gum are cold-swelling materials, whilst carrageenan and LBG are hot-swelling materials.

Gums fulfill several functions in meat products.

- By forming a gel or acting as a thickener (depending on the type of gum) they help to reduce cooking loss and therefore assist in increasing yield
- The formation of gel assists in obtaining texture in a meat product.
- A higher yield results in a more succulent product.
- Gums assist against syneresis in the finished product.
- Gums do not interfere with the activation of protein within meat products.

Curing of meats; may be defined as the addition of salt (Sodium chloride), sugar and nitrate or nitrite to the meat, which results in conversion of the meat pigments into the characteristic cured meat pigments imparting the characteristic cured meat colour and production of characteristic meat flavour.The process of meat curing is currently valued as a means of imparting organoleptic qualities to the cured products, though it originally was introduced as a means of preserving meat.

Apart from chacteristic colour and flavour, the meat packing industry is concerned with the following attributes which also help by curing: **Preservation, Tenderness and Yield**

Nitrites and nitrates (E 249 – E 252) are added to meat like ham and bacon and other cured meats to keep their pink colour and develop flavour, but also to prevent growth of harmful bacteria such as clostridium botulinum. In addition, nitrite also inhibits the oxidation of lipids in meat products and thus prevents rancidity (off flavor)

According to the Food Standard Agency (FSA) around 5% of dietary nitrates and nitrites come from their use as a food additive. Nitrate is also converted into nitrite by the bacteria in 'the deep crypts' of our tongue and our stomach. "Nitrates and nitrites in meat have been added as part of the curing process and will undergo chemical reactions with proteins to form nitrosamines. These are released into our bodies as our digestive systems break down the meat into amino acids to allow them to be absorbed as energy sources." Nitrosamines are harmful to health and can create colon cancer. High nitrite concentrations, on the other hand, are extremely dangerous for infants since they can develop an infant's methemoglobinemia

Nitrite is a strong oxidizing agent and can cause pinking in non-cured meat products at levels as low as 3–5 ppm of nitrite per kilogram of meat product. Occasionally, potassium nitrite is utilized in applications such as low-sodium products. Based on the difference in molecular weight, around 30% more potassium nitrite has to be applied if the same impact on colour development is to be achieved compared with sodium nitrite.

Nitrate (NO_3^-) is the salt of nitric acid (HNO_3) and is also readily soluble in water. In meat products, potassium nitrate (KNO_3) is the most commonly applied source of nitrate but, having said that, in a large percentage of all cured meat products, nitrite is the material of choice. Potassium nitrate dissociates into K^+ and NO_3^- ions and is still sometimes introduced in products such as fermented salami dried for a long time as well as cured air-dried products. Nitrate does not contribute directly to the formation of the red curing colour and nitrite is the active component regarding the formation of the desired red curing colour. If nitrate is applied, it has to be reduced to nitrite, which then forms the curing colour in conjunction with myoglobin, the colour of meat. Nitrite is utilized in meat products for the following reasons.

- It promotes the red curing colour.
- It provides the curing flavour.
- It has a bacteriostatic impact.
- It also acts as an antioxidant.

In order to obtain a strong and stable curing colour in cooked cured meat products, around 30–50 ppm of nitrite are required per kilogram of meat product. Nitrite also acts as a preservative against bacteria such as *Salmonella* spp. and *Staphylococcus aureus* and especially against *Clostridium botulinum*. A concentration of 80–140 ppm of nitrite per kilogram of meat product is an effective hurdle against the growth of those bacteria especially in canned and retorted products. However, nitrite has relatively little impact against *Micrococcus* spp., *Lactobacillus* spp. and *Enterococcus* spp.

Alveograph: The alveograph test provides results that are common specifications used by flour millers and processors to ensure a more consistent process and product. The alveograph is well suited for measuring the dough characteristics of weak gluten wheats. Weak gluten flour with low P value (strength of gluten) and long L value (extensibility) is preferred for cakes and other confectionery products. Strong gluten flour will have high P values and is preferred for breads.

The alveograph test measures and records the force required to blow and break a bubble of dough.

- ***P Value*** is the force required to blow the bubble of dough. It is indicated by the maximum height of the curve and is expressed in millimeters (mm).
- ***L Value*** is the extensibility of the dough before the bubble breaks. It is indicated by the length of the curve and is expressed in millimeters (mm).
- ***P/L Ratio*** is the balance between dough strength and extensibility.
- ***W Value*** is the area under the curve. It is a combination of dough strength (P value) and extensibility (L value) and is expressed in joules.

Weak gluten flour has lower P values than strong gluten flour.

Extensigraph: Extensigraph test are useful in determining the gluten strength and bread-making characteristics of flour. The effect of fermentation time and additives on dough performance can also be evaluated.

Falling Number: The level of enzyme activity measured by the falling number test affects product quality. Yeast in bread dough, for example, requires sugars to develop properly and therefore needs some level of enzyme activity in the dough. Too much enzyme activity, however, means that too much sugar and too little starch are present. Since starch provides the supporting structure of bread, too much activity results in sticky dough during processing and poor texture in the finished product. If the falling number is too high, enzymes can be added to the flour in various ways to compensate. If the falling number is too low, enzymes cannot be removed from the flour or wheat, which results in a serious problem that makes the flour unusable.

- The falling number instrument analyzes viscosity by measuring the resistance of a flour-and-water paste to a falling stirrer.
- Falling number results are recorded as an index of enzyme activity (amylases) in a wheat or flour sample and the results are expressed in time as seconds.
- A high falling number (for example, above 300 seconds) indicates minimal enzyme activity and sound quality wheat or flour.

- A low falling number (for example, below 250 seconds) indicates substantial enzyme activity and sprout damaged wheat or flour.
- Silver Nitrate can be used to deactivate enzyme and examine its impact on the flour

Farinograph: The farinograph test is one of the most commonly used flour quality tests in the world. The results are used as parameters in formulation to estimate the amount of water required to make a dough, to evaluate the effects of ingredients on mixing properties, to evaluate flour blending requirements, and to check flour uniformity. The results are also used to predict processing effects, including mixing requirements for dough development, tolerance to over-mixing, and dough consistency during production. Farinograph results are also useful for predicting finished product texture characteristics. For example, strong dough mixing properties are related to firm product texture.

- The farinograph determines dough and gluten properties of a flour sample by measuring the resistance of dough against the mixing action of paddles (blades).
- Farinograph results include absorption, arrival time, stability time, peak time, departure time, and mixing tolerance index.

Mixograph: The mixograph determines dough and gluten properties of flour by measuring the resistance of dough against the mixing action. Mixograph results include water absorption, peak time, and mixing tolerance. The mixograph curve indicates gluten strength, optimum dough development time, mixing tolerance (tolerance to over-mixing), and other dough characteristics. The amount of water added (absorption) affects the position of the curve on the graph paper. Less water increases dough consistency and moves the curve upward. The mixograph test quickly analyzes small quantities of flour for dough gluten strength. Wheat breeders use mixograph results to screen early generation lines for dough gluten strength. Flour water absorption measured by the mixograph often serves as bake absorption in bread baking tests.

Dough Conditioners: While many brands of dough conditioners are available, most contain a mixture of the following ingredients:

- Emulsifiers, such as DATEM and calcium stearoyl-2-lactylate, for increasing water absorption and gluten strength. DATEM stands for diacetyl tartaric acid esters of mono- and diglycerides.
- Salts and acids, such as calcium carbonate or monocalcium phosphate, for optimizing gluten development by adjusting water hardness and pH. Calcium carbonate increases both water hardness and pH; monocalcium phosphate increases water hardness while it decreases pH. Monocalcium phosphate, an acid salt, is also present in many baking powders.
- Maturing agents that strengthen, such as potassium bromate, ascorbic acid, potassium iodate, and azodicarbonamide (ADA), for increasing gluten strength.
- Yeast foods, such as ammonium salts, to improve yeast fermentation.
- Enzymes, such as amylase, to improve yeast fermentation and browning, and to delay staling.

Patent flour: Patent flour is the highest quality of all commercial grades of white flour. Bakers often use the term patent flour to mean patent bread flour, but most flours sold today—whether bread, pastry, or cake—are patent flours. Patent flour is made by combining the first few streams of flour from the milling process. It consists of the innermost part of the endosperm and is essentially free of bran and germ. This makes patent flour lowest in ash and whitest in color. Different grades of patent flours are available, depending on which streams of flour from the milling process are blended. The highest-quality patent flour is called **extra short** or **fancy patent.**

Clear flour: Clear flour is the lowest quality of all commercial grades of flour. It is milled from the outer part of the endosperm, made from flour streams that remain after patent flour is produced. While different grades are available, all clear flours are relatively high in bran, high in protein and ash, and slightly gray in color. A high grade of clear flour, called first clear, remains after the production of hard wheat first patent flour. Clear flour is less expensive than patent flour. While it is higher in total protein than patent flour, the gluten formed from clear flour is typically of lesser quality than that from patent flour. First clear is commonly added to rye and whole grain breads. Its protein provides needed strength to low-gluten grains, while its gray cast is hidden by the dark color of the rye or whole grain.

Straight flour: Straight flour is milled from the entire endosperm. It is made by combining all usable streams of flour from the milling process and contains bran and germ particles that are not easily separated from the endosperm. Straight flour is not commonly used by the baking industry in North America. French bakers, however, use a type of straight flour in breads.

Wheat Flour Terms: The Food and Drug Administration inspects and approves the use of flour treatments and additives that are used to improve the storage, appearance and baking performance of flour. The treatment additives are in no way harmful.

- **Enriched"** flour supplemented with iron and four B-vitamins (thiamine, niacin, riboflavin and folic acid) and may be with calcium. Reconstituting the nutritional status of a processed food ingredient to match that of the original raw materials.
- **"Fortified"** implies that something is added to a product that makes its nutritional status higher than the product made from "unprocessed" raw materials. i.e. Cereals.
- **"Pre-sifted"** flour is sifted at the mill, making it unnecessary to sift before measuring.
- **"Bromated"** flour is largely discontinued in the United States. Ascorbic acid is now being added to strengthen the flour for bread dough's.
- **"Bleached"** refers to flour that has been bleached chemically to whiten or improve the baking qualities. No change occurs in the nutritional value of the flour and no harmful chemical residues remain. It is a process which speeds up the natural lightening and maturing of flour.
- **"Unbleached"** flour is aged and bleached naturally by oxygen in the air. It is more golden in color, generally more expensive and may not have the consistency in baking qualities that bleached flour does. Unbleached is preferred for yeast breads because bleaching affects gluten strength.
- **"Patent"** flour, bleached or unbleached, is the highest grade of flour. It is lower in ash and protein with good color. Market-wise, it is considered the highest in value and mostly used by bakers. Patent flour is whitest flour and highest of quality.
- **"Organic"** or chemical-free flour is not standardized, so its definition varies from state to state. It may be grown and stored without the use of synthetic herbicides or insecticides. It may also mean no toxic fumigants were used to kill pests in the grain and no preservatives were added to the flour, packaging, or food product.
- **"Gluten"** is a protein formed when water and wheat flour is mixed. Gluten gives bread dough elasticity, strength and gas-retaining properties. Wheat is the only grain with sufficient gluten content to make raised or leavened loaf of bread.

Accelerated freeze drying: This is a process of food dehydration for certain foods such as peas, prawns and coffee. The process involves placing prepared pieces of quick-frozen food under vacuum and gently heating. As a result, 'sublimation' takes place where crystals of ice turn to water vapour without melting. On completion of the process, the food has a brittle and sponge-like texture. Foods treated in this way have a much longer shelf life providing the packaging is kept intact. When water is added to the product, it enters much faster than with conventional dried products. Furthermore, when reconstituted (or re-hydrated), the food is similar in nature to that of the original food. Re-hydrated foods should be treated in the same way as fresh foods.

'Best before' date: This is a system of marking food products with a specific date before which the food will retain its original quality or 'shelf life'. The system is generally applied to low risk foods, some of which have long shelf-lives, such as canned goods, drinks, biscuits and other dry products.

Blast chilling and freezing: Blast chilling is the process of using a fan-assisted refrigeration cabinet or room which lowers the temperature of cooked food very quickly to around 5°C prior to going into refrigerated storage. In order to prevent bacterial multiplication, the process should be completed within 90 minutes. Attention must be paid to the specific size of the food commodities being chilled, particularly in the case of meat joints. Ideally these joints should be no more than 2.5 kg in weight and regularly shaped. Blast freezing takes place in similar manner to blast chilling. Here hot cooked food is quickly reduced to between –18°C and –22°C before being put into refrigerated storage.

Botulism: This is the disease condition caused by the toxin of *Clostridium botulinum* which, in many cases, attacks the central nervous system. This micro-organism is associated with a range of foods including canned fish, certain pastes and bottled vegetables. The disease has an incubation period of 18 to 36 hours and initial symptoms are characterized by diarrhoea, headache and an overall tiredness. In serious cases, these symptoms may be followed by double vision, loss of balance, constipation and speech difficulties which, in some cases, can be fatal. Patients take a long time to recover and this recovery may be incomplete.

There are seven types of botulism (A to G), each of which is recognised by the toxin produced in each strain, types A, B, E and F causing botulism in humans. Death may result due to disturbances of various brain centres, particularly that regulating the control of breathing. Many foods are associated with the micro-organism, principally those with a pH above 4.5. Those which are common are poorly processed or contaminated bottled or canned products, which provide the anaerobic conditions necessary. Contamination of meat and fish may also arise since spores of the organism are widely spread.

Clean as you go: It is a policy about keeping the work area clean and tidy at all times whilst working.

This may include cleaning up spills, wiping down the surfaces, removing wastes to bins and generally keeping the work area tools and equipments and person to the required level of hygiene to produce safe food products for consumption.

Cleaning out of place: It is method of cleaning equipment items by removing them from their operational area and taking them to a designated cleaning station for cleaning. It requires dismantling an apparatus or equipment, washing it in central washing area using an automated system and checking it at re-assembly.

Cleaning in place: It is a method of cleaning the interior surfaces of pipes, vessels, process equipments, filters and associated fittings without disassembly . typical food and beverage applications cleansed using an automated CIP system are product transfer lines, processing tanks, homogenizers, mixers, blenders and fillers.

Clostridium botulinum is a gram-positive, rod-shaped, anaerobic, spore-forming, motile bacterium with the ability to produce botulinum toxin, which is a neurotoxin. It can survive at high temperatures.

Cold chain: A term used to describe the continuing and uninterrupted storage requirements of certain high risk chilled foods from the final production stage to actual consumption. The cold chain incorporates a number of stages of storage, including that after production, during transport and at the premises of wholesalers, retailers and ultimate consumers.

Coliforms: Coliforms or, more correctly, faecal coliforms are a group of bacteria commonly found in the colon (large intestine) and include *Eischerichia coli* (*E. coli*), *Vibrio cholerae* and *Shigella dysenteriae*. Evidence of their presence in food may be an indication of sewage contamination. Coliforms are also responsible for much food spoilage, causing the production of 'off' flavours.

Colony count: A microbiological technique which, fundamentally, involves counting the number of colonies of micro-organisms present in or on a particular food sample after a specified period of time.

Cook-chill: This is a method of mass food preparation used by hospitals, airlines and supermarkets, in particular, where there is a high demand for ready-prepared meals on a continuing basis. In this process food is prepared, cooked to a core temperature of 70°C and then chilled rapidly to 3°C. It is then stored at that temperature and, on demand, regenerated (reheated) to 70°C. The success of this process is dependent on effective temperature control at all stages. This entails regular temperature checks using probe thermometers and should the food, during its storage period, reach 5°C, it must then be consumed within 12 hours. Where the food commodity temperature reaches 10°C, it must be rejected. This is, fundamentally, a five day process although some operators of the system may reduce this time. The storage period lasts three days with a further day for regeneration and eventual consumption on the fifth day.

Corrective action: Corrective action implies any form of action directed at preventing contamination of food and is an important feature of the HACCP process. Other food safety monitoring techniques, such as food safety risk assessments, food hygiene inspections and audits, may identify deficiencies in cleaning procedures, inadequate storage temperatures and other breaches of food hygiene legislation. Inspection reports should specify corrective action required and the time scale for such action.

Deep freeze: This is the process of storing a range of foods at – 18 °C and below at which the growth of many micro-organisms is virtually reduced and the shelf life greatly increased. However, storage at these temperatures does not necessarily kill pathogenic bacteria and, on thawing, bacteria will commence to multiply. Spoilage enzymes are also inhibited at these temperatures, but long term storage may result in loss of quality.

Endotoxin: These are hazardous toxic substances which are released from the cells of bacteria and other micro-organisms, including various fungi. They remain within the cell during its normal life and it is only after the death of the cell, damage to the cell wall or during the formation of spores, that they may be released. Endotoxins are associated with *Escherichia coli*, *Salmonellae* and *Clostridium perfringens* and the symptoms of infection include diarrhoea, fever and local tissue shock.

Enterotoxin: These are poisonous waste products which attack the stomach and intestine linings causing diarrhoea and vomiting. Both endotoxins and exotoxins fall within this group. Enterotoxins are particularly poisonous and resistant to heat, being capable of surviving at a temperature of 100°C for 30 minutes. However, the bacteria which produce enterotoxins, such as *Staphylococcus aureus*, are less heat-resistant and the presence of bacteria in a food product is not vital for illness to arise.

E-numbers: The term 'E-number' applies to the incorporation in food of a range of additives, such as antioxidants, colours, emulsifiers, stabilisers, flavour enhancers, flavourings, preservatives and sweeteners. Where a food additive is identified by an E-number, this implies it has been tested for food safety and is approved for use throughout the European Union. This approval is monitored, reviewed and amended in the light of new scientific data.

Escherichia coli (E.coli): This micro-organism takes a number of strains and is found in the intestines of man, farm animals, dogs and cats. It is commonly found in raw foods, such as meat, poultry and fish and their by-products. It is easily destroyed by heat, through pasteurization and effective cooking. The presence of *E. coli* is generally an indicator of poor standards of hygiene and/or inadequate processing of food. Whilst the majority of strains are harmless, some strains cause a range of ill health conditions due to the release of an enterotoxin, (which causes an illness similar to cholera in symptoms) and the invasion of the lining of the intestine (which causes an illness with symptoms similar to dysentery). Infection from *E. coli* food poisoning has an incubation period of 8 to 72 hours and the illness may last for 1 to 7 days. Maximum growth of the organism takes place between 10°C and 40°C. Symptoms include watery or blood-stained diarrhea, abdominal pain, vomiting and fever.

Extrinsic contamination: This is the contamination arising from sources other than the raw food itself, namely external sources of contamination, such as foreign bodies. During manufacturing and catering processes, food can be exposed to extrinsic contamination from items such as glass particles, wood splinters, hairs, small personal items, such as pens, rings and hair grips, rodent droppings, dead insects, cigarette ends, plastic items and metal objects falling from badly-maintained plant and equipment. Contamination may also be associated with poor standards of building maintenance resulting in flaking paintwork, rust from overhead pipes and contaminated water leaking from pipes, all of which could enter the product at some stage of preparation. Food safety management systems should explore the potential for extrinsic contamination at the various stages of processing.

Food poisoning (food-borne illnesses): Food-borne illnesses are defined as diseases; usually either infectious or toxic in nature, caused by agents that enter the body through the ingestion of food (WHO).Consumption of infectious or toxic food most commonly results in food poisoning. Food poisoning is an acute illness of sudden onset caused by the consumption of contaminated food or food which may contain some form of poisonous agent. The symptoms of food poisoning typically begin several hours after ingestion and, depending on the agent involved, can include one or more of the following body effects: *a*) nausea; *b*) abdominal pain; *c*) vomiting, *d*) diarrhea; *e*) fever; *f*) headache; or *g*) tiredness.

Food storage: Most foods will deteriorate if not stored correctly and, in many cases, at the correct temperature. Deterioration may be associated with the food losing its moisture content, as with bread and confectionery products, *i.e.* the process of staling; food absorbing odours from chemicals, such as disinfectants; or bacterial spoilage resulting in gradual decomposition, particularly in the case of meat, fruit and vegetables.

Fumigation is a method of pest control or the removal of harmful microorganisms by completely filling an area with gaseous pesticides, or fumigants, to suffocate or poison the pests within. It is used to control pests in buildings (structural fumigation), soil, grain, and produce. Fumigation is also used during the processing of goods for import or export to prevent the transfer of exotic organisms.

Gas Fumigation: Gas fumigation uses liquid chemical which will be converted into gaseous state. This method requires enclosed chambers or at least we have to make sure that the place covered with gas-proof material such as tarpaulin. Examples are; Methyl Bromide, Bromo Bromide, Sulfuryl Fluoride and Phosphine.

Solid Fumigation: Solid fumigation requires solid fumigant such as pellets, tablets, or powders, which its quantity measured by the area. This method is the most effective way of fumigation because it kills insects in all stages, from eggs, larvae, pupae, and adults. Examples are Hydrogen Phospide, and Calcium cyanide etc.

Liquid Fumigation: Liquid fumigation requires sprayers to spread the liquid to the whole area. You have to mix the liquid and water with precise measurement. Then you can start to spray it thoroughly. Examples Ethylene chloride, Chloroform, Carbon tetra-chloride and Ethylene dichloride.

Different Types of Fumigation Treatments

1. Chlorine Dioxide Fumigation Treatments, 2. Sulfuryl Fluoride Fumigation Treatments
3. Methyl Bromide Fumigation Treatments, 4. Formalin Fumigation Treatments

Discontinued or rarely used

- Ethylene dibromide, carcinogenic
- dazomet (methyl isothiocyanate precursor)
- formaldehyde, carcinogenic and explosive
- iodoform, expensive vs methyl bromide
- Methallyl chloride, carcinogenic
- DBCP
- hydrogen cyanide, extremely toxic
- methyl isocyanate

High risk foods: Those foods, typically with a high moisture and protein content, that are at particular risk of contamination by bacterial spoilage or the action of pathogens. High risk foods will, under favourable conditions, support the growth of pathogenic bacteria. High risk foods include:

- meat, fish, eggs and prepared products incorporating these foods, together with smoked or cured meat which has been sliced and cured fish
- soft cheeses ripened with moulds or micro-organisms
- smoked and cured fish
- prepared vegetable salads
- fresh cream and artificial cream cakes
- ice cream and frozen desserts
- milk-based desserts
- cooked cereals, such as rice, beans and vegetables
- sandwiches

Strict temperature control is required with respect to these foods. Such foods should be stored at below 8°C or above 63°C.

Hydrogen swell: The buildup of hydrogen gas in canned goods arising from internal corrosion of the can and resulting in 'blowing' of one or both ends of a can. Hydrogen swell is particularly common with acidic canned fruits and tomatoes.

Layout of food premises: The term 'layout' refers to the space available for people working in a particular room or area and the situation of plant, machinery and equipment, etc in relation to the operator and the tasks performed. Well-designed layouts in food manufacturing and catering premises contribute significantly to the avoidance of various forms of contamination. Ideally, raw materials are introduced at one end of the premises and finished products leave at the other end, with the intermediate stages of storage, preparation, production/cooking and assembly taking place in a sequential flow between these two points. An efficient layout should make a material contribution to preventing or reducing overcrowding, minimising the effort required to perform operations, expediting the process in an orderly and sequential flow, and ensuring maximum hygiene and safety standards throughout, together with facilitating the cleaning process. Above all, the working areas should be large enough for the processes carried out, a problem encountered with many restaurant kitchens, for example.

Mycotoxins are naturally occurring toxins produced by certain moulds (fungi) and can be found in food. The moulds grow on a variety of different crops and foodstuffs including cereals, nuts, spices, dried fruits, apples and coffee beans, often under warm and humid conditions. Mycotoxins can cause a variety of adverse health effects and pose a serious health threat to both humans and livestock. The adverse health effects of mycotoxins range from acute poisoning to long-term effects such as immune deficiency and cancer. A scientific expert committee jointly convened by WHO and the Food and Agriculture Organization of the United Nations (FAO) – called JECFA – is the international body responsible for evaluating the health risk from natural toxins including mycotoxins. International standards and codes of practice to limit exposure to mycotoxins from certain foods are established by the Codex Alimentarius Commission based on JECFA assessments.

Neurotoxin: A toxic substance which attacks the central nervous system and the most dangerous biotoxin known. They are produced by several organisms. Common neurotoxins are exotoxins produced by *Staphylococci, Clostridium botulinum* and ciguatoxin (*Ciguatera)* from dinoflagellates.

pH value: The logarithm to the base 10 of the hydrogen ion concentration of a substance and, fundamentally, the degree of acidity or alkalinity of a substance. The pH values below 7 are acidic, above 7 alkaline, with a pH of 7 representing neutrality. Most foods support bacterial multiplication and the relative acidity or alkalinity of a food is an intrinsic factor in the growth of bacteria. Most bacteria grow best at or near a neutral pH and, to this extent, high or low pH can have a serious effect on such growth. Bacterial spores, on the other hand, can survive at any level, but germination will only take place at a pH of 4.5 and above. The way a food is manufactured, processed and stored can have the effect of lowering the pH, thereby inhibiting bacterial growth except in the case of certain moulds which thrive at low pH values.

Rancidity: Rancidity is a cause of unfitness in fatty foods, such as dairy products and oils. It is associated with the formation of substances causing odours and off-flavours in the products concerned, such as butter. It is a chemical process that occurs when fats and oils in food oxidize. Rancid foods can be unsafe to eat.

Risk assessment: The identification of hazards, the measurement and evaluation of the risks arising from hazards, and the implementation of preventive and protective measures to prevent or control exposure to those hazards.

Rotaviruses: This type of virus is responsible for several forms of gastro-enteritis, particularly in young children, resulting in severe diarrhea, vomiting, fever and dehydration. Man is the source, together with sewage-contaminated water. Onset is within one to three days and the duration, four to eight days. Foods commonly associated with Rotavirus are salad, vegetables and raw shellfish.

Salmonellae: *Salmonella* is a Gram-negative, non-spore forming, short rod-shaped bacterium which is widely distributed in humans and animals. Their effects can vary widely and there are nearly 3,000 known serotypes. *Salmonellae* can be classified into three principal groups:

a. those that infect only people and which can be transmitted through food, *e.g. Salmonella Typhi* and *Salmonella Paratyphi*;

b. host-adapted strains, some of which are human pathogens and which can be transmitted by food, *e.g. Salmonella Dublin*; and

c. certain strains which do not have a particular host, but which may have pathogenic effects on people and animals.

The most common causes of food poisoning are those associated with *Salmonella Typhimurium* and *Salmonella Enteriditis* which result in the condition known as 'salmonellosis' The symptoms include sickness, fever, diarrhoea and severe abdominal pain lasting as long as seven days in some cases. A person suffering from salmonellosis excretes the bacteria in the faeces and may transmit the disease to others.

Salmonellae multiply quickly at a temperature between 7°C and 45°C and the route of infection is through raw animal products, such as milk, poultry, eggs and egg-based products and raw meat. They can also be carried on insects, rodents, birds and animal pets, together with water and sewage.

Prevention of infection is based on the maintenance of high standards of personal hygiene, thorough cleaning and disinfection of food processing areas, prevention of cross contamination, strict control of the time-temperature relationship in the preparation of high risk foods and effective pest control procedures.

Shelf life: The period within which food is both at its best quality and safe for human consumption. Shelf life means:

a. in relation to food with respect to which an indication of maximum durability is required in accordance with regulation 20 of the Food Labelling Regulations 1996 (form of indication of minimum durability), the period up to and including the date required to be included in that indication;

b. in relation to food with respect to which a 'use by' date is assigned in the form required in accordance with regulation 21 of the Food Labelling Regulations 1996 (form of indication of 'use by' date), the period up to and including that date; and

c. in relation to food which is not required to bear an indication of minimum durability or a 'use by' date, the period for which the food can be expected to remain fit for sale if it is kept in a manner which is consistent with food safety.

Shigella: A group of Gram-negative non-sporing bacteria found in the intestine of man and other animals, responsible for bacillary dysentery or shigellosis. Shigellosis is common in many tropical countries, being associated with sewage-polluted water supplies, and is commonly known as 'Delhi belly' and 'gyppy tummy'. The disease has an incubation period of 12 to 48 hours and symptoms include diarrhoea, vomiting, fever, abdominal pain and cramps. Severe cases may manifest pus and blood in the faeces.

Spoilage of food: Food spoilage is the process of change in physical, chemical, microbial and sensory properties of the food so that it becomes unfit for human consumption. Food spoilage is any undesirable change in food and such change can be detected by smell, test, touch or sight.

Most of the natural foods have a limited shelf life. Short life span as they contain high amount of moisture. Other food kept for considerable longer time (low moisture) but may get decomposed eventually. **Spoilage is the process in which originally nutritional value , texture , flavors etc. of food are damaged.** Such food ultimately become unacceptable for consumption. Hence it's essential to process or preserve foods after harvesting or slaughtering to reduce the problem of foods spoilage.

Ultra-high temperature processing (UHT), **ultra-heat treatment**, or **ultra-pasteurization** is a food processing technology that sterilizes liquid food by heating it above 140 °C (284 °F) – the temperature required to kill bacterial endospores – for two to five seconds. UHT is most commonly used in milk production, but the process is also used for fruit juices, cream, soy milk, yogurt, wine, soups, honey, and stews. UHT milk was first developed in the 1960s and became generally available for consumption in the 1970s. The heat used during the UHT process can cause Maillard browning and change the taste and smell of dairy products. An alternative process is flash pasteurization, in which the milk is heated to 72 °C (162 °F) for at least fifteen seconds.

Ultra-high-temperature processing is performed in complex production plants, which perform several stages of food processing and packaging automatically and in succession:

- Flash heating
- Flash cooling
- Homogenization
- Aseptic packaging

Flash pasteurization, also called **"high-temperature short-time" (HTST)** processing, is a method of heat pasteurization of perishable beverages like fruit and vegetable juices, beer, wine, and some dairy products such as milk. Compared with other pasteurization processes, it maintains colour and flavour better, but some cheeses were found to have varying responses to the process.

Flash pasteurization is performed to kill spoilage microorganisms prior to filling containers, in order to make the products safer and to extend their shelf life compared to the unpasteurised foodstuff. For example, one manufacturer of flash pasteurizing machinery gives shelf life as "in excess of 12 months".It must be used in conjunction with sterile fill technology (similar to aseptic processing) to prevent post-pasteurization contamination.

The liquid moves in a controlled, continuous flow while subjected to temperatures of 71.5 °C (160 °F) to 74 °C (165 °F), for about 15 to 30 seconds, followed by rapid cooling to between 4 °C (39.2 °F) and 5.5 °C (42 °F).

Microwave Heating: In microwave and radio-frequency processing, the electromagnetic waves of certain frequency are used to heat food products. Generally two frequencies (915 and 2,450 MHz) for microwave food processing and three frequencies (13.56, 27.12, and 40.68 MHz) for radio-frequency processing are used.

There are two main mechanisms by which microwaves product heat in dielectric materials: ionic polarization and dipole rotation. Ionic polarization occurs when ions in solution move in response to an electric field. Kinetic energy is given up to the ions by the electric field. These ions collide with other ions, converting kinetic energy into heat. When the electric field is rotating at 2.45×10^9 Hz, numerous collisions occur, generating a great deal of heat. However, the dipole rotation mechanism is more important. It is dependent on the existence of polar molecules. The most common polar material found in foods is water. Water molecules are randomly oriented under normal conditions. In the presence of an electric field, the polar molecules line up with the field. Heat is generated by dielectric and ionic mechanisms. Dielectric heating is due to the oscillations of the water molecules in the food. Oscillatory migration of ions in the food also generates heat under the influence of the oscillating electric field.

These provide rapid heating and thus require less time to bring the product to the desired temperature. These also provide relatively more uniform heating compared to conventional hot air heating. Equilibration of the product following heating can help to level the temperature distribution and improve uniformity.

Radio-Frequency Heating: Radio frequency (RF) heating involves the transfer of electromagnetic energy directly into the product, therefore inducing volumetric heating due to frictional interaction between molecules . In RF heating the food is placed between two capacitor plates, where it plays the role of a *dielectric* to which a high-frequency alternating electric field is applied. Such field will force polar molecules (*e.g.*, water) to constantly realign themselves with the electric field. This molecular movement is very fast due to the high frequency of the field and will provoke generation of heat within the food by energy dissipation caused by molecular friction. RF waves (as well as microwaves) are both within the radar range and this strongly limits the frequencies that can be used for applications other than communications. The allowed frequencies for RF applications are 13.56, 27.12, and 40.68 Mhz.

As compared with conventional heat-processing technologies, RF heating presents similar advantages to ohmic and microwave heating that are essentially due to the generation of heat throughout the volume of the material to be processed. However, there are some specific advantages of RF over those alternative volumetric technologies, namely:

- there is no need for electrodes contacting the food (in contrast with, *e.g.*, ohmic heating), allowing RF to be easily applied to both solid and liquid foods;
- due to the longer wavelength of RF, its power will penetrate more deeply in the foods as compared to microwave power;
- the construction of large RF heating systems is simpler than their microwave counterparts, and their application to continuous processes is straightforward; it is a technology particularly suited to large industrial applications.

RF's main disadvantages are:

- the higher equipment and operating costs for an equivalent power output when compared to conventional heating systems and also to ohmic heating;
- the reduced power density when compared to microwave heating, meaning that larger RF heating systems are needed for the same power rating and also that slower heating rates are achieved with RF as compared to microwaves;
- the so far limited research efforts regarding, for example, the determination of food RF dielectric properties.

Active Packaging: It is defined as

- Active packaging refers to those technologies intended to interact with the internal gas environment and/or directly with the product, with a beneficial outcome.
- Active packaging is intended to sense internal or external environmental change and to respond by changing its own properties or attributes and hence the internal package environment.
- Active packaging changes the condition of the packaged food to extend shelf life or to improve safety or sensory properties, while maintaining the quality of the packaged food.
- Active packaging is an intelligent or smart system that involves interactions between package or package components and food or internal gas atmosphere and complies with consumer demands for high-quality, fresh-like, and safe products.

Active packaging is a packaging system that possesses extra processing functions that do not exist in conventional barrier packaging. Due to these extra functions, active packaging performs its special task during storage, distribution, and consumption. Therefore, active packaging can be a very special non-thermal processing application. More effective technology to enhance the performance of the packaging system has been developed and will continue to be advanced in the future. Active packaging has many advantages and applications for the food industry. The biggest market of active packaging applications is in the area of antimicrobial packaging and oxygen-scavenging packaging. For producers and processors, better protection by extended shelf life and more convenient systems by reduction in process time and skilled labor would be preferred for the successful utilization of active packaging development and applications. For consumers, fresher quality of products and more convenient use of the products will be attractive. New active packaging materials or systems may have a large market in the food industry if the cost-to-benefit ratio is favorable. Since current packaging is not always optimum for many different food products, there are still many opportunities for packaging improvement and consequently the quality and safety management of packaged foods.

Intelligent Packaging: The term "intelligent" implies that the package has an indicator that monitors the conditions (*e.g.*, quality) of food products, while the "active" in active packaging indicates the procedures that consistently accommodate active interaction of the package with internal atmosphere or the package food. While active packaging changes the condition of the packaged food to give extended shelf life, improved safety, and desirably maintained quality, intelligent packaging monitors the condition of packaged foods to provide information about the quality of the foods during transportation and storage. Intelligent packaging may sense the condition of packaged foods specifically or respond to the changes of the food condition.

Lard is a semi-solid white fat product obtained by rendering the fatty tissue of a pig. It is distinguished from tallow, a similar product derived from fat of cattle or sheep.

Tallow is a rendered form of beef or mutton suet, primarily made up of triglycerides. In industry, tallow is not strictly defined as beef or mutton suet. In this context, tallow is animal fat that conforms to certain technical criteria, including its melting point. Commercial tallow commonly contains fat derived from other animals, such as lard from pigs, or even from plant sources. Tallow contains mainly saturated acids (50%): palmitic acid (26%), stearic acid (14%), and myristic acid (3%). It also contains monounsaturated acids (42%), especially oleic acid (47%) and palmitoleic acid (3%), and polyunsaturated acids (4%), especially linoleic acid (3%) and linolenic acid (1%). Also present are odd-chain, branched-chain, and trans-fatty acids, and cholesterol (0.08%–0.14% in beef tallow and 0.23%– 0.31% in mutton tallow).

Butter: Butter, a water-in-oil emulsion, comprises of > 80% milk fat, but also contains water in the form of tiny droplets, perhaps some nonmilk fat, with or without salt (sweet butter); texture is a result of working/kneading during processing at appropriate temperatures, to establish a fat crystalline network that results in desired smoothness (compare butter with melted and recrystallized butter). It is used as a spread, a cooking fat, or a baking ingredient. Salt, flavorings, or preservatives are sometimes added to butter. When refrigerated, butter remains a solid, but softens to a spreadable consistency at room temperature, and melts to a thin liquid consistency at 32°C–35°C. Butter generally has a pale yellow color, but varies from deep yellow to nearly white. As a water-in-oil emulsion it contains 80%–82% milk fat and 18%–20% of an aqueous phase. Butterfat is very complicated in its fatty acid and triacylglycerol composition. In addition to the usual C16 and C18 acids, it contains short-chain and medium-chain acids (C4–C14), a range of trans monoene acids, mainly 18:1, and oxygenated and branched-chain acids. The trans acids represent 4%–8% of the total acids.65 Butter contains some cholesterol (0.2%–0.4%). Spreads with lower levels of fat are also available. Butter that spreads directly from the refrigerator is made by removing some of its higher melting glycerol esters or by blending with a vegetable oil.

Ghee: Ghee is a solid fat-based product made in India from cow- or buffalo-ripened milk. It is less perishable than butter and, therefore, more suitable for a tropical climate. Milk is curdled. The curd is then manually churned until it precipitates butter and leaves behind some whey. The butter is then heated on a low flame until a layer of white froth covers the surface. This state indicates the end of the process, and the liquid obtained on filtering the suspension is pure ghee. Ghee is made by simmering unsalted butter in a large pot until all water has boiled off and protein has settled to the bottom. The cooked and clarified butter is then spooned off to avoid disturbing the milk solids on the bottom of the pan. Unlike butter, ghee can be stored for extended periods without refrigeration, provided it is kept in an airtight container to prevent oxidation and remains moisture-free.

Fortification: Fortification usually refers to the addition of nutrients to foods from which they were either absent, or present in unimportant amounts. This is carried out because deficiencies or potential deficiencies have been shown in the population. It also includes additions to fulfil the role of another food in the diet. Thus margarine is fortified with vitamin A in many countries to replace that 'lost' when margarine is substituted for butter. Vitamin D is added at higher levels than are found in butter as a public health measure, since extra is considered necessary for the population as a whole.

Restoration: Restoration is self-evident, involving the replacement, in full or in part, of losses incurred in processing (*e.g.* loss of B vitamins and iron in milling of cereals to low extraction rates; loss of vitamin C in the preparation of instant potato). It should be noted that, up to now, restoration has been limited; for example, white bread has thiamin, niacin and iron added back, although other vitamins such as pantothenate, folate, pyridoxine and tocopherol are also partly lost in the milling process. Similarly, fruit juices might have vitamin C added back, but juices also supply folate and thiamin. In some countries, calcium and riboflavin are also added to bread: this is fortification, since wheat contains only small amounts of these two nutrients.

Enrichment: Enrichment is increasing the level of nutrients present to make the food a 'richer' source. Enrichment has frequently been interchanged with restoration and fortification as a general term. However, for labelling purposes the use of the term 'enriched' is controlled.

Standardization: Standardization is sometimes used to mean additions to compensate for natural or seasonal variations in nutrient content.

Substitution: Substitution is the nutrient addition to a substitute product to the levels found in the food which it is designed to resemble in appearance, texture, flavour and odour and which it is intended to replace partially or completely. An example is the addition of vitamins A and D to fat replacers.

Supplementation: Supplementation is the supply of nutrients (normally micronutrients) singly or in combination in a quantified dose form. Supplements can take a variety of forms such as tablets, capsules, pastilles, measured amounts of liquid or small sachets of powder.

Colloidal system in food

A colloid is a heterogeneous system in which substance is dispersed (called dispersion phase) as very fine particle in another substance called dispersion medium.

Colloids are common in everyday life. Some examples include whipped cream, mayonnaise, milk, butter, gelatin, jelly, muddy water, plaster, colored glass, and paper.

Table-1: Various colloidal systems in food

System	Disperse phase	Continuous phase	Products
Sol	Solid	Liquid	Uncooked custard, unset jelly
Gel	Liquid	Solid	Jelly and jam
Emulsion	Liquid	Liquid	Mayonnaise, milk
Solid emulsion	Liquid	Solid	Butter, margarine
Foam	Gas	Liquid	Whipped cream, whisked egg white
Solid foam	Gas	Solid	Meringue, bread, cake, ice cream

Colloidal systems give structure, texture and mouthfeel to many different products, for example: jam, ice cream, mayonnaise etc. The functions of colloidal systems can be used in a variety of ways in order to produce food products.

Functions of colloidal systems in food products: Most colloids are stable, but the two phases may separate over a period of time because of an increase in temperature or by physical force. They may also become unstable when frozen or heated, especially if they contain an emulsion of fat and water.

Main types of colloidal system

Sols and gels: Sols and gels are both liquid loving (lyophilic) colloids. A sol is a liquid colloid or mixture in which solid particles are dispersed in a liquid phase. The disperse phase is attracted to molecules of the continuous phase. Sometimes the mixture needs to be heated and stirred. When this solution cools, the sol changes into a gel, which resembles a solid rather than a liquid. Both protein and starch can be used in the formation of a sol or gel.

When a jelly is made, gelatine is dispersed into a liquid and heated to form a sol. As the sol cools, protein molecules unwind forming a network that traps water and forms a gel. If cornflour is mixed with water and heated, the starch granules absorb water until they rupture, the starch then disperses in the water and the mixture becomes more viscous and forms a gel on cooling.

Other types of gel are formed with pectin and agar. Pectin, a form of carbohydrate found in fruits, is used in the production of jam to help it set. However, for it to gel there must be at least 50% sugar and conditions should be acidic. Agar is a polysaccharide extracted from seaweed which is capable of forming gels. If a gel is allowed to stand for a time, it starts to 'weep'. This loss of liquid is known as syneresis.

Emulsions: An **emulsion** is a colloid of two or more immiscible liquids where one liquid contains a dispersion of the other liquids. In other words, an emulsion is a special type of mixture made by combining two liquids that normally don't mix. The word emulsion comes from the Latin word meaning "to milk" (milk is one example of an emulsion of fat and water). The process of turning a liquid mixture into an emulsion is called **emulsification.**

There are three types of emulsions:

1. Water-in-oil (W/O), 2. Oil-in-water (O/W), 3. Complex emulsions such as water in oil-in-water (W/O/W).

- Oil and water mixtures are emulsions when shaken together. The oil will form drops and disperse throughout the water.

Butter is an emulsion of water in oil.

Familiar foods illustrate examples: milk is an oil in water emulsion; margarine is a water in oil emulsion; and ice cream is an oil and air in water emulsion with solid ice particles as well.

A stable emulsion is formed when two immiscible liquids are held stable by a third substance, called an emulsifying agent.

Emulsifier: A substance that stabilizes an emulsion is called an *emulsifier* or *emulgent*. Emulsifiers work by increasing the kinetic stability of a mixture. Surfactants or surface active agents are one type of emulsifiers. Detergents are an example of a surfactant. Other examples of emulsifiers include lecithin, mustard, soy lecithin, sodium phosphates, diacetyl tartaric acid ester of monoglyceride (DATEM), and sodium stearoyl lactylate.

Foams: Foams are composed of small bubbles of gas (usually air) dispersed in a liquid, *e.g.* egg white foam. As liquid egg white is whisked, air bubbles are incorporated. The mechanical action causes albumen proteins to unfold and form a network, trapping the air. If egg white is heated, protein coagulates and moisture is driven off. This forms a solid foam, *e.g.* a meringue. Ice cream, bread and cake are other examples of solid foams.

Fluids flow in foods

Rheology of fluid food, fermented food is concerned with science and technology of these fluids which largely depend on fluid mechanics. Resistance of a fluid to flow is a necessity of the viscosity and varies with temperatures.

Viscosity: Fluids possess many properties such as density, specific heat, thermal conductivity, etc. One of the important property is viscosity. This property is on account of cohesion and interaction between its molecules, which cause resistance to tangential or shear stress. All fluids possess viscosity though to varying degree. Opposite to viscosity is *fluidity.*

Classification of Fluids

The fluids may be classified into the following types depending upon the presence of viscosity.

(*i*) **Ideal fluids (Inviscid).** An ideal or perfect fluid is one in which only pressure forces exist, whether the fluid is at rest or in motion, and does not possess properties like viscosity, surface tension and compressibility. Such a fluid will not offer any resistance to displacement of surfaces in contact (*i.e.* $\tau = 0$). Ideal fluid is only an imaginary fluid as all the fluids, which exist, have some viscosity, etc.

(*ii*) **Real fluids.** A real or practical or actual fluid is that which possess properties like viscosity, surface tension and compressibility. Such a fluid will always resist displacement.

(*iii*) **Newtonian fluids.** A real fluid, in which the shear stress is directly proportional to the rate of shear strain (or $\tau \propto$ velocity gradient θ, a linear relationship), *i.e.*, obeys the Newton's law of viscosity, is known as Newtonian fluid. Most engineering fluids such as water, glycerine, molten metal, air, etc. are treated as the Newtonian fluids.

(*iv*) **Non-Newtonian fluids.** A real fluid, in which the shear stress is not directly proportional to the rate of shear strain, (non-linear relation) *i.e.*, does not obey the Newton's law of viscosity, is known as non-Newtonian fluid. Blood, grease, chyawanprash (health care food), tar, polymers and sugar solutions are examples of some common non-Newtonian fluids.

There are also some substances in between solids and fluids, they are called *viscoelastic fluids*. They behave in a manner similar to Newtonian fluids under time-invariant conditions but if shear stress changes suddenly behave as if plastic. Fluids whose viscosity is very small (negligible) are called the *inviscid fluids* (or ideal fluids having zero shear stress). A fluid in which the shear stress is more than the yield value is known as *plastic fluid.* For an ideal plastic fluid shear stress remains constant whereas for *bingham plastic* the shear stress is proportional to the rate of shear strain.

The general equation for rheological substances can be expressed by $\tau = A(du/dy)^n + B$, where A, B and n are constants. For Newtonian fluids $n = 1$, $B = 0$ with $A = \mu$, the fluid equation reduces to Newton's law. For ideal fluids $A = 0$, $B = 0$ and $n = 0$. The constant $B = 0$ for all fluids except *Bingham.* For Dilatants (shear thickening fluid, *i.e.,* butter, printing ink), $n > 1$. For *Binghams* (sewage sludge, drilling muds, tooth paste and jellies), $n = 1$. These fluids require a certain minimum shear stress, known as yield stress, before they start flowing. For *pseudoplastic* (paper pulp, blood, milk, rubber suspension paints, mud), $n < 1$. Most non-Newtonian fluids fall into this group. The time variant viscosity fluids are *thixotropic fluids* (lipstic, certain paints and enamels) and *rheopectic* (bentonic solution). In the former fluids the apparent viscosity increases with time whereas in the later type of fluids the apparent viscosity decrease with time. Ostwald-de-Waele suggested an empirical equation to express steady state shear stress as a function of velocity gradient. It is given as

$$\tau_{yx} = A\left(\frac{du}{dy}\right)^{n-1}\frac{du}{dy}$$

The term $A\left(\frac{du}{dy}\right)^{n-1}$ is referred to as the *apparent viscosity.*

For $n = 1$, the equation reduces to Newton's law of viscosity with $A = \mu$. Most non-Newtonian fluids have apparent viscosities that are relatively high compared with the viscosity of water.

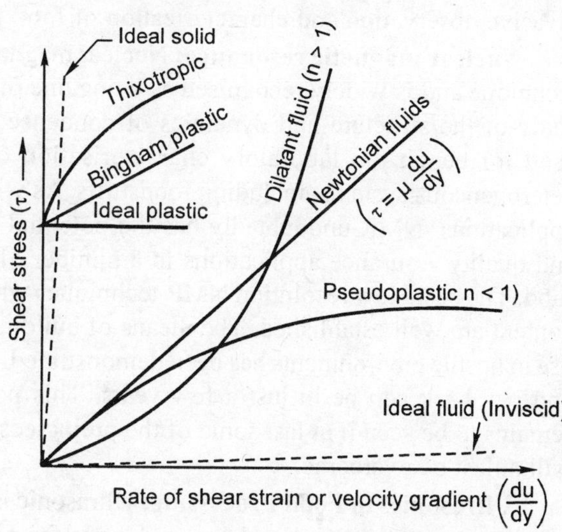

Fig. 1: Classification on rheological behaviour

Fig. 1 shows a classification of substances based on their *rheological* behaviour (*i.e.* shear stress *vs* rate of strain behaviour).

Fluid density, compressibility and surface tension are important properties for fluids at rest and viscosity is an important property when fluids are in motion. At reduced pressure, vapour pressure accounts for phase change. For flow of fluids in vapour and gas phases, thermodynamic properties such as gas constants and specific heats are essential.

Magnetic resonance imaging in Food: The magnetic resonance (MR) phenomenon, and its utilization in exploring the properties of food materials, depends on the inherent magnetic properties of certain atomic nuclei in a magnetic field. The hydrogen nucleus, a proton, behaves as a spinning charged particle; it possesses angular momentum and generates a polar field. In the earth's weak magnetic field, incoherent motion caused by thermal energy prevents any significant population of protons from aligning with the magnetic field. Little difference exists between energy levels of the numbers of protons aligned with or against the field; thermal energy equalizes the two populations.

Placing hydrogen nuclei in a stronger magnetic field imposes a larger difference in energy levels between protons aligned with and those aligned against the field. Thermal motions still tend to equalize the populations, but the population of nuclei aligned with the magnetic field will vary slightly outnumber those aligned against it. A sudden pulse of energy at a frequency and amplitude precisely adjusted for a given nucleus will move the protons from the lower energy level (aligned with) to the higher level (aligned against). MRI offers a versatile, noninvasive, nondestructive experimental technique to study food processing. Its advantages stem from the ability to study and quantify any phenomenon which generates contrast, *i.e.*, change in signal intensity. Magnetic resonance imaging derives many of its attributes from mobility, and not coincidentally MRI techniques have found use in quantifying dynamic processes from the molecular to the macro level. MRI in food applications for the study of freezing and crystallisation, diffusion, emulsions, syneresis, and flow, and hopefully supplied enough theory to allow an intuitive grasp of the possibilities. Realisation of the potential of MRI techniques for non-invasive observation and characterization of food processes has only begun.

Nuclear magnetic resonance: Nuclear magnetic resonance (NMR) is now a mature spectroscopic technique and is widely recognised as being one of the most powerful spectroscopies available for the study of the structure and dynamics of condensed matter. These simple techniques are now widely used for bench top laboratory characterisation of the physical state and composition analysis of heterogeneous systems, including foodstuffs. As will be seen, they form the basis of most on line NMR applications. NMR undoubtedly has the potential to be used successfully for on line process control and quality assurance applications in a nimiber of environments and for various industries including food. The basic low resolution NMR techniques which can be used to determine, for example, moisture content are well established. The means of building large and unusually shaped magnets and coils for use in hostile environments has been demonstrated. The cost, although expensive, need not be exorbitant and pay back can be in just a few years. This potential has been recognised many times before. It remains to be seen if at last some of the prejudices which have prevented NMR being widely taken up will at last be overcome.

Ultrasonics in Food Processing: Ultrasonic is a one of the fast, versatile, emerging, and promising non-destructive green technology used in the food industry from last few years. The ultrasound is being carried out in various areas of food technology namely crystallization, freezing, bleaching, degassing, extraction, drying, filtration, emulsification, sterilization, cutting, etc. Ultrasound is being applied as an effective preservation tool in many food-processing fields viz. vegetables and fruits, cereal products, honey, gels, proteins, enzymes, microbial inactivation, cereal technology, water treatment, diary technology, etc.

Ultrasound are sound waves having frequency beyond the audible range of human capacity (~20 kHz). It has a variety of applications with many advantages as compared to conventional methodologies used in food industries. Ultrasound is similar to 'normal' (audible) sound based on physical properties. Ultrasound is one of the emerging technologies that were developed to minimize processing, maximize quality and ensure the safety of food products. It is one of the new technologies which increases and ensures quality and reduces the time of processing and cost of the food products. So ultrasound is used in food technology for processing, preservation and extraction steps. It makes use of physical and chemical phenomena which marks the difference with conventional techniques. It offers great advantage in various fields like productivity, yield, better quality, less time and being environmental friendly.

Staling: Staling is a common issue that occurs with baked goods, particularly bread, pastries, and cakes. Staling refers to the process in which baked goods lose their freshness and become dry and hard over time. Staling control involves techniques and ingredients used to prolong the freshness and softness of baked goods, ensuring they remain enjoyable for a longer period.

Several factors contribute to the staling of baked goods. One of the main factors is the retrogradation of starch molecules, which occurs when the starch in the baked goods crystallizes and recrystallizes, leading to a loss of moisture and a firming of the texture. Another factor is the migration of moisture from the interior of the baked goods to the crust, causing the interior to dry out and become stale. Additionally, the presence of fats and sugars in baked goods can also contribute to staling by interacting with the starch molecules and accelerating the retrogradation process.

Techniques that can be used to control staling and prolong the freshness of baked goods (1) to wrap the baked goods in airtight packaging, such as plastic wrap or a sealed container, to prevent moisture loss and keep the goods soft. (2_)to store the baked goods in a cool, dry place, as heat and humidity can accelerate the staling process. Additionally, reheating the baked goods in an oven or microwave can help to restore some of their moisture and freshness.

Retrogradation: The process of re-association of the starch granules on cooling of the gelatinized starch or the starch paste is called retrogradation. It depends on the relative proportions of amylose and amylopectin in starch as linear amylose molecules re-associate faster than the highly branched amylopectins. Reheating starchy foods also influences this process. The digestibility of starch in the small intestine is reduced by the degree of processing and retrogradation. The staling of bread is due to retrogradation of starch and the rate of staling is temperature dependent.

Gelatinization: On heating starch in the presence of water, the crystalline structure of the starch granules is lost irreversibly by a process called gelatinization. It is due to absorption of water by starch granules and turning into a jelly like substance. In this process, amylopectin forms the gel and amylase comes into solution. When heating is continued in excess water, more soluble components of starch come into solution and a paste results. In the food processing, the starch granules are not completely dissolved however, their partial gelatinization is sufficient to allow a good part of the starch to be digested rapidly. In the steaming of food, the process of gelatinization occurs to a small extent whereby a large proportion of slowly digestible starch is preserved.

PCR (Polymerase Chain Reaction):

- In 1985, Kary Mullis invented the process known as polymerase chain reaction (PCR),
- PCR is a technique used to rapidly amplify (make many copies of) a specific segment of DNA.
- It involves repeated cycles of heating and cooling, allowing DNA polymerase to replicate the target DNA sequence.
- PCR is used in various applications, including gene cloning, sequencing, and disease diagnosis.
- During the PCR process, the DNA sample is denatured, primers anneal to the template DNA, and DNA polymerase extends the primers, resulting in a million-fold amplification of the target DNA.

Calorimeter:

- A calorimeter is an instrument used to measure heat changes in a chemical or physical process.
- It can be used to determine the amount of heat absorbed or released during a reaction.
- Differential Scanning Calorimetry (DSC) can be used to study the thermal reactions that accompany the PCR process.

Tensiometer:

- A tensiometer is an instrument used to measure surface tension, which is the force that causes liquid surfaces to contract.
- It is used in various applications, including measuring the surface tension of liquids and studying the properties of interfaces.

Chromatography is an important biophysical technique that enables the separation, identification, and purification of the components of a mixture for qualitative and quantitative analysis. Chromatography techniques can be broadly classified into liquid chromatography (LC) and gas chromatography (GC), with variations based on the separation mechanism, stationary phase, and mobile phase.

I. Based on Mobile Phase: Liquid Chromatography (LC):

- **High-Performance Liquid Chromatography (HPLC):** A powerful technique for separating and analyzing complex mixtures, often used in analytical chemistry.
- **Column Chromatography:** Separates compounds based on their affinity for a stationary phase within a column.
- **Thin-Layer Chromatography (TLC):** A simple, planar technique used for separating and identifying compounds.
- **Paper Chromatography:** A basic form of chromatography using paper as the stationary phase.
- **Ion Exchange Chromatography:** Separates compounds based on their charge.
- **Size Exclusion Chromatography (SEC):** Separates compounds based on their size.
- **Affinity Chromatography:** Separates compounds based on specific binding interactions.
- **Adsorption Chromatography:** Separates compounds based on their adsorption to the surface of a stationary phase.
- **Partition Chromatography:** Separates compounds based on their distribution between two immiscible phases.

Gas Chromatography (GC):

- **Gas Chromatography (GC):** Separates volatile or thermally stable compounds by passing them through a column in a gaseous state.

II. Based on Separation Mechanism:

- **Ion Exchange Chromatography:** Separates compounds based on their charge.
- **Size Exclusion Chromatography (SEC):** Separates compounds based on their size.
- **Affinity Chromatography:** Separates compounds based on specific binding interactions.
- **Adsorption Chromatography:** Separates compounds based on their adsorption to the surface of a stationary phase.
- **Partition Chromatography:** Separates compounds based on their distribution between two immiscible phases.

III. Other Notable Types:

- **Supercritical Fluid Chromatography (SFC):** Combines the benefits of gas and liquid chromatography.
- **Flash Chromatography:** A faster version of column chromatography.
- **Fast Protein Liquid Chromatography (FPLC):** A type of HPLC specifically designed for protein purification.
- **Reversed-Phase Chromatography:** A type of liquid chromatography where the stationary phase is non-polar and the mobile phase is polar.
- **Hydrophobic Interaction Chromatography:** Separates proteins based on their hydrophobicity.

MODEL PAPERS-1

1. The processing of the removal of solids particles from a fluid by passing through a filtering medium is called
   (a) cleaning (b) washing (c) filtration (d) scrubbing
2. In a ball mil, most of the size reduction is achieved by
   (a) shearing (b) cutting (c) crushing (d) impact
3. The food is preserved by
   (a) cooling (b) heating (c) boiling (d) all the above
4. Holding time under HTST milk pasteurizer is
   (a) 1.0 min (b) 45 s (c) 30 s (d) 15 s
5. In thermal processing of food, destruction of microorganisms is governed by a ________ order equation.
   (a) zero (b) first (c) second (d) third
6. Rittinger's law is applicable in the process of
   (a) Sieve analysis (b) size reduction (c) freezing (d) drying
7. In freezing, which principle is followed?
   (a) Condensation (b) crystallization (c) drying (d) all of the above
8. The reverse process of freezing is called
   (a) osmosis (b) thawing (c) chilling (d) heating
9. Which is example of cryogenic agent?
   (a) CO (b) CO_2 (c) N_2 (L) (d) None
10. Temperature range of chilling of fruits and vegetables is
    (a) –1 to 8 °C (b) 4-8 °C (c) –18 to –196 °C (d) below 45°C
11. Size reduction is also known as
    (a) Crushing (b) Comminution (c) Separation (d) Screening
12. The force applied at a time with a hammer to the material is known as
    (a) Compression (b) Stress (c) Impact (d) Shear
13. The grinding laws are based on the energy required to reduce the ________ of material to create new surface.
    (a) Texture (b) structure (c) size (d) roundness
14. Ribbon mixer are generally used for blending
    (a) liquid (b) solids (c) dough (d) all of the above
15. Planetary mixer and kneader are generally used in
    (a) Fruit industry (b) bakery industry (c) meat industry (d) dairy industry

16. Solids particles of different densities from a mixture could be separated by
    (a) Sink and Float method (b) Differential settling methods
    (c) Both (a) & (b) (d) None
17. Food irradiation is used to
    a) Precooked Foods (b) kills insect
    (c) Kill microorganisms (d) increase nutritive value
18. Freezing point depression is measured by
    a) Beckmann's method (b) Rast's camphor method
    (c) both above (d) None of these
19. A semi permeable membrane allows the passage of _________ through it.
    (a) Solvent only (b) Solute only (c) Above both (d) None of (a) & (b)
20. Smoke used a colour enhancer in
    (a) Meat (b) milk (c) vegetable (d) cereals
21. Parboiling of rice is originated in
    (a) Pakistan (b) India (c) Bhutan (d) USA
22. Flaked rice is made from
    (a) Raw rice (b) Brown rice (c) Parboiled rice (d) Bulgur
23. Terminal velocity of particle is equal to air velocity for which
    (a) Particle remains in the bottom (b) Particles are carried away
    (c) Particle remains in suspended state (d) None of these
24. Scalping is also known as
    (a) Grading (b) Rough cleaning (c) Separating (d) Dust removal
25. In dry milling process prior to treatment with oil, the following operation is done
    (a) Grading (b) polishing (c) conditioning (d) pitting
26. Removal of bran layer from the brown rice is done by
    (a) Polisher (b) Bran aspirator (c) Whitener (d) both (a) and (c)
27. Horizontal jet pearler is used in paddy milling for
    (a) Polishing (b) Whitening (c) Pearling (d) None of them
28. After the oil treatment, the pulses are kept for about 12 hours to allow proper penetration take place in the pulse kernel is called
    (a) Conditioning (b) Oil penetration (c) Tempering (d) Saponification
29. The LSU is a
    (a) Evaporator (b) Drier (c) Washer (d) Polisher
30. Grading refers to
    (a) Classification of cleaned product (b) Classification of uncleaned product
    (c) Separation of cleaned product (d) Separation of large impurities

31. Screening is a method of separating grains into two or more fractions according to
(a) Size alone (b) Shape alone
(c) Colour alone (d) Texture alone

32. Removal of bran from the brown rice is called
(a) Grading (b) Polishing (c) Bran aspiration (d) Bran separation

33. The effectiveness of which screen is higher than others.
(a) Rotary screen (b) Horizontal screen (c) Revolving screen (d) Vibratory screen

34. Moisture content of substance is expressed in
(a) ml (b) litre (c) gm (d) percentage

35. A machine which removes surface moisture from grain after washing by centrifugal force and impact is called
(a) Hammer mill (b) Ball mill (c) Whizzer (d) Degermer

36. Solid particles of differing densities from a mixture could be separated by
(a) Sink and float method (b) Differential settling method
(c) Both 'a' and 'b' (d) None of these

37. In a ball mill or pebble mill, most of the size reduction is achieved by:
(a) Shearing (b) Cutting (c) Crushing (d) Impact

38. The food is preserved by
(a) Cooling (b) Heating (c) Boiling (d) All of the above

39. Separation of grain by screening is done on the basis of
(a) Size (b) Colour (c) Texture (d) None of the above

40. Rittinger's law is applicable in the process of
(a) Sieve analysis (b) Size reduction (c) Freezing (d) Drying

41. One of the following is not a physical property of food materials.
(a) Porosity (b) Specific gravity (c) Specific heat (d) Frontal area

42. Mechanical damage to seeds and grains which occurs during
(a) Harvesting (b) Threshing (c) Handling (d) All of the above

43. Mechanical damage to seed and grains seriously affect the
(a) Viability and germination power (b) Growth vigour
(c) Insects and fungi attack (d) Quality of the final products
(e) All of them

44. Which physical properties are necessary to evaluate aerodynamic properties of food in case of terminal velocity?
(a) Density size (b) Shape
(c) Drag coefficient (d) All of the above

45. The thermal processing may include
(a) Heating (b) Cooling (c) Drying (d) Freezing
(e) All
46. Heat or cooling of agricultural products may be accomplished by the method of
(a) Convection (b) Conduction (c) Radiation (d) All of them
47. The water activity for high moisture foods such as fruits , vegetables, meat etc is more than
(a) 0.75 (b) 0.85 (c) 0.97 (d) 0.95
48. The water activity of intermediate moisture foods varies from
(a) 0.20-0.36 (b) 0.40-0.50 (c) 0.60-0.90 (d) 0.90-0.95
49. The water activity of non-fat dry milk should be below
(a) 0.35 (b) 0.40 (c) 0.50 (d) 0.60
50. The plot of equilibrium moisture content of a food material versus relative humidity of the environment at a given temperature is referred to as
(a) Sorption-desorption isotherms (b) Drying curve
(c) Psychometric chart (d) Freezing curve
51. Those properties having to do the behavior of the material under applied force is known as
(a) Frictional properties (b) Mechanical properties
(c) Rheological properties (d) All of the above
52. A science devoted to the study of deformation and flow is called
(a) Rheological properties (b) Dielectrical properties
(c) Optical properties (d) Mechanical properties
53. A damage to plant tissue by external forces causing physical change in texture and/or eventual chemical alteration of colour, flavour and texture is known as
(a) Abrasion (b) Bruising (c) Distortion (d) Crack
54. A change in shape of an intact fruits or vegetables which is not characteristics for the variety is referred as
(a) Abrasion (b) Bruising (c) Distortion (d) none
55. The shape which is formed when an ellipse rotates about its minor axis like a grape fruits is called
(a) Prolate spheroid (b) Elliptical
(c) Oblate spheroid (d) Right circular cone
56. The volume of prolate spheroid (V) is expressed as if 'a' and 'b' is major and minor axis, respectively as follows
(a) $4/3\ (\pi ab^2)$ (b) $4/3\ (\pi ab)^2$ (c) $4/3\ (\pi a)\ b^2$ (d) $4/3\ (\pi ab)^3$
57. The volume of oblate spheroid (*V*) is expressed as if 'a' and 'b' is major and minor axis, respectively as follows
(a) $4/3\ (\pi ab)^2$ (b) $4/3\ (\pi b)a^2$ (c) $4/3\ (\pi a^2 b)$ (d) $4/3\ (\pi ab)^3$

58. A fast and accurate method for determining volume and weight density of food material is accomplished by

(a) Platform balance (b) Specific gravity balance

(c) Specific gravity gradient tube (d) Air compression pycnometer

59. Air compression pycnometer is used to measure the

(a) Weight (b) Volume (c) Specific gravity (d) Temperature

60. Which method is not used to measure the specific gravity of fruit and vegetables?

(a) Pycnometer method (b) Platform balance

(c) Specific gravity gradient tube (d) Specific gravity balance

61. Dimension of viscosity of liquid is

(a) $M^{-1}L^{-1}T^{-1}$ (b) $ML^{-1}\ T$ (c) $M^{-1}LT^{-1}$ (d) $ML^{-1}T^{-1}$

62. Which physical properties are necessary to evaluate aerodynamic properties of food in case of terminal velocity?

(a) Density size (b) Shape (c) Drag coefficient (d) All of the above

63. Those properties having to do the behavior of the material under applied force is known as

(a) Frictional properties (b) Mechanical properties

(c) Rheological properties (d) All of the above

64. A science devoted to the study of deformation and flow is called

(a) Rheological properties (b) Dielectrical properties

(c) Optical properties (d) Mechanical properties

65. A damage to plant tissue by external forces causing physical change in texture and/or eventual chemical alteration of colour, flavour and texture is known as

(a) Abrasion (b) Bruising (c) Distortion (d) Crack

66. A change in shape of an intact fruits or vegetables which is not characteristics for the variety is referred as

(a) Abrasion (b) Bruising (c) Distortion (d) Puncture

67. Fruits on the basis of respiration can be classified as

(a) Non climacteric (b) Parthenocarpic

(c) Climacteric (d) Climacteric and Non climacteric

68. The water displacement method is used for the measurement of

(a) porosity (b) roundness (c) volume (d) hardness

69. The fruits and vegetables are cleaned by

(a) screen and aspirators (b) wet cleaning or washing

(c) both wet and dry cleaning (d) none of them

70. Which of the following is a climacteric fruit?

(a) avacad (b) grape (c) lemon (d) pineapple

71. Generalized storage life of leafy vegetables at 21°C is
(a) 1-7 days (b) 1-2 days (c) 7-20 days (d) none of them

72. Most fresh vegetables and fruits are high in
(a) Water (b) protein (c) Fat (d) all of them

73. Which one of the following is a heat resistance enzyme in vegetables?
(a) Catalase (b) peroxidase (c) both (a) and (b) (d) none

74. Which one is not a physical property?
(a) specific gravity (b) specific heat (c) spherecity (d) surface roughness

75. The frontal area are essential to estimate the
(a) terminal velocity (b) drag coefficient
(c) Reynold's number (d) all the above

76. The property that affect the behavior of the fruit and vegetables under the applied force.
(a) optical property (b) dielectric property
(c) mechanical property (d) frictional property

77. Which one is not a physical method of determination of harvest maturity indices of fruits and vegetables?
(a) T-stage (b) weight (c) specific gravity (d) juice content

78. What are the maturity indices of cabbage?
(a) spear length (b) head solidity (c) firmness (d) netting

79. Which is not a pre-cooling method of fruit and vegetables?
(a) hydro cooling (b) contact icing (c) cold air cooling (d) freezing

80. Lye peeling of fruits and vegetables is done in
(a) sulphuric acid (b) caustic soda (c) KMS (d) Citric acid

81. Copra may be cured by
(a) sun drying (b) kiln drying
(c) combination (a) and (b) (d) None

82. Keeping quality of copra depends upon its
(a) Size (b) oil content (c) Moisture (d) variety

83. The average energy content of coconut biomass on a moisture free basis is
(a) 3500 kcal/kg (b) 4000 kcal/kg (c) 4200kcal/kg d) 4500 kcal/kg

84. Percentage of bran received from paddy is
(a) 2 (b) 5 (c) 8 (d) 10

85. Particle board can be made from
(a) coir pith (b) paddy straw (c) bagasse (d) all of the above

86. Briquetting process with binder materials requires __________ pressure.
(a) high (b) low (c) equal (d) ultra high

87. In activated carbon, the basic requirement is
(a) porous and more surface area (b) compact and more surface area
(c) compact and less surface area (d) porous and less surface area

88. Briquetting ________________ ash content after combustion.
(a) increases (b) decreases (c) stabilizes (d) slightly alter

89. Calorific value of paddy husk is approximately __________________ kcal/kg.
(a) 3000-3500 (b) 4000-4500 (c) 4500-5000 d) 5000-6000

90. Paddy husk can be used to produce
(a) activated carbon (b) silicon tetra chloride
(c) sodium silicate (d) all of the above

91. Mango leather prepared from
(a) pulp (b) skin (c) stone (d) all of the above

92. Mango kernel is a good source of
(a) starch (b) fat (c) both (a) and (b) (d) protein

93. During the production of vinegar from mango waste, the extract of peel or stone is fermented by
(a) yeast (b) molds (c) bacteria (d) virus

94. Banana peel is a rich source of
(a) starch (b) crude protein (c) crude fat (d) total dietary fibre

95. Burning of rice husk in ambient atmosphere leaves a residue called
(a) rice husk ash (b) burned silica (c) bran (d) rice bran

96. Silica content in rice husk ash is about
(a) 1-4 % (b) 4-6% (c) 20-24% (d) 87-97%

97. Which one is not a comound of rice husk ash
(a) Al_2O_3 (b) Fe_2O_3 (c) $KMnO_4$ (d) MgO

98. Rice husk is mostly used as a fuel in
(a) tray drier (b) boiler (c) diesel engine (d) steam engine

99. The chief by product of sugar industry is/are
(a) bagasse (b) molasses (c) filter mud (d) all of the above

100. Filter mud is mainly used for
(a) fertilizer (b) cattle feed (c) marine feed (d) alcohol

ANSWER KEY

(Model paper 1)

Q.	Ans.	Q.	Ans.	Q.	Ans.	Q.	Ans.	Q.	Ans.
1.	C	21.	B	41.	C	61.	D	81.	D
2.	D	22.	C	42.	D	62.	D	82.	C
3.	D	23.	C	43.	E	63.	B	83.	C
4.	D	24.	B	44.	D	64.	A	84.	B
5.	B	25.	D	45.	E	65.	B	85.	D
6.	B	26.	D	46.	D	66.	C	86.	B
7.	B	27.	B	47.	C	67.	D	87.	A
8.	B	28.	C	48.	C	68.	C	88.	B
9.	C	29.	B	49.	D	69.	C	89.	A
10.	A	30.	A	50.	A	70.	A	90.	D
11.	B	31.	A	51.	B	71.	B	91.	A
12.	C	32.	B	52.	A	72.	A	92.	C
13.	C	33.	B	53.	B	73.	C	93.	A
14.	B	34.	D	54.	C	74.	B	94.	D
15.	B	35.	A	55.	C	75.	D	95.	A
16.	C	36.	C	56.	A	76.	C	96.	D
17.	C	37.	D	57.	C	77.	A	97.	C
18.	C	38.	D	58.	C	78.	B	98.	B
19.	A	39.	A	59.	B	79.	D	99.	D
20.	A	40.	B	60.	A	80.	B	100.	A

MODEL PAPERS-2

1. In thin layer drying, the thickness of grain is normally up to
   (a) 15-20 cm (b) 20-25 cm (c) 25-30 cm (d) 30-35 cm
2. LSU dryer is a ___________ type dryer.
   (a) continuous mixing (b) non mixing
   (c) thin layer (d) deep bed
3. Holding of grain between two drying passes is termed as
   (a) stabilizing (b) tempering (c) cooling (d) equalizing
4. In drying process, the removal of moisture takes place by
   (a) radiation (b) conduction (c) diffusion (d) convection
5. In drying, end of constant rate period and start of falling rate period is known as
   (a) critical moisture content (b) final moisture content
   (c) equilibrium moisture content (d) initial moisture content
6. Drying takes place in
   (a) fruits (b) vegetables (c) food grains (d) all of the above
7. The Chung-pfost equation fits grain EMC data is over
   (a) 0-20% RH (b) 20-40% RH (c) 15-30% RH (d) 20-90% RH
8. One of the following is not improved grain storage structure.
   (a) Pusa bin (b) Bunker storage
   (c) cover and plinth storage (d) muda
9. In winter season, grains stored in bin will be spoiled at
   (a) Top (b) bottom (c) centre (d) near walls of bin
10. Grain is spoiled in bin due to accumulation of
   (a) temperature (b) heat (c) relative humidity (d) moisture
11. The process of removal of moisture from moist air is known as
   (a) humidification (b) cooling (c) dehumidification (d) drying
12. When dry bulb and wet bulb temperature are same, the RH of air will be
   (a) 0 % (b) 50 % (c) 100 % (d) 70 %
13. The universal moisture meter measures ___________ of the grain at given compaction.
   (a) electrical conductivity (b) electrical resistance
   (c) diffusivity (d) thermal conductivity
14. BET equation is used for measuring the __________________ of the foods.
   (a) moisture content (b) EMC c) water activity (d) dry matter

15. Deep bed drying system has been analyzed by
(a) Hukill (b) Henderson (c) Jenssion (d) Pasteur
16. Shedd's chart is used for calculation of
(a) energy consumption (b) temperature measurement
(c) static pressure drop (d) flow measurement
17. The EMC of a food grain is dependent upon
(a) temperature (b) relative humidity
(c) variety and maturity of grain (d) all the above
18. The ratio of (M-Me)/(Mo-Me) is known as
(a) moisture ratio b) drying ratio (c) drying rate (d) EMC
19. One of the following is not the example of radiation drying
(a) sun drying (b) infrared dying (c) dielectric drying (d) none
20. The size of food grain is represented by
(a) length (b) width (c) diameter (d) equivalent diameter
21. The pearler is also called
(a) Degermer (b) Dehusker (c) Polisher (d) Debranner
22. In sugar mills, cane juice is evaporated in
(a) Horizontal tube evaporator (b) Long vertical tube evaporator
(c) Short vertical tube evaporator (d) Flash evaporator
23. In work study, the symbol ⇨ implies
(a) Delay (b) Transport (c) Operation (d) Inspection
24. In work study, the symbol ▽ implies
(a) Delay (b) Operation (c) Inspection d) Temporary storage
25. The heart of homogenizer is
(a) Pump (b) Body (c) Source of power (d) None
26. An optimum arrangement of different facilities including human resource, plant and machinery, materials etc. refers to as
(a) Flow pattern (b) Plant design (c) Plant layout (d) Process design
27. Which one is not included in basic type of flow pattern
(a) I-flow (b) L-flow (c) U-flow (d) Z-flow
28. Which of the following is true?
(a) LTLT is batch process (b) LTLT is continuous process
(c) HTST is both process (d) None of these
29. The addition of water to the bran and endosperm of wheat grain refers to
(a) Tempering (b) Parboiling (c) Drying (d) Canning

30. The grinding of wheat is done between pairs of
(a) Grinder (b) Disc (c) Degermer (d) Rolls

31. The classification of commodities into various fractions depending on commercial value and usage is known as
(a) Scalping (b) Grading (c) Sorting (d) Cleaning

32. Grading is used for
(a) Fruits and vegetables (b) Processed products
(c) Grains (d) All of these

33. In rice mills, the paddy separator is fitted just below the
(a) Pre cleaner (b) Rubber roll sheller
(c) Husk aspirator (d) Cone polisher

34. Which of the dryer is used for drying liquid food?
(a) Drum dryer (b) Tray dryer (c) Tunnel dryer (d) None

35. Which of the following vegetable is usually not blanched?
(a) Onion (b) Cabbage (c) Potato (d) None

36. Which of the following process is also known as Appertization?
(a) Blanching (b) Pasteurization (c) Canning (d) None

37. SMP stands for
(a) Solid milk powder (b) Skim milk powder
(c) Sweetened milk products (d) Standard milking practices

38. Which of the following heat exchanger are mostly common in milk pasteurization?
(a) Shell and tube (b) Plate type
(c) Steam injected type (d) Steam infusion type

39. Which of the following is not considered for selection of site for a food processing plant?
(a) Availability of water (b) Availability of labour
(c) Availability of power (d) None of these

40. Which of the following is related to process form of layout?
(a) Line flow process (b) Intermitted process
(c) Single storied layout (d) Multistoried layout

41. The basic requirement of parboiling in paddy is done by
(a) Increase the moisture content (b) Minimize breakage during milling
(c) Minimize the recovery of head rice (d) None of them

42. Glazing is done to rice for
(a) Polishing (b) whitening (c) transparent look (d) Pearling

43. The efficiency of gota machine for pulse in single pass is to about
(a) 50 % (b) 60 % (c) 80 % (d) 90 %

44. The LSU is a
(a) evaporator (b) dryer (c) washer (d) polisher

45. Which of the following is not a method of edible oil milling?
(a) Bullock driven ghani (b) Mechanical expression
(c) Chemical lye method (d) Solvent extraction method

46. The oils and fats are composed of different mixture of
(a) glycerin (b) glucose (c) glycerides (d) glycerol

47. The differential speed of the break rolls are
(a) 1:2 (b) 2:1 (c) 2.5:1 (d) 1:1

48. Capacity of bucket elevator may vary from
(a) 10-20 t/h (b) 2-1000 t/h (c) 200-500 t/h (d) 1000-3000 t/h

49. Belt speed of high capacity belt conveyor is around
(a) 2.5 m/s (b) 2.8 m/s (c) 3.5 m/s (d) 4.5 m/s

50. The vertical lift of the bucket elevator may range between
(a) 10-15 m (b) 20-40 m
(c) Few meter to 50 m (d) More than 100 m

51. In belt conveyor, trough angle from paddy grain is
(a) 10° (b) 40° (c) 30° (d) 20°

52. The shape of trough in screw conveyor is used as
(a) L shaped (b) U shaped (c) V shaped (d) J shaped

53. The vertical lift of bucket elevator may range between
(a) 10-15 m (b) 20-40 m
(c) Few meter to 50 m (d) More than 100 m

54. The removal of colour of rice is called
(a) blanching (b) bleaching (c) parboiling (d) polishing

55. The recommended value of oil consumption in India per annum per capita is about
(a) 6 MT (b) 19.4 MT (c) 5 kg (d) 18 kg

56. Moisture of paddy during milling should be
(a) 20-22% (b) 10-12% (c) 12-14% (d) 15-20%

57. Separation of broken and head rice is known as :
(a) Scalping (b) Screening (c) Sorting (d) Grading

58. In solvent extraction of edible oil, the solvent is
(a) n-haxane (b) iso-butane (c) n-butane (d) hot water

59. The kernel of paddy is enclosed by
(a) Hull (b) Germ (c) Bran (d) Both a and c

60. The oil treatment in pulses is done to loosen the
(a) Bran (b) Germ (c) Husk (d) Aleurone layer

61. ISO 9000 represents.
(a) Quality system (b) Safety system
(c) Quality and safety (d) Environment management system

62. Agmark is implemented in the year
(a) 1927 (b) 1937 (c) 1947 (d) 1857

63. HACCP is a systematic approach to assure
(a) Food safety (b) Food quality
(c) Both (a) and (b) (d) All the above

64. Who is responsible for implementation of HACCP?
(a) Farmers (b) Processors
(c) Government (d) Both (b) and (c)

65. Fruit product order is started in the year
(a) 1936 (b) 1955 (c) 1965 (d) 1975

66. A value that defines the difference between acceptable and unacceptable is defined as
(a) Critical limit (b) Critical control point
(c) HACCP (d) Hazard

67. FDA is termed as
(a) Fruit and drug administration (b) Food and drug administration
(c) Fruit and dietary allowance (d) Foundation of Drug administration

68. Airtight storages are normally used
(a) To arrest the insect infestation (b) To protect the wet grain from old attack
(c) To decrease the oxygen content (d) Both (a) and (b)

69. A good quality storage structure should be
(a) Structurally adequate (b) Durable and hygienic
(c) Gas sealable for fumigation (d) All the above

70. The capacity of CAP storage structure is
(a) 10 tonnes (b) 100 tonnes (c) 1000 tonnes (d) 2000 tonnes

71. The potential to cause harm to consumer and/or the product and can be biological or physical is called
(a) Critical limit (b) CCP (c) HACCP (d) Hazard

72. To conduct a planned sequence of observations or measurement to assess the control of CCP
(a) Corrective action (b) Monitoring (c) Hazard (d) Critical limit

73. Those action to be taken when monitoring of a CCP induced a loss of control is
(a) Corrective action (b) Monitoring (c) Hazard (d) Critical limit

74. In field experiment, the commonly used design is
(a) CRD (b) RBD (c) LSD (d) none
75. FSSAI was established in the year
(a) 1986 (b) 1996 (c) 2006 (d) 2016
76. ISO standard is
(a) Mandatory (b) Non mandatory (c) Obligatory (d) Compulsory
77. PFA stands for
(a) Prevention of food adulteration (b) Prevention of food administration
(c) Protection of Food admix (d) All the above
78. Panelist evaluates three samples, and one of them is marked as reference. The test is called
(a) Due-Trio test (b) Triangle test
(c) 9 point hedonic scale (d) All the above
79. Panelists evaluate three samples, two are identical and one if different, the test is termed as
(a) Due-Trio test (b) Triangle test
(c) Paired comparison test (d) None
80. Why use sensory analysis to evaluate food products?
(a) To evaluate or improve the quality (b) To determine market value
(c) To determine shelf life (d) All the above
81. Blanching refers to
(a) Inactivate the enzyme (b) Cooking the food
(c) Sterilization of food (d) Drying of food
82. The Process of preservation of fruits and vegetables with common salt and vinegar is called
(a) Pickling (b) Fermentation (c) Steeping (d) Asepsis
83. Lactic acid forming bacteria is beneficial and grown in
(a) Sauce (b) Ketchup c) Jelly (d) Pickle
84. Controlled atmosphere storage (CAS) of fruits and vegetables is done to
(a) Maintain higher concentration of ethylene than the normal atmosphere
(b) Maintain higher concentration of CO_2 than the normal atmosphere
(c) Maintain higher concentration of N_2 than the normal atmosphere
(d) None of these
85. Cryo-preservation is done in liquid nitrogen at a temperature of
(a) –196°C (b) 0°C (c) 200°C (d) 50 °C
86. The 'Campaigne' is a type of
(a) Juice (b) Wine (c) Beverage (d) Pod

87. Wine is preserved at
a) 10 % alcohol b) 14 % alcohol c) 8 % alcohol d) 5% alcohol

88. The freeze drying generally works at pressure of
a) 2 mm to about 0.1 mm Hg b) 3 mm to about 1.0 mm Hg
c) 1 mm to about 0.3 mm Hg d) None

89. Kiln dryer is used for drying of
a) Vegetables slices b) Potato slices c) Cereals d) Apple slices

90. Which metal foil is used for food packaging?
a) Iron b) Zinc c) Aluminium d) Copper

91. Food Packaging can be classified into
a) Primary packaging (b) Secondary packaging
(c) Tertiary packaging (d) All the above

92. Most important general requirements of food packaging are
a) Non toxic b) Protect against contamination
c) Act as barrier d) All the above

93. Sulphur dioxide are used in food to prevent
a) Microbial load b) Prevent enzymatic /non enzymatic reactions
c) Discolouration of some foods d) All the above

94. Optimum temperature of sharp freezing used to frozen the food is
a) – 23.3°C (b) – 45.6°C (c) – 17.8°C (d) 34.4°C

95. Most commercial storage freezer are used
a) At or above –18°C b) Above –18°C
c) At 18°C d) At –10°C

96. The father of canning is
a) Spllanzani b) Nicolous Appeart
c) Robert Koch d) Louise Pasteur

97. Leafy vegetables is recommended as?
a) Highly perishable b) Semi perishable c) Perishable d) Non-perishable

98. Food packaging foils consists of pure
a) Iron b) Aluminium c) Zinc d) Lead

99. Which is not used as food preservative?
a) KMS b) Sodium benzoate c) Acetic acid d) Bandate

100. Toddy is prepared from
a) Grape b) Apple c) Coconut d) Cashew

ANSWER KEY

(Model paper 2)

Q.	Ans.	Q.	Ans.	Q.	Ans.	Q.	Ans.	Q.	Ans.
1.	A	21.	C	41.	B	61.	B	81.	A
2.	A	22.	B	42.	C	62.	B	82.	A
3.	B	23.	B	43.	A	63.	A	83.	D
4.	C	24.	D	44.	B	64.	D	84.	B
5.	A	25.	A	45.	C	65.	B	85.	A
6.	C	26.	C	46.	C	66.	A	86.	B
7.	D	27.	D	47.	C	67.	B	87.	B
8.	D	28.	A	48.	B	68.	D	88.	A
9.	A	29.	A	49.	C	69.	D	89.	D
10.	D	30.	D	50.	C	70.	C	90.	C
11.	C	31.	B	51.	D	71.	D	91.	D
12.	C	32.	D	52.	B	72.	B	92.	D
13.	B	33.	C	53.	C	73.	A	93.	D
14.	C	34.	A	54.	B	74.	B	94.	A
15.	A	35.	A	55.	C	75.	C	95.	A
16.	C	36.	C	56.	C	76.	B	96.	B
17.	D	37.	B	57.	D	77.	A	97.	A
18.	A	38.	B	58.	A	78.	A	98.	B
19.	C	39.	D	59.	D	79.	B	99.	D
20.	D	40.	B	60.	C	80.	D	100.	C

MODEL PAPERS-3

1. Which of the following microorganism use H_2S as the electron donor to reduce carbon dioxide
   (a) *Chromatium* (b) *Chlorobium* (c) Both A and B (d) *Rhodomicrobium*
2. The microorganism that is referred to as sewage fungus is
   (a) *Methanococcus* sp. (b) *Phytophthora infestans*
   (c) *E. coli* (d) *Sphaerotilus natans*
3. Q fever is caused by
   (a) *Coxiella burnetii* (b) *Treponema pallidum* (c) *Rotavirus* (d) *Corynebacterium*
4. Indicator organism in milk is
   (a) *E. coli* (b) lactic acid bacteria (c) *Coxiellaburnetii* (d) *Propionibacterium*
5. Amoeba belongs to which of the following groups of eukaryotic organisms?
   (a) Protozoa (b) Archaea (c) Fungi (d) Algae
6. BOD of most of food wastes. is
   (a) Considerable more than domestic sewage (b) Less than domestic sewage
   (c) Considerable less than domestic sewage (d) Equal to domestic sewage
7. Archaea are
   (a) Gram -ve (b) Gram +ve (c) Gram variable (d) None of these
8. Indicator organism in water is
   (a) *E. coli* (b) Lactic acid bacteria
   (c) *Coxiella burnetii* (d) *Propionibacterium*
9. Which of the following organisms is used in the production of cheese?
   (a) *Propionibacterium shermanii* (b) *Acteobacter aceti*
   (c) *Giardia* (d) *Fusobacterium*
10. Hammer mills works on the principle of
    (a) Centrifugal (b) Impact (c) Abrasive (d) Gravitational
11. Biological oxygen demand (BOD) of safe drinking water must be
    (a) 0 (b) 10 (c) 50 (d) 100
12. The method adopted for removing, bushes, branches, debris etc from water is known as
    (a) Sedimentation (b) Coagulation (c) Screening (d) Filtration
13. The velocity of flow in any sedimentation tank should not exceed
    (a) 0.05 mm/sec (b) 0.5 mm/sec (c) 5.0 mm/sec (d) 50 mm/sec
14. During the process of composting of organic wastes, the pathogenic microorganisms are killed in
    (a) Mesophilic phase (b) Thermophilic phase (c) Maturity phase (d) Cooling phase
15. The destruction of all microorganisms and their endospores is referred to as
    (a) Disinfection (b) Degermation (c) Sanitization (d) Sterilization
16. Actinomycetes are
    (a) Gram +ve (b) Biofilm forming (c) N fixers (d) Macrofauna
17. Biological action is used in
    (a) Screens (b) Sedimentation tanks (c) Trickle filter (d) All the above

18. Organism used in commercial production of citric acid
    (a) *Rhizopus nigricans* (b) *Aspergillus niger*
    (c) *Penicillium roqueforti* (d) *Fusarium oxysporum*
19. Many peptic ulcers are due to
    (a) *Salmonella typhi* (b) *Helicobacter pylori*
    (c) *Shigellaboydii* (d) *Salmonella enteric*
20. *Azotobacter* was first discovered by
    (a) M. W. Beijerinck (b) Winogradsky (c) Ruinen (d) Hiltner
21. Safe storage of grain is essential
    (a) To prevent losses and diseases
    (b) To prevent from birds, pest and microorganisms
    (c) To maintain good quality of products (d) All the above
22. The essential losses of total food grains of India due to insect is about
    (a) 1-3 % (b) 5-10 % (c) 10-15 % (d) 20-40 %
23. Morai structure is generally suitable for
    (a) Paddy, maize and sorghum (b) Paddy, potato and tobacco
    (c) Mustard, soybean and wheat (d) Maize, bajra and oat
24. 'Kanaj' is a type of
    (a) Grain storage structure (b) Drying method
    (c) Food products (d) Grain separator
25. For enumeration of coliform organisms, the method used is
    (a) IMViC reaction (b) MPN (c) Standard plate count (d) None of these
26. Recommended perforation of aeration in grain storage shall be
    (a) 10% (b) 15% (c) 20% (d) 35%
27. The capacity of screw conveyor varies with
    (a) Screw diameter (b) Inclination of screw blade
    (c) Speed of blade (d) All the above
28. Material handling is concerned with
    (a) Movement (b) Time and place (c) Quantity and space (d) All the above
29. Centrifugal discharge is used in
    (a) Belt conveyor (b) Bucket conveyor (c) Pneumatic conveyor (d) Screw conveyor
30. CAS stands for
    (a) Controlled atmosphere storage (b) Continuous atmosphere storage
    (c) Cold atmosphere storage (d) Controlled ambient storage
31. The main gas used in MAP is
    (a) O_2 (b) CO_2 (c) N_2 (d) Argon
32. How much grain is contaminated by rodents of own actual weight?
    (a) Two times (b) Five times (c) Ten times (d) Twenty times
33. One of the following structures has inverted truncated cone shape.
    (a) Bukhari (b) Kothari (c) Pusa bin (d) Morai

34. One of the following is not a grain storage structure.
(a) Kuthla (b) Kanaj (c) Muda (d) Bellows
35. The size of an open area space on top of Pusa bin for loading should be
(a) 60 cm × 60 cm (b) 50 cm × 50 cm (c) 50 mm × 50 cm (d) No open space
36. The capacity of CAP storage structure is
(a) 10 tonnes (b) 100 tonnes (c) 1000 tonnes d) 2000 tonnes
37. Methyl bromide or phosphine are used as
(a) germicide (b) pesticide (c) fungicide (d) fumigant
38. The pitch of idler in belt conveyor is determined by
(a) the idler rating or carrying capacity of each idler
(b) sag of the belt between idlers
(c) belt tension and belt speed (d) all of the above
39. Generally, for grain conveying by belt conveyor, the belt speed is recommended as
(a) 1.5-1.75 m/s (b) 2.0-2.25 m/s (c) 2.5-2.8 m/s (d) 3.0-3.5 m/s
40. *Rhizopus oligosporus* is used in the production of
(a) Tempeh (b) Wine (c) Vinegar (d) Pickle
41. A group of bacteria predatory on other bacteria
(a) Spirochetes (b) Rickettsias (c) Bdellovibrios (d) Mycoplasmas
42. The group of bacteria commonly found in activated sludge
(a. Sheathed bacteria (b) Appendaged bacteria
(c) Gliding bacteria (d) Budding bacteria
43. Deoxyribose is a
(a) Carbohydrate (b) RNA (c) Proteins (d) DNA
44. Microbial component found numerously in soil is
(a) Bacteria (b) Virus (c) Fungi (d) Phages
45. Absent in Gram positive bacteria
(a) Peptidoglycan layer (b) Murein layer
(c) Outer lipid membrane (d) None of the above
46. Toxicity to oxygen is found in
(a) Aerotolerant bacteria (b) Strictaerobes
(c) Anaerobic bacteria (d) None of the above
47. BOD is high when there is
(a) Noeutrophication (b) High purity (c) High eutrophication (d) None of the above
48. Causative agent of Brain fever is
(a) Virus (b) Prion (c) Viroids (d) Capsids
49. Which of the following is a property of Psychrophiles?
(a) Salt loving (b) High temperature loving
(c) Cold temperature loving (d) Low pH loving
50. Protoplast is generated by
(a) Cellulose (b) Lipase (c) Lysozyme (d) Protease

51. Example of fixed cost
(a) Direct productive labour (b) Depreciation
(c) Direct materials (d) Direct expenses

52. Breakeven point is used to determine
(a) Effect of change in price (b) Effect of change in cost
(c) Safety margin (d) All the above

53. '——▸◂——' is the symbol of
(a) Valve (b) Operation (c) Storage (d) Heat exchanger

54. Methylene blue test is carried to check the purity
(a) Water (b) Mushroom
(c) Milk (d) Cheese

55. Cleaning and ________ should be considered an integral part of food process design and food processing operation.
(a) Sanitation (b) CIP (c) Fouling (d) Flow pattern

56. CIP system involves
(a) Pre-rinsing and alkali wash (b) Acid rinse and final water rinse
(c) Rinse with sanitizing solution (d) All the above

57. The creating and maintaining hygienic and healthful condition in food industry is termed as
(a) CIP (b) Sanitation (c) Fouling (d) None

58. A material dried from 80% moisture to 50% moisture. The percent weight reduction will be
(a) 60 % (b) 50 % (c) 40 % (d) 30 %

59. The unit of energy in SI system is
(a) BTU (b) Kcal (c) Watt (d) Joule

60. The moisture content on wet basis is 20%, then what would be the moisture content on dry basis?
(a) 18 % (b) 20 % (c) 22 % (d) 25 %

61. Which of the following is a natural circulation type freezer?
(a) Air blast freezer (b) Plate type freezer
(c) Chest freezer (d) Fluidized bed freezer

62. During cooking of meat, collagen is softened and converted to
(a) Elastin (b) pectin (c) Gelatin (d) None of the above

63. Which of the following is a unit of drying constant?
(a) hour^{-1} (b) kg/h (c) m^{-1} (d) no unit

64. Efficiency of pasteurizer is measured by which test
(a) Phosphatase test (b) MBR test (c) Reductase test (d) Resazurine test

65. Commercial sterile mean
(a) Kill all microorganisms but some are unable to grow during storage
(b) Completely destruction of all microorganisms
(c) Partial killing of microorganisms by thermal treatment.
(d) Any one (b) or (c)

66. A secondary package contains a number of primary packages, which of the following materials can be a secondary packaging material.
a) Corrugated case (b) Metal cans (c) Glass bottle (d) None of above

67. A ________ package is made up of a number of secondary packages.
(a) quaternary (b) tertiary (c) Secondary (d) None of above

68. LDPE has________ branching than HDPE
a) More (b) Less (c) Same (d) Half

69. LDPE has maximum heat resistance of
a) 60°c (b) 80°c (c) 100°c (d) 120°c

70. Steels used for metals cans are usually
a) Low carbon steel (b) Medium carbon steel
c) High carbon steel (d) Stainless steel

71. Solids food materials are generally
(a) Elastic (b) Plastic (c) Visco-elastic (d) Visco-plastic

72. C:N ratio of microorganism to sustain is
(a) 24:1 (b) 100:1
(c) 1:1 (d) 1.5:5

73. D-value depends upon
(a) Temperature (b) Number of microorganisms
(c) Heating time (d) Death rate constant

74. Most of the bacteria are killed at temperature range of
(a) 80-90°C (b) 82-93°C (c) 95-100°C (d) 100-105°C

75. The water activity equal to
(a) $\frac{T}{100}$ (b) $RH \times 100$ (c) $T \times 100$ (d) $\frac{RH}{100}$

76. The effect of water activity on microorganisms in foods is influenced by
(a) pH and Temperature (b) oxygen
(c) Nutritional concentration (d) All of the above

77. The symbol 'D' in thermo-bacteriology is indicated for
(a) Dehydration (b) Vitamin D
(c) Diffusion (d) Decimal reduction time

78. Air blast freezing in food is done at
(a) –17.8 to –34.4°C (b) –15 to –29°C
(c) –23.5 °C (d) –17.8 to –45.6°C

79. Case hardening in food takes place by
(a) Freezing (b) Improper drying (c) Chilling (d) drying

80. Molds are important in the preparation of
(a) Pickles (b) Jam
(c) Cheese and oriental foods (d) vinegar

81. The side effect of food additives on human heath are
(a) Raised blood pressure (b) Cancer problems
(c) Allergies (d) all the above
82. Cuvette used in spectrophotometer is ______________ in shape.
(a) Square (b) Circular (c) Rectangular (d) Triangle
83. The detector used in NIR spectroscopy is
(a) PbS (b) Silicon Based CCDs (c) InGaAs (d) all the above
84. Second law of thermodynamics related to
(a) Heat (b) work (c) entropy (d) Internal energy
85. Food can be cooked quicker in a pressure cooker because
(a) Due to metal body (b) less heat lost
(c) steam remains within the cooker (d) high temperature
86. Plank's law is applicable to
(a) Conduction (b) convection (c) Radiation (d) Diffusion
87. Heat energy from sun reaches to earth by
(a) Conduction (b) convection (c) Radiation (d) Diffusion
88. When $n > 1$, the fluids are called
(a) Pseudoplastic (b) Newtonian (c) Dilitant (d) Thixotropic
89. Isoelectric point (pH) of milk is
(a) 4.6 (b) 4.8 (c) 5.0 (d) 4.9
90. Thickness of aluminium foil is
(a) 4-150 micron (b) 50-100 micron
(c) 10-100 micron (d) 1-100 micron
91. One thousand tonnes of potatoes at 5°C gives off heat about
(a) 10 kW (b) 12 kW (c) 14 kW (d) 16 kW
92. To prevent sprouting and shrinkage, the potatoes should be kept at
(a) 3°C (b) 4°C (c) 4.4°C (d) 5.4°C
93. Storage life of non-perishable fruits exceeds
(a) 6 week (b) 8 week (c) 10 week (d) 12 week
94. Canned fruits juices are stored at temperature of
(a) 3.5°C (b) 4.4°C (c) 5.5°C (d) 6.5°C
95. Black tea if crushed becomes
(a) bright brown colour (b) black colour
(c) dull brown colour (d) white colour
96. The permanent taste in ginger is due to
(a) oil (b) mineral (c) resin (d) starch
97. The quality of coffee mainly depend upon
(a) harvesting (b) processing
(c) physiological maturity (d) ripening

98. The amount of saturated fatty acids in coconut oil is
(a) 60 % (b) 70 % (c) 75 % (d) 80 %

99. In solvent extraction, the amount of oil left in cake is about
(a) 2-3 % (b) 1.5-2.0 % (c) 1.0 % (d) 0.75 %

100. The relative humidity will be reduced to half of its original value if the temperature of air is increased
(a) 21°C (b) 15°C (c) 11°C (d) 8°C

101. Photosynthetic pigment in bacterium is
(a) Chlorophylla (b) Chlorophyllb (c) Rubisco (d) Phycobilisome

102. Protein particles which are infectious are known as
(a) Viroids (b) Prions (c) Capsomere (d) Virion

103. Soil organisms abundant in terms of biomass
(a) Bacteria (b) Actinomycetes (c) Cyanobacteria (d) Fungi

104. The function of ruminants is to:
(a) Digest cellulosic materials into organic acids which can be used as energy sources.
(b) Construct cellulose from organic acids and use the cellulose as an energy source.
(c) Produce methane gas and increase global warming.
(d) Reduce carbon to H_2O and CO_2.

105. Which of the following is the most complete definition of fermentation?
(a) Oxidation of glucose with organic molecules serving as electron acceptors
(b) Complete catabolism of glucose to CO_2 and H_2O
(C) Production of energy by substrate-level phosphorylation
(D) Production of ethyl alcohol from glucose

106. Cyanobacteria have:
(a) a gram-positive cell wall (b) a gram-negative cell wall
(c) Neither A. nor B. (d) No cell wall

107. Penicillin G is also known as
(a) hydroxy benzyl penicillin (b) phenoxy methyl penicillin
(c) benzyl penicillin (d) 2-pentenyl penicillin

108. Vinegar is a fermentative food product containing not less than:
(a) 4% acetic acid (b) 15% acetic acid (c) 25% acetic acid (d) 6% acetic acid

109. Anaerobic degradation of proteins is referred to as:
(a) Rancidity (b) Fermentation (c) Oxidation (d) Putrefication

110. An example of a pigment producing yeast genus:
(a) Rhodotorula (b) Torulopsis (c) Saccharomyces (d) Candida

111. An example for a heterofermentative micro-organism is
(a) *Leuconostoc mesenteroides* (b) *Lactobacillus delbrueckii*
(c) *Lactobacillus bulgaricus* (d) *Lactobacillus pentose*

112. This organism is used in the microbial production of citric acid:
(a) *Penicillin notatum* (b) *Rhizopus nigrificins*
(c) *Aspergillus niger* (d) *Lactobacillis delbrueckii*

113. Generation time of *Escherichia coli* is
(a) 20 minutes (b) 20 hours (c) 20 days (d) 200 hours

114. Which of the following methods is used to sterilize heat labile solutions?
(a) Dry heat (b) Autoclave
(c) Membrane filtration (d) Pasteurization

115. The enzyme responsible for the light emitted by luminescent bacteria is
(a) Coenzyme Q (b) Luciferase (c) Luciferin (d) Carboxylase reductase

116. Food pyramids illustrate the fact that
(a) The total number of organisms tends to decrease as one travels up trophic levels
(b) The total number of organisms tends to increase as one travels up trophic levels
(c) The greatest amount of energy in the food chain is dispersed at the upper trophic level, or pyramid point
(d) Most organisms are very selective as to what they consume

117. The following method is an exception for the motility of members of Protozoa
(a) flagella (b) gliding by slime secretion
(c) cilia (d) pseudopodia

118. Intestinal bacteria can grow in the presence of:
(a) bile salts (b) low concentration of various dyes
(c) sugars (d) low levels of nitrogen

119. Agar is used for solidifying culture media because:
(a) it is not affected by the growth of bacteria
(b) it does not add to the nutritive properties of the medium
(c) the melting and solidifying points of agar solution are not the same
(d) all of the above

120. Which type of microbe is most likely to grow in the canned food if a canning procedure is not properly followed?
(a) Obligate Aerobe (b) Acidophile
(c) Mesophile (d) Obligate Anaerobe

121. A microbial based polysaccharide used in food industry is:
(a) Guar (b) Xanthan (c) Neither A nor B (d) Both A & B

122. An example for ionizing radiation used in food preservation:
(a) UV rays (b) Gamma rays (c) Microwave rays (d) Infrared rays

123. The red coloured pigment found in actinorhizal nodules is
(a) Phycocyanin (b) Phycoerythrin (c) Anthocyanin (d) Leghaemoglobin

124. A dye used in bacteriological examination of milk:
(a) Resazurin (b) Congo red (c) Safranin (d) Both B and C

125. What is the order of reagents used in the Gram stain?
(a) Crystal violet, iodine, safranin, decolorizer
(b) Crystal violet, iodine, decolorizer, safranin
(c) Safranin, crystal violet, decolorizer, iodine
(d) Crystal violet, safranin, iodine, decolorizer

126. One of the following test is used to detect the production of acetoin:
(a) Citrate test (b) Voges-Proskauer test
(c) Methyl red test (d) Indole test

127. Which of the following is used to grow bacterial cultures continuously?
(a) Chemostat (b) Coulter Counter
(c) Haemostat (d) Petroff-Hausser chamber

128. The enzyme that can easily destroy the cell walls of many gram positive bacteria is:
(a) Lipase (b) Lysozyme (c) Pectinase (d) Peroxidase

ANSWER KEY

(Model paper 3)

Q.	Ans.	Q.	Ans.	Q.	Ans.	Q.	Ans.	Q.	Ans.	Q.	Ans.	Q.	Ans.
1.	C	21.	D	41.	C	61.	C	81.	D	101.	D	121.	B
2.	D	22.	A	42.	B	62.	C	82.	C	102.	B	122.	B
3.	A	23.	A	43.	A	63.	A	83.	D	103.	D	123.	D
4.	C	24.	A	44.	A	64.	A	84.	C	104.	A	124.	A
5.	A	25.	B	45.	C	65.	A	85.	C	105.	A	125.	B
6.	A	26.	B	46.	C	66.	A	86.	C	106.	B	126.	B
7.	C	27.	D	47.	C	67.	B	87.	C	107.	C	127.	A
8.	A	28.	D	48.	A	68.	A	88.	C	108.	A	128.	B
9.	A	29.	B	49.	C	69.	C	89.	A	109.	D		
10.	B	30.	A	50.	C	70.	A	90.	A	110.	A		
11.	A	31.	D	51.	B	71.	C	91.	C	111.	A		
12.	C	32.	C	52.	D	72.	A	92.	C	112.	C		
13.	C	33.	D	53.	A	73.	A	93.	D	113.	A		
14.	B	34.	D	54.	C	74.	B	94.	B	114.	C		
15.	D	35.	B	55.	A	75.	D	95.	C	115.	B		
16.	A	36.	C	56.	D	76.	D	96.	C	116.	A		
17.	C	37.	D	57.	B	77.	D	97.	B	117.	B		
18.	B	38.	D	58.	A	78.	A	98.	B	118.	A		
19.	B	39.	C	59.	D	79.	B	99.	C	119.	D		
20.	A	40.	A	60.	D	80.	C	100.	C	120.	D		

MODEL PAPERS-4

1. Standards on weight and measurement act, 1976 comes under
   A. Ministry of Health and Family Welfare
   B. Ministry of Food Processing Industries
   C. Department of Agriculture and Cooperation
   D. Department of Legal Metrology
2. Export (Quality control and inspection) act, 1963 comes under
   A. Department of Consumer Affairs, Govt., of India
   B. Directorate of Marketing and Inspection
   C. Export Inspection Council of India
   D. Department of Legal Metrology
3. Pasteurization is the process of heating milk
   A. Above 121 °C B. Above boiling point
   C. Below boiling point D. Above 150 °C
4. FSSAI was established in the year
   A. 2006 B. 2008 C. 2011 D. 2007
5. AGMARK can be seen on which product?
   A. Butter B. Turmeric powder C. Rice D. All of these
6. The AGMARK Head Office is located at
   A. Faridabad B. New Delhi C. Bangalore D. Kolkata
7. The permeability is related as
   A. permeability = solubility / diffusivity B. permeability = diffusivity/ solubility
   C. permeability = solubility × diffusivity D. permeability = solubility × $(\text{diffusivity})^2$
8. The gas chromatography is used for measurement of
   A. pressure B. volume C. temperature D. concentration
9. The gas filled thermometer is based on the principle of
   A. Charle's law B. Boyle's law C. Pascal's law D. Plank's law
10. Balometer is used for measurement of
    A. flow rate B. temperature C. Current D. Volt
11. Mohr stress diagram is a plot between
    A. shear stress and pressure B. shear stress and angle of repose
    C. angle of internal friction and angle of repose D. none of these

12. For truly homogeneous mass
    A. angle of repose> angle of internal friction
    B. angle of repose= angle of internal friction
    C. angle of repose< angle of internal friction
    D. none of these
13. Angle of repose is low when particles are
    A. sticky B. very fine C. smooth and round D. rough
14. The crushing efficiency is the ratio of
    A. surface energy created by crushing to energy absorbed by solid
    B. energy absorbed by solid to surface energy created by crushing
    C. energy absorbed by solid to that fed to machine
    D. energy fed to machine to energy absorbed by solid
15. Eggs, milk, and meat are usually classified as good sources of
    A. carbohydrates. B. protein. C. fat. D. None of these
16. Fruits and vegetables are usually considered as good sources of
    A. protein. B. vitamins & minerals.
    C. unsaturated fats. D. none of these
17. _________ is an example of a hydrogenated fat.
    A. Butter B. Margarine C. Olive oil D. Ghee
18. This nutrient is needed for making hormones, healthier skin, and to make cell membranes:
    A. Fat B. Carbohydrate C. Fiber D. Vitamin B_{12}
19. This mineral is essential for healthy red blood cells and a deficiency might cause anemia.
    A. Iron B. Magnesium C. Iodine D. Chromium
20. Which of these nutrients is the preferred energy source for the body?
    A. B Complex Vitamins B. Carbohydrates
    C. Fats D. Fiber
21. Which of the following nutrients is needed to build and maintain the structural components of the body?
    A. Carbohydrates B. Protein C. Fat D. Fiber
22. The bread, cereal, rice and pasta group is a good source of _______?
    A. Carbohydrate B. Vitamin C C. Calcium D. Vitamin D
23. A substance needed by the body for growth, energy, repair and maintenance is called a ________.
    A. nutrient B. carbohydrate C. calorie D. fatty acid
24. Which of the following test is used for detection of Neutralizers in milk? ?
    A. Keris test B. Rosalic acid test C. Hal- phen test D. Foam test

25. Which of the following causes souring of milk ?
(A) Bacillus bulgaricus (B) Bacillus alkalesence
(C) Bacillus coil (D) Sarcines flava

26. Clostridium bacteria is responsible for spoilage of
(A) Canned food (B) Frozen food
(C) Dehydrated food (D) None of the above

27. Waxing of fruits and vegetables help in
(A) Reduction in rate of respiration (B) Reduction in loss of moisture
(C) Increase in shelf life (D) All of the above

28. If you cut and wash a fruit or vegetable which of the following vitamin are lost ?
(A) A and D (B) C and D (C) A and B (D) B and C

29. Food safety and Standards Act, 2006 operationalised on
(A) 5th August, 2007 (B) 5th August, 2011
(c) 5th August, 2012 (D) 5th August, 2013

30. Texture analyzer is a device that tests
(A) Strength and texture properties of food material
(B) Dimension of food material
(C) Optical characteristics of food materials
(D) TSS of the fruits

31. Which of the following in not a key element of Food Safety Management System ?
(A) GHP (B) GCLP (C) HACCP (D) GMP

32. The mandate assigned to the food authority is
(A) Laying down science based standards for articles of food
(B) To facilitate food safety
(C) To regulate manufacture, store, distribution, sale and import of food
(D) All of the above

33. Quality of milk can be observed by following test
(A) Urate test (B) Biuret test
(C) MBRT test (D) None of the above

34. Caramelin are possessing following taste
(A) Sweet (B) Sour (C) Bitter (D) Salty

35. Food processing wastes are generally
(A) Stronger than sewage (B) Similar to sewage
(C) Weaker than sewage (D) None of these

36. Which metal is unsuitable for the manufacture of food containers?
(A) Copper (B) Lead (C) Zinc (D) All of above

37. The declaration of " Best before date" for consumption shall not be applicable to
(A) Bread (B) Milk (C) Beverages (D) Wines and liquors

38. Who can send the food sample for analysis in laboratory ?
(A) Consumer (B) Food business operator
(C) Designated officer (D) All of these

39. As per section 46 of FSSA, 2006 the food analysts shall send the analysis report of the food sample within
(A) 14 days (B) 40 days (C) 4 days (D) 14 working days

40. Turmeric powder is commonly adulterated by
(A) Lead chromate (B) Date husk (C) Starch (D) Chicory

41. F.P.O. stands for
(A) Fruit Production Operation (B) Fruit Product Order
(C) Flavour Production Office (D) Fruit Procurement Order

42. Under ordinary conditions food safety officer should collect, how many parts of sample
(A) 5 (B) 6 (C) 3 (D) 4

43. According to FSSA, 2006 the State Food Authority is
(A) Commission of food safety (B) Designated officer
(C) Food analyst (D) Food safety officer

44. Section 23 of FSSA, 2006 deals with
(A) Labeling of foods (B) Packing of food
(C) Both (A) and (B) (D) None of these

45. Cold sterilization refers to the preservation of food by
(A) Refrigeration (B) Radiation
(C) Dehydration (D) Lyophilisation

46. Phosphatase test is used in the analysis of
(A) Water (B) Tea (C) Milk (D) None of these

47. Which is colour of the symbol of vegetarian food ?
(A) Blue (B) Green (C) Brown (D) Red

48. Chemical hazard is
(A) Salmonella (B) Broken glass piece
(C) Zinc (D) Dioxins

49. Natural toxin in food is
(A) Scrombotoxin (B) Aflatoxin (C) Solanine (D) All of these

50 Scombrotoxin is a food borne toxin that is associated with the consumption of
(A) Fish (B) Fruits (C) Vegetables (D) Milk

51. Section 35 of FSSA, 2006 deals with
(A) Food recall (B) Food poisoning (C) Food business (D) Food standards

52. Function of Food Safety Officer
(A) Taking sample of food article for analysis (B) Registration of food business operators
(C) Inspection of food premises (D) All of above

53. The Indian standard specification for polythene in contact with food stuff is
(A) IS : 10142 (B) IS : 10151 (C) IS : 10910 (D) IS : 10146

54. The principle of processing food by heat is known as
(A) Freezing (B) Sublimation
(C) Chemical preservation (D) Pasteurization

55. The most widely used flavor enhancer is
(A) Sodium hyprochlorite (B) Mono sodium glutamate
(C) Sorbic acid (D) Butylated hydroxy anisole

56. Which of these is not an International Standards and Statutes ?
(A) Codex Alimentarius Commission (CAC) (B) European Union Standards (EU Standards)
(C) Food and Agriculture Organization (FAO) (D) Bureau of Indian Standards

57. As per Food Safety and Standards Act, FSMS stands for
(A) Food Security Management System (B) Food Safety Management System
(C) Food Standards Management System (D) Food Safety Mechanization System

58. Which of the following food item has been exempted from labeling?
(A) On the spot food like bakery items (B) Ready to eat food
(C) Food served on plane/vending machine (D) All of these

59. The compound responsible for hotness of black pepper is
(A) Cadulanine (B) Piperine (C) Capsachin (D) None of these

60. Development of a plan for how to make a product is called as
(A) Operation process chart (B) Processing blocks
(C) Work development activities (D) None of these

61. The selection committee for selection of Chairperson and members of FSSAI
(A) Secretary in-charge of the ministry (B) Chairman of public enterprises selection board
(C) Emineul food technologist (D) Cabinet secretary

62. The most appropriate signs of meat spoilage is
(A) Sour taste (B) Softening and rotting
(C) Darkening and sour odor (D) Slimy coating on the surface

63. Which constituent of whole milk is not available in milk powder?
(A) Protein (B) Fat (C) Vitamins (D) Carbohydrate
64. According to FSSAI, 2006, licensing and registration of food business is mandatory for
(A) Manufacturers (B) Distributer (C) Packers (D) All of these
65. The word " AGMARK" is derived from
(A) Agricultural Marketing (B) Agricultural Plantation
(C) Consumer forum (D) None of the above
66. The proportion of women member in the composition of Food Safety and Standards Authority of India
(A) 1/3 (B) ½ (C) 2/3 (D) 1/4
67. It is important to prepare food safely because
(A) It helps to prevent food poisoning (B) Prepared food looks better
(C) Prepared food tastes better (D) None of the above
68. From which plant source is gluten derived?
(A) Soyabean (B) Corn (C) Rice (D) Wheat
69. Food irradiation is used to
(A) Kill insects (B) Kill micro-organisms
(C) Both (A) and (B) (D) None of these
70. Salt is a better preservative than sugar because it
(A) Has lower molecular weight
(B) Lower the vapour pressure of food water by a larger extent
(C) Kills micro-organism better
(D) Reduces pH
71. Bureau of Indian Standards Act, 1986 comes under
(A) Department of Consumer Affairs, Government of India
(B) Department of Marketing and Inspection
(C) Export Inspection of Legal Metrology
(D) Department of Legal Metrology
72. The FSSAI has its headquarters at
(A) New Delhi (B) Guwahati (C) Mumbai (D) Cochin
73. The date which signifies the end of the estimate period under any stated storage conditions after which the food shall not be sold means
(A) Best before (B) Date of manufacture
(C) Date of packaging (D) Expiry date
74. How many Acts are repealed by Food Safety and Standards Act, 2006?
(A) 4 (B) 5 (C) 7 (D) 8

75. Coffee is adulterated with

(A) Sawdust (B) Chicory

(C) Ghee (D) All of these

76. The AGMARK standard is set by

(A) Central Committee for Food Surveillance (B) Central Committee for Food Standards

(C) Directorate of Marketing and Inspection (D) Bureau of Indian Standard

77. To remove field heat from vegetable immediately after harvesting, vegetable should be

(A) Pre-cooled (B) Refrigerated

(C) Stored at ambient temperature (D) Kept open

78. All of the following will come under the FSSAI Scanner except

(A. GM food (B) Proprietary food

(C) Organic foods (D) Raw agriculture product

79. pH of packaged drinking water shall be between

(A) 6.0 to 8.0 (B) 6.5 to 7.5 (C) 6.5 to 8.5 (D) 6.5 to 8.0

80. BIS stands for

(A) Bharat Import Standards (B) Bureau of Indian Standards

(C) Bureau of International Standards (D) Bureau of Indian System

81. The date on which the food becomes the product as described means

(A) Best before (B) Date of manufacture

(C) Date of packaging (D) Expiry date

82. The most important quality attributes which responsible for colour of the potato chips is

(A) Starch (B) Proteins (C) Reducing sugars (D) Vitamin C

83. A substance intentionally added that affects the nature and quality of food is called

(A) Food poison (B) Food adulterant

(C) Food contaminant (D) Food material

84. Which stage does adulteration take place in ?

(A) Producer (B) Distributor

(C) Retailer (D) All of the mentioned

85. ________ help in maintaining/controlling the acidic/alkaline changes during food processing and hence maintain flavor and stability.

(A) Buffering agents (B) Sequesterants

(C) Anti-caking agents (D) Anti-foaming agents

86. The quick freezing of food products is done by

(A) Air blast freezing (B) Indirect contact freezing

(C) Immersion freezing (D) All of above

87. Union minister for Health and Family Welfare, Shri J.P. Nadda has launched which project for the safety standards of food on the streets?

(A) Safe street food (B) Clean street food

(C) Hygienic street food (D) None of the above

88. How many members are there in Food Authority of FSSA, 2006?

(A) 22 (B) 23 (C) 12 (D) 11

89. All the following techniques are household preservation technique except

(A) Smoking (B) Lyophilisation (C) Dehydration (D) Salting

90. The Food Safety and Standards Authority of India (FSSAI) has issued a set of guidelines regarding the recall of ________________ from the market.

(A) unsafe drinking water (B) unsafe food products

(C) unsafe labelling (D) unsafe packaging

91. What has been banned for tea bag products by FSSAI from 2018?

(A) use of stapler pins (B) thread for dipping

(C) cloth bag containing the tea leaves (D) herbal tea leaves

92. Which is the main type of micro-organism responsible for food poisoning?

(A) Bacteria (B) Fungus (C) Virus (D) Parasite

93. Which of the following is an adulterant?

(A) Urea (B) Pesticides

(C) Iron filings in tea (D) All of the mentioned

94. Methods for detection of common adulterants are

(A) Visual tests (B) Chemical tests

(C) Physical tests (D) All of the mentioned

95. Who has been appointed as CEO of FSSAI on 22nd December, 2015?

(A) Prem Kumar Singh (B) Pawan Kumar Agarwal

(C) Ashok Singh Malik (D) Ashish Bahuguna

(Current CEO is Arun Singhal)

96. What percentage of moisture is required for the safe storage of food grains?

(A) More than 18% (B) Less than 14%

(C) 15% (D) 20%

97. Section 25 of FSSA, 2006 deals with __________.

(A) Export of food products (B) Import of food products

(C) Both (A) and (B) (D) None of these

98. Food safety and standards acts, 2006 passed by Indian parliament and notified on

(A) 24th July, 2006 (B) 24th June, 2006

(C) 24th August, 2006 (D) 24th November, 2006

99. Which of these are responsible for the implementation of FSSAI?
(A) Ministry of Health And Family Welfare
(B) Ministry of Food Processing Industries
(C) Department of Agriculture and Co-Operation
(D) Directorate General of Health Services

100. Hunter L, a, b calorimeter is used to measure
(A) pH value (B) Electrode potential (C) Colour (D) None of these

ANSWER KEY

(Model paper 4)

Q.	Ans.	Q.	Ans.	Q.	Ans.	Q.	Ans.	Q.	Ans.
1.	D	21.	B	41.	B	61.	D	81.	B
2.	C	22.	A	42.	D	62.	D	82.	C
3.	C	23.	A	43.	A	63.	B	83.	B
4.	A	24.	B	44.	C	64.	D	84.	D
5.	D	25.	A	45.	B	65.	A	85.	A
6.	A	26.	A	46.	C	66.	A	86.	A
7.	C	27.	D	47.	B	67.	A	87.	B
8.	D	28.	D	48.	D	68.	D	88.	A
9.	A	29.	B	49.	D	69.	C	89.	B
10.	B	30.	A	50.	A	70.	B	90.	B
11.	A	31.	B	51.	B	71.	A	91.	A
12.	B	32.	D	52.	D	72.	A	92.	A
13.	C	33.	C	53.	D	73.	D	93.	D
14.	A	34.	C	54.	D	74.	D	94.	D
15.	B	35.	A	55.	B	75.	B	95.	B
16.	B	36.	D	56.	C	76.	C	96.	C
17.	B	37.	D	57.	B	77.	A	97.	C
18.	A	38.	D	58.	D	78.	D	98.	C
19.	A	39.	A	59.	B	79.	B	99.	A
20.	B	40.	A	60.	A	80.	B	100.	C

MODEL PAPERS-5

1. Deficiency of iodine may cause
   (A) Frequent abortion (B) Mentally retarded child
   (C) Both (A) and (B) (D) None of these
2. Micronutrients include which of the following?
   (A) Cholesterol (B) Vitamins (C) Minerals (D) Both (B) and (C)
3. Removal of bran layer from the brown rice is done by
   (A) Polisher (B) Bran separator (C) Whitener (D) Both (A) and (C)
4. Flavouring component for butter is
   (A) Acetyl methyl carbinol (B) Diacetyl
   (C) Lactic acid (D) Protein
5. All of the following are needed for strong bones except
   (A) Thiamin (B) Calcium (C) Magnesium (D) Vitamin D
6. Which of the following bacteria can grow in alkaline pH?
   (A) Lactobacilli (B) Vibrio cholera (C) Salmonella (D) Staphylococcus
7. Citrus fruits are an excellent source of
   (A) Calcium (B) Vitamin C (C) Vitamin B (D) Calories
8. Richest source of riboflavin is
   (A) Papaya (B) Mango (C) Bael (D) Karonda
9. Vitamin C and vitamin E, BHA and BHT and sulfites are all
   (A) Flavour enhancer (B) Antimicrobial agent
   (C) Incidental food agent (D) Antioxidant
10. Cider is the product obtained from
    (A) Fermentation of plum (B) Fermentation of peach
    (C) Fermentation of apple (D) Distillation of wine
11. Saliva contain______________ enzyme to digest the food.
    (A) Invertase (B) Galactosidase (C) Amylase (D) Permease
12. The vegetable oil rich in monounsaturated fatty acids is
    (A) Peanut oil (B) Gingelly oil (C) Coconut oil (D) Olive oil
13. The sugar present in the milk is
    (A) Sucrose (B) Lactose (C) Glucose (D) Maltose
14. The egg shell membranes are made up of
    (A) Proteins and polysaccharide (B) Lipids and polysaccharide
    (C) Proteins and Lipids (D) Lipids and amino acids

15. Milk is a poor source of
(A) Iron (B) Calcium (C) Potassium (D) Sodium

16. Body temperature of normal person is
(A) 89.4 °F (B) 90.5 °F (C) 98.4 °F (D) 101.3 °F

17. Number of kidney present in human beings
(A) One (B) Two (C) Three (D) Four

18. More or less nutrient both are ______________ for human.
(A) Useful (B) Harmful (C) Tasty (D) All of the above

19. Pellagra disease is caused by deficiency of
(A) Riboflavin (B) Folic acid (C) Niacin (D) Toccopherol

20. Which of the following has more fibre in it?
(A) Wheat (B) Rice (C) Milk (D) Butter

21. Energy value of 1 gm fat is
(A) 9.3 kcal (B) 2.5 kcal (C) 7 kcal (D) 4.1 kcal

22. Which substance will be given in less amount for jaundice patient?
(A) Calories (B) Protein (C) Carbohydrate (D) Fat

23. Which food does not belong to milk food group?
(A) Chocolate milk (B) Ice cream (C) Yogurt (D) Salad dressing

24. Which one of the following acid is present in tomato sauce?
(A) Oxalic acid (B) Citric acid (C) Lactic acid (D) Acetic acid

25. The egg white is mainly rich in
(A) Carbohydrate (B) Minerals (C) Proteins (D) None of these

26. All of the following are nutrients found in food except
(A) Plasma (B) Proteins (C) Carbohydrate (D) Vitamin

27. The method of enhancing nutritive value of food is
(A) Germination (B) Fermentation (C) Combination (D) All of these

28. Fruits and vegetables are usually considered as good source of
(A) Proteins (B) Vitamins and minerals
(C) Unsaturated fat (D) Carbohydrates

29. In healthy diet pyramid, fruits and vegetables are at the
(A) Level -1 (B) Level -2 (C) Level -3 (D) Level -4

30. Across age, basal metabolic rate
(A) Changes (B) Remains constant (C) Increases (D) Decreases

31. The type of amino acids present in proteins are
(A) 22 (B) 32 (C) 42 (D) 52

32. World food day is celebrated on
(A) 16th October (B) 5th September (C) 3rd January (D) 7th April

33. Vitamins that are soluble in fats are the following except
(A) A (B) D (C) B (D) E

34. Pasteurization of egg should be done at the temperature of
(A) 60-62 °C (B) 60-65 °C (C) 40-50 °C (D) 70-75 °C

35. Rennin used in cheese manufacturing is a
(A) Antibiotic (B) Alkaloid (C) Enzyme (D) Inhibitor

36. In which food product, sorbic acid is used as inhibitor to control the growth of mold?
(A) Mushroom (B) Cheese (C) Leafy vegetables (D) Fruits

37. Mold infection in bread can be prevented by adding of
(A) Salt (B) Sugar
(C) Sodium benzoate (D) Sodium and calcium propionate

38. Which among the following is not a monosaccharide?
(A) Glucose (B) Lactose (C) Galactose (D) Ribose

39. Arginine is
(A) Essential amino acid (B) Saturated fatty acid
(C) Volatile fatty acid (D) Mannose

40. The optimum temperature (degree Celsius) of an enzyme of human body is
(A) 22 (B) 25 (C) 37 (D) 47

41. Enzymes are chemically
(A) Protein (B) Carbohydrate (C) Fat (D) None

42. Carrot is good source of
(A) Vitamin A (B) Vitamin B (C) Vitamin C (D) None of above

43. Which of the following vitamins are obtained from fats?
(A) Vitamin B and C (B) Vitamin B complex
(C) Vitamin A and D (D) All

44. Suggested daily intake of zinc for an adult male is
(A) 5 mg (B) 12 mg (C) 20 mg (D) 35 mg

45. A slice of bread with 2 gm of fat, 10 gm of carbohydrate and 2 gm of protein contains
(A) 42 kcal (B) 57 kcal (C) 66 kcal (D) 82 kcal

46. The pulse that contain more protein and good source of iron and calcium is
(A) Red gram (B) Green gram (C) Cow pea (D) Soyabean

47. $C_{12}H_{22}O_{11}$ is general formula of
(A) Monosaccharide (B) Polyaccharide (C) Disaccharide (D) Trisaccharide

48. If iodine is applied to glycogen rich food, resulting colour will be
(A) Violet (B) Blue –black (C) Red (D) Brown

49. Which coarse grain is sufficient for macronutrient requirement of rural people of the country?
(A) Wheat (B) Rice (C) Maize (D) Ragi

50. Methods for detection of common adulterants are
(A) Visual test (B) Chemical test (C) Physical test (D) All of these

51. Which one of the following is very necessary to digest the food stuff?
(A) Air (B) Water (C) Enzyme (D. Mineral

52. Which among the following is used to test fat in milk?
(A) Lactometer (B) Anemometer (C) CRO (D) Milk tester

53. The percentage of water in cow's milk is approximately
(A) 80 % (B) 90% (C) 87% (D) 50%

54. Aseptic packaging is used after which among the following processing method?
(A) Pasteurization (B) UHT pasteurization
(C) Freezing (D) Drying

55. Consumption of raw soyabeans can be harmful to health because of the presence of following anti nutritional factor.
(A) Phytic acid (B) Tannins (C) Oxalates (D) Trypsin inhibitor

56 Which solvent is commonly used to determine fat content?
(A) Ethyl alcohol (B) Hexane (C) Acetone (D) Benzene

57. Which of the following is an adulterant?
(A) Urea (B) Pesticides (C) Iron filling in tea (D) All of these

58. Which of the adulterant is commonly used in honey?
(A) Fruit juice (B) Molasses
(C) HFCS (*high-fructose corn syrup*) (D) Saccharine

59. Damage to liver cells leads to increase in bilirubin resulting in
(A) Necrosis (B) Cirrhosis
(C) Fatty globulation (D) Jaundice

60. An example of berry spices
(A) Black pepper (B) Cinnamon (C) Onion (D) Garlic

61. Which one of the following is considered as complete protein?
(A) Green gram protein (B) Egg protein
(C) Peanut protein (D) Millet protein

62. Cause of pernicious anaemia in pregnant women
(A) Vitamin C (B) Folic acid (C) Pantothenic acid (D) Vitamin B_{12}

63. Hemoglobin contains the following elements
(A) Protein and minerals (B) Protein and iron
(C) Iron and minerals (D) Vitamin B_{12} and folic acid

64. Energy value of 1 gm protein is
(A) 3.2 kcal (B) 4.1 kcal (C) 8 kcal (D) 9.3 kcal

65. Milk and milk products are good source of protein
(A) True (B) Wrong
(C) No protein in milk (D) None of the above

66. Sea weed is richest source of
(A) Iron (B) Potassium (C) Iodine (D) All of the above

67. Green tea is rich in
(A) Antioxidant (B) Polyphenol (C) Flavonoids (D) All of these

68. Digestion of both starch and protein is done by
(A) Gastric juice (B) Gastric lipases (C) Pancreatic juice (D) Ptyalin enzyme

69. Which of the following vitamins serves an antioxidant function and has a relation to selenium metabolism?
(A) Vitamin A (B) Vitamin C (C) Vitamin D (D) Vitamin E

70. Which of these is not considered a nutrient?
(A) Vitamin (B) Minerals (C) Fibre (D) Fat

71. Which toxic constituent is found in cotton seed?
(A) Saponins (B) Phytoalexins (C) Gossypol (D) Cytogens

72. This mineral is essential for healthy red blood cells and deficiency might cause anaemia
(A) Iron (B) Magnesium (C) Iodine (D) Chromium

73. Which of the following nutrients is known as the sunshine vitamin?
(A) Vitamin C (B) Vitamin A (C) Vitamin K (D) Vitamin D

74. Basal metabolic rate shall be measured while a person is
(A) Jogging (B) Going to work (C) Resting (D) Sweating

75. If biuret solution is added to egg white, resulting colour will be
(A) Blue (B) Black (C) Red (D) Violet

76. Balanced diet includes at least gram of vegetables
(A) 300 gm (B) 200 gm (C) 100 gm (D) 400 gm

77. CIAE is located at
(A) Nagpur (B) Ludhiana (C) Bhopal (D) Budhani

78. Permissible limit of SO_2 in jam is
(A) 300 ppm (B) 40 ppm (C) 70 ppm (D) 100 ppm

79. The chilling temperature for any food is selected on the basis of
(A) Kind of food (B) Time of storage
(C) Condition of storage (D) All

80. Sorbets are more effective than sodium benzoate at pH value above
(A) 2 (B) 4 (C) 6 (D) 7

81. The oxidation of fats and oils may be catalyzed by
(A) Metals and rays (B) Moisture
(C) Microorganisms (D) All of the above

82. The best source of energy supplying food group is
(A) Meat, egg and fish (B) Fats, oils and sweets
(C) Bread and cereals (D) Milk and cheese

83. The nutrient needed for a healthy immune system and strong connective tissue is
(A) Fibre (B) Vitamin K
(C) Vitamin C (D) Fluoride

84. Amylases in saliva begin the breakdown of carbohydrate into
(A) Fatty acid (B) Polypeptides (C) Amino acid (D) Polysaccharides

85. A ____________ is a unit of energy that indicates the amount of energy contained in food.
(A) Label (B) Food guide pyramid
(C) Calorie (D) Basket

86. Food like fruit, honey and sugarcane are all good example of
(A) Mineral (B) Starches (C) Sugar (D) All of these

87. Excess carbohydrates are stored in the body as
(A) Body fat (B) Glycogen (C) (A) and (B) (D) None of these

88. Proteins are broken down into _____ whereas fats are digested mostly into _____.
(A) amino acids, sugars (B) amino acids, fatty acids
(C) fatty acids, sugars (D) glucose, vitamins

89. The unit of measure that is used in nutrition science that expresses the amount of energy provided by a food is :
(A) calorie. (B) nutrient.
(C) nutrient-dense food. (D) unit of glucose.

90. Which PCR tool is used in testing COVID-19 in India?
(A) RACE PCR (B) Inverse PCR
(C) Real time RT PCR (D) Nested PCR

91. Substances found in plant foods that are not essential nutrients but may have health-promoting properties are

(A) amino acids. (B) dietary supplements.

(C) phytochemicals. (D) zoochemicals.

92. Foods that have health-promoting and/or disease-preventing properties beyond basic nutritional functions are called

(A) essential foods. (B) fortified foods.

(C) functional foods. (D) phytochemicals

93. All of the following are macronutrients except

(A) carbohydrate. (B) lipids.

(C) proteins. (D) vitamins.

94. All of the following are examples of lipids except

(A) cholesterol. (B) saturated fat.

(C) sugars. (D) unsaturated fat.

95. With the exception of _______, all the classes of nutrients are involved in forming and maintaining the body's structure.

(A) carbohydrates (B) lipids (C) minerals (D) vitamins

96. A deficient intake of _______ is known to produce osteoporosis.

(A) calcium (B) iron (C) Vitamin A (D) Vitamin C

97. Nutrition recommendations are developed to:

(A) address the nutritional concerns of the population.

(B) evaluate the nutrient intake of populations.

(C) help individuals meet their specific nutrient needs.

(D) All of these are true.

98. Which of the following substances is not absorbed by the human body?

(A) Amino acids (B) Fatty acids

(C) Fiber (D) Sugars

99. When needed glycogen $(C_6H_{10}O_5)_n$ can be easily hydrolyzed to

(A) starch (B) galactose (C) glucose (D) lactose

100 Glucose $(C_6H_{12}O_6)$ converted to glycogen $(C_{24}H_{42}O_{21})$ may be stored in

(A) muscles (B) liver

(C) pancreas (D) both (A) and (B)

ANSWER KEY

(Model paper 5)

Q.	Ans.	Q.	Ans.	Q.	Ans.	Q.	Ans.	Q.	Ans.
1.	C	21.	A	41.	A	61.	B	81.	D
2.	D	22.	B	42.	A	62.	D	82.	C
3.	D	23.	D	43.	C	63.	B	83.	C
4.	B	24.	B	44.	B	64.	B	84.	D
5.	A	25.	C	45.	C	65.	A	85.	C
6.	B	26.	A	46.	D	66.	D	86.	C
7.	B	27.	D	47.	C	67.	D	87.	C
8.	C	28.	B	48.	D	68.	C	88.	B
9.	D	29.	C	49.	D	69.	D	89.	A
10.	C	30.	A	50.	D	70.	C	90.	C
11.	C	31.	A	51.	C	71.	C	91.	C
12.	D	32.	A	52.	D	72.	A	92.	C
13.	B	33.	C	53.	C	73.	D	93.	D
14.	A	34.	A	54.	B	74.	C	94.	C
15.	A	35.	C	55.	D	75.	D	95.	D
16.	C	36.	B	56.	B	76.	A	96.	A
17.	B	37.	D	57.	D	77.	C	97.	D
18.	B	38.	B	58.	C	78.	B	98.	C
19.	C	39.	A	59.	D	79.	D	99.	C
20.	A	40.	C	60.	A	80.	B	100.	D

MODEL PAPERS-6

1. Denaturation and even coagulation of proteins takes place at the temperature above:
   a) 40°C b) 50°C c) 60°C d) 70°C
2. Ripening of fruits and vegetables is accompanied with production of
   a) Acetylene b) Carbon-dioxide
   c) Carbon monoxide d) Propylene
3. Microwave frequency which is permitted for commercial application in food processing in India
   a) 2450 MHz b) 2.450 MHz c) 2540 MHz d) 2.540 MHz
4. Coefficient of friction between granular materials is:
   a) Cumulative effect of free shrinkage
   b) Free shrinkage exerted by the adjacent cells
   c) Tangent of the angle of internal friction for that material
   d) Changes with depth in drying bin
5. Size of irregular shaped food grains is represented by:
   a) Total diameter b) Average diameter
   c) Perimeter d) Equivalent diameter
6. Which property of milk is not effected due to pasteurization process:
   a) Rheological b) Organoleptic
   c) Chemical d) Textural
7. Which of the following information must be stated on a food label:
   a) Unit price of food b) Manufacturing & expiry date
   c) Type of free gift offered d) Calorie content of food
8. The radiation dose used for shelf-life extension of fruits and vegetables is:
   a) < 1 kgy b) 1-10 kgy c) 100y d) > 100 kgy
9. Textural property of 'paneer' can be best represented by:
   a) Hardness b) Gumminess c) Springiness d) Chewiness
10. Cooking quality of rice is judged on the basis of:
    a) Time of cooking b) Swelling capacity and expansion ratio
    c) Gruel quality and pastiness d) All of the above
11. How much water should be evaporated from milk of 15% concentration to form 40% concentration:
    a) 0.225 kg water/kg feed b) 0.60 kg water/kg feed
    c) 0.625 kg water/kg feed d) 0.825 kg water/kg feed
12. The dimension of thermal diffusivity of a food is:
    a) MLT^2 b) $M^\circ L^2T^{-1}$ c) $M^{-1}LT$ d) $M^\circ LT$

13. Increasing the temperature of drying air will cause:
 a) Increase its absolute humidity b) Decrease its absolute humidity
 c) Not change in its absolute humidity d) Change the absolute humidity marginally
14. Relationship between water activity and equilibrium moisture content of food at a constant temperature is:
 a) Drying curve b) Moisture sorption isotherm
 c) Stability curve d) Death rate curve
15. Which of the following is a permitted preservative for use in fruit juices and beverages
 a) Ascorbic acid b) Citric acid
 c) Nitric acid d) Hydrochloric acid
16. The application of heat to food, either before or after sealing in a hermetically sealed container is:
 a) Microfiltration b) Pasteurization
 c) Minimal thermal process d) Irradiation
17. The destruction of all microorganisms in food by thermal processing is known as
 a) Pasteurization b) Sterilization
 c) Blanching d) Scalding
18. Decimal reduction time in microbial destruction is inversely proportional to:
 a) Z-value b) Reaction rate
 c) Initial concentration d) Universal gas constant
19. Thermal degradation in quality of food material during thermal processing follows kinetic of the following order:
 a) First b) Second
 c) Third d) Zero
20. The amount of moisture in air is measured by
 a) Thermistor b) Spectrophotometer
 c) Sling psychrometer d) Orsat apparatus
21. Grade of stainless steel used in the manufacturing of food processing equipments is
 a) SS-403 b) SS-315
 c) SS-304 d) SS-513
22. While designing a heat exchanger, we consider the following because temperature of fluids change from point to point along length of travel
 a) Mean temperature difference b) Log mean temperature difference
 c) Temperature of hot fluid. d) Temperature of cold fluid
23. While laying out a food processing plant, one must consider
 a) Geographical location of site b) Provision for expression of plant
 c) Proximity of terminal market d) All of the above

24. Colour code recommended for potable water in a plant is

a) Dark blue b) Aqua
c) Olive green d) Violet

25. The level of contamination of waste water from foods processing plant is measured in terms of

a) Chemical oxygen demand b) Biological oxygen demand
c) pH value d) Concentration of colloidal

26. Which one of the following is related to safety standard in manufacturing chain

a) FPO b) HACCP
c) AGMARK d) FAO

27. Packaging technique wherein package and food are made sterile separately and packaged thereafter under sterile conditions is

a) Canning b) Modified atmosphere packaging
c) Aseptic packaging d) Controlled atmosphere packaging

28. The shelf life of agriculture produce can be extended appreciably by

a) Maintaining aerobic respiration at low level
b) Maintaining aerobic respiration at high level
c) Allowing anaerobic respiration
d) Increasing the temperature of storage to high level

29. Which type of package is used for retailing single unit of food product

a) Tertiary b) Primary
c) Secondary d) None of above

30. While transporting fruits and vegetable, transpiration process can be slowed down by

a) Maintaining a low relative humidity in storage
b) Controlling permeability of produce by waxing
c) Not packaging than in polymeric film
d) Maintaining sufficiently high temperature difference between evaporator coil and produce

31. Packaging a food serves the following

a) Protects the food b) Contain the food
c) Enhances marketability d) All of the above

32. FSSAI is governed by

a) Ministry of Agriculture b) Ministry of Law & Justice
c) Ministry of Health and Family Welfare d) Ministry of Food Processing Industries

33. Codex alimentarius commission was established in the year

a) 1968 b) 1970
c) 1960 d) 1961

34. ISO-14000 deals with
 a) Iron and steel industries b) Environmental management
 c) Food industries d) Population control

35. In size reduction of a material into a fine powder, which the following laws is more applicable
 a) Kicks law b) Rittingers law
 c) Bonds law d) All of the above

36. For the selection of location for a food industry this is not an important criteria
 a) Availability of water b) Availability of power
 c) Availability of labour d) None of the above

37. FSSAI was implemented in ________
 a) 2003 b) 2011 c) 2005 d) 2006

38. Various hazards in food industries are
 a) Physical b) Biological
 c) Chemical d) All of the above

39. Deterioration of food grains during storage occurs due to
 a) Microorganisms b) Rodents
 c) Environmental factors d) All of the above

40. Consumer protection act was passed in the year
 a) 1946 b) 1966 c) 1986 d) None of the above

41. Cream seperation is done by
 a) Centrifuging b) Evaporation
 c) Sedimentation d) Crystalisation

42. In miik, fat is present in state
 a) Emulsion b) Colloidal c) Solution d) Foam

43. Pulsed electric field involves treating foods placed between electrodes by high voltage pulse in the order of:
 a) 10-40 kV b) 20-80 kV c) 10-20 kV d) 10-50 kV

44. Starch is insoluble in
 a) Distilled water b) Hot water
 c) Cold water d) None of the above

45. In canning of fruits & vegetables, 'flats sour' refers to
 a) Bulging of cans b) Overfilling of cans
 c) High acid formation d) Flat can

46. During lag-phase of a growth curve of micro organism, the mass
 a) Increases b) Decreases c) Remains same d) Just doubles

47. Calcium hydroxide react with grain moisture to produce
 a) O_2 b) H_2O c) Ethylene d) H_2

48. Thermal processing of food material should be based on the heat senstivity of the

a) Spores of fungi
b) Vegetative cells of fungi
c) Spores of bacteria
d) Vegetative cells of bacteria

49. Textural property of 'paneer' can be best represented by:

a) Hardness
b) Gumminess
c) Springiness
d) Chewiness

50. Packaging technique wherein package and food are made sterile separately and packaged thereafter under sterile conditions is

a) Canning
b) Modified atmosphere packaging
c) Aseptic packaging
d) Controlled atmosphere packaging

51. Dielectric properties of food products depend on which of following

a) Temperature of food
b) Texture of food
c) Moisture content of food
d) Shape of the food sample

52. If there is a uniform shrinkage in material, it is all dimensions of the

a) Anisotropic shrinkage
b) Isotropic shrinkage
c) Isenotropic shrinkage
d) Positive shrinkage

53. Protein in millk is present in which of the following state

a) Emulsion
b) Colloidal
c) Solute
d) Foam

54. In miik, fat is present in the state

a) Emulsion
b) Colloidal
c) Solution
d) Foam

55. Which property of milk is not effected due to pasteurization process:

a) Rheological
b) Organoleptic
c) Chemical
d) Textural

56. Dry ice is known as

a) Solidified water kept in moisture free environment
b) Solidified freon
c) Solidified carbon-dioxide
d) Solidified nitrogen

57. Which of the following is the primary refrigerant

a) Sodium chloride
b) Calcium chloride
c) Water
d) Ammonia

58. Height of declaration made on package should not be less than

a) 2 mm
b) 1 mm
c) 3 mm
d) none of the above

59. Which of the following is a permitted preservative for use in fruit juices and beverages

a) Ascorbic acid
b) Citric acid
c) Nitric acid
d) Hydrochloric acid

60. Cream separation is done by
a) Centrifuging
b) Evaporation
c) Sedimentation
d) Crystalisation

61. According to FSSAI, 2006, licensing and registration of food busines is mandatory for
a) Manufacturers
b) Distributer
c) Packers
d) All of these

62. Bureau of Indian Standard Act, 1986 comes under
a) Department of Consumer Affairs, Government of India
b) Department of Marketing and Inspection
c) Export Inspection of Legal Metrology
d) Department of Legal Metrology

63. During storage of grams, fungi grows in the temperature ranging between
a) 20-40 °C
b) 0-20 °C
c) 3-7 °C
d) 7-50 °C

64. In refining of crude oil to edible oil, winterizaition refers to
a) Removal of free fatty acid
b) Removal of odorous matters
c) Removal of coloring matters
d) Removal of soft wax

65. In general , insects in stored grains are killed when oxygen level in the Inter granular air falls to about
a) 2 % by volume
b) 2 % by weight
c) 1 % by volume
d) 1 % by weight

66. Codex Alimentarius Commission was established in the year
a) 1968
b) 1970
c) 1960
d) 1961

67. The sensory evaluation method to determine textural characteristics of a food is method of following nature
a) Objective
b) Repeatable
c) More compatible
d) Subjective

68. While transporting fruits and vegetables, transpiration process can be slowed down by
a) Maintaining a low relative humidity in storage
b) Controlling permeability of product by waxing
c) not packaging them in polymeric film
d) None of the above

69. Environmental protection act was formulated in the year
a) 1966
b) 1937
c) 1986
d) 1926

70. The most favorable location for a food processing plant is one which ensures
a) Availability of raw material
b) Prompt marketability of finished product
c) Lowest unit cost in producing and distributing the products to consumers
d) Availability of labour force

71. In freeze drying, drying time is directly proportional to- of the material

a) Thickness b) Square the thickness

c) Cube of thickness d) 4th power of thickness

72. HDPE is commonly recycled and has the identification code number in its recycling symbol

a) 1 b) 2 c) 3 d) 4

73. LDPE contains the chemical element

a) Carbon and hydrogen b) Carbon hydrogen and oxygen

c) Carbon hydrogen and nitrogen d) Carbon hydrogen oxygen and nitrogen

74. Most dairy equipment are made up of 18:8 stainless steel what does 18:8 stand for

a) 18% chromium and 8% tin b) 18% chromium and 8% nickel

c) Aluminium and 8% nickel d) 18% nickel and 8% chromium

75. The common fumigant for storage of cereals is

a) Zinc Phosphine b) Ethylene dibromide

c) Aluinium posphide d) DDT

76. Transfer of heat from liquids to gas follows

a) Conduction b) Convection

c) Radiation d) All of the above

77. Freeze drying is also called as

a) Sublimation b) Lyophilisation

c) Both d) None

78. Salt and sugar are added to preserve food for

a) Killing microorganisms b) Increasing acidic

c) Binding water d) All of the above

79. The capacity of CAP storage structure is

a) 10 tonnes b) 100 tonnes

c) 1000 tonnes d) 2000 tonnes

80. Moulds are of ______ type

a) Facultative b) Aerobic

c) Anerobic d) All of the above

81. Osmotic pressure is calculated by

a) Raoult's law b) Henry's law

c) Fick's law d) None

82. Liquid with capillary effect is governed by

a) Poisuille equation b) Stoke's equation

c) Reynolds number d) Bernoulli equation

83. Ripening of fruits and vegetables is accompanied with production of

a) Acetylene b) Carbon-dioxide

c) Carbon monoxide d) Propylene

84. The phenomena that moisture moves in the same direction as heat flows is known as
   a) Moisture migration b) Thermo moisture conductivity
   c) Thermo moisture diffusivity d) None of the above

85. Hygrometer measures
   a) Relative Humidity b) Temperature
   c) Specific gravity d) Viscosity

ANSWER KEY

(Model paper 6)

Q. Ans.	Q. Ans.	Q. Ans.	Q. Ans.	Q. Ans.
1) b	2) b	3) a	4) c	5) d
6) b	7) b	8) b	9) c	10) d
11) c	12) b	13) c	14) b	15) b
16) c	17) b	18) a	19) a	20) c
21) c	22) b	23) b	24) a	25) b
26) b	27) c	28) a	29) b	30) b
31) d	32) c	33) d	34) b	35) b
36) d	37) b	38) d	39) d	40) c
41) a	42) a	43) b	44) c	45) c
46) c	47) d	48) c	49) c	50) c
51) c	52) c	53) b	54) a	55) b
56) c	57) d	58) b	59) b	60) a
61) d	62) a	63) a	64) d	65) a
66) d	67) d	68) b	69) c	70) a
71) b	72) b	73) a	74) b	75) a
76) b	77) c	78) c	79) c	80) c
81) d	82) a	83) a	84) b	85) a

MODEL PAPERS-7

FSSAI Act, 2006

1) According to FSSAI, improvement notice means any notice issued under section ________ of act

a) 32 b) 35
c) 30 d) 31

2) If a licence is not issued within _____ months from the date of making the application or his application is not rejected, the applicant may start his food business after expiry of the said period

a) 1 b) 2
c) 3 d) 6

3) According to FSSA, Any person who, whether by himself or by any other person on his behalf, manufactures for sale or stores or sells or distributes or imports any article of food for human consumption which is unsafe, shall be punishable – where such failure or contravention results in death, with following imprisonment and fine.

a) 6 years and 5 lakh rupees
b) 7 years and 5 lakh rupees
c) 7 years to life imprisonment and fine not less than 5 lakhs
d) 7 years to life imprisonment and fine not less than 10 lakhs

4) According to FSSA, Punishment for interfering with seized items shall be imprisonment up to ________ and fine up to _________.

a) 6 months and 1 lakh rupees b) 6 months and 2 lakh rupees
c) 1 year and 1 lakh rupees d) 1 year and 3 lakh rupees

5) Food Analyst after receiving the sample from the Food Safety Officer shall analyse the sample and send the analysis report mentioning method of sampling and analysis within _______ days to Designated Officer with a copy to Commissioner of Food Safety

a) 7 b) 14
c) 21 d) 30

6) According to FSSA, Any person who, whether by himself or by any other person on his behalf, manufactures for sale or stores or sells or distributes or imports any article of food for human consumption which is unsafe, shall be punishable – where such failure or contravention does not result in injury, with following imprisonment and fine.

a) 3 months and 1 lakh rupees b) 6 months and 2 lakh rupees
c) 6 months and 1 lakh rupees d) 1 year and 2 lakh rupees

7) The head office of the Food Standard Authority is located at

a) Mumbai b) New Delhi
c) Hyderabad d) Noida

8) If any petty manufacturer commits an offence under FSSA, payment of a sum of money by way of composition of the offence can be collected by

a) Food Safety Officer b) Designated Officer

c) Commissioner d) FSSAI

9) According to FSSA, appeal against the report of Food Analyst shall life before the

a) Food Safety Officer b) Designated Officer

c) Commissioner d) FSSAI

10) According to FSSA, the penalty for selling food not of the nature or substance or quality demanded, shall not exceed ________

a) 2 lakh rupees b) 3 lakh rupees

c) 5 lakh rupees d) 10 lakh rupees

11) According to FSSA, Penalty for misbranded food may extend to

a) 2 lakh rupees b) 3 lakh rupees

c) 5 lakh rupees d) 10 lakh rupees

12) According to FSSA, Penalty for contraventions for which no specific penalty is provided, shall be liable to a penalty which may extend to

a) 2 lakh rupees b) 3 lakh rupees

c) 5 lakh rupees d) 10 lakh rupees

13) According to FSSA, Any person who, whether by himself or by any other person on his behalf, manufactures for sale or stores or sells or distributes or imports any article of food for human consumption which is unsafe, shall be punishable

a) 2 lakh rupes b) 3 lakh rupes

c) 5 lakh rupes d) 10 lakh rupes

14) ___________ is appointed under section 37 of FSSA

a) Food Safety Officer b) Designated Officer

c) Commissioner d) Food Authority

15) According to FSSA, Any person who, whether by himself or by any other person on his behalf, manufactures for sale or stores or sells or distributes or imports any article of food for human consumption which is unsafe, shall be punishable – where such failure or contravention results in a non-grievous injury, with following imprisonment and fine.

a) 6 months and 1 lakh rupees b) 6 months and 2 lakh rupees

c) 1 year and 1 lakh rupees d) 1 year and 3 lakh rupees

16) Section 97 of FSSA, 2006 deals with

a) Reward by State Government b) Recovery of Penalty

c) Repeal and Savings d) Power to remove difficulties

17) The ____________ of Food Safety shall, if he so deems fit decide, within the period prescribed by the Central Government, as per the gravity of offence, whether the matter be referred to,-- ordinary jurisdiction or special court.

a) Food Safety Officer b) Assistant Commissioner

c) Commissioner d) Food Authority

18) According to section 42 of FSSA, __________ after scrutiny of the report of Food Analyst shall decide as to whether the contravention is punishable with imprisonment or fine only and in the case of contravention punishable with imprisonment, he shall send his recommendations within fourteen days to the Commissioner of Food Safety for sanctioning prosecution.
a) Food Safety Officer
b) Designated Officer
c) Adjudicating Officer
d) Both a & c

19) A single licence may be issued by the __________ for one or more articles of food and also for different establishments or premises in the same area
a) Food Safety Officer
b) Designated Officer
c) Commissioner
d) Food Authority

20) Guidelines relating to food recall procedures as the Food Authority may specify by regulations should be followed by
a) Manufacturer
b) Retailer
c) Distributor
d) Every food business operator

21) According to FSSA, _______ means an article of food for which standards have not been specified but is not unsafe:
a) Proprietary food
b) Novel food
c) Organic food
d) Both a & b

22) Food Safety and Standards act, 2006 contains ______ number of chapters
a) IX
b) X
c) XI
d) XII

23) According to FSSA, Any person who, whether by himself or by any other person on his behalf, manufactures for sale or stores or sells or distributes or imports any article of food for human consumption which is unsafe, shall be punishable – where such failure or contravention results in a grievous injury, , with following imprisonment and fine.
a) 1 year and 3 lakh rupees
b) 2 years and 5 lakh rupees
c) 6 years and 5 lakh rupees
d) 7 years and 5 lakh rupees

24) According to FSSA, Food Analyst should cause to be analyzed the samples and shall send the four copies of report to
a) Food Safety Officer
b) Designated Officer
c) Commissioner
d) FSSAI

25) According to FSSA, _______, in relation to any article of food, means a process consisting of three components, *i.e.* risk assessment, risk management and risk communication;
a) Risk Assessment
b) Risk
c) Risk Analysis
d) Risk Communication

26) According to FSSA, _______ means the interactive exchange of information and opinions throughout the risk analysis process concerning risks, risk-related factors and risk perceptions, among risk assessors, risk managers, consumers, industry, the academic community and other interested parties, including the explanation of risk assessment findings and the basis of risk management decisions;
a) Risk Assessment
b) Risk Management
c) Risk Analysis
d) Risk Communication

27) The Food Authority shall consist of a Chairperson and the following _____ number of members
a) 18
b) 20
c) 22
d) 25

28) According to FSSA, Any person who whether by himself or by any other person on his behalf manufactures for sale or stores or sells or distributes or imports any article of food for human consumption which is sub-standard, shall be liable to a penalty which may extend to _______.
a) 2 lakh rupees
b) 3 lakh rupees
c) 5 lakh rupees
d) 10 lakh rupees

29) The Food Authority shall contain _______ number of member/(s) food industries
a) 1
b) 2
c) 3
d) 5

30) According to FSSA, Compensation to consumer in case of injury to costumer other than death and grievous shall not exceed
a) 1 lakhs
b) 2 lakhs
c) 3 lakhs
d) 4 lakhs

31) According to FSSA, Compensation in case injury of death of consumer, an interim relief shall be paid to the next of the kin within _____ days of the incident
a) 3 days
b) 7 days
c) 15 days
d) 30 days

32) According to FSSA, Compensation shall be paid at the earliest and in no case later than _______ months from the date of occurrence of the incident:
a) 1
b) 3
c) 6
d) 12

33) First recommendation for One comprehensive legislation on food with Food Regulatory Authority concerning both domestic and export market made by Prime Minister's Council on Trade and Industry in the year:
a) 1992
b) 1995
c) 1998
d) 2004

34) The _________ shall have administrative control over the officers and other employees of the Food Authority
a) Chairperson
b) Chief Executive Officer
c) Central Advisory Committee
d) All of these

35) Establishment of limits for use of food additives, crop contaminants, pesticide residues, residues of veterinary drugs, heavy metals, processing aids, myco-toxins, antibiotics and pharmacological active substances and irradiation of food is of:
a) Chairperson
b) Chief Executive Officer
c) Central Advisory Committee
d) Food authority

36) According to FSSA, No insecticide shall be used directly on article of food except fumigants registered and approved under the act:

a) FSSA
b) Insecticides Act, 1968
c) Pesticide Residue act, 1969
d) Pesticide & Fumigants act, 1969

37) The Commissioner of Food Safety for the State for efficient implementation of food safety and standards is appointed by

a) Food Authority
b) Central Government
c) State Government
d) Chairperson of FSSAI

38) A person can commence or carry on any food business except under a licence is

a) Petty food manufacturer
b) Person serving food to religious gathering
c) Dabba wala
b) None of These

39) As stated in Schedule – I of FSSA, Maharashtra state falls under ________ zone

a) 1st
b) 2nd
c) 3rd
d) 4th

40) _________ is appointed under section 36 of FSSA

a) Food Safety Officer
b) Designated Officer
c) Commissioner
d) Food Authority

41) As per FSSA, An appeal against the order of rejection for the grant of licence shall lie to the ___________ of Food Safety

a) Food Safety Officer
b) Designated Officer
c) Commissioner
d) Food Authority

42) The need to converge (combine) all food laws to have a single regulatory body was emphasized by Joint Parliamentary Committee on Pesticide Residues in its report in the year:

a) 1992
b) 1995
c) 1998
d) 2004

43) Standard Committee of Parliament on Agriculture in its 12th Report submitted in ______ desired that much needed legislation on integrated Food Law should be Expedited.

a) April 1998
b) April 2004
c) April 2005
d) April 2006

44) According to FSSA, _______ shall be responsible for inspection of food business, drawing samples and sending them to Food Analyst for analysis.

a) Food Safety Officer
b) Designated Officer
c) Assistant Commissioner
d) Commissioner

45) According to FSSA, _______, in relation to any article of food, means the probability of an adverse effect on the health of consumers of such food and the severity of that effect, consequential to a food hazard;

a) Risk Assessment
b) Risk
c) Risk Analysis
d) Risk Communication

46) _______ has the power for Recognition and accreditation of laboratories, research institutions and referral food laboratory

a) Food Safety Officer
b) Assistant Commissioner
c) Commissioner
d) Food Authority

47) According to FSSA, _______ means food products that have been produced in accordance with specified organic production standards.

a) Proprietary food
b) Novel food
c) Organic food
d) Both b & c

48) According to FSSA, Food Safety Officer should send _______ parts of sample to Designated Officer

a) 0
b) 1
c) 2
d) 3

49) According to FSSA, _______ means a scientifically based process consisting of the following steps : (*i*) hazard identification, (*ii*) hazard characterisation; (*iii*) exposure assessment, and (*iv*) risk characterisation;

a) Risk Assessment
b) Risk Management
c) Risk Analysis
d) Risk Communication

50) According to FSSA, Penalty for misleading advertisement may be extended to

a) 2 lakh rupees
b) 3 lakh rupees
c) 5 lakh rupees
d) 10 lakh rupees

51) If the test reports for the sample of analysis are found to be at variance, the report of _______ shall be considered as final.

a) FSSAI
b) Central laboratory
c) Referral laboratory
d) Food Analyst

52) According to FSSA, Penalty for food containing extraneous matter may be extended to

a) 1 lakh rupees
b) 2 lakh rupees
c) 3 lakh rupees
d) 5 lakh rupees

53) According to FSSA, Penalty for failure to comply with the directions of Food Safety Officer may be extended to

a) 1 lakh rupees
b) 2 lakh rupees
c) 3 lakh rupees
d) 5 lakh rupees

54) If any petty manufacturer commits an offence under FSSA, payment of a sum of money by way of composition of the offence and the payment should not be more than _______

a) 1 lakh
b) 2 lakh
c) 3 lakh
d) 5 lakh

55) According to FSSA, Penalty for unhygienic or unsanitary processing or manufacturing of food may extend to

a) 1 lakh rupees
b) 2 lakh rupees
c) 3 lakh rupees
d) 5 lakh rupees

56) According to FSSA, Penalty for possessing adulterant for a person who whether by himself or by any other person on his behalf, imports or manufactures for sale, or stores, sells or distribute any adulterant shall be liable: where such adulterant is not injurious to health, to a penalty not exceeding

a) 1 lakh rupees
b) 2 lakh rupees
c) 3 lakh rupees
d) 5 lakh rupees

57) According to FSSA, Penalty for possessing adulterant for a person who whether by himself or by any other person on his behalf, imports or manufactures for sale, or stores, sells or distribute any adulterant shall be liable: where such adulterant is injurious to health, to a penalty not exceeding

a) 2 lakh rupees
b) 3 lakh rupees
c) 5 lakh rupees
d) 10 lakh rupees

58) The responsibilities to organize Training programmes in food safety and standards for persons who are or intend to become involved in food businesses lies to:

a) Food Safety Officer
b) Designated Officer
c) Commissioner
d) Food Authority

59) Notwithstanding anything contained in FSSA, no court shall take cognizance of an offence under this Act after the expiry of the period of _______ from the date of commission of an offence:

a) 1 month
b) 3 months
c) 6 months
d) 1 year

60) NABL stands for

a) National Analytical Board for Laboratories
b) National Accreditation Board for Testing and Certification of Laboratories
c) National Analytical Board for Testing and Calibration of Laboratories
d) National Accreditation Board for Testing and Calibration of Laboratories

61) According to FSSA, Food Safety audit and checking compliance with Food Safety Management systems required under this act and regulations can be done by

a) FSSAI authority only
b) Accreditation body only
c) Certification bodies only
d) Any organization recognized by authority

62) Any sample taken by Food Safety Officer should be divided into _______ parts

a) 2
b) 4
c) 6
d) 8

63) Commissioner of Food Safety may, for reasons to be recorded in writing, approve prosecution within an extended period of up to three years.

a) 1 year
b) 2 years
c) 3 years
d) 5 years

64) Food Authority shall prepare its budget for the every ________ financial year

a) 1 b) 2

c) 3 d) 5

65) FSSA has its Overriding effect of over

a) Consumer protection act b) Prevention of Food Adulteration Act

c) Food Product Order d) all other food related laws

66) ________ has the power to make rules under FSSA.

a) FSSAI b) Central Government

c) State Government d) Both b & c

67) ________ has power to make regulations under FSSA.

a) FSSAI b) Central Government

c) State Government d) Both b & c

68) ________ may empower the Commissioner of Food Safety to order payment of reward to be paid to a person who renders assistance in the detection of the offence or the apprehension of the offender, from such fund and in such manner as may be prescribed by the State Government

a) FSSAI b) Central Government

c) State Government d) Both b & c

69) Recovery of penalty under FSSA, if it is not paid, can be done as an arrears of

a) Land revenue b) Equipment revenue

c) Raw material revenuer d) All of these

70) State Govt. may appoint ________ of food safety for implementation of food safert and stndards and other requirements.

a) Food Safety Officer b) Designated Officer

c) Commissioner d) Food Authority

71) ________ means an article of food offered or promoted for sale with false, misleading or deceptive claims either;

a) Prohibited food b) Deceptive food

c) Misleading food d) None of these

72) According to FSSA, Food Safety Officer should retain _____ part/(s) of sample with him

a) 0 b) 1

c) 2 d) 3

73) According to FSSA, _______ means the process, distinct from risk assessment, of evaluating policy alternatives, in consultation with all interested parties considering risk assessment and other factors relevant for the protection of health of consumers and for the promotion of fair trade practices, and, if needed, selecting appropriate prevention and control options;

a) Risk Assessment b) Risk Management

c) Risk Analysis d) Risk Communication

74) Notwithstanding anything contained in sub-section (2) of section 31, the ______ may search any place, seize any article of food or adulterant, if there is a reasonable doubt about them being involved in commission of any offence relating to food

a) Food Safety Officer
b) Designated Officer
c) Commissioner
d) Food Authority

75) Appeal: Any person aggrieved by a decision or order of a Special Court may, on payment of such fee as may be prescribed by the Central Government and after depositing the amount, if any, imposed by way of penalty, compensation or damage under this Act, within ________ from the date on which the order was served, prefer an appeal to the High Court:

a) 30 days
b) 45 days
c) 60 days
d) 90 days

76) According to FSSA, Punishment for carrying out a business without licence shall be punishable with imprisonment for a term which may extend to ________ and also with a fine which may extend to ________

a) 6 months and 1 lakh rupees
c) 1 year and 2 lakh rupees
c) 6 months and 5 lakhs
d) 1 year and 5 lakhs

77) According to FSSA, Compensation in case injury of death of consumer shall be not less than

a) 3 lakhs
b) 5 lakhs
c) 10 lakhs
d) 20 lakhs

78) According to FSSA, Compensation to consumer in case of grievous injury shall be not less than

a) 2 lakhs
b) 3 lakhs
c) 5 lakhs
d) 1 lakhs

79) According to FSSA, _______ include the parent compounds or their metabolites or both in any edible portion of any animal product and include residues of associated impurities of the veterinary drugs concerned.

a) Residues of veterinary drugs
b) Insecticide residue
c) Pesticide residues
d) Toxicants

80) According to section 42 of FSSA, Designated Officer after scrutiny of the report of Food Analyst shall decide as to whether the contravention is punishable with imprisonment or fine only and in the case of contravention punishable with imprisonment, he shall send his recommendations within ______ days to the Commissioner of Food Safety for sanctioning prosecution.

a) 7
b) 14
c) 21
d) 30

81) Food Safety and Standards act, 2006 contains ______ number of sections

a) 83
b) 97
c) 101
d) 113

82) According to FSSA, ________ shall not be below the rank of a Sub-Divisional Officer, to be in-charge of food safety administration in such area as may be specified by regulations.
 a) Food Safety Officer b) Designated Officer
 c) Assistant Commissioner d) Commissioner

83) It is not compulsory to have a member of Food Authority to be from following ministry
 a) Agriculture b) Consumer affairs
 c) Finance d) Legislative affairs

84) ________ numbers of members of food authority comes from consumer organizations
 a) 1 b) 2
 c) 3 d) 4

85) The Food Authority shall establish scientific panels up to the number
 a) 5 b) 17
 c) 22 d) No limit

86) Food Safety and Standards Act was passed on
 a) 16th October 2006 b) 16th August 2006
 c) 23rd October 2006 d) 23rd August 2006

87) IMS stands for
 a) Integrated Modified Standards b) Internationally Modified Standards
 c) Integrated Management system d) International Management system

88) Which of the following has/have the power to cancel the licence?
 a) Food Safety Officer b) Designated Officer
 c) Adjudicating Officer d) All of these

89) If the sample of article sent to Food Analyst is lost or damaged, on a requisition made by him, ________ should dispatch one of the parts of sample to Food Analyst
 a) Food Safety Officer b) Designated Officer
 c) Adjudicating Officer d) All of these

90) Any purchaser can send the sample to Food Analyst for getting analyzed provided that:
 a) He should inform to FBO b) He should inform FSO
 c) He should inform to FSSAI d) He should inform to Designated Officer

91) If any sample sent by purchaser for analysis to Food Analyst and does not compliance with the FSSA regulations then Food Analyst should:
 a) Return the fee of analysis b) Forward report to Designated officer
 c) Bring it to notice of FSO d) Both a & b

92) According to section 42 of FSSA, ________ shall be responsible for inspection of food business, drawing samples and sending them to Food Analyst for analysis.
 a) Food Safety Officer b) Designated Officer
 c) Adjudicating Officer d) Both a & c

93) __________ is appointed under section 30 of FSSA

a) Food Safety Officer
b) Designated Officer
c) Commissioner
d) Food Authority

94) The Food Analyst after receiving the sample from the Food Safety Officer shall analyse the sample and send the analysis report mentioning method of sampling and analysis within fourteen days to Designated Officer with a copy to ________.

a) Food Safety Officer
b) Adjudicating Officer
c) Assistant Commissioner
d) Commissioner

95) The member of Food Safety and Standard Authority of India should not be below the rank of

a) Commissioner
b) Designated officer
c) Joint Secretary
d) Secretary

96) The maximum age limit for the chairperson of Food Authority is _____ years

a) 60
b) 62
c) 63
d) 65

97) Punishment for false information shall be imprisonment up to ________ and fine up to ________.

a) 3 months and 1 lakh rupees
b) 3 months and 2 lakh rupees
c) 6 months and 1 lakh rupees
d) 1 year and 2 lakh rupees

98) According to FSSA, Punishment for obstructing or impersonating a Food Safety Officer, shall be punishable with imprisonment for a term which may extend to ______ and also with fine which may extend to _________.

a) 3 months and 1 lakh rupees
b) 3 months and 2 lakh rupees
c) 6 months and 1 lakh rupees
d) 1 year and 2 lakh rupees

99) According to FSSA, _______ means any specified substance in food resulting from the use of a pesticide and includes any derivatives of a pesticide, such as conversion products, metabolites, reaction products and impurities considered to be of toxicological significance and also includes such residues coming into food from environment;

a) Residues of veterinary drugs
b) Insecticide residue
c) Pesticide residues
d) Toxicants

100) If the test reports for the sample of analysis are found to be at variance, then designated officer shall send one part of sample to ___________.

a) FSSAI
b) Central Laboratory
c) Referral Laboratory
d) Food Analyst

101) ________ has the power for Recognition of organisation or agency for food safety audit.

a) Food Safety Officer
b) Assistant Commissioner
c) Commissioner
d) Food Authority

102) The Food Safety and Standards Authority of India (FSSAI) has issued a set of guidelines regarding the recall of __________ from the market?

a) Unsafe drinking water
b) unsafe food products
c) unsafe labelling
d) unsafe packaging

103) What has been banned for tea bag products by FSSAI from 2018?
a) Use of stapler pins b) Thread for dipping
c) Cloth bag containing the tea leaves d) Herbal tea leaves

104) FSSAI has come out with draft regulations for ____ food products.
a) Grain b) Inorganic
c) Organic d) Vegetarian

105) FSSAI has launched which logo for fortified foods?
a) Square with an F and a + sign with a ring b) Circle with an F and a + sign with a ring
c) Rectangle with an F and a + sign with a ring d) None of the above

106) FSSAI has set up a scientific panel on ______
a) Final regulations on food fortification
b) Preparing strategies to address malnutrition
c) Boosting production and consumption of fortified foods
d) All of the above

107) FSSAI has issued an advisory banning the use of which material for wrapping and packaging of food items?
a) Newspaper b) Plastic
c) Polythene d) None of the above

108) Regulator FSSAI has joined hands with which organisation to check misleading ads in the foods and beverages sector?
a) ASCI b) ASDI
c) ASOI d) ASBI

109) Who has been appointed as CEO of FSSAI on 22nd December 2015?
a) Prem Kumar Singh b) Pawan Kumar Agarwal
c) Ashok Singh Malik d) Ashish Bahugana
(In 2022 CEO is Arun Singhal)

110) FSSAI is located in 5 regions with head office located at
a) Hyderabad b) Mumbai
c) Bangalore d) New Delhi

111) As per Section 3 of Food Safety & Standards Act 2006, if food article sold in the market contains any inferior or cheaper substances whether wholly or partly which is injurious to health then such products can be called as
a) Sub-standard b) Unsafe
c) Misbranded d) Partly sub-standard

112) As per section 22 of FSS Act 2006, Foods for special dietary uses or functional foods or neutraceuticals or health supplements does not include
a) Botancial extracts b) Vitamin supplements
c) Parenterals d) Probiotics

113) Food Safety and Standards Act, 2006 - passed by Indian Parliament and notified on:
a) 24th July, 2006 b) 24th June, 2006
c) 24th August, 2006 d) 24th November, 2006

114) Food Safety and Standards Act, 2006 - operationalised on:
a) 5th August, 2007 b) 5th August, 2011
c) 5th August, 2012 d) 5th August, 2013

115) How many acts are repealed by Food Safety and Standards Act, 2006
a) 4 b) 5 c) 7 d) 8

116) Which of these are responsible for the implementation of FSSAI:
a) Ministry of Health & Family Welfare b) Ministry of Food Processing Industries
c) Department of Agriculture & Cooperation d) Directorate General of Health Services

117) Agencies involved behind "Plant Quarantine (Regulation of Import into India) Order, 2003"
a) Ministry of Health & Family Welfare b) Ministry of Food Processing Industries
c) Department of Agriculture & Cooperation farmers welfare
d) Directorate General of Health Services

118. How many section FSSAI contains in 12 chapters.
a) 101 b) 83 c) 150 d) 65

119. How many principal regulation are in FSSAI Act.
a) Eight b) Six c) Five c) Ten

120. The molisch test is a chemical test that determines the presence of
a) All carbohydrates b) Sucrose c) Fructose d) Glucose

121. Iodine test for starch is mainly performed to test the presence of
a) carbohydrates *b*) Proteins *c*) Vitamins d) None

- **Purple book in FSSAI : -** The purple Book is a handbook on general recommendations on diets for common medical conditions such as diabetes, hypertension, cancer and so on. It has been developed as a resource for hospitals, clinics and medical centres.
- **Pink book :-** The book has nine sections namely, buying food, storing food, preparing and cooking food, serving food, eating healthy food, managing leftover food, packaging food, maintaining hygiene & sanitation in the kitchen and managing waste. It provides useful tips, dos and don'ts, methods and practices that are recommended for Indian kitchens
- **Golden rules in FSSAI 12 golden rules**

Yellow Book in FSSAI :- FSSAI launched 'The Yellow Book – your guide to safe and nutritious food at school', that provides age appropriate content which can be adopted across schools through State education machineries as part of their curricular and co-curricular activities.

Green Book :- Your Companion on Safe and Nutritious Food @ Home'. This would have useful and practical tips and information about food safety and nutrition that Indian households need on a day-to-day basis.

The Orange Book :- 'Safe and Nutritious Food at Workplace' is a nation-wide campaign to help people eat safe and eat right while at work. With the rising incidence of diet-related diseases, we need to be more conscious and mindful of our diets. This initiative, therefore, educates people on safe and healthy diets. Further, the campaign would help to develop an overall ecosystem for safe and nutritious food in workplaces. The Orange Book is organized in 3 parts. First part is meant for HR/Administration. Second part is for the canteen or cafeteria establishment. Third part is for employees stay healthy at the workplace.

ANSWER KEY
(Model paper 7)

Q.	Ans.	Q.	Ans.	Q.	Ans.	Q.	Ans.	Q.	Ans.
1.	a	21.	d	41.	c	61.	d	81.	c
2.	b	22.	d	42.	d	62.	b	82.	b
3.	d	23.	c	43.	c	63.	c	83.	c
4.	b	24.	b.	44.	a	64.	a	84.	c
5.	b	25.	c	45.	b	65.	d	85.	d
6.	c	26.	d	46.	d	66.	b	86.	d
7.	b	27.	c	47.	c	67.	a	87.	c
8.	b	28.	c	48.	c	68.	c	88.	c
9.	b	29.	b	49.	a	69.	a	89.	b
10.	c	30.	a	50.	d	70.	c	90.	a
11.	b	31.	a	51.	d	71.	d	91.	d
12.	a	32.	c	52.	a	72.	b	92.	a
13.	c	33.	d	53.	b	73.	b	93.	c
14.	a	34.	b	54.	a	74.	b	94.	d
15.	d	35.	d	55.	a	75.	b	95.	c
16.	c	36.	b	56.	b	76.	c	96.	d
17.	c	37.	b	57.	d	77.	b	97.	b
18.	b	38.	d	58.	d	78.	b	98.	a
19.	b	39.	a	59.	d	79.	a	99.	c
20.	d	40.	b	60.	d	80.	b	100.	c
101.	d	102.	b	103.	a	104.	c	105.	a
106.	d	107.	a	108.	a	109.	b	110.	d
111.	b	112.	c	113.	c	114.	b	115.	d
116.	a	117.	c	118.	a	119.	b	120.	a
121.	a								

MODEL PAPERS-8

(RPPSC Food Safety Officer 2019)

1. Example of Gel is—
(*a*) Smoke (*b*) Fog (*c*) Milk (*d*) Butter
2. Which BIS standard is compulsory for Packaged drinking water?
(*a*) IS 14243 (*b*) IS 14543 (*c*) IS 13543 (*d*) IS 14534
3. What is the limiting value of water activity for the growth of any microorganism?
(*a*) A_W 0.75 (*b*) A_W 0.88 (*c*) A_W 0.60 (*d*) A_W greater than 0.91
4. Aflatoxin is produced by—
(*a*) *Aspergillus* species (*b*) *Salmonella* species
(*c*) *Fusarium* species (*d*) *Streptococcal* species
5. Which of the following bacteria produce alpha toxin?
(*a*) *Salmonella typhi* (*b*) *Listeria monocytogenes*
(*c*) *Clostridium perfringens* (*d*) *Toxicoplasma gondii*
6. Methods for estimation of nitrogen are—
(*a*) Dumas and Carius method (*b*) Kjeldahl's and Carius method
(*c*) Dumas and Kjeldahl's method (*d*) Carius method
7. Saurkraut is generally prepared from—
(*a*) Tomato (*b*) Pumpkin (*c*) Cauliflower (*d*) Cabbage
8. The micro-organism ______ is responsible for the formation of beer and wine and its fermented end product is______.
(*a*) Saccharomyces cerevisiae, ethanol (*b*) Saccharomyces cerevisiae, acetic acid
(*c*) Lactobacillus plantarum, ethanol (*d*) Lactobacillus plantarum, lactic acid
9. Which of the following is fermented by Koji?
(*a*) Barley (*b*) Millet (*c*) Soyabean (*d*) Zea mays
10. Number of GTP (Guanosine tri phosphate) formed after complete aerobic oxidation of one molecule of Glucose:—
(*a*) 02 (*b*) 36 (*c*) 30 (*d*) 16
11. *Agaricus bisporus* is—
(*a*) A food stuff (*b*) Useful in beer making
(*c*) A pathogenic bacteria (*d*) A human parasite
12. Fatty acids are oxidised by—
(*a*) Alpha (α) and beta (β) oxidation (*b*) Delta (Δ) oxidation
(*c*) Sigma (σ) oxidation (*d*) Gamma (γ) oxidation
13. Captafol is a/an—
(*a*) Algaecide (*b*) Fungicide (*c*) Protein (*d*) Food colour

14. Which of the following vitamin is antihaemorrhagic?
(*a*) Vitamin A (*b*) Vitamin C (*c*) Vitamin E (*d*) Vitamin K

15. What is the general mechanism of an enzyme?
(*a*) It acts by decreasing the activation energy. (*b*) It acts by increasing the activation energy.
(*c*) It actss by decreasing the pH. (*d*) It acts by increasing the pH.

16. Methyl and ethyl alcohol are detoxified in the human body by—
(*a*) Oxidation (*b*) Reduction (*c*) Conjugation (*d*) Sulphurisation

17. Consumption of raw egg white causes deficiency of—
(*a*) Folic Acid (*b*) Biotin (*c*) Niacin (*d*) Pyridoxine

18. Which is not included in the five kingdom system of classification?
(*a*) Viruses, Viriods and Lichens (*b*) Slime moulds
(*c*) Bacteria (*d*) Phycomycetes

19. Match **List I** (Minerals) with **List II** (Functions) and choose correct answer—

List I	***List II***
A. Calcium	I. Blood coagulation
B. Sodium	II. Maintenance of electrical equilibrium between intracellular fluid
C. Iron	III. Anaemia
D. Iodine	IV. Formation of Thyroid hormone

(*a*) A-IV, B-I, C-II, D-III (*b*) A-III, B-IV, C-II, D-I
(*c*) A-I, B-II, C-III, D-IV (*d*) A-II, B-III, C-I, D-IV

20. What is not true about prokaryotes?
(*a*) No nuclear membrane or nucleoli (*b*) Presence of mitochondria
(*c*) 70s ribosomes present (*d*) Usually single chromosome

21. Which one of the following is the scientific name of cat fish?
(*a*) Catla catla (*b*) Labeo rohita (*c*) Cirrihina mrigala (*d*) Wallago attu

22. Which one of the following blood clotting factors is known as "Factor"?
(*a*) Factor X (*b*) Factor XII (*c*) Factor VIII (*d*) Factor II

23. Match **List I** (Connective tissue) with **List II** (Examples) and choose correct answer—

List I	***List II***
A. Loose connective tissue	I. Tendons Ligaments
B. Dense regular connective tissue	II. Mesenchyme
C. Embryonic connective tissue	III. Bone, Cartilage, blood
D. Specialized mature connective tissue	IV. Adipose tissue

(*a*) A-III, B-II, C-I, D-IV (*b*) A-IV, B-II, C-III, D-I
(*c*) A-IV, B-I, C-II, D-III (*d*) A-II, B-IV, C-I, D-III

24. If lipid is the respiratory substrate respiratory quotient will be—
(*a*) One (*b*) Less than one (*c*) More than one (*d*) Zero

25. In addition to thyroxin (T_4) and triiodothyronine (T_3) thyroid gland secretes—
(*a*) Thyroid stimulating hormone (*b*) Noradrenaline
(*c*) Calcitonin (*d*) Gonadotropic hormone

26. In tissue culture, Callus is—
(a) A tissue that forms embryo
(b) An insoluble carbohydrate
(c) A tissue that grows to form embryoid
(d) An unorganized activity dividing mass of cell manitained tissue culture

27. What is true about Bt-toxin?
(a) The concerned bacteria has antitoxin.
(b) The inactive protoxin gets converted into active form in the pest gut due to its alkaline pH.
(c) The activated toxin enters the overies of pest to sterilize it and thus prevents its multiplication.
(d) Bt-toxin protein exists as active toxin in bacteria.

28. The proteolytic enzyme of the stomach is—
(a) Pepsin (b) Bile (c) Lactose (d) Amylase

29. An increase in concentration of the toxicants which are neither metabolized nor excreted and get deposited at successive trophic levels is called—
(a) Biomonitoring (b) Biomineralization (c) Biomagnification (d) Bioremediation

30. The use of micro-organisms to degrade environmental pollutants is called—
(a) Microremediation
(b) Nanoremediation
(c) Bioremediation
(d) Biocoenose

31. What is the mean, median and mode of the following data?

Class interval	*Freqency*
30 – 40	18
40 – 50	37
50 – 60	45
60 – 70	27
70 – 80	15
80 – 90	08

	$(\overline{X})$	(M)	(Z)
(a)	55.53,	53.08,	54.44
(b)	54.44,	53.08,	55.53
(c)	53.08,	54.44,	55.53
(d)	55.53,	54.44,	53.08

32. Lactoferrin gene has been used for commercial production of which of the following transgenic animals?
(a) Cow (b) Mice (c) Fish (d) Chicken

33. Relation between demand and price is—
(a) Positive correlation
(b) Negative correlation
(c) Perfect correlation
(d) No correlation

34. Agro-forestry system involving agricultural and forest crops—
(*a*) Agri-silviculture system (*b*) Silvi-pastoral system
(*c*) Horti-pastoral system (*d*) Agri-silvi-postoral system

35. Which of the following is a bunch type variety of groundnut?
(*a*) AH-334 (*b*) RG-382 (*c*) RG-425 (*d*) Girnar-2

36. Formula for standard deviation is—

(*a*) $\sigma = \frac{\sum(X \times \overline{X})}{N}$ (*b*) $\sigma = \sqrt{\frac{\sum(X - \overline{X})^2}{N}}$

(*c*) $\sigma = \sqrt{\frac{\sum(X \times \overline{X})}{N}}$ (*d*) $\sigma = \sqrt{\frac{\sum X}{N}}$

37. Which variety of Mango is susceptible to spongy tissue?
(*a*) Chausa (*b*) Fazli (*c*) Alphonso (*d*) Gulab Khas

38. Which of the following variety of onion produces white coloured bulbs?
(*a*) Bhima Raj (*b*) Bhima Shubhra (*c*) Pusa Madhavi (*d*) Arka Kalyan

39. 'Arka Rakshak' is an important variety of—
(*a*) Brinjal (*b*) Chilli (*c*) Tomato (*d*) Okra

40. As per basic Animal Husbandry Statistics DAHD & F, GOI milk production in India in the year 2017-18 was __________ million tonnes.
(*a*) 140 – 150 (*b*) 130 – 139 (*c*) 160 – 165 (*d*) 170 – 180

41. 'Pant Ragini' is variety of—
(*a*) Cumin (*b*) Fennel (*c*) Fenugreek (*d*) Coriander

42. Parasitic weed associated with mustard is—
(*a*) Striga (*b*) Orobanche (*c*) Cuscuta (*d*) Loranthus

43. Rajasthan ranks __________ in per capita milk availability in India (2017-18).
(*a*) 1st (*b*) 2nd (*c*) 3rd (*d*) 4th

44. In India, maximum amount of milk is utilized in __________
(*a*) Ghee making (*b*) Khoa making (*c*) Liquid milk (*d*) Powder making

45. Gestation period of cow is ________ days.
(*a*) 300 – 320 (*b*) 280 – 285 (*c*) 150 – 200 (*d*) 250 – 260

46. Rate of feeding colostrum to a new born calf is —
(*a*) 10 % of the body weight (*b*) 20 % of the body weight
(*c*) 30 % of the body weight (*d*) 40 % of the body weight

47. Normally __________ is used for packaging of butter.
(*a*) Parchment paper (PVP) (*b*) Polyethylene
(*c*) Aluminium foil (*d*) Polypropylene

48. Causative agent of haemorrhagic septicaemia is __________
(*a*) *Pasteurella multocida* (*b*) *Clostridium chauvoei*
(*c*) *Brucella abortus* (*d*) *Mycobacterium bovis*

49. The husk : seed ratio of 'Isabgol' by weight is—
(a) 25 : 75 (b) 50 : 50 (c) 75 : 25 (d) 40 : 60

50. Microbes that have beneficial effect on health of the consumers are called ________.
(a) Prebiotics (b) Probiotics (c) Synbiotics (d) Antibiotics

51. Food Safety and Standards Authority of India (FSSAI) Act in parliament was established in the year ________ and impemented in the year ________.
(a) 1954 and 1979 (b) 1995 and 2015 (c) 2006 and 2011 (d) 1984 and 2002

52. Pneumonia in animals occurs due to faulty administration of drugs is ________.
(a) Interstitial pneumonia (b) Gangrenous pneumonia
(c) Parasitic pneumonia (d) Drenching pneumonia

53. Which of the following is used as 'Ethylene scrubber' in storage of fruits?
(a) Potassium permanganate (b) Calcium chloride
(c) Sodium chloride (d) Citric acid

54. Indian Food Safety & Standards Act, 2006 contains ________ number of sections—
(a) 83 (b) 97 (c) 101 (d) 113

55. Fat content of whipping cream ranges from ________.
(a) 10 – 20 % (b) 15 – 20 % (c) 30 – 40 % (d) 40 – 50 %

56. The most commonly used chemical for preservation in food is—
(a) Sodium Benzoate (b) Sodium Bromide
(c) Potassium Permanganate (d) Sodium Phosphate

57. According to standards, a fruit squash should contain at least ______ fruit juice/pulp.
(a) 0 – 05 % (b) 15 – 20 % (c) 5 – 10 % (d) 20 – 30 %

58. The type of Can which is used for canning of acidic red fruits—
(a) R–enamel (b) C–enamel (c) S–enamel (d) A–enamel

59. The enzymatic browning in cut surface of fruits and vegetables is due to—
(a) Oxidation of phenols (b) Maillard reaction
(c) Caramelization (d) Putrefaction

60. Which of the following is a 'Climacteric fruit'-grows between 16 – 26 °C and in soil pH 6-7?
(a) Strawberry (b) Grapes (c) Avocado (d) Lime

61. Remains of fortification have been recovered from which chalcolithic site?
(a) Ahar (b) Balathal (c) Ganeshwer (d) Gilund

62. "AGMARK Act 1937" comes under—
(a) Department of Consumer Affairs, Government of India
(b) Directorate of Marketing and Inspection
(c) Department of Agriculture and Cooperation
(d) Department of Legal Meterology

63. During the fiscal year 2022, which state produced the largest share of vegetable in India?
(a) Maharashtra (b) Uttar Pradesh (c) West Bengal (d) Bihar

64. Which of the following committee is not related with poverty?
(*a*) Rangrajan Committee (*b*) Lakdawala Committee
(*c*) Tendulker Committee (*d*) R. Swaminathan Committee

65. Second Nuclear Power Plant of Rajasthan is proposed at—
(*a*) Jodhpur (*b*) Bikaner (*c*) Banswara (*d*) Alwar

66. FSSAI is the Regulating Body for Food Safety in India. In the October 2019, on the occasion of World Food Day FSSAI started many initiatives, which of the following was not among them?
(*a*) Food Safety Mitra Scheme was launched.
(*b*) A smart jacket was introduced for field staff to keep their devices.
(*c*) A reusable cloth bag was introduced to replace plastic bag for shopping.
(*d*) To increase shelf life of processed food, an agreement was executed with an American firm.

67. At Yokohama, Japan FAO has its : —
(*a*) Headquarters (*b*) Regional Office
(*c*) Sub-regional Office (*d*) Liaison Office

68. Read the following statement about Abiy Ahmad Ali and choose the correct answer code:
(A) He is the President of Ethiopia who earlier served as an army officer.
(B) He was awarded the Nobel Peace Prize 2019.
(*a*) Only (A) statement is correct.
(*b*) Only (B) statement is correct.
(*c*) Neither (A) or (B) statement is correct.
(*d*) Both (A) and (B) are correct.

69. The place where the Indian Prime Minister and American President met in September 2019 is—
(*a*) India (*b*) France (*c*) Germany (*d*) America

70. NCERT has started a national level programme for the holistic advancement of school heads and teachers. The abbreviated name of this programme is—
(*a*) PRATISHTHA (*b*) PARIKSHA (*c*) NISHTHA (*d*) ISHTHA

71. An aircraft of Indian Air Force crashed in Gwalior on 25 September 2019.— The aircraft was the
(*a*) Mirage – 2000 (*b*) Sukhoi Su – 30 (*c*) MiG – 21 (*d*) MiG – 29

72. Identify the city, where the largest Business Incubator of India, "Bhamashah Techno Hub" has been established by the Government of Rajasthan—
(*a*) Jodhpur (*b*) Jhalawar (*c*) Ajmer (*d*) Jaipur

73. Agricultural and Processed Food Products Export Development Act which was passed by Parliament in December 1985, came into effect from—
(*a*) 13th February, 1986 (*b*) 13th January, 1986
(*c*) 1st March, 1986 (*d*) 1st April, 1986

74. BIS Hallmark is used as an Indian Standard for : —
(*a*) Industrial products (*b*) Agricultural products
(*c*) Medical products (*d*) Gold and Silver products

75. pH of milk is—

(*a*) 7.4 (*b*) 6.8 (*c*) 6.4 (*d*) 5.0

76. pKa value of Acetic Acid is—

(*a*) 4.76 (*b*) 5.65 (*c*) 3.76 (*d*) 3.67

77. Value of K_W at 298 K is—

(*a*) 1×10^{-14} M^2 (*b*) 1×10^{-7} M (*c*) 1×10^{-14} M (*d*) 1×10^{-9} M^2

78. Unit of rate constant for second order reaction is—

(*a*) S^{-1} (*b*) mol L^{-1} S^{-1} (*c*) mol^{-1} L S^{-1} (*d*) mol L S^{-1}

79. The molecular geometry of ClF_3 is—

(*a*) Linear (*b*) Tetrahedral (*c*) T-shape (*d*) Bend

80. $R-\overset{\overset{O}{||}}{C}-H + 2H \xrightarrow{\text{Pt or Pd}}$ main product—

(*a*) $R-\underset{\underset{H}{|}}{CH}-OH$ (*b*) $R-\overset{\overset{R}{|}}{\underset{\underset{R}{|}}{C}}-OH$ (*c*) $R-\overset{\overset{R}{|}}{\underset{\underset{H}{|}}{C}}-OH$ (*d*) R – O – R

81. 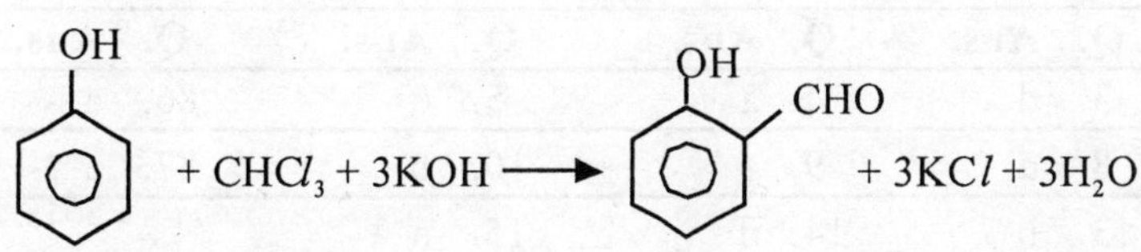

Above reaction is—

(*a*) Reimer-Tiemann (*b*) Kolbe's reaction

(*c*) Friedel-Craft's reaction (*d*) Williamson synthesis

82. Chemical formula of Gammaxane is—

(*a*) C_6Cl_6 (*b*) $C_6H_5Cl_7$ (*c*) $C_6H_4Cl_8$ (*d*) $C_6H_6Cl_6$

83. $R-\overset{\overset{O}{||}}{C}-O-H + H-O-\overset{\overset{O}{||}}{C}-R \xrightarrow[\text{Conc.}H_2SO_4]{P_2O_5/}$ Main product is—

(*a*) Anhydride (*b*) Ketone (*c*) Carboxylic Acid (*d*) Aldehyde

84. Tilden reagent is—

(*a*) Nitrosyl chloride (*b*) Acetyl chloride

(*c*) Pyridine (*d*) Per acid

85. Chemical structure of Pinacol is—

(*a*) 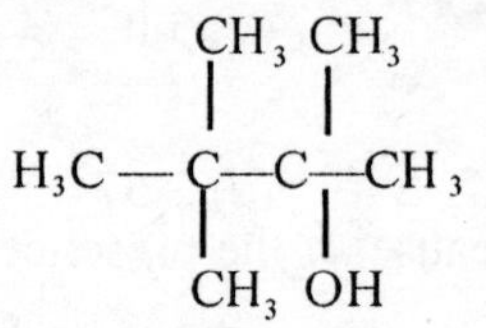

(*b*) 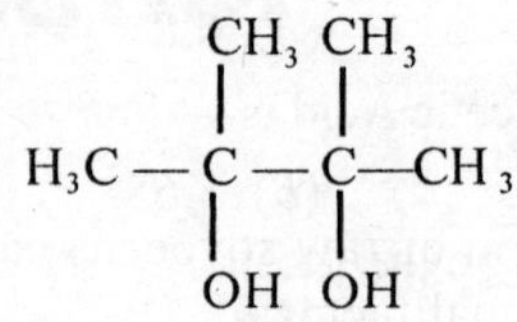

(*c*) 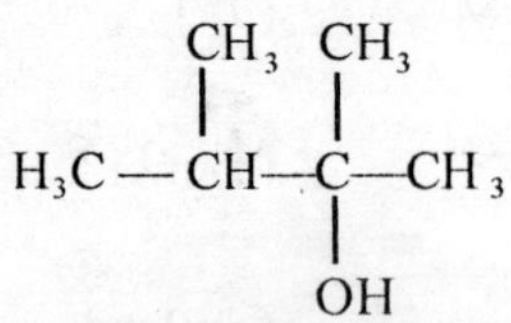

(*d*) 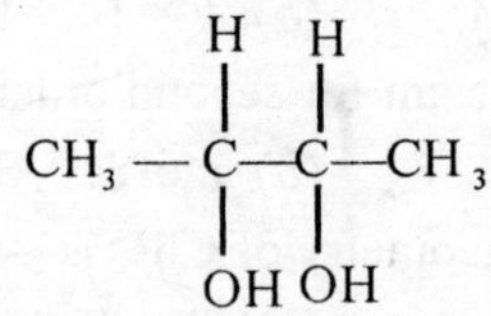

86. Which international commission is responsible for the publication of microbial load in foods?

(a) ICMSF (b) HACCP (c) FDA (d) FSSAI

87. Which one of the following microbial indicators is detected and correlates with food quality in fruit juices?

(a) Diacetyl (b) Putrescine (c) Histamine (d) Lactic acid

ANSWER KEY

(Model paper 8)

Q. Ans.	Q. Ans.	Q. Ans.	Q. Ans.	Q. Ans.	Q. Ans.
1. d	2. b	3. d	4. a	5. c	86. a
6. c	7. d	8. a	9. c	10. b	87. a
11. a	12. a	13. b	14. d	15. a	
16. a	17. b	18. a	19. c	20. b	
21. d	22. b	23. c	24. b	25. c	
26. d	27. b	28. a	29. c	30. c	
31. d	32. a	33. c	34. a	35. d	
36. b	37. c	38. b	39. c	40. d	
41. c	42. b	43. b	44. b	45. b	
46. a	47. a	48. a	49. a	50. b	
51. c	52. d	53. a	54. c	55. c	
56. a	57. b	58. d	59. a	60. c	
61. c	62. b	63. b	64. d	65. c	
66. a	67. d	68. d	69. d	70. c	
71. c	72. d	73. a	74. d	75. b	
76. a	77. c	78. a	79. c	80. a	
81. a	82. d	83. a	84. b	85. b	

MODEL PAPERS-9

(Kerala Food Safety Officer Exam, 2015)

1. Consumption of raw soybeans can be harmful to health because of the presence of following anti-nutritional factor:
   (A) Phytic acid (B) Tannins (C) Oxalates (D) Trypsin inhibitor
2. In a standard fruit jam preparation the content of total soluble solids should not be less than:
   (A) 68% w/w (B) 45% w/w (C) 65% w/w (D) 70% w/w
3. The safe level of irradiation for foods, which presents no toxicological hazard is:
   (A) 5.0 kGy (B) 10.0 kGy (C) 7.0 kGy (D) 25.0 kGy
4. Subjecting rice to higher degree of polishing is associated with following:
   (A) Better nutritional density and easy digestibility
   (B) Better glycemic index and suitability for diabetics
   (C) Lowered nutritional and better cooking characteristics
   (D) Higher bioavailable nutrients and lowered sensory quality
5. The browning occurring in cut apples on aeration is due to the presence of:
   (A) Polyphenolases (B) Oxidoreductases (C) Polymeric oxidases (D) Polyhydrogenases
6. FSSAI stands for:
   (A) Fire Safety and Security Association of India
   (B) Food Safety and Standards Authority of India
   (C) Fire Safety and Standards Arrangements Incorporation
   (D) Food Safety and Security Association of India
7. Identify the correct group of stimulating constituents present in tea :
   (A) Theobromine, triphylline, catechol (B) Caffein, tricantenol, trimethylamine
   (C) Theonitrile, caffeicol, theophylline (D) Caffeine, theobromine, theophylline
8. Acceptable daily intake level of additives is derived from following :
   (A) No observed adverse effect level of compound and uncertainty factor
   (B) Level at which toxicity may not occur in humans
   (C) Levels likely to be used in foods
   (D) Chemical nature of the compound
9. Identify the cluster of essential fatty acids for humans from the following :
   (A) Myristic, arachidonic and capric acids (B) Linolenic, linoleic and arachidonic acid
   (C) Stearic, malic and acetic acid (D) Linolenic, stearic and cholic acid
10. Aseptic packaging refers to :
    (A) Use of sterile packaging containers
    (B) Heating the food to make it sterile and then pack
    (C) Packaging sterile food in sterile atmosphere in sterile packaging
    (D) Using ultra high temperature for processing

11. The latest indicator organism for proper pasteurisation is :
(A) Coxiella burnetti (B) Mycobacterium tuberculosis
(C) Bacillus anthrasis (D) FMD virus
12. Rasagolla is prepared using :
(A) Paneer (B) Channa (C) Khoa (D) Condensed Milk
13. Aseptic packaging is used after which among the following processing method?
(A) Pasteurisation (B) UHT Pasteurisation (C) Freezing (D) Drying
14. The water percentage of cow milk is approximately :
(A) 80% (B) 90% (C) 87% (D) 50%
15. Which among the following practice reduces the occurrence of Mastitis?
(A) Feeding concentrate (B) Urea molasses lick
(C) Teat dipping (D) Automatic water bowl
16. Which among the following is used to test fat in milk?
(A) Lactometer (B) Anemometer (C) CRO (D) Milkotester
17. The bacterial culture used to prepare Yoghurt contains Streptococcus thermophilus and
(A) Lactobacillus bulagaricus (B) Yersinia enterocolitica
(C) Alcaligenes viscolactis (D) Escherichia coli
18. Which among the following is used to sterilize milk cans in dairies?
(A) Steam (B) Iodophore solution (C) Autoclaving (D) All the above
19. The base material for preparing Shrikhand is :
(A) Chakka (B) Channa (C) Curd (D) Cheese
20. 'Outlines of Dairy Technology' is written by :
(A) Jagadish Prasad (B) N.S.R. Shastry (C) Sukumar De (D) Tufail Ahamed
21. The pink colour characteristic of cured meat is due to :
(A) Myoglobin (B) Nitrosyl myoglobin
(C) Haemoglobin (D) Nitrosyl haemochrome
22. Natural casing for sausage preparation is derived from :
(A) Intestinal submucosa (B) Collagen (C) Intestinal mucosa (D) Cellulose
23. PSE condition of pork is caused due to :
(A) Short term pre-slaughter stress (B) Chronic stress
(C) Rapid decline of muscle pH (D) Both (A) and (C)
24. The vitamin which is ABSENT in chicken egg :
(A) Vitamin C (B) Vitamin B_{12} (C) Vitamin A (D) Vitamin E
25. The bacterium known as "terror of the deep" due to the sea food poisoning it causes with the highest fatality rate of any food borne bacterium :
(A) *Salmonella enteritidis* (B) *Vibrio vulnificus*
(C) *Vibrio parahaemolyticus* (D) *Clostridium botulinum*

26. The stunning method recommended for slaughter of adult cattle :
(A) Electric stunning (B) Penetrative captive bolt pistol
(C) Carbon dioxide gas stunning (D) All of the above

27. The dressing percentage for pigs is approximately :
(A) 53% (B) 65% (C) 75% (D) 88%

28. ________ is used for testing the effectiveness of bleeding of carcass.
(A) Sodium nitrate (B) Malachite green
(C) Sodium ascorbate (D) All of the above

29. The larval nematode worm seen in striated muscle of pigs infecting human beings after ingestion of such infected pork is :
(A) *Trichinella spiralis* (B) *Toxoplasma gondii*
(C) *Tichuristrichiura* (D) *Taenia solium*

30. Pick out the WRONG statement:
(A) The first transgenic cow, "Rosie", produced human protein-enriched milk
(B) Green rot in eggs is mainly caused by *Pseudomonas fluorescens*
(C) Bloom is the term used for preservation of meat using salt
(D) Pork and poultry meat are more susceptible to rancidity as they are richer in unsaturated fatty acids than other meats

31. In a complaint against several accused, if the complainant withdraws his complaint against one accused, the Magistrate can :
(A) Convict that particular accused
(B) Acquit all the accused
(C) Acquit the particular accused against whom the complaint is so withdrawn
(D) Convict all the accused

32. An application for bail under Section 438 Cr.P.C. can be filed before :
(A) Any Court (B) First Class Magistrate Court/Metropolitan Court
(C) Trial Court (D) High Court or Court of Session

33. In a trial before a Court of Session, Prosecution shall be conducted by :
(A) Magistrate (B) Public Prosecutor (C) Amicus Curie (D) Advocate General

34. Private Complaint can be filed before the Court under Section ________ of Cr.P.C.
(A) 190 (B) 191 (C) 195 (D) 313

35. Examination of Complainant by the Magistrate taking cognizance of an offence is not required, if :
(A) He is a public servant (B) He is private complainant
(C) He is a doctor (D) A Court has made the complaint

36. Admissibility of documents procured by illegal means under Indian Evidence Act is:
(A) Admissible (B) Not Admissible
(C) Admissible if relevant and its genuineness proved (D) None of these

37. Primary Evidence under Sec.61 of Indian Evidence Act means :
(A) Certified copies. of documents
(B) Photostat copies attested by the Gazetted Officer
(C) Original documents produced before the Court
(D) None of these
38. Unlicensed sale of food shall be punishable with:
(A) Imprisonment upto 6 months
(B) Imprisonment upto 6 months and fine upto Rs. 5 lakhs
(C) Fine upto Rs. 2 lakhs
(D) Imprisonment upto 1 year and fine upto Rs. 10 lakhs
39. Death caused due to consumption of any food purchased from a seller, is liable to be compensated with :
(A) Not less than Rs. 5 lakhs (B) Not less than Rs. 10 lakhs
(C) Not exceeding Rs. 3 lakhs (D) Rs. 7 lakhs
40. The maximum penalty to be imposed on a person who sells any food which is not in compliance with the provisions / regulations of Food Safety Act, is :
(A) Rs. 10 lakhs (B) Not Exceeding Rs.2 lakhs
(C) Not Exceeding Rs.5 lakhs (D) Rs.25,000
41. Energy yield per unit weight of food is known as :
(A) Calorific value (B) Energy density (C) Both (A) & (B) (D) None of these
42. R.Q. of fats is less than carbohydrates because :
(A) Fats have lesser oxygen content (B) Carbohydrates have lesser oxygen content
(C) Fats have higher oxygen content (D) None of these
43. Specific Dynamic Action refers to :
(A) Energy required for physical activity
(B) Increased heat production following intake of food
(C) Extra energy for exercising
(D) Energy requirement by a person for dynamic activites
44. ________ is an essential amino acid.
(A) Aspartic acid (B) Glutamic acid (C) Proline (D) Threonine
45. Which of the following has the lowest iodine number?
(A) Soybean oil (B) Cotton seed oil (C) Beef fat (D) Corn oil
46. Scurvy can be cured by the administration of :
(A) Folic acid (B) Glutamic acid (C) Fumaric acid (D) Ascorbic acid
47. Dietary fibre represents the following nutrient group :
(A) Lipids (B) Carbohydrates (C) Proteins (D) None of these
48. The one which is not used as a clarifier :
(A) Phosphoric acid (B) Lead nitrate
(C) Phosphotungstic acid (D) Lead acetate

49. Ionisation technique not used in mass spectrometry :
(A) Fast atom bombardment (B) Field desorption
(C) Laser desorption (D) Radiation
50. Inhomogeneity of flow velocities and path lengths around packing particles in column chromatography leads to:
(A) Partition (B) Retention (C) Eddy diffusion (D) None of these
51. The protective agent used in cryopreservation of bacterial cells :
(A) EDTA (B) DMSO (C) SDS (D) NADP
52. Staining of specimens using uranyl acetate has been used in :
(A) Atomic force microscope (B) Confocal Scanning Laser Microscope
(C) Transmission Electron Microscope (D) Phase Contrast Microscope
53. Which of the following is a type of food intoxication?
(A) Botulism (B) Salmonellosis (C) Cholera (D) Gastroenteritis
54. *Ashbya gossypii* is used commercially for the production of :
(A) L-glutamic acid (B) Invertase (C) Cyanocobolamine (D) Riboflavin
55. Enrichment of lakes due to high concentration of organic nutrients :
(A) Humus formation (B) Biomagnification
(C) Eutrophication (D) Nitrosification
56. The sanitizer commonly used for treatment of drinking water :
(A) Sodium nitrate (B) Sodium hypochlorite
(C) Sodium sorbate (D) Sodium metabisulphite
57. Which of the following is a semi perishable food?
(A) Fish (B) Egg (C) Milk (D) Potato
58. Temperature used in HTST pasteurization is :
(A) 161°F (B) 145°F (C) 154°F (D) 175°F
59. Which of the following is not involved in the fermentation of Sauerkraut?
(A) *Leuconostoc mesenteroides* (B) *Lactobacillus plantarum*
(C) *Leuconostocdelbruekii* (D) *Streptococcus faecalis*
60. Enzyme used for the clarification of fruit juice:
(A) Invertase (B) Pectinase (C) Protease (D) Lipase
61. Tapping and aroma are maturity indices of :
(A) Jack fruit (B) Water melon (C) Tomato (D) Mango
62. Evaporative cooling system saturated with water is used in :
(A) Onion storage (B) Zero energy cool chamber
(C) Cold stores (D) Irradiation
63. "W" and "O" emulsions are used in:
(A) Storage of fruits and vegetables (B) Field spray of fruits and vegetables
(C) Waxing of fruits and vegetables (D) None of the above

64. The most destructive of all field rats is :
(A) *Mus booduga* (B) *Rattus rattus*
(C) *Rattus norvegicus* (D) *Bandicota bengalensis*

65. Aflatoxin is the mycotoxin produced by :
(A) Aspergillus flavus (B) Fusarium spp.
(C) Claviceps purpurea (D) Aspergillus clavatus

66. Khapra beetle is a serious pest of stored :
(A) Rice (B) Wheat (C) Pulses (D) Fruits

67. Most widely used chronic poison in rodent control :
(A) Thallium sulphate (B) Barium carbonate
(C) Warfarin (D) Zinc phosphide

68. *Callosobruchus chinensis* is a storage pest of :
(A) Wheat (B) Rice (C) Fruits (D) Pulses

69. Commercially the most viable mushroom world over is :
(A) Button mushroom (B) Oyster mushroom
(C) Paddy straw mushroom (D) Milky mushroom

70. The best disinfectant for the empty store is the use of :
(A) DDVP (B) Aluminium phosphide
(C) Malathion (D) Gamma-BHC

71. Temple Entry Proclamation in Travancore issued on :
(A) 12 Nov. 1936 (B) 24 Nov. 1936
(C) 12 Jan. 1936 (D) 24 Jan. 1936

72. Which of the following story was written by Lalithambika Antharjanam?
(A) Mudra (B) Thamarathoni
(C) Gosayi Paranja Katha (D) Marappavakal

73. Revolt of 1857 was started at :
(A) Delhi (B) Meerut (C) Nepal (D) Kanpur

74. "Kaneerum Kinavum" was the autobiography of :
(A) E.V. Krishnapillai (B) G. Sankarakurup
(C) V.T. Bhattathirippadu (D) Changampuzha

75. Who was the founder of Samathva Samagam?
(A) Ayyan Kali (B) Sree Narayana Guru
(C) Dr.Palpu (D) Vaikunda Swamikal

76. Leader of Bardoli Sathyagraha:
(A) Nehru (B) Sardar Vallabhai Patel
(C) Gandhiji (D) Dr. Ambedkar

77. Who was the first General Secretary of Nair Service Society?
(A) C. Kesavan (B) K. Kelappan
(C) T.K. Madhavan (D) Mannathu Padmanabhan

78. Who was known as the father of Local self Government in India?
(A) Lord Rippon (B) Lord Litton
(C) Lord Minto (D) Lord Dalhousie

79. Who was the founder of Indian National Congress?
(A) Lord Duffrin (B) A.O. Hume
(C) Dadabhai Naoroji (D) Gandhiji

80. Who was known as "Kerala Gandhi"?
(A) A.K. Gopalan (B) M.C. Joseph
(C) K. Kelappan (D) P.K.Chathan Master

81. What is the next number in the series 6, 10, 9, 13, 12, ______?
(A) 15 (B) 6 (C) 16 (D) 11

82. Sum to infinity of the series 1/2 + 1/4 + 1/8 +.....?
(A) 1 (B) 1/4 (C) 2 (D) infinity

83. 2015 September 24 is Monday. After 61 days it will be :
(A) Wednesday (B) Thursday (C) Tuesday (D) Saturday

84. Fill in the blanks :
Train :Staton : Ship : ______
(A) Sea (B) Harbour (C) Backwater (D) Anchor

85. Ajith is in the East of Manu and he is also in the north of Akshay. If Raju is in the South of Akshay, then in which direction of Ajith is Raju?
(A) North (B) South (C) South East (D) South West

86. Synonym of the word 'Nupitals' :
(A) Wedding (B) Death (C) Birth (D) Disaster

87. Which is the odd one in the following?
(A) 63 (B) 28 (C) 124 (D) 215

88. If the surface area of a cube is 294 cm^2, what is the volume of the cube?
(A) 216 (B) 176 (C) 294 (D) 343

89. If the word 'INSPECTOR' is coded as 987654321, what is the code for 'INSPECTION'?
(A) 987654321 (B) 9876543928
(C) 9876543289 (D) 9876543288

90. If $x/5 = y/3$ then $x + 5 : y + 3 =$:
(A) 3 : 5 (B) 5 : 7 (C) 5 : 3 (D) 7 : 5

91. This clause of FDA enacted in 1958 in response to public concern about cancer
(A) Delaney clause (B) PFA (C) HACCI (D) All of these

ANSWER KEY
(Model paper 9)

Q.	Ans.	Q.	Ans.	Q.	Ans.	Q.	Ans.	Q.	Ans.	Q.	Ans.	Q.	Ans.
1	d	16	d	31	c	46	d	61	a	76	b	91	a
2	a	17	a	32	d	47	b	62	b	77	d		
3	b	18	d	33	b	48	a	63	c	78	a		
4	c	19	a	34	a	49	d	64	d	79	b		
5	a	20	c	35	d	50	c	65	a	80	c		
6	b	21	d	36	c	51	b	66	b	81	c		
7	d	22	a	37	c	52	c	67	c	82	a		
8	a	23	d	38	b	53	a	68	d	83	d		
9	b	24	a	39	a	54	d	69	a	84	b		
10	c	25	b	40	c	55	c	70	b	85	d		
11	a	26	b	41	d	56	b	71	a	86	a		
12	b	27	c	42	a	57	d	72	c	87	b		
13	b	28	b	43	b	58	a	73	b	88	d		
14	c	29	a	44	d	59	c	74	c	89	b		
15	c	30	c	45	c	60	b	75	d	90	c		

EXPLANATION

Q.7. Best known is caffeine, a potent stimulant that you can also get from coffee, soft drinks, and energy drinks. Tea also contains two substances related to caffeine: theobromine and theophylline. Finally, it provides a rather unique amino acid called L-theanine, which has some very interesting effects on the brain.

Q. 11. Pasteurization defined by the Codex Alimentarius Committee for Food Hygiene as ‘a microbial heat treatment aimed at reducing the number of any pathogenic microorganisms in milk and liquid milk products, if present, to a level at which they do not constitute a significant health hazard. Pasteurization conditions are designed to effectively destroy the organisms *Mycobacterium tuberculosis* and *Coxiella burnetii*. C. burnetii is the cause of Q fever, recognized in 1935 as an occupational disease for workers in Australia. It is new type of Rickettsia isolated from tiles, that was able to pan through Filters The first description was published in 1925.

Q.16. **Milko Tester:** The instrument is used for fat determination in milk. It can analyse 80-120 samples/ hour and require very small sample of milk (1.6 ml). The instrument gives results which are comparable to reference method. The instrument determine the fat content on the basis of scattering of light by a diluted sample of milk. Calcium chelating agent eliminate the turbidity caused by the casein micelles, hence the scattering of light is due to the presence of fat globules. The size and number of fat globules influence the result therefore the sample is homogenized in a 4-stage homogenizer to reduce the size of the globules to a specific size.

Q. 21. Nitric oxide binds to myoglobin and changes fresh meat color to a bright red known as nitroslymyoglobin. **Subsequent heating of meat containing the NO-myoglobin complex causes chemical reactions and changes myoglobin to a compound known as nitrosylhemochrome.** This produces the characteristic pink color of cured meats.

Q. 23. **Pale, Soft, Exudative meat**, or **PSE meat**, describes a carcass quality condition known to occur in pork, beef, and poultry. It is characterized by an abnormal color, consistency, and water holding capacity, making the meat dry and unattractive to consumers. The condition is believed to be caused by abnormal muscle metabolism following slaughter, due to an altered rate of glycolysis and a low pH within the muscle fibers. A mutation point in the ryanodine receptor gene (*RYR1*) in pork, associated to stress levels prior to slaughter are known to increase the incidence of PSE meat. Although the term "soft" may look positive, it refers to raw meat. When cooked, there is higher water loss and the final product is hard, not juicy.

Q. 42. Respiratory Quotient," the Ratio of Carbon Dioxide Production to Oxygen Utilization, can Be Used to Estimate Fat and Carbohydrate Utilization

When carbohydrates are metabolized with oxygen, exactly one carbon dioxide molecule is formed for each molecule of oxygen consumed. This ratio of carbon dioxide output to oxygen usage is called the *respiratory quotient*, so the respiratory quotient for carbohydrates is 1.0. When fat is oxidized in the body's cells, an average of 70 carbon dioxide molecules are formed for each 100 molecules of oxygen consumed. The respiratory quotient for the metabolism of fat therefore averages 0.70. When proteins are oxidized by the cells, the average respiratory quotient is 0.80. The reason that the respiratory quotients for fats and proteins are lower than those for carbohydrates is that a portion of the oxygen metabolized with these foods is required to combine with the excess hydrogen atoms present in their molecules, so less carbon dioxide is formed in relation to the oxygen used.

Q.43. **Meaning of Specific Dynamic Action (S.D.A):** All foodstuffs, after being ingested, increase the rate of heat production though the subject is in a basal state. This increased heat production due to ingestion above the basal metabolic rate (B.M.R) is known as Specific Dynamic Action (S.D.A) or calorigenic action of foods. It can be expressed at cost of metabolism of the various food substances.

Q. 51. **DMSO :-** Dimethyl Sulfoxide is used as protection agent because of its membrane penetrating and water displacement properties. It is added to cell culture media to reduce ice formation and thereby prevent cell death.

Q. 54. The industrial production of riboflavin mostly relies on the microbial fermentation of flavinogenic microorganisms and *Ashbya gossypii* is the main industrial producer of the vitamin. Accordingly, bioengineering strategies aimed at increasing riboflavin production in *A. gossypii* are highly valuable for industry.

Q.59. Historically, four species of lactic acid bacteria (LAB) have been identified as organisms that are present in sauerkraut fermentations: *Leuconostoc mesenteroides*, *Lactobacillus brevis*, *Pediococcus pentosaceus*, and *Lactobacillus plantarum*.

Q. 63. When oil and water are mixed powerfully, they form either oil-in-water (o/w) or water-in-oil (w/o) emulsions. In o/w emulsions, oil is dispersed in a continuous water phase, while in w/o emulsions, **water droplets are dispersed in oil.**

MODEL PAPERS-10

(Gujarat Food Safety Officer Exam, 2021)

1. Adulteration of Maida with stones and sand can be inferred by—
(*a*) Total Ash (*b*) Acid insolube ash (*c*) Total solids (*d*) Crude fibre

2. Unsafe food means—
1. Injurious to health 2. Genetically modified
3. Presence of any colouring matter other than specified
4. Containing extraneous matter
(*a*) 2, 3 and 4 (*b*) 1, 2 and 3 (*c*) 1, 3 and 4 (*d*) 1, 2 and 4

3. The Headquarters of world Health Organization is based at ________.
(*a*) Rome (*b*) Paris (*c*) Geneva (*d*) New York

4. The heaviest naturally occurring elements is—
(*a*) Thorium (*b*) Uranium (*c*) Mercury (*d*) Polonium

5. ________ food drink may contain added "Caffeine"—
(*a*) Tea (*b*) Coffee (*c*) Chicory (*d*) Energy Drink

6. Which of the following is not a bacterium?
(*a*) *Pandoraea* (*b*) *Pantoea* (*c*) *Moraxella* (*d*) *Mucor*

7. As per the provisions of the FSS (Food Products Standards and Food Additives) Regulations, 2011 ____ solvent extracted flour can contain lowest protein content.—
(*a*) Solvent Extracted Coconut Flour (*b*) Solvent Extracted Groundnut Flour
(*c*) Solvent Extracted Soybean Flour (*d*) Solvent Extracted Sesame seed Flour

8. The atomic number of an element represents.—
(*a*) Number of neutrons in the nucleus (*b*) Number of protons and neutrons in the nucleus
(*c*) The valency of the element (*d*) Number of protons in the nucleus

9. The acidity of the extracted fat pressed from Grated Desiccated Coconut is expressed as ________.
(*a*) Oleic acid (*b*) Palmitic acid (*c*) Lauric acid (*d*) Acetic acid

10. Glucose molecules are linked with _____ linkage in cellulose.
(*a*) β 1-4 (*b*) β 1-6 (*c*) α 1-4 (*d*) α 1-6

11. Stable, liquid form of water is due to the presence of ________.
(*a*) Van der waals forces (*b*) Ionic bond
(*c*) Covalent bond (*d*) Hydrogen bond

12. Size and shape of the grains is measured by—
(*a*) Spindle (*b*) Scale (*c*) Stalagnometer (*d*) Vernier Cliper

13. A person handling less than ______ litres per day milk would be considered as "Petty Food Manufacturer" per FSS (Licensing and Registration of Food Businesses), Regulations 2011.
(*a*) 100 (*b*) 500 (*c*) 200 (*d*) 1000

14. Reverse of swelling of gei is known as.—
(*a*) Sorption (*b*) Thixotropy (*c*) Syneresis (*d*) Leakage

15. The sodium content in table salt is ______.
(a) 60.66 % (b) 39.34 % (c) 22.99 % (d) 35.5 %
16. NIN is situated at.—
(a) New Dehli (b) Bhopal (c) Hyderabad (d) Bangalore
17. The Agricltural and Processed Food Products Export Development Authority Act was promulgated in the year.—
(a) 1971 (b) 2006 (c) 1998 (d) 1986
18. pH value of acidic solution is.—
(a) < 7 (b) > 7 (c) 7 (d) 0
19. Basicity of sulphuric acid is.—
(a) 1 (b) 2 (c) 4 (d) 3
20. Which of the following enzyme is basis for checking the adequacy of pasteurization?
(a) Phosphatase (b) Catalase (c) Lipase (d) Peroxidase
21. Which is statement is not true considering provision for proprietary food as per FSS (Food Products Standards and Food Additives) Regulations, 2011?
(a) Proprietary food shall use only such additives and at such levels, as specified for the Category or Subcategory under Appendix A
(b) Proprietary food shall comply with the microbiological requirements as specified in Appendix B
(c) Proprietary food includes function foods
(d) Proprietary food means an article of food that has not been standarlized under these regulations FSS (Food Products Standards and Food Additives) Regulations, 2011
22. Which of the following compounds does NOT undergo muterotation?
(a) Glucose (b) Sucrose (c) Ribose (d) Fructose
23. ISO 22000 was last revised in the year ______.
(a) 2020 (b) 2018 (c) 2019 (d) 2005
24. Red litmus paper is changed into blue in solution of.—
(a) Base (b) Acid (c) Salt (d) Neutral
25. __________ is used for determination of heavy metal contamination in food.
(a) Electrophoresis (b) X-ray diffraction
(c) ELISA (d) Inductively Coupled Plasma spectroscopy
26. According to the Act, which are the categories of food, which does not meet to the specified standards?
1. Sub-standard food 2. Mis-leading 3. Misbranded
4. Organic food 5. Unsafe food 6. Proprietary food
(a) 1, 2, 5 (b) 1, 3, 5 (c) 1, 3, 4 (d) All of the above
27. World Food Safety Day is celebrated on ______.
(a) 7th June (b) 5th June (c) 26th November (d) 28th February
28. Which of the following is not the authority regarding Food Safety in India?
(a) Food Safety Officer (b) Designated Offiicer
(c) Food Welfare Officer (d) Food Analyst

29. The red colour of beet is due to the presence of ______ pigment.
(*a*) Lycopene (*b*) Beta carotene (*c*) Curcumin (*d*) Betalain

30. Which of the following metals is not attacked by the environment?
(*a*) Silver (*b*) Copper (*c*) Gold (*d*) Iron

31. As per the Legal Metrology Rules the compounding charges for "Selling of products beyond MRP" are rupees.—
(*a*) 2000-10000 (*b*) 2000-5000 (*c*) 5000-25000 (*d*) 10000-25000

32. Which of the following is a primary standard for use in standardizing bases?
(*a*) Acetic acid (*b*) Sulfuric acid
(*c*) Potassium hydrogen phthalate (*d*) Ammonium hydroxide

33. As per the provisions of FSS (Laboratory and Sample Analysis) Regulations, 2011, the approximate quantity of sample to be sent to the Food Analyst for Whole Spices, Condiments and Mixed Masala is.—
(*a*) 500 g (*b*) 100 g (*c*) 200 g (*d*) 1000 g

34. The principal protein of rice is.—
(*a*) Oryzenin (*b*) Zein (*c*) Glutenin (*d*) Gliadin

35. Benzoic acid is an example of ______.
(*a*) Antioxidant (*b*) Salt (*c*) Chelating agent (*d*) Preservative

36. The heat stability of milk is judged by.—
(*a*) Freezing point (*b*) COB (Clot on Boiling) (*c*) MBRT (*d*) Lactometer

37. The FSSAI notified Referral laboratory for Gujarat state is situated at ______.
(*a*) Kolkata (*b*) Ghaziabad (*c*) Ahmedabad (*d*) Mysore

38. Which liquid has highest viscosity?
(*a*) Honey (*b*) Milk (*c*) Water (*d*) Cooking oil

39. The "Radura" logo is used for ______.
(*a*) Organic food (*b*) Fortified food (*c*) Imported food (*d*) Irradiated food

40. The principal sugar/carbohydrate in milk is.—
(*a*) Lactose (*b*) Glucose (*c*) Sucrose (*d*) Maltose

41. In the gas chromatograhpic technique, separation of molecule occurs on the basis of ______.
(*a*) Polarity (*b*) Molecular weight
(*c*) Polarity and Molecular weight (*d*) Chirality

42. Which of the following is the most common naturally occurring form in which silicon is found?
(*a*) Nitride (*b*) Sulfide (*c*) Oxide (*d*) Fluoride

43. As per the FSS (Labelling and Display) Regulations, 2020 mandatory declaration "Polyols may have laxative effect" shall be there on every package of polyol containing food, if it contains ______.
(*a*) 5 % or more polyol (*b*) 1 % or more polyol
(*c*) 10 % or more polyol (*d*) 2 % or more polyol

44. The yellow colour of milk products like ghee is due to.—
(*a*) Cholesterol (*b*) Carotene (*c*) Riboflavin (*d*) Xanthophylls

45. The maximum permissible limit for Free and Total gossypol is specified for ______ in FSS (Food Products Standard and Food Additives) Regulations, 2011.—
(*a*) Solvent Extracted Groundnut Flour
(*b*) Solvent Extracted coconut Flour
(*c*) Solvent Extracted Sesame Flour
(*d*) Solvent Extracted Cotton Seed Flour

46. Procedure by which an authoritative body gives formal recognition to an organization is competent to perform specific tasks is called as.—
(*a*) Accreditation (*b*) Certfication (*c*) Peer review (*d*) Inspection

47. The full form of NABL is ______.
(*a*) National Advisory Board for Testing and Calibration Laboratories
(*b*) National Analytical Board for Testing and Calibration Laboratories
(*c*) National Accreditation Board for Testing and Inspection Laboratories
(*d*) National Accreditation Board for Testing and Calibration Laboratories

48. _____ helps in identifying the product or brand and describe several things about the products.—
(*a*) Labelling (*b*) Packaging (*c*) Store branding (*d*) Supplying

49. As per the FSS (Food Products Standards and Food Additives) Regulations, 2011, the instant coffee chicory mixture the percent coffee shall not be less than ______.
(*a*) 50 % (*b*) 70 % (*c*) 51 % (*d*) 20 %

50. Kumiss is a type of.—
(*a*) Fermented milk
(*b*) Ice cream
(*c*) Cheese
(*d*) Fermented soy product

51. Which of the following statement regarding dietary fibre is not true?
(*a*) Their degree of polymerization (DP) is greater than 3.
(*b*) Psyllium husk is a source of dietary fibre.
(*c*) They are digestible by pancreatic enzyme.
(*d*) They are acted upon by gut microbiota.

52. In electrolysis current in solution is carried by.—
(*a*) Molecules (*b*) Atoms (*c*) Electrons (*d*) Ions

53. As per the provision of FSS (Food Products Standards and Food Additives) Regulations, 2011 total urea content in the milk shall not be more than _______ ppm.—
(*a*) 1000 (*b*) 70 (*c*) 700 (*d*) 800

54. Which of the following type of spectroscopy is a light scattering technique?
(*a*) Nuclear magnetic resonance
(*b*) Ultraviolet visible
(*c*) Raman
(*d*) Infrared

55. As per the provision of FSS (Food Products Standards and Food Additives) Regulations, 2011, yogurt starter culture must contain ______.
(*a*) *Lactobacillus bulgaricus, Streptococcus thermophilus*
(*b*) *Lactobacillus acidophilus, Streptococcus thermophilus*
(*c*) *Lactobacillus bulgaricus, Bifidobacterium bifidum*
(*d*) *Lactobacillus bulgaricus, Saccharomyces boulardii*

56. Which of the following is an example of non-climacteric fruit?
(*a*) Pear (*b*) Pomegranate (*c*) Kiwifruit (*d*) Sapota

57. This solution can be used to detect presence of strach in khoa, milk, etc.
(*a*) Nitric acid (*b*) Iodine (*c*) Wijs' (*d*) Fehling's

58. Kaizen means—
(*a*) Continuous production (*b*) Continuous management
(*c*) Continuous improvement (*d*) Continuous process

59. FSSAI has been mandated by the FSS Act, 2006 for performing the following functions, except ______.
(*a*) Framing of Regulations to lay down the Standards and guidelines in relation to articles of food.
(*b*) Laying down mechanisms and guidelines for accreditation of certification bodies engaged in certification of FSMS.
(*c*) Promotion of food export.
(*d*) Promotion general awareness about food safety and food standards.

60. Which is newly adopted system by FSSAI for licensing and registrations?
(*a*) FoSCoS (*b*) FLRS
(*c*) FSSAI_ Lic. Reg. Portal (*d*) Food Safety and registration for all

61. In a workplace conteen the frozen food shall be stored at ______.—
(*a*) –2 °C or below (*b*) –18 °C or below (*c*) –5 °C or below (*d*) – 10 °C or below

62. Minimum Requirement of degree brix (°brix) in apple juice is.—
(*a*) 14 (*b*) 12 (*c*) 15 (*d*) 16

63. The statement regarding PFA Act, 1954 is not true.—
(*a*) There is direct prosecution by court.
(*b*) Focus of the act is on finding adulteration.
(*c*) There is no provision for improvement notice.
(*d*) Implementation of GMP or GHP was mandatory.

64. Redox Dye used in the determination of Vitamin C in fruit juice is.—
(*a*) 2, 6 di chloro phenol indophenols (*b*) Resazurin
(*c*) Methylene blue (*d*) Resorufin

65. Karl Fischer titration methods is used for determination of ______.
(*a*) Fat (*b*) Acidity (*c*) Protein (*d*) Moisture

66. A substance intentionally added that preserves flavor and improves taste is called.—
(*a*) Food material (*b*) Food contaminat (*c*) Food adulteration (*d*) Food additive

67. As per the Consumer Protection Act, 2019, the rights of the consumer includes except______.
(*a*) The right to consumer awareness (*b*) The right to be informed
(*c*) The right to be heard (*d*) The right to be insured

68. Green tea is.—
(*a*) Unfermented tea (*b*) Semi fermented tea
(*c*) Fermented tea (*d*) None of the above

69. Bureau of Indian Standards works under_______.
(*a*) Ministry of Consumer Affairs, Food & Public Distribbution
(*b*) Ministry of Health and Family Welfare
(*c*) Ministry of Commerce
(*d*) Ministry of Food Processing Industry

70. The HACCP records should.—
(*a*) Not contain the data and time of the activity reflected on the entry
(*b*) Not contain the signture or initials of the employee making the entry
(*c*) Have the information entered on the record at the time it is being observed
(*d*) Not contain actual observations or data values obtained

71. GDA in relation to Nutritional labelling stands for.—
(*a*) Gross Daily Amount (*b*) Guideline Daily Amount
(*c*) Guideline Daily Advise (*d*) Grouped Daily Amount

72. Oxalic acid is found in.—
(*a*) Spinach (*b*) Beans (*c*) Almonds (*d*) Spices

73. The provisions of Schedule 4 (part 3) FSS (Licensing and Registration of Food Businesses) Regulations 2011 pertains to_______.
(*a*) General hygienic and sanitary practices to be followed by FBO licensee - Milk and milk products
(*b*) General hygienic and sanitary practices to be followed by FBO licensee - Slaughter house and meat processing
(*c*) General hygienic and sanitary practices to be followed by FBO licensee - Fish processing unit
(*d*) General hygienic and sanitary practices to be followed by FBO licensee - Catering

74. Rennet is used in processing of.—
(*a*) Cheese (*b*) Ice cream (*c*) Butter (*d*) Ghee

75. As per provisions of FSS (Labelling and Display) Regulations, 2020 a product still remians marketable and safe even if it has passed its _______.
(*a*) Expiration date (*b*) Used by date (*c*) Expiry date (*d*) Best before date

76. A single substance that exists in two or more form is called.—
(*a*) Amorphous (*b*) Isomorphous (*c*) Monomorphous (*d*) Polymorphous

77. As per the provision of FSS (Food Products Standards and Food Additives) Regulations, 2011 "Low lactose milk" shall have less than ______ % lactose.
(*a*) 0.1 (*b*) 2 (*c*) 1.0 (*d*) 0.2

78. This principal flavoring compound in clove is.—
(*a*) Eugenol (*b*) Cinnamaldehyde (*c*) Ethyl Maltol (*d*) Anethole

79. This is not an example of group of antibiotics.—
(*a*) Tetracyclines (*b*) β lactams (*c*) Alkaloids (*d*) Macrolides

80. Milk SNF does not include.—
(*a*) Fat (*b*) Sugar (*c*) Protein (*d*) Mineral

81. The acidity of vinegar is expressed in trems of ______.
(a) Percent malic acid (b) Percent lactic acid
(c) Percent tartaric acid (d) Percent acetic acid

82. Goitrogen is present in.—
(a) Tomato (b) Cabbage (c) Plums (d) Onion

83. The H–O–H bond angle in water is about ______.
(a) 100° (b) 105° (c) 109° (d) 102°

84. Name of the first commercially synthesized colour is.—
(a) Lycopene (b) Annato (c) Mauve (d) β-carotene

85. The characteristic pigment present in the turmeric powder is.—
(a) Asthaxanthin (b) Beta carotene (c) Curcumin (d) Gamma carotene

86. HACCP standards were developed by.—
(a) NASA (b) ISRO (c) DRDO (d) CFTRI

87. Presence of ______ in ghee indicates adulteration with plant oils.
(a) Cholesterol (b) Phospholipid (c) Phytosterol (d) Cholesterol ester

88. The word AGMARK is derived form the words.—
(a) Agricultural manufacturing (b) Agricultural marketing
(c) Agricultural management (d) Agricultural money

89. The Specific Migration Limit (SML) in relation to food packaging material is expressed in terms of ______ of substance per kg of food simulants.
(a) Microgram (b) mg (c) Picogram (d) g

90. Name the initiative of the Government of India and the Food Safety and Standards Authority of India (FSSAI) to transform the country's food system in order to ensure safe, healthy and susteinable food for all Indians.—
(a) Save food: everyone's responsibility (b) Food and Indian Nation
(c) Eat Right India (d) Eat Smart, Eat Healthy

91. Upon receipt of sample by Food Analyst, he is liable to finish the analysis and send the report of analysis of sample within ______ days to Designated officer.
(a) 7 (b) 30 (c) 14 (d) 10

92. What are Sequestrants?
(a) They keep the food oxidized (b) Added for colour
(c) Form a complex ion with metals like copper, iron etc
(d) They are added to keep the food stable

93. Turmeric adulterated sella rice forms ______ colour upon spraying lime water on it.
(a) Red (b) White (c) Blue (d) Gray

94. Which is used as preservative during the sampling?
(a) 40 % KOH (b) 40 % NaCl
(c) 40 % Formaldehyde (d) 40 % any disinfectant

95. Lovibond scale is used for________.
(*a*) Colour measurement in Baudouin test
(*b*) Colour measurement in Halphens test
(*c*) Colour measurement in Phytosterol acetate test
(*d*) Colour measurement in Pensky Martin test

96. Which microorganism represents coliform group of microorgaanism?
(*a*) *E. coil* (*b*) *S. aureus* (*c*) Yeasts (*d*) All Probiotics

97. As per the FSS (Food Products Standards and Food Additives) Regulations, 2011, the melting point as determined by the capillary slip method shall not exceed _______ °C in case of bakery shortening.—
(*a*) 45 (*b*) 30 (*c*) 41 (*d*) 37

98. Limiting essential amino acid in wheat is—
(*a*) Phenylalanine (*b*) Isoleucine (*c*) Leucine (*d*) Lysine

99. The food most likely to contain mercury, dioxins, or PCBs is ________.
(*a*) Municipal water supply (*b*) Vegetables and fruits grown with pesticides
(*c*) Milk from transgenic dairy cattle (*d*) Fish from rivers, streams, and lakes

100. Out of the following which one is an example of emulsion?
(*a*) Soap solution (*b*) Milk (*c*) Blood (*d*) Air

101. The *Kjeldahl* factor used for conversion of nitrogen percentage into protein for the Malted Milk Food and Malt based food is ________.
(*a*) 6.25 (*b*) 5.85 (*c*) 5.71 (*d*) 6.38

102. Maximum residue limit (MRL) for contaminant in food products is given by—
(*a*) FSSAI (*b*) CAC (*c*) BIS (*d*) ISO

103. Monosodium Glutamate is an example of ________.
(*a*) Emulsifier (*b*) Stabilizer (*c*) Flavour enhancer (*d*) Thickener

104. Six Sigma is a—
(*a*) Process quality control (*b*) Statistical quality control
(*c*) Sampling control (*d*) Production control

105. Crysocope can be used to detect adulteration of milk with ________.
(*a*) Water (*b*) Neutralizers (*c*) Strach (*d*) Prseervatives

106. Which of the following defines "FOOD" according to the Act?
1. Intended for human consumption 2. Genetically modified or engineered food
3. It can include any animal feed 4. It can include narcotic or psychotropic substances
(*a*) 1, 2, 3, 4 (*b*) 1, 2, 3 (*c*) 1 and 2 only (*d*) 3 and 4 only

107. If the pH of a solution is 4. Its $[H^+]$ concentration is ________.
(*a*) 0.04 M (*b*) 10^{-4} M (*c*) 4 M (*d*) 10^4 M

108. The test used for detection of starch.—
(*a*) Glucose test (*b*) Iodine test (*c*) Sodium test (*d*) Salt test

109. When put in water pure honey _______.

(*a*) Floats on water (*b*) Does not disperse in water

(*c*) Immediately dissolves in water (*d*) Makes foam

110. Kimchi is a fermented product of.—

(*a*) Cucumber (*b*) Vegetables and milk

(*c*) Vegetables and rice (*d*) Mixed vegetable in Chinese cabbage

111. As per the provision of the FSS (Food Products Standards and Food Additives) Regulations, 2011, the Sucrose content in Refined suger shall not be lass than _______.—

(*a*) 99.0 per cent by weight (*b*) 98.0 per cent by weight

(*c*) 99.5 per cent by weight (*d*) 98.5 per cent by weight

112. According to FSSA, standardized milk should contain.—

(*a*) 5.0 % fat & 8.5 % SNF (*b*) 4.5 % fat & 8.5 % SNF

(*c*) 5.0 % fat & 9.5 % SNF (*d*) 4.5 % fat & 9.5 % SNF

113. The maximum permissible limit for Aflatoxin M1 in milk as per the provision of the FSS (Contaminants, Toxins and Residues) Regulations, 2011 is _______.

(*a*) 0.5 μg/kg (*b*) 30 μg/kg (*c*) 50 μg/kg (*d*) 20 μg/kg

114. Which is the major acid in lemon?

(*a*) Citric acid (*b*) Tartaric acid (*c*) Malic acid (*d*) Quinic acid

115. _______ is an example of gluten free grain.—

(*a*) Buckwheat (*b*) wheat (*c*) Barley (*d*) Oats

116. The natural enzyme present in fruit that hydrolyze pectin is.—

(*a*) Pectin ethyl peroxidase (*b*) Pectin methyl peroxidase

(*c*) Pectin ethyl esterase (*d*) Pectin methyl esterase

117. The purity of water is judged by measuring its_______.

(*a*) Refractive Index (*b*) Conductivity

(*c*) Density (*d*) Acidity

118. Most important monosaccharide in biological system is.—

(*a*) Fructose (*b*) Galactose (*c*) Glucose (*d*) Xylose

119. _______ is 600 times sweeter than surcose.—

(*a*) Sucralose (*b*) Aspartame (*c*) Saccharin (*d*) Stevia

120. Which of the following elements will have the lowest electron affinity?

(*a*) Phosphorus (*b*) Nitrogen (*c*) Chlorine (*d*) Fluorine

121. This statement is not true regarding Codex standards.—

(*a*) They are science based. (*b*) They are mandatory.

(*c*) They facilitate international trade.

(*d*) They are not a substitute for national legislation.

122. Lathyrism is caused by eating.—

(*a*) Kesari dal (*b*) Chick pea (*c*) Black gram (*d*) Green gram

123. The statement regarding enzymes is not true.—

(*a*) They are protein in nature. (*b*) They are destroyed by moist heat at 100 °C.
(*c*) They are signification inactive at 0°C. (*d*) They are not affected by extreme pH.

124. Which additives are used for the purpose of restoring nutrients lost or degraded during production?

(*a*) Nutritional additives (*b*) Processing agents
(*c*) Preservatives (*d*) Sensory agents

125. The statement regarding responsiblity of Food Safety Supervisor (FSS) is not true.—

(*a*) To maintain the medicals records of food handlers.

(*b*) Food Vendors, canteen operators, workplace kitchen are compliant to provisions of schedule 4 of FSS (Licensing and Registration) 2011.

(*c*) Encouraging employees for exercise

(*d*) Food vendors, canteen operators, workplace kitchen are having FSSAI lincense ans registration.

126. Reference method for estimation of protein in food products is.—

(*a*) Lawry's (*b*) Dye binding (*c*) Micro Kjeldhal (*d*) Dumas

127. _______ is an example of anticaking agent.—

(*a*) Cl_2 (*b*) Calcium silicate (*c*) Sorbitol (*d*) EDTA

128. NABL is an autonomous body under the aegis of.—

(*a*) Dept. of Science and Technology (*b*) Dept. of Biotechnology
(*c*) Quality Council of India (*d*) Ministry of Food Processing Industries

129. _______ is considered National Standards Body of India.—

(*a*) AGMARK (*b*) APEDA
(*c*) Food Safety and Standards Authority of India (*d*) Bureau of India Standards

130. Tempeh is a fermented soybean product prepared by using.—

(*a*) Bacteria (*b*) Mold (*c*) Yeast (*d*) Virus

131. _______ is amino acid based sweetener.—

(*a*) Sucralose (*b*) Aspartame (*c*) Saccharin (*d*) Stevia

132. Atomic Absorption Spectrometry is generally used for the estimation of.—

(*a*) Antibiotics (*b*) Pesticides
(*c*) Trace and ultra trace metals (*d*) Toxins

133. The most deficient essential amino acid in cereal proteins is_______.

(*a*) Lysine (*b*) Histidine (*c*) Methionine (*d*) Glutamic acid

134. Host country for Codex committee on Spices and Culinary herbs is.—

(*a*) Norway (*b*) India (*c*) China (*d*) Eypt

135. "Jago Grahak jago" is a campaign run as a part of_______.

(*a*) BIS Act, 2016 (*b*) FSS Act, 2006
(*c*) Consumer Protection Act, 2019 (*d*) Legal Metrology Act, 2009

136. Nodal office for Codex Alimentarius Commission in India is.—

(*a*) BIS (*b*) APEDA (*c*) AGMARK (*d*) FSSAI

137. _______ is an example of antioxidant.—
(*a*) Butylated Hydroxy Anisole (*b*) Citrulline
(*c*) Poly Glycerol Poly Ricinoeate (*d*) Sulphur dioxide

138. ISO established in the year_______.
(*a*) 1958 (*b*) 1947 (*c*) 1980 (*d*) 1985

139. Indiscriminate use of monosodium glutamete is associated with _______ disease.
(*a*) Anemia (*b*) Chinese restaurant syndrome
(*c*) Diabetes (*d*) Goiter

140. Milko tester used in the estimation of milk fat is based on the principle of.—
(*a*) Light absorption (*b*) Light scattering
(*c*) Light penetration (*d*) Light refraction

141. Fats liquid at room temperature can be made more solid by the process of_______.
(*a*) Emulsification (*b*) Hydrogenation (*c*) Calcification (*d*) Esterification

142. Total soluble solids in beverages is measured by using.—
(*a*) Referactometer (*b*) Viscometer (*c*) Stalagnometer (*d*) Pycnometer

143. An example of Omega-3 fatty acid is _______.
(*a*) Linolenic acid (*b*) Linoleic acid (*c*) Arachidonic acid (*d*) Oleic acid

144. Accoding to new Act regarding Food Safety, the post of food inspector is remaned as_______.
(*a*) Food Welfare Officer (*b*) Foos Safety Mitre
(*c*) Food Safety Officer (*d*) Designated Officer

145. Fruits and vegetable to be consumed as raw shall be washed with _______ followed by potable water.—
(*a*) 50 ppm chlorine solution (*b*) 500 ppm chlorine solution
(*c*) 100 ppm chlorine solution (*d*) 5 ppm chlorine solution

146. The detection of adulteration of milk with water is done by.—
(*a*) Total acidity (*b*) Alcohol-Alizarin test (*c*) Lactometer (*d*) Ethanol test

147. The size of nano particles ranges between_______.
(*a*) 100-200 nm (*b*) 200-500 nm (*c*) 1-100 nm (*d*) 500-1000 nm

148. Suger added in milk is considered as.—
(*a*) Preservative (*b*) Additive (*c*) Adulterant (*d*) Thickener

149. Which food would provide least calories?
(*a*) A cup of black coffee (*b*) A cup of sweetened dahi
(*c*) A cup of plain milk (*d*) A cup of flavoured milk

150. Hedonic scale is used in.—
(*a*) Sensory analysis (*b*) Chemical analysis
(*c*) Physical analysis (*d*) Texture analysis

151. ISO 22000 standards are related to _______.
(*a*) Food Safety Monitoring System (*b*) Food Security Management System
(*c*) Food Safety Management System (*d*) Food Safety Monitoring Scheme

152. Anthocyanins are found in.—
(*a*) Carrots (*b*) Capsicum (*c*) Banana (*d*) Blueberries

153. As per the provision of FSS (Prohibition and Restrictions on Sales) Regulations, 2011, mixture of coffee and any other substance expect _______ is not permitted.
(*a*) Chicory (*b*) Sugar (*c*) Chocolate (*d*) Milk

154. Advanced instrument used to measure the colour of food products.—
(*a*) Rheometer (*b*) Rancimat (*c*) Hunter LAB (*d*) Instron

155. Maillard browning is result of interaction between _______.
(*a*) Protein and mineral (*b*) Protein and Carbohydrates
(*c*) Carbohydrates and mineral (*d*) Protein and Lipids

156. Prevention of Food Adulteration Act (PFA) is formulated by.—
(*a*) CAC (*b*) CCFS (*c*) FAO (*d*) WHO

157. _______ yeast species is used in the bread making process.—
(*a*) *Saccharomyces boulardii* (*b*) *Saccharomyces cerevisiae*
(*c*) *Zygosaccharomyces rouxii* (*d*) *Saccharomyces rouxii*

158. A substance intentionally added that affects the nature and quality of food is called.—
(*a*) Food adulterant (*b*) Food poison (*c*) Food contaminant (*d*) Food material

159. The Butyro-refractometer reading of ghee is measured at _______.
(*a*) 25 °C (*b*) 30 °C (*c*) 35 °C (*d*) 40 °C

160. ISO stands for.—
(*a*) Indian Standardization Organization
(*b*) International Standardization Organization
(*c*) International Organization for Standardization
(*d*) Indianl Organization for Standardization

161. Central Agmark Laboratory is situated at_______.
(*a*) Mumbai (*b*) New Dehli (*c*) Faridabad (*d*) Nagpur

162. Most accurate method for detection of adulteration of water is.—
(*a*) Freezing point method (*b*) Lactometer method
(*c*) Hydrometer method (*d*) Boiling point method

163. The Food Safety and Standards Act, 2006 received the assent of the President of India in the month of ____, 2006.—
(*a*) July (*b*) January (*c*) August (*d*) December

164. What has been banned for tea bag products by FSSAI from 2018?
(*a*) Use of stapler pins (*b*) Thread for dipping
(*c*) Cloth bag containing the tea leaves (*d*) Herbal tes leaves

165. ______ is part of micronutrient fraction of food.—
(*a*) Magnesium (*b*) Zinc (*c*) Calcium (*d*) Sodium

166. Which of the following bacteria is most active in microbial spoilage of canned foods?
(*a*) Psychrophillic (*b*) Mesophillic (*c*) Thermophillic (*d*) None of the above

167. Polarimetry is generally used for analysis of ______.
(*a*) Fats (*b*) Sugars (*c*) Minerals (*d*) Proteins

168. Which of the following is a major ingredient for curing?
(*a*) Nitrite (*b*) Nitrate (*c*) Sugar (*d*) NaCl

169. The Food Safety and Standards Authority of India comprises of _____ memebers and a Chariman.
(*a*) 15 (*b*) 20 (*c*) 10 (*d*) 22

170. Which of the following lacks vitamin D?
(*a*) Plants products (*b*) Milk (*c*) Egg (*d*) Fish liver oil

171. The Unit of refractive index is _______.
(*a*) Dyne/cm (*b*) Unit less (*c*) Mho/cm (*d*) Poise

172. Gum Arabic is a type of.—
(*a*) Microbial gum (*b*) Seed gum (*c*) Seaweed gum (*d*) Exudate gum

173. As per the provisions of Food Safety And Standard Act (FSSA), 2006 the misleading advertisment would attract penalty of.—
(*a*) Rs. 10 lakh (*b*) Rs. 5 lakh (*c*) Rs. 2 lakh (*d*) Rs. 1 lakh

174. Total charge on protein molecule at isoelectric point is.—
(*a*) +1 (*b*) –1 (*c*) 0 (*d*) +2

175. As per the FSS (Food Products Standards and Food Additives) Regulations, 2011, the margarine shall contain not les than _____ percent of its weight of Til oil.—
(*a*) 10 (*b*) 1 (*c*) 5 (*d*) 2

176. Number of carbon atom present in palmitic acid.—
(*a*) 10 (*b*) 12 (*c*) 14 (*d*) 16

177. Export Inspection Council certification is mandatory for export of ______.
(*a*) Cocoa (*b*) Coffee (*c*) Honey (*d*) Sugar cane

178. The unit of current is.—
(*a*) Ohm (*b*) Ampere (*c*) Faraday (*d*) Volt

179. As per provisions of FSS (Food Products Standards and Food Additives) Regulations, 2011 Dehydrated Green Leafy Vegetables should not contain sulpur dioxide more than ______.
(*a*) 1000 ppm (*b*) 2000 ppm (*c*) 100 ppm (*d*) 200 ppm

180. Black pepper is commonly adulterated with.—
(*a*) Mustard seeds (*b*) Anne seeds (*c*) Papaya seeds (*d*) Poppy seeds

181. As per the provisions of FSS (Labelling and Display) Regulations, 2020 the Recommended Dietary Allowance (RDA) provided by ______ organization shall be applicable for the product marketed in India.—
(*a*) Indian Council of Medical Research (*b*) Indian Dietetic Association
(*c*) Indian Medical Association (*d*) USFDA

182. FSSAI has issued an advisory banning the use of which material for wrapping and packaging of food items?
(*a*) Newspaper (*b*) Plastic (*c*) Polythene (*d*) Aluminium foil

183. The concentration of formaldehyde in formalin solution is ______.
(*a*) 10 % vol/vol (*b*) 50 % vol/vol (*c*) 30 % vol/vol (*d*) 40 % vol/vol

184. AGMARK standards are approved by—
(*a*) Directorate of Marketing and Inspection (*b*) Department of Legal Metrology
(*c*) Department of Agriculture & Cooperation
(*d*) Department of Consumer Affairs, Govt. of India

185. Bureau of Indian Standard Certification Mark is mandatory for the ______ product as per the provisions of FSS (Prohibition and Restrictions on Sales) Regulations, 2011.
(*a*) Mineral water (*b*) Fruit nectars (*c*) Vegetable nectars (*d*) Butter milk

186. Which of these are responsible for the implenetation of FSSAI?
(*a*) Directorate General of Health Services (*b*) Ministry of Food Processing Industries
(*c*) Department of Agriculture & Cooperation (*d*) Ministry of Health & Family Walfare

187. For the Nutritional declaration per single consumption pack of the product and per serve percentage (%) contribution to Recommended Dietary Allowance is calculated on the basis of ______ kcal energy per day.
(*a*) 1500 (*b*) 2500 (*c*) 2000 (*d*) 3000

188. Grain is a unit of.—
(*a*) Volume (*b*) Density (*c*) Mass (*d*) Viscosity

189. The "Indian Standards Institution" was established in the year.—
(*a*) 1946 (*b*) 1953 (*c*) 1947 (*d*) 1952

190. Which of the following is the non crystalline solid?
(*a*) Rubber (*b*) Lead iodide (*c*) Zinc sulphide (*d*) Mercury sulphide

191. A carbon isotopic analysis is used for.—
(*a*) Moisture content of honey (*b*) Confirming origin of honey
(*c*) Ash content of honey (*d*) Lipoidal material

192. Unit of the osmotic pressure is.—
(*a*) K (*b*) Pa (*c*) T (*d*) R

193. Ergot specified in standards of Oats are related to ______.
(*a*) Protozoa (*b*) Bacteria (*c*) Virus (*d*) Fungi

194. Main objective of quality assurance programme in food industry is.—
(*a*) To preserve food (*b*) To protect consumers health
(*c*) To maintain the standards (*d*) To process the product

195. The strongest chemical force among the following is ______.
(*a*) Van der Waals forces (*b*) Covalent bond
(*c*) Hydrogen bonds (*d*) Hydrophobic interaction

196. Odour is perceived by.—
(*a*) Tongue (*b*) Olfactory (*c*) Tactile (*d*) Nose

197. Apo-enzyme refers to ______.
(*a*) The protein part of the enzyme (*b*) The prosthetic group of enzyme
(*c*) The cofactors of enzyme (*d*) The catalytic site of enzyme

198. Naturally occurring sugars are mostly.—
(*a*) Pentoses (*b*) Heptoses (*c*) Octoses (*d*) Hexoses

199. β-galactosidase belong to the _____ class of enzymes.—
(*a*) Transferases (*b*) Hydrolases (*c*) Oxidoreductase (*d*) Lyases

200. Diamond is.—
(*a*) A compound (*b*) An element (*c*) A mixture (*d*) A liquid

ANSWER KEY

(Model paper 10)

Q.	Ans.	Q.	Ans.	Q.	Ans.	Q.	Ans.	Q.	Ans.	Q.	Ans.	Q.	Ans.	Q.	Ans.
1	b	26	b	51	c	76	d	101	a	126	c	151	c	176	d
2	c	27	a	52	d	77	c	102	b	127	b	152	d	177	c
3	c	28	c	53	c	78	a	103	c	128	c	153	a	178	b
4	b	29	d	54	c	79	c	104	b	129	d	154	c	179	b
5	d	30	c	55	a	80	a	105	a	130	b	155	b	180	c
6	d	31	b	56	b	81	d	106	c	131	b	156	b	181	a
7	a	32	c	57	b	82	b	107	b	132	c	157	b	182	a
8	d	33	a	58	c	83	b	108	b	133	a	158	d	183	d
9	c	34	a	59	c	84	c	109	b	134	a	159	d	184	a
10	a	35	d	60	a	85	c	110	d	135	c	160	c	185	a
11	d	36	b	61	b	86	a	111	c	136	d	160	d	186	d
12	d	37	d	62	b	87	c	112	b	137	a	162	a	187	c
13	b	38	a	63	d	88	b	113	a	138	b	163	c	188	c
14	c	39	d	64	a	89	b	114	a	139	b	164	a	189	c
15	b	40	a	65	d	90	c	115	a	140	b	165	b	190	a
16	c	41	c	66	d	91	c	116	d	141	b	166	c	191	b
17	d	42	c	67	d	92	b	117	b	142	a	167	b	192	b
18	a	43	c	68	a	93	a	118	c	143	a	168	d	193	d
19	b	44	b	69	a	94	c	119	a	144	c	169	d	194	b
20	a	45	d	70	c	95	a	120	a	145	a	170	a	195	b
21	c	46	a	71	b	96	a	121	b	146	c	171	b	196	b
22	b	47	d	72	a	97	c	122	a	147	c	172	d	197	a
23	b	48	a	73	a	98	d	123	d	148	c	173	a	198	d
24	a	49	c	74	a	99	d	124	a	149	a	174	c	199	b
25	d	50	a	75	d	100	b	125	c	150	a	175	c	200	b

MODEL PAPERS-11

Food Safety Officer, 2024

[Solved]

Maximum Marks: 300 *Total time: 3 hrs*

Note: **Question from 1 to 150 are from Food Technology. Question from 151 to 200 are from general studies.**

1. Mold inhibitor used in bread is:
   (A) Sodium/Calcium propionate (B) Sodium chloride
   (C) Calcium carbonate (D) None of these

2. Who developed the process of canning:
   (A) Nicolas Appert (B) Louis Pasteur
   (C) Norman Borlaug (D) Walter Hesse

3. Nisin is used as:
   (A) Antimicrobial agent (B) Emulsifier
   (C) Stabilizer (D) Sweetener

4. Iodized salt contains iodine in the form of:
   (A) I_2 (B) KIO_3
   (C) KI (D) NaI

5. The first synthetic sweetening agent used was:
   (A) Saccharine (B) Cyclamates
   (C) Aspartame (D) Sucralose

6. Jam, jellies and preserves can be preserved by adding sugar at concentration of:
   (A) 65% (B) 70%
   (C) 40% (D) 30%

7. After drying moisture content in vegetables should be:
   (A) 6-8% (B) 8-10%
   (C) 10-15% (D) 15-20%

8. Agar-agar is used as:
   (A) Stabilizer and thickener (B) Antibiotic
   (C) Colour ingagent (D) Nutrient supplement

9. Frozen storage is generally operated at temperature of:
   (A) –0°C (B) –18°C
   (C) –50°C (D) –60°C

10. Toco pherol is an example of:
(A) Anticaking agent
(B) Antioxidant
(C) Flavouring agent
(D) None of these

11. Bitterness in colocasia is due to:
(A) Calcium oxalate
(B) Calcium chloride
(C) Potassium oxalate
(D) Calcium carbonate

12. In high temperature short time method of pasteurization, milk is heated at temperature:
(A) 72°C for 15 seconds
(B) 62°C for 15 seconds
(C) 72° C for 30 minutes
(D) 62°C for 30 minutes

13. Butylated Hydroxyanisole (BHA) is:
(A) Chelating agent
(B) Antioxidant
(C) Stablizer
(D) Emulsion

14. BIS Headquarters is situated in:
(A) Pune
(B) Chennai
(C) New Delhi
(D) Ajmer

15. Germination affects nutritive value of legumes by:
(A) Increase in vitamin C content
(B) Decrease in tryps in inhibitor activity
(C) Increase in enzyme activity
(D) All of these

16. Pineapple variety suitable for canning is:
(A) Queen
(B) Kew
(C) Mauritius
(D) Cayenne

17. Richest source of Riboflavin is :
(A) Papaya
(B) Mango
(C) Bael
(D) Karonda

18. Which of the following is non-Climacteric type of fruit?
(A) Pineapple
(B) Litchi
(C) Grape
(D) All of these

19. Emission of Ethylene during transportation of cut flowers causes a disorder called:
(A) Bud opening
(B) Sleepiness
(C) Bentneck
(D) Calyx splitting

20. Which is the precursor of Ethylene?
(A) Tryptophane
(B) Methionine
(C) ABA
(D) IAA

21. Cauliflower curds can be stored for a month at:
(A) 0°C with 85-90% RH (B) 15°C with 60-80% RH
(C) 15 °C with 60-65% RH (D) 20 °C with 50-70% RH

22. For curing, sweet potato are kept for 10 days at:
(A) 25°C and 85% RH (B) 40°C and 70% RH
(C) 80°C and 30% RH (D) 30°C and 80% RH

23. Tomato fruits for canning are harvested at:
(A) Mature green stage (B) Red ripe stage
(C) Immature green stage (D) Half-ripe/pink stage

24. Which chemical is used for controlling sprouting of onions in storage?
(A) Maleic Hydrazide (MH) (B) Ethylene (C_2H_4)
(C) GA (D) All of these

25. For Low Sugar content, potato tubers are stored at:
(A) 5°C (B) 10°C
(C) 15°C (D) 20°C

26. For longer storage of cucumber fruits, the temperature should be:
(A) 5°C (B) 10°C
(C) 20°C (D) 25°C

27. The limiting Amino acid in green vegetables is:
(A) Arginine (B) Lysine
(C) Methionine (D) Tryptophan

28. Which is the staple vegetable in Indian diet?
(A) Tomato (B) Cauliflower
(C) Potato (D) Chilli

29. Which bean is used for extraction of gum?
(A) Broad bean (B) Cluster bean
(C) French bean (D) Hyacinth bean

30. Chillies are rich source of:
(A) Vitamin A (B) Vitamin C
(C) Vitamin A and C (D) Vitamin E

31. Vegetables are subjected to drying after:
(A) Sulfuring (B) Sulphitation
(C) Blanching (D) None of these

32. Yellow coloured vegetables are rich source of:
(A) Vitamin A (B) Vitamin B
(C) Vitamin C (D) Vitamin D

33. Toddy from coconut is prepared by :
(A) Deep Frying (B) Fermentation
(C) Hydrogenation (D) Oxidation

34. According to FPO, the maximum limit of SO_2 allowed in squashes and cordials is:
(A) 350 ppm (B) 500 ppm
(C) 1000 ppm (D) 600 ppm

35. The toxicity of SO_2 increases at:
(A) Low temperature (B) High temperature
(C) Moderate temperature (D) No effect of temperature

36. Concentration of SO_2 in concentrated juice is:
(A) 500 ppm (B) 1000 ppm
(C) 1500 ppm (D) 350 ppm

37. Enzyme responsible for converting pectin into pectic acid is:
(A) Pectinase (B) Proto-peclinase
(C) Pectic Methyl Esterase (PME) (D) Poly Galucturonase

38. The term 'Climacteric' was first used by:
(A) Gane (1934) (B) Kidd and West (1927)
(C) Cruess (1912) (D) Bleekar (1929)

39. O_2 requirement for Apple storage in Controlled Atmosphere (CA) is:
(A) 2% (B) 3%
(C) 5% (D) 7%

40. Storage temperature for Asparagus is:
(A) 0-5°C (B) 5-7°C
(C) 7-11°C (D) 10-15°C

41. Vegetable which is not blanched before drying:
(A) Cauliflower (B) Palak
(C) Onion (D) Tomato

42. Moisture content in dried vegetable is:
(A) 2% (B) 3%
(C) 5% (D) 6%

43. Vitamin which is not found in Fruits and Vegetables:

(A) Vitamin A (B) Vitamin B_1

(C) Vitamin B_6 (D) Vitamin B_{12}

44. Best maturity index of orange is:

(A) TSS (B) Sugar%

(C) Acid% (D) Brix:acid ratio

45. Bacteria which is used to absorb ethylene from storage chamber is:

(A) *Agro bacterium* (B) *Mycobacterium*

(C) *Bacillus* (D) *Azotobacter*

46. Toughening effect on canned bean is due to:

(A) K (B) Ca

(C) S (D) None of these

47. Agriculture Produce (Grading and Marketing) Act (1937) is also:

(A) PFA Act (B) FPO Act

(C) Agmark Act (D) ISI Act

48. The term "three quarterful or full three quarter" is used to denote fruit maturity in:

(A) Banana (B) Mango

(C) Tomato (D) Pineapple

49. During controlled atmospheric storage composition of which of the following set of gases is controlled:

(A) $O_2 + N_2$ (B) $CO_2 + N_2$

(C) $C_2H_4 + N_2$ (D) $CO_2 + O_2$

50. At which pH fruits and vegetables are divided into acidic and non-acidic for thermal processing:

(A) 4.5 (B) 5.5

(C) 6.5 (D) 7.5

51. In pre-cooling, water is mostly removed by:

(A) Convection (B) Conduction

(C) Radiation (D) None of these

52. Albinism is an important physiological disorder of:

(A) Plum (B) Peach

(C) Strawberry (D) Cherry

53. Calliper grade is the maturity measurement for:
(A) Apple (B) Mango
(C) Banana (D) Pineapple

54. Formation of abscission layer is maturity index of:
(A) Tomato (B) Leafy vegetables
(C) Melons (D) Onion

55. What is the maturity index for Avocado?
(A) Sugar content (B) Acid content
(C) TSS (D) Oil content

56. Which of the following is biodegradable plastic?
(A) Poly propylene (B) LDPE
(C) Polythene (D) Polyhydroxy butyrate

57. As fruits mature, the specific gravity will:
(A) Increase (B) Decrease
(C) Remains constant (D) None of these

58. 'Solidity' is the maturity index for:
(A) Root vegetables (B) Seed vegetables
(C) Leafy vegetables (D) Cucurbits

59. Which of the following plant hormone is considered as ripen?
(A) Cytokinin (B) GA_3
(C) Ethylene (D) IAA

60. Maximum density of water is at a temperature of:
(A) 0°C (B) 4°C
(C) 4°C (D) –7°C

61. Guava fruit is botanically known as:
(A) Drupe (B) Sorosis
(C) Berry (D) Pome

62. In onion pink colour is due to:
(A) Anthocyanin (B) Carotene
(C) Xanthophyll (D) Quercitin

63. Secondary metabolites:
(A) are essential to microbe function
(B) are by-products of metabolism that are not important to microbe function
(C) are products that require additional processing before they can be packaged
(D) are harvested during the exponential phase of growth

64. Hen and Chicken disorder is associated with:
(A) Mango (B) Tomato
(C) Grapes (D) Guava

65. The membrane lipid hypothesis was given by:
(A) Kidd & West (B) James Harrison
(C) Raison & Lyons (D) Graham & Patterson

66. The point at which the dried products just become lumpy is known as?
(A) Danger Point (B) Saturated Point
(C) Critical Point (D) Safety Point

67. What is the percentage of sugars in Honey?
(A) 42% (B) 82%
(C) 65% (D) 62%

68. Fungus which mostly grown on grapes:
(A) *Geotrichum* (B) *Penicillium*
(C) *Botrytis* (D) *Colletotrichum*

69. Vitamin D is chemically known as:
(A) Retinol (B) Cobalamin
(C) Calciferol (D) Tocopherol

70. Lye peeling is done at a temperature of:
(A) 75°C (B) 84°C
(C) 93°C (D) 105°C

71. Which of the following is associated with 'browning' disorder?
(A) Apple (B) Cabbage
(C) Cauliflower (D) Citrus

72. What is the threshold level of ethylene in fruit and vegetables?
(A) 0.01 μL/L (B) 0.02 μL/L
(C) 0.03 μL/L (D) 0.04 μL/L

73. Which of the following is a rapid precooling method?
(A) Forced air cooling (B) Hydro Cooling
(C) Vacuum Cooling (D) Evaporative Cooling

74. In cucumber, chilling- injury symtoms occur at:
(A) < 7°C (B) 7°C
(C) 10°C (D) >10°C

75. Degreening is not applicable in:
(A) Banana (B) Guava
(C) Mango (D) Citrus

76. Under normal conditions Orchid can be stored upto 2 weeks at:
(A) 2-4°C (B) 5-7°C
(C) 7.5-10°C (D) >10°C

77. What is the operating principle behind oven drying for determining moisture content of foods?
(A) Colour change is measured (B) Loss of weight represents loss of water
(C) Change in refractive index is measured (D) Change in light absorbance is measured

78. Which of the following packages is an example of aseptic packaging?
(A) Tetra Pak drinking boxes (B) Paper bag
(C) Milk carton (D) Plastic bread bag

79. Which of the following ingredients in chocolate milk comes from seaweed?
(A) Carrageenan (B) Cocoa
(C) Sucrose (D) Glucose

80. Which microorganism is commonly associated with fecal contamination?
(A) *Clostridium botulinum* (B) *Campylobacter jejuni*
(C) *Bacillus cereus* (D) *Trichinella spiralis*

81. Which of the following analytical methods can be used to distinguish flavour compounds?
(A) Hydrometry (B) Near infrared spectroscopy
(C) Polarimetry (D) Gas chromatography

82. Which of the following microorganisms cannot tolerate oxygen?
(A) *Clostridium botulinum* (B) *Staphylococcus aureus*
(C) *Penicillium roquefortii* (D) *E. coli*

83. Which of the following methods is a quick test for sugar content during the early stages of the brewing process for beer?
(A) Hydrometry (B) Babcock test
(C) Wet ashing (D) Soxhlet extraction

84. Which of the following processing methods involves heating foods at high temperatures for short periods of time in order to reduce the risk of food poisoning?
(A) Blanching (B) Ohmic heating
(C) Irradiation (D) Pasteurization

85. Which of the following does not have antimicrobial activity?
(A) Chlorophyll (B) Organic acids
(C) Spice extracts (D) Hydrogen peroxide

86. What is the percent of acetic acid in commercially available vinegar?
(A) 2% (B) 4%
(C) 6% (D)10%

87. Which of the following is not an intrinsic factor in food spoilage?
(A) pH (B) Moisture
(C) Temperature (D) Available nutrients

88. Lyophilization is synonymous with:
(A) Freeze-drying (B) Pasteurization
(C) Filteration (D) Spoilage

89. Antibiotics tend to be:
(A) Primary metabolites (B) Secondary metabolites
(C) Tertiary metabolites (D) Quaternary metabolites

90. Amino acids are used as food additives for which of the following reasons?
(A) As natural antibiotics (B) As natural growth inhibitors
(C) For nutritive purposes (D) As antioxidants

91. Grinding and mixing of foods such as sausage and hamburger:
(A) Increase the food surface area
(B) Alter cellular structure
(C) Distribute contaminating microorganisms throughtout the food
(D) All of the above

92. Louis Pasteur established the modern era of food microbiology in 1857 when he showed that microorganisms cause _______ spoilage:
(A) Beer (B) Wine
(C) Juice (D) Milk

93. Despite efforts to eliminate spoilage organisms during canning, sometimes canned foods are spoiled. This may be due to:
(A) Spoilage before canning
(B) Underprocessing during canning
(C) Leakage of contaminated water through can seams during cooling
(D) All of the above.

94. The effectiveness of many chemical preservatives depends primarily on the food:
(A) Temperature (B) pH.
(C) Water content (D) Acidity.

95. Which type of fermentation is used to produce yogurt?
(A) Mesophilic (B) Thermophilic
(C) Therapeutic (D) Yeast-lactic fermentations

96. Which of the following refers to the addition of microorganisms to the diet in order to provide health benefits beyond basic nutritive value?
(A) Antibiotics (B) Prebiotics
(C) Probiotics (D) All the above

97. Moisture content in intermediate moisture food (IMF) is:
(A) 10-20% (B) 20-25%
(C) 20-40% (D) 15-50%

98. Deep frying of potato chips lead to generation of carcinogen:
(A) Acrylamide (B) Acefamide
(C) Formamide (D) Antioxidants

99. Which of the amino acid is not essential in diet:
(A) Tyrosine (B) Tryptophan
(C) Phenylalanine (D) Lysine

100. Material suitable for micro-wave heating:
(A) EPP (B) LDPE
(C) PET (D) DAIP

101. Baking powder contains:
(A) NaCl (B) $NaHCO_3$
(C) Na-benzoate (D) NaI

102. FSSAI stands for:
(A) Food Safety and Standards Authority of India
(B) Food Security and Standards Authority of India
(C) Food Safety and Security Authority of India
(D) Food Safety and Standards Agency of India

103. Which one of the following is not a food preservative?
(A) Acetic acid (B) Propionic acid
(C) Butyric acid (D) Sorbic acid

104. Which out of the following is a non reducing sugar?
(A) Fructose (B) Glucose
(C) Mannose (D) Sucrose

105. In cooking oils, the antioxidant added to prevent rancidity is:
(A) Tocopherol (B) Ascorbic acid
(C) BHT (D) TBHQ

106. Most common toxicogenic spoilage in stored groundnuts is:
(A) *Aspergillus flavus* (B) *Aspergillus niger*
(C) *Aspergillus oryzae* (D) *Aspergillus albus*

107. Sauerkraut is the fermented product of:
(A) Cabbage
(B) Turnip
(C) Raddish
(D) Beetroot

108. Argemone oil is used to adultrate:
(A) Mustard oil
(B) Milk
(C) Tea
(D) Milk

109. "C" enamel cans are used for:
(A) High acidic food
(B) Non-acidic foods
(C) Medium-acidic foods
(D) Fat rich foods

110. AGMARK was promulgated in:
(A) 1937
(B) 1954
(C) 1935
(D) 2009

111. Cold test of fat is a measure of:
(A) Freezing point of oil
(B) Viscosity of oil at temperature just above its freezing point
(C) Resistance of oil to crystallization
(D) Total saturated fat

112. For manufacturing of pasta, wheat variety used is:
(A) Soft wheat
(B) Hard wheat
(C) Durum wheat
(D) White wheat

113. Which of the following is produced with the combination of apoenzyme and coenzyme?
(A) Holoenzyme
(B) Enzyme substrate complex
(C) Prosthetic group
(D) Enzyme product complex

114. The enzyme which hydrolyses starch to maltose is:
(A) Protease
(B) Amylase
(C) Lactase
(D) Maltase

115. Enzymes having slightly different molecules structure but performing identical activity are:
(A) Apoenzymes
(B) Isoenzymes
(C) Holoenzymes
(D) Coenzymes

116. Ribozyme is:
(A) RNA without phosphate
(B) RNA with sugar
(C) RNA with enzyme activity
(D) RNA with extra phosphate

117. Human insulin is being commercially produced from a transgenic species of:
(A) *Escherichia*
(B) *Saccharomyces*
(C) *Rhizobium*
(D) *Mycobacterium*

118. Example of a typical homopolysaccharide is:
(A) Lignin (B) Suberin
(C) Inulin (D) Starch

119. Which of the following is not a conjugated protein?
(A) Peptone (B) Phosphoprotein
(C) Lipoprotein (D) Chromoprotein

120. The "Repeating Unit" of glycogen is:
(A) Fructose (B) Mannose
(C) Glucose (D) Galactose

121. The catalytic efficiency of two different enzymes can be compared by the:
(A) Molecular size of the enzyme (B) The pH optimum value
(C) The Km value (D) Formation of the product

122. High value of BOD (Biochemical Oxygen Demand) shows:
(A) Water is normal (B) Water is highly polluted
(C) Water is less polluted (D) None of these

123. Which of the following is fermentation process?
(A) Batch process (B) Continuous process
(C) Both a and b (D) None of these

124. Who showed that *Sacchaaromyces cerevisiae* causes fermentation forming products such as beer and buttermilk?
(A) Louis Pasteur (B) Alexander Fleming
(C) Selman Waksman (D) Schatz

125. A bioreactor is:
(A) Hybridoma
(B) Culture containing radioactive isotopes
(C) Culture for synthesis of new chemicals
(D) Fermentation tank

126. Humulin is:
(A) Carbohydrate (B) Protein
(C) Fat (D) Antibiotics

127. Enzyme immobilisation is:
(A) Conversion of an active enzyme into inactive form
(B) Providing enzyme with protective covering
(C) Changing a soluble enzyme into insoluble state
(D) Changing pH so that enzyme is not able to carry out its function

128. Vinegar is obtained from molasses with the help of:
(A) *Rhizopus* (B) *Acetobacter*
(C) Yeast (D) Both b and c

129. Which of the following statements is incorrect regarding Gram negative bacteria:
(A) Cell wall has a thin peptidoglycan layer (B) Cell wall lipid content is very low
(C) Lipopolysaccharide layer is present (D) All of these
(Peptidoglycan is a polymer of sugars and amino acids that forms a mesh-like layer outside the plasma membrane of most bacteria, forming the cell wall)

130. Common food poisoning microbes are:
(A) *Clostridium* and *Salmonella* (B) *Clostridium* and *E.coli*
(C) *E.coli* and *Salmonella* (D) *Clostridium* and *Streptococcus*

131. Clostridium perfingens poisoning is associated with:
(A) Meat products (B) Vegetables
(C) Canned foods (D) Fish products

132. Salmonellosis involves:
(A) An enterotoxin and exotoxin (B) An enterotoxin and cytotoxin
(C) An exotoxin and cytotoxin (D) A cytotoxin only

133. The lipid with the lowest energy value for human nutrition is:
(A) Cardiolipin (B) Olestra
(C) Margarine (D) Olive oil

134. One serving of Cheddar cheese (28g) provides ______% of the RDA of calcium:
(A) 10 (B) 50
(C) 75 (D) 20

135. Which of the following is a Class II poduct?
(A) Frozen desert (B) Butter
(C) Fluid milk (D) Cheese

136. Class IV milk includes milk used to...
(A) Produce hard cheese and cream cheese (B) Fluid Milk
(C) Fluid cream and cottage cheese (D) Butter and any product in dried form

137. A food must contain less than _______ grams of fat per serving to be considered a low fat food:
(A) 8 (B) 6
(C) 3 (D) 7

138. _______ is a protein in milk that contains all the essential amino acids:
(A) Casein (B) Gluten
(C) a and b both (D) Whey protein

139. _______ is a defect in milk that is described as tasting papery:
(A) Bitter (B) Flat
(C) Oxidized (D) Salty

140. _______ is the general name for a class of bacteria that causes mastitis in dairy cattle:
(A) *Lactobacilus* (B) *E.coli*
(C) *Staphylococcus* (D) *Lactococcus*

141. Most UHT pasteurized milk has a shelf life of _____ days:
(A) 10 (B) 120
(C) 180 (D) 50

142. During malting, barley and other grains are broken down by:
(A) Heating to 95°C (B) Lagering
(C) Amylases (D) Yeasts

143. Milk fermentation to produce cheese is done initially by inoculating with:
(A) *Saccharomyces cerevisiae*
(B) *Streptococcus lactis and Lactobacillus ssp.*
(C) *Acetobacter and Gluconobacter*
(D) *Lactobacillus bulgaricus and Streptococcus thermophilus*

144. Nitrates maintain the red color of preserved meats and:
(A) Are among the most widely used preservatives
(B) Inhibit germination of botulism spores
(C) Maintain a high osmotic pressure to kill microorganisms
(D) Prevent mold

145. Salting, as a preservative:
(A) Retards growth of Staphylococcus aureus
(B) Plasmolyzes bacteria and fungi
(C) Is used to prevent growth of halophiles
(D) All of the above

146. In batch fermentation:
(A) Substrates are added to the system all at once and runs until product is harvested
(B) Nutrients are continuously fed into the reactor and the product is siphoned off during the run
(C) New batches of microorganisms are screened for increased yield
(D) Small-scale production is used to synthesize product

147. The technique first described to determine the incipient spoilage in meat was:
(A) Homogenate Extract Volume (HEV) (B) Agar Plate Count (APC)
(C) Extract Release Volume (ERV) (D) None of the above

148. Which of the following is responsible for a musty or earthy flavour?
(A) Actinomycetes (B) Flavobacterium
(C) Both a and b (D) Pseudomonas syncyanea

149. Molds causing spoilage of eggs include species of:
(A) *Cladosporium* (B) *Mucor*
(C) *Thamnidium* (D) All of these

150. Vacuum packaged meats are spoiled by:
(A) *B. thermosphacta* (B) *Lactobacilli*
(C) Both *a* and *b* (D) None of these

151. Which of the following pairs is not correctly matched?
(A) X-ray: Roentgen (B) Radioactivity: Becquerel
(C) Microscope: Galileo (D) Oxygen: Joseph Priestley

152. What is the correct sequence of Planets in terms of decreasing size?
(A) Saturn, Earth, Neptune, Mars (B) Earth, Saturn, Mars, Neptune
(C) Earth, Mars, Saturn, Neptune (D) Saturn, Neptune, Earth, Mars

153. Which of the following is incorrect about Nobel Prize 2014?
(A) The Prize in Physics was awarded for invention of efficient blue light emitting diodes
(B) The Prize in Medicine was given for discovery of cells constituting positioning system in brain
(C) Kailash Satyarthi became first Indian to receive Noble Peace Prize
(D) Malala Yousafjai became the youngest ever Noble Peace Prize winner

154. Which of the following is a Kharif crop?
(A) Tobacco (B) Barley
(C) Potato (D) Maize

155. Which of the following countries does not have Coastline?
(A) Zimbabwe (B) Cambodia
(C) North Korea (D) Finland

156. Name the first Vice President of India who was given Bharat Ratna:
(A) Sarvapalli Radhakrishnan (B) Gyani Zail Singh
(C) Dr. Rajendra Prasad (D) APJ Abdul Kalam

157. The maximum duration for which President of India's Office can remain vacant:
(A) 2 months (B) 3 months
(C) 6 months (D) It cannot remain vacant

158. Which of the following pair (National Park: State) is incorrect?
(A) Simlipal: Orissa (B) Nokrek: Meghalaya
(C) Tadoba: Maharashtra (D) Guindy: Karnataka

159. Which body part gets affected in Cirrhosis?
(A) Heart (B) Liver
(C) Kidney (D) Lungs

160. Which of the following teams did not play Semi Finals of inaugural edition of Hero Indian Super League?
(A) Kerala Blasters (B) Chennaiyin FC
(C) FC Goa (D) United North East

161. In Jainism 'Kaivalya' means:
(A) Perfect Knowledge (B) Meditation
(C) Nirvan (D) Ratna

162. Pulmonary artery originates from:
(A) Right ventricle (B) Right auricle
(C) Left auricle (D) Left ventricle

163. Which of the following means "by what authority"?
(A) Mandamus (B) Quo Warranto
(C) Certiorari (D) Habeas Corpus

164. Model Code of conduct comes into force during election from:
(A) Date of Notification
(B) Last date of filing nomination
(C) Date of announcement of election schedule by ECI
(D) Date of Nomination

165. Who was known as 'Little Corporal'?
(A) Bismark (B) Adolf Hitler
(C) Napolean Bonaparte (D) Lord Curzon

166. Which of the following states have only one representatives each in Lok Sabha?
(A) Nagaland, Mizoram (B) Goa, Nagaland
(C) Arunachal Pradesh, Tripura (D) Meghalaya, Mizoram

167. Beighton Cup is associated with:
(A) Badminton (B) Polo
(C) Kabaddi (D) Hockey

168. Average blood volume in a normal human being is:
(A) 5-6 litres
(B) 3-4 litres
(C) 2-3 litres
(D) 8-10 litres

169. Which of the following pairs is incorrect?
(A) Bora-Adriatic Sea
(B) Mistral-Gulf of Lion
(C) Harmattan-Gulf of Guinea
(D) Tocopherol

170. Which of the following pair (river: origin place) is incorrect?
(A) Chambal: Janapav
(B) Son: Amarkantak
(C) Tapi: Multai
(D) Godavari: Mahabaleshwar

171. What is the name of position in which Earth and Sun are nearest?
(A) Perihelion
(B) Aphelion
(C) Apogee
(D) Perigee

172. Who said that 'Education is the manifestation of perfection already in man'?
(A) Swami Vivekanand
(B) Sri Aurobindo
(C) Ravindranath Tagore
(D) Subhash Chandra Bose

173. INDICA was written by:
(A) Ban Bhatt
(B) Kalidas
(C) Chanakya
(D) Megasthenese

174. World's only floating National Park is located in:
(A) India
(B) West Indies
(C) Malaysia
(D) Australia

175. Jet Streams are:
(A) Wind System with a pronounced seasonal reverse in direction
(B) Winds blowing from subtropical High Pressure belts towards sub-polar low pressure belts
(C) Winds blowing from sub-polar low pressure belts towards subtropical High Pressure belts
(D) Narrow meandering bands of swift winds which blow in the mid latitudes near the tropopause and encircle the globe

176. What is the missing number in the series:
2,7,28,63,126,_____
(A) 215
(B) 245
(C) 276
(D) 296

177. A man starts walking from his house towards south. After walking 5 km, he turned to his left and walked 6 km. Then he walked further 5 km after turning left. Then he turned to his left and continued to walk for 9 km. How far is he from his house?
(A) 3 km
(B) 4 km
(C) 5 km
(D) 6 km

178. A man pointing to a lady said, "The son of her only brother is the brother of my wife". The lady is related to the man as:
(A) Mother-in-law
(B) Grand Mother
(C) Mother's sister
(D) Sister of Father-in-law

179. Which of the following country became first member of European Union to recognise the State of Palestine?
(A) Hungary
(B) Sweden
(C) Poland
(D) Iceland

180. The first border haat (market) facility on Indo-Bangladesh International border in Tripura was recently opened at:
(A) Sylhet-Chittagong border
(B) Srinagar-Ramgarh border
(C) Khulna-Rajshahi border
(D) Rangpur-Dhaka border

181. International 'Internet Day' is celebrated on:
(A) 27 August
(B) 28 September
(C) 29 October
(D) 30 November

182. Maya Rao who died recently was a renowned:
(A) Kathak dancer
(B) Bihu dancer
(C) Odishi dancer
(D) Kuchipudi dancer

183. The lifespan of Red Blood Cells (RBCs) is:
(A) 60 days
(B) 120 days
(C) 180 days
(D) 200 days

184. Biosensor is used to measure:
(A) Body pH
(B) Blood Glucose level
(C) Haemoglobin
(D) Salinity in urine

185. Which are primary colours?
(A) White, Black, Blue
(B) Red, Yellow, Orange
(C) Red, White, Green
(D) Red, Green, Blue

186. The percentage (%) of Carbon in atmosphere, by volume, is:
(A) 0.03
(B) 3
(C) 13
(D) 21

187. Which organization releases 'World Investment Report' every year?
(A) UNCTAD
(B) WTO
(C) IMF
(D) World Bank

188. Right to Property, according to Indian Constitution is a:
(A) Legal Right
(B) Social Right
(C) Fundamental Right
(D) Statutory Right

189. The book 'Planning and the Poor' was authored by:
(A) Gunnar Myrdal
(B) Amartya Sen
(C) David Ricardo
(D) B.S. Minhas

190. Which of the following pair (Country: Capital) is incorrect?
(A) Cambodia: Vientin
(B) Philippines: Manila
(C) Syria: Damascus
(D) Estonia: Tallin

191. Total number of High Courts in India is:
(A) 20
(B) 22
(C) 24
(D) 25

192. Which one of the following is the correct chronological order in which the Grand Slam Tennis Tournaments are held every year?
(A) US Open-French Open-Australian Open-Wimbledon
(B) Australian Open-French Open-Wimbledon-US Open
(C) French Open-Australian Open-US Open-Wimbledon
(D) Wimbledon-French Open-US Open-Australian Open

193. Which article of the Indian Constitution relates to "Right to Education"?
(A) Article 45
(B) Article 26A
(C) Article 21
(D) Article 15

194. When was Manipuri language added to 8th Schedule of Indian Constitution?
(A) 1992
(B) 1998
(C) 2001
(D) 2004

195. Which of the following pairs is not correctly matched in respect of Manipur?
(A) Nongeen: State bird
(B) Pengba: State fish
(C) Sangai: State animal
(D) Orchid: State flower

196. The components of Human Development Index are:
(A) Life Expectancy, Per Capita GDP and Sex Ratio
(B) Sex Ratio, Educational Attainment and Pure Drinking Water
(C) Life Expectancy, Per Capita GDP and Educational Attainment
(D) Per Capita GDP, Sex Ratio and Infrastructure

197. What is Potlei?
(A) A transparent and thin veil thrown over the head
(B) Ras costume of Sri Radhika and the Gopis
(C) Golden ring round the head
(D) An Embroidered brightly coloured silk skirt

198. 21st Commonwealth Games in 2022 will be hosted by:

(A) Australia (B) South Africa

(C) Cameroon (D) England

199. Irang, Maku and Tuivai are important tributaries of:

(A) Barak river (B) Imphal river

(C) Yu river (D) Chakpi river

200. Thabal Chongba is integral part of which festival?

(A) Yaoshang (B) Ningol Chakouba

(C) Heikru Hidongba (D) Cheiraoba

ANSWERS SHEET

1. (*a*)	2. (*a*)	3. (*a*)	4. (*c*)	5. (*a*)	6. (*a*)	7. (*a*)	8. (*a*)	9. (*b*)
10. (*b*)	11. (*a*)	12. (*a*)	13. (*b*)	14. (*c*)	15. (*d*)	16. (*b*).	17. (*c*)	18. (*d*)
19. (*d*)	20. (*b*)	21 (*a*)	22. (*c*)	23. (*b*)	24. (*a*)	25. (*b*)	26. (*b*)	27. (*c*)
28. (*c*)	29. (*b*)	30. (*c*)	31. (*c*)	32. (*c*)	33. (*b*)	34. (*a*)	35. (*c*)	36. (*c*)
37. (*a*)	38. (*b*)	39. (*a*)	40. (*a*)	41. (*c*)	42. (*d*)	43. (*d*)	44 (*d*)	45. (*b*)
46. (*b*)	47 (*c*)	48. (*a*)	49. (*d*)	50. (*a*)	51. (*a*)	52. (*c*)	53. (*c*)	54. (*c*)
55. (*d*)	56. (*d*)	57. (*a*)	58. (*c*)	59. (*c*)	60. (*b*)	61. (*c*)	62. (*a*)	63. (*b*)
64. (*c*)	65. (*c*)	66. (*c*)	67. (*b*)	68. (*c*)	69. (*c*)	70. (*c*)	71. (*a*)	72. (*a*)
73. (*b*)	74. (*a*)	75. (*b*)	76. (*b*)	77. (*b*)	78. (*a*)	79. (*a*)	80. (*c*)	81. (*a*)
82. (*a*)	83. (*a*)	84. (*d*)	85. (*d*)	86. (*a*)	87. (*d*)	88. (*a*)	89. (*b*)	90. (*c*)
91. (*a*)	92. (*c*)	93. (*d*)	94. (*d*)	95. (*b*)	96. (*c*)	97. (*d*)	98. (*a*)	99. (*a*)
100. (*c*)	101. (*b*)	102. (*a*)	103. (*c*)	104. (*d*)	105. (*c*)	106. (*a*)	107. (*a*)	108. (*a*)
109. (*a*)	110. (*a*)	111. (*c*)	112. (*c*)	113. (*a*)	114. (*b*)	115. (*b*)	116. (*c*)	117. (*a*)
118. (*d*)	119. (*a*)	120. (*c*)	121. (*b*)	122. (*b*)	123. (*a*)	124. (*a*)	125. (*d*)	126. (*b*)
127. (*a*)	128. (*b*)	129. (*b*)	130. (*b*)	131. (*a*)	132. (*b*)	133. (*b*)	134. (*d*)	135. (*a*)
136. (*d*)	137. (*c*)	138. (*a*)	139. (*c*)	140. (*c*)	141. (*c*)	142. (*a*)	143. (*d*)	144. (*c*)
145. (*a*)	146. (*a*)	147. (*c*)	148. (*a*)	149. (*d*)	150. (*b*)	151. (*c*)	152. (*d*)	153. (*b*)
154. (*d*)	155. (*a*)	156. (*a*)	157. (*a*)	158. (*d*)	159. (*b*)	160. (*b*)	161. (*a*)	162. (*a*)
163. (*b*)	164. (*b*)	165. (*c*)	166. (*a*)	167. (*d*)	168. (*a*)	169. (*d*)	170. (*d*)	171. (*a*)
172. (*a*)	173. (*d*)	174. (*a*)	175. (*a*)	176. (*a*)	177. (*b*)	178. (*d*)	179. (*b*)	180. (*a*)
181. (*c*)	182. (*a*)	183. (*b*)	184. (*c*)	185. (*d*)	186. (*a*)	187. (*a*)	188. (*a*)	189. (*d*)
190. (*a*)	191. (*a*)	192. (*b*)	193. (*a*)	194. (*a*)	195. (*d*)	196. (*c*)	197. (*b*)	198. (*a*)
199. (*a*)	200. (*a*)							

35. The toxicity of SO_2 increases with increasing relative humidity. In an atmosphere of 96% RH, SO_2 is more than 20 times as effective as at 75% RH. The toxicity also increases about 1.5 times for each 10°C rise in temperature between 0-30°C.

Additional Important Points

- Gluicidic foods are foods that contain carbohydrates and can raise blood sugar lvels.
- The Glycemic Index is a rating system that ranks carbohydrates on a scale of 1 to 100 based on how much they raise blood sugar. Processed foods such as candy, breads, cake, and cookies have a high GI, while whole foods such as unrefined grains, non-starchy vegetables, and fruits tend to have a lower GI.
- Partially seaming of lid of cans is known as clinching
- Bitter taste of fenugreek is due toTrigonellen (allkaloid)
- Basil plant contains phenolic compounds anethole and methyl chavicol.
- Sweet taste in fennel is due to anethole
- Cloves are good source of eugenol, clove buds contain 45-70% of eugenol.
- Eugenol has therapeutic potential against many diseases.
- Cinnamon bark and leaves also contain eugenol but in lower conc.
- Soyabean is rich source of Isoflavanols.
- Pectinol enzyme is widely used for clarification of juices
- Flute is common to describe the properties and structure of material being used in the packaging, especially corrugated cardboard boxes. A packaging flute plays an important role in the environmental impact, durability, and performance of the packaging.
- Flute types are based on different thicknesses and sizes. The common types are mentioned below:

  A-Flute: A type of flute with a thickness of up to 5/32 inches or 4mm, offering ideal cushioning to fragile products.

  B-Flute: B flute is thinner than A flute, providing a balance between cushioning and strength. Thickness is 3/16 inches or 4.8mm, which is the ideal flute sheet for packing electronics, food, and consumer goods.

  C-Flute: It is the most common flute type, ensuring excellent strength and cushioning. C flute thickness is 9/32 inches or 7mm, perfect for heavy-duty boxes for shipping products.

  E-Flute: E flutes are thinner than A, B, and C flutes. Moreover, the flute thickness is 1/16 or 1.6mm, ideal for retail-ready boxes, ensuring a fabulous visual appearance. E flute vs B flute can be used to pack smaller products.

  F-Flute: One of the thinner kinds of flute with a thickness of 1/32 inches or 0.8mm. A durable and lightweight option for retail packaging
- **Maturity indices of various fruits and vegetable crops**

  Avocado- Oil Contents

  Sapota- Change of fruit peel to potato colour

  Guava - green mature stage - or Half mature stage for long distaance s

  Ideal TSS for processing grapes- 150°Brix

  For Export purpose - TSS more than 180 °brix

  Ideal TSS of Raisin grapes-; 22-23 °Brix

  Mango ; Slight colour development on the shoulders.

Mango-When one or two ripe fruits fall from the tree naturally (tapka method).

Papaya- Light green with tinge of yellow at apical end. For canning and distant markets-Fully matured

Apple: TSS of Fruit pulp and Starch Index should be 1-2

Pear; Fruit colour, starch Index and Pulp firmness in the fruit

Plum: Fruit colour and firmness TSS 12.5 °brix for european plum

Peach; full bloom, firmness, change of ground colour, from green to yellow or red.

Almond : Change of colour from green to yellow with cracks

Jack fruit Flatenning of spines on the rind and the thickening of latex

Mangostem: Green brown to dark brown

FRUIT BEVERAGES

* Fruit beverages are categorized into two types

(A) **Unfermented beverages:** Fruit juices which do not undergo alcoholic fermentation are called as unfermented beverage. These are under-

1. **Sweetened juice**: It contain 85% natural juice and 10% soluble solids.
2. **RTS (Ready to serve):** It contain 10% fruit juice, 10% soluble solids and 0.3% acid. It is diluted before serving.
3. **Nectar:** It contain 20% fruit juice, 10% soluble solids and 0.3% acid. It is also diluted before serving. It is prepared from Mango, Papaya, Beal and Aonla.
4. **Cordial:** It is a clear fruit juice having no trace of pulp and other soluble substances. It contain 25% juice, 30% TSS, 1.5% acid and 350 ppm solphuric acid. It is prepared from lime and lemon.
5. **Squash:** It contain 25% fruit juice or pulp and 40-45% TSS. It is diluted before serving. It is prepared from Mango, Orange and Pineapple on commercial scale.
6. **Crush:** It contain 25% fruit juice or pulp and 55% TSS. It is also diluted before serving.
7. **Syrup:** It contain 25% fruit juice or pulp, 65% TSS and 1-3 to 15% acid.
8. **Fruit juice concentrate:** It is a kind of beverage with almost no amount of water. Water is removed by heating or freezing. It contain pure juice with at least 32% TSS.
9. **Fruit juice powder:** Fruit juice is converted into free flowing and highly hygrooscopic powder. It tends to retain about 95% of nutritional content of the fruit. It has zero fibre content.
10. **Barley water:** Barley water is a drink made from water that has been cooked with barley . Fruit juice is added to make it a healthy drink. It contain 25% fruit juice, 30% TSS, 0.25% barley starch and 1% acid. It is prepared from lime, lemon and grape fruit.

(B) **Fermented beverages:** Fruit juices which undergo alcoholic fermentation by yeasts or other microbers are called *fermented beverages*.

1. **Wine:** It is prepared from fermentation of Grape juice by yeast. Light wine have 7 to 9% alcohol, medium wine have 9 to 16% alcohol and strong wine have 10 to 21% alcohol.Red wine is prepared from coloured grape (skin intact) white white wine is prepared from white/ green grapes (skin removed)
2. **Feni:** Spiritous liquor. It is prepared from Cashew apple.
3. **Cider:** Alcoholic beverage. It is prepared from Apple.
4. **Champaigne:** It is sparkling wine made in France.

Fruit Beverages FPO specification

Sr.No.	*Product*	*Fruit Juice %*	*TSS%*	*Acidity %*	*SO_2 (ppm)*
1.	Unsweetened juice	100	—	—	—
2.	Sweetened Juice	85	10	—	—
3.	RTS	10	10	0.3	—
4.	Nectar	20	15	0.3	—
5.	Cordial	25	30	1.5	350
6.	Squash	25	40-50	1.0	350
7.	Crush	25	55	1.0	350
8.	Syrup	25	65	1.3 to 1.5	350
9.	Fruit Juice concentrate	—	32	—	—
10.	Barley water	25	30	1.0	—

5. **Port:** It is fortified sweet red wine made originally in Portugal.
6. **Tokay:** It is a fortified wine made originally in Hungary.

* Aging or maturation time for wine is 6 to 8 months.
* Optimum temperature for fermentation of grape wine is 22 to 28°C.
* Common yeast used in wine is *saccharomyces cerevisiae* var. ellipsoideus (20 ml/kg of grape).
* Common yeast used in Cider is *saccharomyces carlsbergensis.* Bael, Jamun, Phalsa and Aonla are also used for preparation of cider.
* CO_2 concentration in cold drinks and beverages is 6-8 g/litre (3-4 Volumes)

Post Harvest Products of Fruits

JAM

❖ It is a product made by boiling fruit pulp with sufficient amount of sugar to a reasonable thick consistency as to hold tissue in original position.

* Jam contain 0.5 to 0.6% acid and 40% invert sugar. Crystallization of Jam occurs when sugar is less than 30%. Sticky or Gummy Jam is due to high TSS. Premature setting of Jam is due to low TSS and high pectin. Generally TSS in jams is minimum 65%(w/w) Sugar content is 60-70% is ok. Maximum limit of sulphur dioxide in form of KMS is 40 ppm. Jam is prepared from Mango, Pear, Apple, Sapota, Peach, Papaya, Tomato, Muskmelon, Raspberry. End point of Jam can be determined by Jelmeter Test.

JELLY

❖ It is a semi-solid product prepared by boiling fruit juice, a clear stained solution from pectin containing fruit extract free from pulp after addition of sugar and acid.

* A perfect Jelly should have original flavour of fruit. It contain minimum 65% TSS. pH of final jelly should be 3.2. Jelly require at least 0.5% pectin. Sugar 60-65%, Fruit acid -1% and water 33-38%. Pectin is the most important constituent of Jelly. Guava is most suitable for Jelly preparation. Jelly is prepared from Guava, Sour-Apple, Plum, Wood Apple, Gooseberry, Papaya and Loquat. Firm ripe fruits are most suitable for Jelly making. Premature gelation happens due to excess of pectin. Pectin content is determined by Alcohol or Telmeter test. Cirtic acid (2 g/kg of fruit) is commonly used as acid in Jelly preparation. The phenomenon of spontaneous exudation of fluid from a gel is called *syneresis* or *weeping Jelly.*
* **Defects in jelly:** 1. Crystal in jelly, 2. Cloudy jelly, 3. Failure to gel, 4. Tough jelly. 5. Weeping jelly

MARMALADE

- As per FSSAI marmalade means a product prepared by boiling sound fruits with peel, pulp and juice with or without water.
- It is prepared from citrus fruit slices suspended in sugar solution.
  - Cooking temperature for marmalade is 103 to 105°C. Cooling temperature for marmalade is 82-88°C. End point is minimum 65% TSS (w/w) at 105°C. Browning is common problem in marmalade. Browning of marmalade is prevented by addition of KMS (0.09 g/kg of marmalade). Sweet orange peel is most commonly used in preparation of marmalade.

CANDY (Confectionary)

- A fruit or vegetable impregnated with cane sugar syrup and subsequently draining of syrup leaving it dried is called candy. Mainly sucrose from sugar cane or sugar beets are major constituent. Other sweeteners in candy are corn syrup, honey, molasses and maple sugar. Milk is used in concentrated or dried form. Milk contributes flavor, colour, texture to candy. Fats in candy are primarily used to supply textural and mouth feel. They are also used to control crystallization and to impact plasticity. Colloids as gelatin and pectin and egg albumin are used as emulsifying agents.

❖ Boiling point ranges of some common sugar confectionery products

Type of confectionery	*Boiling Temperature (°C)*	*Informations*
Non Crystalline candies- Amorphous candies in contrast, have a heterogenous structure and crack into pieces rather than be cut with a knife (*e.g.*, toffee and brittles).		
Hard-boiled sweets	149-166	Four stages involved (1) preparation of the raw materials (2) cooking to the desired consistency (3) cooling and cutting into shapes (4) packing. The chief function of this stage is to bring about emulsification of fat.
Hard toffee	146-154	
Crystalline candies- consistency of sugar syrup to enable the sugar to crystallize to induce crystallization by seeding or agitation and addition of small amounts of other materials which will prevent formation of large crystals.		
Fudge	116	Prepared from brown sugar.Sucrose crystallizes less readily. Fudge ripens during storage and becomes soft and velvetty after 24 hr storage.
Fondant	116-121	A good fondant should be snowy white in colour, the crystals soft enough to be plastic and velvety.
Caramels and regular toffee	118-132	Non crystalline candy.To prevent crystallization of sucrose, larger amounts of invert sugar (or) corn syrup are added. Product texture depend on the quantity of corn syrup, molasses (or) invert sugar

❖ Caramelization temperatures of common carbohydrates

Sugar	*Temperature*
Fructose	110° C
Galactose	160° C
Glucose	160° C
Maltose	180° C
Saccharose	160° C

❖ Some dairy products and organisms used

S. No.	Fermented product	Organisms used
1.	Cultured buttermilk	*Streptococcus lactis* subsp. *cremoris, S. lactis* subsp. *lactis, Leuconostoc mesenteroides*
2.	Bulgarian buttermilk	*Lactobacillus delbrueckii* subsp. *bulgaricus*
3.	Kefir (made from cow, sheep, goat milk)	Mainly *Lactobacillus brevis,* yeasts
4.	Kumiss (made from mare's milk)	LAB and yeasts
5.	Taette	*Streptococcus lactis*

❖ Spoilage characteristics of dairy products

S. No.	Fermented product	Spoilage
1.	Fermented milk	Vessels or equipment if contaminated with Coliforms and lactose-fermenting yeasts may result in gas production and bad odour
2.	Cheese	
2.1	During manufacturing	Use of raw milk might cause gas formation and off flavor, Spores of Clostridium can also cause gas formation
	Cheddar cheese: Holes or openness	*Leuconostoc* spp.
	Slimy cheese	*Pseudomonas, P. fragi, Alcaligenes metalcaligenes*
2.2	During ripening	'Late Gas' formation by heterofermentative LAB, *Clostridium* spp.
	Bitterness in cheese	Streptococci, coliforms
	Putrefaction	*Clostridium tyrobutyricum, C. sporogenes, C. lentoputrescens*
	Cheddar cheese: Rusty spots	*Lactobacillus plantarum* var. *rudensis L. brevis* var. *rudensis*
2.3	Finished cheese	Moulds: *Oospora* (*Geotrichum*) spp.*Cladosporium* spp. *Penicillium* spp. *Monilia* spp.
	"Dairy mold"	*Oospora* (*Geotrichum*) *lactis*
	"Cheese cancer"	*O. caseovorans*
	Dark coloured cheese	*Cladosporium herbarum*
	Spots on rind (Yellowish brown)	*Penicillium casei*
	Spots on rind (black) on hard cheese	*Monilia nigra*

❖ **Fermented products with their substrates and related organisms**

Sl. No.	Fermented product	Substrate	Organisms used
1.	*Sinki*	Radish	*Lactobacillus plantarum, L. brevis, L. fermentum*
2.	*Kinema*	Soybean	Natural fermentation: *Bacillus subtilis, Enterococcus faecium*
3.	*Soibum/Soidon*	Bamboo-shoot *Dendrocalamus* sp., *Melocana bambusoide, Bambusa* sp.	*Lactobacillus plantarum, L. brevis, L. coryniformis, L. delbrueckii, L. lactis, Leuconostoc falllax, L. mesentroides, Enterococcus durans, Streptococcus lactis, Bacillus subtilis, B. licheniformis, B. coagulans, Candida* sp., *Saccharomyces* sp., *Torulopsis* sp.
4.	*Mesu*	Bamboo-shoot	*Lactobacillus plantarum, L. brevis* and *L. pentosaceus.*
5.	*Apong*	Rice	*Saccharomyces cerevisiae, Hanseniaspora* sp., *Kloeckera* sp., *Pichia* sp., *Candida* sp.
6.	*Sake* (Rice beer)	Rice	*Aspergillus oryzae, Saccharomyces* spp.
7.	*Sonti* (Rice beer/wine)	Rice	*Rhizopus sonti*
8.	Pulque	Agave	*Zymomonas mobilis*
9.	Rum (Distilled liquors)	Sugarcane: juice or molasses,	*Saccharomyces cerevisiae* var. *ellipsoideus* (distillers' yeasts)
10.	Whiskey (Distilled liquors)	Grains like: rye, corn, wheat	*Saccharomyces cerevisiae* var. *ellipsoideus* (distillers' yeasts)

❖ **Defects in Pickle and their causes**

Defect	Cause
Floaters/ bloaters result in floating/Bloating	Heterofermentative LAB, *L. plantarum,* yeasts, or coliforms produce CO_2
Slippery pickle: Slipperiness, sliminess	Air exposure, Growth of film yeast on brine surface
Soft pickle: Degradation of pectin	Pectinolytic enzymes from *Penicillium,Fusarium, Cladosporium,* and *Alternaria,* less salt, too low acidity, faulty fermentation, high temperature
Black pickle: H_2S production	Black color due to reaction of H_2S with iron resulting in Ferrous sulfide Low acidity, growth of *Bacillus nigrificans*
Fish eye in ripe olives	*Bacillus subtilis, Bacillus pumilus*

❖ Spoilage of Canned foods:

Spoilage	Microorganism responsible	Characteristics
Sulfide spoilage	*Clostridium nigricans, Desulfotomaculum nigricans*	Produces 'H_2S' gas & 'rotten egg' smell, blackening
Flat sour spoilage	*Bacillus coagulans*	Sour taste, Off flavor,Cloudy appearance of food inside can Spoilage can't be detected unless the can is opened as there is no swelling
Putrefactive anaerobic spoilage	*Clostridium sporogenes*	Swelling, putrid odor
Thermophilic anaerobic spoilage	*Clostridium thermosaccharolyticum*	Swelling of can, production of H_2 and CO_2, Can might burst open, sour & cheesy taste, butyric smell

❖ Average Air Composition

S. No.	Air components	Symbol	Volume (dry air)
1	Nitrogen %	N_2	78.08
2	Oxygen %	O_2	20.95
3	Argon %	Ar	0.93
4	Carbon dioxide (ppm)	CO_2	350
5	Neon (ppm)	Ne	18.2
6	Helium (ppm)	He	5.24
7	Methane (ppm)	CH_4	2
8	Krypton (ppm)	Kr	1.1
9	Hydrogen (ppm)	H_2	0.5
10	Nitrous oxide (ppm)	N_2O	0.3
11	Xenon (ppm)	Xe	0.08
12	Carbon monoxide (ppm)	CO	0.05-0.2
13	Ozone (ppm)	O_3	0.02-0.03

*Dry atmosphere below 80 Km (ppm = parts per million)

Quick Review

Most important essential fatty acid is	Linoleic acid
Amino acid converted in body to Niacin	Tryptophan
Pyridoxine is vitamin	B_6
Most sensitive tool for evaluating iron status of body	Serum ferritin
Trace element having vitamin E like action	Selenium
Food standards in India are based on the standards of	Codex alimentarius
Carbohydrate reserve in human body	400-500 gm of glycogen
RDA of **proteins** for adult Indian	0.83 gm/kg/day
Iodine dose in pregnancy	250 mcg per day
Semi essential amino acids are	Histidine, Arginine
Daily requirement of vitamin K	55 mcg/d
Daily dose of iron for adult man	19 mg per day
Acceptable fluoride concentration in drinking water	1 ppm
Expected level of iodine in iodized salt at production level is	> 30 ppm
Expected level of iodine in iodized salt at consumer level is	> 15 ppm
Iodine requirement	150 mcg per day (< 1 teaspoon for entire lifetime)
Salt containing compound potassium iodide is called	Iodised salt
Salt containing compound potassium iodide is termed as	Iodated salt
RDA of calcium in normal adult male	1000 mg/d
Iron recommended intake of adult woman per day	29 mg per day
Richest source of vitamin-A and D is	Halibut liver oil (50 mg of Vit A and 80 μg of Vit. D.
Richest source of vitamin-C	Amla (Indian Gooseberry)
Optimum level of fluorine intake	0.5-0.8 ppm (mg/L)
Richest source of iron among nuts	Pistachio nuts
Phosphatase test is done for	Efficiency of pasteurization
Milk is poor in	Vitamin C and iron
Toxin in Lathyrism	BOAA
Pulses with highest protein content	Soya bean (43%)
Methionine is limiting amino acid in	Pulses
Highest content of saturated fatty acids is in	Coconut oil
Maize is pellagrogenic due to excess of	Leucine

Pulse proteins are poor in	Methionine
Biological value of rice protein	67
1 gram of Twin fortified salt' provides	40 mcg iodine + 1 mg iron
First indicator of PEM	Under-weight for age
Order in Nalgonda technique for defluoridation	Lime + Alum
Amino acid deficient in wheat	Threonine and Lysine
Defluoridation of water is done by technique	Nalgonda technique
Parboiling of rice reduce disease	Beriberi
BOAA (β-N-oxalylamino-L-alanine) toxin responsible for Neuroplathyrism, contains amino acid	Alanine
Lathyrism is due to consumption of	Khesari dhal
First sign of vitamin A deficiency is	Conjunctival xerosis (Dry eye)
Kanawati index is used for	Protein energy malnutrition
Most common nutritional problem in India	Iron deficiency anaemia
Limiting amino acid in soya bean is	Methonine
Meat is poor source of	Calcium
Fish is a poor source of	Carbohydrates
Egg is poor source of	Vitamin C and Carbohydrates
Gingelly Seeds (Seasame) are richest source of	Vitamin B_1 (Thiamine)
Ragi is rich source of	Calcium
Richest source of Essential fatty acid	safflower
Omega 3 Fatty acids are shown to reduce incidences of	Coronary Heart Diseases
Essential Fatty acids were earlier known as	Vitamin F
Protein contains approximately 16% nitrogen by weight, so 1 gram of nitrogen represents	6.25 grams of protein
RDI (Recommended Dietary Intake) (Vitamin B_{12}) for adults	2.4 µg
RDI (Recommended Dietary Intake) (Vitamin C) for adults women	71 µg
RDI (Recommended Dietary Intake) (Vitamin C) for adult men	90 µg
RDI (Recommended Dietary Intake) (Vitamin C) for smokers	125 µg (36 meg more)

NUTRITIONAL REQUIREMENTS : NEW NUTRITIONAL GUIDELINES (2020-21)

	Iron mg/day	*Folic acid mcg/day*	*Calcium mg/day*	*Vitamin A mcg/day*	*Vitamin D IU/dayMa*
Man	19	300	1000	1000	600
Woman	29	220	1000	840	600
Pregnancy	40	570	1000	900	600
Lactation	23	330	1200	950	600

RECOMMENDED DAILY ENERGY AND PROTEIN INTAKE (NEW GUIDELINE (2021)

Group	*Particulars*	*Energy (kcal/(d)*	*Proteins (g/(d)*
Adult Male	Sedentary worker	2100	54
	Moderate worker	2700	54
	Heavy worker	3500	54
Adult Female	Sedentary worker	1700	54.7
	Moderate worker	2100	45.7
	Heavy worker	2700	45.7
	Pregnancy	+350	+9.5, +22
	Lactation (0-6 m)	+600	+17
	Lactation (6-12 m)	+520 kcal/d	8.1
Infants	0-6 months	550 kcal/d	8.1
	6-12 months	670 kcal/d	10.5

Specific dynamic action (SDA) or (thermic effect of food (TEF) or Dietary induced thermogenesis (DIT)

- TEF is the amount of energy expenditure above the basal metabolic rate due to the cost of processing food for use and storage.
- TEF is the energy required for digestion, absorption, and disposal of ingested nutrients.
- TEF magnitude depends on the composition of food consumed; Protein (20-30% of energy consumed > Carbohydrates (5-15%) > Fat: (at most 5-15%).
- A thermic effect of 30% for proteins means that 100 calories of protein only end up as 70 usable calories.

Amino acids most deficient in proteins of a food item are 'Limiting amino acids'.

Food items	*Limiting amino acid(s)*
Cereals	Threonine (& Lysine)
Pulses	Methionine (& Cysteine)
Maize	Tryptophan (& Lysine)

Essential amino acids (EAA): Amino acids which are not synthesized in adequate amounts in the human body; so they have to be supplemented in diet from outside to prevent deficiency.

There are 10, EAA, namely, Phenylalanine, Valine, Threonine, Tryptophan, Isoleucine, Methionine, Histidine, Arginine, Leucine, Lysine.

The **glycemic index** is a measure used to determine how much a food can affect your blood sugar levels. Several factors affect the glycemic index of a food, including the ripeness, nutrient composition, and cooking method.

Glycemic index of various food items:

Carbohydrate foods that break down quickly during digestion have the highest glycemic index. The benchmark is white bread, which has a GI of 100.

Low GI (Less than 55): Most Fruits and vegetables(Except Potato/watermelon/sweet potato) Whole grains, beans, pasta, lentils and wheat)

Medium GI (GI 56-69): Sucrose, Basmati rice, Brown rice

High GI (GI greater than 70): Corn flakes, baked potato, white bread, candy bar, syrupy foods, jasmine rice and all sugary foods.

Fatty Acid Content of Different Fats (%)

Fats	*SFA*	*MUFA*	*PUFA*
Coconut Oil	92	6	2
Safflower oil	10	15	75
Sunflower seed oil	8	27	65
Soya bean oil	14	24	62
Margarine	25	25	50
Groundnut oil	19	50	31
Palm Oil	46	44	3
Mustard oil	12	60	21

SFA (Saturated Fatty Acids, MUFA: Mono saturated Fatty Acids and PUFA: Poly-unsaturated Fatty Acids) Monounsaturated and polyunsaturated fats — lower disease risk. Unsaturated fat remains the healthiest type of fat.

Essential Fatty Acids (EFA): Are those that cannot be synthesized in human body; they can only be derived from the food.

The most important EFA is Linoleic Acid, which serves as a basis for production of other EFA

Dietary sources of EFA:

EFA	*Dietary source*	*% Content*
Linoleic Acid	Safflower oil	73
	Corn oil	57
	Sunflower oil	56
	Soyabean oil	51
Arachidonic Acid	Meat, Eggs	0.5
	Milk (fat)	0.5
Linolenic Acid	Soyabean oil	7
Elcosapentaenoic Acid	Fish oil	10

❖ List of compounds approved by FSSAI as prebiotics

1. Polydextrose
2. Soya poly-saccharides and soya oligosaccharides
3. Isomalto-oligosaccharides
4. Fructo-oligosaccharides
5. Gluco-oligosaccharides
6. Xylo-oligosaccharides
7. Inulin
8. Isomaltulose
9. Gentio-oligosaccharides
10. Lactulose

❖ List of strains approved by FSSAI as probiotics (live microorganisms)

1. *Lactobacillus acidophilus*
2. *Lactobacillus plantarum*
3. *Lactobacillus reuteri*
4. *Lactobacillus rhamnosus*
5. *Lactobacillus salivarius*
6. *Lactobacillus casei*
7. *Lactobacillus brevis*
8. *Lactobacillus johnsonii*
9. *Lactobacillus delbrueckii* (sub-sp. *bulgaricus*)
10. *Bacillus coagulans*
11. *Lactobacillus fermentum*
12. *Lactobacillus caucasicus*
13. *Lactobacillus helveticus*
14. *Lactobacillus lactis*
15. *Lactobacillus amylovorus*
16. *Lactobacillus gallinarum*
17. *Lactobacillus delbrueckii*
18. *Bifidobacterium bifidum*
19. *Bifidobacterium lactis*
20. *Bifidobacterium breve*
21. *Bifidobacterium longum*
22. *Bifidobacterium animalis*
23. *Bifidobacterium infantis*
24. *Streptococcus thermophilus*
25. *Saccharomyces boulardii*
26. *Saccharomyces cerevisiae*
27. *Lactobacillus paracasei*
28. *Lactobacillus gasseri*
29. *Bacillus clausii*
30. Established probiotic strains of *'Bacillus subtilis'*

This list may be updated by the Food Authority to add any new strain of microorganism that possesses probiotic properties, after proper scientific evaluation. Probiotic preparations may contain added prebiotics permitted under these regulations.

SUPPLEMENT TO COMPETITION BOOK FOR FOOD SAFETY OFFICER

FSSAI

- Present Chairperson of FSSAI is- **Rajesh Bhushan, IAS**
- Present Chief Executive Officer of FSSAI is - **G. Kamala Vardhana Rao, IAS**
- Headquarters of FSSAI is located at **New Delhi**
- Total Zones of FSSAI - **(Five) 5 (North Zone, South Zone, East Zone, West Zone, North East Zone)**
- Total Regional Offices - **8 (Eight) (Delhi, Chennai, Kolkata, Mumbai, Chandigarh, Lucknow, Guwahati and Kochi)**
- FSS act 2006 has **12 chapters and 101 sections.**

Chapter 1: Preliminary (Section 1 to 3) - 1. Short title, 2. Declaration, 3. Definitions

Chapter 2: FSSAI (Section 4 to 17)

Chapter 3: General Principles of Food Safety (Section 18) - 18. General Principles to be followed in administration of Act

Chapter 4: General provisions as to articles of Food (Section 19 - 24)

Chapter 5: Provisions relating to import (Section 25) - 25. All imports of articles of food to be subject to this Act.

Chapter 6: Special responsibilities as to food safety (Section 26 - 28) - 26. Responsibilities of the food business operator, 27. Liability of the manufacturers, packers, wholesalers, distributors and sellers, 28. Food recall procedures.

Chapter 7: Enforcement of the act (Section 29 - 42)

Chapter 8: Analysis of food (Section 43 to 47)

Chapter 9: Offences and Penalties (Section 48 to 67)

Chapter 10: Adjudication and food safety appellate tribunal (Section 68 to 80) -

Chapter 11: Finance, Accounts, Audits and reports (Section 81 to 84) - 81. Budget of Food Authority, 82. Finances of the Food Authority, 83. Accounts and audit of Food Authority, 84. Annual report of Food Authority.

Chapter 12: Miscellaneous (Section 85 to 101)

- According to FSSAI, Penalty for unhygienic processing or manufacturing of food may extend to 1 lakh rupees.
- According to FSSAI, Punishment for interfering with seized items shall be imprisonment up to 6 months and fine up to 2 lakh rupees
- Adjudicating Officer have the power of Civil Court and all proceedings before him shall be deemed to be judicial proceedings under India Panal Code.
- Appeal against special court can be filed in high court within 45 days from the date on which order was served, after payment of fee.
- Appeal against tribunal order can be filed in high court within a period of 60 days of decision/order.
- **Food safety officer** - Inspection of premises, sample drawn and sending to food analyst.

Duties

The Commissioner of Food Safety shall appoint such persons as he thinks fit, having the qualifications prescribed by the Central Government, as Food Safety Officers for such local areas as he may assign to them for the purpose of performing functions under this Act and the rules and regulations.

The Commissioner of Food Safety may, by notification, appoint such persons as he thinks fit, having the qualifications prescribed by the Central Government, to be Food Analysts for such local areas as may be assigned to them by the Commissioner of Food Safety.

The Food Safety and Standards Act, 2006 (Definitions) Section 3

(1) "Adulterant" means any material which is or could be employed for making the food unsafe or sub-standard or mis-branded or containing extraneous matter;

(2) "advertisement" means any audio or visual publicity, representation or pronouncement made by means of any light, sound, smoke, gas, print, electronic media, internet or website and includes through any notice, circular, label, wrapper, invoice or other documents;

(3) "Chairperson" means the Chairperson of the Food Authority;

(4) "Claim" means any representation which states, suggests, or implies that a food has particular qualities relating to its origin, nutritional properties, nature, processing, composition or otherwise;

(5) "Commissioner of Food Safety" means the Commissioner of Food Safety appointed under section 30;

(6) "Consumer" means persons and families purchasing and receiving food in order to meet their personal needs;

(7) "Contaminant" means any substance, whether or not added to food, but which is present in such food as a result of the production (including operations carried out in crop husbandry, animal husbandry or veterinary medicine), manufacture, processing, preparation, treatment, packing, packaging, transport or holding of such food or as a result of environmental contamination and does not include insect fragments, rodent hairs and other extraneous matter;]

(8) "Designated Officer" means the officer appointed under section 36;

(9) "Extraneous matter" means any matter contained in an article of food which may be carried from the raw materials, packaging materials or process systems used for its manufacture or which is added to it, but such matter does not render such article of food unsafe;

After test or analysis the certificate there of shall be supplied to off with to sector in Form B. Fees of certificate Rs. 1000 per sample certificate must be signed by Director.

(10) "Food" means any substance, whether processed, partially processed or unprocessed, which is intended for human consumption and includes primary food, genetically modified or engineered food or food containing such ingredients, infant food, packaged drinking water, alcoholic drink, chewing gum, and any substance, including water used into the food during its manufacture, preparation or treatment but does not include any animal feed, live animals unless they are prepared or processed for placing on the market for human consumption, plants, prior to harvesting, drugs and medicinal products, cosmetics, narcotic or psychotropic substances:

Provided that the Central Government may declare, by notification in the Official Gazette, any other article as food for the purposes of this Act having regards to its use, nature, substance or quality;

(11) "food additive" means any substance not normally consumed as a food by itself or used as a typical ingredient of the food, whether or not it has nutritive value, the intentional addition of which to food for a technological (including organoleptic) purpose in the manufacture, processing, preparation, treatment, packing, packaging, transport or holding of such food results, or may be reasonably expected to result (directly or indirectly), in it or its by-products becoming a component of or otherwise affecting the characteristics of such food but does not include "contaminants" or substances added to food for maintaining or improving nutritional qualities;

(12) "Food business" means any undertaking, whether for profit or not and whether public or private, carrying out any of the activities related to any stage of manufacture, processing, packaging, storage, transportation, distribution of food, import and includes food services, catering services, sale of food or food ingredients;

(13) "Food business operator" in relation to food business means a person by whom the business is carried on or owned and is responsible for ensuring the compliance of this Act, rules and regulations made thereunder;

(14) "Food laboratory" means any food laboratory or institute established by the Central or a State Government or any other agency and accredited by **National Accreditation Board for Testing and Calibration Laboratories** or an equivalent accreditation agency and recognised by the Food Authority under section 43;

(15) "Food safety" means assurance that food is acceptable for human consumption according to its intended use;

(16) "Food safety audit" means a systematic and functionally independent examination of food safety measures adopted by manufacturing units to determine whether such measures and related results meet with objectives of food safety and the claims made in that behalf;

(17) "Food Safety Management System" means the adoption of Good Manufacturing Practices, Good Hygienic Practices, Hazard Analysis and Critical Control Point and such other practices as may be specified by regulation, for the food business;

(18) "Hazard" means a biological, chemical or physical agent in, or condition of, food with the potential to cause an adverse health effect;

(19) "Improvement notice" means a notice issued under section 32 of this Act;

(20) "Infant food" and "infant milk substitute" shall have the meanings assigned to them in clauses (*f*) and (*g*) of sub-section (1) of section 2 of the Infant Milk Substitutes, Feeding Bottles and Infant Foods (Regulation of Production, Supply and Distribution) Act, 1992 (41 of 1992), respectively;

(21) "Ingredient" means any substance, including a food additive used in the manufacture or preparation of food and present in the final product, possibly in a modified form;

(22) "Label" means any tag, brand, mark, pictorial or other descriptive matter, written, printed, stencilled, marked, embossed, graphic, perforated, stamped or impressed on or attached to container, cover, lid or crown of any food package and includes a product insert;

(23) "Licence" means a licence granted under section 31 of the act;

(24) "Local area" means any area, whether urban or rural, notified by the Commissioner of Food Safety, to be a local area for the purposes of the Act;

(25) "Manufacturer" means a person engaged in the business of manufacturing any article of food for sale and includes any person who obtains such article from another person and packs and labels it for sale or only labels it for such purposes;

(26) "Member" includes a part-time Member and the Chairperson of the Food Authority;

(27) "misbranded food" means an article of food–'

(A) if it is purported, or is represented to be, or is being–

(*i*) offered or promoted for sale with false, misleading or deceptive claims either;

(*a*) upon the label of the package, or (*b*) through advertisement, or

(*ii*) sold by a name which belongs to another article of food; or

(*iii*) offered or promoted for sale under the name of a fictitious individual or company as the manufacturer or producer of the article as borne on the package or containing the article or the label on such package; or

(B) if the article is sold in packages which have been sealed or prepared by or at the instance of the manufacturer or producer bearing his name and address but–

(*i*) the article is an imitation of, or is a substitute for, or resembles in a manner likely to deceive, another article of food under the name of which it is sold, and is not plainly and conspicuously labelled so as to indicate its true character; or

(*ii*) the package containing the article or the label on the package bears any statement, design or device regarding the ingredients or the substances contained therein, which is false or misleading in any material particular, or if the package is otherwise deceptive with respect to its contents; or

(*iii*) the article is offered for sale as the product of any place or country which is false; or

(C) if the article contained in the package–

(*i*) contains any artificial flavouring, colouring or chemical preservative and the package is without a declaratory label stating that fact or is not labelled in accordance with the requirements of this Act or regulations made thereunder or is in contravention thereof; or

(*ii*) is offered for sale for special dietary uses, unless its label bears such information as may be specified by regulation, concerning its vitamins, minerals or other dietary properties in order sufficiently to inform its purchaser as to its value for such use; or

(*iii*) is not conspicuously or correctly stated on the outside thereof within the limits of variability laid down under this Act

(28) "notification" means a notification published in the Official Gazette;

(29) "Package" means a pre-packed box, bottle, casket, tin, barrel, case, pouch, receptacle, sack, bag, wrapper or such other things in which an article of food is packed;

(30) "Premises" include any shop, stall, hotel, restaurant, airline services and food canteens, place or vehicle or vessel where any article of food is sold or manufactured or stored for sale;

(31) "Prescribed" means prescribed by rules made by the Central Government or the State Government, as the case may be under this Act;

(32) "Primary food" means an article of food, being a produce of agriculture or horticulture or animal husbandry and dairying or aquaculture in its natural form, resulting from the growing, raising, cultivation, picking, harvesting, collection or catching in the hands of a person other than a farmer or fisherman;

(33) "Prohibition order" means an order issued under section 33 of this Act;

(34) "Risk", in relation to any article of food, means the probability of an adverse effect on the health of consumers of such food and the severity of that effect, consequential to a food hazard;

(35) "Risk analysis", in relation to any article of food, means a process consisting of three components, *i.e.* risk assessment, risk management and risk communication;

(36) "Risk assessment" means a scientifically based process consisting of the following steps: (*i*) hazard identification, (*ii*) hazard characterization; (*iii*) exposure assessment, and (*iv*) risk characterization;

(37) "Risk communication" means the interactive exchange of information and opinions throughout the risk analysis process concerning risks, risk-related factors and risk perceptions, among risk assessors, risk managers, consumers, industry, the academic community and other interested parties, including the explanation of risk assessment findings and the basis of risk management decisions;

(38) "Risk management" means the process, distinct from risk assessment, of evaluating policy alternatives, in consultation with all interested parties considering risk assessment and other factors relevant for the protection of health of consumers and for the promotion of fair trade practices, and, if needed, selecting appropriate prevention and control options;

(39) "Sale" with its grammatical variations and cognate expressions, means the sale of any article of food, whether for cash or on credit or by way of exchange and whether by wholesale or retail, for human consumption or use, or for analysis, and includes an agreement for sale, an offer for sale, the exposing for sale or having in possession for sale of any such article, and includes also an attempt to sell any such article;

(40) "Sample" means a sample of any article of food taken under the provisions of this Act or any rules and regulations made thereunder;

(41) "Standard", in relation to any article of food, means the standards notified by the Food Authority;

(42) "Substance" includes any natural or artificial substance or other matter, whether it is in a solid state or in liquid form or in the form of gas or vapour;

(43) "Sub-standard" - an article of food shall be deemed to be sub-standard if it does not meet the specified standards but not so as to render the article of food unsafe;

(44) "Unsafe food" means an article of food whose nature, substance or quality is so affected as to render it injurious to health:—

(*i*) by the article itself, or its package thereof, which is composed, whether wholly or in part, of poisonous or deleterious substances; or

(*ii*) by the article consisting, wholly or in part, of any filthy, putrid, rotten, decomposed or diseased animal substance or vegetable substance; or

(*iii*) by virtue of its unhygienic processing or the presence in that article of any harmful substance; or

(*iv*) by the substitution of any inferior or cheaper substance whether wholly or in part; or

(*v*) by addition of a substance directly or as an ingredient which is not permitted; or

(*vi*) by the abstraction, wholly or in part, of any of its constituents; or

(*vii*) by the article being so coloured, flavoured or coated, powdered or polished, as to damage or conceal the article or to make it appear better or of greater value than it really is; or

(*viii*) by the presence of any colouring matter or preservatives other than that specified in respect thereof; or

(*ix*) by the article having been infected or infested with worms, weevils, or insects; or

(*x*) by virtue of its being prepared, packed or kept under insanitary conditions; or (*xi*) by virtue of its being mis-branded or sub-standard or food containing extraneous matter; or

(*xii*) by virtue of containing pesticides and other contaminants in excess of quantities specified by regulations.

4. Establishment of Food Safety and Standards Authority of India. This section seeks to provide for establish and incorporation of an authority to be called the Food Safety and Standards Authority of India. The head office of the Authority shall be at Delhi. However, the Authority is empowered to establish its offices at any other places in India.

5. Composition of Food Authority and qualifications for appointment of its Chairperson and other Members.

6. Selection Committee for selection of Chairperson and Members of Food Authority.–(1) The Central Government shall, for the purpose of selection of the Chairperson and the Members other than *ex officio* Members of the Food Authority, constitute a Selection Committee consisting of–

(*a*) Cabinet Secretary–Chairperson,

(*b*) Secretary-in-charge of the Ministry or the Department responsible for administration of this Act as the convener–Member,

(*c*) Secretary-in-charge of the Ministries or the Departments of the Central Government dealing with Health, Legislative and Personnel–Members,

(*d*) Chairman of the Public Enterprises Selection Board–Member,

(*e*) An eminent food technologist to be nominated by the Central Government–Member.

7. Term of office, salary, allowances and other conditions of service of Chairperson and Members of Food Authority.–(1) The Chairperson and the members other than ex officio Members shall hold office for a term of three years from the date on which they enter upon their offices, and shall be eligible for re-appointment for a further period of three years.

8. Removal of Chairperson and Members of Food Authority: This section lays down the various grounds on which the Chairperson and Members of the Food Authority can be removed from office such as on the grounds of insolvency, physical or mental incapacity conviction in an offence involving moral turpitude or having an interest prejudicial to his functions as a Member or abuse of position.

9. Officers and other employees of Food Authority. This section provides for appointment of a Chief Executive Officer and other officers and employees of the Food Authority. It provides that salaries and allowances payable to and other conditions of service of Chief Executive Officer and other officers and employees shall be determined by regulations made by the Food Authority with the approval of the Central Government.

10. Functions of the Chief Executive Officer. This section prescribes that the Chief Executive Officer of the Food Authority, who shall be in the rank of Additional Secretary to the Government of India, shall be appointed by the Central Government and he shall be the legal representative of the Food Authority.

11. Central Advisory Committee. This section provides for establishment of a Central Advisory Committee by the Food Authority consisting of representatives specified therein and the Chief Executive officer shall be its *ex officio* Chairperson.

12. Functions of Central Advisory Committee. This section enumerates functions of Central Advisory Committee such as ensuring close co-operation between the Food Authority and the enforcement agencies and to advise the Food Authority on drawing up of Authority's work programmes, prioritisation of work, identifying potential risks, pooling of knowledge and such other functions as may be specified. It shall meet at least three times in a year.

13. Scientific Panels. This section seeks to provide for establishment of Scientific Panels consisting of independent scientific experts, with representation of industry and consumer organizations for deliberations.

14. Scientific Committee. This section seeks to provide for constitution of Scientific Committee consisting of the Chairpersons of the Scientific Panels and six independent scientific experts not belonging to any of the Scientific Panels.

15. Procedure for Scientific Committee and Scientific Panel. This section prescribes the general procedure for the appointments of the members of the Scientific Committee and Scientific Panels and empowers the Food Authority to lay down procedure for the operation and co-operation of the Scientific Committee and Scientific Panel.

16. Duties and functions of Food Authority. This section enumerates in detail the duties and functions of the Food Authority. It shall be the duty of the Food Authority to regulate and monitor the manufacture, processing, distribution, sale and import of food and shall specify by regulations, the standards and guidelines in relation to articles of food; the mechanisms and guidelines for accreditation of certification bodies engaged in certification of food business and laboratories and notify the accredited laboratories, etc. It shall also provide scientific advice and technical support to the Central and State Governments in matters of framing the policy and rules in areas which have a direct or indirect bearing on food safety; contribute to the development of international technical standards for food, sanitary and phyto-sanitary standards and to undertake any other task assigned by the Central Government to carry out the objects of the Act. The Food Authority shall make it public without undue delay, the opinions of the Scientific Committee and Scientific Panels public immediately after adoption.

17. Proceedings of Food Authority. This section provides for the procedures in regards to meetings of the Food Authority, the transaction of business at its meetings and procedure of voting by the Members etc.

General Principle to be followed in the Act (Section 18)

18. General principles to be followed in administration of Act. This section seeks to provide for the general principles to be followed in administration of the Act by the Central Government, the Food Authority, the State Governments and other agencies, as the case may be, while framing regulations and specifying food safety standards or while enforcing or implementing the provisions of the Act.

Articles of Food

19. Use of food additive or processing aid. – No article of food shall contain any food additive or processing aid unless it is in accordance with the provisions of this Act and regulations made thereunder.

20. Contaminants, naturally occurring toxic substances, heavy metals, etc.– No article of food shall contain any contaminant, naturally occurring toxic substances or toxins or hormone or heavy metals in excess of such quantities as may be specified by regulations.

21. Pesticides, Veterinary drugs residues, antibiotic residues and microbiological counts.– (1) No article of food shall contain insecticides or pesticides residues, veterinary drugs residues, antibiotic residues, solvent residues, pharmacological active substances and micro-biological counts in excess of such tolerance limit as may be specified by regulations.

(2) No insecticide shall be used directly on article of food except fumigants registered and approved under the Insecticides Act, 1968 (46 of 1968).

22. Genetically modified foods, organic foods, functional foods, proprietary foods, etc.– Save as otherwise provided under this Act and regulations made thereunder, no person shall manufacture, distribute, sell or import any novel food, genetically modified articles of food, irradiated food, organic foods, foods for special dietary uses, functional foods, neutraceuticals, health supplements, proprietary foods and such other articles of food which the Central Government may notify in this behalf.

This section provides that no person shall manufacture, process or sell genetically modified articles of food, irradiated food, organic foods, functional foods, neutraceuticals health supplements, proprietary foods and similar foods except in accordance with the provisions contained in the Act and rules and regulations made thereunder.

23. Packaging and labelling of foods. This section provides that no person shall manufacture, distribute, sell or expose for sale or dispatch or deliver to any agent or broker for the purpose of sale, any packaged food products which are not marked and labelled in the manner as may be specified. Every food business operator shall ensure that the labelling and presentation of food does not mislead consumers.

24. Restrictions of advertisement and prohibition as to unfair trade practices. This section provides for restriction on advertisement of any food which misleads or contravenes the provisions of the Act or the rules and regulations made thereunder. It also provides for prohibition as to any unfair trade practice for the purpose of promoting sale, supply, use and consumption of articles of food or adoption of any unfair or deceptive practice to mislead the public regarding the standards, quality, quantity, usefulness or giving of any guarantee of the efficacy that is not based on an adequate or scientific justification thereof.

25. All imports of articles of food to be subject to this Act. This section make all imports of articles of food to be subject to the provisions of Act. It provides that no person shall import into India any article of food in contravention of the Act or any rules and regulations made thereunder. It also provides that the Central Government shall, while prohibiting, restricting or otherwise regulating import of articles of food under the Foreign Trade (Development and Regulation) Act, 1992 (22 of 1992), follow the standards laid down by the Food Authority under the provisions of this Act and the rules and regulations made thereunder.

Special Responsibilities As To Food Safety

26. Responsibilities of the Food business operator.– (1) Every food business operator shall ensure that the articles of food satisfy the requirements of this Act and the rules and regulations made thereunder at all stages of production, processing, import, distribution and sale within the businesses under his control.

(2) No food business operator shall himself or by any person on his behalf manufacture, store, sell or distribute any article of food–

(*i*) which is unsafe; or
(*ii*) which is misbranded or sub-standard or contains extraneous matter; or
(*iii*) for which a licence is required, except in accordance with the conditions of the licence; or
(*iv*) which is for the time being prohibited by the Food Authority or the Central Government or the State Government in the interest of public health; or
(*v*) in contravention of any other provision of this Act or of any rule or regulation made thereunder.

(3) No food business operator shall employ any person who is suffering from infectious, contagious or loathsome disease.

(4) No food business operator shall sell or offer for sale any article of food to any vendor unless he also gives a guarantee in writing in the form specified by regulations about the nature and quality of such article to the vendor:

Provided that a bill, cash memo, or invoice in respect of the sale of any article of food given by a food business operator to the vendor shall be deemed to be a guarantee under this section, even if a guarantee in the specified form is not included in the bill, cash memo or invoice.

(5) Where any food which is unsafe is part of a batch, lot or consignment of food of the same class or description, it shall be presumed that all the food in that batch, lot or consignment is also unsafe, unless following a detailed assessment within a specified time, it is found that there is no evidence that the rest of the batch, lot or consignment is unsafe:

27. Liability of manufacturers, packers, wholesalers, distributors and sellers.– (1) The manufacturer or packer of an article of food shall be liable for such article of food if it does not meet the requirements of this Act and the rules and regulations made thereunder.

(2) The wholesaler or distributor shall be liable under this Act for any article of food which is–

(*a*) Supplied after the date of its expiry; or
(*b*) Stored or supplied in violation of the safety instructions of the manufacturer; or
(*c*) Unsafe or misbranded; or
(*d*) Unidentifiable of manufacturer from whom the article of food have been received; or
(*e*) Stored or handled or kept in violation of the provisions of this Act, the rules and regulations made thereunder; or
(*f*) Received by him with knowledge of being unsafe.

(3) The seller shall be liable under this Act for any article of food which is–

(*a*) Sold after the date of its expiry; or
(*b*) Handled or kept in unhygienic conditions; or
(*c*) Misbranded; or
(*d*) Unidentifiable of the manufacturer or the distributors from whom such articles of food were received; or
(*e*) Received by him with knowledge of being unsafe.

28. Food recall procedures. This section contains the provisions relating to food recall procedures. If a food business operator considers or has reason to believe that a food which it has processed, manufactured or distributed is not in compliance with the provisions of the Act and the rules and regulations made thereunder, it shall immediately initiate procedures to withdraw the food in question from the market and the consumers and inform the competent authorities and co-operate with them, if he considers or has reasons to believe that a food which he has placed on the market may be injurious to human health and shall inform the competent authorities of the action taken to prevent risks to the consumer.

29. Authorities responsible for enforcement of Act.– (1) The Food Authority and the State Food Safety Authorities shall be responsible for the enforcement of this Act.

(2) The Food Safety Officers shall enforce and execute within their area the provisions of this Act with respect to which the duty is not imposed expressly or by necessary implication on some other authority.

30. Commissioner of Food Safety of the State. This section empowers the State Government to appoint Commissioner of Food Safety for the State for efficient implementation of food safety and standards and other requirements laid down under the Act or the rules and regulations made thereunder.

31. Licensing and registration of food business. This section provides for licensing the registration of food business. It provides that no person shall commence or carry on any food business except under a licence issued by a Designated Officer authorised by the Commissioner of Food Safety. An appeal against the order of the Designated Officer shall lie with the Commissioner of Food Safety. Sub-clause (8) of the Act provides that every petty manufacturer who himself manufactures and sell any article of food, retailer, hawker, itinerant vendor, temporary shall holder shall only register their business with the concerned municipality or the Panchayat the case may be.

32. Improvement notices. This section contains provisions for issuing improvement notices to the food businesses which fails to comply with the requirements of the Act. The Designated Officer may serve an improvement notice if he has reasonable grounds for believing that the proprietor or a food business operator has failed to comply with any regulations and in the event of failure to comply with such improvement notice, the licence may be suspended or cancelled. Any person who is aggrieved by an improvement notice may appeal to Commissioner of Food Safety whose decision thereon shall be final.

33. Prohibition orders. This section empowers the court to issue prohibition orders in cases where the food business operator is convicted of an offence under the Act; and the court by or before which he is so convicted is satisfied that the health risk exists with respect to that business. Any person who knowingly contravenes such an order shall be guilty of an offence and be punishable with a fine which may extend to rupees three lakhs.

34. Emergency prohibition notices and orders. This section empowers the Commissioner of Food Safety to serve emergency prohibition notices and orders to the food business operators if the Designated Officer is satisfied that the health risk condition exist with respect to any food business, and on an application made by him to the Commissioner of Food Safety for imposing the appropriate prohibition.

35. Notification of food poisoning. The Food Authority may, by notification, require registered medical practitioners carrying on their profession in any local area specified in the notification, to report all occurrences of food poisoning coming to their notice to such officer as may be specified

36. Designated Officer. The Commissioner of Food Safety shall, by order, appoint the Designated Officer, who shall not be below the rank of a Sub-Divisional Officer, to be in-charge of food safety administration in such area as may be specified by regulations

37. Food Safety Officer. (1) The Commissioner of Food Safety shall, by notification, appoint such persons as he thinks fit, having the qualifications prescribed by the Central Government, as Food Safety Officers for such local areas as he may assign to them for the purpose of performing functions under this Act and the rules and regulations made thereunder.

(2) The State Government may authorise any officer of the State Government having the qualifications prescribed under sub-section (1) to perform the functions of a Food Safety Officer within a specified jurisdiction.

38. Powers and Duties of Food Safety Officer.

The duties of food safety officer are:

- The Food Safety Officer may take a sample of food and can seize any article of food which appears contravention of this Act. Where any sample is taken, its cost calculated at the rate at which the article is usually sold to the public shall be paid to the person from whom it is taken.
- The Food Safety Officer may enter and inspect any place where the article of food is manufactured, or stored for sale, or stored for the manufacture of any other article of food, or exposed or exhibited for

sale and where any adulterant is manufactured or kept, and take samples of such articles of food or adulterant for analysis.

- Where any article of food seized is of a perishable nature and the Food Safety Officer is satisfied that such article of food is so deteriorated that it is unfit for human consumption, the Food Safety Officer may, after giving notice in writing to the food business operator, cause the same to be destroyed.
- The Food Safety Officer shall, in exercising the powers of entry upon, and inspection of any place under this section.
- Any adulterant found in the possession of a manufacturer or distributor any article of food may be seized by the Food Safety Officer and a sample of such adulterant submitted for analysis to a Food Analyst.
- The Commissioner of Food Safety may from time to time issue guidelines with regard to exercise of powers of the Food Safety Officer, which shall be binding. Provided that the powers of such Food Safety Officer may also be revoked for a specified period by the Commissioner of Food Safety.

39. Liability of Food Safety Officer in certain cases.– Any Food Safety Officer exercising powers under this Act or the rules and regulations made thereunder who–

(*a*) vexatiously and without any reasonable ground seizes any article of food or adulterant; or

(*b*) commits any other act to the injury of any person without having reason to believe that such act is necessary for the execution of his duty, shall be guilty of an offence under this Act and shall be liable to a penalty which may extend to one lakh rupees:

40. Purchaser may have food analysed. This section enables the purchaser of any article of food to get analyzed such food from the Food Analyst after informating the food business operator at the time of purchase of his intention to have such article so analyzed. In case the Food analyst finds the sample in contravention of the provisions of the Act, he shall follow the procedure prescribed under the Act for prosecution.

41. Power of search, seizure, investigation, prosecution and procedure thereof. This section empowers the Food Safety Officer to search any place, seize any article of food or adulterant, if there is a reasonable doubt about them being involved in commission of any offence relating to food.

42. Procedure for launching prosecution. This section lays down procedure for launching prosecutions, if provides that the Designated Officer, after scrutiny of the report of Food Analyst shall decide as to whether the contravention is punishable with imprisonment or fine only and in the case of contravention punishable with imprisonment, he shall send his recommendations within fourteen days to Commissioner of Food Safety for sanctioning prosecution.

ANALYSIS OF FOOD

43. Recognition and accreditation of laboratories, research institutions and referral food laboratory. This section contains the provisions relating to recognition and accreditation of laboratories, research institutions and referral food laboratory. It empowers the Food Authority to, recognize any food laboratory and research institution as accredited by National Accreditation Board for Testing and Calibration Laboratories (NABL) or similar accreditation agency for the purposes of carrying out analysis of samples by the Food Analysts; establish or recognize one or more referral food laboratory or laboratories to carry out the functions entrusted to the referral food laboratory, frame regulations specifying the functions of food laboratory and referral food laboratory, the procedure for submission of samples of articles of food to the laboratory for analysis or tests.

44. Recognition of organisation or agency for food safety audit. This section provides for recognition of organisation or agency for food safety audit by the food authority for the purposes of food safety audit and checking compliance with safety management systems required under the Act or the rules or regulations made thereunder.

45. Food Analysts. This section empowers the Commissioner of Food Safety of the State to appoint Food Analysis for such local areas as may be assigned to them. However, no person who has any financial interest in the manufacture or sale of any article of food shall be appointed as a Food Analyst.

46. Functions of Food Analyst.

Duties of Food Analyst:

- On receipt of a package containing a sample for analysis from a Food Safety Officer or any other person, the Food Analyst shall compare the seal on the container and the outer cover with specimen impression received separately and shall note the conditions of the seal there on.
- Provided that in case a sample container received by the Food Analyst is found to be in broken condition or unfit for analysis, he shall within a period of 7 days from the date of receipt of such sample inform the Designated Officer about the same and send requisition to him for sending second part of the sample.
- The Food Analyst shall cause to be analysed such samples of article of food as may be sent to him by Food Safety Officer or by any other person authorized.
- The Food Analyst shall, within a period of fourteen days from the date of receipt of any sample for analysis, send Designated Officer, four copies of the report indicating the method of sampling and analysis.
- Where such sample is received under purchaser, a copy of the report indicating the method of sampling and analysis to the person who had purchased such article of food with a copy to the Designated Officer.
  - If in case the sample cannot be analysed within fourteen days of its receipt, the Food Analyst shall inform the Designated Officer and the Commissioner of Food Safety giving reasons for delay.
  - An appeal against the report of Food Analyst shall lie before the Designated Officer who shall, if he so decides, refer the matter to the referral food laboratory as notified by the Food Authority for opinion.
  - **License granted** under FSSAI act and regulations shall be valid for a period of 1 to 5 years.
  - **FSSAI issues license of food business for Registration:** For firms which have a turnover of less than Rs. 12 Lakh.
  - **FSSAI issues license of food business for State License:** For firms with turnover between Rs. 12 Lakh to Rs. 20 Crore.
  - **FSSAI issues license of food business for Central License:** For firms with turnover of above Rs. 20 Crore.

47. Sampling and analysis. This section provides for the procedures for sampling and analysis of articles of foods. When a sample of any article of food or adulterant is taken the Food Safety Officer shall, by the immediately succeeding working day, send the sample in accordance with the rules prescribed for sampling to the Food Analysts for the area concerned. An article of food or adulterant seized, unless destroyed, shall be produced before the Designated Officer as soon as possible and in any, case not later than seven days after the receipt of the report of the Food Analyst.

OFFENCES & PENALTIES

48. General provisions relating to offences.– (1) A person may render any article of food injurious to health by means of one or more of the following operations, namely:–

(*a*) adding any article or substance to the food;
(*b*) using any article or substance as an ingredient in the preparation of the food;
(*c*) abstracting any constituents from the food; or
(*d*) subjecting the food to any other process or treatment, with the knowledge that it may be sold or offered for sale or distributed for human consumption.

49. General provisions relating to penalty.–While adjudging the quantum of penalty under this Chapter, the Adjudicating Officer or the Tribunal, as the case may be, shall have due regard to the following:–

(*a*) the amount of gain or unfair advantage, wherever quantifiable, made as a result of the contravention,
(*b*) the Amount of loss caused or likely to cause to any person as a result of the contravention,
(*c*) the repetitive nature of the contravention,
(*d*) whether the contravention is without his knowledge, and
(*e*) any other relevant factor.

50. Penalty for selling food not of the nature or substance or quality demanded.– Any person who sells to the purchaser's prejudice any food which is not in compliance with the provisions of this Act or the regulations made thereunder, or of the nature or substance or quality demanded by the purchaser, shall be liable to a penalty not exceeding five lakh rupees:

Provided that the persons covered under sub-section (2) of section 31, shall for such non-compliance be liable to a penalty not exceeding twenty-five thousand rupees.

51. Penalty for sub-standard food.– Any person who whether by himself or by any other person on his behalf manufactures for sale or stores or sells or distributes or imports any article of food for human consumption which is sub-standard, shall be liable to a penalty which may extend to five lakh rupees.

52. Penalty for misbranded food.– (1) Any person who whether by himself or by any other person on his behalf manufactures for sale or stores or sells or distributes or imports any article of food for human consumption which is misbranded, shall be liable to a penalty which may extend to three lakh rupees.

53. Penalty for misleading advertisement.– Any person who publishes, or is a party to the publication of an advertisement, which–

(*a*) falsely describes any food; or

(*b*) is likely to mislead as to the nature or substance or quality of any food or gives false guarantee, shall be liable to a penalty which may extend to ten lakh rupees.

54. Penalty for food containing extraneous matter.– Any person whether by himself or by any other person on his behalf manufactures for sale or stores or sells or distributes or imports any article of food for human consumption containing extraneous matter, shall be liable to a penalty which may extend to one lakh rupees.

55. Penalty for failure to comply with the directions of Food Safety Officer.– If a food business operator or importer without reasonable ground, fails to comply with the requirements of this Act or the rules or regulations or orders issued thereunder, as directed by the Food Safety Officer, he shall be liable to a penalty which may extend to two lakh rupees.

56. Penalty for unhygienic or unsanitary processing or manufacturing of food.– Any person who, whether by himself or by any other person on his behalf, manufactures or processes any article of food for human consumption under unhygienic or unsanitary conditions, shall be liable to a penalty which may extend to one lakh rupees.

57. Penalty for possessing adulterant. This section provides penalty for manufacture, sales, distribution or import of any adulterant.

58. Penalty for contraventions for which no specific penalty is provided.– Whoever contravenes any provisions of this Act or the rules or regulations made thereunder, for the contravention of which no penalty has been separately provided in this Chapter, shall be liable to a penalty which may extend to two lakh rupees.

59. Punishment for unsafe food.– Any person who, whether by himself or by any other person on his behalf, manufactures for sale or stores or sells or distributes or imports any article of food for human consumption which is unsafe, shall be punishable,

60. Punishment for interfering with seized items.– If a person without the permission of the Food Safety Officer, retains, removes or tempers with any food, vehicle, equipment, package or labelling or advertising material or other thing that has been seized under this Act, shall be punishable with imprisonment for a term which may extend to six months and also with fine which may extend to two lakh rupees.

61. Punishment for false information.– If a person, in connection with a requirement or direction under this Act, provides any information or produces any document that the person knows is false or misleading, he shall be punishable with imprisonment for a term which may extend to three months and also with fine which may extend to two lakh rupees.

62. Punishment for obstructing or impersonating a Food Safety Officer.– If a person without reasonable excuse, resists, obstructs, or attempts to obstruct, impersonate, threaten, intimidate or assault a Food Safety Officer in exercising his functions under this Act, he shall be punishable with imprisonment for a term which may extend to three months and also with fine which may extend to one lakh rupees.

63. Punishment for carrying out a business without licence.– If any person or food business operator (except the persons exempted from licensing under sub-section (2) of section 31 of this Act), himself or by any person on his behalf who is required to obtain licence, manufacturers, sells, stores or distributes or imports any article of food without licence, shall be punishable with imprisonment for a term which may extend to six months and also with a fine which may extend to five lakh rupees.

64. Punishment for subsequent offences. This section seeks to provide punishment for subsequent offences and makes the offender liable to twice the punishment which might have been imposed on a first conviction, subject to the punishment being maximum provided for the same offence; and a further fine on daily basis which may extend upto one lakh rupees, where the offence is a continuing one, and cancellation of his licence.

65. Compensation in case of injury or death of consumer.– (1) Without prejudice to the other provisions of this Chapter, if any person whether by himself or by any other person on his behalf, manufactures or distributes or sells or imports any article of food causing injury to the consumer or his death, it shall be lawful for the Adjudicating Officer or as the case may be, the court to direct him to pay compensation to the victim or the legal representative of the victim, a sum—

(*a*) not less than five lakh rupees in case of death;
(*b*) not exceeding three lakh rupees in case of grievous injury; and
(*c*) not exceeding one lakh rupees, in all other cases of injury:
(*d*) Recovery of penalty under FSSAI if not paid can be recovered from Land revenue.

66. Offences by companies

67. Penalty for contravention of provisions of this Act in case of import of articles of food to be in addition to penalties provided under any other Act.

68. Adjudication,

69. Power to compound offences

70. Establishment of Food Safety Appellate Tribunal

71. Procedure and powers of the Tribunal

72. Civil court not to have jurisdiction

73. Power of court to try cases summarily

74. Special courts and Public Prosecutor

75. Power to transfer cases to regular courts

76. Appeal

77. Time limit for prosecutions

78. Power of court to implead manufacturer, etc.,

79. Magistrate's power to impose enhanced punishment

80. Defences which may or may not be allowed in prosecution under this Act.

Table 1: Recommended quantity of sample to be sent to the Food Analyst for Analysis

S. No.	Article of Food	Approximate Quantity
1.	Milk	500 ml
2.	Sterilized Milk / UHT Milk	500 ml
3.	Malai / Dahi	200 gms
4.	Yoghurt / Sweetened Dahi	500 gms
5.	Chhana / Paneer / Khoya / Shrikhand	250 gms
6.	Cheese / Cheese spread	200 gms
7.	Evaporated Milk / Condensed Milk	200 gms
8.	Ice-Cream / Softy / Kulfi / Icecandy / Icelolly	300 gms
9.	Milk Powder / Skimmed Milk Powder	250 gms
10.	Infant Food / Weaning Food	500 gms
11.	Malt Food / Malted Milk Food	300 gms
12.	Butter / Butter Oil / Ghee / Margarine / Cream / Bakery Shortening	200 gms
13.	Vanaspati, Edible Oils / Fats	400 gms
14.	Carbonated Water	3 litres

15.	Baking Powder	100 gms
16.	Arrow root / Sago	250 gms
17.	Corn flakes / Macaroni Products / Corn Flour / Custard Powder	200 gms
18.	Spices, Condiments and Mixed Masala (Whole)	500 gms
19.	Spices, Condiments and Mixed Masala (Powder)	500 gms
20.	Nutmeg / Mace	250 gms
21.	Asafoetida	100 gms
22.	Compounded Asafoetida	150 gms
23.	Saffron	20 gms
24.	Gur/jaggery, Icing Sugar, Honey, Synthetic Syrup, Bura	250 gms
25.	Cane Sugar / Refined Sugar /Cube Sugar, Dextrose, Misri /Dried Glucose Syrup	200 gms
26.	Artificial Sweetener	100 gm.
27.	Fruit Juice / Fruit Drink / Fruit Squash	1 ltr.
28.	Tomato Sauce / Ketch up / Tomato Paste, Jam / Jelly / Marmalade / Tomato Puree / Vegetable Sauce	300 gms
29.	Non Fruit Jellies	200 gms
30.	Pickles and Chutneys	250 gms
31.	Oilseeds / Nuts / Dry Fruits	250 gms
32.	Tea / Roasted Coffee / Roasted Chicory	500 gms
33.	Instant Tea / Instant Coffee / Instant Coffee-Chicory Mixture	100 gms
34.	Sugar Confectionery / Chewing Gum / Bubble Gum	20 gms
35.	Chocolates	200 gms
36.	Edible Salt	200 gms
37.	Iodised Salt / Iron Fortified Salt	200 gms
38.	Food Grains and Pulses (Whole and Split)	1 kg
39.	Atta / Maida /Suji / Besan/Other Milled Product /Paushtik Fortified Atta /Maida	500 gms
40.	Biscuits and Rusks	200 gms
41.	Bread / Cakes / Pasties	250 gms
42.	Gelatin	150 gms
43.	Catechu	150 gms
44.	Vinegar / Synthetic Vinegar	300 gms
45.	Food Colours	25 gms
46.	Food colour preparation Solid/100 gm (Solid/Liquid) /100 ml liquid	
47.	Natural Mineral Water / Packaged Drinking Water 4000 ml in three minimum original sealed packs.	
48.	Silver Leafs	2 gm
49.	Prepared Food	500 gms
50.	Proprietary Food, (Non Standardized Foods)	500 gms
51.	Canned Foods	6 Sealed cans
52.	Food not specified	500 gms

After test or analysis the certificate thereof shall be supplied forth with to sender in Form B. Fees of certificate is Rs. 1000/- per sample certificate must be signed by Director.

- **SOFTEL** - Strengthening of Food Testing Laboratories Information Bank.

Six initiatives of the schemes

1. Support Mobile Food labs.
2. Strengthen referral Food Testing Laboratory.
3. Strengthen State Food Testing Laboratory.
4. Develop Food testing culture in schools/colleges.
5. Capacity building of Food Testing personnel.
6. Incentivize state to use facilities available in FSSAI notified private labs.

- Receiving temperature of potentially high risk foods should be at 5 °C or below or above 60 °C to avoid danger zone.
- Working surface of vending carts shall be placed at least 60 to 70 cm from above ground to clean it easily (According to FSSAI).
- The temperature in fridge for refrigeration should be in the range of 4 ° C to 6 °C.
- Raw milk must be brought to a dairy plant by a producer within four hours of milking for safe quality of milk.
- Stunning methods induce temporary loss of consciousness and rely on prompt and accurate sticking procedures to cause death. Two most commonly employed electrical stunning methods are: **head-to-body induction head-to-body, head-to-forelegs or split electric stunning.**
- Stunning is done prior to slaughter is a statutory requirement for animal welfare.
- **Three main types of stunning for pigs:** 1. Mechanical, 2. Electrical and 3. Gas.
- Cooked food must be served hot and should be kept at a temperature of at least 60 °C to prevent microbial growth.
- Reheated food must reach a minimum internal temperature of 74 °C to serve.
- Chopping instruments should be cleaned with hot water at a temperature of 82 °C.
- **Thawing** is process of warming of food that has been frozen so that food can be eaten or prepared to be served for eating. Thawing of food should never be done under danger zone of 40°F - 140°F (5 °C - 60 °C). Bacteria can grow rapidly under these temperature.
- **Thawing** can be done by
  1. Defrosting food in Refrigerator, 2. Defrosting in the microwave, 3. Defrosting food under cool running water, 4. Defrosting as a part of cooking
- Thawing in running water should not exceed 90 minutes.
- After thawing product must be used within 12 hours time.
- Aflatoxins are colourless, odourless and tasteless chemicals which are invisible to naked eye
- Aflatoxins are produced by fungus, *Aspergillus fungus* or *Aspergillus parasite*
- Aflatoxin in all articles of food has a limit of 4-30 mg/kg for human consumption
- Aflatoxin M_1 in milk as per FSSAI has a maximum limit of 0.5 mg/kg.
- Aflatoxins limits for cereals, cereal products, pulses, nuts and nuts for further processing is 15 μg/kg
- Limit of 10 μg/kg for **ready to eat products, dried figs** while 30 μg/kg for spices and oil seeds for further processing limit is set at 15 μg/kg.
- **Cream cheese, coulommiers, cottage, ricotta** and **cheese** comes under soft unripened cheese.
- **Samsoe, Emmentaler, Cheshire** and **Cheddar** are hard ripened cheese.
- Can used for canning of acid red fruit - AR enamel
- **Can used for non-acidic foods** - C-enamel
- Tin containers are preferred over - **glass containers**
- **Exhausting** is the process of removing all the air from the can before sealing to create anaerobic environment and also retain quality. Exhaustion is prescribed at 82-87°C temperature of water for 6-10 minutes.
- **Rigid packaging** - Metal can, Corrugated fibre board and Glass container.
- **Semi rigid packaging includes** - Folding carton, Line carton and Aseptic carton.
- **Flexible packaging** - Aluminium, Aluminium foil, Paper, Paper board and Plastic.
- **Thermoplastic** - These are polymers that can be melted and recast almost indefinitely. They are molten when heated and harden upon cooling. When frozen, however, thermoplastic becomes glass-like and subject to fracture.

- **Thermoset** - Thermoset are typically hard and rigid plastic. Keep their form and remain solid under heat once cured.
- **Controlled Atmosphere Packaging** - Controlling the known gas composition in the packaging or storage room environment such as O_2, CO_2, water vapour and ethylene concentration which reduce spoilage and contamination thus extending shelf life of the product.
- **Modified Atmosphere Packaging** - Three main gases used in MAP are CO_2, O_2 and N_2 either singly or combined. Modifies the internal package atmosphere of food and helps to preserve packaged food.
- **Intelligent packaging:** A packaging system that is capable of carrying out intelligent functions (such as detecting, sensing, recording, tracing, communicating, and applying scientific logic) to facilitate decision making to extend shelf life, enhance safety, improve quality, provide information and warn about possible problems.
- Codex Alimentarius commission was created in the year 1963.
- Codex Alimentarius commission was created by joint efforts of WHO and FAO.
- Right to Information Act (RTI) was passed b parliament on Oct 2005.
- AGMARK was promulgated in 1937.
- AGMARK Act 1937 comes under Department of Agriculture and Cooperation.
- National Horticultural Board was set up by Government of India in April 1984. With Headquarters at Gurugram, Haryana.

Cyanogenic glycosides are natural plant toxins which occur is at least 2000 plant species. Amygdalin is the most common. It occur as glycosides which are stored in the vacuole.

Bacteria are single celled microorganisms found in nearly all environments.

Viruses are extremely small parasites and they require living cells of human or animals or bacteria for growth.

Food with a fuzzy or cottony appearance is likely mold a type of fungus which make food unfit for consumption.

Yeast refer to fungi which are not filamentous but are avoid or spherical and which reproduce by budding of fission. Currently 1,500 species of yeast are recognized.

Mycotoxins are toxins produced by moulds or fungi

Most commonly used chemical for preservation of food is **sodium Benzoate.**

FSSAI regulations permit **urea content** in milk shall not be more than 700 ppm.

Major quality tests of milk

Name of test	*Purpose*	*Remark*
Acidity	Final acceptance /rejections of milk	As platform test
Ethanol(alcohol test)	To determine heat stability	As platform test
Alcohol-alizarin	To determine heat stability and pH of milk	As platform test
COB(clot on boiling)	To determine heat stability	As platform test
Dye reduction test(MBR)	To determine the extent of bacterial contamination and growth in milk	As platform test
DMC(direct microscopic count	To identify the types of microorganism present in milk	As laboratory test
SSPC (standard plate count)	To determine the extent bacterial contamination growth in milk	As laboratory test
Lactometer test	To determine adulteration of milk with water	As platform test

Additional Abbreviations

- **ASABE** : American Society of Agricultural and Biological Engineers.
- **ASHRAE** : American Society of Heating, Refrigerating and Air Conditioning Engineers.
- **IDF** : International Dairy Federation.
- **EFFCA** : European Food & Fermentation Cultures Association (Formed in 1994)
- **EFSA** : European Food Safety Authority
- **FAO** : Food andAgriculture Organization.
- **WHO** : World Health Organization.
- **FSSAI** : Food Safety and Standards Authority of India.
- **CAC** : Codex Alimentarius Commission.
- **SPS** : Sanitary and Phytosanitary Measures.
- **TBT** : Technical Barriers to Trade.
- **JECFA** : Joint Expert Committee on Food Additives.
- **JMPR** : Joint Meetings on Pesticide Residues.
- **JEMRA** : Joint Expert Meeting on Microbiological Risk Assessment.
- **JEMNU** : Joint Expert Meeting on Nutrition.
- **IPPC** : The International Plant Protection Convention.
- **ICMSF** : International Commission on Microbiological Specifications for Foods.
- **OIE** : World Organisation for Animal Health.
- **QPS** : Qualified Presumption of Safety.
- **QRAC** : Quantitative Risk Analysis Committee
- **IPCC** : Inter Governmental Panel on Climate Change (HQ at Geneva Switzerland) (1988)
- **NOEL** : No Observable Effect Level
- **PAGE** : Polyacrylamide Gel Electrophoresis
- **HPLC** : High-Performance Liquid Chromatography
- **TLC** : Thin-Layer Chromatography
- **GPC** : Gel Permeation Chromatography

International Organization

- **CCFA** : Codex Committee on Food Additives
- **CCCF** : Codex Committee on Contaminants in Foods
- **CCFH** : Codex Committee on Food Hygiene
- **CCFICS** : Codex Committee on Food Import and Export Inspection and Certification Systems
- **CCFL** : Codex Committee on Food Labelling
- **CCGP** : Codex Committee on General Principles
- **CCMAS** : Codex Committee on Methods of Analysis and Sampling
- **CCFSDU** : Codex Committee on Nutrition and Foods for Special Dietary Uses
- **CCPR** : Codex Committee on Pesticide Residues
- **CCRVDF** : Codex Committee on Residues of Veterinary Drugs in Foods
- **CCCPL** : Codex Committee on Cereals, Pulses and Legumes
- **CCFFV** : Codex Committee on Fresh Fruits and Vegetables
- **CCFO** : Codex Committee on Fats and Oils
- **CCPFV** : Codex Committee on Processed Fruits and Vegetables
- **CCSCH** : Codex Committee on Spices and Culinary Herbs

Food Science and Technology (2025)

1. Red muscle fibres have ____________ myoglobin than white muscle fibre.
   (A) higher (B) lower
   (C) dense (D) thin
2. Foaming is a functional property attributed to the ____________ component of food.
   (A) protein (B) fat
   (C) minerals (D) sugars
3. Pectin is primarily composed of ____________.
   (A) galactose and glucose (B) fructose
   (C) galacto-pyranosyl uronic acid (D) amylose
4. Candling of egg reveals the presence of ____________.
   (A) blood spot (B) hazards
   (C) vitelline membrane (D) microorganisms
5. The standard weight of extra large size grade hen eggs, ranges ____________ g.
   (A) 38- 44 (B) More then 60
   (C) 53- 59 (D) 45- 52
6. The major microorganism responsible for food transmitted through eggs is ____________.
   (A) *E.coli* (B) *Salmonella*
   (C) *Pseudomonas* (D) *Clostridium botulinum*
7. Match List I with List II

List I *Cake defects*	*List II* *Causes*
(a) Too light crust	(I) Too high baking temperature
(b) Dense texture	(II) Too much shortening
(c) Too dark crust	(III) Too little sugar
(d) Crumbly texture	(IV) Too much liquid

   Choose the **most appropriate** answer from the options given below:
   (A) (a)-(I), (b)-(II), (c)-(III), (d)-(IV) (B) (a)-(I), (b)-(III), (c)-(II), (d)-(IV)
   (C) (a)-(I), (b)-(II), (c)-(IV), (d)-(III) (D) (a)-(III), (b)-(IV), (c)-(I), (d)-(II)
8. Match List I with List II

List I *Ingredients for bread manufacture*	*List II* *Role of ingredients*
(a) Shortening	(I) Texture
(b) Yeast	(II) Flavour
(c) Sugar	(III) Loaf volume
(d) Flour	(IV) Fermentation substrate

   Choose the **most appropriate** answer from the options given below:
   (A) (a)-(II), (b)-(III), (c)-(IV), (d)-(I) (B) (a)-(I), (b)-(III), (c)-(II), (d)-(IV)
   (C) (a)-(I), (b)-(II), (c)-(IV), (d)-(III) (D) (a)-(III), (b)-(IV), (c)-(I), (d)-(II)

9. The term "GRAS" stands for :
(A) Generally Recognized As Stable
(B) Generally Recommended As Safe
(C) Generally Regarded As Stable
(D) Generally Recognized As Safe

10. Match List I with List II

List I *Product*	*List II* *Property*
(a) Biscuit	(I) Low sugar and fat
(b) Cracker	(II) Flat crisp
(c) Hard dough biscuit	(III) Partially developed gluten
(d) Soft dough biscuit	(IV) Flowy dough

Choose the **most appropriate** answer from the options given below:
(A) (a)-(II), (b)-(I), (c)-(III), (d)-(IV)
(B) (a)-(I), (b)-(III), (c)-(II), (d)-(IV)
(C) (a)-(I), (b)-(II), (c)-(IV), (d)-(III)
(D) (a)-(III), (b)-(IV), (c)-(I), (d)-(II)

11. The sequence of biscuit manufacturing process generally involves:
(a) Cooling and packing
(b) Forming
(c) Baking
(d) Mixing
Choose the **most appropriate** answer from the options given below:
(A) (d), (b), (c), (a)
(B) (a), (b), (c), (d)
(C) (b), (a), (d), (c)
(D) (c), (b), (d), (a)

12. The process for the development of cocoa mass follows a sequence of
(a) Cooling and packing
(b) Cleaning and roasting
(c) Breaking and winnowing
(d) Fermentation of dried beans
Choose the **most appropriate** answer from the options given below:
(A) (a), (b), (c), (d)
(B) (d), (b), (c), (a)
(C) (b), (a), (d), (c)
(D) (c), (b), (d), (a)

13. Syneresis or weeping is a defect in ______________.
(A) Jelly
(B) Pickles
(C) Juices
(D) Jam

14. Arrange the processing steps of Jelly marmalade in a proper sequence :
(a) Selection and preparation of fruit
(b) Preparation of sherds and peels
(c) Boiling and cleaning of pectin
(d) Canning and sterilization
Choose the **most appropriate** answer from the options given below:
(A) (a), (b), (d), (c)
(B) (a), (b), (c), (d)
(C) (a), (c), (b), (d)
(D) (c), (b), (d), (a)

15. Natural carotenes can be extracted from ______________.
(A) Saffron
(B) Soyabean
(C) Beans
(D) Pear

16. The process of yoghurt manufacture involves the following sequence :
(a) Homogenization of milk
(b) Standardization of milk
(c) Pasteurization, cooling followed by addition of starter culture
(d) Fermentation, packaging and storage

Choose the **most appropriate** answer from the options given below:

(A) (c), (a), (b), (d) (B) (b), (c), (a), (d)

(C) (b), (a), (c), (d) (D) (a), (b), (c), (d)

17. Toxic constituent in Vicia faba may cause __________ pathological disorder.

(A) Favism (B) Lathyrism

(C) Rickets (D) Blindness

18. Which of the following legume is considered as the poor man's pulse?

(A) Field bean (B) Horse gram

(C) Green gram (D) Lentil

19. Which of the following are polyunsaturated fatty acids (n-6)?

(a) Linolic (b) γ- Linoleic

(c) Arachidonic (d) Oleic

Choose the **most appropriate** answer from the options given below :

(A) (a), (b) and (d) only (B) (a), (b) and (c) only

(C) All of the above (D) (b), (c) and (d) only

20. Durum wheat is used for the making of __________ .

(A) Pasta (B) Cake

(C) Pastry (D) Cookies

21. Freshly milled wheat flour used for bread making is matured for __________ months during storage.

(A) 3 to 4 (B) 2 to 3

(C) 1 to 2 (D) 5 to 6

22. The yellow colour of the cow milk is due to the presence of __________ .

(A) sterols (B) albumin

(C) phospholipids (D) carotenoids

23. Sequentially arrange the processing steps involved in the manufacturing of **cheddar cheese**

(a) Standardization (b) Pre-heating

(c) Addition of starter culture (d) Pasteurization

Choose the **most appropriate** answer from the options given below:

(A) (a), (b), (d), (c) (B) (a), (b), (c), (d)

(C) (b), (a), (d), (c) (D) (c), (b), (d), (a)

24. Foods which are specially processed or formulated to satisfy a particular dietary requirement which exists due to a disease or disorder are known as __________ .

(A) Healthy foods (B) Nutraceuticals

(C) Balanced foods (D) Special foods

25. The rate of food spoilage is not dependent on __________ .

(A) Water activity (B) Package size

(C) OR potential (D) Temperature

26. Match List I with List II

List I *Raw Foods*	*List II* *Storage temperature range (°C)*
(a) Banana	(I) 13-15.6
(b) Lemon	(II) 0-2.2
(c) Nuts	(III) 12.8-14.4
(d) Tomato	(IV) 4.4-10

Choose the **most appropriate** answer from the options given below:

(A) (a)-(I), (b)-(II), (c)-(III), (d)-(IV) (B) (a)-(I), (b)-(III), (c)-(II), (d)-(IV)
(C) (a)-(I), (b)-(II), (c)-(IV), (d)-(III) (D) (a)-(III), (b)-(IV), (c)-(I), (d)-(II)

27. What does the term "JECFA" stands for :
(A) Joint Expert Committee on Food Additives
(B) Joint Excellence Committee on Food Allergens
(C) Joint Excellence Committee on Food Analysis
(D) Joint Export Committee on Food Additives

28. Which of the following criteria that are used for screening of the New Food Product ideas? **cheese**
(a) Marketability (b) Technical feasibility
(c) Manufacturing capacity (d) Financial capability
Choose the **most appropriate** answer from the options given below:
(A) (a), (b) and (d) (B) (a), (b) and (c)
(C) All of the above (D) (b), (c) and (d)

29. In chiffon cakes, leavening occurs mainly by whipping of the ____________.
(A) Egg yolk (B) Citric acid
(C) Egg white (D) Ascorbic acid

30. Hypobaric storage represents storage at ____________.
(a) Low pressure (b) High pressure
(c) Low pressure and high humidity (d) Low pressure and low humidity
Choose the **most appropriate** answer from the options given below:
(A) (a) and (b) only (B) (c)
(C) All of the above (D) (b), (c) and (d) only

31. Which of the following is commonly used as oxygen scavenger in food packaging?
(A) Powered iron (B) Calcium
(C) Potassium permanganate (D) Chlorine

32. Match List I with List II

List I *Methods*	*List II* *Process*
(a) Rigor mortis	(I) Papain
(b) Tenderization of meat	(II) Muscle stiffness
(c) Evisceration	(III) Removal of feathers
(d) Scalding	(IV) Inspection of viscera

Choose the **most appropriate** answer from the options given below:

(A) (a)-(I), (b)-(II), (c)-(III), (d)-(IV) (B) (a)-(I), (b)-(III), (c)-(II), (d)-(IV)

(C) (a)-(II), (b)-(I), (c)-(IV), (d)-(III) (D) (a)-(III), (b)-(IV), (c)-(I), (d)-(II)

33. The penetration of fat within the muscle fibre when an animal is well fed, is called as ____________.

(A) Stabilization (B) Marbling

(C) Ageing (D) Rigor mortis

34. The molten mixture of sand, soda, limestone for the development of glass is called as ____________.

(A) Mold (B) Gob

(C) Curing (D) Annealing

35. Application of silicone on the glass bottle surface during their manufacturing helps in

(a) Maintaining glossy appearance (b) Prevents breakage

(c) Decreases the noise on contact (d) Prevents spoilage

Choose the **most appropriate** answer from the options given below:

(A) (a), (b) and (d) only (B) (a), (b) and (c) only

(C) All of the above (D) (b), (c) and (d) only

36. Sugarcane gur (jaggery) contains ____________ % sucrose.

(A) 65 to 85 (B) 20 to 30

(C) 35 to 40 (D) 50 to 60

37. During processing the characteristic flavour is developed in cocoa :

(A) Cooking (B) Roasting

(C) Boiling (D) Frying

38. Increase in volume of bread during baking is known as ____________.

(A) Sheen (B) Oven spring

(C) Bloom (D) Rising

39. ____________ are responsible for the flavour and aroma of bread.

(A) Propanol and Maltol (B) Flavanol and Isomaltol

(C) Maltol and Isomaltol (D) Maltose and Galactose

40. Match List I with List II

List I	*List II*
Food	*Toxicant*
(a) Peas	(I) Hemagglutinins
(b) Soyabean	(II) Saponins
(c) Spinach	(III) Prussic acid
(d) Almond	(IV) Oxalic acid

Choose the **most appropriate** answer from the options given below:

(A) (a)-(II), (b)-(I), (c)-(IV), (d)-(III) (B) (a)-(I), (b)-(III), (c)-(II), (d)-(IV)

(C) (a)-(I), (b)-(II), (c)-(IV), (d)-(III) (D) (a)-(III), (b)-(IV), (c)-(I), (d)-(II)

41. A flexible pouch capable of with standing temperature of about 120 °C is known as ________.

(A) High barrier plastic
(B) Microwave-ovenable package
(C) Retortable pouch
(D) Aseptic pouch

42. Match List I with List II

List I *Can Name*	*List II* *Dimension*
(a) 62	(I) 307 × 409
(b) No. 2	(II) 203 × 308
(c) No. 10	(III) 303 × 406
(d) 303	(IV) 603 × 700

Choose the **most appropriate** answer from the options given below:

(A) (a)-(I), (b)-(II), (c)-(III), (d)-(IV)
(B) (a)-(II), (b)-(I), (c)-(IV), (d)-(III)
(C) (a)-(I), (b)-(II), (c)-(IV), (d)-(III)
(D) (a)-(III), (b)-(IV), (c)-(I), (d)-(II)

43. Which of the following is NOT a type of "**Difference test**"?

(A) Duo-trio test
(B) Triangle test
(C) Paired-comparison test
(D) Hedonic test

44. QRAC stands for :

(A) Qualitative Risk Analyzing Committee
(B) Qualitative Risk Assessment Committee
(C) Quantitative Risk Assessment Committee
(D) Qualitative Risk Analyzing Committee

45. The instrument used to measure plasticity of bread dough is known as

(A) *Penetrometer*
(B) *Fibrograph meter*
(C) *Tenderometer*
(D) *Brabender Farinograph*

46. The "AGMARK" standard was set up by

(A) Ministry of Health and Family Welfare
(B) Ministry of Agriculture
(C) Directorate of Marketing and Inspection
(D) Directorate of Quality and Inspection

47. The **Codex Alimentarius Commission** was established under the authority of

(a) World Health Organization
(b) World Trate Organization
(c) Food and Agriculture Organization
(d) International Organization for Standardization

Choose the **most appropriate** answer from the options given below:

(A) (a), (b) and (c) only
(B) (a) and (d) only
(C) (a) and (c) only
(D) (b), (c) and (d) only

48. The chemical agents most suitable for deflocculation process are

(a) Sodium metasilicate
(b) Sodium tripolyphosphate
(c) Sodium decaphosphate
(d) Sodium sesquisilicate

Choose the **most appropriate** answer from the options given below:

(A) (a) and (d) only (B) (a), (b) and (d) only

(C) (a), (b) and (d) only (D) (c) and (d) only

49. NOEL stands for

(A) Non-Observable Effluent Limit (B) No Observable Effluent Limit

(C) Non-Observable Effect Level (D) No Observable Effect Level

50. The instrument used to measure the salt percentage of pickles is ___________.

(A) Polari meter (B) Brino graph

(C) Salt meter (D) Lono graph

51. A type of freezing where resistance to heat transfer is minimized due to intimate contact between food or package and refrigerant

(A) Indirect contact freezing (B) Air freezing

(C) Immersion freezing (D) Fluidized-bed freezing

52. The process of 'Hot-break' is commonly used in the manufacturing of products like

(a) Orange squash (b) Tomato paste

(c) Orange juice (d) Tomato juice

Choose the **most appropriate** answer from the options given below:

(A) (b) and (d) only (B) (a), (b) and (c) only

(C) All of the above (D) (c) and (d) only

53. During the process of ripening of fruits, the transition of pectic substance occurs in the following order:

(a) Protopectin (b) Pectin

(c) Pectic acid (d) Pectic acid

Choose the **most appropriate** answer from the options given below:

(A) (a), (c), (b), (d) (B) (b), (a), (c), (d)

(C) (b), (c), (d), (a) (D) (c), (b), (d), (a)

54. The soft and fragile food products, having delicate flavours and colours, are best dried by which of the following method :

(A) Drum drying (B) Vacuum drying

(C) Tray drying (D) Freeze drying

55. Which of the following is used as an antioxidant in facts and oils?

(A) BHA (B) BHF

(C) HBT (D) HBA

56. The correct order of unit operations carried out in the *Canning* of vegetables is:

(A) Sorting ------ Retorting ------ Exhausting ------ Filling ------ Sealing

(B) Retorting ------ Filling ------ Exhausting ------ Processing ------ Sealing

(C) Retorting ------ Filling ------ Processing ------ Exhausting ------ Sealing

(D) Sorting ------ Filling ------ Exhausting ------ Sealing ------ Retorting

57. An example of hard and ripened cheese is :

(A) Roquefort cheese (B) Cottage cheese

(C) Cheddar cheese (D) Camembert cheese

58. The alkali treatment of cocoa to enhance its colour and flavour is known as :

(A) French process
(B) Dutch process
(C) Enrobing
(D) Tempering

59. The enzyme used in isomerization of corn starch during the making of **High Fructose Corn Syrup** is/ are:

(a) Alpha-amylase
(b) Glucoamylase
(c) Glucose isomerase

Choose the **most appropriate** answer from the options given below:

(A) (a) and (b) only
(B) (b) and (c) only
(C) (b) only
(D) (a), (b) and (c)

60. Match List I with List II

List I *Type of sugar*	*List II* *Application*
(a) Icing	(I) Common sweetening ingredient
(b) HFCS	(II) Cake preparation
(c) Sugar cubes	(III) Candies
(d) Granulated	(IV) Tea service

Choose the **most appropriate** answer from the options given below:

(A) (a)-(II), (b)-(III), (c)-(IV), (d)-(I)
(B) (a)-(I), (b)-(II), (c)-(III), (d)-(IV)
(C) (a)-(IV), (b)-(II), (c)-(I), (d)-(III)
(D) (a)-(III), (b)-(IV), (c)-(I), (d)-(II)

61. Match List I with List II

List I *Fat type*	*List II* *Manufacturing*
(a) Lard	(I) Ripening
(b) Butter	(II) Rendering
(c) Margarine	(III) Emulsion
(d) Mayonnaise	(IV) Partial hydrogenation

Choose the **most appropriate** answer from the options given below:

(A) (a)-(II), (b)-(I), (c)-(IV), (d)-(III)
(B) (a)-(I), (b)-(II), (c)-(III), (d)-(IV)
(C) (a)-(IV), (b)-(II), (c)-(I), (d)-(III)
(D) (a)-(III), (b)-(IV), (c)-(I), (d)-(II)

62. Identify the correct sequence of product/ by-product formation during cocoa and chocolate processing/ manufacturing :

(a) Cocoa powder
(b) Chocolate liquor
(c) Cocoa butter
(d) Nibs

Choose the **most appropriate** answer from the options given below:

(A) (a), (b), (c), (d)
(B) (a), (b), (d), (c)
(C) (d), (b), (c), (a)
(D) (c), (b), (d), (a)

63. The drier that can be used for carrying out the instantizing or agglomeration process is:

(A) Drum drier
(B) Spray drier
(C) Tunnel drier
(D) Kiln drier

64. The major microorganism that the food handler's may harbour as part of the body's flora is :

(A) *Staphylococcus aureus* (B) *Bacillus thermophilus*

(C) *Clostridium botulinum* (D) *Bacillus cereus*

65. The basic functions of a food package are :

(a) Containment (b) Fortification

(c) Adulteration (d) Communication

Choose the **most appropriate** answer from the options given below:

(A) (a) and (d) only (B) (a), (b) and (d)

(C) All of the above (D) (b), (c) and (d)

66. Examples of active packaging includes:

(a) MAP (b) Ethlyene scavenger

(c) Antioxidant release film (d) Moisture absorbents

Choose the **most appropriate** answer from the options given below:

(A) (a), (b) and (d) only (B) (a), (b) and (c) only

(C) All of the above (D) (b), (c) and (d)

67. Match List I with List II

List I *Irradiation dose range, kGy*	*List II* *Objectives*
(a) 0.05-0.15	(I) Elimination of specific pathogens
(b) 35.60	(II) Insect disinfestation
(c) 3.0-13	(III) Inhabitation of sprouting
(d) 0.1-0.5	(IV) Sterilization of foods

Choose the **most appropriate** answer from the options given below:

(A) (a)-(I), (b)-(II), (c)-(III), (d)-(IV) (B) (a)-(III), (b)-(IV), (c)-(I), (d)-(II)

(C) (a)-(I), (b)-(II), (c)-(IV), (d)-(III) (D) (a)-(I), (b)-(IV), (c)-(III), (d)-(II)

68. The industrial High Pressure Processing setup consists of the following components :

(a) Pressure pump (b) Pressure agitator

(c) Pressure chamber (d) Pulse chamber

Choose the **most appropriate** answer from the options given below:

(A) (a), (b) and (d) only (B) (a) and (d) only

(C) (a) and (c) only (D) (b), (c) and (d) only

69. Match List I with List II

List I *Foods*	*List II* a_w *values*
(a) Flour	(I) 0.96
(b) Dry fruits	(II) 0.75-0.80
(c) Jam	(III) 0.55-0.80
(d) Bread	(IV) 0.67-0.87

Choose the **most appropriate** answer from the options given below:

(A) (a)-(IV), (b)-(III), (c)-(II), (d)-(I) (B) (a)-(I), (b)-(II), (c)-(III), (d)-(IV)

(C) (a)-(I), (b)-(II), (c)-(IV), (d)-(III) (D) (a)-(III), (b)-(IV), (c)-(I), (d)-(II)

70. Which of the following statements is/ are correct with reference to composition of fats and oils;

(a) The chain length and degree of saturation control the properties that are found within the fatty acids and lipids

(b) Fatty acids typically contains an even number of carbon atoms.

(c) The saturated acids have higher melting points than unsaturated acids of corresponding size.

Choose the **most appropriate** answer from the options given below:

(A) (a) and (c) only (B) (b) and (c) only

(C) (a) and (b) only (D) (a), (b) and (c)

Answers

1. A	2. A	3. C	4. A	5. B	6. B	7. D	8. C	9. D	10. A
11. A	12. B	13. A	14. B	15. A	16. C	17. A	18. B	19. B	20. A
21. C	22. D	23. A	24. D	25. B	26. B	27. A	28. C	29. C	30. C
31. A	32. C	33. B	34. B	35. B	36. A	37. B	38. B	39. C	40. A
41. C	42. B	43. D	44. C	45. D	46. C	47. C	48. A	49. D	50. C
51. C	52. A	53. A	54. D	55. A	56. D	57. C	58. B	59. D	60. A
61. A	62. C	63. B	64. A	65. A	66. D	67. B	68 C.	69. A	70. D

Food Analysis and Testing

1. Ion exchange chromatography is used for________

a. Vitamin analysis
b. Pesticide analysis
c. Air & water pollution analysis
d. Organic acid analysis
e. All of these

2. At present, the primary use for a mass spectrometer by the food analyst is as a

a. Detector for GC
b. Detector for HPLC
c. Detector for paper chromatography
d. Detector for NMR

3. Electropheric mobility of molecule is defined as

a. Migration of molecule per unit time
b. Migration of molecule per unit area of membrane
c. Migration of molecule per unit polarity of solute
d. Migration of molecule per unit field strength

4. Beer's and Lambert's laws are principle law in the following

a. Dialysis
b. Spectrophotometry
c. Polarimeter
d. Bomb caloriemeter

5. Why is it important to avoid air bubbles in the column during chromatography?

a. The air in the bubbles might react with the compounds being separated
b. Bubbles cause the samples to travel unevenly down the column and thus the components might not separate
c. Bubbles may destroy the column
d. Both b and c

6. Radioactivity of substance is determined by

a. Isoelectric pH
b. Conductivity method
c. Isotopic method
d. None of the above

7. Which of these effects results from slow injection of a large sample volume?

a. Increased resolution
b. Non-linear detector response
c. Decreased resolution
d. None of the above

8. Syringe pump, in HPLC, is a type of

a. Reciprocating pump
b. Gradient pump
c. Positive displacement pump
d. None of the above

9. Which of the following is an HPLC detector

a. UV absorption detector
b. Teflon Detector
c. RI detector
d. Both a and c

10. Which of the following is NOT the detector for GC

a. FID
b. RID
c. ECD
d. TCD

11. What does the selectivity factor describe?
    a. The proportional difference in widths of two chromatographic peaks
    b. The maximum number of different species which a column can separate simultaneously
    c. The relative separation achieved between two species
    d. Both a and b
12. Which of the following relationships between absorbance and %Transmittance is INCORRECT?
    a. A = 2 - log10 %T
    b. A = log10 100 / %T
    c. A = 1 - log10 1 / %T
    d. A = log10 1 / %T
13. Rutter technique is
    a. Horizontal chromatography
    b. Two dimensional chromatography
    c. Thin Layer Chromatography
    d. None of the above
14. In HPLC, isocratic elution occurs when solvent is __________ throughout entire separation process
    a. Kept constant
    b. Kept decreasing
    c. Kept increasing
    d. None of these
15. In preparative electrophoresis, thick slabs of buffer soaked into an appropriate medium is
    a. Horizontal
    b. Vertical
    c. Cross sectional
    d. None of these
16. ________ filter is recommended in HPLC for organic solvents
    a. Micorporons
    b. Cellulose acetate
    c. Pellicular
    d. Teflon
17. Gas Chromatography is used to analyse following substances
    a. Volatile
    b. Sugars
    c. Organic acid
    d. None of the above
18. The point at which three phases solid, liquid and gas coexists is ________
    a. Critical point
    b. Triple point
    c. Freezing point
    d. Boiling point
19. In spectrophotometer, A compound with high molar absorbtivity
    a. Have a higher limit of detection than a compound with low molar absorbtivity
    b. Have a lower limit of detection than a compound with low molar absorbtivity
    c. Have a constant limit of detection than a compound with low molar absorbtivity
    d. None of the above
20. Texture profile analysis is determined by ________
    a. Hakke's Viscometer
    b. Tintometer
    c. Texturometer
    d. Brookfield viscometer
21. Technique of separation of leaf pigment was first used by
    a. Russian Botanist (Mikhail Tsvet)
    b. Martin
    c. John Smith
    d. Fedrick

22. Incase of HPLC mobile phase is
    a. He
    b. H_2
    c. Organic solvent
    d. Air
23. Dialysis used to separate macromolecule from micro moleclule
    a. On the basis of size
    b. On the basis of molecular weight
    c. On the basis of concentration
    d. Both a and b
24. Application of ion exchange chromatography
    a. Toxilogy
    b. Air and water pollution analysis
    c. Industrial hygiene
    d. All of the above
25. Relative movement of protein through polyacrylamide gel do not depend upon
    a. Size
    b. Charge
    c. Polarity
    d. Mol. Weight
26. Which of the following method can be used for hydrolysis of peptide for determination of total amino acid in milk
    a. Acid hydrolysis
    b. Enzymic hydrolysis
    c. Alkaline hydrolysis
    d. All of the above
27. Proteins show greatest absorbance at
    a. 480 nm
    b. 240 nm
    c. 360 nm
    d. 280 nm
28. Electropheric mobility of molecule is defined as
    a. Migration of molecule per unit time
    b. Migration of molecule per unit polarity of solute
    c. Migration of molecule per unit field strength
    d. Migration of molecule per unit area of membrane
29. Isotopic method of analysis is based on
    a. Polarity of substance
    b. Conductivity of substance
    c. Isoelectric pH of substance
    d. Radioactivity of substance
30. Volatile substances can be separated using
    a. HPLC
    b. TLC
    c. Gel electrophoresis
    d. GC
31. Which of the following supporting medium has advantage of transparency
    a. Agar gel
    b. Silica
    c. PAGE
    d. Cellulose acetate
32. A molecule when absorbs energy
    a. Vibrates faster
    b. Vibrates with positive acceleration
    c. Vibrates with greater amplitude
    d. None of the above
33. The energy associated with visible and ultavoilet regions are
    a. 40-400 Kcal/mole
    b. 40-440 Kcal/mole
    c. 30-350 Kcal/mole
    d. 40-140 Kcal/mole

34. Best % of a solution that obeys Beer's law for most accurate reading
   a. 39.5%
   b. 29.5%
   c. 30.5%
   d. 36.87%

35. If the light through entire visible spectrum is absorbed in part, the object appears to be
   a. White
   b. Black
   c. Grey
   d. Opaque

36. Isoelectric focusing is a type of
   a. Electrophoresis
   b. Ultrafiltration
   c. Dialysis
   d. None of these

37. GPC means
   a. Gas Phase Chromatography
   b. Gold phase Chromatography
   c. Gel Permeation Chromatography
   d. Gas Permeation Chromatography

38. Why is it important to avoid air bubbles in the column during chromatography?
   a. the air in the bubbles might react with the compounds being separated
   b. bubbles may destroy the column
   c. bubbles cause the samples to travel unevenly down the column and thus the components might not separate
   d. Both b and c

39. A column chromatography procedure for the separation of a polar and a non-polar compound calls for sequential elution with the following two solvents: methylene chloride and hexanes Which solvent should be used first?
   a. methylene chloride
   b. It does not matter which solvent is used first
   c. Hexanes
   d. None of these

40. The point at which both liquid and gas phase coexist is
   a. Critical point
   b. Triple point
   c. Freezing point
   d. Boiling point

41. Which type of column has the greater efficiency and resolution
   a. Packed
   b. Both have the same
   c. Capillary
   d. None of the above

42. The response from a Flame Ionization Detector is
   a. Affected by changes in mobile phase flow rate
   b. Affected or not affected depending upon the sample
   c. Not affected by changes in mobile phase flow rate
   d. None of the above

43. Which of these effects results from slow injection of a large sample volume?
   a. Increased resolution
   b. Decreased resolution
   c. Non-linear detector response
   d. None of the above

44. Phenomenon occurring to ampholytes in a pH gradient influenced by an electric field is
   a. Electrofocusing
   b. Disc electrofocusing
   c. Isoelectric focusing
   d. Both a and b

45. Coulometric titrations are based on
   a. Ohm's law b. Coulson's law
   c. Faraday's law d. Cann's law

46. In preparative electrophoresis, thick slabs of buffer soaked into an appropriate medium is
   a. Horizontal b. Cross sectional
   c. Vertical d. None of These

47. Major component(s) of mass spectrometer is/are
   a. Ion source b. Detector
   c. Analyzer d. All of the above

48. At present, the primary use for a mass spectrometer by the food analyst is as a
   a. Detector for HPLC
   b. Detector for paper chromatography
   c. Detector for GC
   d. Detector for NMR

49. Which of the following is the basic unit(s) of NMR spectrometer
   a. Magnet b. Rf detector
   c. Rf oscillator d. All of above

50. _______ fields, all at right angles to each other are required for NMR
   a. 2 fields b. 4 fields
   c. 3 fields d. None of the above

51. Physical principle in thin layer chromatography is
   a. Adsorption b. Gel permeation
   c. Partition d. Ion exchange

52. Rf value is
   a. Distance of solvent movement Distance of solute movement
   b. Distance of solvent movement Standard reference of solvent movement
   c. Distance of solute movement Distance of solvent movement
   d. Distance of solute movement Standard reference of solute movement

53. HPLC stands for
   a. High Performance Liquid Chromatography b. High Pressure Liquid Chromatography
   c. High Paper Liquid Chromatography d. Both a and b

54. _____ filter is recommended in HPLC for organic solvents
   a. Micorporons b. Pellicular
   c. Cellulose acetate d. Teflon

55. Syringe pump, in HPLC, is a type of
   a. Reciprocating pump b. Gradient pump
   c. Positive displacement pump d. None of the above

56. In HPLC, isocratic elution occurs when solvent is ________ throughout entire separation process

a. Kept constant
b. Kept increasing
c. Kept decreasing
d. None of these

57. Particles type of HPLC column packaging is

a. None porous
b. Macroporous
c. Circular
d. Fully porous

58. Which of the following is an HPLC detector

a. UV absorption detector
b. RI detector
c. Teflon Detector
d. Both a and b

59. Which of the following is NOT the type of liquid chromatography

a. Liquid – Solid chromatography
b. Gel permeation chromatography
c. Paired ion chromatography
d. None of the above

60. Ligands are used in

a. High Performance Liquid Chromatography
b. Gel Filtration
c. Ion Exchange chromatography
d. Affinity chromatography

61. ______ is associated with the amount of flour produced per unitweight of wheat

a. Weight
b. Hectolitre weight
c. density
d. Vitreosity

Hectolitre weight (or weight per unit volume) is the weight of 100 litres of wheat and is the simplest criteria of wheat quality. It gives us a rough index of flour yield.

62. Which of these regulators are not permitted for use in foods by FSSAI

a. Malic acid
b. Citric acid
c. Succinic acid
d. Lactic acid

63. If you are asked by FSO to indicate whether the sample is Khandsari Sugar (Sulphur Sugar) Khandsari sugar (desi), which method you will use

a. Sulphated ash estimation
b. Conductivity method
c. LC-MS/MS
d. ICP-MS

64. Analysis of the proline content of honey is a measure of its

a. Ripeness
b. Shelf life stability
c. Added Sugar
d. None of above

65. Test used to detect insect infestation in cereals and their products is

a. Peroxidase test
b. Barfoed's test
c. Uric acid test
d. Baudouin test

Bolder grains such as: Wheat/Maize/Barley/Whole pulses: 50 gm

Smaller grains such as: Rice/Split pulses/millets: 20gm

66. The extent to which an instrument replicates its result when measurements are taken repeatedly on the same unit is called;

a. Real bias
b. Precision
c. Accuracy
d. True value

67. The CAS (Chemical Abstract Service) registery number of a chemical is

a. a rating of toxicity
b. a unique identifying number for each chemical
c. a rating of flammability
d. None of the above

68. The quality standard for the laboratory accrediting body in India National Accredition Board for testing and callibration NEW DELHI is;

a. ISO 9001
b. ISO 15189
c. ISO 17011
d. None of these

69. Which of the following test is a quick test for sugar content during the early stages of the brewing process for beer

a. Hydrometer
b. Babcock test
c. Wet ashing
d. Soxhlet extraction

10. A 3000 mg sodium diet has approximately how many meq of sodium?

a. 69
b. 77
c. 117
d. 130

ANSWER KEY

Q. No.	Ans.	Q. No.	Ans.	Q. No.	Ans.	Q. No.	Ans.	Q. No.	Ans.	Q. No.	Ans.
1	d	13	b	25	c	37	c	49	d	61.	b
2	a	14	a	26	d	38	c	50	c	62.	c
3	d	15	a	27	d	39	c	51	a	63.	b
4	c	16	d	28	c	40	d	52	c	64.	a
5	b	17	a	29	d	41	c	53	d	65.	c
6	b	18	b	30	d	42	c	54	c	66.	b
7	c	19	b	31	c	43	b	55	c	67.	b
8	c	20	c	32	b	44	c	56	a	68.	b
9	d	21	a	33	c	45	c	57	d	69.	a
10	b	22	c	34	d	46	a	58	d	70.	d
11	c	23	d	35	b	47	d	59	d		
12	d	24	d	36	a	48	c	60	d		

Milk and Milk Products

1. Average ove run in Butter is ________.
(a) 40% (b) 20% (c) 5% (d) 35%
2. Danedar type of khoa is used for preparation of ________.
(a) Basundi (b) Pedha (c) Gulabjamun (d) Kalakand
3. Rasagulla is best prepared by using ________.
(a) Channa (b) Paneer (c) Cheese (d) Sandesh
4. Rennet is used in preparation of ________.
(a) Paneer (b) Icecream (c) kulfi (d)Cheese
5. Citric acid is used for preparation of ________.
(a) Cheese (b) Paneer (c) Icecream (d) Kulfi
6. Chakka is used for prepation of ________
(a) Kalakand (b) Pedha (c) Shrikhand (d) Chamcham
7. Average fat content of Butter is ________
(a) 80% (b) 99% (c) 40% (d) 8.5%
8. Yellow colour to Cow milk is because of ________ pigment.
(a) Xanthopyll (b) Chlorophyll (c) Carotene (d) Lecithin
9. Dhap type of khoa is used for preparation of ________
(a) Sandesh (b) Gulabjamun (c) Pedha (d) Rasgulla
10. Volumetric capacity of ISI specified sampling dipper is _____ ml.
(a) 30 ml (b) 20 ml (c) 80 ml (d) 120 ml
11. Composite sample should not be less than ________.
(a) 200 ml (b) 175 ml (c) 100 ml (d) 500 ml
12. Sampling of cold canned milk should be ________.
(a) 20-22°C (b) 40-45°C (c) 10-15 °C (d) 32-40 °C
13. Sample can be preserved by using ________ as preservative.
(a) Formalin (36%) (b) NaOH (c) Phenolphthalin (d) H_2SO_4
14. Milk is agitated by using ________ before sampling
(a) Butyrometer (b) Sampling dipper (c) Sampling plunger (d) Sampling bottle
15. Microbial standard of raw milk is tested by ________test
(a) COB Clot on boiling
(b) Methyl blue reduction test (MBR) or Resazurin test
(c) Fat test
(d) Sediment test

16. Total acidity and heat stability of raw milk is checked by ________ test
(a) Sediment test (b) MBR test (c) COB (d) Alcohol test
17. Colostrum milk can be detected by ________ platform test.
(a) COB test (b) Alcohol test (c) Sediment test (d) MBR test
18. Dirt, dust and physical impurities of raw milk are estimated by ________ test.
(a) MBR test (b) Alcohol test (c) Sediment test (d) COB test
19. Price fixation of raw milk in is mostly done on basis of ________and ________ reading.
(a) Fat and SNF % (b) pH and Acidity
(c) Sediment and MBR reading (d) Fat and protein %
20. Gerber centrifuge revolves at speed of ________ to________ rpm.
(a) 5000-6000 rpm (b) 1100-1200 rpm (c) 100-200 rpm (d) 500-600 rpm
21. Specific gravity of sulphuric acid (H_2SO_4) used in fat estimation is ________.
(a) 0.99 (b) 0.46 (c) 1.84 (d) 1.00
22. Charring of fat in acid milk mixture is avoided by ________ during fat estimation.
(a) NaOH (b) Amyl Alcohol (c) H_2O_2 (d) KOH
23. Volumetric capacity of milk pipette used for fat estimation is ______ ml capacity.
(a) 10ml (b) 5ml (c) 10.75ml (d) D 20ml
24. Specific gravity of milk can be determined by using ________
(a) Butyrometer (b) Lactometer
(c) Hortvets cryoscope (d) Sediment tester
25. Average specific gravity of cow milk is ________ to________ .
(a) 0.99-1.00 (b) 1.84-2.00 (c) 1.028-1.030 (d)1.47-1.58
26. ISI lactometr is calibrated at temp of ________°C used for milk test.
(a) 40 °C (b) 27 °C (c) 15.5 °C (d) 45 °C
27. Formula of specific gravity = ________ .(CLR = Correct Lactometer Reading)
(a) =CLR+1 (b) = CLR/1000+1 (c) 1+CLR/1000 (d) =CLR-1/1000
28. Specific gravity of pure milk fat is ________.
(a) 0.99 (b) 1.00 (c) 1.35 (d) 1.99
29. Sodium hydroxide (NaOH) used as alkali for determination of acidity by titration of raw milk has strength of ________N.
(a) 1 N (b) 0.1 N (c) 10 N (d) 100 N
30. Indicator used in acidity determination by titration is ________.
(a) Phenolphthalin (b) NaOH (c) H_2SO_4 (d) Amyl alcohol
31. Total acidity of raw milk should not be more than ________.
(a) 1.20% (b) 10% (c) 2% (d) 20%
32. Pearson's square method is used in process of ________ of milk and milk products.
(a) Standardization (b) Neutralization
(c) Acidity (d) Total solid estimation

33. Double tonned milk contain ________% fat.
(a) 3.0% (b) 6.5% (c) 1.5% (d) 4.5%
34. Tonned milk contain ________% fat.
(a) 3.0% (b) 6.5% (c) 1.5% (d) 4.5%
35. Speed of centrifugal cream separator machine is ________ rpm.
(a) 1100-1200 (b) 5000-6000 (c) 100-200 (d) 2000-3000
36. Milk fat density is ________g/cm^3.
(a) 1.047 (b) 1.00 (c) 0.93 (d) 1.82
37. Skim milk density is ________.
(a) 1.036 (b) 1.048 (c) 1.00 (d) 1.028
38. Skim milk contains ________% fat.
(a) 9.0% (b) 0% (c) 3.5% (d) 6.5%
39. Bottom disc of cream separator machine also called as ________disc.
(a) Separating disc (b) Bowl hood (c) Bowl cove (d) All of the above
40. Urea in milk can be treated as 'added urea'. If urea content are found more than ________ in the sample.
(a) 50mg/100 ml (b) 20mg/100ml (c) 70 mg/100 ml (d) 100mg/100ml
41. Normal fresh mille has pH of approx.
(a) 7.5 – 8.5 (b) 6.5 – 7.5 (c) 4.5 – 5.5 (d) 2.5 – 3.5
42. Freezing point of milk ranges from
(a) – 535°C – 0.550°C (b) – 0.225°C – 0.250°C
(c) – 0.350°C – 0.375°C (d) None of these
43. Boiling point of the both cow and Buffalo milk range from
(a) 100.2°C – 101°C (b) 98.2°C – 100°C (c) 101°C – 102°C (d) None of these
44. Sampling of cream is done at temperature
(a) 105°C (b) 40°C (c) 50°C (d) Any of these

ANSWER KEY

1. (b)	2. (d)	3. (a)	4. (d)	5. (b)	6. (b)	7. (a)	8. (c)
9. (c)	10. (c)	11. (b)	12. (d)	13. (a)	14. (b)	15. (b)	16. (d)
17. (a)	18. (c)	19. (a)	20. (b)	21. (c)	22. (b)	23. (c)	24. (b)
25. (c)	26. (b)	27. (c)	28. (c)	29. (b)	30. (a)	31. (a)	32. (a)
33. (c)	34. (a)	35. (b)	36. (a)	37. (a)	38. (c)	39. (b)	40. (c)
41. (b)	42. (a)	43. (a)	44. (b)				

Points to Ponder

- Post-harvest unit operations involve handling, processing, and storage of agricultural produce after harvest.
- Cleaning removes dirt, dust, and foreign materials from produce.

FOOD PROCESSING

- Sorting separates produce based on quality, size, or maturity.
- Grading classifies products into categories based on standards.
- Washing improves appearance and reduces microbial load.
- Peeling removes the outer skin of fruits and vegetables.
- Blanching inactivates enzymes before freezing or drying.
- Drying removes moisture to increase shelf life.
- Dehydration reduces water content to safe storage levels.
- Size reduction improves processing efficiency and uniformity.
- Centrifugation separates components based on density.
- Preservation techniques (like canning, freezing) extend shelf life.
- Winnowing separates lighter particles using air flow.
- Sieving classifies grains based on size using screens.
- Dehusking removes the outer husk from paddy or other grains.
- Dehulling separates bran layers from grains like pulses.
- Milling converts grains into flour or semolina.
- Polishing improves grain appearance by removing outer layers.
- Tempering adjusts moisture content before milling for better efficiency.
- Conditioning softens grain kernels prior to processing.
- Aspiration removes light impurities using air suction.
- Food grain processing involves converting raw grains into edible and usable products.
- Fortification adds essential nutrients to processed grains.
- Extrusion produces ready-to-eat cereal and snack products.
- Heat transfer efficiency is a key factor in designing thermal processing equipment.
- Proper insulation minimizes energy loss in processing machinery.
- Ergonomic design improves operator comfort and reduces fatigue to workers.
- Processing machinery should comply with food safety standards and regulations.
- Agitator design depends on viscosity and mixing requirements.
- Energy efficiency is a major consideration in modern machinery design.
- Equipment should be designed to avoid dead zones where food can accumulate.
- Computer-aided design (CAD) is widely used for precise equipment design.
- Material handling involves movement, storage, control and protection of materials during processing.

- Efficient handling reduces product loss and improves productivity.
- Screw conveyors are suitable for handling semi-solid and powdered materials.
- Pneumatic conveying uses air pressure to transport powders through pipelines.
- Sanitary design is essential to prevent contamination in food handling systems.
- Vibratory conveyors are suitable for fragile and delicate food products.
- Forklifts and pallet systems are used for bulk material movement in warehouses.
- Cold chain transport maintains temperature-sensitive food quality.
- Process plant design involves planning layout, equipment, and operations for efficient production.
- **Cohesive Arch** forms when smaller particles (fine powders) possess enough cohesive strength to bond together.
- **Mechanical/Interlocking Arch** occurs when particles are large relative to the outlet size and lock together, bridging the opening.

FOOD PACKAGING/ FOOD STORAGE

- Packaging protects products from contamination and damage.
- Food packaging protects products from physical, chemical, and biological damage.
- Food packaging extends shelf life by preventing moisture, oxygen, and microbial contamination.
- Modified Atmosphere Packaging (MAP) slows down spoilage by altering gas composition.
- Vacuum packaging removes air to inhibit microbial growth.
- Active packaging interacts with food to enhance shelf life.
- Smart packaging monitors food quality and safety conditions.
- Edible packaging reduces environmental waste.
- Biodegradable packaging helps in sustainable waste management.
- Nanotechnology improves strength and barrier properties of packaging materials.
- Storage engineering focuses on safe preservation of food and agricultural products.
- Temperature control is critical for maintaining product quality.
- Relative humidity affects moisture content and shelf life of stored materials.
- Controlled atmosphere storage regulates oxygen, carbon dioxide, and nitrogen levels.
- Cold storage is widely used for perishable commodities like fruits and vegetables.
- Grain storage structures include silos, bins, and warehouses.
- Hermetic storage prevents oxygen entry and pest infestation.
- Proper ventilation avoids condensation and heat buildup.
- Modern storage uses automation and IoT for efficient management.
- Proper storage minimizes quantitative and qualitative losses.
- Stack management ensures proper airflow and prevents damage.
- Storage losses can be reduced through proper hygiene and sanitation.
- **Proper site selection considers util**ities, transport, and environmental factors.
- Piping and instrumentation diagrams (P&IDs) provide details for control in piping systems.
- Hygienic design is essential to prevent contamination in food plants.

- Waste management systems must be included in plant design.
- Safety measures such as fire protection and hazard control are mandatory.
- Packaging influences consumer attraction and product perception.
- On-farm storage structures are used to store agricultural produce at the farm level.
- Traditional storage structures include mud bins, bamboo bins, and underground pits.
- Metal bin provides better protection against rodents and moisture.
- Pusa bin is an improved farm-level storage structure in India.
- Kothar is used in rural areas for grain storage.
- Elevated storage structures protect grains from flooding and pests.
- Crib is used for storing maize cobs.
- GSM stands for Grams per Square Meter. It measures the weight of a paperboard per square meter of area. Simply put, GSM indicates how heavy the board is?
- 200 GSM board weighs 200 grams per square meter.350 GSM board weighs 350 grams per square meter
- Higher GSM generally suggests higher material density, but not necessarily greater thickness.
- Thickness of paper board, also known as caliper, measures how thick the board is physically. It is typically measured in microns (μm) or millimeters (mm).
- Thickness of paper board directly impacts:Structural strength,Folding performance,Cushioning ability.Perceived premium feel
- Two boards with the same GSM can have different thickness levels depending on fiber quality, pulp composition, and manufacturing process.

- Storage preserves quality under controlled conditions.
- Transportation ensures safe movement of produce to markets.
- Storage in silos protects grains from moisture, pests, and spoilage.
- Fumigation controls insect infestation during storage.

- Flaking converts grains into flat products like oats.
- Modern processing improves shelf life, digestibility, and market value.

MILK PROCESSING

- Milk processing involves treatment of raw milk to ensure safety and quality.
- Standardization of milks adjusts fat and solids-not-fat (SNF) content.
- High-Temperature Short-Time (HTST) pasteurization heats milk at 72°C for 15 seconds.
- Ultra-High Temperature (UHT) processing treats milk at about 135–150°C for a few seconds.
- Homogenization reduces fat globule size to prevent cream separation.
- Cream separation is done using centrifugal separators.
- Cooling slows down microbial growth after milk processing.
- Fermentation converts milk into products like curd and yogurt.
- Coagulation is the basis for cheese and paneer production.

- Spray drying converts milk into milk powder.
- Condensation produces sweetened condensed milk.
- Fortification adds vitamins like A and D to milk for better value
- Processed milk products include butter, cheese, ghee, and ice cream.

VEGETABLE PROCESSING

- Cutting and slicing of fruits and vegetables prepare produce for further processing.
- Blanching inactivates enzymes before freezing or drying.
- Canning preserves produce by heat processing in sealed containers.
- Osmotic dehydration of fruits and vegetables uses sugar or salt solutions for partial drying.
- Fermentation produces products like pickles and sauerkraut.
- Design of processing machinery focuses on efficiency, safety, and product quality.
- Equipment design should allow easy cleaning and sanitation in place (CIP/SIP systems).

MEAT PROCESSING

- **Meat processing** involves converting raw meat into safe, palatable, and value-added products.
- Slaughtering is the first step, ensuring humane killing and proper bleeding.
- Rigor mortis affects meat tenderness and occurs due to ATP depletion.
- Aging improves tenderness and flavor through enzymatic breakdown of proteins.
- Curing involves adding salt, nitrates, or nitrites to preserve meat.
- Smoking enhances flavor and extends shelf life by antimicrobial action of compound in wood smoke.
- Tenderization can be done mechanically or using enzymes like papain.
- Comminution refers to grinding or chopping meat into smaller pieces.
- Emulsified meat products like sausages require stable fat-water-protein systems.
- Packaging of meat methods include vacuum packaging and modified atmosphere packaging (MAP).
- By-products of meat like bones and blood are utilized in rendering and other industries.
- Marination enhances flavor, tenderness, and juiciness of meat.
- Meat grading is based on quality attributes like marbling, color, and texture.
- Food Consumer Science studies consumer behavior related to food choices and consumption.
- Food preferences are shaped by culture, tradition, and personal experiences.
- Consumer perception of food quality includes taste, safety, and nutritional value.
- Nutritional awareness influences healthier food selection among consumers.
- Branding and advertising significantly affect food purchasing behavior.
- Convenience foods are increasingly preferred due to busy lifestyles.
- Price sensitivity affects the demand for various food products.

CONSUMER SCIENCE

- Sensory evaluation helps understand consumer acceptance of food products.
- Social media has become a major driver of food trends.
- Food claims (organic, low-fat, gluten-free) impact buying behavior.

- Demographic factors such as age and income affect food consumption patterns.
- Consumer satisfaction determines repeat purchase and brand loyalty.

MICROBIOLOGY

- Bacteria, yeasts, and molds are the main microbes involved in food systems.
- Microorganisms can cause both food spoilage and foodborne diseases.
- Beneficial microbes are used in fermentation processes.
- Salmonella is a major cause of food poisoning.
- Escherichia coli can indicate fecal contamination in food.
- Listeria monocytogenes can grow at refrigeration temperatures.
- Lactobacillus is widely used in dairy fermentation.
- Molds can produce toxins known as mycotoxins in food.

WASTE AND ENERGY

- Composting converts agricultural waste into nutrient-rich manure.
- Vermicomposting uses earthworms to decompose organic residues.
- Biogas production generates energy from agricultural waste.
- Biofuel other produced from crop residues and other by-products.
- 'Rice husk can be used for energy generation and also as a building material.
- Sugarcane bagasse is widely used in paper and power industries.
- Fruit and vegetable peels can be processed into animal feed.
- Agricultural waste can be used for mushroom cultivation.
- Silage is prepared from crop residues for livestock feeding.
- Pyrolysis converts biomass into biochar and energy.
- Biochar improves soil fertility and carbon sequestration.
- Agro-waste can be used in making biodegradable packaging materials.
- Utilization of agricultural waste supports sustainable farming systems.
- Recycling farm waste reduces dependence on chemical fertilizers.

AUTOMATION

- PID controller uses proportional, integral, and derivative actions for control.
- Feedback control system continuously adjusts output based on measured values.
- Open-loop control system operates without feedback from output.
- SCADA enables real-time monitoring and control of processes.
- Flow measurement devices include orifice meters, venturi meters, and rotameters.
- Process automation improves efficiency, safety, and reduces human intervention.

FOOD CHEMISTRY

- Carbohydrates are the primary source of energy for the human body.
- Proteins are essential for growth, repair, and maintenance of body tissues.
- Fats provide concentrated energy and help in absorption of fat-soluble vitamins.
- Vitamins are organic compounds required in small amounts for metabolism.

- Minerals are inorganic nutrients essential for various physiological functions.
- Water is the most vital nutrient for maintaining body functions.
- Dietary fiber aids digestion and prevents constipation.
- Calories represent the energy value of food.
- Glycemic index measures how quickly foods raises blood glucose levels.
- Antioxidants help protect the body from oxidative damage.
- Arching (or bridging) in hoppers occurs when cohesive bulk materials form a stable, compacted bridge over the discharge outlet, stopping flow.
- **Eliminating Arching give Flow Promotion** installing flow aids, such as vibrators, air pads, or air cannons, to break the bridge.
- Rat holing in a hopper occurs when cohesive, powdery, or fine materials stick to the walls, forming a narrow, stable core (or "pipe") through which material flows, leaving the surrounding material stagnant.
- **Cleated belt conveyors** are vital for transporting materials on steep inclines or declines, providing secure, non-slip movement that prevents product loss and optimizes floor space.
- Cleats can be designed in various heights, shapes (*e.g.*, L-shape, V-shape, or chevron patterns), and spacings to match the specific product being moved.

FOOD PROCESSING AND TESTING

- Specific heat of food indicates how much energy is required to raise its temperature, which explains why water-rich foods like soup heat up slowly, while foods like ice cream warm and melt more quickly.
- Thermal conductivity determines whether the food article stays hot in the box or loose heat and becomes soggy by the time it is delivered.
- Porosity is not a flaw; it is the structural property that gives bread its fluffiness and makes snack foods light and crispy.
- Rheology governs how substances flow, determining whether ketchup pours smoothly or resists flowing out of the bottle.
- Sphericity measures how closely the shape of foods like peas or potatoes approaches a sphere, which affects their rolling behaviour during processing.
- Angle of repose determines how materials like flour accumulate in a pile, indicating their flow ability and stability.
- Viscosity describes the resistance to flow in liquids, helping maintain the desired consistency of sauces and batters.
- Young's modulus indicates how much a material, such as a cookie, deforms under stress, reflecting its stiffness and crispiness.
- Moisture content is not just the amount of water present; it plays a crucial role in controlling shrinkage, cracking, and shelf life of food products.
- Electrical conductivity influences how food interacts with microwave energy, affecting the uniformity of heating and the occurrence of cold spots.
- Destructive testing determines quality changes, such as browning in apples, by breaking down the sample during analysis.

- Hyperspectral imaging non-destructively examines the internal quality of produce, similar to an X-ray for assessing freshness.
- Destructive microbial testing involves sacrificing a few samples to ensure the safety of the remaining batch.
- Penetration tests are destructive methods that measure firmness by applying force until the food structure breaks.
- Destructive testing determines quality changes, such as browning in apples, by breaking down the sample during analysis.
- Hyperspectral imaging non-destructively examines the internal quality of produce, similar to an X-ray for assessing freshness.
- Destructive microbial testing involves sacrificing a few samples to ensure the safety of the remaining batch.
- An electronic nose detects spoilage non-destructively by sensing volatile compounds, eliminating the need for sensory tasting.
- Penetration tests are destructive methods that measure firmness by applying force until the food structure breaks.
- Near-infrared spectroscopy non-destructively measures sugar content in fruits quickly and accurately.
- Machine vision systems is a technology combining imaging hardware and software to automate inspection and identification tasks non-destructively and sort fruits like apples based on color and surface defects during processing.
- Compression testing is a destructive method used to evaluate texture by applying force until the sample deforms or breaks.
- Ultrasound waves non-destructively assess internal structure and detect voids within food materials.
- Titration for acidity is a destructive method that determines acid content by chemically reacting with the sample.
- Thermal imaging non-destructively detects temperature variations and defects in foods such as meat.
- Raman spectroscopy non-destructively analyzes molecular composition in foods like oils and spices.
- X-ray CT scanning non-destructively reveals internal defects such as cavities or infestations in fruits.
- Non-destructive techniques preserve sample integrity, reduce waste, and enable quality assessment without damage.
- Ball mill works on the principle of impact and attrition.
- Hammer mill works on the principle of impact crushing.
- Burr mill works on the principle of shearing and crushing material (Such as coffee beams and grains).
- Heat transfer explains why hot coffee cools down, while mass transfer governs the movement of aroma compounds to the surroundings.

- In drying, heat transfer supplies energy, while mass transfer removes moisture from the product.
- Thermal diffusivity indicates how quickly temperature changes propagate through a food during heating.
- In frying, mass transfer occurs as water evaporates and oil is absorbed into the food.
- During freezing, heat transfer removes energy, causing water to undergo phase change into ice.

OTHERS

- The heat transfer coefficient determines the rate at which heat is transferred between a surface and its surroundings.
- A psychrometric chart is used to analyze the relationship between temperature, humidity, and air properties in food processing.
- During sterilization, effective heat transfer ensures that the coldest point reaches the required temperature to destroy microorganisms.
- Evaporator coils absorb heat from the cold storage environment as the refrigerant evaporates.
- Condenser coils release heat to the surroundings as the refrigerant condenses back into liquid form.
- Air conditioning does not create cold; it removes heat from indoor air and transfers it outside.
- In food cold chains, refrigeration preserves quality and prevents spoilage of perishable products like milk and fish.
- The expansion valve reduces pressure, causing the refrigerant to cool rapidly.
- Blast freezing removes heat quickly, forming small ice crystals that preserve texture in foods like shrimp.
- Refrigerant acts as the heat-transfer medium, carrying heat away without contacting the food.
- Chilled water systems provide large-scale cooling for food processing facilities.
- Controlled atmosphere storage combines refrigeration and gas control to extend the shelf life of fruits like apples.
- Fluid dynamics governs how liquids such as tomato sauce flow during processing and dispensing.
- In pumping viscous foods like ketchup, flow behaviour depends on viscosity and flow rate.
- Bernoulli's principle explains the increase in fluid velocity when pressure is applied, such as squeezing a juice pouch.
- Fluid dynamics ensures proper circulation of oil for uniform frying of foods like French fries.
- Turbulent flow enhances mixing efficiency in processes such as blending spices into sauces.
- Drag force determines the energy required to pump viscous foods through pipelines.
- In spray drying, fluid dynamics controls droplet formation and movement to produce fine powder.
- Fluid flow design prevents dead zones in equipment like pasteurizers, ensuring uniform heating.
- In extrusion cooking, high-pressure flow shapes products like snacks and pasta.
- Rheology and fluid dynamics together determine the flow and texture of products like ice cream.
- Clean-in-Place (CIP) systems use turbulent flow to effectively clean processing equipment without disassembly.